The Sund
State Scho

The Sunday Times State Schools Book

The definitive guide to over 500 state schools throughout the country

BLOOMSBURY

The information in this book was correct to the best of the Editor's and Publisher's belief at the time of going to press. While no liability can be accepted for errors or omissions of any kind, the editor and publisher would welcome corrections and suggestions for material to include in subsequent editions of this book.

First published in 1997 by Bloomsbury Publishing Plc
38 Soho Square, London W1V 5DF

A copy of the CIP entry for this book is available from the British Library

ISBN 0 7475 3406 3

10 9 8 7 6 5 4 3 2 1

Text design by AB3
Typeset by Hewer Text Composition Services, Edinburgh
Printed and bound in Great Britain by Clays Ltd, St Ives plc

This edition is dedicated to my father-in-law Stanley Hughes, with many thanks for his unstinting help and hard work – without which it could never have been completed – and to his daughter, Susan, granddaughter, Lucy (anxiously awaiting her A-level results) and grandson, Thomas.

Contents

Introduction   ix

Schools
  England, Wales and Northern Ireland
    (arranged by rank)   1
  Scotland
    (arranged alphabetically)   395

Indexes
  (i)   *by school name*   407
  (ii) *by location*   415
  (iii) *by education authority*   425

Introduction

Education, education, education. Tony Blair's triple endorsement of what the new Labour Government promises will be its top priority bodes well for parents whose children are enjoying – or, in some cases, enduring – free schooling in the state system.

Even more heartening than the rhetoric of an election campaign, though, have been the actions of the new administration. Far from dismantling the structural reforms of their Tory predecessors, Labour ministers appear determined to swallow some of their past criticisms and ensure the advances of the past decade are protected and strengthened by being made to work more efficiently for a greater number of families.

Consequently, *The State Schools Book*, now in its fifth edition, will remain a valuable tool for parents wanting to give their children a head start without resorting to the privileges associated with the independent sector. A decent education for those who want it should never be regarded as a privilege to be granted only to those who can afford it.

With details of more than 500 of the country's best schools, *The State Schools Book* is established as the best and most authoritative parents' guide to the best and most challenging schools available to all children.

Last year, I wrote: 'Parents can rest assured that every school in this edition has achieved enviable examination results. But each has something unique to offer. And that is where the future of schools lies: the promise of excellence and distinction.

'Increasingly, schools are specialising and selecting – responding to the market forces unleashed by the reforms of recent years. Similarly, parents are becoming more sophisticated, better informed, more aware of the difficult-to-define differences between schools.'

Thankfully, it appears the same will hold true under Tony Blair: the continuing 'hit lists' of failing schools requiring urgent action; the publication of even more detailed and useful information about examination results, national curriculum tests and 'value added' academic performances; an emphasis on basic skills such as reading, writing and mathematics. As a result, the state system will continue to become more diverse, with schools better-placed to shape themselves to the needs of individual pupils of all ages and the demands of parents from all backgrounds.

The real test of New Labour's commitment to education will be its attitude to bad teachers (they should be sacked not suffered), the rewarding of outstanding teachers (they should be paid much more and encouraged to stay in the classroom, not to seek promotion into administration), and the length of the school day (it should be longer) and school holidays (they should be shorter so that valuable assets such as school buildings are not left idle for up to three months a year).

As I suggested in the introduction to the fourth edition, the performance of primary schools – good and bad – will be thrown into ever sharper focus. In a welcome move, local authorities will be required to produce their own primary school league tables and to publish them quickly so that they can be of most use to parents.

For the first time, secondary schools in this edition of *The State Schools Book* were asked to name the primary schools from which they drew the most pupils. For some – for example, grammar schools in rural areas – this was an impossible task; for others, however, the replies provide useful pointers to parents with young children who want to plan several years ahead. Too often, parents exercise their right to choose schools only at secondary level, possibly in the belief that most primary schools are more or less the same. They aren't – as the results of tests for seven-year-olds and 11-year-olds have shown.

All the secondary schools in this book have their strengths; few are without weaknesses. And none are foolish enough to be complacent. Indeed, this year's entries again provide more than enough evidence that the schools in the 'premier league' of the state system are striving to become ever more successful.

As ever, all the entries in this book are intended only to be a starting point for parents wanting the best for their children. Importantly, they reflect to a significant extent how the schools regard themselves and how they would like others to see them. In common with previous practice, I have used quotations from the schools themselves whenever seemed appropriate, particularly concerning matters of opinion rather than fact.

Schools are ranked according to examination results achieved in the summer of 1996. The primary criterion is the proportion of pupils gaining five or more GCSE 'pass' grades A–C; others are the proportion of A-level entries resulting in grades A or B and A–E. Previous years' rankings and statistics are given in brackets. Other statistics include the proportion of sixth-formers going on to higher education (along with the number of pupils winning places at Oxford or Cambridge).

As previously, Scottish schools are listed alphabetically, partly because headteachers and education authorities remain reluctant to volunteer the necessary information despite this year's renewed attempts to overcome such resistance. In Scotland, schools were asked about the proportion of pupils gaining five or more Standard Grades 1–2 and 1–4, and the proportion gaining five or more Higher Grades A–C.

As ever, though, this book could never have been produced without the cooperation of the hundreds of schools approached for detailed information within demanding deadlines. Headteachers, staff and pupils of the nation's best schools deserve the accolade this book aims at providing. They are your future and mine. May many more follow their example in the years to come.

Greg Hadfield
August 1997

England, Wales and Northern Ireland

ERMYSTED'S GRAMMAR SCHOOL

Gargrave Road
Skipton
North Yorkshire BD23 1PL
Tel (01756) 792186
Fax (01756) 793714

- National ranking 1 (40, 33, 6, 100)
- GCSE 100% (99%)
- A-levels 74% (A/B); 99% (A/E)
- Higher education 95% (Oxford 2, Cambridge 9)

- Boys' grammar
- Pupils 578
- Boys (11–18) 578
- Girls *Not applicable*
- Sixth form 148 (26%)
- Education authority *North Yorkshire*

Headteacher David Michael Buckroyd, 58, appointed in September 1982. Staff 37 (men 34, women 3).

Motto Suivez la raison (Follow the right path).

Background Founded circa 1492 by Peter Toller as a Chantry school in Skipton parish church; refounded in 1548 on different site by William Ermysted, Canon Residentiary of St Paul's Cathedral, London. The school moved to its current green and wooded site near centre of the Yorkshire Dales market town in 1876, celebrating its quincentenary in 1992 with a visit by the Princess Royal. All buildings are stone; small swimming pool and new sports hall; boarding ceased in 1989. Selection procedures identify top 30% of ability range. About half of places remain for extra-district applicants, who outnumber supply by a ratio of three to one. Well-equipped in technology and art; competitive sport supported by strong house tradition; other strengths include drama, public speaking and music. Inter-school fixtures in rugby, cricket, cross-country, athletics, tennis, orienteering and golf. Voluntary-aided; Christian ethic predominates, with daily assemblies and links with Skipton Parish Church.

Alumni William Petyt, first Keeper of National Records in Tower of London, c.1690; Iain McLeod, Conservative statesman and former chancellor; Blake Morrison, poet, author and former literary editor of *Independent on Sunday*.

Streaming Boys wishing to continue with Latin beyond year 7 are put together from year 8.

Approach to discipline 'A well-established and sensitive pastoral system seeks to spot difficulties before they arise. But when and if necessary boys are detained at lunchtime and after school.' For more serious and repeated offences, pupils recalled on Saturday morning after parental consultation.

Uniform Navy blazer with school badge, white/grey shirt, house or colours tie, grey flannel trousers, dark shoes. Standard uniform worn by all boys.

Homework Average 11-year-old, seven hours 30 minutes; 14-year-old, 10 hours; 16-year-old, 12 hours 30 minutes.

Vocational qualifications *None*

Inspection December 1994: 'A good school with some outstanding features. A highly-intelligent, well-motivated pupil body is assisted by a committed staff and strong governor support. They work in an ethos which demands continuing success born of traditional approaches. Pupils are consequently well-nurtured to produce impeccable examination results and performances, especially on the sports field.'; 'The gaining of knowledge rightly enjoys a crucial place in a school which is noted for its academic success, but too few opportunities are provided for pupils to express their sensitivity and their growing understanding of humanity.'

Primary schools Selective arrangements in 19 local primary schools and 'innumerable' out-of-district schools identify the top 28% of the ability range.

NEWSTEAD WOOD SCHOOL FOR GIRLS

Avebury Road
Orpington
Kent BR6 9SA
Tel (01689) 853626
Fax (01689) 853315
E-mail: newstead@rmplc.co.uk
Internet: http://www.rmplc.co.uk/eduweb/
              sites/newstead/index.html

- National ranking 2 (33, 6, 8, 3)
- GCSE 100% (99%)
- A-levels 72% (A/B); 100% (A/E)
- Higher education 97% (Oxford 6, Cambridge 2)

- Grant-maintained
- Girls' grammar
- Pupils 825
- Boys *Not applicable*
- Girls (11–18) 825
- Sixth form 253 (31%)
- Education authority *Bromley*

Headteacher Barbara Gibbs, 51, appointed in April 1994. Staff 57 (men 12, women 45).

Motto Fortitudine crescamus (In strength, we grow).

Background Originally Orpington Girls' Grammar School, founded in 1957; pupils aim at university and a range of demanding careers. Buildings are 'modern, sunlit and airy' in extensive grounds with woods nearby. Facilities include accommodation for computing, design technology, music and science as well as two libraries, drama studio, gymnasium and games hall. Sixth-form block has its own common rooms and snack bar. Heavily over-subscribed, with six applications per place. Success in national mathematics contests; poet-in-residence scheme attracts leading practitioners; six in 10 learn musical instruments; athletics, skiing and trampolining among sports; curriculum enrichment and enhancement programmes.

Alumni Emma Johnson, clarinettist, former Young Musician of the Year; Christine Hancock, general secretary of Royal College of Nursing; Lorraine McAslan, violinist; Susan Tebby, sculptress; Jennifer Keaveney, winner of 1986 BBC *Mastermind* quiz with record 20 points for general knowledge; Gillian Doubleday, 1989 *Mastermind* runner-up.

Streaming Only in mathematics in years 9 to 11.

Approach to discipline High standards of courtesy, self-discipline and responsibility for others; good staff–student relationships; supportive pastoral network and regular contact with parents 'enable us to achieve a lively and friendly environment'.

Uniform Green skirt, green-and-white striped shirt, green V-neck jumper with logo, green or black coat. No exceptions made in years 7 to 11. Sixth-formers are not required to wear uniform.

Homework Average 11-year-old, seven hours 30 minutes a week; 14-year-old, 10 + hours; 16-year-old, 15 hours.

Vocational qualifications Foreign Languages at Work (French, Spanish, German); Community Sports Leaders' Award; GNVQ Advanced Information Technology.

Inspection April 1996: 'This is a first-class girls' grammar school. The pupils, all of high ability, respond very well to the high quality of teaching provided, obtain excellent results in public examinations, and almost all go on to higher education.'; 'Teachers have high expectations of the pupils, who have high expectations of themselves.'; 'Pupils' attitudes to their studies are also very good. This is reflected not only in their diligence, but also in their generally good behaviour, both in and out of classrooms, and their excellent records of attendance.'; 'A minority of parents are dissatisfied with the amount and quality of information they receive about their daughters' progress, and with responses by some teachers to questions put or matters raised.'; 'The management and leadership of the school are generally good. The strengths are many.'

Primary schools More than 40 feeder schools.

THE HENRIETTA BARNETT SCHOOL

Central Square
Barnet
London NW11 7BN
Tel (0181) 458 8999
Fax (0181) 455 8900

- National ranking 3 (32, 1, 61, 125)
- GCSE 100% (99%)
- A-levels 69% (A/B); 98% (A/E)
- Higher education 91% (Oxford 3, Cambridge 3)

- Girls' grammar
- Pupils 662
- Boys *Not applicable*
- Girls (11–18) 662
- Sixth form 200 (30%)
- Education authority *Barnet*

Headteacher E. Jane de Swiet, 54, appointed in September 1989. Staff 45 (men 11, women 34).

Motto *None*

Background Voluntary-aided school founded by Dame Henrietta Barnett in 1911 at centre of the Hampstead Garden Suburb she created. Shares building, designed by Lutyens, with adult education institute. Hugely over-subscribed: 850 applications for 93 places in 1996. Limited facilities but notable physical education department: athletics, sailing, outdoor pursuits. The school has its own field centre in Wiltshire. Thriving classics department. Clubs include public speaking, Jewish Club, dance, gym, chess; two orchestras. Strong school council which discusses curriculum, uniform, discipline and other issues. Peer Education programme has won national recognition; European work-experience in France, Sweden and Germany. Named as 'outstanding school' in 1996 Ofsted annual report.

Streaming *None*

Approach to discipline Policy on discipline, with detailed guidelines: 'The policy is based on expectations we have of all members of the school community, staff and students alike. We prefer not to have 'school rules', but all members of the community are made aware of the behaviour which is expected and the sanctions which may have to be imposed in the rare occurrence of misdemeanours.'

Uniform Navy skirt/trousers, white/light-blue shirt, regulation navy knitwear in four styles with stripes at neck and wrists. Sixth-formers do not wear uniform.

Homework Average 11-year-old, 10 hours a week; 14-year-old, 15 hours; 16-year-old, 25 hours.

Vocational qualifications *None*

Inspection February 1994: 'The school has a good reputation that is well-deserved. Standards of achievement in external examinations are excellent. Achievement in relation to the pupils' ability is also consistently high.'; 'In most departments there are examples of outstanding teaching and learning. In a very small proportion of lessons the quality is below par where teaching styles are limited and unchallenging.'; 'Pupils are helpful, courteous and mature, and relationships between pupils and staff are good. Pupils are well aware of the high expectations held of them and respond accordingly.'

Primary schools More than 100 feeder schools.

CHELMSFORD COUNTY HIGH SCHOOL FOR GIRLS

Broomfield Road
Chelmsford
Essex CM1 1RW
Tel (01245) 352592
Fax (01245) 345746
E-mail: cghs@rmplc.co.uk

- National ranking 4 (4, 2, 3, 4)
- GCSE 100% (100%)
- A-levels 67% (A/B); 99% (A/E)
- Higher education 99% (Oxford 7, Cambridge 7)

- Grant-maintained
- Girls' grammar
- Pupils 702
- Boys *Not applicable*
- Girls (11–18) 702
- Sixth form 210 (30%)
- Education authority *Essex*

Headteacher Bernice McCabe, 44, appointed in September 1990. Staff 50 (men 11, women 39).

Motto Vitai lampada ferimus (We bear the torch of life).

Background One of the first secondary girls' schools in Essex, founded in 1907. Traditional red-brick buildings, much extended: new classrooms, technology laboratory, multi-skills centre; two fully-equipped computer rooms. New £850,000 science block opened in September 1994. Development Appeal launched in 1995 for performing arts and sixth-form accommodation improvements, and artificial pitch. The school is close to the town centre but in spacious playing fields with its own swimming pool. Over-subscribed, taking top 112 pupils who pass 11-plus examination and name school as first choice; over three years an average of seven applications per place. All girls take separate sciences, German and French from year 7; Latin is added in year 8. Emphasis on extra-curricular provision; over 50 activities each week: 13 musical groups, including two orchestras, wind bands, jazz band, chamber groups and choirs, compete nationally; many pupils in youth orchestras, including National Children's Orchestra. Junior and senior drama groups and productions; junior and senior public-speaking and debating. Twenty sports teams; long-standing tradition of success in hockey at national and territorial levels; athletics and netball represented at national level; also swimming, tennis, fencing and Duke of Edinburgh Award. Academic results are 'top priority for forward-looking but traditional school'. Identified by Ofsted in 1996 as an 'outstandingly successful' school.

Alumni Dame Margaret Anstey, diplomat and first woman under-secretary-general to the United Nations; Deborah Poplett, actress; Deborah Bushnell, England discus-thrower; Dianne Stradling, television presenter.

Streaming Pupils banded 'according to pace rather than ability' in mathematics, years 9 to 11.

Approach to discipline 'High expectations of self-discipline and courtesy.' Detailed code of conduct emphasises consideration for others, self-discipline.

Uniform Navy blazer with badge and motto, long-sleeve white blouse, school tie, grey pleated skirt. Dress code for sixth-formers, who wear their own clothes.

Homework Average 11-year-old, six hours a week; 14-year-old, eight hours; 16-year-old, nine hours 50 minutes.

Vocational qualifications Foreign Languages at Work (French).

Inspection May 1994: 'Chelmsford County High School is a very good school. The standards of achievement, the quality of teaching and learning are very high.'; 'Pupils are interested and take great pride in the quality and presentation of their work.'; 'Standards of behaviour, discipline and attendance are exemplary. Expectations by teachers of their pupils are high and the quality of relationships within the school is good. Pupils behave in a mature fashion and show courtesy and consideration for others.'

ST OLAVE'S GRAMMAR SCHOOL

Goddington Lane
Orpington
Kent BR6 9SH
Tel (01689) 820101
Fax (01689) 897943

- National ranking 5 (5, 51, 126, 30)
- GCSE 100% (100%)
- A-levels 67% (A/B); 98% (A/E)

- Higher education 99% (Oxford 5, Cambridge 5)

- Grant-maintained
- Boys' grammar
- Pupils 698
- Boys (11–18) 698
- Girls *Not applicable*
- Sixth form 192 (28%)
- Education authority *Bromley*

Headteacher Anthony Jarvis, 51, appointed in September 1994. Staff 48 (men 34, women 14).

Motto *None*

Background Founded more than 400 years ago by voluntary efforts of Southwark parishioners; one of first governors was Robert Harvard, whose son, probably a pupil at the school, went on to found Harvard University. Occupied various sites in Bermondsey, most recently by Tower Bridge, before moving to Orpington on edge of Kent countryside in 1967; 20 acres of tree-fringed playing fields. Buildings include chapel, 25-metre indoor swimming pool, squash and Eton fives court, Great Hall. Over-subscribed, with more than six applications per place; to expand to four-form entry in 1997. A £2m building programme, including new science block completed in 1997. Sporting achievements include national success in rugby, basketball, athletics, swimming, Eton fives, chess and debating. Instrumental ensembles have been among winners in National Chamber Music competition in 1983, 1986, 1987, 1993 and 1994; pupils in National Youth Orchestra and choir; finalists on several occasions in National Chamber Music Competition; school provides trebles for Queen's Chapel of the Savoy. Gold and bronze medallists in both physics and mathematics Olympiads. Domestic and foreign work-shadowing and work-experience. Exchanges with schools in France, Germany and Spain. Christian ethos. Sixth-form Festival week. Series of subscription concerts well-established; recent performances have included Julian Lloyd-Webber and Stephen Kovacevich.

Alumni Sir Leon Bagrit, pioneer of automation; Baron Hill of Luton, former BBC chairman; Sir Alan Marre, former Parliamentary Commissioner for Administration (Ombudsman); Abba Eban, Israeli politician and writer; Roy Marsden, actor; Sir John

Smith, deputy commissioner of Metropolitan Police.

Streaming In mathematics from year 9.

Approach to discipline 'Firm, with an emphasis on commitment, loyalty, courtesy and concern for others.'

Uniform Black blazer with badge, grey/black trousers, white shirt, school tie, grey/black socks, black shoes. Suits in sixth form.

Homework Average 11-year-old, six hours a week; 14-year-old, up to 10 hours; 16-year-old, 12 to 15 hours.

Vocational qualifications Institute of Linguists.

Inspection November 1996: 'A good school with some outstanding features.'; 'In sport, individual and team performances are of a very high standard as are levels of individual and group ensemble work in extra-curricular music.'; 'Pupils' attitudes to their work are very good. This is a strength of the school. They concentrate well in lessons, are conscientious about completing homework and show very good behaviour in class and around the school.'; 'The overall standard of teaching is good. Teachers are well-qualified and their knowledge of the subjects they are teaching at examination level is good. The working relationships in most lessons are good. Teachers motivate pupils effectively. There are some weaknesses in lesson planning at Key Stage 3 and some inconsistencies in the quality of teaching which need to be addressed.'; 'The headteacher gives very good leadership and the positive results of changes to the staffing structure, curriculum and aspects of management which he has initiated in the two years since his appointment are evident.'

Primary schools Warren Road Primary; Crofton Junior; Highfield Primary; Pickhurst Junior; Dulwich Hamlet Primary; Worsley Bridge Primary. More than 70 feeder schools.

COLCHESTER COUNTY HIGH SCHOOL FOR GIRLS

Norman Way
Colchester
Essex CO3 3US
Tel (01206) 576973
Fax (01206) 769302
E-mail: colchigh@rmplc.co.uk

- National ranking 6 (13, 7, 1, 2)
- GCSE 100% (100%)
- A-levels 66% (A/B); 97% (A/E)
- Higher education 95% (Oxford 4, Cambridge 9)

- Grant-maintained
- Girls' grammar
- Pupils 680
- Boys *Not applicable*
- Girls (11–18) 680
- Sixth form 181 (27%)
- Education authority *Essex*

Headteacher Dr Aline Mary Black, 60, appointed in September 1987. Staff 41 (men 12, women 29).

Motto Wisdom giveth life.

Background Out of origins in the early 1900s, it became a girls' grammar school in about 1944; moved to current site on outskirts of Colchester in 1958. Well-maintained building 'boasts much glass but little architectural merit'. Heavily over-subscribed, with five applications for each place: 'It is now bursting at the seams.' Extensive grounds with fine old trees, netball and tennis courts, athletics track and outdoor swimming pool. 'If the technology lab is unmistakably 1990s, summer lunch hours in the grounds have a nostalgic Edwardian charm.' County-wide reputation for drama, sport and music (two orchestras, many choirs and instrumental groups). High proportion go on to higher education to become scientists, engineers, medical students and veterinary surgeons. School-leavers have recently won examination board prizes for top papers in biology, history and Spanish. Strong careers guidance. Strong language and orchestral exchange links with partner school in Germany.

Streaming Irrelevant, because of initial selection procedure.

Approach to discipline Courteous and civilised behaviour expected: 'achieved as a natural result of the happy, well-motivated student atmosphere'. Emphasis on individual responsibility.

Uniform Dark-blue skirt and pullover, pale-blue blouse. Uniform not worn in sixth form 'despite omnipresent denim'.

Homework Average 11-year-old, five hours a week; 14-year-old, seven hours; 16-year-old, as long as necessary!

Vocational qualifications *None*

Inspection December 1995: 'A very good school with many outstanding features.'; 'Overall, taking age into account, pupils achieve excellent standards in all year-groups. They also achieve levels which are very appropriate for their high abilities, with a significant proportion achieving impressive levels in this respect.'; 'The quality of education is good and, in particular, the quality of learning is consistently high and often outstanding. Pupils are highly-motivated, enthusiastic and intellectually lively.'

Primary schools 'Our highly-selective intake from a wide geographical area means that students are drawn from a very large number of primary schools in both the state and independent sectors.'

READING SCHOOL

Erleigh Road
Reading
Berkshire RG1 5LW
Tel (0118) 926 1406
Fax (0118) 935 2755
E-mail: secretary@readingschool.i-way.co.uk

- National ranking 7 (1, 42, 62, 38)
- GCSE 100% (100%)
- A-levels 65% (A/B); 94% (A/E)
- Higher education 99% (Oxford 8, Cambridge 4)

- Grant-maintained
- Boys' grammar
- Pupils 763
- Boys (11–18) 763
- Girls *Not applicable*
- Sixth form 225 (29%)
- Education authority *Berkshire*

Headteacher Dr Peter Mason, 47, appointed in September 1990. Staff 53 (men 43, women 10).

Motto *None*

Background One of the 10 oldest schools in England, it was founded in 1125; moved to current site near centre of Reading in 1870 when the Waterhouse-designed buildings were completed. Stands in 16 acres, with further playing fields about a quarter of a mile away. The school, which also takes boarders, describes itself as 'a characteristic

English grammar school'. Fine cricket square attracts first-class fixtures between Berkshire and Middlesex each season. Cricket, hockey and rugby are main team sports. Community service on timetable for all pupils not in Combined Cadet Force. Vigorous house system. Substantially over-subscribed, with four applications per place. Mathematics and science are among strengths of a school that aims at 'all-round academic excellence'; about 80% of pupils take mathematics and/or science to A-level. Humanities have grown over recent years, while Classics undergoing resurgence in the middle school. Drama and music flourish throughout.

Alumni Archbishop William Laud, Archbishop of Canterbury beheaded in 1645; Sir George Pinker, Queen's former surgeon-gynaecologist and president of the Royal Society of Medicine.

Streaming In years 7 and 8, only in mathematics; in mathematics, science and French from year 9.

Approach to discipline High expectations and clear, detailed guidance based on respect. Detentions held twice weekly.

Uniform Grey suit with house tie.

Homework Average 11-year-old, seven to eight hours a week; 14-year-old, eight to 10 hours; 16-year-old, 12 to 15 hours.

Vocational qualifications *None*

Inspection February 1993: 'Reading School is a successful selective school at which many pupils achieve impressively high standards. A well-qualified and committed staff work hard to ensure consistency of standards in most areas of the school's work.'; 'The quality of pupils' learning is exceptionally high. It was satisfactory or better in 90% of the lessons inspected, and good or very good in 60%. Pupils demonstrate excellent powers of concentration, assimilation, recall and inquisitiveness.'; 'This highly-popular school offers its pupils a challenging but supportive community.' October 1996: 'An excellent school with an outstanding record of success in public examinations.'; 'Almost all students make consistently sound progress, and for over a third progress is very good.'; 'Higher-attaining students make exceptional progress and achieve outstanding results.'; 'Information technology is not yet fully used across the curriculum.'; 'All teachers are well-qualified and have a secure

command of the subjects they teach.';
'Homework is regularly given and marking
is constructive and encourages students to
improve their standards.'; 'Careers education
and guidance has a very positive impact on
the personal development of students.';
'There is a long-term plan for the maintenance, redecoration and refurbishment of
the buildings and, although much work
has been accomplished, there remains a
considerable amount of accommodation in
a poor state of repair which has a detrimental
effect upon the quality of provision.'

Primary schools More than 120 feeder
schools.

COLCHESTER ROYAL GRAMMAR SCHOOL

Lexden Road
Colchester
Essex CO3 3ND
Tel (01206) 577971/2/3
Fax (01206) 549928
E-mail: colch.royalgramsch@campus.
bt.com
Internet: http://www.campus.bt.com/
CampusWorld/orgs/org1124/crgs

- National ranking 8 (29, 50, 32, 29)
- GCSE 100% (99%)
- A-levels 64% (A/B); 96% (A/E)
- Higher education 98% (Oxford 4, Cam-
  bridge 6)

- Grant-maintained
- Boys' grammar
- Pupils 665
- Boys (11–18) 665
- Girls Not applicable
- Sixth form 186 (28%)
- Education authority Essex

Headteacher Stewart Francis, 59, appointed in
January 1985. Staff 42 (men 36, women 6).

Motto Vitae corona fides (Loyalty is the
crown of life).

Background Directly descended from 'town-
school' of 1206; granted royal charters by
Henry VIII and Elizabeth I; voluntary-controlled; became grant-maintained September
1993. Heavily over-subscribed at 11, with
five applications per place; occasional vacancies at 13+; admits external entrants
from state and independent schools into

sixth form. County-wide catchment area,
also attracts pupils from neighbouring Suffolk. In 'delightful' grounds in residential
area of Colchester: extensive playing fields,
pavilion, changing rooms, grass and hard
tennis courts within walking distance. Com-
prehensively redecorated and refurbished;
mixture of new and older buildings, remodelled art and technology block, school hall,
large stage, pipe organ; swimming pool,
indoor cricket school; new computer suite
and satellite system in 1997. Successful and
developing boarding house attracts full-time
and weekly sixth-form boarders from
throughout UK and overseas. Classics 'vigorously retained', with Greek sponsored by
Greek government; single sciences at GCSE;
pioneered A-levels in Classical Civilisation;
broad 'minorities course' jointly with girls'
high school. Strong musical provision: orchestras, choirs, ensembles, jazz. 'Richly
varied' drama programme. Regular fixtures
for rugby, cricket (more than 100 a season)
and hockey. Hosts of Royal Grammar
Schools' cricket festival every five years.
Success at national level in music, cricket,
chess, public speaking, croquet, Worldwise
Quiz, Citizen Foundation's mock trials, Capital Choices competitions, and Arthur An-
dersen Links with Industry. Parent-teacher
Association. Old Colcestrian Society. Member of upper-sixth selected to represent
United Kingdom in 1995 International
Mathematical Olympiad. Several awards
from examining boards to 1995 and 1996
A-level students for exceptional performance. Building plans include sixth-form
centre, lecture theatre and exterior of music, art and drama facilities.

Alumni Dr William Gilberd, chief physician to
Elizabeth I and James I; Sir George Biddell
Airy, former Astronomer Royal; Dr Samuel
Harsnett, former Archbishop of York; Pro-
fessor Tim Congdon, economist and Treas-
ury adviser; Mike Baker, BBC Television
education correspondent; Dr Geoffrey Mar-
tin, former Keeper of Public Records; Robert
Fulford, former world croquet champion;
Nicholas Elam, ambassador to Luxem-
bourg; Giles Smith, Daily Telegraph educa-
tion correspondent; Jim Acheson, triple-
Oscar-winning costume designer; Richard
Merriweather, round-the-world yachtsman.

Streaming Pupils put in sets in French and
mathematics in years 10 and 11.

Approach to discipline 'Rigorous and humane.

Courtesy and consideration for others are expected and insisted upon. Code of conduct issued to pupils and a copy sent to all parents. A commendation system rewards academic achievement and service to the school. Annual prize-giving reintroduced. Confident about resolving behavioural problems by firm, fair and consistent approaches by staff and close co-operation between school and parents.

Uniform School blazer and tie, white shirt, dark-grey trousers. Sixth-formers wear suit or jacket and trousers, with a tie: 'smart, individual, adult dress'. Regulations enforced firmly and consistently.

Homework Average 11-year-old, seven hours a week; 14-year-old, nine to 10 hours; 16-year-old, 12 to 14 hours.

Vocational qualifications *None*

Inspection December 1993: 'The school is a happy, well-ordered community. The pupils are well-mannered and co-operative, and display a relaxed and refreshing maturity. Relationships between teachers and pupils, and between the boys themselves, are excellent. Parental expectations, particularly on the academic front, are largely met.'; 'Communication with parents is effective. Accommodation is scattered and varied, but the school makes good use of its premises and fields.'; 'Standards in cricket, rugby, football and hockey are excellent. All these extra-curricular activities contribute to a strong *esprit de corps*.'

Primary Schools Very selective intake from wide catchment area and large number of primary and preparatory schools.

KING EDWARD VI CAMP HILL GRAMMAR SCHOOL FOR BOYS

Vicarage Road
Kings Heath
Birmingham
West Midlands B14 7QJ
Tel (0121) 444 3188
Fax (0121) 441 2796
Internet: http://www.icafe.co.za/mirage/kechb

- National ranking 9 (31, 9, 2, 43)
- GCSE 100% (99%)
- A-levels 61% (A/B); 97% (A/E)
- Higher education 90% (Oxford 4, Cambridge 3)

- Grant-maintained
- Boys' grammar
- Pupils 647
- Boys (11–18) 647
- Girls *Not applicable*
- Sixth form 183 (28%)
- Education authority *Birmingham*

Headteacher Mervyn Brooker, 43, appointed in September 1995. Staff 40 (men 34, women 6).

Motto Spartam nactus es: hanc exorna (You have reached Sparta: do it credit).

Background One of the five grant-maintained grammar schools of the King Edward VI Foundation in Birmingham. Founded in 1883 on its original site at Camp Hill in the centre of the city. Moved to current site in King's Heath, in southern Birmingham, in 1956. Typical 1950s buildings surrounded by playing fields and wooded areas. Entry strictly on academic merit based on results of verbal-reasoning, non-verbal-reasoning tests and mathematics tests. Applicants from Birmingham and areas such as Solihull, Redditch and Bromsgrove. Heavily over-subscribed, with 780 first-choice applications for 93 places. Shares competition-class swimming pool with Camp Hill Girls' School. Rugby, hockey and cricket among sporting achievements; fixtures against all leading schools in Midlands. Musical productions; art and chess among extra-curricular strengths. School prides itself on breadth of social composition: more than one in five pupils from ethnic minorities.

Streaming Pupils put in sets in French and mathematics in years 10 and 11.

Approach to discipline Firm discipline to produce orderly atmosphere crucial to education and learning. 'The school also believes that boys respond best to encouragement and praise rather than criticism and denigration. Standards of behaviour are good because both pupils and staff share a common purpose.'

Uniform Navy blazer with badge, grey trousers, white/grey/pale-blue shirt, black/grey/brown shoes. All pupils, including sixth-formers, required to comply.

Homework Average 11-year-old, seven hours 30 minutes a week; 14-year-old, 10 hours; 16-year-old, 12 hours 30 minutes.

Vocational qualifications BTEC Level 3, Mathematics.

Inspection December 1994: 'A successful school with many good features. Standards are high. Across all subjects and in nearly all lessons, they appropriately reflect the high ability of the intake; in a third of the lessons, they are high in relation to pupils' ability.'; 'Much of the teaching is good and some is very good, especially in the sixth form.'; 'There is some inconsistency in the application of the attendance policy, but it works effectively. Overall, the school manages its day-to-day activities well'; 'This is an orderly and happy community where relationships are good and pastoral care is well-developed.'

Primary schools Wheelers Lane Primary; Colmore Primary; Moseley CE Primary; Hall Green Primary; King David Primary; Kings Heath Primary.

LANCASTER ROYAL GRAMMAR SCHOOL

East Road
Lancaster
Lancashire LA1 3EF
Tel (01524) 32109
Fax (01524) 847947
E-mail: lrgs@ednet.lancs.ac.uk
Internet: http://www.ednet.lancs.ac.uk/lrgs

- National ranking 10 (10, 48 =, 21, 31)
- GCSE 100% (100%)
- A-levels 59% (A/B); 96% (A/E)
- Higher education 96% (Oxford 4, Cambridge 5)

- Grant-maintained
- Boys' grammar
- Pupils 910
- Boys (11–18) 910
- Girls *Not applicable*
- Sixth form 265 (29%)
- Education authority *Lancashire*

Headteacher Peter John Mawby, 56, appointed in September 1983. Staff 60 (men 55, women 5).

Motto Praesis ut prosis (Lead in order to serve).

Background One of the oldest and best-known state schools in the northwest of England. Records suggest it existed long before its endowment in 1472; in middle of 19th century school received royal charter and moved to current site overlooking city of Lancaster and Morecambe Bay with views to Lake District and Pennines. Over-subscribed, with 2.3 applications per place. Pupils include 190 boarders in three boarding houses. Recent building improvements: mathematics (1993), English and drama (1994), and design and technology (1995); senior boarding house. Facilities include sports hall, swimming pool, library, technology and information technology centres. Mathematics, science and technology are academic strengths, recognised by award of Technology College status. National representatives in cricket, rugby, rowing, swimming, athletics and water polo. Voluntary Combined Cadet Force; four flying scholarships in 1996; also sailing, flying, sub-aqua, rock-climbing.

Alumni Baron Parkinson of Carnforth, former Conservative Party chairman; Don Foster, Liberal Democrat MP for Bath, education spokesman; William Whewell, scientist, philosopher and Master of Trinity College, Cambridge, from 1841. Inventor of the word 'scientist'; Sir Richard Owen, palaeontologist and founder of Natural History Museum, president of British Association, coined the word 'dinosaur'; Sir Edward Frankland, co-discoverer of valency; Sir Ronald Halstead, deputy chairman of British Steel; Air Vice-Marshal George Colin Lamb, businessman and international rugby referee.

Streaming In mathematics from age of 13.

Approach to discipline Firm but understanding and purposeful. School expects highest standards in personal and corporate behaviour. Pastoral system through form-masters, heads of lower and upper school/sixth form, and for boarders through Housemasters. Almost half senior boys given opportunity to exercise responsibility in day-to-day running of school.

Uniform Navy blazer, grey/white/blue shirt, blue/black tie, grey trousers. Sixth-formers wear sports jacket and trousers, with distinctive tie. Regulations enforced 'exactly'; smart alternatives for sixth-formers tolerated.

Homework Average 11-year-old, five hours a week; 14-year-old, seven hours 30 minutes; 16-year-old, 15 hours.

Vocational qualifications Cambridge Certificate in Information Technology.

Primary schools Boys drawn from more than 100 primary schools.

WYCOMBE HIGH SCHOOL

Marlow Hill
High Wycombe
Buckinghamshire HP11 1TB
Tel (01494) 523961
Fax (01494) 510354
E-mail: wycombeh@aol.com
Internet: http://www.rmplc.co.uk/
　　　　　eduweb/sites/whshw/index.html

- National ranking 11 (79, 41, 33, 47)
- GCSE 100% (97%)
- A-levels 58% (A/B); 98% (A/E)
- Higher education 94% (Oxford 9, Cambridge 4)

- Girls' grammar
- Pupils 1,266
- Boys *Not applicable*
- Girls (12–18) 1,266
- Sixth form 380 (30%)
- Education authority *Buckinghamshire*

Headteacher Muriel Pilkington, 56, appointed in September 1986. Staff 69 (men 10, women 59).

Motto Fortiter, fideliter, feliciter (Bravely, faithfully, happily).

Background A popular and successful school dating from 1901. It moved to its current 26-acre landscaped site on Marlow Hill, near to M40, in 1956. Accommodation includes sixth-form block, technology block, music centre, drama studio and sports complex. Voluntary-controlled; consistently good examination results. There is an average of three applications per place; school expanded to 1,300 places from September 1993, with appointment of more than 20 extra staff. Nearly 30 A-level subjects. Two orchestras; regular music concerts and choral recitals. Fourteen different sports taught; hockey, tennis and netball teams regularly in regional or national finals; under-18 hockey team were national champions in 1991.

Alumni Heather Angel, wildlife photographer and former president of Royal Photographic Society; Penelope Jamieson, Anglican Bishop of Dunedin (New Zealand).

Streaming Pupils in sets for mathematics and French in years 9 to 11, and in science in years 10 and 11.

Approach to discipline Firm. Behaviour described as very good. Rules and regulations negotiated with girls through school council. School has own behaviour policy.

Uniform Navy skirt, navy/white striped blouse, navy jumper with school crest (years 8 and 9), burgundy jumper with crest (years 10 and 11). No uniform for sixth-formers, but trousers not allowed. Regulations enforced in full, including PE kit and coats.

Homework Average 12-year-old, eight hours a week; 14-year-old, 12 hours; 16-year-old, 15 hours.

Vocational qualifications City and Guilds, Information Technology; Foreign Languages at Work. Diploma of Achievement.

Primary schools Hamilton Combined; Stokenchurch Middle; St Augustine's RC Combined; Godstowe Preparatory; Tylers Green Middle.

ST PATRICK'S GIRLS' ACADEMY

35 Killymeal Road
Dungannon
County Tyrone BT71 6LJ
Tel (01868) 722474
Fax (01868) 753148

- National ranking 12 (7, 46, 77, 54)
- GCSE 100% (100%)
- A-levels 57% (A/B); 99% (A/E)
- Higher education 71%

- Girls' grammar
- Pupils 827
- Boys *Not applicable*
- Girls (11–18) 827
- Sixth form 245 (30%)
- Education authority *Southern Education and Library Board*

Headteacher Joan McParland, appointed in April 1996. Staff 49 (men 14, women 35).

Motto Ad Jesum per Mariam (To Jesus through Mary).

Background History traced from 1894 when Sisters of Mercy came to Dungannon from Dundalk. In early 20th century St Patrick's Academy built on site near parish church, home for almost 75 years. In 1960s temporary classrooms to cope with increasing numbers until negotiations completed for new site on the Killymeal Road, with new school opening in 1975. 'Outstanding' record in fostering Irish language and culture; frequent winners of Ashbourne Shield for proficiency in spoken Irish. Over-subscribed, with 1.5 applications per place. Successful Irish-language debating team. Extra-curricular activities: athletics, traditional music, folk group, choir (both English and Irish), orchestra, modern language society, European society, mini-enterprise, public speaking club, science club, environment clubs; video-active club, first-aid club. Represented Northern Ireland in United Kingdom Mock Trial Competition; featured in Home Truths documentary; winners of Northern Ireland Home Accident Prevention Public Speaking competition. Charity fundraising of more than £8,000. Annual musical production. Education for Mutual Understanding; winners of Spirit of Enniskillen Bursary and Coca-Cola International Work-experience bursaries. European Awareness programme: exchange visits to Germany, France and Spain. Languages taught include Irish, French, Spanish, German and Japanese.

Alumni Bernadette McAliskey (formerly Devlin), former Independent Unity MP for Mid-Ulster; Sally O'Neill, Assistant Director of Trocaire, Catholic third-world charity; Deirdre Fox, managing director of Ex-Lingua international language school.

Streaming *None*

Approach to discipline 'We believe that the best discipline is self-discipline and encouragement is the keynote. We work hard to develop sound relationships between staff and students, and stress that discipline is the responsibility of all staff.'

Uniform Blue blazer, blue blouse, navy skirt, navy socks/tights. Very strictly enforced; regular checks, with two teachers having overall responsibility.

Homework Average 11-year-old, seven hours 30 minutes to 10 hours a week; 14-year-old, 10 hours; 16-year-old, 13 to 15 hours.

Vocational qualifications RSA.

Inspection October 1992: 'This school has a strong sense of community, which is shared by the pupils and a very caring, committed staff. The teachers are hard-working and effective; they show in their work a full sympathy with the aims of the school.'; 'The pupils are polite, courteous and well-

behaved; the quality of relationships between them is universally strong. The climate in classrooms is open, and the pupils are confident of receiving a sympathetic response from teachers and peers.'

Primary schools St Patrick's Primary, Dungannon; Primate Dixon Primary, Coalisland; Holy Trinity Primary, Cookstown; Edendork Primary; St Patrick's Primary, Mullinahoe.

KENDRICK GIRLS' SCHOOL

London Road
Reading
Berkshire RG1 5BN
Tel (01734) 585959
Fax (01734) 505539
E-mail: ar82@dial.pipex.com
Internet: http://www.i-way.co.uk/
homepage/thames_valley_info/
schools/kendrick

- National ranking 13 (2, 3, 19, 1)
- GCSE 100% (100%)
- A-levels 57% (A/B); 94% (A/E)
- Higher education 92% (Oxford 2, Cambridge 3)

- Girls' grammar
- Pupils 677
- Boys *Not applicable*
- Girls (11–18) 677
- Sixth form 198 (29%)
- Education authority *Berkshire*

Headteacher Marsha Marilyn Elms, 49, appointed in January 1993. Staff 43 (men 7, women 36).

Motto Dum spiro spero (While I breathe, I hope).

Background An endowment by John Kendrick to the town in 1624 was the origin of this non-denominational girls' school, which moved to its current site in the heart of Reading town centre in 1927. Increasingly over-subscribed, with more than six applications for each place. Indoor swimming pool; synchronised swimming team is one of top two in the country; two orchestras, two choirs, ensembles. In addition to national curriculum, pupils have chance to study three separate sciences, two modern languages and Latin. Aim is not to be 'an exam factory,' but to offer an all-round education. Identified in 1995 Ofsted report as 'outstandingly successful' school.

Alumni Janet Reger, women's underwear designer; Beryl Cooke, artist.

Streaming Some setting in mathematics from year 8.

Approach to discipline Self-discipline is the watchword within 'a very pleasant, happy atmosphere'. Highest standards expected; teachers report excellent relationships with, and between, girls: 'We simply do not have discipline problems.'

Uniform Kendrick red sweater, white blouse, mid-grey skirt, grey/black coat. No uniform for sixth-formers but 'acceptable' standard demanded. 'Very strictly enforced.'

Homework Average 11-year-old, eight hours a week; 14-year-old, 11 hours; 16-year-old, 14 hours.

Vocational qualifications Information Systems; French and German for Business; Business Studies.

Inspection March 1995: 'This is an outstanding school which sets and achieves very high standards in all aspects of its work. The education provided allows pupils to achieve excellence in both their academic performance and their personal development. The school's reputation with parents and the local community is justifiably high.'; 'Pupils work hard and acquire an outstanding range of learning skills as they progress through the school.'; 'Standards of teaching are very high; staff are committed, well-qualified and hard-working.'; 'The school is very well managed and benefits from strong and effective leadership.'

Primary schools More than 100 feeder schools.

COLYTON GRAMMAR SCHOOL

Colyford
Colyton
Devon EX13 6HN
Tel (01297) 552327
Fax (01297) 553853
Internet: http://www.c-g-s.demon.co.uk

- National ranking 14= (43, 38, 40=, 121)
- GCSE 100% (99%)
- A-levels 54% (A/B); 98% (A/E)
- Higher education 98% (Oxford 4, Cambridge 5)

- Grant-maintained
- Mixed grammar
- Pupils 682
- Boys (11–18) 314
- Girls (11–18) 368
- Sixth form 130 (19%)
- Education authority *Devon*

Headteacher Barry Sindall, 51, appointed in January 1991. Staff 47 (men 23, women 24).

Motto Esse quam videri (To be rather than seem to be).

Background Only state grammar within 50-mile radius, with rural 12-acre site in Axe Valley, East Devon; founded in 1546. Pupils drawn from Devon, Somerset and Dorset; takes top 25% of the ability range. Sports facilities: sports hall, open-air swimming pool, floodlit all-weather pitch for hockey and tennis. One of the first schools to become grant-maintained in 1989; since then improvements have included £1m science and technology centre, music suite, drama studio, and sixth-form centre. Modern languages wing and new library and information technology centre. Over-subscribed, with four applications for each place. Prides itself on broad, balanced curriculum: three foreign languages, separate sciences at GCSE, and a choice of 18 A-levels and range of AS-levels. Work-shadowing for all year 11 pupils, and work-experience for all sixth-formers, including European work placements for modern linguists; Duke of Edinburgh Award Scheme; Young Enterprise; British Association of Young Scientists. Other clubs include orchestra, choir, jazz band, drama, and art workshops. Identified by Ofsted in 1996 as 'outstandingly successful'.

Alumni Sir Rex Richards, former chancellor of Exeter University, president of Royal Society of Chemistry (1990–2); James May, Olympic gymnast.

Streaming Only in mathematics and modern languages.

Approach to discipline High standards, high expectations through good relationships and recognition of achievement rather than sanctions. 'Work and behaviour detentions are used sparingly but with consistency.'

Uniform Navy blazer, white shirt, navy-and-gold tie. 'Correct uniform is mandatory.'

Homework Average 11-year-old, six hours a

week; 14-year-old, nine hours; 16-year-old, 10 hours.

Vocational qualifications City and Guilds, Foreign Languages at Work (German).

Inspection September 1993: 'A good school offering an effective education.'; 'Work of high quality is produced in all areas of the curriculum. Pupils' attitudes are very positive, with motivated children who concentrate and cooperate well. Pupils often show that they enjoy lessons. The relationship between pupils and teachers is very good. These qualities are found in nearly all lessons.'; 'The school is a well-ordered community: pupils respond positively to high expectations of behaviour.'

Primary schools Axminster Primary; Colyton Primary; Seaton County Primary; St Nicholas CE Junior, Sidmouth; West Hill Primary, Ottery St Mary.

WOLVERHAMPTON GIRLS' HIGH SCHOOL

Tettenhall Road
Wolverhampton
West Midlands WV6 0BY
Tel (01902) 312186
Fax (01902) 715834

- National ranking 14 = (8, 12 = , 13, 14)
- GCSE 100% (100%)
- A-levels 54% (A/B); 98% (A/E)
- Higher education 98% (Oxford 3, Cambridge 1)

- Grant-maintained
- Girls' grammar
- Pupils 660
- Boys *Not applicable*
- Girls (11–18) 660
- Sixth form 160 (24%)
- Education authority *Wolverhampton*

Headteacher D. James, 47, appointed in September 1997. Staff 45 (men 5, women 40).

Motto Ludus supra praemium (The game above the prize).

Background Opened in 1911 as county school for girls from Wolverhampton and Staffordshire. Large red-brick building in 40,000 square metres in urban area of west Wolverhampton; new technology building opened in 1993; new science block in 1995; six tennis courts, two hockey pitches; three netball courts. Over-subscribed, with five applications per place. Russian taught from year 7; Chinese in year 12. Town and county representation in athletics, hockey, netball, swimming and tennis. Music a strength: wide range of instrumental lessons available; choirs, musical groups and ensembles, from senior orchestra to quartets and trios. Drama, public speaking, chess, and dance clubs; wide range of trips abroad. Successful Young Enterprise teams in 1994, including national finals; economics group came third in national final of *Financial Times* Pro-share Competition. Vocal ensemble in National Festival of Music for Youth. 'Traditional ethos that prepares girls for future full of change.'

Alumni Rachel Heyhoe-Flint, broadcaster, journalist and former England women's cricket captain; Baroness Perry, president, Lucy Cavendish College; Pamela Hodgson, broadcaster and writer; Winifred Mantle, author; Judith Flower, author; Gwen Berryman, actress; Jean Barrington, opera singer; Marilyn Troth, opera singer; Helene Hayman, chairman of Whittington Hospital NHS Trust.

Streaming *None*

Approach to discipline Simple but effective rules, which are strictly enforced. 'Pupils are sanctioned when work or conduct is unsatisfactory, and rewarded for excellence.'

Uniform Navy blazer and skirt, with pale-blue shirt and school tie. Strictly enforced; uniform to be worn at all times.

Homework Average 11-year-old, 10 hours a week; 14-year-old, 13 hours; 16-year-old, 18 hours.

Vocational qualifications RSA, Computer Literacy and Information Technology; Foreign Languages at Work.

Inspection October 1995: 'The school sets high standards and achieves them.'; 'With few exceptions, pupils achieve levels which are at least appropriate for their ability.'; 'Throughout the curriculum, pupils are very competent readers, write well and have good skills of speaking and listening. Numeracy skills are well-developed and applied in a range of other subjects as well as mathematics.'; 'The quality of education is predominantly good and sometimes outstanding.'; 'Levels of concentration, motivation and interest are sustained remarkably well throughout lessons. Pupils' enjoyment of learning, however, is frequently diminished by the cumulative quantity of written work and homework which they feel compelled to complete in order to match their own and the school's high expectations. The often challenging teaching contributes significantly to the quality of learning and to high standards.'

Primary schools Uplands Primary; Newbridge Preparatory; Woodthorne Primary; Woodfield Primary; Perton Middle; Elston Hall Primary.

THE ROYAL GRAMMAR SCHOOL

Amersham Road
High Wycombe
Buckinghamshire HP13 6QT
Tel (01494) 524955
Fax (01494) 510604
E-mail: rmp.9045404.d4w@dialnet.co.uk
Internet: http://www.rmplc.co.uk/eduweb/sites/rgshiwyc/

- National ranking 16 (14, 5, 20, 16)
- GCSE 100% (100%)
- A-levels 54% (A/B); 96% (A/E)
- Higher education 95% (Oxford 13, Cambridge 16)

- Grant-maintained
- Boys' grammar
- Pupils 1,160
- Boys (12–18) 1,160
- Girls *Not applicable*
- Sixth form 400 (34%)
- Education authority *Buckinghamshire*

Headteacher David Roger Levin, 47, appointed in September 1993. Staff 83 (men 64, women 19).

Motto *None*

Background Chartered by Queen Elizabeth I in 1562, the school is set on 22-acre site a mile from High Wycombe centre. Buildings are a blend of traditional and modern. In past six years, £2.5m has been spent on new accommodation including library, information technology centre, sports hall, sixth-form centre, dining hall, technology centre and classrooms. School has up to 60 boarders; serves all south Buckinghamshire, with pupils from 15-mile radius. 'Nicely full', with 311 first-choice applications. Every year for

the past decade, the school has had at least half a dozen United Kingdom or England representatives in rugby, hockey, fencing, tennis or rowing; 14 sports offered, including Eton Fives and shooting. Total of 24 subjects at A-level, more than 30 school societies. Combined Cadet Force, and a Voluntary Service Unit.

Alumni Professor Michael Zander, professor of law at London School of Economics; Professor Roger Scruton, philosopher; Lord McIntosh of Haringey, Labour peer; David Ashby, Conservative MP for Leicestershire North-West; Peter Fry, Conservative MP for Wellingborough.

Streaming Regarded as unnecessary, but setting in mathematics and modern languages in years 10 and 11. Teaching groups based mainly on tutorial groups or option choices.

Approach to discipline 'Courteous but firm, based on respect for others and good manners.' Prefectorial system; few sanctions have to be imposed.

Uniform Navy blazer, charcoal-grey trousers, white shirt, black shoes. For sixth-formers, plain dark-grey suit acceptable. Regulations enforced 'totally'.

Homework Average 12-year-old, 10 hours a week; 14-year-old, 12 hours 30 minutes; 16-year-old, 14 hours.

Vocational qualifications *None*

Inspection March 1995: 'The Royal Grammar School is a popular school with a deserved reputation for high academic performance. Test and examination results show that standards of achievement are high throughout the school and results compare favourably with other selective schools nationally.'; 'Pupils learn quickly and effectively. The quality of the great majority of teaching is sound or better. In many cases it is good and sometimes it is outstanding.'; 'A wide range of subjects is provided, although the time allocated to some subjects is insufficient. The curriculum is enriched by a programme of extensive extra-curricular activities.'; 'Behaviour is good. Pupils are proud of their school, motivated to work and have confidence in themselves.'; 'Pupils write accurately, spell well and have a good understanding of grammar and punctuation. Note-making and recording is well done, but writing for imaginative purposes is more limited.'

Primary schools 'The school has a policy not to give information that could allow comparison between primary schools.'

NEWPORT GIRLS' HIGH SCHOOL

Wellington Road
Newport
Shropshire TF10 7HL
Tel (01952) 811040
Fax (01952) 820054

- National ranking 17 (22, 27, 11, 11)
- GCSE 100% (100%)
- A-levels 54% (A/B); 95% (A/E)
- Higher education 95%

- Girls' grammar
- Pupils 226
- Boys *Not applicable*
- Girls (11–18) 226
- Sixth form 62 (27%)
- Education authority *Shropshire*

Headteacher Kaye Harrison, 46, appointed in January 1992. Staff 17 (men 2, women 15).

Motto *None*

Background The main building dates from the 1920s, when the school opened in the Shropshire market town. Extra mobile classrooms have been added over the years. The school is over-subscribed, with 160 applications for 32 places. New technology room and art room in September 1995. Other recent additions include four new classrooms. All sports facilities are contained within the school's grounds, but use is also made of the National Sports Centre at Lilleshall. A drama club is run by sixth-formers; there is a strong house system; charity fund-raising is regarded as an integral part of school life. There is two weeks' work-experience for year 11 pupils; work-experience abroad is arranged for year 12. The school values its industrial links. 'Academic results are excellent, but of equal importance is that strangers are made to feel welcome and able to participate in a thriving environment. Relationships between the home and school are strong, with a flourishing parent-teacher association.'

Streaming *None*

Approach to discipline 'Within this small community of generally sociable, responsible and well-maturated young women, there is seldom any necessity for discipline. However guidelines to enable the smooth functioning of the school are given. Emphasis is upon self-discipline.'

Uniform Years 7 to 11: navy skirt and jumper/cardigan, white blouse, school tie. Sixth form: navy skirt, white blouse, sixth-form tie for special occasions. Regulations enforced tightly in lower school; navy skirt always enforced in sixth form.

Homework Average 11-year-old, seven hours 30 minutes a week; 14-year-old, 10 hours; 16-year-old, 12 hours 30 minutes.

Vocational qualifications *None*

Inspection Feburary 1997

Primary schools Priority given to Newport area girls.

STRATFORD-UPON-AVON GRAMMAR SCHOOL FOR GIRLS

Shottery Manor
Stratford-upon-Avon
Warwickshire CV37 9HA
Tel (01789) 293759
Fax (01789) 261450

- National ranking 18 (89, 8, 63, 71)
- GCSE 100% (97%)
- A-levels 53% (A/B); 97% (A/E)
- Higher education 90% (Oxford 1)

- Girls' grammar
- Pupils 492
- Boys *Not applicable*
- Girls (11–18) 492
- Sixth form 171 (35%)
- Education authority *Warwickshire*

Headteacher Roger Stanbridge, 48, appointed in April 1991. Staff 29 (men 6, women 23).

Motto Aequam memento servare mentem (Remember to keep a balanced mind).

Background The school opened in 1958 and is set in what was once the orchard and gardens of Shottery Manor, a restored 14th-century house around which a modern school has been built. The school is a mile from the centre of Stratford in the quiet residential hamlet of Shottery. Generous playing fields. Substantially over-subscribed, with about seven applications for every place; admits 60 girls a year. House and form system central to school organisation; community links through social services programme; links with local business through Young Enterprise Scheme, school bank and work-experience. Duke of Edinburgh Award Scheme. Charity fund-raising includes sponsorship of children at Thandigudi school in southern India. Termly newsletters and school magazine.

Alumni Jane Barker, financial director of Stock Exchange.

Streaming *None*

Approach to discipline 'There is a code of conduct that girls are expected to follow.'

Uniform Full purple-and-blue uniform for years 7 to 11. Sixth-form dress, based on navy and white, with 'smart, professional look'. High standard expected.

Homework Average 11-year-old, seven hours a week; 14-year-old, 11 hours; 16-year-old, 15 hours.

Vocational qualifications *None*

Inspection October 1995: 'A very good school which enables pupils to achieve high standards. It is a well-ordered community where the quality of relationships is excellent and the progress and esteem of all its members are nurtured. The school is characterised by warmth, friendliness, care and respect for others, and courtesy and mutual support are the norm. The school has very many strengths, not least those that the pupils themselves bring to the school.'

PATE'S GRAMMAR SCHOOL

Princess Elizabeth Way
Cheltenham
Gloucestershire GL51 0HG
Tel (01242) 523169
Fax (01242) 232775

- National ranking 19 (3, 10, 5, 17)
- GCSE 100% (100%)
- A-levels 53% (A/B); 96% (A/E)
- Higher education 98% (Oxford 7, Cambridge 10)

- Grant-maintained
- Mixed grammar
- Pupils 920
- Boys (11–18) 460
- Girls (11–18) 460

- Sixth form 319 (35%)
- Education authority *Gloucestershire*

Headteacher David Barnes, 57, appointed in February 1986. Staff 54 (men 32, women 22).

Motto Patebit tum quod latuit (So shall be revealed that which is hidden).

Background Elizabeth I granted estates in 1574 to Richard Pate to endow the first school in Cheltenham. By 1905 Pate's Foundation had grown to a boys' grammar and a separate grammar school for girls; in 1986 a single co-educational school was established in Princess Elizabeth Way; became grant-maintained in September 1990. Over-subscribed, with 5.8 applications for each place. Total new school constructed in September 1995. Winner of first European Young Enterprise competition in 1990; two sixth-formers in England team for 1991 World Schools' Debating competition; national debating finalists in 1995; continental work-experience; 'very strong' music and drama; Duke of Edinburgh Award Scheme and combined Cadet Force. International representatives in rugby (1995), badminton, modern pentathlon (1995), football (1996), diving (1996) and chess (1996). Girls' hockey team were national finalists in 1990; girls' netball team national finalists in 1996 and 1997.

Alumni Gustav Holst, composer; Desmond Wilcox, television producer and film-maker; Brian Jones, member of Rolling Stones; Felicity Lott, soprano; Sarah Walker, mezzo-soprano; Elaine Donnelly, actress; Sir Frederick Handley Page, aircraft constructor; Gilbert Jessop, former Gloucestershire and England cricketer; Sue Limb, journalist and writer; Pat Smythe, international show jumper; Sir Benjamin Baker, engineer and designer of Forth railway bridge, Aswan Dam and London Underground.

Streaming *None*

Approach to discipline Proud of reputation. 'We encourage good discipline by setting a tone that makes for constructive and purposeful conduct, and that lays stress on courtesy and consideration for others.'

Uniform Black blazer with badge, school tie, scarlet sweater (optional), grey trousers/skirt. Sixth form has its own uniform. Enforced 'firmly but fairly'.

Homework Average 11-year-old, five hours 30 minutes a week; 14-year-old, eight to 10 hours; 16-year-old, 15 hours.

Vocational qualifications *None*

Inspection March 1995: 'A high-achieving school with many excellent characteristics.'; 'Good achievements are spread across the curriculum.'; 'An essentially orderly, purposeful and happy community.'; 'The pupils are very well motivated. They have enquiring minds and combine intellectual curiosity with genuine enthusiasm for their work. Pupils throughout the school are extremely well-behaved.'; 'In view of the excellent standards of achievement alongside prudent financial stewardship, the school offers very good value for money.'

Primary schools Two-thirds of 60 feeder schools send pupils each year.

AYLESBURY HIGH SCHOOL

Walton Road
Aylesbury
Buckinghamshire HP21 7ST
Tel (01296) 415237
Fax (01296) 415237
E-mail: aylhigh@aol.com
Internet: http://www.member.aol.com/aylhigh

- National ranking 20 (44, 16 = , 49, 21)
- GCSE 100% (99%)
- A-levels 52% (A/B); 96% (A/E)
- Higher education 97% (Oxford 7, Cambridge 4)

- Girls' grammar
- Pupils 1,100
- Boys *Not applicable*
- Girls (12–18) 1,100
- Sixth form 380 (35%)
- Education authority *Buckinghamshire*

Headteacher Elizabeth Jane Wainwright, 46, appointed in September 1992. Staff 63 (men 13, women 50).

Motto *None*

Background Founded in 1959 on wooded parkland 10 minutes' walk from Aylesbury town centre. The school has grown steadily, adding a Technology Centre in 1993; drama studio and extra classrooms will open in 1997. 'Broad and balanced curriculum'; up to GCSE, girls follow National Curriculum plus expressive arts and humanities subjects. Sixth-formers' supplementary studies include information technology, humanities, communication skills, religious studies and community service. Emphasis on contributing to outside community. Close links with neighbouring Aylesbury Grammar School for boys. Waiting list for places.

Alumni Lynda Bellingham, actress (Oxo mum, *All Creatures Great and Small*); Margaret Campbell, flautist.

Streaming Small amount of setting, including mathematics in years 10 and 11.

Approach to discipline 'Relaxed but firm.' Few rules, strong pastoral system, emphasis on mutual respect between staff and students.

Uniform Navy skirt, navy jumper, white shirt/ blouse. No uniform for sixth-formers and variety of colours offered in year 11.

Homework Average 12-year-old, seven hours 30 minutes a week; 14-year-old, eight hours; 16-year-old, 10 hours 30 minutes.

Vocational qualifications *None*

Primary schools Bedgrove Middle; Broughton Middle; Haddenham Middle; Turnfurlong Middle; Wendover CE Middle; Weston Turnville CE Combined.

DR CHALLONER'S GRAMMAR SCHOOL

Chesham Road
Amersham
Buckinghamshire HP6 5HA
Tel (01494) 721685
Fax (01494) 721862
E-mail: dcgrammar@aol.com
Internet: http://www.members.aol.com/ dcgrammar/school/dcgsmain.htm

- National ranking 21 (39, 63, 46, 28)
- GCSE 100% (99%)
- A-levels 52% (A/B); 95% (A/E)
- Higher education 96% (Oxford 18, Cambridge 4)

- Boys' grammar
- Pupils 1,086
- Boys (12–18) 1,086
- Girls *Not applicable*
- Sixth form 380 (35%)
- Education authority *Buckinghamshire*

Headteacher Graham Chadwick Hill, 55, appointed in January 1993. Staff 65 (men 45, women 20).

Motto Ad astra, per aspera (To the stars, through toil).

Background In 1624, Dr Robert Challoner provided in his will for the building of a free grammar school in Amersham, a small town in south Buckinghamshire on the edge of the Chilterns and convenient for London (close to Metropolitan Line station). The school was in Old Amersham until it moved to its current site in 1903. Since the 1950s, there have been regular and extensive building programmes. Since 1980: 11 science laboratories, three language laboratories, four computer networks, art and pottery rooms, design and technology centre, sixth-form centre; new history and geography suites plus drama studio opened in 1995/6. Over-subscription results in about four applications for every place. Expeditions in 1996 to Ecuador, Egypt, eastern Mediterranean and Ethiopia; skiing trip to Canada. Sport is 'very impressive', with county, national and international competitors: under-16 soccer team were national champions in 1993. Old Challoners' Society; active parent-teacher association known as Friends. Identified in 1995 Ofsted report as 'outstandingly successful'.

Streaming Pupils banded in mathematics and foreign languages for GCSE. Some pupils take GCSE French and mathematics a year early.

Approach to discipline 'Firm but fair. One of the key aims of the school is to provide a caring environment in which pupils feel that sensitive and sympathetic help and advice are readily available.' Form-tutors responsible for day-to-day care; year-tutors deal initially with disciplinary matters; after-school detention is normal punishment for serious offences.

Uniform Years 8 to 11: grey/black trousers, navy blazer, white/grey/light blue shirt, school tie, black/grey/navy V-neck pullover, 'conventional' shoes. Sixth-formers wear conventional suit, or sports jacket and trousers, sixth-form tie.

Homework Average 12-year-old, four to five hours a week; average 14-year-old, six to seven hours; 16-year-old, eight to nine hours.

Vocational qualifications *None*

Inspection Spring 1994: 'Dr Challoner's Grammar School is a very successful school, which is highly regarded by parents and the wider community. It sets, and achieves, high academic standards in lessons and in public examinations. The pupils are attentive, motivated by their work and have well-developed learning skills. The quality of teaching is a strength of the school. Teachers have a good command of their subjects.'

Primary schools The Beacon School, Amersham; Butlers Court Combined, Beaconsfield; Chalfont St Giles Middle; Chalfont St Peter CE Middle; Chartridge Combined; Chesham Preparatory; Elangeni Middle; Gayhurst School, Gerrards Cross; Gerrards Cross CE Middle; Little Chalfont Combined; Prestwood Middle; Robertswood Combined; The Russell Primary, Chenies; Thorpe House, Gerrards Cross; Woodside Middle, Amersham; St Mary's CE Combined, Amersham.

ST MICHAEL'S CATHOLIC GRAMMAR SCHOOL

Nether Street
North Finchley
London N12 7NJ
Tel (0181) 446 2256
Fax (0181) 343 9598
E-mail: stmichael@rmplc.co.uk

- National ranking 22 (27, 32, 50, 6)
- GCSE 100% (100%)
- A-levels 50% (A/B); 96% (A/E)
- Higher education 98% (Oxford 2)

- Grant-maintained
- Girls' grammar
- Pupils 630
- Boys *Not applicable*
- Girls (11–18) 630
- Sixth form 152 (24%)
- Education authority *Barnet*

Headteacher Ursula Morrissey, 47, appointed in March 1995. Staff 43 (men 12, women 31).

Motto Quis ut deus (Who is like unto God).

Background The school grew from a boarding school started in 1906 by The Sisters of the Poor Child Jesus; became voluntary-aided Catholic girls' grammar. Compact school comprising four adjacent buildings of widely-contrasting styles: sixth-form centre is The Grange, adapted 19th-century private house with conservatory, lawn, and surrounded by trees; lower school, stone building from early 1900s; main school built in 1950s. Tennis courts and small playing field. Over-subscribed, with three applications per place. Sporting achievements in badminton, trampolining, athletics, tennis and netball. Girls normally take 10 or 11 GCSEs; all sixth-formers take three A-levels or two A-levels and two AS-levels and complementary studies. Strong music tradition; range of modern languages. 'The school is first and foremost a Catholic school. We aim to see that Christian values permeate all aspects of the school including discipline, curriculum and general attitudes.'

Streaming Only in mathematics.

Approach to discipline Girls expected to treat others with respect: 'Anything else is unacceptable.' Firm discipline without regimentation. 'In lessons the atmosphere is generally warm but firm and well-organised. The pace is fast. Punctuality is important.'

Uniform Years 7 to 11: purple kilt-style skirt, purple jumper, mauve blouse, blazer with crest. Sixth-formers required to wear 're spectable dress'. Very strictly enforced.

Homework Average 11-year-old, 10 hours a week; 14-year-old, 10 hours; 16-year-old, 20 hours.

Vocational qualifications RSA, Typing, Computer Literacy and Information Technology.

Inspection March 1995: 'St Michael's is a high-achieving school where relationships are excellent. The pupils are happy and well cared for morally, socially and spiritually. The school's national reputation in the Catholic community is justifiably high.'; 'All pupils read accurately, expressively and with understanding. They read widely. The pupils write accurately and are articulate. They are highly numerate. The pupils' ability to use information technology in a wide range of contexts is good.'; 'The pupils' attitudes to learning are exemplary.'

Primary schools St Vincent's RC Primary; St Monica's RC Primary; St Bernadette's RC Primary, Harrow; St George's RC Primary, Enfield; Our Lady of Muswell RC Primary.

SKIPTON GIRLS' HIGH SCHOOL

Gargrave Road
Skipton
North Yorkshire BD23 1QL
Tel (01756) 792115
Fax (01756) 701068
E-mail: sghscholl@aol.com

- National ranking 23 (42, 19, 15, 34)
- GCSE 100% (99%)
- A-levels 49% (A/B); 97% (A/E)
- Higher education 90% (Cambridge 3)

- Girls' grammar
- Pupils 618
- Boys *Not applicable*
- Girls (11–18) 618
- Sixth form 166 (27%)
- Education authority *North Yorkshire*

Headteacher Diana Chambers, 54, appointed in September 1987. Staff 38 (men 10, women 28).

Motto Qui s'estime petyt, deviendra grand (He who considers himself small shall become great).

Background Set in pleasant grounds on edge of Skipton, the original buildings date from founding in 1886 from the Petyt Trust; additions include hall, gymnasium, laboratories and classrooms, with new extension completed 1993; new dance-drama studio opened by Dame Judi Dench in May 1996; library re-furbished in 1997. Sixth-form centre in West Bank, Edwardian house on opposite side of Gargrave Road. The school takes top 30% of ability range, substantially over-subscribed from outside local area; girls travel from West Yorkshire and Lancashire; pressure growing annually. All in-district children tested, plus 120–130 from out of district, for 87 places. Strengths include art and music, dance/drama: orchestra, choir, and madrigals. Flourishing Old Girls' Guild. 'Very strong' Duke of Edinburgh Award Scheme.

Alumni Elizabeth Harwood, opera singer.

Streaming Pupils are only in sets in mathematics, from year 9 and in English, from year 10.

Approach to discipline Discipline seen to be of prime importance and as a 'partnership' between pupils, parents and staff. 'Dealt with by form teachers and, if necessary, senior staff. Serious offences such as bullying or truancy are rare; if they occur, they are dealt with by head or deputies in consultation with parents.'

Uniform Navy skirt/trousers, white blouse, navy-and-gold tie, navy jumper/school sweatshirt. Strictly enforced.

Homework Average 11-year-old, five hours; 14-year-old, six hours 30 minutes; 16-year-old, 10 hours. (Up to five hours per subject at A-level.)

Vocational qualifications *None*

Inspection March 1994: 'Skipton Girls' High School is a very good school. Pupils achieve high standards which reflect their capabilities and the high expectations of parents, pupils, teachers and the wider community.'; 'The school is a very orderly community where pupils are respected and supported as individuals. The school has clear and well-established values, and pupils are able to communicate their beliefs very successfully. Good relationships exist at every level in the school and it is highly valued by the local community.'

Primary schools Water Street Primary; Carleton CE Primary; Embsay CE Primary; Parish CE Primary; Bradley Primary; St Stephen's Primary; Grassington CE Primary; Threshfield Primary.

STRATHEARN SCHOOL

188 Belmont Road
Belfast BT4 2AU
Tel (01232) 471595
Fax (01232) 650555
E-mail: strathearn@schools.class–ni.org.uk

- National ranking 24 (12, 111, 82, 91)
- GCSE 100% (100%)
- A-levels 48% (A/B); 97% (A/E)
- Higher education 78% (Oxford 2)

- Girls' grammar
- Pupils 750
- Boys *Not applicable*
- Girls (11–18) 750
- Sixth form 203 (27%)
- Education authority *Belfast Education and Library Board*

Headteacher David Manning, appointed in September 1997. Staff 54 (men 11, women 43).

Motto *None*

Background Founded in 1929 following the purchase of Strathearn House and its 18-acre grounds. First assembly hall added to original building in 1933; preparatory department transferred to Penrhyn House, close to main school, in 1953; first science block completed in 1954, with an extension completed in 1971; additional laboratories added in 1995. Sixth-form centre built in 1972; arts and careers suite in 1985. New technology and information technology centre opened in January 1996. Purpose-built sports hall houses facilities for many sports, including indoor hockey, badminton (five courts), volleyball, netball and indoor tennis.

Alumni Anne Gregg, travel writer and broadcaster; Ingrid Surgenor, international accompanist.

Streaming *None*

Approach to discipline Copy of responsibility code sent to parents on enrolment. Aim to create environment 'in which the growth of individual values, attitudes and beliefs is fostered together with an awareness of personal responsibility and standards of accepted behaviour'.

Uniform 'Distinctive, comfortable, serviceable.'

Homework Average 11-year-old, two to three hours a week; 14-year-old, four to five hours; 16-year-old, six hours.

Vocational qualifications *None*

Primary schools Penrhyn (Strathearn Preparatory Department): Strandtown Primary; Holywood Primary; Strand Primary; Gilnahirk Primary.

BISHOP WORDSWORTH'S SCHOOL

11 The Close
Salisbury
Wiltshire SP1 2EB
Tel (01722) 333851
Fax (01722) 325899

- National ranking 25 (56 = , 23, 39, 36)
- GCSE 100% (98%)
- A-levels 48% (A/B); 93% (A/E)
- Higher education 97% (Oxford 1, Cambridge 2)

- Grant-maintained
- Boys' grammar

- Pupils 763
- Boys (11–18) 763
- Girls *Not applicable*
- Sixth form 197 (26%)
- Education authority *Wiltshire*

Headteacher Clive D. Barnett, 47, appointed in September 1992. Staff 46 (men 35, women 11).

Motto Veritas in caritate (Truth in a caring society).

Background Founded in 1890 by John Wordsworth, Bishop of Salisbury (1885–1911). Grant-maintained since April 1994; formerly voluntary-controlled, with church playing important part: monthly cathedral services, Church of England chaplain. Most school buildings on a site in the northeast corner of the Cathedral Close, bordered by the Close Wall. They include an early Tudor manor house, late Victorian chapel block and more modern buildings that house laboratories, classrooms, gymnasium, music school and library. Three applications for each place. Curriculum enrichment project for sixth-formers. Swimming pool on site; games fields half a mile away. Rugby a particular strength: fixtures against independent schools, finalists in national cup competition in 1991; under-14 cricket team were 1992 and 1994 county champions. Traditional and academic curriculum: notable for quality of English, history, modern languages and science.

Alumni Andrew Harvey, BBC Television newsreader; John Shaw, England hockey captain; Ralph Fiennes, actor; Hamish Milne, concert pianist; Bishop Mervyn Alexander, Roman Catholic Bishop of Clifton; Richard Hill, England rugby international; Colin Sharman, KPMG senior partner.

Streaming In French and mathematics from year 9; in science from year 10, but only with creation of a top set.

Approach to discipline Traditional, with clear rules and moral standards. 'As a boy matures, we feel he should take more and more responsibility for his actions within this context.'

Uniform Dark-blue blazer with school crest, dark trousers, white/grey shirt, school tie. Strictly enforced, with limited relaxation in sixth form.

Homework Average 11-year-old, seven hours

30 minutes a week; 14-year-old, 10 hours; 16-year-old, 15 hours.

Vocational qualifications *None*

Inspection March 1996: 'Despite inadequate accommodation, Bishop Wordsworth's School provides a good quality of education for its pupils, who achieve high standards.'; 'The quality of teaching is good across most of the curriculum, with a very low proportion of unsatisfactory teaching. As with learning, teaching quality is higher at Key Stage 4 and in the sixth form. Teachers' expectations of pupils are invariably high and the school has considerable expertise at its disposal, though a minority of lessons at Key Stage 3 could be improved by clearer objectives and more appropriate tasks.'; 'The quality of the school's senior management is generally good, but more variable at the level of middle management. The headmaster provides strong leadership for a committed and experienced staff.'; 'Pupils respond well to the emphasis that is placed on personal responsibility and most behave well in an over-crowded site.'

Primary schools St Mark's CE Junior; Harnham Junior; Swan Preparatory. More than 80 feeder schools.

THE SKINNERS' SCHOOL

St John's Road
Tunbridge Wells
Kent TN4 9PG
Tel (01892) 520732
Fax (01892) 549356

- National ranking 26 (81, 48=, 37, 37)
- GCSE 100% (97%)
- A-levels 45% (A/B); 96% (A/E)
- Higher education 90% (Oxford 3, Cambridge 1)

- Grant-maintained
- Boys' grammar
- Pupils 708
- Boys (11–18) 708
- Girls *Not applicable*
- Sixth form 192 (27%)
- Education authority *Kent*

Headteacher Peter Braggins, 51, appointed in January 1992. Staff 43 (men 35, women 8).

Motto In Christo fratres (Brothers in Christ); To God only be all glory (motto of the Skinners' Company).

Background Founded by the Skinners' Company, one of the 'Great 12' City of London livery companies, in 1887. A voluntary-aided boys' grammar from 1944, it became grant-maintained in April 1992. Close to the centre of Tunbridge Wells, two impressive Victorian buildings give character to the school's accommodation. New technology and art block, including six classrooms. Extensive playing fields of more than 20 acres are 15 minutes' walk from main site. Significantly over-subscribed at 11, with 1.5 applications per place. Rugby and other team and individual sports are strong; 20 teams play inter-school fixtures; under-15s were 1992 national rugby cup-winners and under-16s are All-England seven-a-side champions. Music a strength, with touring orchestra; large Combined Cadet Force; established record of community service. Duke of Edinburgh Award Scheme.

Alumni Bob Woolmer, former Kent and England cricketer, Warwickshire coach; Alec McCowen, actor; Christopher Hogwood, musician and conductor.

Streaming Pupils streamed in mathematics from year 8, and in French from year 9.

Approach to discipline General code of conduct. 'Discipline is set by example with guidance from teachers, especially form-teachers who exercise pastoral responsibility.' Exclusions, temporary or indefinite, are rare.

Uniform Blazer, dark-grey trousers, house tie for younger boys. Grey suit for older pupils.

Homework Average 11-year-old, seven hours 30 minutes a week; 14-year-old, 10 hours; 16-year-old, minimum of 12 hours 30 minutes.

Vocational qualifications Foreign Language in Commerce; City and Guilds, Information Technology.

Primary schools Claremont Primary; St John's CE Primary; St James's Primary; Pembury Primary; Langton Green Primary.

KING EDWARD VI FIVE WAYS

Scotland Lane
Bartley Green
Birmingham
West Midlands B32 4BT
Tel (0121) 475 3535
Fax (0121) 477 8555

Internet: http://www.rmplc.co.uk/eduweb/sites/ke5ways

- National ranking 27 (20, 88, 131, 127)
- GCSE 100% (100%)
- A-levels 45% (A/B); 91% (A/E)
- Higher education 88% (Oxford 4, Cambridge 3)

- Grant-maintained
- Boys' grammar (mixed from September 1998)
- Pupils 702
- Boys (11–18) 648
- Girls (16–18) 54
- Sixth form 220 (31%)
- Education authority *Birmingham*

Headteacher John Geoffrey Knowles, 49, appointed in April 1990. Staff 43 (men 36, women 7).

Motto Dieu et mon droit (God and honour).

Background One of seven Schools of King Edward VI in Birmingham, with financial support from the King Edward Foundation. Opened in 1883 at Five Ways, just south of the city centre; moved in 1958 to 30-acre site on southwest tip of Birmingham, bordering Bartley Reservoir and looking out to Frankley Beeches. Design centre added in 1986; £500,000 sixth-form centre in 1991; extensive alterations to main building; new music school, including recording studio, opened in 1992; substantial conversion to provide centre for teaching Classics and social sciences. Library refurbished in 1994, followed by science laboratories and classrooms; new sports hall in 1996. Over-subscribed, with more than 1,000 applications for 96 places; since 1994, entry no longer restricted to boys living within Birmingham; applications welcomed from parts of Hereford and Worcester, and the Black Country. Established reputation for use of information technology throughout the curriculum. Main team sports: rugby, hockey, netball, cross-country, cricket, sailing and tennis. From September 1998, the school will take a mixed intake of 150 pupils a year, making it the only mixed grammar in the Birmingham area; £2.5 million building programme including increased provision for art and technology, science, modern languages and English.

Alumni Sir Michael Checkland, former director-general of BBC; Professor David Cannadine, historian; Keith Fielding, England rugby player.

Streaming *None*

Approach to discipline 'Care and concern for the individual is paramount; anti-social behaviour is not tolerated. There is a limited set of rules and standing orders that define the school's disciplinary policy. All pupils may apply to be prefects and are involved in ensuring the school runs smoothly.'

Uniform Black blazer with badge, dark-grey trousers, white shirt, school tie, black 'polished' shoes. Sixth-formers wear 'business dress' (jacket and tie). 'Very strictly enforced.'

Homework Average 11-year-old, five hours a week; 14-year-old, 10 hours; 16-year-old, 15 hours.

Vocational qualifications *None*

Inspection October 1995: 'Five Ways is a school with many good and some excellent features. It serves its pupils and parents well. There are, however, areas where further development is needed.'; 'The lessons seen revealed evidence of both high achievement in relation to pupils' abilities, and underachievement.'; 'Pupils read competently, but not widely enough. Although most write with an acceptable degree of clarity and accuracy, weaknesses in written work inhibit achievement for a significant minority. The great majority of pupils are fluent and confident as speakers.'; 'Teachers are conscientious and committed to the school. Most give willingly of their free time to promote pupils' interests. Their subject expertise is of a high order and the teaching is, in general, planned carefully and organised efficiently.'

CLITHEROE ROYAL GRAMMAR SCHOOL

York Street
Clitheroe
Lancashire BB7 2DJ
Tel (01200) 423118
Fax (01200) 442177

- National ranking 28 (24, 21, 26, 18)
- GCSE 100% (100%)
- A-levels 43% (A/B); 95% (A/E)
- Higher education 93% (Oxford 1, Cambridge 6)

- Grant-maintained

- Mixed grammar
- Pupils 1,102
- Boys (11–18) 466
- Girls (11–18) 636
- Sixth form 485 (44%)
- Education authority *Lancashire*

Headteacher Stuart Holt, 53, appointed in April 1991. Staff 72 (men 34, women 38).

Motto In saxo condita (Founded on rock).

Background Founded in 1554; previously separate boys' and girls' grammar schools amalgamated in 1985; split-site school, with modernised and re-designed sixth-form centre on site of former boys' school in York Street; became grant-maintained in September 1991. After amalgamation, purpose-built specialist facilities for computing, technology, ceramics and music; new gymnasium. Over-subscribed, with three applicants per place. All pupils take 10 GCSEs; in sixth form, three subjects out of a choice of 26 options; in addition, all students take General Studies A-level and one Additional Studies subject such as PE, Geology, Archaeology, Spanish to GCSE. Young Enterprise Scheme; Sainsbury Engineering Education Scheme; annual three-day Industry Conference for lower-sixth pupils; week-long workshadowing for upper-sixth; Blue Sky Initiative; Venture schemes. Success in competitive sports, with county or national representatives in soccer, cricket, tennis, golf, cross-country, athletics and skiing. Choir, school orchestra and wind band; annual musical production; art, drama and debating. Exchange links with France, Germany and United States.

Alumni Baroness Hart of South Lanark, former Labour MP and minister for overseas development; Pattie Coldwell, television presenter; Jane Forrest, golfer; Cyril Washbrook, former Lancashire and England cricketer; Bryan Cowgill, television producer and former BBC1 controller; Sir Derek Spencer, Solicitor-General and Conservative MP for Brighton Pavilion; Martin Dobson, former Everton and England footballer.

Streaming *None*

Approach to discipline 'School rules are kept to a minimum. These are approached in an atmosphere that is firm but fair and which seeks to promote co-operation and trust.'

Uniform Boys: royal-blue blazer with crest, dark-grey trousers, grey/white shirt, blue-red-and-gold school tie, grey V-neck pull-over, grey socks, black shoes. Girls: royal-blue blazer, dark-grey skirt, white blouse, school tie, royal-blue V-neck pullover, white socks, black shoes. Sixth-formers wear black blazer and black trousers/skirt. Staff vigilant; regulations adhered to 'in spirit of co-operation rather than enforcement'.

Homework Average 11-year-old, five hours 30 minutes a week; 14-year-old, 10 hours; 16-year-old, at least five hours per subject.

Vocational qualifications RSA, Typing, Word-processing.

Inspection January 1997: 'A fine school with many outstanding features and very few weaknesses. It is very well managed; the teaching is good, and pupils' personal and academic achievements are very high.'; 'Pupils' excellent speaking, listening, reading, writing and numerical skills make a very significant contribution to their high attainment and enhance the quality of learning in all subjects.'; 'The strength of the teaching rests on the teachers' good command of their subjects, thorough and careful planning and, above all, on an insistence on high standards. Teachers' relationships with pupils are excellent: praise and encouragement are used effectively.'; 'Good behaviour and self-discipline are underpinned by the consistently high expectations of the staff and the school's clear code of conduct.'; 'The school is very well managed, and the headteacher and senior staff provide far-sighted and strong leadership; they ensure equality of opportunity for all pupils and maintain excellent discipline.'; 'Some of the teaching accommodation is cramped or otherwise inadequate, for example in art, design technology, drama and physical education.'

Primary schools Pendle County Primary; Brookside County Primary; Samlesbury CE Primary; St Leonard's CE Primary; Whalley CE Primary; Read CE Primary; St Mary's CE Primary.

PARKSTONE GRAMMAR SCHOOL

Sopers Lane
Poole
Dorset BH17 7EP
Tel (01202) 697456
Fax (01202) 696268
E-mail: parkstone@lds.co.uk

- National ranking 29 (21, 24, 12, 23)
- GCSE 100% (100%)
- A-levels 42% (A/B); 93% (A/E)
- Higher education 83% (Oxford 6, Cambridge 2)

- Grant-maintained
- Girls' grammar
- Pupils 920
- Boys *Not applicable*
- Girls (12–18) 920
- Sixth form 280 (30%)
- Education authority *Dorset*

Headteacher Janet Susanna Morrison, 44, appointed in September 1997. Staff 54 (men 20, women 34).

Motto The encouragement of excellence.

Background Founded in 1905 as a mixed independent school. Moved to purpose-built school in 1961 on large, pleasant site and playing fields. Extensive refurbishment since it acquired grant-maintained status. New classroom block and specialist accommodation for science, mathematics and technology; large assembly hall, canteen, gymnasium, fitness room and resources centre/library; new drama studio. New sixth-form centre and music studio in December 1997. Takes only top 16% of ability range; waiting list for each year of the school, with 2.5 applications per year 8 place. Musical strengths include three orchestras, three choirs, jazz band, recorder group, string ensemble. Regional and national success in sport, particularly swimming, cricket, volleyball, soccer, athletics, netball, hockey and tennis. Annually, year 10 students spend two weeks on work-experience; annual careers convention; community service scheme. Foreign exchanges and overseas work placements. School's 'mission statement': 'We aim to make the most of our talents in order to serve others and be happy.'

Streaming Setting in mathematics and French.

Approach to discipline Firm but caring; problems solved quickly, with parents called in swiftly. Excellent reputation in the areas of punctuality, litter, uniform and attendance. Bullying, smoking or worse 'are not problems at the school'.

Uniform Black blazer, grey skirt, grey jumper, yellow blouse. The sixth form wear smart working dress with discreet make-up and jewellery.

Homework Average 12-year-old, seven to eight hours a week; 14-year-old, 11 to 12 hours; 16-year-old, 15 to 18 hours.

Vocational qualifications *None*

Inspection February 1996: 'A very good school with some excellent features and some aspects which need further development.'; 'It is a well-ordered community with many strengths, not least those that the pupils themselves contribute to the school.'; 'Many teachers, for example in art, religious education, physical education, modern foreign languages and music, successfully transmit their enthusiasm for the subject and inspire pupils to develop their talents and skills.'; 'There is scope for development in mathematics and in some aspects of science, particularly at sixth-form level, if standards in these subjects are to be improved further.'; 'Standards of behaviour are excellent and pupils respond well to opportunities to take responsibility and to contribute to the life of the school.'

Primary schools Baden Powell and St Peter's CE Middle; Broadstone Middle; Canford Heath Middle; Haymoor Middle; Oakdale Middle; St Michael's CE Middle, Wimborne.

KING EDWARD VI SCHOOL

Church Street
Stratford-upon-Avon
Warwickshire CV37 6HB
Tel (01789) 293351
Fax (01789) 293564

- National ranking 30 (19, 25, 10, 61)
- GCSE 100% (100%)
- A-levels 40% (A/B); 93% (A/E)
- Higher education 81% (Oxford 2, Cambridge 1)

- Boys' grammar
- Pupils 432
- Boys (11–18) 432
- Girls *Not applicable*
- Sixth form 117 (27%)
- Education authority *Warwickshire*

Headteacher Timothy Peter Moore-Bridger, 51, appointed in April 1997. Staff 27 (men 20, women 7).

Motto Age quod agis (What you do, do properly).

Background Although a school existed in Stratford-upon-Avon in the 13th century, first extant charters date from 1482 and 1553 when Stratford Grammar School was renamed and refounded by King Edward VI. Two 15th-century buildings still in use, but most built in 1960s with laboratories, classrooms, gymnasium and heated indoor swimming pool supplementing 1930s additions. Science and technology building added in 1987; new art room and sixth-form common room in 1994; new school hall for music, drama and sports opened in 1997. School site in centre of Stratford and 20-acre playing fields within a mile. Rugby a strength; pupils have represented Great Britain at rowing and fencing. Voluntary-aided; takes top 16% of ability range; over-subscribed, with four applications per place.

Alumni William Shakespeare, playwright; General Sir Richard Gale, commander of sixth airborne division for D-day landings and former deputy supreme commander of Allied forces in Europe; Tim Pigott-Smith, actor; Richard Tracey, Conservative MP for Surbiton and former sports minister; Richard Spender, war poet; Reginald Warneford, VC.

Streaming Pupils in sets for mathematics for years 9 to 11.

Approach to discipline 'Standards are clearly conveyed and consistently upheld within a constantly-developing framework of pastoral care.'

Uniform Blazer with badge, school tie, flannels for years 7 to 11. Blazer and flannels, or grey suit, school tie for sixth-formers. Strictly enforced.

Homework Average 11-year-old, seven hours 30 minutes a week; 14-year-old, seven hours 30 minutes; 16-year-old, 15 hours.

Vocational qualifications *None*

WEALD OF KENT GRAMMAR SCHOOL FOR GIRLS

Tudeley Lane
Tonbridge
Kent TN9 2JP
Tel (01732) 352819
Fax (01732) 770536

- National ranking 31 (65, 101, 40=, 77)
- GCSE 100% (98%)
- A-levels 23% (A/B); 83% (A/E)

- Higher education 51%

- Girls' grammar
- Pupils 830
- Boys *Not applicable*
- Girls (11–18) 830
- Sixth form 200 (24%)
- Education authority *Kent*

Headteacher Susan Ann Rowell, 50, appointed in April 1991. Staff 50 (men 8, women 42).

Motto Encouraging excellence.

Background Started as a girls' technical high school before becoming grammar school in 1978; 30 years on current site in modern compact building in attractive grounds on edge of Tonbridge. Pupils mainly from west Kent. Rapid increase in popularity since 1992; expanded to four-form entry to meet over-subscription: 133 applications for 120 places in 1997. New sixth-form common room and study area; also science laboratory, newly-refurbished computer room and business studies room, additional practice rooms for music, and new mathematics suite; floodlit netball and tennis facilities; also hockey and athletics. Strong junior teams in netball and tennis; two pupils represent Kent at netball; one pupil represents England at karate; one pupil won national award in technology in 1996; several national awards for creative writing. Strong emphasis on high academic achievement and pastoral care of pupils. Commitment to extra-curricular activities: Duke of Edinburgh Award; extensive music provision in liaison with Kent Music School. Investor in People Award.

Streaming Mathematics from year 8; science from year 9; English and languages in years 10 and 11.

Approach to discipline Few rules, but must be obeyed. 'The atmosphere within the school is positive and standards of behaviour are very high.'

Uniform Pale burgundy sweater with cream logo, cream open-neck shirt, navy skirt, navy blazer. New in 1992. Strictly enforced: school stockist, makes and styles specified.

Homework Average 11-year-old, five hours a week; 14-year-old, seven hours 30 minutes; 16-year-old, 10 hours.

Vocational qualifications *None*

Inspection November 1996: 'A very good

school. Strong emphasis is placed on the personal development and academic achievement of pupils. The good behaviour of pupils and the very positive relationship within the school community effectively support learning. The school gives very good value for money.'; 'In lessons and other work, pupils make good progress in all subjects The girls are confident and articulate. They plan well and successfully research information for themselves. Information technology and mathematical skills are applied well in other subjects.'; 'Pupils benefit from high expectations and good teaching. This is a strength of the school. In three-quarters of lessons teaching is good or very good. Teachers have a very strong command of their subject and plan their lessons carefully. However, at times, pupils are insufficiently challenged.'; 'Pupils work hard. Their attitude to learning is extremely positive. They collaborate well and learn successfully together. Behaviour is particularly good.'; 'Some accommodation is inadequate, particularly for design and technology and science.'

Primary schools Woodlands Junior, Tonbridge; Amherst Junior, Sevenoaks; Sevenoaks County Primary; Pembury County Primary; Sussex Road County Primary, Tonbridge.

THE LATYMER SCHOOL

Haselbury Road
Edmonton
London N9 9TN
Tel (0181) 807 4037
Fax (0181) 807 4125
E-mail: latymer_edu@msn.com
Internet: http://schoolsite.edex.net.uk/138

- National ranking 32 (34, 31, 17, 49)
- GCSE 99% (99%)
- A-levels 65% (A/B); 97% (A/E)
- Higher education 95% (Oxford 4, Cambridge 18)

- Grant-maintained
- Mixed grammar
- Pupils 1,297
- Boys (11–18) 648
- Girls (11–18) 649
- Sixth form 386 (30%)
- Education authority *Enfield*

Headteacher Geoffrey Thomas Mills, 61, appointed in September 1983. Staff 81 (men 47, women 34).

Motto Qui patitur vincit (He who endures wins).

Background School founded in 1624 in Edward Latymer's will and moved half a mile to its current site in 1910; became voluntary-aided in 1955; became grant-maintained in 1993; over-subscribed, with nine applications per place; grounds and buildings owned by Latymer Foundation, whose sole purpose is to run the school. Buildings 'sound rather than spectacular'; development plans include refurbishment of science laboratories (eight laboratories already refurbished); improvement to technology accommodation and IT provision via Technology College Initiative under way; good playing fields; 'outstanding' in music. Owns Ysgol Latymer field centre at Cwm Penmachno in North Wales: outdoor pursuits in years 7 and 9; field trips for biology, geography and art. Wide range of extra-curricular activities: four orchestras, four choirs, many ensembles; frequently appear at national and international festivals. House system is very strong, although it is not the basis of pastoral care. Recent increase in Oxbridge places; school has formal links with St John's, Cambridge (Edward Latymer's College) and Corpus Christi (where Latymer's father was a student).

Alumni Bruce Forsyth, entertainer; Johnny Haynes, former Fulham and England soccer player; Eileen Atkins, actress; Margaret Seward, president of British Dental Council; Dr John Horlock, former vice-chancellor of Open University.

Streaming Some setting in mathematics and modern languages.

Approach to discipline 'The emphasis is on self-discipline resulting from the desire to learn and from an awareness of the needs of others. The school is, however, prepared to use sanctions to punish persistent or serious misbehaviour. Parents are always involved in such cases.'

Uniform Boys: navy blazer with school badge, charcoal-grey trousers, white shirt, school tie, navy V-neck pullover, grey/navy/white socks, black shoes. Girls: navy skirt/trousers, white shirt, navy V-neck jumper, school tie, navy/white socks, black shoes. No uniform for sixth form; strictly enforced for years 7 to 11.

Homework Average 11-year-old, six hours 15 minutes a week; 14-year-old, seven hours 30 minutes; 16-year-old, 10 hours.

Vocational qualifications None

Inspection May 1994: 'A good school with several outstanding features.'; 'Pupils are highly-motivated and hard-working. Relationships between pupils and with staff are very good.'; 'Teachers are well-qualified and have an excellent knowledge and command of their subject areas. They work hard with commitment and enthusiasm. However, teachers do not recognise sufficiently either the different learning needs of pupils or pupils' earlier achievements when planning lessons and their further learning.'; 'The traditions and values which the school promotes create loyalty and a sense of belonging in pupils.'

KING EDWARD VI HANDSWORTH SCHOOL

Rose Hill Road
Handsworth
Birmingham
West Midlands B21 9AR
Tel (0121) 554 2342
Fax (0121) 554 3879

- National ranking 33 (16, 14, 44, 74)
- GCSE 99% (100%)
- A-levels 60% (A/B); 97% (A/E)
- Higher education 88% (Oxford 5, Cambridge 3)

- Grant-maintained
- Girls' grammar
- Pupils 877
- Boys Not applicable
- Girls (11–18) 877
- Sixth form 237 (27%)
- Education authority Birmingham

Headteacher Elspeth V. Insch, 48, appointed in September 1989. Staff 53 (men 8, women 45).

Motto Dieu et mon droit (My God and my right).

Background Founded in 1883; moved to current site in 1911; one of seven schools of King Edward in Birmingham. Well-maintained buildings; separate blocks for physical education (with pavilion) and science; two new laboratories in 1992; 'very beautiful and interesting' sixth-form centre completed in

March 1997; intake reflects ethnic mix of the city; school prides itself on relaxed, friendly and well-disciplined atmosphere. Over-subscribed, with nine applications per place. More than half of pupils have instrumental lessons; orchestra, choirs, flute choir, wind band; senior string quartet in 1996 and 1997 finals of National Chamber Music competition. Drama productions, both English and French. Classics, with plays performed in Latin. Winner of NatWest quiz for Birmingham; best Young Enterprise company in Birmingham for two consecutive years; winners of 1995 National Fire Prevention Quiz. Duke of Edinburgh Award Scheme. Sporting achievement, with emphasis on participation and not just winning. Named in Ofsted Chief Inspector's annual report as 'outstandingly successful'.

Alumni Dame Jill Knight, Conservative MP for Edgbaston.

Streaming Pupils divided into five sets for mathematics from year 9.

Approach to discipline 'Firm but fair. We really have very few problems. We aim to contact parents swiftly if a problem arises. We firmly believe in a partnership between pupils, parents and preceptors.' Prides itself on 'very special warm, welcoming atmosphere'.

Uniform Blazer with badge, navy skirt, blue blouse, striped tie, navy jumper with school crest, navy/white socks, black shoes. Very strictly enforced; governors' annual grant of £71 to those on income support or family credit.

Homework Average 11-year-old, five hours a week; 14-year-old, 10 hours; 16-year-old, 12 to 15 hours.

Vocational qualifications *None*

Inspection September 1994: 'A good school.'; 'The school has clearly-stated aims'; 'The quality of teaching and learning is sound, with many good features and no major shortcomings, although learning is inhibited in some cases by short 30-minute lessons. Pupils are well-motivated and are encouraged to achieve their potential.'; 'The school is an orderly and harmonious community providing a secure environment with good standards of behaviour and discipline. The quality of relationships between staff and pupils is built upon mutual respect and co-operation.' *The school has since introduced 25 one-hour lessons.*

Primary schools Cherry Orchard Primary; Deanery CE Primary; Harborne Primary; Maney Hill Primary; Walmley Primary.

TONBRIDGE GRAMMAR SCHOOL FOR GIRLS

Deakin Leas
Tonbridge
Kent TN9 2JR
Tel (01732) 365125
Fax (01732) 359417

- National ranking 34 (11, 47, 35, –)
- GCSE 99% (100%)
- A-levels 60% (A/B); 95% (A/E)
- Higher education 90% (Oxford 5, Cambridge 2)

- Grant-maintained
- Girls' grammar
- Pupils 972
- Boys *Not applicable*
- Girls (11–18) 972
- Sixth form 254 (26%)
- Education authority *Kent*

Headteacher Wendy Carey, 51, appointed in April 1990. Staff 67 (men 16, women 51).

Motto Courage and honour.

Background Founded in 1905; moved in 1913 to current 19-acre site in residential Tonbridge on hill overlooking Kentish Weald; extra buildings added. 'Excellent' facilities for science and technology with new £1.2 million science and technology building opened in October 1996. Extensive playing fields and heated outdoor swimming pool. Grant-maintained since September 1993. Over-subscribed, with 200 applications for 140 places. Broad curriculum. Pupils choose a second language in year 8 from German, Spanish and Latin. Wide choice of A-level and AS-level subjects. High academic achievement. Cultural , sporting and extra-curricular activities. Strengths in drama, art and music; music bursaries available; four choirs, three orchestras, concert band, chamber ensembles. Representative sports teams in hockey, netball, tennis, athletics, swimming, cross-country; ski-teams in various age-groups; also basketball, volleyball, trampoline, rounders and dance. Strong European dimension; visits to France, Germany, Greece, Italy and Spain; work-experience opportunities in Europe. Year 7 residential visit with educational, cultural and social aims in summer term. Keen support by pupils of many charities and strong community links through west Kent Voluntary Service Unit. 'Led by a head who believes strongly in the enabling virtues of single-sex education, the school's aim is to educate and prepare for life able girls from all backgrounds, to allow every girl to realise her full potential in an atmosphere of academic excellence and thereby to develop her self-confidence and self-respect, together with an awareness of her responsibilities to others.' Identified for praise in 1997 Ofsted report.

Alumni Rebecca Stephens, first British woman to climb Everest in 1993; Sarah Wilkinson, first woman fellow at All Souls, Oxford, in 1996; Hayley Allen, Olympic diver; Susan Chandler, England hockey captain; Jacquetta May, actress; Susan Pettett, gold medallist in 1974 Commonwealth Games relay; Jennifer Stinton, international flautist; Shena Mackay, novelist.

Streaming Setting in mathematics and French from year 8.

Approach to discipline 'Firm but supportive. Consultation with parents very important.'

Uniform Tartan skirt, green jersey, polo-neck cotton jumper/white shirt. Sixth-formers can wear their own choice of clothing. Regulations enforced firmly, with letters to parents and reminders to pupils if necessary.

Homework Average 11-year-old, seven hours a week; 14-year-old, eight to nine hours; 16-year-old, 10 hours.

Vocational qualifications Cambridge Information Technology Diploma, in sixth form or earlier.

Inspection March 1996: 'Clear vision and good management, high standards of behaviour in the school, exceptionally good examination results, particularly noteworthy in the three core subjects English, mathematics and science at GCSE, a rich and broad curriculum, and the high levels of confidence and competence reached by the students.'

BANBRIDGE ACADEMY

Lurgan Road
Banbridge
County Down BT32 4AQ

Tel (018206) 23220
Fax (018206) 28122

- National ranking 35 (46, 87, 45, 48)
- GCSE 99% (99%)
- A-levels 59% (A/B); 97% (A/E)
- Higher education 71% (Oxford 2)

- Mixed grammar
- Pupils 1,077
- Boys (11–18) 473
- Girls (11–18) 604
- Sixth form 260 (24%)
- Education authority *Southern Education and Library Board*

Headteacher Raymond Pollock, 47, appointed in March 1996. Staff 61 (men 28, women 33).

Motto Per deum et industriam (Through God and hard work).

Background Founded as private school in 1786; transferred to local authority in 1938; became controlled grammar school in 1973 in dormitory and commercial town of Banbridge (population 12,000) on Upper Bann. Non-denominational; over-subscribed, with average of 1.2 applications per place. Extensive £5m rebuilding programme completed in 1994. On 40-acre estate, formerly owned by local linen family, with generous facilities for hockey, rugby and tennis. Sporting achievements: 1993 Irish schoolboys' hockey champions, represented Ireland in Europe; 1993 Irish schoolgirls' squash champions; 1993 Ulster Schools' Bridge Champions. Council for Education in World Citizenship has raised more than £20,000 for Third World projects. European Studies project.

Alumni Frederick Edward McWilliam, sculptor.

Streaming *None*

Approach to discipline To encourage a co-operative atmosphere; to encourage self-discipline; to enhance self-image and self-esteem.

Uniform Traditional uniform, with petrol-blue, red and black as dominant colours.

Homework Average 11-year-old, six hours 40 minutes a week; 14-year-old, 10 hours; 16-year-old, 10 hours.

Vocational qualifications RSA, Computer Literacy and Information Technology, Word-processing; French for Professional Use; German for Professional Use.

Primary schools Edenderry Primary; Abercorn Primary; Waringstown Primary; Bridge Primary; Dromore Primary; Iveagh Primary; Donacloney Primary; St Mary's Primary; Ballydown Primary; Ballyroney Primary; Maralin Village Primary; Portadown Integrated.

TUNBRIDGE WELLS GIRLS' GRAMMAR SCHOOL

Southfield Road
Tunbridge Wells
Kent TN4 9UJ
Tel (01892) 520902
Fax (01892) 536497

- National ranking 36 (55, 84, 79, –)
- GCSE 99% (98%)
- A-levels 57% (A/B); 98% (A/E)
- Higher education 92%

- Girls' grammar
- Pupils 864
- Boys *Not applicable*
- Girls (11–18) 864
- Sixth form 226 (26%)
- Education authority *Kent*

Headteacher Angela Susan Daly, 48, appointed in April 1993. Staff 51 (men 10, women 41).

Motto Give your best.

Background Moved to current rural site on edge of Tunbridge Wells in 1913, eight years after it was founded. Specialist classrooms, library and assembly hall built in 1950s and 1960s. Major appeal has updated facilities in library, including CD-ROM. Over-subscribed, with 1.5 applications for each place. Some classes are accommodated in old but brightly-coloured and furnished mobile classrooms. Newly-completed extension to music block providing two large rooms, plus 10 practice rooms. Extensive grounds with all-weather courts. Duke of Edinburgh Award Scheme, with 35 involved with Gold, 27 with Silver, and 150 with Bronze. County and national success in netball, hockey, gymnastics, cricket and trampolining. International competition in sailing, riding, gymnastics and athletics. Local, county, and national successes in music.

Alumni Virginia Wade, tennis player; Helen Walker, opera singer. Dame Audrey Emerton, Chief Nursing Adviser to St John's Ambulance Hospital, Jerusalem.

Streaming Flexible grouping in French and mathematics from year 8.

Approach to discipline 'Serious. Highest standards expected and obtained, in and out of school. Mutual teacher–pupil respect means problems are rare. Pastoral care is discreet, supportive and well-regarded.'

Uniform Plaid pleated skirt, plaid tie, white shirt, navy jacket. No sixth-form uniform. Regulations enforced firmly.

Homework Average 11-year-old, five hours a week; 14-year-old, seven hours 30 minutes; 16-year-old, nine hours.

Vocational qualifications *None*

Inspection A very good school. The socio-economic circumstances of the girls are very favourable generally and their attainment on entry into the school is high. The girls make very good progress in their studies, achieving generally high or very high standards compared with national expectations for girls of their ages. Their behaviour and attitudes are excellent.'; 'Girls attain a very high standard in speaking and listening. They are fluent, articulate and confident in a wide range of activities and situations. Standards in reading are high and most girls enjoy reading for pleasure and information.'; 'The quality of teaching is very good throughout the school, with few weaknesses and great strengths.'; 'Teachers generally have high or very high expectations as to what the girls can achieve, which leads to good pace in lessons and demanding work.'; 'The headteacher gives very good and effective leadership.'; 'There are insufficient specialist facilities, but what are available are well used.'

Primary schools Claremont Primary; St John's Primary; St James's Primary; Langton Green Primary; Derwent Lodge Primary, Tonbridge. Plus 36 other feeder schools.

ALTRINCHAM GRAMMAR SCHOOL FOR GIRLS

Cavendish Road
Bowdon
Altrincham
Cheshire WA14 2NL

Tel (0161) 928 0827
Fax (0161) 941 7400

- National ranking 37 = (82, 12 =, 43, 66)
- GCSE 99% (97%)
- A-levels 55% (A/B); 98% (A/E)
- Higher education 91% (Cambridge 2)

- Girls' grammar
- Pupils 1,056
- Boys *Not applicable*
- Girls (11–18) 1,056
- Sixth form 212 (20%)
- Education authority *Trafford*

Headteacher David Henry Welsh, 53, appointed in September 1991. Staff 60 (men 8, women 52).

Motto Fortiter, fideliter, feliciter (Bravely, faithfully, cheerfully).

Background Founded in 1910, the school is set in leafy suburbs 10 miles from Manchester city centre, with a separate sixth-form centre. Strong traditions in music, sport and community service. Specialist accommodation includes two language laboratories, seven science laboratories, three information technology rooms, two libraries and a gymnasium. Two new all-weather hockey pitches, six tennis/netball courts and an artificial athletics track. A new technology block opened in May 1994. Although the school is expanding, places are limited to 168 in each year group; three applications per place; application for grant-maintained status in 1997. The school takes top 35–40% of ability range, significantly wider than many grammar schools. Minimum entry qualification for sixth form is five grade-C GCSEs, grade Bs in proposed A-level subjects, and an interview. England Schools' hockey champions in 1993; England under-16 netball champions in 1994. Competition winners in 1994 for Young Enterprise and for Chemical Analysis (Zeneca Cup). Identified by Ofsted in 1996 as 'outstandingly successful' school.

Streaming Pupils are divided into sets in French and mathematics from year 8.

Approach to discipline Self-discipline and self-motivation, with clear standards of behaviour expected. 'Good behaviour is acknowledged, rules are few, indiscipline is very rare, and parents are consulted if a serious problem arises.'

Uniform White blouse, navy pullover/cardigan and skirt, navy coat/anorak. Navy blazer optional. No uniform in sixth form but smart dress expected. No jeans.

Homework Average 11-year-old, seven hours 30 minutes; 14-year-old, 13 hours 30 minutes; 16-year-old, 15 hours.

Vocational qualifications *None*

Inspection February 1995: 'This is an outstanding school. High achievement, enthusiasm for learning, inspired leadership and a committed staff, a caring ethos and courteous behaviour characterise the school.'; 'Pupils are well-motivated and are extended by their teachers in
an atmosphere of academic excitement.'; 'Teachers are committed and highly competent.'; 'The school's success is achieved despite deficiencies in accommodation.'

Primary schools Bollin Primary; Broadheath Primary; Broomwood Primary; Cloverlea Primary; Elmridge Primary; Heyes Lane Junior; Navigation Primary; Oldfield Brow Primary; Park Road Primary; Stamford Park Junior: Well Green Primary; Willows Primary.

KING EDWARD VI CAMP HILL SCHOOL FOR GIRLS

Vicarage Road
Kings Heath
Birmingham
West Midlands B14 7QJ
Tel (0121) 444 2150
Fax (0121) 444 5123
E-mail: kingedwardcamphill@campus.bt.
com

- National ranking 37 (23, 11, 48, 13)
- GCSE 99% (100%)
- A-levels 55% (A/B); 98% (A/E)
- Higher education 99% (Oxford 6)

- Grant-maintained
- Girls' grammar
- Pupils 700
- Boys *Not applicable*
- Girls (11–18) 700
- Sixth form 209 (30%)
- Education authority *Birmingham*

Headteacher Joan Fisher, appointed in September 1992. Staff 42 (men 14, women 28).

Motto Idem per diversa (Unity through diversity).

Background Moved from original site on Camp Hill in 1958 to leafier Kings Heath; tree-lined approach with extensive playing fields, next to Kings Heath Park on southern edge of city. Became grant-maintained in April 1993 and looks forward to greater security after 'political pressure' in recent years; significant improvements in information technology and library resources; also drama studio and refurbished classrooms; improvements to showers and changing rooms, and reception areas. Over-subscribed, with up to eight applications for each place. Expanding to four-form entry. Building work completed in September 1996 also provides much-needed music accommodation, second computer room, new science laboratories, state-of-the-art classrooms. Flute choir in 1995 National Festival of Music for Youth. Some joint provision of A-level courses with Camp Hill School for Boys; shared sixth-form centre. Tradition of public speaking; 15 part-time instrumental teachers. Netball and hockey strong; sports facilities 'excellent'; under-16 netball team were 1993 West Midlands champions; competition-standard swimming pool. Regular participants in annual International Science Forum in London; 1996 winner of National Science Competition organised by Ministry of Agriculture, Food and Fisheries. Old Girls' Association. Leadership activities increasingly popular; more than half of year 10 girls in Duke of Edinburgh Award Scheme; 'fun' charity events encouraged and successful. 'We are especially keen for girls to develop leadership qualities and encourage sixth-formers to take an active part in the activities of younger girls: through their roles as form prefects, helping with junior charities, being good listeners, organising teams.'

Alumni Claire Russell, member of all-women crew of round-the-world yacht *Maiden*; Dorothy Reynolds, co-writer of *Salad Days* with Julian Slade.

Streaming Setting in Mathematics from year 10.

Approach to discipline Emphasis on positive aspects of reward and praise; sanctions to suit the offence. 'Before admission to year 7 and to the sixth form we make it clear to parents and their daughters that an acceptance of the rules and structures, and a willingness to abide by them, forms an integral part of the basis of their admission to the school.' Code of Conduct published and discussed by pupils at School Council; drugs and sex education policy circulated to parents before acceptance by governors. 'There is a relaxed and friendly atmosphere but high expectations. Governors visit the school to observe lessons, to be available to meet parents at functions, to take assemblies, to judge competitions.'

Uniform Navy and blue uniform. Reasonable flexibility allowed to make uniform available to all families at competitive prices. All girls below sixth form wear uniform; reminders sent from time to time.

Homework Average 11-year-old, six hours 30 minutes a week; 14-year-old, eight hours; 16-year-old, 10 hours.

Vocational qualifications Computer Literacy and Information Technology.

Inspection April 1994: 'Pupils are highly-motivated. Teaching is good and lessons are intellectually stimulating, but the high level of academic expectation places some pressure upon the achievement of more general aims.'; 'Staff are well-qualified and have an excellent command of their subject.'; 'The school is an orderly community and provides a pleasant environment for learning. Pupils are courteous and well-behaved and, when given the opportunity to do so, exercise responsibility with good humour and maturity.'

Primary schools Pupils drawn from total of 93 junior schools.

QUEEN MARY'S GRAMMAR SCHOOL

Sutton Road
Walsall
West Midlands WS1 2PG
Tel (01922) 720696
Fax (01922) 725932
E-mail: qmgs@rmplc.co.uk
Internet: http://www.rmplc.co.uk/eduweb
/sites/qmgs

- National ranking 39 (50, 15, 25, 5)
- GCSE 99% (99%)
- A-levels 54% (A/B); 94% (A/E)
- Higher education 95% (Oxford 6, Cambridge 2)

- Grant-maintained

- Boys' grammar
- Pupils 653
- Boys (11–18) 648
- Girls (16–18) 5
- Sixth form 179 (27%)
- Education authority *Walsall*

Headteacher Stuart Grosvenor Holtam, 48, appointed in September 1995. Staff 39 (men 36, women 3).

Motto Quas dederis solas semper habebis opes (You get out of life only what you put into it).

Background Founded in 1554 by Queen Mary Tudor; current buildings opened by Dean of Westminster in 1966; 12-acre site a mile south of Walsall centre; takes pupils from wide area beyond boundaries of Walsall borough (population 285,000). Indoor swimming pool and a rifle range. Heavily over-subscribed, with seven applications for each of 90 places. Extensive playing fields; strong sporting traditions: rugby, hockey, cricket, cross-country. Chess: *Times* winners in 1983 and 1987. Bridge: *Daily Mail* winners in 1985, and 1993 finalists. Shooting: *Country Life* CCF/ACF winners in 1992 and RAF/CCF Assegai winners in 1988 and 1993. Combined Cadet Force; Duke of Edinburgh Award Scheme. Many outdoor activities at school's own field centre near Dolgellau. Lively drama and choral music. Old Marians.

Alumni Sir Henry Newbolt, poet; Baron Harmar-Nicholls of Peterborough, former Conservative Euro-MP; Baron Ennals of Norwich, former Labour MP, foreign minister and social services secretary; Sir Terence Beckett, former CBI director-general; Sir Richard Powell, former civil servant; Sir Stephen Brown, president of High Court Family Division; Sir Harry Hinsley, official historian of wartime intelligence; Sir Eric Pountain, Tarmac non-executive chairman; Sir Leonard Peach, chairman of Police Complaints Authority; Jan Webster, England rugby player.

Streaming Pupils in sets in French from year 8; in mathematics from year 9.

Approach to discipline 'Discipline is traditional and strict, with a strong prefect system. Parents are very supportive; relations between staff and pupils, while formal, are responsible and relaxed.'

Uniform Navy blazer, mid-grey trousers, white shirt, school tie. Worn throughout the school; special ties and pullovers for sixth form and sports teams.

Homework Average 11-year-old, five hours a week; 14-year-old, 10 hours; 16-year-old, 15+ hours.

Vocational qualifications *None*

Inspection February 1995: 'A successful and happy school which is largely achieving its well-chosen aims. Standards are generally high or very high for pupils of all ages.'; 'Standards of achievement are very high in science, mathematics, modern languages, English, history, design technology, physical education and religious education. In other subjects, standards are high, except in music where they are a little better than sound and in information technology where they are not as good as they should be given the pupils' abilities.'; 'Much of the teaching is of good quality and none is poor.'; 'The school is well-managed. It runs particularly smoothly.'; 'The pupils work hard, attend regularly and punctually, and behave responsibly.'

SIMON LANGTON GRAMMAR SCHOOL FOR BOYS

Langton Lane
Nackington Road
Canterbury
Kent CT4 7AS
Tel (01227) 463567
Fax (01227) 456486
E-mail: slangton@rmplc.co.uk
Internet: http://www.rmplc.co.uk/eduweb/
          sites/slangton

- National ranking 40 (97, 140, 31, 150)
- GCSE 99% (96%)
- A-levels 52% (A/B); 93% (A/E)
- Higher education 90% (Cambridge 4)

- Grant-maintained
- Boys' grammar
- Pupils 845
- Boys (11–18) 845
- Girls *Not applicable*
- Sixth form 180 (21%)
- Education authority *Kent*

Headteacher John Harris, 62, appointed in September 1977. Staff 50 (men 37, women 13).

Motto Meliora sequamur (In pursuit of excellence).

Background Origins go back to the 13th century; formally founded in 1881 in present form; moved to current site in open countryside on outskirts of city in 1959; became grant-maintained in January 1992; over-subscribed, with 1.2 applications per place; new music wing and purpose-built technology block opened in 1994; additional classrooms and laboratories in 1996. Access to Canterbury hockey and rugby clubs, and to Kent County Cricket Club facilities. Parents' Association funded new swimming pool in 1981. Strong sport at all age groups – soccer, cricket, particularly hockey: National Schools' Hockey Association runners-up under-16 (1994, 1995) and under-18 (1995); county champions, under-14 and under-18; national finalists at under-16 and under-14 (1997). Music: full range of orchestra, choir and ensembles, concerts, players in National Youth Orchestra and brass band; regular travel and fieldwork in United Kingdom and abroad. Strength in modern languages: French, Spanish, German, also Russian available. Residential courses: France (year 8), Snowdonia (year 9), exchanges in years 9–13. Annual carol and commemoration services held in Canterbury Cathedral. Strong Parents' Association and Old Boy support. Identified as 'outstandingly successful' in 1997 annual Ofsted report.

Alumni Sir Freddie Laker, founder of Laker Airways; Trevor Pinnock, international conductor and harpsichordist; Sir Alec Rose, round-the-world yachtsman; Raymond Kendall, secretary-general of Interpol.

Streaming Setting in mathematics from year 8 and French from year 9.

Approach to discipline Boys expected to behave responsibly, courteously and in a disciplined way at all times. Close oversight of progress and behaviour by senior pupils, who also serve as form guardians and coach in academic work, sport and activities.

Uniform Special Langton blazer and tie in years 7–11. Other items standard. Sixth-formers dress formally on formal occasions.

Homework Average 11-year-old, five hours a week; 14-year-old, seven hours 30 minutes; 16-year-old, 10 hours.

Vocational qualifications *None*

Inspection November 1995: 'A very good school. Standards are well above average. All aspects of the education provided are at least satisfactory and most are good or very good. Its popularity in the community is fully justified.'; 'Overall, the pupils are achieving higher standards than could be expected, even allowing for their high initial abilities.'

Primary schools Blean County Primary; St Stephen's Junior; Pilgrim's Way County Primary; Herne CE Primary, Herne Bay; Wincheap County Primary; St Peter's Methodist Primary.

THE JUDD SCHOOL

Brook Street
Tonbridge
Kent TN9 2PN
Tel (01732) 770880
Fax (01732) 771661
E-mail: thejuddschool@campus.bt.com
**Internet: http://www.rmplc.co.uk/eduweb/
sites/judd/index.html**

- National ranking 41 (6, 30, 23, 12)
- GCSE 99% (100%)
- A-levels 51% (A/B); 96% (A/E)
- Higher education 90% (Oxford 3, Cambridge 10)

- Boys' grammar
- Pupils 831
- Boys (11–18) 807
- Girls (16–18) 24
- Sixth form 252 (30%)
- Education authority *Kent*

Headteacher Keith Andrew Starling, 53, appointed in September 1986. Staff 52 (men 38, women 14).

Motto Deus dat incrementum (God gives growth).

Background Founded 1888 by The Skinners' Company out of funds provided by the Sir Andrew Judd Foundation. Buildings on current site (which includes some playing fields, with others a mile away) date from 1896. Substantial development of Cohen Building in 1993 for technology, information technology, art, modern languages and science. Music centre opened in 1995. Voluntary-aided; always over-subscribed, with 1.7 applications for each place. Strong in rugby, cross-country and music; three hard tennis courts, rifle range and open-air swimming pool. Combined Cadet Force; Duke of Edinburgh Award Scheme.

Alumni Cecil Powell, Nobel prize-winner for physics; Baron Lewin of Greenwich, Chief of Defence Staff 1979–82; Bernard Hailstone, war artist, royal portrait painter and former president of Royal Society of Portrait Painters; Humphrey Burton, artistic adviser at Barbican Centre, BBC Television head of music and arts.

Streaming Setting in mathematics and French.

Approach to discipline 'Expectation of high standards of appearance, behaviour and courtesy. There is mutual respect and shared objectives.'

Uniform Navy blazer with badge, dark-grey trousers, white/grey shirt, maroon-and-navy school tie. Strictly enforced.

Homework Average 11-year-old, seven hours 30 minutes a week; 14-year-old, 11 hours; 16-year-old, 15 hours.

Vocational qualifications *None*

LANCASTER GIRLS' GRAMMAR SCHOOL

Regent Street
Lancaster
Lancashire LA1 1SF
Tel (01524) 32010
Fax (01524) 846220
E-mail: lggs@ednet.lancs.ac.uk

- National ranking 42 (49, 53, 115, 60)
- GCSE 99% (99%)
- A-levels 47% (A/B); 92% (A/E)
- Higher education 92% (Oxford 2, Cambridge 5)

- Grant-maintained
- Girls' grammar
- Pupils 760
- Boys *Not applicable*
- Girls (11–18) 760
- Sixth form 135 (18%)
- Education authority *Lancashire*

Headteacher Pamela Barber, 50, appointed in January 1987. Staff 47 (men 15, women 32).

Motto *None*

Background Opened in 1907, the main Victorian building is in a quiet conservation area near the centre of Lancaster; the art department is in an older Georgian house. New technology block opened in 1993. Over-subscribed, with three applications for each place; takes top 25% of ability range. Musically strong: 10 instrumental teachers, two orchestras, swing band, choirs, musical groups; parents often take part in concerts with pupils. Schools Curriculum Award; community links; industrial links include at least one teacher-placement each year as well as sixth-form sponsorship. Overseas work-experience; strong language department. Latin taught; A-level subjects include media studies and psychology. Recently gained Technology College status; Investors in People Award.

Alumni Rachel Medd, former world windsurfing champion.

Streaming *None*

Approach to discipline 'We expect and achieve very high standards. Problems are not "hidden" but dealt with as they occur. Parents are kept informed of any discipline problems.'

Uniform Navy skirt, white blouse, navy-and-gold striped tie, navy sweater with school crest (or blazer), navy coat. Enforced 'very strictly'. Sixth-formers do not wear uniform.

Homework Average 11-year-old, five to six hours a week; 14-year-old, eight to 10 hours; 16-year-old, 10 to 12 hours.

Vocational qualifications *None*

Inspection December 1994: 'Lancaster Girls' Grammar School provides a very good education for its pupils. Standards of achievement are consistently high.'; Pupils are committed and enthusiastic learners, having high expectations of themselves.'; 'The staff are committed and demonstrate a high level of specialist subject knowledge and skill.'; 'Pupils are well-behaved and courteous, and the school is a very orderly community. Relationships throughout the school are very good, with care and respect featuring strongly.'

Primary schools Dallas Road Primary; Great Wood Primary; Moorside Primary; Bowerham Primary; Scotforth Primary; Christ Church CE Primary.

AYLESBURY GRAMMAR SCHOOL

Walton Road
Aylesbury
Buckinghamshire HP21 7RP
Tel (01296) 84545
Fax (01296) 84545
E-mail: aylgmscl@rmplc.co.uk
Internet: http://www.rmplc.co.uk/eduweb/
sites/aylgmscl

- National ranking 43 (58, 68 = , 70, 67)
- GCSE 99% (98%)
- A-levels 46% (A/B); 97% (A/E)
- Higher education 90% (Oxford 7, Cambridge 12)

- Boys' grammar
- Pupils 1,100
- Boys (12–18) 1,100
- Girls *Not applicable*
- Sixth form 380 (35%)
- Education authority *Buckinghamshire*

Headteacher Ian P. Roe, 57, appointed in September 1992. Staff 68 (men 48, women 20).

Motto Floreat Aylesburia (May Aylesbury flourish).

Background Founded in 1598, the school moved to its current site in 1907. For many years a co-educational independent school, it became voluntary-controlled in 1952. Seven years later, the girls moved to an adjacent site to become Aylesbury High School, with which the school maintains close links. Main buildings date from 1907, with modern additions including lecture theatre, sixth-form centre, science block, computer centre, library and a geography block. Plans for new technology and art block, a music centre and additional sixth-form studies centre. Takes 27% of cohort by selection. Technology College status in 1997. 'Very strong' sports tradition: indoor swimming pool, squash courts, rifle range. 'The philosophy of the school is to involve as many pupils as possible in teams representing the school as well as competing at the highest level.' Main sports: rugby, hockey, cricket, athletics, cross-country, football, squash and tennis. Clubs: rifle-shooting, karate, fencing. Recent public-speaking honours in the Observer Mace and English Speaking Union competitions; three world champions. Orchestral groups, jazz band (runner-up in Central TV competition) and barber-shop group. Computer science, Business Studies, mathematics, Classics, English and languages among strengths. Identified in 1996 Ofsted report as 'outstandingly successful' school. Expeditions and visits include Costa Rica, Himalayas and Trinidad (cricket tour). Charity fundraising; has supported a link hospital in Malawi for 20 years. School councils for each section of the school, with pupil representatives also on other committees.

Alumni Professor William Mead, emeritus professor of geography, University College, London, and international authority on Scandinavia.

Streaming Setting by ability in some subjects from year 10.

Approach to discipline Very high expectations. 'We believe in encouraging pupils to develop an awareness of what constitutes acceptable and unacceptable behaviour in a community and to develop a sense of pride over appearance and conduct.'

Uniform Black blazer, dark-grey trousers, school tie and badge. 'Strictly enforced.' School shop supplies uniform.

Homework Average 12-year-old, seven hours 30 minutes a week; 14-year-old, 10 hours; 16-year-old, 12 hours.

Vocational qualifications CBI, Basic Competence in Information Technology.

Inspection May 1995: 'This is a good school in which pupils learn effectively and achieve very high standards in a caring and sensitive environment. The school's values are supported overwhelmingly by parents.'; 'Standards are high in English with very good examination results. Most pupils speak and read well; all write with basic competence and many do so fluently.'; 'Standards are generally high in all curriculum areas, although they are variable in history and largely restricted to performance skills in physical education.'; 'The curriculum for all pupils is extended through the provision of an impressive and varied programme of extra-curricular activities and visits.'

Primary schools More than 60 feeder schools.

DEVONPORT HIGH SCHOOL FOR GIRLS

Lyndhurst Road
Peverell
Plymouth
Devon PL2 3DL
Tel (01752) 705024
Fax (01752) 791873

- National ranking 44 (84, 78, 36, 115)
- GCSE 99% (96%)
- A-levels 44% (A/B); 94% (A/E)
- Higher education 90% (Oxford 2, Cambridge 1)

- Girls' grammar
- Pupils 750
- Boys *None*
- Girls (11–18) 750
- Sixth form 190 (25%)
- Education authority *Devon*

Headteacher Elizabeth Barbara Dunball, 57, appointed in September 1991. Staff 43 (men 15, women 28).

Motto Sine labe decus (Honour without dishonour).

Background A three- or four-form entry non-denominational selective school founded in 1911, moving to its current site in 1947. Mellow red-brick buildings face pleasant lawns and playing fields, even though the school lies at the heart of the city. It takes pupils from a large area, including many from across the River Tamar in neighbouring Cornwall. Over-subscribed by about 70 pupils annually, school is full to capacity, with four-form entry for each of the last three years. High proportion of girls learn musical instruments; Latin taught, with French, German, Italian and Spanish; good take-up for A-level science and mathematics; 'excellent' technology facilities. Extensive new sixth-form centre with social and study area. Girls regularly represent the county at hockey and netball; nationally successful basketball teams. Flourishing industrial links.

Alumni Penny Way, three times windsurfing world champion.

Streaming Pupils in sets for mathematics and French in year 9.

Approach to discipline 'Discipline is largely self-imposed. Pupils try hard in lessons and at games because they enjoy their work.'

Uniform Distinctive brown sweater with gold motif, brown skirt, white blouse, school tie. Strictly enforced; sixth-formers do not wear uniform.

Homework Average 11-year-old, five hours a week; 14-year-old, nine hours; 16-year-old, 11 hours.

Vocational qualifications *None*

TUNBRIDGE WELLS GRAMMAR SCHOOL FOR BOYS

St John's Road
Tunbridge Wells
Kent TN4 9XB
Tel (01892) 529551
Fax (01892) 536833
E-mail: twgboys@rmplc.co.uk
Internet: http://www.rmplc.co.uk/eduweb/
sites/twgsboys/index.html

- National ranking 45 (152, 161 =, –, 163)
- GCSE 99% (92%)
- A-levels 43% (A/B); 94% (A/E)
- Higher education 77% (Oxford 1)

- Boys' grammar
- Pupils 905
- Boys (11–18) 905
- Girls *Not applicable*
- Sixth form 206 (23%)
- Education authority *Kent*

Headteacher Derek Ernest Barnard, 52, appointed in September 1988. Staff 52 (men 39, women 13).

Motto Faber est quisque suae fortunae (Each man is the maker of his own fortune).

Background Originally a technical high school, it changed to a grammar in 1982, reflecting increasingly academic curriculum. On a site to the north of Tunbridge Wells on the borders with Southborough (west side of A26), the buildings date from 1962; strong emphasis on technology facilities; sports centre next door for swimming, squash and sports hall. A premier basketball, soccer and chess school; national success for under-19 soccer team. One of the biggest selective boys' schools in Kent; takes four or five forms of entry annually. One in five pupils learns musical instrument; drama a strength: theatre studies offered at A-level.

Alumni Nicholas Brown, Labour MP for Newcastle East; Gary Brazil, soccer player with

Newcastle and Fulham; Christopher Ward, former England chess captain.

Streaming In mathematics in years 9 to 11.

Approach to discipline 'Firm but fair. Uniform worn by all (no earrings, ponytails). Strong pastoral care system. School promotes self-discipline.'

Uniform Black blazer with badge, school tie, charcoal-grey trousers, black shoes. Sixth-formers have choice of blazer without badge or grey suit. Strictly enforced in years 7 to 11.

Homework Average 11-year-old, five hours a week; 14-year-old, nine hours; 16-year-old, 10 to 12 hours. At A-level, five hours a week per subject.

Vocational qualifications *None*

Primary schools Amherst Junior, Sevenoaks; Claremont Primary, Tunbridge Wells; St James's CE Primary, Tunbridge Wells; East Peckham Primary, Paddock Wood; Woodlands Primary, Tonbridge.

RUGBY HIGH SCHOOL

Longrood Road
Rugby
Warwickshire CV22 7RE
Tel (01788) 810518
Fax (01788) 811794
E-mail: rugbyhs@enterprise.net

- National ranking 46 (88, 103, 51, 19)
- GCSE 99% (97%)
- A-levels 40% (A/B); 94% (A/E)
- Higher education 77% (Oxford 2)

- Grant-maintained
- Girls' grammar
- Pupils 672
- Boys *Not applicable*
- Girls (11–18) 672
- Sixth form 224 (33%)
- Education authority *Warwickshire*

Headteacher Margaret Thornton, 58, appointed in September 1988. Staff 38 (men 6, women 32).

Motto *None*

Background Founded by Olive Hands in 1903, it became a county school, known as Arnold High School, in 1919. Moved to current suburban leafy site in 1961; serves Rugby and surrounding villages. It became grant-maintained in April 1993. The Alexander Youngman Music Centre, built in memory of music mistress's husband, was opened in April 1992. Regular competitors in local debating competitions; girls play hockey and netball at county level. The school prides itself on its 'democratic community', with ideas from pupils adopted throughout the school. More than four pupils apply for each place, but many do not achieve the level required in the 12+ examination. Entry at 11 providing extra 90 pupils from September 1996.

Streaming Pupils streamed in mathematics and modern languages in years 10 and 11.

Approach to discipline 'We believe that the only worthwhile discipline is self-discipline. We have a very relaxed atmosphere but do not tolerate behaviour that harms or offends others.'

Uniform Navy skirt and pullover, pale-blue blouse; no uniform in sixth form. 'Minimal requirements, strictly enforced.'

Homework Average 14-year-old, six hours a week; 16-year-old, eight hours.

Vocational qualifications *None*

Inspection October 1994: 'The quality of education is very good. Most teaching is sound or good. It is very good in English, music, religious education and information technology.'; 'Pupils display excellent attitudes to their learning. They concentrate, persevere and enjoy their learning tasks.'; 'Strong and purposeful leadership is displayed by the headteacher and she is well-supported in this by a committed and active governing body.'; 'The pupils enjoy working within a sensitive and safe learning community where excellent relationships exist amongst pupils and between staff and pupils.'

Primary schools Bilton Junior; Rokeby Junior; Paddox Junior; Boughton Leigh Junior; St Marie's RC Junior.

DOVER GRAMMAR SCHOOL FOR BOYS

Astor Avenue
Dover
Kent CT17 0DQ
Tel (01304) 206117
Fax (01304) 206074
E-mail: admin@dgsb.demon.co.uk
Internet: http://www.demon.co.uk/dgsb

- National ranking 47 (53, –, 124, 95)
- GCSE 99% (99%)
- A-levels 33% (A/B); 94% (A/E)
- Higher education 94%

- Grant-maintained
- Boys' grammar
- Pupils 570
- Boys (11–18) 570
- Girls Not applicable
- Sixth form 115 (20%)
- Education authority Kent

Headteacher Neil Arnold Slater, 54, appointed in April 1990. Staff 33 (men 28, women 5).

Motto Fiat lux (Let there be light).

Background The school opened in 1905 as Dover County School and moved to its current imposing buildings in extensive grounds in 1931; name changed in 1944. Overlooks town, port and the Channel; Dover Castle on hill opposite. Over-subscribed, with two applications per place. Works closely with College St Pierre in Calais, with frequent exchanges. Curriculum strengths include Creative and Performing Arts, English, science, computer science and mathematics, sports studies and Classics. Sports facilities 'very good'; soccer success, Kent league champions in 1995.

Alumni R. J. Unstead, historian and author; Baron Cockfield of Dover, former Trade Secretary, Treasury minister and Chancellor of the Duchy of Lancaster; John Russell-Taylor, art critic; David Elleray, soccer referee; Professor David Thomas, Sheffield University.

Streaming Setting in mathematics, from year 8; in French and science, from year 10.

Approach to discipline Policy based on self-discipline; enforces high standards 'firmly and quietly'. School aims to emphasise integrity, consideration for others, decency, straightforwardness, common sense, loyalty, respect, and abhorrence of bullying or intimidation.

Uniform Navy/black blazer, dark-grey/black trousers, white shirt, school tie, dark socks, black shoes. Sixth-formers may wear a suit or conventional jacket and trousers, or school pullover with badge instead of jacket. 'All boys wear the uniform as prescribed.'

Homework Average 11-year-old, five hours a week; 14-year-old, seven hours; 16-year-old, 12 hours.

Vocational qualifications None

Inspection September 1994.

Primary schools St Mary's CE Primary, Dover; River Primary, Dover; Whitfield Primary, Dover; The Downs CE Primary, Walmer; Warden House Primary, Deal; Astor Primary, Dover; Barton Primary, Dover; St Martin's Primary, Dover; St Richard's RC Primary, Dover.

THE NORTON KNATCHBULL SCHOOL

Hythe Road
Ashford
Kent TN24 0QJ
Tel (01233) 620045
Fax (01233) 633668

- National ranking 48 (104, 132, 155, 133)
- GCSE 99% (96%)
- A-levels 32% (A/B); 87% (A/E)
- Higher education 91% (Cambridge 1)

- Boys' grammar
- Pupils 772
- Boys (11–18) 772
- Girls Not applicable
- Sixth form 183 (24%)
- Education authority Kent

Headteacher Philip Gordon Cox, 61, appointed in September 1971. Staff 46 (men 30, women 16).

Motto Benefactorum recordatio iucundissima est (Recollection of things well done is the most pleasing).

Background Founded in 1630 by Sir Norton Knatchbull, school now on its third site, on edge of Ashford with extensive playing fields. Modern buildings completed in three phases: new block in 1992 for information technology, mathematics, languages and careers; new Astroturf hockey and tennis areas. Over-subscribed, with five applications per place. Strong emphasis on extra-curricular activities: award-winning jazz group; county and regional representatives in variety of sports. 'We regard co-operation between teachers and pupils as one of the fundamentals necessary for academic achievement as well as personal development.' Identified as 'outstandingly successful' in 1996 Ofsted annual report.

Alumni Baron Deedes, former editor of the Daily Telegraph (1974–1986); Bob Holness, television personality; Martin Mortimore, television producer (*Tomorrow's World, Hospital Watch*).

Streaming Broad bands in mathematics in year 8; in mathematics and science in years 9 to 11.

Approach to discipline 'The aim of the school is to establish a framework of good social behaviour in which punishment is unnecessary and there is mutual respect between pupil and staff, and pupil and pupil.' Sanctions employed when necessary; high priority given to good order and purposeful study.

Uniform Dark-blue blazer with school badge, dark-grey trousers, white shirt, school tie, dark-grey V-neck pullover. Enforced '100%'.

Homework Average 11-year-old, six hours 30 minutes a week; 14-year-old, eight hours; 16-year-old, 11 hours.

Vocational qualifications *None*

Inspection February 1996: 'A school with high academic and social standards in which learning is valued and excellence is prized. The standards of teaching are sound. Its values of courtesy and respect form the basis of good relationships.'; 'Reading is generally good, but some pupils read little beyond what is required in lessons. Writing is sound, but there is evidence of a lack of attention to detail which results in poor spelling and presentation. The skills of writing for different audiences are being developed and there are good examples in many subjects of extended writing.'; 'The standard of numeracy throughout the school is good with evidence of pupils making good use of their acquired skills.'; 'The school provides pupils with a secure, orderly environment in which learning is valued and excellence is prized.'

Primary schools Willesbrough Primary; Tinterden Primary; Wye Primary; Mersham Primary; St Mary's CE Primary, Ashford; Hopewell Primary.

KING EDWARD VI GRAMMAR SCHOOL

Broomfield Road
Chelmsford
Essex CM1 3SX
Tel (01245) 353510
Fax (01245) 344741

- National ranking 49 (9, 4, 4, 20)
- GCSE 98% (100%)
- A-levels 72% (A/B); 100% (A/E)
- Higher education 95% (Oxford 5, Cambridge 13)

- Grant-maintained
- Boys' grammar
- Pupils 749
- Boys (11–18) 715
- Girls (16–18) 34
- Sixth form 251 (34%)
- Education authority *Essex*

Headteacher Anthony David Tuckwell, 54, appointed in January 1984. Staff 46 (men 31, women 15).

Motto Quidquid agas fortiter ex animo (Whatever you do, do it bravely from the heart).

Background King Edward VI, known locally as KEGS and sited in the centre of Chelmsford, serves an intake from more than 500 square miles of mid-Essex. Founded in 1551, the school has been on its current site since 1892, a quarter of a mile from the cathedral with which it has a choral link. Behind its impressive Victorian frontage, containing a library and administrative area, are substantial additional buildings dating from 1937 and 1963, and a new art and technology block. The foundation owns the 30-acre Bedford Playing Fields and Pavilion in the nearby village of Broomfield; there is a smaller playing field and practice facilities on the main site. All subjects have specialist rooms. Other facilities include two gymnasia, a multi-gym, two computer rooms networked around the school, music rooms, drama studio, spacious hall and stage, seven laboratories. The school is substantially over-subscribed, with 5.5 applications per place. Inter-school and inter-House fixtures: soccer, rugby, hockey, basketball, cross-country, athletics, cricket. Two soccer internationals in 1992, including under-18 captain. Two orchestras, wind band, choir, instrumental ensembles; seven concerts a year. Musical exchange with Max Planck Gymnasium, Schorndorf. Two high-quality drama productions, one touring Australia in 1996. Combined Cadet Force, with Corps of Drums. Duke of Edinburgh Award Scheme. Fleur de Lys Debating and Charity Society. Sports Leadership Award. Chess, bridge, scientific and mathematical teams have achieved success in regional and national competitions. School represents the United Kingdom in Club 92, a school link across the European Union. Many societies, including history, politics and philosophy; Christian Union. Language exchanges and many trips at home and abroad.

Alumni Sir Norman Fowler, former Conservative Party chairman; Peter Joslin, Warwickshire chief constable; Mervyn Day, former West Ham United and England Under-21 goalkeeper; Mike Smith, television personality; Major-General Peter Baldwin, chairman of Radio Authority; Robin O'Neill, diplomat and recently British Ambassador in Brussels and Vienna; Professor John Taylor, professor of neural networks, King's College, London.

Streaming Pupils are divided into sets for mathematics from year 8.

Approach to discipline The school is proud of its reputation for the self-discipline and courtesy of its pupils. Sanctions available include detentions, extra work and, in extreme cases, suspension. 'The school works in partnership with parents on the rare occasions that discipline needs to be imposed.'

Uniform Black blazer, with red edging braid for years 7 to 9, school badge, dark grey trousers/skirts, white shirt (or grey or blue for sixth-formers), dark socks, black shoes (or brown in years 10 to 13). There is a school tie, with a separate design for sixth-formers and specially-presented prefects' ties and service ties (for those who, from year 10, have contributed significantly to school life). 'All pupils are required to wear uniform. The school receives full co-operation from pupils and parents.'

Homework Average 11-year-old, seven hours 30 minutes a week; 14-year-old, 10 hours; 16-year-old, 12 hours (additional private reading expected in sixth form).

Vocational qualifications *None*

Inspection October 1996: 'A very good school. Attainment is very high. High expectations, intellectual challenge and rigour are the norm. The leadership provided by the headteacher is outstanding. He is well supported by an effective senior management team and some good middle-managers. The quality of teaching is high and is a strength of the school. There is a powerful ethos related to a learning culture. Adults and pupils exhibit a sense of corporate purpose and of belonging to the school.'; 'There is a genuine focus on the development of the whole person to which pupils respond very positively and with a commitment to excel.'; 'The quality of teaching is high and is good or very good in 85% of lessons. Teaching rarely has unsatisfactory aspects and it is particularly good in the sixth form. It is a major strength of the school.'; 'The school has formed effective links with parents and has well-established and valued procedures for maintaining them.'; 'The overall ethos of the school is very positive. It is underpinned by a commitment to high achievement within a supportive framework.'; 'The leadership provided by the headteacher is outstanding.'

THE TIFFIN GIRLS' SCHOOL

Richmond Road
Kingston-upon-Thames KT2 5PL
Tel (0181) 546 0773
Fax (0181) 547 0191
Internet: http://www.campus.bt.com/
    campusworld/orgs/org1125/
    index.html

- National ranking 50 (80, 44, 59, 15)
- GCSE 98% (97%)
- A-levels 64% (A/B); 97% (A/E)
- Higher education 98% (Oxford 8, Cambridge 3)

- Girls' grammar
- Pupils 863
- Boys *Not applicable*
- Girls (11–18) 863
- Sixth form 263 (30%)
- Education authority *Kingston-upon-Thames*

Headteacher Pauline Cox, 48, appointed in September 1994. Staff 52 (men 14, women 38).

Motto Sapere aude (Dare to be wise).

Background Developed in 1880 from 17th-century foundation; after 50 years in previous building, also in Richmond Road, moved in 1987 to current site: open grounds of just over nine acres on east of Richmond Road towards northern edge of Kingston-upon-Thames; 12 laboratories and workshops for science and technology, two computer suites, drama studio, music suite, a ceramics room, library connected to expanding resources centre with audio-visual equipment and computers. Two large gymnasia; courts and playing fields on site. Sixth form based in separate building with own common room and study area. Over-subscribed, with 10 applications for each of 120 places; takes top 10% of the ability range. Traditional occasions: Speech Day, Junior Presentation of Awards, carol service, school birthday. Sporting strengths include netball, with teams often reaching national finals. Musical concerts every term; two orchestras, three choirs. Drama productions; impressive charity fund-raising. School Council controls proportion of school fund; school officers appointed after application and interview; 40 elected prefects. 'It is our intention that girls achieve the greatest possible academic success, while acquiring the skills, adaptability and maturity which will help to prepare them for their future careers and for life in the 21st century.'

Streaming Sometimes pupils are put in sets in mathematics and French from year 9.

Approach to discipline 'Girls are encouraged to exercise self-discipline and to act with consideration towards all members of the school community.'

Uniform Teal-blue blazer and sweater, grey skirt, white shirt. Strictly enforced. No uniform for sixth-formers.

Homework Average 11-year-old, five hours a week; 14-year-old, seven hours 30 minutes; 16-year-old, 10 hours.

Vocational qualifications *None*

Inspection November 1995: 'There is a very good working environment at the Tiffin Girls' School in which pupils learn effectively. Standards of achievement overall are high even considering the selective nature of the school and pupils' abilities on entry.'; 'The headteacher leads the school skilfully and sensitively.'; 'Well-qualified and diligent staff ensure consistent levels of pupil achievement in most areas of the school's work.'; 'This justifiably popular school offers its pupils a challenging and pleasant environment for learning. Pupils enjoy and are proud of their school. Relationships are warm and behaviour exemplary.'

BOURNEMOUTH SCHOOL FOR GIRLS

Castle Gate Close
Castle Lane West
Bournemouth
Dorset BH8 9UJ
Tel (01202) 526289
Fax (01202) 548923

- National ranking 51 (36 = , 62, 29, 75)
- GCSE 98% (99%)
- A-levels 59% (A/B); 97% (A/E)
- Higher education 93% (Oxford 3, Cambridge 2)

- Grant-maintained
- Girls' grammar
- Pupils 990
- Boys *Not applicable*
- Girls (11–18) 990
- Sixth form 277 (28%)
- Education authority *Bournemouth*

Headteacher Margaret J. Matthews, 54, appointed in 1984. Staff 64 (men 14, women 50).

Motto *None*

Background Founded in 1918 to provide secondary education for girls in Bournemouth, it moved to current site to the northeast of the town in 1960. Parkland setting. New science facilities opened in 1994; some new technology facilities in 1990. New 12-classroom teaching block in September 1997. Well-equipped library, with 30,000 books and computer-based catalogue system. Unable to accommodate all 'out-of-area' applicants who pass 11 + examination; over-subscribed, with three applications for each place. Traditionally takes top 16% of ability range; girls study 10 subjects, plus IT short course, to GCSE; total of 24 subjects offered at A-level. Top student in AEB English A-levels in 1995; 1996 AEB Certificate of Excellence for performance in A-level Politics; top student in Cambridge Textiles A-levels in 1995; further special award in English. Recent national representatives at athletics, cross-country, judo, netball, skating, squash and trampolining; national swimming finalists in 1996. Representatives in county youth orchestras and ensembles. Duke of Edinburgh Award Scheme; Youth Awards Scheme; Young Enterprise; Da Vinci and ensemble groups for able students; two members of National

Youth Theatre. All girls undertake work experience in year 10, with further work and community experience in sixth form.

Streaming Some setting in mathematics in years 9 to 11.

Approach to discipline 'Clear guidelines within supportive tutorial and pastoral framework.' Parental involvement where appropriate; sanctions such as detention, as appropriate; more serious problems dealt with by year-heads, deputy heads or headteacher.

Uniform French-blue skirt with blue-and-white striped blouse in years 7 to 10. In year 11, skirt and blouse in black and white. Sixth-formers wear own choice of clothes. No jeans or leisure wear.

Homework Average 11-year-old, five hours 40 minutes a week; 14-year-old, eight hours; 16-year-old, 10 to 15 hours.

Vocational qualifications Information Technology Certificate of Competence.

Inspection November 1994: 'A good school with many excellent features. The school is an orderly community where relationships are good, and mutual respect and trust are high. The pupils display natural good manners and friendliness in their responses to each other, to staff and to visitors. They are given and respond well to opportunities to show initiative and take responsibility.'; 'The school serves its pupils well, although pupils of the highest ability do not always have sufficient demands placed upon them.'

Primary schools Bethany CE Junior; Elmrise Primary; Kings Park Primary; Moordown St John's CE Primary; Pokesdown County Primary; St Michael's CE Primary; Summerbee Junior.

WESTCLIFF HIGH SCHOOL FOR GIRLS

Kenilworth Gardens
Westcliff-on-Sea
Essex SS0 0BS
Tel (01702) 76026
Fax (01702) 471328

- National ranking 52 (119, 66, 98, 104)
- GCSE 98% (95%)
- A-levels 58% (A/B); 99% (A/E)
- Higher education 95% (Oxford 5, Cambridge 4)

- Grant-maintained
- Girls' grammar

- Pupils 875
- Boys (16–18) 5
- Girls (11–18) 870
- Sixth form 217 (25%)
- Education authority Essex

Headteacher Patricia Mary Elliott, 54, appointed in January 1990. Staff 62 (men 18, women 44).

Motto Fide et fortitudine (In faith and strength).

Background Moved to current spacious site in 1931; main building 'has considerable character and architectural merit'. New sixth-form facilities with common rooms, study areas, library and careers room. New science block with nine laboratories came into use in February 1995. Outdoor facilities include 14 tennis courts, three hockey pitches, running track, extensive gardens. Over-subscribed, with three applications for each place. Choice of 22 A-level subjects. Music is a strength: orchestra, choirs, chamber music, concerts and annual opera production. Gymnastics team has twice reached national finals. Retains much of traditional grammar school ethos; strong sense of community.

Alumni Baroness Platt of Writtle, former chairperson of Equal Opportunities Commission.

Streaming Pupils put in sets in mathematics from year 8; in science and modern languages from year 9.

Approach to discipline 'Considerable emphasis is placed on responsible behaviour that enhances the life of the school community. Pupils are encouraged to show consideration and respect to each other and to adults. Any breaches of this code of conduct are dealt with firmly.'

Uniform Navy skirt, navy jersey with school logo, light-blue blouse, blazer. Sixth-formers are not required to wear uniform.

Homework Average 11-year-old, five hours 20 minutes a week; 14-year-old, eight hours 40 minutes; 16-year-old, nine hours 30 minutes.

Vocational qualifications RSA, Text-processing.

Inspection December 1993.

Primary schools St Michael's Preparatory; Chalkwell Hall Junior; West Leigh Junior; Leigh Junior; Crowstone Preparatory; Heycroft Primary. Total of 55 feeder schools.

RIPON GRAMMAR SCHOOL

Clotherholme Road
Ripon
North Yorkshire HG4 2DG
Tel (01765) 602647
Fax (01765) 606388
E-mail: ripongs@rmplc.co.uk

- National ranking 53 (56 =, 26, 53, 84)
- GCSE 98% (98%)
- A-levels 57% (A/B); 97% (A/E)
- Higher education 94% (Oxford 1, Cambridge 9)

- Mixed grammar
- Pupils 720
- Boys (11–18) 344
- Girls (11–18) 376
- Sixth form 160 (22%)
- Education authority *North Yorkshire*

Headteacher Alan M. Jones, 50, appointed in January 1992. Staff 44 (men 22, women 22).

Motto Giorne ymb lare ymb diowotdomas (Eager both to learn and to seek after righteousness).

Background Founded in the 14th century, the school claims to be the oldest grammar school in the country; moved to current site on outskirts of Ripon in 1874; Victorian buildings augmented by addition of new blocks when school became co-educational in 1962. Extensive building programme has expanded facilities for sixth form, the library, science, computing and technology; the only state school with boarding provision in Yorkshire: weekly and full boarders in two boarding houses. Over-subscribed, with four applications per place. Classics thrive, with all pupils studying Latin for at least two years; Latin, Greek and Classical Studies offered to GCSE and A-level. Proud of reputation for team sports, with regular success in regional competition; supplies players to area and county sides. 'A traditional co-educational grammar school that seeks to preserve high academic standards in traditional areas while seeking to prepare youngsters for life in the modern world. Expectations of pupils' work, conduct and participation are high. They work hard and play hard.'

Alumni Bruce Oldfield, fashion designer; Peter Squires, rugby player and cricketer; Barbara Holland, former president of All England Women's Hockey Association; Tony Rutherford, embryologist; Peter Toyne, Rector of Liverpool John Moores University.

Streaming In mathematics from year 8 and in French from year 9.

Approach to discipline 'Expectations and regulations are made clear, with the emphasis thereafter being on the school community and the impact of an individual's behaviour (for good or ill) upon that community. Formal sanctions are balanced with individual negotiation in a spirit of cooperation and reasonableness.'

Uniform Navy blazer, grey trousers/navy skirt, white shirt/blouse, school tie. Summer dress for girls includes option of school-pattern dress.

Homework Average 11-year-old, seven hours 30 minutes a week; 14-year-old, at least 10 hours; 16-year-old, at least 10 hours.

Vocational qualifications *None*

Inspection November 1995: 'Ripon Grammar School serves its community well and its reputation is justifiably high. It provides for its pupils an effective education with many outstanding features which results in high academic standards of achievement.'; 'Standards in the school are very high.'; 'Acquisition of basic mathematical skills is good. Standards of reading and writing are well above national expectations. The majority of pupils communicate clearly and audibly. Sixth-form students display great confidence with critical language. Lack of opportunities inhibit some overall achievements in the performing arts.'; 'The broad approach to classics establishes strong links with spiritual, moral, aesthetic and cultural issues. Teachers have a secure knowledge of their subject and the quality of teaching was found to be consistently sound or good in about 98% of lessons.'

Primary schools Holy Trinity CE Junior; Greystone Primary; St Wilfrid's RC Primary; Cathedral CE Primary; Moorside Junior.

THE BLUE COAT SCHOOL

Church Road
Liverpool L15 9EE
Tel (0151) 733 1407
Fax (0151) 734 0982

- National ranking 54 (62, 71 = , 121, 110)
- GCSE 98% (98%)
- A-levels 53% (A/B); 94% (A/E)
- Higher education 98% (Oxford 3)

- Grant-maintained
- Boys' comprehensive
- Pupils 892
- Boys (11–18) 834
- Girls (16–18) 58
- Sixth form 266 (30%)
- Education authority *Liverpool*

Headteacher John Speller, 48, appointed September 1989. Staff 54 (men 42, women 12).

Motto Non sibi sed omnibus (Not for oneself but for everyone).

Background Originally founded in 1708 as a city-centre orphanage, the school moved in 1906 to what was purpose-built accommodation (and is now a Grade 2 listed building) in the then commuter village of Wavertree, which has become a suburb bordering the inner city and more affluent suburbia. Sports ground 200 yards away from school, to which a chapel was added in 1912 and, in the 1960s, a gymnasium, squash courts and heated indoor swimming pool. The voluntary-aided school took in a number of boarders until 1990. It fought off closure in 1985, and was described by the then Sir Keith Joseph, the former education secretary, as 'a school of proven worth'. In 1989, girls were admitted to the sixth form; since 1991, the school expanded from three- to four-form entry. It remains over-subscribed, with four applications for each place. Pupils have achieved national honours in soccer, basketball and swimming; two drama productions annually; school orchestra, brass band and choir.

Streaming Pupils are streamed according to ability in French in years 9 to 11, and mathematics in years 9 to 11.

Approach to discipline 'We expect students to work hard, to allow others to work hard, and to behave at all times in a civilised manner.'

Uniform Blue blazer with badge, blue tie, grey trousers, white/grey shirt, black shoes. Girls allowed to wear grey/blue shirt. Regulations strictly enforced.

Homework Average 11-year-old, five hours 30 minutes; 14-year-old, eight hours; 16-year-old, 10 hours 30 minutes.

Vocational qualifications *None*

Inspection February 1994: 'A very good school which deserves its excellent reputation for high standards of scholarship, for its conern for pupils and for the quality and range of its cultural, social and sporting activities. It is rightly proud of its tradition, which is providing a firm foundation for development. Pupils respond well to the challenge posed by the intellectual rigour of the curriculum. They acquire clear values and a sense of responsibility and are enriched by the breadth of experiences provided.'

Primary schools Booker Avenue Primary; Childwall CE Primary; Rudston Primary; Mosspits County Junior; Gilmour Junior; Sudley Primary; Woolton Primary.

QUEEN MARY'S HIGH SCHOOL

Upper Forster Street
Walsall
West Midlands WS4 2AE
Tel (01922) 721013
Fax (01922) 32387
E-mail: qmarys@rmplc.co.uk
Internet: http://www.rmplc.co.uk/eduweb/
sites/qmarys/index.html

- National ranking 55 (15, 43, 9, 27)
- GCSE 98% (100%)
- A-levels 50% (A/B); 97% (A/E)
- Higher education 92% (Oxford 3)

- Grant-maintained
- Girls' grammar
- Pupils 690
- Boys (16–18) 2
- Girls (11–18) 688
- Sixth form 210 (30%)
- Education authority *Walsall*

Headteacher Ann Denny, 54, appointed in September 1991. Staff 40 (men 10, women 30).

Motto *None*

Background Part of Queen Mary's Foundation, dating from 1554; voluntary-aided school celebrated centenary in 1993; became grant-maintained in September 1993. Occupies Victorian and early 20th-century buildings that once housed both boys' and girls' school on 'cramped site' near centre of Walsall; playing fields 10 minutes' walk away. Recently-refurbished sixth-form area. Substantially over-subscribed, with seven applications for each place. Designated as a Language College in April 1996; Japanese introduced in 1996; new multi-media language learning facilities and new science block from September 1996. Three European languages taught (to equal numbers) from year 7; all girls take a second language from year 8. Latin taught to all girls in lower school. Strong musical tradition; finalists in choir section of National Festival of Music for Youth; large orchestra, with half of all pupils taking instrumental lessons.

Alumni Meera Syal, actress and writer.

Streaming Some setting of pupils in mathematics.

Approach to discipline Minimal rules; self-discipline the aim. 'However, we apply sanctions as appropriate, including detentions.'

Uniform 'Deckchair-stripe' blazer in green, navy and gold, green skirt, green blouse. Sixth-formers do not wear uniform. Rigorously enforced.

Homework Average 11-year-old, seven hours a week; 14-year-old, eight to 10 hours; 16-year-old, 12 to 14 hours.

Vocational qualifications Foreign Languages at Work; Cambridge Certificate in Information Technology; CSLA.

Inspection November 1996.

Primary schools Park Hall Junior; Cooper & Jordan CE Junior; St Mary's RC Primary; Mayfield Preparatory.

CAISTOR GRAMMAR SCHOOL

Church Street
Caistor
Lincoln
Lincolnshire LN7 6QJ
Tel (01472) 851250
Fax (01472) 852248

- National ranking 56= (54, 36, 74, 144)
- GCSE 98% (98%)
- A-levels 49% (A/B); 97% (A/E)
- Higher education 98% (Cambridge 2)

- Grant-maintained
- Mixed grammar
- Pupils 580
- Boys (11–18) 270
- Girls (11–18) 310

- Sixth form 134 (23%)
- Education authority *Lincolnshire*

Headteacher Roger Thomas Hale, 35, appointed in January 1996. Staff 40 (men 24, women 16).

Motto Ever to excel.

Background Founded in 1631 by Francis Rawlinson, Rector of South Kelsey; attractive site on brow of hill close to centre of small market town of Caistor, 24 miles north of Lincoln and 15 miles south of Humber Bridge. School buildings help to form two sides of a close around the parish church; original ironstone school hall still in daily use. Buildings were extended in 19th century, 1930s and, substantially, in 1980s. New technology buildings in 1995. Became grant-maintained in September 1991; over-subscribed, with 209 qualified applicants for 84 places; takes top 25% of the ability range; many pupils come from outside catchment area (six-and-a-half-mile radius). Boarding phased out in 1995. Duke of Edinburgh Award; Young Enterprise Scheme; wide range of sporting, musical and dramatic activity; 'vigorous' House system, which supports considerable inter-school competition. Identified by Ofsted in 1996 as 'outstandingly successful'.

Alumni Sir Henry Newbolt, poet; Dawn French, comedian.

Streaming Pupils mostly in three mixed-ability forms in years 7–9; four groups for technology, physical education and second language; option groups in years 10 and 11. Setting in mathematics in years 9–11; some grouping by ability in French and German in years 10 and 11.

Approach to discipline 'Very high standards of conduct are expected. We try to treat our students with respect and understanding and feel justified by their response.' Pastoral system emphasises role of form tutor and heads of sections (lower, middle and upper school, and sixth form). Senior students, who are prefects, and House officials play prominent part.

Uniform Black blazer with badge (for boys), grey trousers/school skirt, grey/black pullover, white shirt/school blouse, school tie (for boys), white socks (for girls), black shoes. Dark, plain coats. Guidelines for sixth-formers require them to dress like 'young professionals at work'. Firmly enforced in years 7 to 11; 'with persistence and good humour in the sixth form'.

Homework Average 11-year-old, five hours a week; 14-year-old, eight hours; 16-year-old, 12 hours.

Vocational qualifications *None*

Inspection October 1995: 'Caistor Grammar School provides a very good quality of education. Pupils attain high standards of achievement. In recent years the school has made significant improvements. The quality of learning is very good. Pupils relish learning and have high-quality learning skills. Teachers respond well to the talents and abilities of the pupils, providing challenging and stimulating lessons.'; 'The school is well-managed. The governors have played a significant part in establishing the aims and purposes of the school.'; 'Pupils have a strong work ethic. They have excellent standards of behaviour and very positive attitudes to learning.'

Primary schools Caistor Joint CE/Methodist Primary; St Martin's Preparatory, Grimsby; Brigg Preparatory, Brigg; Keelby Primary; Lisle Marsden Junior, Grimsby.

PORTADOWN COLLEGE

Killicomaine Road
Portadown
County Armagh BT63 5BU
Tel (01762) 332439
Fax (01762) 350733

- National ranking 56= (18, 97, 42, 78)
- GCSE 98% (100%)
- A-levels 49% (A/B); 97% (A/E)
- Higher education 86% (Oxford 1)

- Mixed grammar
- Pupils 785
- Boys (14–18) 355
- Girls (14–18) 430
- Sixth form 364 (46%)
- Education authority *Southern Education and Library Board*

Headteacher Thomas William Flannagan, 50, appointed in September 1993. Staff 52 (men 26, women 26).

Motto Fortiter et humaniter (Bravely and courteously).

Background Founded in 1924 as a grammar school; since 1969 has been senior grammar school admitting pupils at 14 +. New school half a mile from town centre built in 1962 on 10-hectare site; extended in 1966, 1973 and 1987 to accommodate increased numbers. Over-subscribed, with up to 380 applications for 210 places. Well-equipped science laboratories, technology workshop/laboratory, computing suites, sixth-form centre, sports hall, on-site playing fields. Emphasis on careers guidance; structured pastoral care system. Represented Northern Ireland in United Kingdom finals of British Association of Young Scientists; A-level pupil named among top five in mathematics in United Kingdom. Air Training Corps. Dramatic society; school choir, orchestra and madrigal group; 'Lifeline', the largest school club, raises substantial amount for charity. Finalists in Northern Ireland Britannic Assurance 1995 Debating Competition. Hockey and rugby success: girls' 1st XI were Ulster Senior Cup champions, while 1st XV reached the final of the Ulster Subsidiary Shield Final in 1995–96.

Alumni Mary Peters, Olympic gold-medallist; Gloria Hunniford, television personality; Stephanie Callister, television presenter; Alexander Walker, film critic and writer; Denys Hawthorne, actor and producer; Rev Professor Ernest Nicholson, provost of Oriel College, Oxford; Michael Bloch, barrister, writer and biographer; Niall Sloane, editor of BBC Television's Match of the Day.

Streaming Pupils are placed in three bands in year 10. All pupils sit eight or nine GCSEs at end of year 11.

Approach to discipline Detailed written policy, signed by parents on behalf of children: straightforward advice to be sensible, considerate and polite. 'Discipline operates at a positive level and mutual trust is developed between pupils and staff; appropriate sanctions are available and used when required. We believe that the best discipline is self-discipline.'

Uniform Black blazer, black trousers/skirt, blue shirt/blouse. Compulsory.

Homework Average 14-year-old, 10 hours a week; 16-year-old, 12 hours.

Vocational qualifications Sixth-formers take some vocational courses in local further education college on word-processing and computer-aided design.

TOWNLEY GRAMMAR SCHOOL FOR GIRLS

Townley Road
Bexleyheath
Kent DA6 7AB
Tel (0181) 304 8311
Fax (0181) 298 7421

- National ranking 58 (74, 76, 75, 89)
- GCSE 98% (98%)
- A-levels 48% (A/B); 96% (A/E)
- Higher education 74% (Cambridge 1)

- Girls' grammar
- Pupils 1,003
- Boys *Not applicable*
- Girls (11–18) 1,003
- Sixth form 215 (21%)
- Education authority *Bexley*

Headteacher Linda C. Hutchinson, 47, appointed in September 1992. Staff 64 (men 13, women 51).

Motto *None*

Background Founded in 1930s as technical school for girls; moved in 1937 to current building, which has been extended regularly on greenfield site a short walk from centre of Bexleyheath. Over-subscribed, with 1.5 applications per place. Tradition of excellence in music, with concerts at least three times a year and school assemblies providing performance opportunities for two choirs, two orchestras, concert band, string and recorder ensembles. Clubs and societies include hovercraft club, science societies, Christian Union, drama clubs. Charity fund-raising. 'The school aims to create a hardworking and academic environment and, at the same time, a lively, caring community within which girls may grow in confidence and independence.'

Alumni Valerie Amos, chief executive of Equal Opportunities Commission; Joan Thirkettle, television journalist.

Streaming Setting in mathematics and French in years 7 to 9; in mathematics, science and modern languages in years 10 and 11.

Approach to discipline 'The school prides itself on the good working atmosphere created by a well-disciplined environment. A high standard of behaviour based on consideration for others and social responsibility is expected at all times.' Parental support sought; early discussion of any difficulties. Any sanctions necessary are chosen to suit individual pupil.

Uniform Grey blazer, grey skirt, grey cardigan/jumper, blue shirt in lower school and white shirt in upper school. Strictly enforced for years 7 to 11; sixth-formers wear school colours.

Homework Average 11-year-old, six hours a week; 14-year-old, 12 hours; 16-year-old, 15 hours.

Vocational qualifications GNVQ Advanced, Business.

Inspection January 1997: 'A very good school with some outstanding features.'; 'Pupils are extremely well motivated, which enables teachers to teach and improve attainment. The majority are articulate and confident when speaking. They listen to teachers and each other extremely well.'; 'The school functions as an orderly community, combining clear expectations of good behavior within a relaxed and friendly environment. Relationships within the school are excellent.'; 'Pupils are fortunate to benefit from teaching which is almost always at least satisfactory, with two-thirds of teaching seen being good or very good. Teachers are well-qualified, have good subject knowledge and most are good practitioners. They know their pupils well and have high and generally appropriate expectations of them.'; 'The school is very ably led by the head. She has a clear vision for its future development, firmly based on raising all aspects of achievement.'

Primary schools Total of 48 feeder schools.

NONSUCH HIGH SCHOOL FOR GIRLS

Ewell Road
Cheam
Surrey SM3 8AB
Tel (0181) 394 1308
Fax (0181) 393 2307
E-mail: 100444.1541@compuserve.com

- National ranking 59 (48, 117, 69, 72)
- GCSE 98% (99%)
- A-levels 47% (A/B); 96% (A/E)
- Higher education 95% (Cambridge 2)

- Grant-maintained
- Girls' grammar
- Pupils 917

- Boys *Not applicable*
- Girls (11–18) 917
- Sixth form 226 (25%)
- Education authority *Sutton*

Headteacher Genefer Espejo, 47, appointed in September 1995. Staff 50 (men 10, women 40).

Motto Serve God and be cheerful.

Background Opened in 1938, the school stands on edge of 22-acre Nonsuch Park, once part of Nonsuch Palace, built 400 years ago by Henry VIII and demolished in the late 17th century. The association is commemorated in school badge with silhouette of palace on Tudor rose. More than five applicants for every place. Total of 27 A-level subjects offered. Music is a particular strength: three orchestras, four choirs, wind band and ensembles. 'Excellent' facilities include new technology wing, new eight-classroom wing, 10 laboratories and 'splendid' new music suite. Extensive playing fields and swimming pool on site. School proud of its 'dynamic combination of tradition and innovation'.

Alumni Marilyn Hill Smith, soprano; Vivien Saunders, British Women's golf champion 1976; Gillian Goodwin (née Gilks), former all-England badminton champion and sportswoman of the year; Lucy Wakeford, harpist; Patricia Berry, author; Christine Lamb, author and journalist; Glenwyn Benson, BBC Head of Adult Education; Susan Arkell, chess master; Sheila Paine, travel writer.

Streaming Pupils taught in form groups for all but practical subjects. Setting in French and Mathematics in years 8 and 9; continues for mathematics up to GCSE.

Approach to discipline Common sense, courtesy and self-discipline are the watchwords. 'A detention system operates for work or behaviour that falls below an acceptable standard. Parents are always kept fully informed.'

Uniform Dark-and-light-blue plaid kilt-style skirt, blue blouse, navy pullover/cardigan with school crest.

Homework Average 11-year-old, seven hours 30 minutes a week; 14-year-old, 10 to 12 hours; 16-year-old, 12 hours.

Vocational qualifications Business Studies; RSA, Computer Literacy; RSA, Foreign Languages

and Information Technology.

Inspection January 1994: 'Nonsuch High School is a very successful school. Of the 240 lessons observed, 96% were deemed to be satisfactory or better, with 50% being good or very good. Written work is of a high standard. Pupils read competently and they are generally confident orally. Pupils' numeracy skills are sound.'; 'The school provides a caring and secure environment within which pupils learn. Standards of behaviour, discipline and attendance are excellent.'

Primary schools Cuddington Croft Primary; St Dunstan's Primary, Cheam; Auriol County Junior; Burlington Junior; The Avenue Primary; Glaisdale School; Lynton Preparatory; Seaton House Preparatory.

INVICTA GRAMMAR SCHOOL

Huntsman Lane
Maidstone
Kent ME14 5DR
Tel (01622) 755856
Fax (01622) 678584
E-mail: invicta@rmplc.co.uk
Internet: http://www.rmplc.co.uk/eduweb/ sites/invicta

- National ranking 60 (51, 60, 88, 108)
- GCSE 98% (99%)
- A-levels 44% (A/B); 97% (A/E)
- Higher education 85% (Cambridge 1)

- Girls' grammar
- Pupils 924
- Boys (16–18) 4
- Girls (11–18) 920
- Sixth form 218 (24%)
- Education authority *Kent*

Headteacher Susan J. Glanville, appointed in September 1993. Staff 52 (men 11, women 41).

Motto *None*

Background Founded in 1940, modern buildings in grounds on eastern outskirts of town, on landscaped campus with access to open parkland; buildings extensively improved and extended in past decade. Recent additions include purpose-built sixth-form block, music suite with auditorium, drama wing, laboratories and technology rooms; new information technology network and 'impressive' resources centre. 'Superb' sports facilities include all-weather sports pitch. Always fully-subscribed; additional form of entry required to meet first-choice demand. School prides itself on wide range of courses, particularly in sixth form. Emphasis on careers education: work-experience in Britain, Germany, France and Spain; local industry supports annual Challenge of Management Conference for year 12 pupils. Music, art and drama also regarded as strong with high reputation. Named in Ofsted Chief Inspector's 1995 and 1996 annual reports as 'outstandingly successful'.

Streaming In mathematics in years 8 to 11.

Approach to discipline Atmosphere of mutual respect. 'Students are encouraged to develop self-discipline, personal and collective organisation, and the ability to work together in teams while developing their potential to the full.'

Uniform Maroon skirt or black trousers and pale-blue blouse with maroon jumper for years 7 to 11. No formal uniform for sixth-formers.

Homework Average 11-year-old, six hours a week; 14-year-old, 12 hours; 16-year-old, 18 hours.

Vocational qualifications *None*

Inspection November 1993: 'The school provides an education of good quality and range. The standards achieved by pupils are good or very good in the great majority of lessons, and in some subjects they are outstanding.'; 'Most of the teaching is soundly based and in some areas it is inspiring.'; 'Relationships between pupils and standards of behaviour are very good. Pupils and parents show a strong commitment to the school, identify with its aims and support its activities.'; 'The school has strong leadership and a clear vision for the future.'

Primary schools Draws from about 50 feeder schools in Maidstone and the surrounding area.

KING EDWARD VI ASTON SCHOOL

Frederick Road
Aston
Birmingham
West Midlands B6 6DJ
Tel (0121) 327 1130
Fax (0121) 328 7020

- National ranking 61 (38, 123, 80, 39)
- GCSE 98% (99%)
- A-levels 44% (A/B); 91% (A/E)
- Higher education 98% (Oxford 1, Cambridge 2)

- Grant-maintained
- Boys' grammar
- Pupils 645
- Boys (11–18) 645
- Girls *Not applicable*
- Sixth form 180 (28%)
- Education authority *Birmingham*

Headteacher Peter Anthony Christopher, 53, appointed in September 1992. Staff 40 (men 29, women 11).

Motto *None*

Background One of five grant-maintained grammar schools of the foundation of schools of King Edward VI in Birmingham. Original 1883 buildings. Site extended: gymnasium, science laboratories and assembly hall added in 1960s; new technology facilities opened in 1991; drama studio and sixth-form study area in 1992. 'Excellent' playing fields half a mile from school on other side of Aston Hall and park. Strong rugby tradition; in athletics, one pupil is current 100m national schools' champion; junior athletics team are Midlands champions; cross-country and basketball strong, and cricket played at all levels. All pupils study three sciences to GCSE; two modern languages until 14. Curriculum links with industry, particularly British Gas. Over-subscribed, with 880 applications for 96 places.

Alumni Ted Allbeury, author and broadcaster; Sir Edgar Britten, first captain of the *Queen Mary*; Sir Edward Downes, conductor and associate music director of Royal Opera House; Bernard Ford, world ice-dance champion; Henry Reed, poet.

Streaming Broad bands in years 7 to 9. Setting in mathematics, modern languages and subject options in years 10 and 11.

Approach to discipline Self-discipline, common sense, and respect for others and their property are the aims. 'Reinforced by clear guidelines and a framework of rewards and sanctions. Senior boys are expected to set the tone and to lead in a well-structured and accepted prefect system.'

Uniform Years 7 to 11: black blazer with school badge, school/house tie/colours or national/county representation tie. Sixth-formers: jacket or suit with tie.

Homework Average 11-year-old, five hours a week; 14-year-old, seven hours 30 minutes; 16-year-old, eight to 10 hours.

Vocational qualifications *None*

Inspection February 1994: 'King Edward VI Aston School provides a good education for its pupils'; 'Teaching and learning are conducted within a calm, purposeful and productive atmosphere and with excellent relationships between all those involved. The timetabled curriculum is enhanced by many additional extra-curricular activities, most notably sport and music.'; 'The courteous, confident and mutually supportive nature of the pupil body is an excellent characteristic of the school. Attitudes of respect for self and others are successfully promoted.'

Primary schools Total of 76 feeder schools throughout the West Midlands.

SIR WILLIAM BORLASE'S GRAMMAR SCHOOL

West Street
Marlow
Buckinghamshire SL7 2BR
Tel (01628) 482256
Fax (01628) 477886
E-mail: enquiries@borlase.marlow.sch.uk
Internet: http://www.borlase.marlow.sch.uk

- National ranking 62 (128, 89, 72, 68)
- GCSE 98% (94%)
- A-levels 41% (A/B); 98% (A/E)
- Higher education 100% (Oxford 1)

- Mixed grammar
- Pupils 854
- Boys (12–18) 433
- Girls (12–18) 421
- Sixth form 312 (37%)
- Education authority *Buckinghamshire*

Headteacher Peter Alan Holding, 42, appointed in April 1997. Staff 52 (men 31, women 21).

Motto Te digna sequere (Follow things worthy of you).

Background Founded in 1624 by Sir William Borlase in memory of his son, Henry, MP for Marlow, who died in that year. Still on original site using some of original build-

ings in one of town's oldest streets in a conservation area; Christian foundation. Additions include classrooms built around a cloister, a chapel, science and technology blocks, gymnasium, music suite, library, sixth-form common rooms. New building programme. Latin taught to all year 9 pupils; French and German exchanges each year; strong links with Marly-le-Roi, Marlow's twin town in France. Over-subscribed to varying degrees each year. Proud of national reputation for sport: five times national champions in hockey; winners of gold and silver medals for rowing. Strong fixture lists for cricket, hockey, netball, rugby and soccer; championship standards for chess, general knowledge and consumer law (1992 national champions). Parents' Association; Old Borlasian Club. Named among top 10 schools in the country in competition to mark 150th anniversary of Institution of Mechanical Engineers.

Alumni Garfield Weston, chairman of Associated British Foods; Paul Daneman, actor; Simon Dutton, actor; David Willey, journalist.

Streaming Setting used in mathematics and modern languages.

Approach to discipline 'The self-discipline of the pupils is uniformly high.' Breaches of disciplinary code dealt with 'firmly and sensitively'.

Uniform Formal uniform, including blazer and tie, worn by all pupils. 'Uniform regulations are respected and adhered to without question.'

Homework Average 12-year-old, at least seven hours 30 minutes a week; 14-year-old, at least 10 hours; 16-year-old, at least 15 hours.

Vocational qualifications *None*

Primary schools Danesfield Combined, Medmenham; St Peter's RC Combined; Spinfield County Combined; Burford Combined, Marlow Bottom; Holy Trinity CE Middle.

CHISLEHURST AND SIDCUP GRAMMAR SCHOOL

Hurst Road
Sidcup
Kent DA15 9AG
Tel (0181) 302 6511
Fax (0181) 309 6596

- National ranking 63 (138, 115, 133, 86)
- GCSE 98% (93%)
- A-levels 40% (A/B); 96% (A/E)
- Higher education 85% (Oxford 1, Cambridge 3)

- Mixed grammar
- Pupils 1,300
- Boys (11–18) 721
- Girls (11–18) 579
- Sixth form 400 (31%)
- Education authority *Bexley*

Headteacher James Andrew Rouncefield, 46, appointed in September 1994. Staff 75 (men 42, women 33).

Motto Abeunt studia in mores (Out of effort, character is formed).

Background Moved to its current parkland site in 1954 as a four-form entry boys' grammar. First girls came to the school in 1973; takes 192 pupils from up to 60 primary schools. Over-subscribed, two applications per place. Substantial investment in information technology hardware and software. New technology suite and science laboratories Academic success is hallmark of school. But teachers 'not interested in producing large numbers of clever but selfish adults'. Also proud of examination success of less able pupils. Art, music and drama also 'outstanding'; strong sporting tradition, particularly in rugby, cricket, athletics and netball.

Streaming Pupils in sets for mathematics in years 8 and 9. Setting widely used from year 10.

Approach to discipline Behaviour policy with guidelines on sanctions: 'The object is to impose such discipline in the early stages of a pupil's time with us as to induce an increasing amount of self-discipline as they proceed into the sixth form.' Emphasis on early consultation, and co-operation, with parents.

Uniform Purple blazer, grey trousers/skirt. Very strictly enforced.

Homework Average 11-year-old, at least five hours a week; 14-year-old, at least seven hours 30 minutes; 16-year-old, at least 15 hours.

Vocational qualifications *None*

Inspection October 1994: 'Pupils have good learning skills. They are enthusiastic and capable of extended research and concentration. However, more responsibility for learning needs to be placed with the pupils themselves so they can develop the independent learning skills necessary for even higher levels of achievement, particularly at A-level'; 'Pupils are courteous and well-behaved. Moral education occurs in some of the subjects of the curriculum.'

Primary schools Total of 70 feeder schools.

SOUTHEND HIGH SCHOOL FOR GIRLS

Southchurch Boulevard
Southend-on-Sea
Essex SS2 4UZ
Tel (01702) 588852
Fax (01702) 587181

- National ranking 64 (93, 20, 71, 69)
- GCSE 98% (97%)
- A-levels 40% (A/B); 94% (A/E)
- Higher education 70% (Cambridge 1)

- Grant-maintained
- Girls' grammar
- Pupils 857
- Boys (16–18) 7
- Girls (11–18) 850
- Sixth form 200 (24%)
- Education authority *Essex*

Headteacher Ruth Alinek, 44, appointed in January 1995. Staff 56 (men 12, women 44).

Motto Ad dei gloriam (To the glory of God).

Background Founded early this century with tradition of academic, musical and sporting achievement. Originally in centre of Southend. Moved in 1950s to current site: modern buildings, landscaped grounds, six science laboratories, home economics, textiles room, two art studios, photographic dark room, two gymnasia, computer studies and office skills rooms; two technology studios; drama studio added in 1992. Separate centre for A-level studies includes common room, IT room, individual study area. New building projects in 1995 included extension to sixth-form centre, two new laboratories and media studies studio. Over-subscribed, with two applications per place. 'Excellent' records in Young Enterprise, Engineering Education, Insight into Industry for year 9, Insight into Management for year 12; also courses on environmental education, and moral and spiritual awareness. Emphasis on music and creative arts. Recent national athletics champions; county champions at tennis and hockey; local champions at netball, cross-country, volleyball and swimming.

Streaming Faster sets in mathematics, science and French from year 9.

Approach to discipline Pupils encouraged to look on school as working environment; appropriate behaviour expected. 'Our school is a place to work and learn. Behaviour that hinders this or makes someone else unhappy is unacceptable.'

Uniform Green blazer, green skirt, green pullover, green-and-white striped blouse. Fully enforced; parental co-operation excellent.

Homework Average 11-year-old, six hours a week; 14-year-old, 11 hours; 16-year-old, 18 hours.

Vocational qualifications RSA, Word-processing; Cambridge Certificate in Information Technology.

Primary schools Bournes Green Primary.

SOUTHEND HIGH SCHOOL FOR BOYS

Prittlewell Chase
Southend-on-Sea
Essex SS0 0RG
Tel (01702) 343074
Fax (01702) 300028
E-mail: shsb@rmplc.co.uk

- National ranking 65 (153, 148, 97, 64)
- GCSE 98% (91%)
- A-levels 40% (A/B); 91% (A/E)
- Higher education 79% (Oxford 1, Cambridge 1)

- Grant-maintained
- Boys' grammar
- Pupils 865
- Boys (11–18) 830
- Girls (16–18) 35
- Sixth form 247 (29%)
- Education authority *Essex*

Headteacher Michael Frampton, 50, appointed in September 1988. Staff 56 (men 45, women 11).

Motto Forti nihil difficile (To the brave, nothing is difficult).

Background The first secondary school in Southend when founded in 1895. It moved to its current site, close to main road with 12 acres of playing fields, in 1939. Latin and Greek taught; separate sciences at GCSE; consistent level of Oxbridge entrants; strong choral tradition; prides itself on music, drama, public speaking and foreign exchanges. Over-subscribed, with up to five applications per place. Local athletics champions for past 20 years, with regional and national success at soccer, hockey and tennis. Strong house and prefectorial system. Old boys' association is one of biggest in the country.

Alumni David and John Lloyd, tennis players; Gary Nelson, soccer player; Air Marshal Sir Frank Holroyd; Robert Lloyd, opera singer; Digby Fairweather, jazz musician; Baron Chilver of Cranfield.

Streaming Pupils in sets in mathematics from year 8, modern languages from year 10.

Approach to discipline Written policy on behaviour includes basic rules, code of conduct and specific regulations; sanctions include detention. Rewards and incentives include 'excellence' awards and house credits scheme.

Uniform Green blazer with school badge, white/grey shirt with house tie, black/dark grey trousers and socks, black shoes. Regulations strictly enforced throughout. Distinctive ties for sixth-formers and prefects.

Homework Average 11-year-old, seven hours 30 minutes a week; 14-year-old, 10 hours; 16-year-old, 12 hours 30 minutes.

Vocational qualifications *None*

Inspection February 1995: 'A good, traditional but outward-looking grammar school. The ethos is purposeful and well-disciplined, emphasising the pursuit of academic excellence and the development of high standards in spiritual, moral, cultural and social development. The school has high expectations of its pupils.'; 'The pastoral system is a strength.'; 'The quality of learning is sound or better in over 90% of lessons at both key stages and in the sixth form. The pupils are polite and courteous and are given excellent opportunities to exercise and develop a sense of personal and corporate responsibility.'

JOHN HAMPDEN GRAMMAR SCHOOL

Marlow Hill
High Wycombe
Buckinghamshire HP11 1SZ
Tel (01494) 529589
Fax (01494) 447714

- National ranking 66 (70, 57, 14, 52)
- GCSE 98% (98%)
- A-levels 39% (A/B); 92% (A/E)
- Higher education 97% (Oxford 4, Cambridge 3)

- Boys' grammar
- Pupils 750
- Boys (12–18) 750
- Girls *Not applicable*
- Sixth form 261 (35%)
- Education authority *Buckinghamshire*

Headteacher Andrew John MacTavish, appointed in January 1983. Staff 48 (men 35, women 13).

Motto Quit ye like men (1 Corinthians 16.13).

Background Founded in 1893 initially to teach science, art and technology, the school rapidly grew in size and stature. Today it is set in its own grounds at the top of Marlow Hill, drawing pupils from a wide area of south Buckinghamshire and adjacent areas of Oxfordshire, Berkshire and Middlesex. School nationally renowned for technology and runs its own week-long exhibition annually. It appears regularly in Wembley finals of Young Engineer for Britain and in Sainsbury Trust Engineering Scheme. Soccer team were joint winners of national under-19 cup in 1986 and finalists in 1992. Strong Christian and moral ethos; over-subscribed. Work completed in January 1996 on £1.7m sixth-form block to provide specialist teaching rooms, private study accommodation, common room and new library. Development gave school a new façade in September 1995. Half entry (60 boys) at 11 from September 1997; full entry at 11 from September 1998.

Alumni Terry Pratchett, novelist; Nick Clarry, oarsman.

Streaming In mathematics, the most able are accelerated.

Approach to discipline Boys referred to as 'gentlemen' and expected to behave as such. 'The staff have high standards and lead by example. For these reasons, the school is a secure and happy place.'

Uniform Black blazer with badge, dark-grey trousers, white shirt, school tie, black shoes. Sixth-formers wear distinctive tie, but not blazer badge. Very strictly enforced.

Homework Average 12-year-old, eight hours a week; 14-year-old, 11 hours; 16-year-old, 14 hours.

Vocational qualifications *None*

Inspection December 1994: 'A successful school. Achievement is good throughout the school with pupils at both key stages and at post-16 consistently attaining good standards both in terms of national norms for their age groups and in relation to their ability.'; 'The quality of education provided by the school is of a consistently good standard.'; 'The school supports the spiritual, moral, social and cultural development of the pupils through a clear set of values which pervade all aspects of its life.'

Primary schools Butlers Court Combined, Beaconsfield; Hamilton Combined, High Wycombe; Great Kingshill CE Combined; Stokenchurch Middle; Tylers Green Middle, Penn; Holy Trinity Middle, Marlow.

WALLINGTON HIGH SCHOOL FOR GIRLS

Woodcote Road
Wallington
Surrey SM6 0PH
Tel (0181) 647 2380
Fax (0181) 773 9884

- National ranking 67 (47, 65, 38, 53)
- GCSE 98% (99%)
- A-levels 38% (A/B); 93% (A/E)
- Higher education 72% (Oxford 1)

- Grant-maintained
- Girls' grammar
- Pupils 927
- Boys *Not applicable*
- Girls (11–18) 927
- Sixth form 278 (30%)
- Education authority *Sutton*

Headteacher Margaret J. Edwards, 52, appointed in September 1992. Staff 53 (men 5, women 48).

Motto Heirs of the past, makers of the future.

Background Founded in 1888 by local residents and clergy as a school for lower-middle-class girls, it opened with only 25 pupils. Now in its fourth set of buildings, set in large grounds on the edge of the green belt. Oversubscribed, with four times as many qualified applicants as places. Strong links with industry; girls encouraged not to be stereotyped.

Alumni Lesley Downer (1960–67), cookery writer and broadcaster; Paula Bott (1967–74), opera singer; Pauline Boty (1949–54), pop artist.

Streaming One top mathematics set and one 'slow' set in years 9 to 11.

Approach to discipline High standards in a happy, supportive environment. 'Each individual is treated with respect, and thus learns to respect the needs of others.'

Uniform Plaid kilt, blue blouse, green jumper/cardigan, navy coat. All girls in years 7 to 11 are expected to wear the correct uniform.

Homework Average 11-year-old, eight to nine hours a week; 14-year-old, nine to 10 hours; 16-year-old, 12 to 13 hours.

Vocational qualifications Foreign Languages at Work.

Inspection February 1994: 'Wallington High School for Girls is a very successful school which provides a high-quality all-round education, equipping its pupils to flourish as lively and confident individuals in the adult world.'; 'The pupils demonstrate a mature attitude to learning and relationships between all members of the school community are very good.'; 'There is significant pressure on the school's accommodation due to rising rolls and changes in the curricular needs.'

Primary schools Barrow Hedges Primary; Stanley Park Junior; Holy Trinity CE Primary; Bandon Hill Primary; Seaton House; Hackbridge Junior.

TORQUAY GRAMMAR SCHOOL FOR GIRLS

30 Shiphay Lane
Torquay
Devon TQ2 7DY
Tel (01803) 613215
Fax (01803) 616724
E-mail: 4114@911-4114.devon.cc.gov.uk

- National ranking 68 (45, 22, 92, 8)
- GCSE 98% (99%)
- A-levels 38% (A/B); 92% (A/E)
- Higher education 75%

- Girls' grammar
- Pupils 809
- Boys *Not applicable*
- Girls (11–18) 809
- Sixth form 244 (30%)
- Education authority *Devon*

Headteacher S. M. Roberts, appointed in September 1996. Staff 44 (men 16, women 28).

Motto Aude sapere (Dare to be wise).

Background Founded in 1915, the school moved in 1939 to its current building, 'The White House on the Hill', described as a typically provincial adaptation of the international modern style, characterised by flat roofs, symmetry and pristine white finish; open aspect to playing fields. Shiphay Manor, rough red sandstone building, became sixth-form centre in 1979. Paddock links principal buildings; sloping parkland with trees. Over-subscribed, with 1.5 applications per place; building programme completed to include 10 more classrooms and art department; opened in 1995 by Baroness P. D. James. Bought own residential centre at Tregourez in Brittany in 1990, European base for work-experience, cross-curricular projects, cultural exchanges. Choir has won national competitions and sung in Salzburg. Sporting success includes regional and county representatives. Team success in Ten Tors expedition.

Alumni Sarah Gomer, tennis player; Vivien Stuart, BBC Radio Two weather presenter; Diana and Bryony Behets, actresses in *Neighbours*, the Australian soap opera; Jenna Ward, actress and singer.

Streaming Only in mathematics from year 8; French and German from year 9; English from year 10.

Approach to discipline High expectations; good relations between staff and pupils. 'Praise and encouragement engender a positive attitude to self-esteem, self-discipline and personal responsibility.' Appropriate sanctions when standards not met; rules and regulations to allow pupils to pursue studies unhindered.

Uniform Years 7 to 11: navy skirt, blue-check

blouse, navy jumper. Sixth-formers wear grey skirts with cream/white/blue/black tops; can also wear green. Strictly enforced.

Homework Average 11-year-old, six hours a week; 14-year-old, nine hours; 16-year-old, at least 12 hours.

Vocational qualifications Business English, French and German; Liverpool enrichment award.

Inspection October 1993: 'The quality of education is high. The pupils' attitude to learning is excellent; they are highly-motivated. Learning skills are well-developed and pupils respond to intellectual and creative challenge. Where teaching strategies do not provide these opportunities, the progress of pupils is more limited.'

CHURSTON GRAMMAR SCHOOL

Greenway Road
Brixham
Devon TQ5 0LN
Tel (01803) 842289
Fax (01803) 846007

- National ranking 69 (66, 107, 111, 145)
- GCSE 98% (98%)
- A-levels 34% (A/B); 94% (A/E)
- Higher education 90%

- Mixed grammar
- Pupils 826
- Boys (11–18) 367
- Girls (11–18) 459
- Sixth form 230 (28%)
- Education authority *Devon*

Headteacher John Robert Parsons, 57, appointed in January 1979. Staff 48 (men 22, women 26).

Motto *None*

Background The only local authority mixed grammar school in Devon and one of only a few in England. Built in 1957 in extensive grounds at southern end of Torbay, with panoramic views towards the River Dart. Serves coastal towns of Brixham, Paignton, Kingswear and Dartmouth, although some pupils travel from much farther afield. New purpose-built art and music block; science and technology areas refurbished and extended; sixth-form block, sports hall, multi-gym and expressive arts centre completed in November 1994. Top 25% of ability range admitted; average of three applications per place. School proud of sporting and extra-curricular achievements: senior basketball team have been twice England champions in recent years; public speaking 'unparalleled', with senior teams in several English Speaking Union finals. School choir and band also notable for success. Priority given to development and welfare of pupils so that their achievements fully match their potential.

Alumni Peter Larter, England rugby international; Gary Lane, international chess master.

Streaming In mathematics, pupils put in sets from year 8.

Approach to discipline 'The school expects students to exercise self-discipline and respond to encouragement. Behaviour is very good and sanctions are rarely needed.'

Uniform Navy sweater with school badge, dark-grey trousers/navy skirt, white shirt/blouse, school tie. No uniform for sixth-formers; smart dress expected. Strictly enforced.

Homework Average 11-year-old, five hours a week; 14-year-old, seven hours 30 minutes; 16-year-old, 10 hours.

Vocational qualifications Foreign Languages at Work; Sports Leadership; Business Studies.

Inspection December 1994: 'Churston Grammar School provides a broad, good education at all levels and the sixth form course is particularly encouraging in offering a broadly-based curriculum which is well-received by pupils. The standards of teaching and learning are generally high.'; 'The school has clear, established values and is an orderly and harmonious community. There are many opportunities for pupils to develop personal responsibility both within the classroom and outside, including a wide range of extra-curricular activities.'

Primary schools Curledge Street Primary, Paignton; Eden Park Primary, Brixham; Oldway Primary, Paignton; Furzeham Primary, Brixham; Galmpton CE Primary, Brixham; White Rock Primary, Paignton; Hayes Primary, Paignton; Roselands Primary, Paignton.

METHODIST COLLEGE BELFAST

1 Malone Road
Belfast BT9 6BY
Tel (01232) 669558
Fax (01232) 666375
E-mail: ranaylor@methody.dnet.co.uk
Internet: http://www.niweb.com/schools/
mcb

- National ranking 70 (83, 95, 90, 81)
- GCSE 97% (97%)
- A-levels 59% (A/B); 94% (A/E)
- Higher education 84% (Oxford 8, Cambridge 13)

- Mixed grammar
- Pupils 2,473
- Boys (11–18) 1,360
- Girls (11–18) 1,113
- Sixth form 548 (22%)
- Education authority *Belfast Education and Library Board*

Headteacher Thomas Wilfred Mulryne, 53, appointed in September 1988. Staff 148 (men 59, women 89).

Motto Deus nobiscum (God be with us).

Background Established in 1868 as a public school for boarders and day pupils irrespective of their denominations; on south side of Belfast, close to university and Ulster Museum. Opposite are Botanic Gardens leading down to River Lagan where college has boathouse for rowing clubs. Two sports fields comprising 50 acres. Over-subscribed, with two applications for each place. Includes two prep schools. Recently-built science and technology block incorporating design rooms equipped with computers. Sporting success includes rugby; winners of Ulster Schools' Rugby Shield. Strong family commitment.

Alumni Barry Douglas, pianist; Professor Ernest Walton, 1951 Nobel prizewinner for physics; Dr Robin Eames, Archbishop of Armagh and Church of Ireland Primate.

Streaming Pupils put in three bands in years 8 and 9 according to courses (for example, whether they are doing a second modern language); in years 10 and 11 pupils put in sets for mathematics and French.

Approach to discipline 'Firm, fair and consistent, implemented through a structured form system.'

Uniform Navy blazer, white shirt/blouse, grey trousers/skirt, navy school tie with white Maltese cross. Strictly enforced.

Homework Average 11-year-old, seven hours 30 minutes a week; 14-year-old, 10 hours; 16-year-old, 12 hours.

Vocational qualifications RSA, Computer Literacy and Information Technology.

Primary schools Fullerton House Preparatory; Downey House Preparatory; Stranmillis Primary; St Bride's Primary; Finaghy Primary; Cairnshill Primary.

DR CHALLONER'S HIGH SCHOOL

Cokes Lane
Little Chalfont
Buckinghamshire HP7 9QB
Tel (01494) 763296
Fax (01494) 766023
E-mail: drchalls@rmplc.co.uk

- National ranking 71 (28, 52, 47, 44)
- GCSE 97% (99%)
- A-levels 55% (A/B); 97% (A/E)
- Higher education 90% (Oxford 6, Cambridge 6)

- Girls' grammar
- Pupils 880
- Boys *Not applicable*
- Girls (12–18) 880
- Sixth form 280 (32%)
- Education authority *Buckinghamshire*

Headteacher Susanne Lawson, 51, appointed in September 1993. Staff 48 (men 5, women 43).

Motto Pro Maleficiis Beneficia (For evil, return good).

Background The school was established in 1962 after the previous co-educational Dr Challoner's Grammar School, founded in 1624, became two single-sex schools. Close contact is maintained with the boys' grammar. The school is sited in wooded surroundings on the outskirts of Little Chalfont, near Amersham. Its buildings were enlarged in 1984 and extensions in 1993 and 1997, including multi-media workshop, additional information technology facilities and a graphics/design and electronics area, new classroom suites for mathematics and English, and a sixth-form study area. Further building in 1997: refurbished art area and sixth-form laboratory; new languages and music wing, plus further laboratory in 1998; planning permission for sports hall. Over-subscribed, with 3.5 applications per place. Extra-curricular activities 'a particular feature of the school, with music, sport and drama being specially strong'. Many activities shared with Dr Challoner's Grammar School, 'with whom we have the closest ties'. Orchestra, string orchestra, woodwind ensemble, swing band, three choirs, recorder group. Duke of Edinburgh Award Scheme. Bridge, chess, computing, Christian Union, public-speaking and swimming. Well-established work-experience scheme supports careers guidance; personal, social and health education programme 'encourages the skills needed to promote the positive self-image of women in the 21st century'.

Streaming Pupils are divided into sets in some subjects for years 10 and 11.

Approach to discipline 'A school code of conduct seeks to ensure a well-ordered but caring environment in which learning can flourish. High standards of behaviour and achievement are expected.'

Uniform Navy skirt, navy school sweatshirt with DCHS emblem, navy-and-white striped blouse.

Homework Average 12-year-old, six hours a week; 14-year-old, nine hours; 16-year-old, 12 hours.

Vocational qualifications *None*

Primary schools Elangeni Middle, Amersham; Little Chalfont Combined; Chalfont St Peter CE Middle; Chalfont St Giles Middle; Maltman's Green School. Total of 25+ feeder schools.

SUTTON COLDFIELD GIRLS' SCHOOL

Jockey Road
Sutton Coldfield
West Midlands B73 5PT
Tel (0121) 354 1479
Fax (0121) 354 9418
E-mail: suttcold@lea.birmingham.gov.uk

- National ranking 72 (103, 61, 54, 65)
- GCSE 97% (96%)
- A-levels 53% (A/B); 97% (A/E)
- Higher education 90% (Oxford 1)

- Girls' grammar

- Pupils 940
- Boys *Not applicable*
- Girls (11–18) 940
- Sixth form 185 (20%)
- Education authority *Birmingham*

Headteacher Jennifer J. Jones, 57, appointed in September 1983. Staff 55 (men 13, women 42).

Motto Not for our own advantage, but for the common good.

Background Founded as a grammar school for girls in 1929, the school briefly became comprehensive in 1975, until becoming a selective school again in 1980. Within walking distance of Sutton Coldfield, and also well-placed for bus and rail links; pupils come from Sutton Coldfield, Lichfield, Tamworth, Walsall, Bromsgrove and Redditch as well as the whole of Birmingham. Over-subscribed with eight applications for each place. New technology and sixth-form blocks planned. Reputation for musical activities: pupils in most of Birmingham orchestras and ensembles; biennial production of a light opera with neighbouring school. Outdoor pursuits, including national and international representatives. Foreign exchanges with Lyon in France, Madrid in Spain, the United States and Australia. Very successful in art competitions. Strong tradition in sport: netball, hockey, cross-country, orienteering, triathlon, tennis, rounders, athletics and swimming. 'Excellent' achievements in art competitions.

Alumni Louise Botting, financial journalist and former presenter of BBC Radio Four's *Moneybox* programme; Mon Pickersgill, president of All England Women's Hockey Association; Estella Hindley, QC, Crown Court recorder; Shona Lindsay, singer and actress; Jane Rossington, actress.

Streaming *None*

Approach to discipline Everyone expected to be polite and considerate, 'producing an atmosphere of firm but fair discipline'. Punishments rare; but used when unsatisfactory behaviour occurs.

Uniform Brown blazer (optional), brown skirt, cream shirt, brown pullover. Dress code for sixth-formers.

Homework Average 11-year-old, five hours 20 minutes a week; 14-year-old, nine hours 20 minutes; 16-year-old, at least 10 hours.

Vocational qualifications *None*

Inspection October 1994: 'A good school with some strong features.'; 'Seldom are standards less than high.'; 'Leadership is thoughtful and sensitive.'; 'The school is orderly and provides a supportive environment for learning. Pupils are courteous and behave well. Common moral values are the accepted norm. Any occasional lapses in behaviour are promptly dealt with by staff. Sixth-formers are good role models and willingly take responsibility, for example, in helping and organising activities for others.'

Primary schools Walmley Junior; Bromford Junior; Whitehouse Common Primary; Harborne Junior; Mayfield Preparatory. Pupils come from a total of 80 feeder schools.

OUR LADY AND ST PATRICK'S COLLEGE, KNOCK

Kingsway Gardens
Belfast BT5 7DQ
Tel (01232) 401184
Fax (01232) 799890

- National ranking 73 (130, 141, 138, 129)
- GCSE 97% (94%)
- A-levels 52% (A/B); 97% (A/E)
- Higher education 87% (Oxford 1)

- Mixed grammar
- Pupils 1,231
- Boys (11–18) 634
- Girls (11–18) 597
- Sixth form 381 (31%)
- Education authority *South Eastern Education and Library Board*

Headteacher Very Rev Patrick McKenna, 53, appointed in January 1987. Staff 78 (men 30, women 48).

Motto Gratias agamus (Let us give thanks).

Background Founded in 1985 with fusion of Sacred Heart of Mary Grammar School, Holywood, County Down, and St Patrick's College, Knock; located in spacious grounds in Cherryvalley suburb of east Belfast, 'thoughtfully-designed, modern and the campus has impressive indoor and outdoor sporting facilities'. Over-subscribed. All Ireland netball champions in 1991, 1992 and 1994. Strong in technology and design; 'state-of-the-art' technology equipment and laboratories; outdoor pursuits; pupils take three A-levels and a 'curriculum enrichment' subject: contemporary European studies, Japanese studies, GCSE Law. A total of 32 subjects are offered. 'Our aim is to provide a school where students are happily and enthusiastically involved in a wide variety of work within a well-structured but flexible framework.'

Alumni Grainne Gunn, Channel swimmer; Angie Phillips, weather presenter.

Streaming *None*

Approach to discipline Subject teachers are 'backbone' of disciplinary structure; counsellors assist individual pupils with difficulties. Students may be referred to class tutor, head of school or vice-principal; head of upper school may refer pupil to disciplinary committee comprising three vice-principals.

Uniform Boys: black blazer with school crest, black trousers, white shirt, grey V-neck jumper with college colours, college tie. Girls: black blazer with school crest, grey skirt, white shirt, college tie, black V-neck jumper with college colours. Very strictly enforced.

Homework Average 11-year-old, at least seven hours 30 minutes a week; 14-year-old, at least 12 hours 30 minutes; 16-year-old, at least 15 hours.

Vocational qualifications RSA Stage 1, Word-processing.

Primary schools St Bernard's Primary, Belfast; St Bride's Primary, Belfast; St Malachy's Primary, Bangor; St Joseph's Primary, Carryduff; St Comgall's Primary, Bangor; St Mary's Primary, Kircubbin; St Mary's Primary, Portaferry; St Patrick's Primary, Holywood; St Michael's Primary, Belfast.

ST LOUIS GRAMMAR SCHOOL

Cullybackey Road
Ballymena
County Antrim BT43 5DW
Tel (01266) 49534
Fax (01266) 630287
E-mail: st_louis@mail.rmplc.co.uk

- National ranking 74 (63 = , 102, 85, 96)
- GCSE 97% (98%)
- A-levels 50% (A/B); 95% (A/E)
- Higher education 62% (Cambridge 1)

- Mixed grammar
- Pupils 966
- Boys (11–18) 454
- Girls (11–18) 512
- Sixth form 227 (23%)
- Education authority *North Eastern Education and Library Board*

Headteacher John Stuart, 55, appointed in September 1987. Staff 59 (men 29, women 30).

Motto Ut sint unum (That we may be one); Dieu le veult (God wills it).

Background Founded in 1924 by the Congregation of the Sisters of St Louis, originally a French order from Monaghan in the Irish Midlands; originally a traditional convent girls' grammar in the Convent House; purpose-built school opened in 1954 for 300 girls; extensions in 1969 and 1983; became co-educational in 1971. First lay principal appointed in September 1987. 'The school is located in a very attractive setting of lawns, shrubs and wooded areas close to the town centre. The various buildings blend harmoniously and provide a stimulating working environment.' Takes the top 30% of the ability range; consistently over-subscribed, with 1.3 applications per place. Wide range of sports: under-17 soccer team won 1989 Northern Ireland Cup. Notable recent examination success in full range of A-level subjects. All sixth-formers in year 12 expected to take additional subject on top of three or four A-level subjects to avoid over-specialism: Spanish, Japanese, French for Business Studies, drama, additional mathematics, information technology and practical electronics. Catholic ethos; strong commitment to academic, cultural and sporting contacts with schools of differing traditions.

Alumni Paul Kearney, author of *The Way to Babylon*; Fionnuala O'Connor, journalist; Michael Hughes, Northern Ireland soccer international.

Streaming Some setting in years 10 and 11.

Approach to discipline 'The emphasis is on self-discipline and self-control in the context of a Christian, caring community. A civilised and orderly atmosphere in which pupils respect each other and all they come into contact with is expected at all times. Discipline is firm, fair and flexible.'

Uniform Boys: black blazer with school crest, dark-grey trousers, grey pullover, pale-blue shirt, school tie. Girls: navy blazer with school crest, navy skirt, navy pullover, pale-blue blouse, pale-blue socks and school scarf. 'Strictly and fairly enforced.'

Homework Average 11-year-old, seven hours a week; 14-year-old, 10 hours; 16-year-old, 15 hours.

Vocational qualifications *None*

Primary schools St Mary's Primary, Portglenone; St Louis' Convent Primary, Ballymena; St Mary's Primary, Ballymena; St Joseph's Primary, Ballymena; Mount St Michael's Primary, Randalstown.

THE ROCHESTER GRAMMAR SCHOOL FOR GIRLS

Maidstone Road
Rochester
Kent ME1 3BY
Tel (01634) 843049
Fax (01634) 818340

- National ranking 75 (98, 29, 107, 111)
- GCSE 97% (96%)
- A-levels 49% (A/B); 96% (A/E)
- Higher education 90% (Oxford 1, Cambridge 3)

- Grant-maintained
- Girls' grammar
- Pupils 870
- Boys *Not applicable*
- Girls (11–18) 870
- Sixth form 206 (24%)
- Education authority *Kent*

Headteacher Jane Price, 53, appointed in January 1989. Staff 50 (men 9, women 41).

Motto Sub umbra alarum tuarum (Under the shadow of thy wings).

Background The school was founded in 1888 by the Wardens of Rochester Bridge. Based in original Victorian building until 1990, when it moved to another site with new buildings on open site about a mile out of Rochester. Over-subscribed, with two applications per place. New sports hall, all-weather pitch and playing fields among 'excellent' sports facilities. One computer for every nine pupils; six new science laboratories. All pupils study Latin from year 8, with German and French. Total of 17 subjects offered up to GCSE and 20 at A-level.

Mathematics, Classics and music among strengths. New technology block in 1995; new Performing Arts block in 1997.

Alumni Dame Sybil Thorndyke, actress.

Streaming Setting in mathematics from year 9, when taught in smaller groups.

Approach to discipline Seeks to work with pupils and parents by adopting a pastoral system based on year-groups. All pupils and parents issued with school rules when they enter school.

Uniform Navy blazer, royal-blue kilt and pullover, blue blouses, navy coat, black/brown shoes. No jewellery. Strictly enforced. Sixth-formers wear own choice of clothes.

Homework Average 11-year-old, six hours a week; 14-year-old, nine hours; 16-year-old, 10 hours.

Vocational qualifications RSA, Computer Literacy and Information Technology; Foreign Languages at Work (French and German); Sports Leadership Award.

Inspection December 1993: 'Standards of achievement are at least satisfactory and in the majority of subjects they are good.'; 'The quality of learning is good in the majority of lessons. Pupils are motivated, highly-committed and enthusiastic. Teaching is good and provides challenge and high expectation. The school has clear and established values which promote good relationships within an orderly and caring environment.'

Primary schools St Andrew's Preparatory; Spinnen's Acre Primary; Balfour Primary; Delce Primary; Tunbury Primary.

BOURNEMOUTH SCHOOL

East Way
Bournemouth
Dorset BH8 9PY
Tel (01202) 512609
Fax (01202) 516095
E-mail: jg@bmthsch.demon.co.uk

- National ranking 76= (35, 34, 22, 59)
- GCSE 97% (99%)
- A-levels 48% (A/B); 95% (A/E)
- Higher education 86% (Oxford 5, Cambridge 5)

- Grant-maintained
- Boys' grammar

- Pupils 970
- Boys (11–18) 970
- Girls *Not applicable*
- Sixth form 300 (31%)
- Education authority *Dorset*

Headteacher John Granger, 47, appointed in September 1996. Staff 62 (men 50, women 12).

Motto Pulchritudo et salubritas (Beauty and health).

Background Founded in 1901 and has always been a grammar school for the most able boys in the area; on north side of Bournemouth, three miles from town centre; surrounded on three sides by large copse that forms natural playground; 33 acres of adjoining playing fields: rugby, soccer, hockey, tennis, cricket and athletics. Over-subscribed, with up to three applications for each place. In 1995, 100% pass rate in 17 A-levels, including art and design, biology, business studies, economics, electronics, English, further mathematics, French, German, music, physics, religious studies and technology; designated Technology School. 'Excellent' sporting reputation: 1992 English Schools' Junior Freestyle Relay champions; South-West England Tennis Pairs champions; South-West England under-13 tennis champions. Full range of competitive sports; dramatic and musical productions; school orchestra, two choirs, big band, jazz band, numerous clubs and societies. Combined Cadet Force.

Alumni Sir David English, chairman and editor-in-chief of Associated Newspapers; Sir Paul Fox, former managing director of BBC Network Television; Christian Bale, film star; Gavin Stewart, 1988 Oxford University boat team captain and Olympic rower.

Streaming Pupils put in sets for mathematics and science.

Approach to discipline Even balance of rewards and sanctions. 'Incidents of indiscipline are rare, but when they occur they are dealt with firmly. Great emphasis is placed on the work ethic, mutual respect and high personal standards.'

Uniform Grey suit for years 7 to 11; dark business suit for sixth-formers. Very strictly enforced.

Homework Average 11-year-old, seven hours 30 minutes a week; 14-year-old, seven hours

30 minutes to 10 hours; 16-year-old, 10 hours.

Vocational qualifications GNVQ Advanced, Business Studies

Inspection November 1992: 'Bournemouth School provides a broad and largely balanced curriculum for its pupils. It is a well-organised, firmly-managed and efficient school. Standards of teaching and learning are generally good with some work of excellence being produced. The school operates within a well-ordered, civilised working atmosphere, characterised by good relationships between staff and pupils.'; 'The school is popular with parents and is justifiably valued for the general quality of the educational experience that it provides for its pupils.'

Primary schools King's Park Junior; Summerbee Junior; Moordown St John's CE Primary; The Park Primary; St Thomas Garnett's School; St Michael's CE Primary.

QUEEN ELIZABETH'S GRAMMAR SCHOOL

West Street
Horncastle
Lincolnshire LN9 5AD
Tel (01507) 522465
Fax (01507) 527711
E-mail: 9255411.04W@dialnet.co.uk

- National ranking 76= (135, 112, 28, –)
- GCSE 97% (93%)
- A-levels 48% (A/B); 95% (A/E)
- Higher education 89%

- Grant-maintained
- Mixed grammar
- Pupils 678
- Boys (11–18) 287
- Girls (11–18) 391
- Sixth form 160 (24%)
- Education authority Lincolnshire

Headteacher Timothy James Peacock, 47, appointed in September 1986, Staff 39 (men 23, women 16).

Motto None

Background Foundation dates from 1571: moved to current site on outskirts of Horncastle in 1908; subsequent development due to expansion. Recent additions to buildings include a new electronics and physics block and a technology centre. Extensive playing fields on site. School serves wide rural catchment area, stretching as far as Lincoln and Boston, including much of central Lincolnshire. Wide range of sporting and extra-curricular activities: music, drama, outdoor pursuits, community service, traditional team games. Numerous educational trips and visits each year, at home and abroad. Well-established links with local industry. Young Enterprise. 'Above all, the school is a friendly and caring place. It enjoys excellent support from parents and from the community it serves.'

Streaming Pupils are setted by ability in mathematics from year 9.

Approach to discipline 'The school's approach to discipline is traditional. Emphasis is placed upon a sense of responsibility to the whole school community and upon self-discipline, but a range of sanctions can be employed as required.'

Uniform Maroon blazer, white shirt, grey trousers/navy skirt or trousers, school tie. Separate uniform for sixth-formers.

Homework Average 11-year-old, five hours a week; 14-year-old, seven hours 30 minutes; 16-year-old, 12 hours 30 minutes.

Vocational qualifications None

Primary schools Horncastle Primary; St Andrew's CE Primary; Wragby County Primary; Coningsby CE County Primary; Tetford County Primary.

TORQUAY BOYS' GRAMMAR SCHOOL

Shiphay Manor Drive
Torquay
Devon TQ2 7EL
Tel (01803) 615501
Fax (01803) 614613
E-mail: torquayboysgrammsch@
campus.bt.com

- National ranking 76= (126, 70, 95, 83)
- GCSE 97% (94%)
- A-levels 48% (A/B); 95% (A/E)
- Higher education 90% (Oxford 4, Cambridge 1)

- Grant-maintained
- Boys' grammar
- Pupils 973
- Boys (11–18) 973

- Girls *Not applicable*
- Sixth form 259 (27%)
- Education authority *Devon*

Headteacher Roy Ernest Pike, 49, appointed in September 1986. Staff 58 (men 46, women 12).

Motto Aude sapere (Dare to be wise).

Background Original grammar school opened in 1914 and moved to new premises in attractive grounds in November 1983. The two-storey brick building, opened by Sir John Fieldhouse, is on the outskirts of Torquay in south Devon, within easy reach of Dartmoor National Park. It was the first grammar school built in Britain after the Second World War. The school is over-subscribed, with at least two applications per place. New purpose-built science and technology centre, media studies and music and expressive arts suite in 1994/5. At least 100 pupils leave for university each year; mathematics, science and technology notably popular. School band has released second cassette recording; under-12 and under-15 chess teams won London Invitation Tournament; Devon Lords Taverners under-15 cricket champions; 1991 national soccer champions; national swimming and water-polo finalists; 1995 Young Consumer of the Year champions, represented United Kingdom in the United States; 1995 Young Film-makers Award; 1995 UK skiing champions.

Alumni Mike Sangster, tennis professional; Malcolm Windeatt, six times British swimming champion; Brian Southwood, head of space and atmospheric physics group, Imperial College, London.

Streaming *None*

Approach to discipline Life of school revolves around five houses for academic, sports, extra-curricular and charitable activities; 40 societies 'an especial strength'. Positive reward and sanction policy negotiated through school council. 'A short, sharp sentence is usual action for misdemeanours.'

Uniform Years 7 to 11: grey V-neck pullover, grey trousers, navy blazer with house badge and tie. Years 12 and 13: sober-coloured pullover, grey trousers, black blazer with house badge and tie.

Homework Average 11-year-old, five hours a week; 14-year-old, eight hours 30 minutes;

16-year-old, 10 hours.

Vocational qualifications Courses in foreign languages, marketing, design, technology, media skills; Young Enterprise.

Inspection January 1997.

Primary schools About 50 feeder primary schools each year, with numbers varying annually and according to size of schools.

TIFFIN SCHOOL

Queen Elizabeth Road
Kingston-upon-Thames
Surrey KT2 6RL
Tel (0181) 546 4638
Fax (0181) 546 6365
E-mail: dradempsey@aol.com

- National ranking 79 (30, 85, 18, 62)
- GCSE 97% (99%)
- A-levels 48% (A/B); 92% (A/E)
- Higher education 93% (Oxford 4, Cambridge 8)

- Grant-maintained
- Boys' grammar
- Pupils 973
- Boys (11–18) 973
- Girls *Not applicable*
- Sixth form 318 (33%)
- Education authority *Kingston-upon-Thames*

Headteacher Dr Anthony Michael Dempsey, 52, appointed in September 1988. Staff 58 (men 49, women 9).

Motto Faire sans dire (Action not words).

Background Founded in 1638 by the Tiffin brothers, leading to new school in 1880 at Fairfield, and in 1929 rebuilding on current tree-lined site in centre of Kingston-upon-Thames: main building (built 1929); south building (1980s); creative studies centre (1991); Elmfield, renovated listed building (1790s); central garden area. Playing fields at Hampton Court. New sports hall. Substantially over-subscribed, with nine applications per place. Strong house system, mounting 14 competitions annually from public speaking to table tennis. Sporting strengths include rugby, cricket, athletics and rowing; also music and drama (links with National Youth Music Theatre).

Alumni John Bratby, painter and writer; Alec

Stewart, cricketer; Neil Bennett, journalist; Peter Hillmore, journalist; Mark Feltham, cricketer.

Streaming *None*

Approach to discipline 'Firm with understanding. Clear guidelines, clear system, sanctions if necessary, solutions found to solve problems.'

Uniform Tiffin striped blazer in years 7 to 10; navy blazer in years 11 to 13. Grey trousers, plain white/grey shirts, black shoes. Strict enforcement.

Homework Average 11-year-old, seven hours 30 minutes a week; 14-year-old, 10 hours; 16-year-old, 15 hours.

Vocational qualifications *None*

Inspection November 1996: 'Tiffin is a very good school. The pupils make good progress in their studies and attain high standards. Their behaviour is very good and they are highly motivated to learn and willing to take on responsibilities. Attendance at the school is excellent. This success reflects good teaching and an appropriate and demanding curriculum. However, teachers sometimes rely too much on long talks and some pay too little attention to pupils' individual needs.'; 'There is not enough monitoring of departments and teaching.'; 'The school is well-managed. High standards are promoted through clear aims which are pursued by the strong leadership of the headteacher and the governing body.'

Primary schools Total of 78 feeder schools.

HIGHWORTH GRAMMAR SCHOOL FOR GIRLS

Quantock Drive
Ashford
Kent TN24 8UD
Tel (01233) 624910
Fax (01233) 612028
E-mail: 100751.1313@compuserve.com
Internet: http://www.ourworld.compuserve.
   com/homepages/highworth

- National ranking 80 (99, 96, 118, 76)
- GCSE 97% (96%)
- A-levels 47% (A/B); 97% (A/E)
- Higher education 85% (Cambridge 1)

- Girls' grammar
- Pupils 868

- Boys *Not applicable*
- Girls (11–18) 868
- Sixth form 198 (23%)
- Education authority *Kent*

Headteacher Lesley Lee, 51, appointed in September 1994. Staff 52 (men 13, women 39).

Motto Ad caelestia sequere (Follow to the stars).

Background Founded in 1904 as Ashford County School for Girls; moved to current site on edge of Ashford, close to M20, in 1928; later became Ashford Grammar School for Girls, then Highworth School for Girls in 1973, before changing to the current name in 1994. Substantial building programme in 1992 with completion of three-storey block including language suite, laboratory and world satellite system, and fully-equipped performing arts studio. Further plans for expansion including technology suite, in 1998. Extensive grounds include all-weather Astroturf sports pitch, grass pitches, hard-court areas, 20-metre outdoor swimming pool. Over-subscribed, with nearly three first-choice applications per place. Total of 16 subjects up to GCSE; 22 at A-level (many of them modular); six at AS-level. Kent Music School shares the site, and up to 150 pupils have instrumental lessons. Student management team plays important role and runs the House system. Extensive range of clubs, teams and societies. Two information technology rooms with computer network throughout school; IT encouraged in all subjects. Friends of Highworth (for parents) and Past Student Association. Identified for praise in 1997 annual Ofsted report. 'The curriculum is broad and designed to enable students to become independent and responsible members of the community. The emphasis is on achieving academic excellence while at the same time developing an awareness of others and fostering moral and spiritual values.'

Alumni Patsy Byrne, actress.

Streaming Pupils in sets for mathematics in years 8 to 11.

Approach to discipline Encourages thoughtful and sensible behaviour in disciplined environment; guidelines indicating good practice. Heads of year, pastoral co-ordinator, form prefects attached to classes in years 7 to 10.

Uniform Grey skirt/trousers, pale-blue blouse and house tie, grey V-neck pullover. Sixth-formers expected to dress 'appropriately' according to code. Standards monitored closely and parents notified if regulations breached.

Homework Average 11-year-old, five hours 30 minutes a week; 14-year-old, eight hours 30 minutes; 16-year-old, 11 hours.

Vocational qualifications French for Business; German for Business; Computer Literacy and Information Technology.

Primary schools Willesborough Junior; Tenterden CE Junior; St Mary's CE Primary; Hopewell Primary; Kennington Junior; Goddington Primary. Total of 36 feeder schools, with a wide urban and rural catchment area.

SOUTH WILTS GRAMMAR SCHOOL FOR GIRLS

Stratford Road
Salisbury
Wiltshire SP1 3JJ
Tel (01722) 323326
Fax (01722) 320703
E-mail: swgs@rmplc.co.uk

- National ranking 81 (25, 74, 100, 24)
- GCSE 97% (100%)
- A-levels 46% (A/B); 95% (A/E)
- Higher education 86% (Cambridge 1)

- Grant-maintained
- Girls' grammar
- Pupils 824
- Boys *Not applicable*
- Girls (11–18) 824
- Sixth form 210 (25%)
- Education authority *Wiltshire*

Headteacher Marian Freeman, 51, appointed in September 1991. Staff 51 (men 16, women 35).

Motto Onwards.

Background Old E-shaped red-brick building, with two quadrangles, opened in 1927; additional buildings after 1945 when the school expanded rapidly. Large open site within walking distance of centre of Salisbury. Playing fields include all-weather running track; outdoor swimming pool; pupils have gained county honours in variety of sports. Music is dominant art form: choirs, choral society, orchestra, string orchestra, wind bands, recorder groups, jazz band, and A Cappella Choir. Three applicants for each place.

Alumni Penny Tranter, BBC weather forecaster.

Streaming In mathematics from year 8; in science in years 10 and 11.

Approach to discipline 'The school expects an orderly atmosphere, a respect for others and an appreciation of the right of individuals to have different talents.'

Uniform Winter uniform: tartan kilt, white blouse, green sweater with school logo. Summer uniform is similar but of lighter material and short-sleeve blouse. Sixth-form expected to 'dress appropriately'. Lapses regarded as breaches of discipline.

Homework Average 11-year-old, seven hours 30 minutes a week; 14-year-old, 10 hours; 16-year-old, 10 to 12 hours.

Vocational qualifications *None*

Inspection Autumn 1993: 'The school provides an education of high quality.'

Primary schools Applications from 90 primary schools; places offered to pupils from 54 schools, 23 of which are direct feeder schools.

RAINHAM MARK GRAMMAR SCHOOL

Pump Lane
Rainham
Gillingham
Kent ME8 7AJ
Tel (01634) 364151
Fax (01634) 260209
E-mail: superg@rmgs.rmplc.co.uk
Internet: http://www.rmplc.co.uk/eduweb/
                sites/rmgs

- National ranking 82 (118, 37, 24, 101)
- GCSE 97% (95%)
- A-levels 46% (A/B); 92% (A/E)
- Higher education 80% (Cambridge 3)

- Grant-maintained
- Mixed grammar
- Pupils 1,129
- Boys (11–18) 642
- Girls (11–18) 487
- Sixth form 302 (27%)
- Education authority *Kent*

Headteacher Peter Limm, 47, appointed in September 1996. Staff 58 (men 33, women 25).

Motto *None*

Background The school began in Rochester before the Second World War, moving to Gillingham in the 1950s; current 22-acre site with river view in Rainham dates from 1965. New buildings after it became co-educational in 1972; became grant-maintained in 1992, enabling refurbishment of older buildings, new drama facilities and laboratories. New English block in 1995. Over-subscribed, with two applications per place. Music strong: orchestra, choirs, wind band. Soccer and netball teams for all years; tennis, athletics, dance, gymnastics, trampoline, basketball, girls' soccer; Saturday sports club; national representatives in soccer, netball and hockey. Curriculum strengths include English, modern languages, mathematics and economics.

Streaming Fast sets for mathematics for pupils taking GCSE early, followed by Statistics in fifth year. Similar sets for modern languages take up to three GCSEs in French, German and Spanish.

Approach to discipline 'We recognise good behaviour and praise it. There are sanctions: unsupervised access to facilities such as the computer room or music rooms might be denied if these are misused.' Mild rebuke or short detention usually suffices; unused formal system beyond that. Parents involved.

Uniform Black blazer with badge, grey trousers/skirt, white shirt, school tie, black shoes. Sixth-formers have negotiated dress code: no jeans, no t-shirts. Regulations enforced 'tactfully but fully'.

Homework Average 11-year-old, seven hours 30 minutes a week; 14-year-old, 10 hours; 16-year-old, 15 hours.

Vocational qualifications City & Guilds, Information Technology (modular).

Inspection April 1994: 'The ethos of the school is excellent. There is a strong sense of purpose and a supportive community atmosphere. Rainham Mark Grammar School has achieved a balance between the demands of an academically rigorous and successful institution and the aim to create a caring and mutually respectful community.'

Primary schools Fair View Junior; St Margaret's CE Junior; Thamesview Junior; Twydall Junior; Park Wood Junior; Hempstead Junior; Wakeley Junior.

BEACONSFIELD HIGH SCHOOL

Wattleton Road
Beaconsfield
Buckinghamshire HP9 1RR
Tel (01494) 673043
Fax (01494) 670715

- National ranking 83 (36 = , 45, 7, 46)
- GCSE 97% (99%)
- A-levels 45% (A/B); 97% (A/E)
- Higher education 99% (Oxford 5, Cambridge 1)

- Grant-maintained
- Girls' grammar
- Pupils 900
- Boys *Not applicable*
- Girls (11–18) 900
- Sixth form 280 (31%)
- Education authority *Buckinghamshire*

Headteacher Penny Castagnoli, appointed in April 1996. Staff 49 (men 7, women 42).

Motto Disciplina et doctrina (Discipline and learning).

Background Set on attractive greenfield site near M40 in Beaconsfield old town, the school opened in 1966. Became grant-maintained in 1991 and is consistently over-subscribed, with 3.5 applications per place. New £750,000 technology block from September 1993. Instrumental service provides extensive opportunities, with girls regularly in national orchestras. Evidence of sporting strength, with netball team All-England finalists for third successive year in 1994. School council and prefect system allows responsibility to be devolved to pupils. Latin and Classics taught. National and regional competition successes include Shakespeare on Platform, Sega marketing competition, and Young Enterprise.

Streaming Some setting in French and mathematics.

Approach to discipline 'Expectations of girls are high and generally achieved. Extensive and supportive pastoral system. Girls encouraged to take responsibility. Firm approach when necessary.'

Uniform Royal-blue V-neck pullover, grey skirt. Sixth-formers required to wear smart 'business-like' dress.

Homework Average 14-year-old, eight hours a week; 16-year-old, 11 hours 30 minutes.

Vocational qualifications Pitman, Certificate in Information Technology (the school had the three highest results in the country in 1992 examination); Oxford and Cambridge Diploma, Sports Leaders.

Primary schools Holtspur Combined; Butlers Court Combined; Chalfont St Peter CE Middle; Farnham Primary; High March Primary; St Bernard's Primary; Langley Manor Primary.

POOLE GRAMMAR SCHOOL

Gravel Hill
Poole
Dorset BH17 7JU
Tel (01202) 692132
Fax (01202) 606500

- National ranking 84 (146, 54, 30, 32 =)
- GCSE 97% (92%)
- A-levels 44% (A/B); 92% (A/E)
- Higher education 80% (Oxford 12, Cambridge 2)

- Grant-maintained
- Boys' grammar
- Pupils 844
- Boys (12–18) 844
- Girls *Not applicable*
- Sixth form 275 (33%)
- Education authority *Dorset*

Headteacher Alexander Arthur John Clarke, 51, appointed in April 1990. Staff 54 (men 41, women 13).

Motto Finis opus coronat (The task is crowned by its completion).

Background Opened as co-educational grammar school in 1904; 1939 expansion led to creation of separate girls' grammar (Parkstone Grammar School). In 1966, the school moved to new purpose-built buildings on wooded heathland on northern edge of Poole. New technology block and two specialist art rooms opened in 1993, along with sixth-form study base; new tennis courts in 1995; further extensions being designed include drama/music studios and science laboratories. Became grant-maintained in April 1994. Takes top 16% of ability range. The school reports a big increase in demand for places from out-of-area families.

Although an average of 1.3 academically-successful pupils apply for each place, most have been accommodated by providing extra classes. Some pupils travel up to 25 miles to attend. Physics, chemistry and biology compulsory as separate sciences to GCSE. Strong sporting achievements in rugby, soccer, tennis and cricket; holds own sailing regatta; flourishing curricular and extra-curricular drama; extensive music interests include Dixieland Band that has appeared twice in School Proms at Albert Hall. A-level linguists undertake work-experience in France and Germany.

Streaming *None*

Approach to discipline 'Firm but supportive.' Clear rules and expectations of effort, conduct and courtesy. Sanctions imposed for misdemeanours. Pupils congratulated and interviewed personally by headteacher for academic improvement and high achievement.

Uniform Blazer, school tie and grey trousers in years 8 and 9; school pullover may be worn instead of blazer in years 10 and 11. No set uniform for sixth-formers; guidelines include a tie, but exclude denim and 'extremes of fashion'.

Homework Average 12-year-old, six hours a week; 14-year-old, eight hours; 16-year-old, 13 hours.

Vocational qualifications *None*

Inspection April 1996: 'Poole Grammar School provides a very good education for all its pupils. It promotes high standards of achievement for pupils at Key Stage 3 and has achieved good results at GCSE for several years.'; 'In lessons achievement is good or very good across the whole range of subjects. In the rare case where it is less than satisfactory, this is almost entirely due to the teachers' misjudgment of the rate at which pupils are able to learn rather than to their attitude or motivation.'; 'Pupils are strong in all the basic skills. They speak confidently and well on informal and formal occasions. They sustain complex and detailed discussions both with teachers and amongst themselves.'; 'The governing body makes an effective contribution to the management of the school alongside the good leadership provided by the senior management group.'

Primary schools Baden Powell and St Peter's CE Middle; Canford Heath Middle; Oakdale

Middle; Haymoor Middle; Broadstone Middle; St Michael's CE Middle, Colehill; Castle Court Preparatory; Dumpton Preparatory.

DARTFORD GRAMMAR SCHOOL

West Hill
Dartford
Kent DA1 2HW
Tel (01322) 223039
Fax (01322) 291426
E-mail: root@dartfordg.rmplc.co.uk
Internet: http://www.rmplc.co.uk/eduweb/sites/isdgs

- National ranking 85 (59, 35, 66, 119)
- GCSE 97% (98%)
- A-levels 41% (A/B); 95% (A/E)
- Higher education 81% (Oxford 3, Cambridge 1)

- Grant-maintained
- Boys' grammar
- Pupils 960
- Boys (11–18) 944
- Girls (16–18) 16
- Sixth form 266 (28%)
- Education authority *Kent*

Headteacher Anthony John Smith, 49, appointed in April 1986. Staff 56 (men 38, women 18).

Motto Ora et labora (Pray and work).

Background After its foundation in 1576, Dartford Grammar School moved to its current site to the west of the town centre in 1866. Buildings constructed at various times from then until 1989; 11 acres of sports fields close to main site. Technology block opened in 1989; new sports centre; performing arts centre to be established in 1995. Over-subscribed, with 3.1 applications per place. Music a particular strength; offers 15 sports, with inter-school competition in 10; total of 29 county representatives in seven sports in 1993. European links and many opportunities to travel abroad; average of seven foreign trips each year. Emphasis on community service; works closely in the sixth forms with Dartford Grammar School for Girls.

Alumni Mick Jagger, rock singer with The Rolling Stones; Sidney Keyes, poet; Sir George Jefferson, businessman and former chairman of British Telecom; Thomas Pullinger, motor industry pioneer; Minal Patel, cricketer.

Streaming *None*

Approach to discipline Based on trust and goodwill, with intention that boys develop self-discipline. 'Staff intervene firmly and positively when a lack of self-discipline is evident.'

Uniform Dark-blue blazer, blue shirt, maroon-and-gold school tie, dark-grey trousers, black shoes. Enforced 'very strictly'.

Homework Average 11-year-old, seven hours 30 minutes a week; 14-year-old, 10 hours; 16-year-old, 12 hours 30 minutes.

Vocational qualifications *None*

Inspection March 1995: 'This is a successful and popular school in which high standards are valued and promoted.'; 'Standards are particularly good in technology, business studies, English, music, history and classics.'; 'Pupils generally have positive attitudes and are enthusiastic and well-motivated. Learning is effective throughout the school, with pupils taking responsibility and supporting each other. In some cases standards could be even higher if learning opportunities were more clearly matched to the capabilities of individual pupils and more independent learning was encouraged.'; 'Teaching is generally good and in many lessons is characterised by effective planning, challenging tasks and appropriate pace. Relationships between pupils and teachers are very good. Pupils are well supported and make good progress.'

Primary schools West Hill County Primary; Hextable County Primary; Old Bexley County Primary; Merton Court Primary; St Anselm's RC Primary.

OLD SWINFORD HOSPITAL

Heath Lane
Stourbridge DY8 1QX
Tel (01384) 370025
Fax (01384) 441686

- National ranking 86 (131, 131, 135, 124)
- GCSE 97% (94%)
- A-levels 39% (A/B); 92% (A/E)
- Higher education 99% (Cambridge 1)

- Grant-maintained
- Boys' comprehensive
- Pupils 560
- Boys (11–18) 560
- Girls *Not applicable*

- Sixth form 190 (34%)
- Education authority *Dudley*

Headteacher Christopher Frederick Rendall Potter, 57, appointed in September 1978. Staff 43 (men 35, women 8).

Motto Ut prosim, vince malum bono (To serve, conquer evil with good).

Background Founded on model of Christ's Hospital in 1670 by Thomas Foley, a local industrialist. Primarily a boarding school, taking a limited number of day boys each year, on elevated site to south of Stourbridge. Richly-endowed; one of the first grant-maintained schools in the country. Parents pay only for the boarding costs (£1,525 a term); 'market leader' in boarding provision for boys from wide range of backgrounds and broad geographical area at 'comparatively modest cost'. Rapid expansion in past 12 years: four new boarding houses; new classroom wing in 1997; single study-bedrooms for sixth-form boarders. Increasingly oversubscribed, with three applications for each place. Two weeks' work-experience at end of GCSE year. Craft, design, technology centre; new science laboratories, computer centre and network, music school, earth sciences centre. Sports facilities include: squash courts, tennis courts, playing fields on site. School owns local golf course; new climbing wall. 'Excellent' record at cricket and rugby; many other sports available; wide variety of clubs and societies; strong music and drama; Duke of Edinburgh Award Scheme.

Streaming Setting of pupils according to ability in mathematics, English, French and Latin.

Approach to discipline Clear standards; emphasis on reward; belief that prevention is better than cure. 'School rules are precisely defined so every boy knows where he stands. When punishment has to be administered, emphasis is on community service benefiting the house or school as a whole.' Prefectorial system.

Uniform Blazer, grey trousers, school/house tie. Boys may wear sports jackets from age of 13; sixth-formers may wear suits. 'Precisely defined and firmly enforced.'

Homework Average 11-year-old, minimum of six hours a week; 14-year-old, minimum of 10 hours; 16-year-old, minimum of 12 hours.

Vocational qualifications *None*

Inspection November 1993: 'The school provides a very good quality of education with an exceptionally wide range of extra-curricular activities. The standards achieved by pupils are high in virtually all subject areas.'; 'Standards of behaviour are excellent. Pupils' spiritual, moral, social and cultural development is strongly supported by the school's traditional ethos and boarding environment. The school is strongly led and well organised; resources are used efficiently. Teaching accommodation, though efficiently employed, is inadequate, posing health and safety risks in some subject areas.' *The school reports that the opening of a new classroom wing has since addressed the accommodation issue raised by the inspection report.*

Primary schools Because Old Swinford Hospital is a boarding school, pupils come from schools across the country.

THE KING'S SCHOOL

Brook Street
Grantham
Lincolnshire NG31 6RP
Tel (01476) 563180
Fax (01476) 590953
E-mail: kingssch@campus.bt.com

- National ranking 87 (69, 75, 110, 136)
- GCSE 97% (98%)
- A-levels 39% (A/B); 90% (A/E)
- Higher education 91% (Cambridge 4)

- Grant-maintained
- Boys' grammar
- Pupils 850
- Boys (11–18) 850
- Girls *Not applicable*
- Sixth form 216 (25%)
- Education authority *Lincolnshire*

Headteacher Stephen Burton Howarth, 45, appointed in September 1995. Staff 57 (men 45, women 12).

Motto Honi soit qui mal y pense (Shame on him who thinks evil of it).

Background A grant-maintained day and boarding school that traces its history from medieval times. Most important refoundation in 1528, when Bishop Foxe endowed the school; original stone school house, a Grade 1 listed building, still used as school library. Occupies two-acre site in the town centre; Gonerby House, the boarding house for 70 boys, is set in own 'delightful' grounds a mile from the main school. Playing fields 500 yards from school: tennis courts, rifle range, indoor cricket nets. Over-subscribed, with 150 applications for 120 places. New building for physical and natural sciences, computing, information technology and design; economics and business studies suite as well as a creative and performing arts faculty. Water-polo among sporting achievements, with teams consistently qualifying for national finals. Combined Cadet Force. Duke of Edinburgh Award Scheme. Named in Ofsted Chief Inspector's 1996 annual report as 'outstandingly successful'.

Alumni Sir Isaac Newton; Lord Burghley, Lord Treasurer to Queen Elizabeth I; Bishop Wand; Albert Ball VC.

Streaming Setting in mathematics and modern languages from year 8.

Approach to discipline 'Fair, firm and consistent; friendly within a structured environment; high standards of behaviour and dress expected.'

Uniform Black blazer with school badge, medium-grey or dark-grey trousers, white shirt, black-and-maroon striped tie, grey socks, black shoes. Maroon blazers for 'full colours'.

Homework Average 11-year-old, six to seven hours 30 minutes a week; 14-year-old, eight to 10 hours; 16-year-old, 10 to 13 hours.

Vocational qualifications *None*

Inspection Autumn 1993.

Primary schools The National CE Junior, Gonerby Hill Foot CE Primary; Cliffedale County Primary; Long Bennington CE Primary; Barrowby CE Primary.

THE NORTH HALIFAX GRAMMAR SCHOOL

Moorbottom Road
Illingworth
Halifax HX2 9SU
Tel (01422) 244625
Fax (01422) 245237
E-mail: maslen@nhgs.co.uk

- National ranking 88 (166, 119, 165, 179)
- GCSE 97% (84%)
- A-levels 37% (A/B); 96% (A/E)
- Higher education 65%

- Grant-maintained
- Mixed grammar
- Pupils 903
- Boys (11–18) 404
- Girls (11–18) 499
- Sixth form 202 (22%)
- Education authority *Calderdale*

Headteacher Graham Maslen, 43, appointed in September 1996. Staff 53 (men 31, women 22).

Motto Nisi dominus frustra (Without God all is in vain).

Background Built in the 1960s, the school building has undergone ambitious re-cladding since award of grant-maintained status; transformed previous 'uninspiring environment'. The school, on an open site with panoramic views four miles out of Halifax towards Keighley, was formed in 1985 from amalgamation of Highlands School and Princess Mary School, well-established grammar schools. Over-subscribed, with 2.5 applications for each place; pupils from broad range of backgrounds; numbers increasing. Music tuition at modest cost to pupils; five choirs, concert band, orchestra, guitar ensemble, recorder group; Latin, Russian, German and French taught; physics, chemistry, biology plus balanced science. School proud of flourishing links with business: 'Challenge of Business Management' conference alternates with Careers Convention. Traditional formality 'combines with easy but respectful relationships': morning assemblies, grace at lunchtime, Speech Day, carol services. Prefects. International links building slowly. Highlighted for praise in 1994 annual report by the Office for Standards in Education as one of 52 'beacons of excellence'; identified in 1996 as one of 32 'outstandingly successful' schools.

Streaming Some setting for mathematics in year 9. Mathematics, English and, sometimes, French in years 10 and 11.

Approach to discipline Staff 'endlessly patient' in supporting pupils: 'High standards of work, personal and social behaviour are expected, and these high expectations determine outcomes'. Close knowledge of pupils' strengths and weaknesses. Sanctions range from litter-picking and cleaning to appearing before governors (in a few very serious cases).

Uniform Years 7 to 11: girls wear red knitwear and boys wear grey blazers. Dress code for sixth-formers is less formal. Regulations enforced 'to the letter'.

Homework Average 11-year-old, eight hours a week; 14-year-old, 12 hours; 16-year-old, 15 to 20 hours.

Vocational qualifications RSA Stage II, Desktop Publishing.

Inspection March 1994: 'This is a good school with many outstanding features.'; 'The school provides a broad and balanced curriculum. Opportunities for using information technology across the curriculum are variable. The overall quality of teaching is consistently good, but a wider range of teaching approaches would enrich the experience of pupils.'; 'Homework is set consistently and it is both rigorous and effective in practice.'; 'There is a strong school ethos which promotes high standards of achievement. The behaviour of pupils is excellent and the school is very orderly.'

Primary schools Lightcliffe CE Primary; Holy Trinity CE Primary; St Mary's RC Primary; Bowling Green Primary; Bradshaw Primary.

ADAMS' GRAMMAR SCHOOL

High Street
Newport
Shropshire TF10 7BD
Tel (01952) 810698
Fax (01952) 812696
E-mail: admin@agsn.demon.co.uk

- National ranking 89 (113, 124, 137, 92)
- GCSE 97% (95%)
- A-levels 37% (A/B); 90% (A/E)
- Higher education 98% (Oxford 3, Cambridge 2)

- Grant-maintained
- Boys' grammar
- Pupils 680
- Boys (11–18) 640
- Girls (16–18) 40
- Sixth form 200 (29%)
- Education authority *Shropshire*

Headteacher James Michael Richardson, 48, appointed in January 1994. Staff 43 (men 32, women 11).

Motto Serve and obey.

Background Founded as a free grammar school in 1656 by William Adams, a haberdasher; one of eight Haberdashers' Company Schools. Still occupies 17th-century site in centre of small market town of Newport, near Telford. Also has Longford Hall, an 18th-century mansion, as a boarding house for 100 boarders, surrounded by 100 acres of playing fields, woodland, adventure area and fishing pool. Became grant-maintained in September 1990. Technology College status in 1996, with new 'outstanding' fully-networked computing facilities; new technology and science block, drama room, language laboratory and music recording studio. Girls admitted to sixth form from September 1993; takes top 25% of the ability range; over-subscribed, with three applications for each place. Pupils drawn from Newport, Telford, Shrewsbury, Stafford and Wolverhampton, and boarders from a wider area. Sciences taught separately; German and French taught throughout school; mathematics and physics among A-level strengths. Because it is a boarding school, there is a wide range of activities: five rugby pitches, three hockey pitches, two cricket squares, shooting range, swimming pool. Highly-successful sporting record. Large orchestra and choir, with string, wind and brass ensembles; about one in three pupils have instrumental tuition. Annual music festival. Combined Cadet Force. Competitive spirit. House system.

Alumni Sir Oliver Lodge, 19th-century physicist who succeeded in detecting radio waves two years before Marconi; Simon Bates, BBC Radio One disc jockey; Jeremy Corbyn, Labour MP for Islington North; Sir Peter Roberts, former Conservative MP.

Streaming *None*

Approach to discipline To guide boys to exercise common sense, good manners, and consideration for others. 'As far as possible, school rules are "life rules" and are applied with the consent of the governed.'

Uniform Maroon blazer with crest, grey trousers, white shirt, school tie, black shoes. Sixth-formers wear dark-blue blazers, sixth-form or prefects' tie. 'Uniform is expected and every boy wears it.'

Homework Average 11-year-old, seven hours 30 minutes a week; 14-year-old, eight hours 30 minutes; 16-year-old, 10 hours.

Vocational qualifications *None*

Inspection Spring 1994: 'Standards are above average in most subjects, but more needs to be done to cater for the needs of the most able, particularly in Key Stage 3.'; 'The school is an orderly community of highly-motivated pupils who are proud to be part of a school with long-established traditions. The quality of learning is good, but pupils are capable of taking on far more responsibility for their own learning.'

Primary schools Newport CE Junior; Moorfield County Primary; Lilleshall County Primary; Tibberton CE Primary; St Peter's CE Primary, Edgmond; St Lawrence CE Primary, Enosall; Market Drayton Junior; Christchurch Junior, Wolverhampton; Brewood Middle; Priorslee County Primary, Telford; Castle House Preparatory; Birchfield Preparatory. About 80 other feeder schools.

WIRRAL COUNTY GRAMMAR SCHOOL FOR GIRLS

Heath Road
Bebington
Wirral L63 3AF
Tel (0151) 644 8282
Fax (0151) 643 1332

- National ranking 90 (140, 122, 136, 99)
- GCSE 97% (93%)
- A-levels 36% (A/B); 84% (A/E)
- Higher education 83% (Oxford 1, Cambridge 1)

- Girls' grammar
- Pupils 998
- Boys *Not applicable*
- Girls (11–18) 998
- Sixth form 243 (24%)
- Education authority *Wirral*

Headteacher Alice Margaret-Mary Wakefield, 54, appointed in September 1994. Staff 66 (men 16, women 50).

Motto Monumentum aere perennius (A monument more lasting than bronze).

Background Founded in 1931, the school was administered until 1974 by Cheshire education authority; since then, it has been the responsibility of Wirral education committee, local governors, and the Department for Education. In Bebington in the centre of the Wirral, it draws on pupils

from the Wirral, Cheshire, and elsewhere in the northwest. On average, there are 1.2 pupils who pass the entrance examination applying for each place. National reputation in several sports, with individual pupils being national representatives in lacrosse, netball and volleyball. More than 200 girls receive musical instrument tuition, with choirs and orchestras giving regular concerts. Drama studio is base for regular stage productions. New technology room was built in 1994. New information technology facilities in 1996.

Alumni Jean Boht, actress.

Streaming As this is a selective school, further grouping by ability is considered unnecessary, except in French and mathematics from year 8.

Approach to discipline School rules kept to minimum. 'Punishments are few and there is the ACE Award Scheme, through which girls are awarded points for achievement, helping the community, or for effort.'

Uniform Navy skirt, blue shirt and tie. Sixth-formers expected to wear smart, appropriate dress. Regulations enforced 'firmly'.

Homework Average 11-year-old, seven hours 30 minutes; 14-year-old, eight hours 15 minutes; 16-year-old, up to 10 hours.

Vocational qualifications RSA, Community Sports Leaders.

Inspection October 1993: 'This is a successful and happy school, providing education of good quality.'

Primary schools Higher Bebington Junior School; Poulton Lancelyn Primary; Stanton Road Primary, Bebington; Brackenwood Junior, Bebington; Woodchurch Road Primary, Birkenhead.

KESTEVEN AND GRANTHAM GIRLS' SCHOOL

Sandon Road
Grantham
Lincolnshire NG31 9AU
Tel (01476) 563017
Fax (01476) 593037

- National ranking 91 = (150, 144, 109, 143)
- GCSE 97% (92%)
- A-levels 35% (A/B); 91% (A/E)

- Higher education 84% (Oxford 1, Cambridge 2)

- Girls' grammar
- Pupils 1,021
- Boys *Not applicable*
- Girls (11–18) 1,021
- Sixth form 243 (24%)
- Education authority *Lincolnshire*

Headteacher Ann Hopkinson, 52, appointed in April 1989. Staff 62 (men 16, women 46).

Motto Veras hinc ducere voces (From this source draw true inspiration).

Background Opened in 1910 on extensive site overlooking Grantham; original fine buildings well-maintained and recently refurbished. Substantial extensions as well as modifications over the years. Over-subscribed, with 2.1 applications per place. Sporting success at local, regional and national level. Lower-sixth public-speaking team won 1993 national finals. Music: three choirs, guitar groups, recorder and other chamber groups, recorder orchestra, wind band, full orchestra; many pupils receive instrumental tuition and attend Grantham Music School, based at school, on Saturdays; pupils in county youth orchestra. Community service. House system. Parents', Teachers' and Friends' Association.

Alumni Baroness Thatcher of Kesteven, former Conservative prime minister.

Streaming Mixed-ability teaching groups in years 7 to 9; pupils reorganised for mathematics from year 8; alternative smaller groupings for technology and creative/expressive arts. More fluid groupings for options after year 9.

Approach to discipline 'Behaviour policy is based upon the expectation that every student will demonstrate a sense of responsibility for herself, consideration towards others and loyalty to the school.'

Uniform Navy blazer or V-neck pullover, navy skirt, saxe-blue shirt, navy tie. Dress code for sixth-formers. 'Girls are expected to demonstrate their full commitment to the school in relation to its uniform.'

Homework Average 11-year-old, seven hours 30 minutes a week; 14-year-old, eight hours 30 minutes; 16-year-old, at least 10 hours.

Vocational qualifications *None*

Inspection March 1995: 'Students throughout the school achieve standards which are appropriate or better in relation to their age and sound or good in relation to their ability.'; 'Apart from English, there are insufficient instances of students achieving really high standards, and there is some under-achievement, particularly by the most able.'; 'Teachers have good academic knowledge and adopt a caring approach to the welfare and progress of students.'; 'The headteacher provides sound leadership.'

Primary schools The National CE Junior; Cliffedale Primary; Long Bennington CE Primary; Gonnerby Hill Foot CE Primary; Huntingtower Road Primary.

THE HARVEY GRAMMAR SCHOOL

Cheriton Road
Folkestone
Kent CT19 5JY
Tel (01303) 252131
Fax (01303) 220721
E-mail: the_harvey_grammar_edu
@msn.com

- National ranking 91 = (52, 143, 83, 105)
- GCSE 97% (99%)
- A-levels 35% (A/B); 91% (A/E)
- Higher education 92% (Oxford 1, Cambridge 1)

- Boys' grammar
- Pupils 880
- Boys (11–18) 880
- Girls *Not applicable*
- Sixth form 210 (24%)
- Education authority *Kent*

Headteacher John Edwards, 54, appointed in January 1986. Staff 48 (men 40, women 8).

Motto Temeraire, Redoutable et Fougueux (ships from the Battle of Trafalgar involving Admiral Harvey).

Background The school was founded in 1674 through the will of Dr William Harvey, the physician who discovered the circulation of the blood and who was born in Folkestone in 1578. The main buildings, within sight of the North Downs and the Channel Tunnel terminal, were completed in 1913 and have been substantially extended. Additions include an £800,000 science and technology centre (1990), a modern languages suite with satellite link, and a music room. Facilities have also been improved for the sixth form and for information technology. A sports complex opened in March 1996 to supplement 10 acres of on-site playing fields. Long sporting tradition has resulted in school being represented in more county cricket and soccer cup finals than any other in Kent. Other sports range from table tennis to skiing. Language exchange schemes in France and Germany; foreign work-experience; ski trips, football tours to United States, cricket tours to west country, and visits to Moscow and St Petersburg. The school selects the top 23% of the ability range and recently has received increasing applications from outside immediate catchment area, expanding from a three-form entry to a five-form entry to meet demand. Curriculum strengths include mathematics and English, in which examination pass rates often reach 100%.

Alumni Sir Peter Imbert, former Metropolitan Police commissioner; Sir George Gardiner, Conservative MP for Reigate; Gerald Sinstadt, television sports commentator; Les Ames, former England wicketkeeper and batsman; Andrew Brownsword, greetings card magnate.

Streaming In mathematics in years 10 and 11.

Approach to discipline Self-discipline and appreciation of responsibilities are the aim. 'Pupils are expected to behave courteously and with consideration for others. Sanctions include additional work, detention after school or on Saturday mornings, suspension or expulsion.' High expectations are generally met, but when necessary the school takes firm and appropriate action.

Uniform Black blazer with school badge, formal dark-grey trousers, plain white/grey shirt, school tie, dark socks, black shoes. Distinctive ties for sixth-formers and prefects. 'Any pupil not conforming with uniform requirements would be sent home to change.'

Homework Average 11-year-old, seven hours 30 minutes a week; 14-year-old, seven hours 30 minutes; 16-year-old, 10 hours.

Vocational qualifications French for Business, Business Studies, Understanding Industry.

Inspection December 1994: 'A very good school which provides an education of high quality.'; 'Pupils are keen to learn and their learning skills are developing well. Their attitude to learning is very good throughout the school.'; 'Teaching is competent in all departments.'; 'The ethos of the school is supportive to pupils, but also rigorous and purposeful. Pupils are well-mannered and feel a strong sense of identification and commitment to the school. Behaviour and relationships are excellent and there is a high level of order and courtesy.'

Primary schools Saltwood CE Primary; Sandgate Primary; Park Farm Primary; St Mary's CE Primary; Hawkinge Primary; Dymchurch Primary; New Romney Primary.

THE CROSSLEY HEATH SCHOOL

Savile Park
Halifax HX3 0HG
Tel (01422) 360272
Fax (01422) 349099

- National ranking 93 (155, 94, 153, 57)
- GCSE 97% (91%)
- A-levels 35% (A/B); 89% (A/E)
- Higher education 90% (Oxford 2)

- Grant-maintained
- Mixed grammar
- Pupils 790
- Boys (11–18) 392
- Girls (11–18) 408
- Sixth form 155 (20%)
- Education authority *Calderdale*

Headteacher John Trevor Bunch, 52, appointed in September 1991. Staff 46 (men 23, women 23).

Motto Omne bonum ab alto (Everything good comes from on high).

Background The school was formed in 1985 by the amalgamation of Heath Grammar School (founded 1585) and Crossley and Porter School (founded 1864). It is currently housed in the Victorian building of the latter on a site in Savile Park, two miles from the town centre. The school, which has four applicants for every place, became grant-maintained in April 1991. Laboratory refurbishment in 1994; house system strong feature of school life.

Alumni Lawrence Sterne, writer; Ronald Lewin, military historian and author; Richard Belling, electrical goods manufacturer.

Streaming Setting only in mathematics in GCSE years.

Approach to discipline Tutorial and pastoral

system. 'A range of rewards and sanctions operates to reinforce good behaviour and discourage bad conduct.'

Uniform Boys: black blazer, white/grey shirt, school tie, grey trousers. Girls: school jumper, white shirt/blouse, school tie, grey skirt (trousers optional in sixth form). Regulations applied 'firmly but sensibly'.

Homework Average 11-year-old, five hours a week; 14-year-old, seven to nine hours; 16-year-old, 10 to 12 hours.

Vocational qualifications *None*

Inspection November 1992: 'The Crossley Heath School provides education which is generally satisfactory and at best is good.'; 'Lessons are carefully planned with a high level of specialist knowledge of subjects. However, a limited range of teaching styles is used, which restricts the development of some skills and constrains the degree of challenge for more able pupils.'; 'This is a school in which an atmosphere of healthy competition and striving to do well is complemented by a trusting and orderly environment in which pupils are well known. Relationships between teachers and pupils are good and standards of behaviour are excellent.' October 1996: 'The Crossley Heath School building is impressive architecturally and reflects its original charitable foundation.'; 'The educational standards achieved in the school are very good indeed and have been improving in the past two years.'; 'The progress made by all pupils, including high-attainers and those with special educational needs, is good. Pupils' behaviour and their attitudes to work are good.'; 'All teachers have considerable subject expertise. They plan lessons well and their delivery is clear. They have high expectations of pupils. Class control is excellent.'; 'The headteacher and governors provide clear direction for the school.'

Primary schools All Saints CE Primary; Holy Trinity CE Primary; Warley Road Primary; Lindley Junior, Huddersfield; Lightcliffe CE Primary; Holywell Green Primary; Savile Park Primary; Shade Primary, Todmorden.

BOURNE GRAMMAR SCHOOL

South Road
Bourne
Lincolnshire PE10 9JE

Tel (01778) 422288
Fax (01778) 394872

- National ranking 94 (71, 153, 58, 147)
- GCSE 97% (98%)
- A-levels 31% (A/B); 93% (A/E)
- Higher education 76%

- Mixed grammar
- Pupils 773
- Boys (11–18) 364
- Girls (11–18) 409
- Sixth form 135 (17%)
- Education authority *Lincolnshire*

Headteacher John Nicholson, 61, appointed in 1974. Staff 48 (men 26, women 22).

Motto Vigila et ora (Watch and pray).

Background Founded in 1636, voluntary-controlled school occupying pleasant site with extensive playing fields to south of Bourne since 1922. Substantial extension and rebuilding completed in 1992, along with new teaching block; new sports hall in 1995. New sixth-form facilities in 1996; substantially upgraded information technology facilities in 1997; additional technology (graphics) area complete in September 1997. Admits top 25% of ability range through selection tests; catchment area includes parts of Leicestershire and Cambridgeshire as well as south Lincolnshire, with children from more than 40 primary schools. Over-subscribed, with about 400 applications for 140 places. Languages: French, German, Latin and Spanish. All three sciences at GCSE. Art and drama are popular, with school providing venue for professional touring companies. Pupils have competed at national level in cross-country, athletics and other sports; Roleplay Club; quiz teams competing in national competitions. Sixth-form work-experience in Germany and with Eurotunnel; exchanges with French, Spanish and German students; links with school in Denmark; annual ski trip. Impressive charity fundraising.

Streaming Banding and setting in year 9; full setting in years 10 and 11.

Approach to discipline 'We expect and get a very high standard of cooperation. The approach is firm, fair and friendly with appropriate use of minor sanctions, credit for success, and close relationships between the pastoral staff and parents.'

Uniform Years 7 to 11. Boys: black blazer with school badge, dark-grey trousers, white/grey shirt, school tie, black/dark-grey V-neck pullover, black/dark-grey socks, black shoes. Girls: dark-green skirt, white blouse, blazer/cardigan, brown/black shoes. No denim. Sixth form: 'no uniform but standard of dress required as for many in commerce (collar and tie, and equivalent for girls)'.

Homework Average 11-year-old, five hours a week; 14-year-old, 10 hours; 16-year-old, 12 hours.

Vocational qualifications RSA.

Inspection March 1994: 'The ethos and value of the school are good and conducive to study. Pupils' behaviour and attitudes are very good. They work and play well. The general atmosphere enhanced by a new well-equipped teaching block is good and the school runs smoothly on a day-to-day basis.'; 'The standards of courtesy to visitors and non-teaching staff is high.'; 'Levels of attendance are excellent.'

Primary schools Bourne Abbey (GM) Primary; Westfield County Primary; Thurlby County Primary, Thurlby; Sir Malcolm Sargent (GM) Primary, Stamford. Another 38 feeder schools in Lincolnshire, Cambridgeshire and Leicestershire.

GRAVESEND GRAMMAR SCHOOL FOR GIRLS

Pelham Road
Gravesend
Kent DA11 0JE
Tel (01474) 352896/327296
Fax (01474) 331195

- National ranking 95 (129, 79, 55, 58)
- GCSE 97% (94%)
- A-levels 31% (A/B); 91% (A/E)
- Higher education 80%

- Grant-maintained
- Girls' grammar
- Pupils 846
- Boys *Not applicable*
- Girls (11–18) 846
- Sixth form 196 (23%)
- Education authority *Kent*

Headteacher Susan Court, 53, appointed in January 1987. Staff 52 (men 13, women 39).

Motto Per aspera ad astra (To the stars through toil).

Background Founded in 1893, the school moved to its current site in 1926. Main building, with impressive frontage and distinctive quadrangle, surrounded by playing fields in centre of residential area 10 minutes from centre of Gravesend. Interior modified to meet curriculum needs. Expansion resulted in 'excellent' facilities for drama, music, sport, science and technology; healthy social mix of pupils. Over-subscribed as a four-form entry school; it has admitted five-form entry in all but one of past five years; two applications per place. Grant-maintained since January 1996. Strong community links, and ties with industry and commerce. Extensive use of information technology; range of modern languages; pioneering developments in work-shadowing, European work-experience and industry-linked curriculum projects. One student gained one of top five marks in A-level Government and Politics in 1993. Recent school inspection report: 'The overall school ethos was characterised by courtesy, good humour and civility. A clear code of conduct underpinned the well-ordered society of the school.'

Streaming Pupils grouped according to ability in mathematics after first term of intake.

Approach to discipline 'Reward and praise are emphasised rather than criticism and punishment.' Goals are mutual respect, self-discipline and acceptance of responsibility for actions.

Uniform Navy skirt, pale-blue blouse, navy knitwear with school stripes of pink, mauve and dark-green, school tie. Dress code for sixth-formers. Enforced strictly in main school.

Homework Average 11-year-old, seven hours 30 minutes a week; 14-year-old, 10 hours; 16-year-old, 12 hours.

Vocational qualifications *None*

Inspection April 1997.

Primary schools Meopham County Primary; Painter's Ash County Primary; Riverview Junior; Shears Green Junior; St Joseph's Convent Preparatory.

HECKMONDWIKE GRAMMAR SCHOOL

High Street
Heckmondwike
West Yorkshire WF16 0AH
Tel (01924) 402202
Fax (01924) 411345
E-mail: hecknet@hecknet.poptel.org.uk

- National ranking 96 (109, 110, 112, 156)
- GCSE 97% (96%)
- A-levels 25% (A/B); 90% (A/E)
- Higher education 80% (Cambridge 1)

- Grant-maintained
- Mixed grammar
- Pupils 850
- Boys (11–18) 410
- Girls (11–18) 440
- Sixth form 190 (22%)
- Education authority *Kirklees*

Headteacher Mark Tweedle, 42, appointed in January 1990. Staff 50 (men 26, women 24).

Motto Nil sine labore (Nothing without toil).

Background Founded in 1898; original buildings extended in 1930s, 1960s and 1990s; became grammar school following 1944 Education Act; became grant-maintained in 1989, one of the first in the country. Heavily over-subscribed, with five applications for each place. Specialist accommodation includes technology suite and information technology facilities. About one in three pupils receives individual instrumental music tuition; 'impressive record' of success in Associated Board examinations. Identified by Ofsted in 1996 as 'outstandingly successful' school.

Alumni Professor John Fozard, designer of Harrier jump jet and director of National Air and Space Museum, Washington; Sir Hubert Houldsworth, former chairman of National Coal Board and vice-chancellor of Leeds University; Michael McGowan, Labour Euro-MP for Leeds.

Streaming Pupils put in sets in mathematics, science, modern languages and English from year 8 or 9.

Approach to discipline 'Firm but fair. Rules are deliberately few in number because at all times, both inside and outside school, pupils are expected to show consideration for others and conduct themselves in a manner that could give no grounds for criticism.' For minor breaches, up to one-hour detention at lunchtime or after school, or on Saturday mornings for persistent offenders. For more serious breaches, parents and senior staff involved; possible short or, rarely, permanent exclusion.

Uniform Brown blazer, black trousers/brown skirt, brown-and-gold tie. Regulations enforced rigorously.

Homework Average 11-year-old, six to seven hours a week; 14-year-old, eight to nine hours; 16-year-old, 10 to 12 hours.

Vocational qualifications RSA, Information Technology (as part of sixth-form general studies programme).

Inspection April 1995: 'A very good school. The quality of education is high with many outstanding features. Standards of achievement in public examinations are high and steadily improving. The school's reputation in and beyond the local community is justifiably high.'; 'Management and administration are of a high standard. The headteacher and senior management team provide powerful and effective leadership. There is a strong unity of purpose in the school and a high level of staff commitment, with both good subject leadership and effective pastoral support for pupils.'

Primary schools More than 40 feeder schools throughout north Kirklees.

THE FOLKESTONE SCHOOL FOR GIRLS

Coolinge Lane
Folkestone
Kent CT20 3RB
Tel (01303) 251125
Fax (01303) 221422

- National ranking 97 (148, 128, 52, 123)
- GCSE 96% (92%)
- A-levels 61% (A/B); 98% (A/E)
- Higher education 98% (Oxford 1, Cambridge 1)

- Grant-maintained
- Girls' grammar
- Pupils 882
- Boys *Not applicable*
- Girls (11–18) 882
- Sixth form 200 (23%)
- Education authority *Kent*

Headteacher Shan Mullett, 51, appointed in

September 1989. Staff 52 (men 15, women 37).

Motto *None*

Background Hillside site overlooking sea, with extensive grounds. Facilities include specialist laboratories, mathematics rooms, technology suite, languages and humanities rooms, business studies and information technology suite; art and design rooms include dark room and pottery; music rooms include practice rooms and high-technology recording studio; two libraries, two gymnasia, two halls, drama room, sixth-form common rooms. Fully-subscribed; all pupils successful in the Kent selection test are offered places. Pupils perform at local, county, national and international level in wide variety of extra-curricular activities 'too numerous to mention'.

Alumni Professor Dame Sheila Sherlock, gastro-enterologist and professor of medicine, Royal Free Hospital School of Medicine; WPC Helen Phelps, BBC *Crimewatch*.

Streaming In year 9 two sets continue with Latin as well as French and German; some streaming in years 10 and 11 in mathematics, science and modern languages.

Approach to discipline Highest standards expected in all areas, not just academic; general rules to ensure acceptable behaviour. 'We insist upon courtesy and consideration for others at all times, and expect every girl to be polite and thoughtful in her dealings with other people.'

Uniform Years 7 to 9: plaid kilt, blue blouse, blue sweater with logo; in years 10 and 11 kilt replaced by blue skirt. Summer uniform is lightweight blue skirt and white polo-shirt. General guidelines for sixth-formers. Strictly enforced.

Homework Average 11-year-old, seven hours a week; 14-year-old, 10 hours; 16-year-old, 12 hours.

Vocational qualifications GNVQ Level 3, Business, Health and Social Care; RSA, Word-processing, Computer Literacy and Information Technology.

Inspection November 1993.

Primary schools Park Farm Primary; Harcourt Primary; All Souls' CE Primary.

WOODFORD COUNTY HIGH SCHOOL

High Road
Woodford Green
Essex IG8 9LA
Tel (0181) 504 0611
Fax (0181) 506 1880

- National ranking 98 (124, 18, 68, 85)
- GCSE 96% (94%)
- A-levels 60% (A/B); 97% (A/E)
- Higher education 90% (Oxford 2, Cambridge 1)

- Girls' grammar
- Pupils 784
- Boys *Not applicable*
- Girls (11–18) 784
- Sixth form 184 (23%)
- Education authority *Redbridge*

Headteacher Helen Cleland, 46, appointed in September 1991. Staff 47 (men 11, women 36).

Motto Laeti gratias deo agimus (Joyfully we give thanks to God).

Background Founded as girls' grammar in 1919, it is housed in characterful building, the former manor of Highams (built 1768) in extensive grounds designed by Humphrey Repton. New buildings and refurbishment include art and technology centre, sixth-form centre, and extra laboratories and classrooms. Size increased from three-form entry to four-form in September 1992, catering for catchment area that includes whole of Redbridge and into Waltham Forest and Essex. Heavily over-subscribed, with 10 applications per place; voluntary selection test administered by local education authority; more than 1,000 applicants for 120 places. All pupils receive work-experience and community placements. Strengths include art, music and sport; regular individual and team successes at county and national level.

Alumni Sue Bonner, BBC radio producer.

Streaming In mathematics from year 9 and in science from year 10.

Approach to discipline 'Firm but fair.' Simple code of behaviour agreed by girls on entry. 'Staff and governors would take a serious view of anyone unable to observe this.'

Uniform Blue-and-white striped blouse, navy kilt, white socks. Navy sweater, blazer and outdoor coat. Sixth-formers do not wear uniform but 'expected to dress appropriately on formal occasions'. Regulations 'closely observed'.

Homework Average 11-year-old, six hours 40 minutes a week; 14-year-old, nine hours 20 minutes; 16-year-old, 10+ hours.

Vocational qualifications RSA, Word-processing, Office Practice; Business German and Business Spanish may enrich A-level courses.

Inspection October 1994: 'A very good school. The standards of achievement and the quality of both teaching and learning are good.'; 'Work of real excellence is done in many subjects.'; 'The excitement of learning in many classes produces genuine intellectual debate of a high order. However, where there is less challenge standards of achievement and the quality of learning are adversely affected.'; 'Standards of behaviour are exemplary, yet pupils are not suppressed. The ethos of the school makes unspoken demands on pupils, to which they respond positively. Discipline and attendance are very good.'

Primary schools Pupils are drawn from more than 50 feeder schools.

ILFORD COUNTY HIGH SCHOOL

Fremantle Road
Barkingside
Ilford
Essex IG6 2JB
Tel (0181) 551 6496
Fax (0181) 503 9960

- National ranking 99 (86, 67, 93, 112)
- GCSE 96% (97%)
- A-levels 57% (A/B); 92% (A/E)
- Higher education 80% (Oxford 1, Cambridge 8)

- Boys' grammar
- Pupils 803
- Boys (11–18) 803
- Girls Not applicable
- Sixth form 203 (25%)
- Education authority Redbridge

Headteacher Stuart Ian Devereux, 47, appointed in September 1993. Staff 49 (men 38, women 11)

Motto None

Background Originally one of several selective schools in Redbridge, the school was the only one for boys that was retained in the 1970s; Woodford County High School is the girls' selective school. Main two-storey building dates from 1930s. Lower level includes assembly hall, modern language rooms, chemistry laboratories, music rooms, and a humanities wing (1990), housing geography, history, economics and business studies. Further extension in 1996; enhanced facilities for design and technology, and electronics. Well-equipped gymnasium and heated indoor swimming pool. Upper level: biology and physics laboratories, art rooms, mathematics rooms, computer rooms, careers room, sixth-form common room and library. Also rooms for religious education and classics. Four-classroom English block, opened in September 1993; on-site tennis courts, basketball court, and playing fields for football, rugby, hockey, cricket and athletics. Final building phase in September 1998: additional science laboratory, classrooms, new library and sixth-form study areas. Over-subscribed, with 10 applications per place: about 1,200 boys sit the voluntary 11-plus selection test for 120 places. Ten GCSEs in year 11. Extra-curricular activities include music and drama, sailing, jazz band, brass band, chess, debating, computing, orchestra. Also strong reputation in sport: soccer is main winter game; also inter-school matches in basketball, badminton, rugby, swimming, waterpolo, athletics and cricket. 'We endeavour to combine keen competition and a desire to win with a sport-for-all philosophy.' Duke of Edinburgh Award Scheme; Parents' Association; Old Parkonians, with old boys' clubhouse next to Redbridge Sports Centre, less than 10 minutes from the school.

Alumni Lord Sheppard, chairman and chief executive of Grand Metropolitan; Trevor Brooking, former West Ham and England footballer.

Streaming None

Approach to discipline 'We aim to foster self-discipline through a disciplinary system that is firm yet fair. We expect good behaviour both within school and on the journey to and from school.' Uniform, punctuality, politeness and hard work among the requirements. Sanctions range from verbal reprimand to official detention; commendation system considered to be equally important. 'Very occasionally' it is necessary to exclude a boy from the school for a serious offence.

Uniform Maroon blazer, grey trousers, school tie, grey V-neck pullover (optional), black shoes. Dark blue blazer in sixth form. Strictly enforced, but with concessions to sixth-formers, who are allowed to wear their own ties.

Homework Average 11-year-old, five to seven hours a week; 14-year-old, nine to 12 hours; 16-year-old, at least 15 hours.

Vocational qualifications *None*

Inspection December 1993: 'The school provides effective education and pupils reach good standards of achievement in most subjects. Their standards of work are also good in the areas of reading, writing, numeracy, speaking and listening. The teaching is, in general, effective in helping pupils to learn, although the range of teaching styles is somewhat limited. Pupils attend to their studies with interest and enthusiasm, and participate in lessons keenly and readily. The school day is short, and this constrains the range, depth and balance of the curriculum.'; 'Behaviour in lessons and around the school is of a high standard. The ethos in the school is of good work and behaviour. There are clear and high expectations for pupils' conduct. The pupils generally relate well to each other and to adults, and show respect for the environment.' The school has since lengthened teaching time to 25 hours a week as part of action plan in response to inspectors' comments and to 'further enhance the range, depth and balance in the curriculum'. *The school reports it has introduced a 25-hour week.*

Primary schools Total of more than 50 feeder schools.

CRANBROOK SCHOOL

Waterloo Road
Cranbrook
Kent TN17 3JD
Tel (01580) 712163
Fax (01580) 715365

- National ranking 100 (112, 90, 101, 102)
- GCSE 96% (95%)
- A-levels 56% (A/B); 98% (A/E)
- Higher education 91% (Oxford 3, Cambridge 2)

- Grant-maintained
- Mixed grammar
- Pupils 706
- Boys (13–18) 403
- Girls (13–18) 303
- Sixth form 269 (38%)
- Education authority *Kent*

Headteacher Peter A. Close, 53, appointed in 1988. Staff 59 (men 37, women 22).

Motto Maiora tento praesentibus aequus (We are equal to present tasks and striving for greater things).

Background Founded in 1518 by John Bluebery, the school has occupied the same site in the Wealden town of Cranbrook for 450 years. Queen Elizabeth I granted its royal charter in 1574; grant-maintained, co-educational grammar for day and boarding pupils. Six boarding houses in 70 acres of grounds. Facilities include 400-seat theatre, suite of music practice rooms, and a recently-built sports centre with Astroturf playing surface. More than two applicants for each place. Many students study four or five A-level/AS-level subjects. Sports include lacrosse, basketball, hockey, cricket, rugby, tennis, netball and athletics. Pupils currently represent England in shooting, hockey and athletics.

Alumni Hammond Innes, novelist; Peter West, BBC commentator; Phil Edmonds, cricketer; Georgina Henry, journalist; Piers Sellers, NASA astronaut.

Streaming Banding based on previous experience in French and Classics in year 9; setting by ability in mathematics. Years 10 and 11: setting by ability in mathematics, French and in some option subjects.

Approach to discipline Self-discipline encouraged within clear guidelines. 'Wide-ranging opportunities are offered to students to make choices and decisions, and to exercise responsibility along with realisation that they will be held responsible for their actions.'

Uniform Boys: charcoal-grey trousers, brown tweed jacket, school tie. Girls: grey skirt/kilt, white blouse, maroon jumper. Compulsory for all except sixth-formers.

Homework Average 14-year-old, 12 hours a week; 16-year-old, 20 to 24 hours.

Vocational qualifications Business French.

Inspection April 1993: 'Standards achieved in

most subjects are good, occasionally outstanding: overall standards are commensurate with the ability range within the school.'; 'Academic studies are complemented by a wide range of extra-curricular activities where pupils are expected to, and do, make a contribution. The quality of teaching provided is almost always at least satisfactory and often good, and pupils are highly-motivated, enthusiastic and well-organised.'; 'Relationships are positive and behaviour is very good.' February 1997: 'A very successful school. In addition to good academic achievement, the pupils are developing into responsible, confident and caring members of society. Behaviour in school is very good, relationships are warm and friendly and all staff and pupils work hard. The headteacher gives clear and effective leadership and direction. He is very well supported by the senior staff, governing body, all other staff and the vast majority of parents.'

HIGH SCHOOL FOR GIRLS

Denmark Road
Gloucester
Gloucestershire GL1 3JN
Tel (01452) 543335
Fax (01452) 549862
E-mail: hsfg@aol.com

- National ranking 101 (108, 129 = , 99, 32 =)
- GCSE 96% (96%)
- A-levels 51% (A/B); 95% (A/E)
- Higher education 96%

- Girls' grammar
- Pupils 702
- Boys (16–18) 3
- Girls (11–18) 699
- Sixth form 169 (24%)
- Education authority *Gloucestershire*

Headteacher Margaret A. Bainbridge, 47, appointed in September 1992. Staff 42 (men 6, women 36).

Motto In honour preferring one another.

Background The school opened for 50 pupils in 1883; moved to current site with 200 pupils in 1908; Grade 2 listed building in extensive tree-lined grounds in residential area to north of Gloucester. More recent additions include classrooms, science block and gymnasium. Second gymnasium, new

suite of science laboratories and substantial refurbishment, including new sixth-form centre in 1996. Over-subscribed, with four applications per place. Sixth-formers take on considerable responsibility in helping organisation and leadership of school. 'The school preserves the best elements of a traditional grammar school while seeking to be at the forefront of all educational initiatives and developments.'

Alumni Monica Sims, director of production of the Children's Film and Television Foundation and formerly BBC Radio's director of programmes; Sir Robin Day (in nursery department).

Streaming In mathematics after year 7; in science in year 10.

Approach to discipline 'The school's approach is firm. A code of conduct is insisted upon, based on good manners and consideration for others.'

Uniform Navy skirt, blue-and-white striped blouse, school tie, school blazer, navy cardigan/jumper, navy/black jacket or coat. Strictly enforced.

Homework Average 11-year-old, six hours a week; 14-year-old, eight hours; 16-year-old, more than 12 hours.

Vocational qualifications *None*

MAIDSTONE GRAMMAR SCHOOL

Barton Road
Maidstone
Kent ME15 7BT
Tel (01622) 752101
Fax (01622) 753680
E-mail: mgsone@mail.rmplc.co.uk

- National ranking 102 (110, 68 = , 65, 51)
- GCSE 96% (95%)
- A-levels 50% (A/B); 98% (A/E)
- Higher education 85% (Oxford 2, Cambridge 3)

- Boys' grammar
- Pupils 1,243
- Boys (11–18) 1,200
- Girls (16–18) 43
- Sixth form 360 (29%)
- Education authority *Kent*

Headteacher Neil Anthony Turrell, 51, appointed in September 1992. Staff 72 (men 54, women 18).

Motto Olim meminisse iuvabit (One day it will please us to remember).

Background A royal charter established the school in 1549; moved to current 16-acre site in 1930. Voluntary-controlled since 1994. Main neo-Tudor-style block built around cloistered quadrangle; newer wings date from early 1960s; second quad completed with opening of large sixth-form and arts block in 1981. Library and art room recently extended. Entry was at 13+ and 16+, but 11+ entry returned in 1993. Routinely over-subscribed. Outstanding record in GCSE mathematics, with most candidates earning top grade; high proportion study mathematics at A-level. Total of 24 A-level candidates achieved three or more A grades in 1996. Outstanding results in sciences and media studies. Wide-ranging work-experience scheme. Combined Cadet Force. National success in chess. Winner of Schools Challenge quiz in three consecutive years. Regional success in hockey and bridge.

Alumni Lord Beeching, former chairman of British Rail; James Burke, television personality; Professor Geoffrey Hosking, professor of Russian History, London University, and Reith lecturer; Christopher Smart, poet; William Golding, novelist and Nobel prize-winner, taught briefly at the school; Stuart Miles, *Blue Peter* presenter; Tommy Pearson, Music Machine presenter on Radio Three.

Streaming Some streaming in mathematics to allow some pupils to take GCSE early, and go on to AO level in year 11. One form of outstanding students in each of years 10 and 11. International Baccalaureate as well as A-levels from September 1997.

Approach to discipline Respect for authority of staff; prefect system; punctuality and fulfilment of obligations; range of sanctions for misbehaviour. 'Students are given greater freedom as they move up the school. Individual responsibility is the keynote.'

Uniform Black blazer with badge, grey/sober-coloured trousers, white/grey/pale-coloured shirt; sixth-formers may wear a suit or sports jacket, with school tie.

Homework Average 11-year-old, five hours a week; 14-year-old, seven hours; 16-year-old, 10 hours.

Vocational qualifications *None*

Inspection November 1993.

Primary schools 'We regularly draw our students from around 70 schools over a wide area in mid-Kent.'

DARTFORD GRAMMAR SCHOOL FOR GIRLS

Shepherds Lane
Dartford
Kent DA1 2NT
Tel (01322) 223123
Fax (01322) 294786
E-mail: **dggs@dggs.demon.co.uk**

- National ranking 103 (72, 55, 94, 56)
- GCSE 96% (98%)
- A-levels 50% (A/B); 96% (A/E)
- Higher education 86%

- Grant-maintained
- Girls' grammar
- Pupils 872
- Boys *Not applicable*
- Girls (11–18) 872
- Sixth form 237 (27%)
- Education authority *Kent*

Headteacher Jillian Hadman, 61, appointed in 1986. Staff 56 (men 16, women 40).

Motto In quietness and confidence.

Background The first county grammar school for girls in Kent and one of earliest state secondary schools for girls in the country. In 1912, moved to current purpose-built building in residential area of west Dartford; imposing facade with central tower and coat of arms. New technology centre opened in 1994; seven science laboratories, language laboratory, outdoor swimming pool and grass tennis courts. Full range of expressive arts, including dance and theatre studies, among strengths; two AL Certificates of Excellence in 1995 for top marks in Art and Design Textiles; student performer in Schools Prom. Five languages taught: Russian, French, German, Spanish and Italian; also Arabic, Gujerati, Bengali and Modern Greek through extra-curricular open learning. More than 31 A-level subjects. Many foreign exchanges and overseas work-experience: Switzerland, Netherlands, Germany and Australia. Strong industry links, with sponsor governors. Average of 3.75 applicants per place. Admits top 25% of ability range. School's good practice featured in two 1997 publications: Managing Financial Resources Effectively, an Ofsted publication, and The State of the Arts, published by Exeter University on behalf of the Gulbenkian/Hamlyn Foundations.

Alumni Sheila Hancock, actress; Diana Quick, actress; Anne Swithinbank, gardener and broadcaster; Andrea Vogler, national percussion finalist in 1994 BBC Young Musician of the Year.

Streaming Setting only in mathematics from Year 8; Science and English from year 10.

Approach to discipline 'Positive approach.' No prescribed set of rules; shared expectations made clearly known; encouragement of self-discipline, individual and corporate responsibility. Sanctions include reprimand, community service within school or detention.

Uniform Dark-green skirt and jumper, green-and-white striped blouse, dark-green/black coat, which is bought from one designated outfitter. Sixth-formers do not wear uniform.

Homework Average 11-year-old, six hours 15 minutes a week; 14-year-old, 10 hours; 16-year-old, at least 15 hours.

Vocational qualifications RSA, Information Technology, Business Russian, Business Italian, Business Spanish; Foreign Languages at Work (French and German); Foreign Languages into Commerce (Chinese).

Inspection January 1997: 'Dartford Grammar School for Girls provides a broad, stimulating, high-quality learning experience. In addition to achieving good results in GCSE and A-level examinations, the girls are being extremely well prepared for the demands of life outside of school and into the 21st century. Behaviour is very good, relationships are warm and friendly, and staff and pupils work hard. The senior staff, governing body and all other staff give first-class support to the excellent and visionary leadership of the headteacher.'; 'The work of pupils in the sixth form is good overall and is very good in English, music, art and science. Pupils' personal studies in art history are outstanding as is the competency of some students in foreign languages.'; 'Achievement in modern languages is exceptional. For example, girls have learnt to speak and write confidently in Russian by the end of year 8. They have an exceptionally wide repertoire of writing skills in English.'; 'Teaching is good in 55% of lessons and

very good in a further 10%. There is no unsatisfactory teaching. All teachers are well-qualified, have very secure and deep knowledge of their subject, and they present their lessons with a high degree of confidence and enthusiasm.'; 'The opportunities for pupils to extend their interests through extra-curricular activites are excellent.'

Primary schools Fleetdown County Primary; Our Lady's RC Primary; St Anselm's RC Primary; Sutton-at-Hone CE Primary; Horton Kirby CE Primary; Maypole County Primary; Old Bexley CE Primary; Hextable County Primary.

ABBEY GRAMMAR SCHOOL

Courtenay Hill
Newry
County Down BT34 2ED
Tel (01693) 63142
Fax (01693) 62514

- National ranking 104 (162)
- GCSE 96% (87%)
- A-levels 48% (A/B); 92% (A/E)
- Higher education 76%

- Boys' grammar
- Pupils 836
- Boys (11–18) 836
- Girls *Not applicable*
- Sixth form 173 (21%)
- Education authority *Southern Education and Library Board*

Headteacher Dermot McGovern, 42, appointed in May 1995. Staff 49 (men 37, women 12).

Motto Facere et docere (To do and to teach).

Background Established by the Irish Christian Brothers in 1851, the school derives its name from historic location in grounds of Cistercian Abbey founded by St Malachy in 1144; current building is 30 years old, but constantly expanded and upgraded. Facilities include modern gymnasium, state-of-the-art fitness room, computerised library with CD-ROM, technology suite, two computer rooms, seven science laboratories, language laboratory, music room, drama room, resources room, sixth-form common room and study. Over-subscribed, with 1.5 applications per place. 'While the development of the individual and the pursuit of excellence are central to the school's philosophy, students are expected to display genuine Christian concern for the welfare of others exemplified through exceptional commitment to charity fund-raising and community projects.' Extra-curricular involvement 'strongly encouraged'. Success in inter-school competitions: notably, Gaelic football, golf, swimming, Irish drama and science. Winners of Irish and European Young Scientist of Year Awards in 1993 and 1995; first prize in UK Environmental Science contest in 1995. Scientific expedition to Ecuador in 1996. European dimension underlined by regular exchanges with, and trips to, schools in France, Belgium and Spain. 'Vibrant' past pupils' and parent-teacher associations.

Alumni Seamus Mallon, MP for Newry and Mourne; Frank Aiken, Tanaiste; Professor Art Cosgrove, president of University College, Dublin; Ronan Rafferty, Ryder Cup golfer; Raymond Burns, Walker Cup golfer; Sean O'Neill, Gaelic footballer; D.J. Kane, Gaelic footballer.

Streaming Additional mathematics group in year 11; mixed-ability groups elsewhere.

Approach to discipline 'Simple and effective discipline code and structure clearly understood by pupils, parents and staff. The application of sanctions is obviated by a pastoral system of rewards and credits.'

Uniform Black blazer with school crest, black trousers, grey shirt (years 7 to 11)/white shirts (sixth form), school tie (black with red-and-amber diagonal stripes), grey V-neck pullover, black/grey socks, black shoes. Sixth-formers may substitute black sweatshirt with school crest for blazer. Regulations 'rigidly enforced'.

Homework Average 11-year-old, seven hours 30 minutes a week; 14-year-old, 10 hours; 16-year-old, 15 hours. Study timetables designed by pupils.

Vocational qualifications None

Primary schools St Colman's Abbey Primary; St Peter's Primary, Warrenpoint; St Malachy's Primary; Cloughoge Primary; St Patrick's Primary; St Mary's Primary, Mullaghbawn.

ALTRINCHAM GRAMMAR SCHOOL FOR BOYS

Marlborough Road
Bowdon
Altrincham
Cheshire WA14 2RS
Tel (0161) 928 0858
Fax (0161) 929 5137

- National ranking 105 (41, 71=, 91, 128)
- GCSE 96% (99%)
- A-levels 43% (A/B); 94% (A/E)
- Higher education 90% (Oxford 2, Cambridge 1)

- Grant-maintained
- Boys' grammar
- Pupils 925
- Boys (11–18) 925
- Girls *Not applicable*
- Sixth form 187 (20%)
- Education authority *Trafford*

Headteacher Bryan Purvis, 49, appointed in September 1993. Staff 54 (men 36, women 18).

Motto Labor omnia vincit (Toil conquers all).

Background Established in 1912 on 28-acre site in leafy suburb to south of Manchester, bordering Cheshire countryside; extended in 1938 and again in 1960; 20 acres of playing fields. Conservation area containing pond and small wood within school grounds. Traditional grammar school that also offers new technological disciplines; only state school in Manchester area to offer Latin and Greek to A-level; strong science department; music flourishing in school. Over-subscribed, with four applications per place. School prides itself on charity fund-raising of more than £5,000 annually; full programme of social action, regularly helping elderly and handicapped. 'Deeply etched into the ethos of the school is a sense of friendliness, a strong feeling for the school as a community and an awareness of its role in the wider community.' Active Parents' Association.

Alumni Antony Hopkins, composer and conductor; Bill Canaway, author; Ronald Gow, playwright; Paul Allott, Staffordshire cricketer; Ian Livingstone and Steve Jackson, authors and games compilers; Paul Watson, television director; Ian Hargreaves, editor of *New Statesman*; John Morrill, Reader in Early Modern History and Vice-Master of Selwyn College, Cambridge; Peter Bamford, managing director of W.H. Smith; Father Barnabas Lindars, former Rylands Professor of Biblical Criticism and Exegesis, Manchester University.

Streaming Pupils are put in sets in mathematics.

Approach to discipline 'Our watchword is co-operation. Our rules are brief but enforced. We couch our discipline in a spirit of common purpose. It works! Discipline extends to appearance as well as manners.'

Uniform Green blazer with school badge, grey trousers, white shirt, green tie with crests, black shoes. Strictly enforced; sixth-formers wear suit with school tie.

Homework Average 11-year-old, five hours a week; 14-year-old, seven hours 30 minutes; 16-year-old, 10 hours.

Vocational qualifications *None*

Inspection October 1994: 'A very good school with considerable strengths in many areas. The school values learning and achievement, and provides an effective education for its pupils.'; 'Pupils have a natural curiosity and enthusiasm for learning. They show a persistent determination to understand and are prepared to work hard. Progress in lessons observed was most effective where pupils were given the freedom to explore and extend their learning. The quality of learning observed was particularly good in the sixth form.'; 'The inadequate accommodation is a major impediment to the further development of the school. It may not lie within the power of the school and governors to resolve this problem alone.'

Primary schools Heyes Lane Junior; Stamford Park Junior; Bowdon CE Primary; Well Green Primary; Cloverlea Primary.

WEST KIRBY GRAMMAR SCHOOL FOR GIRLS

Graham Road
West Kirby
Wirral
Merseyside L48 5DP
Tel (0151) 632 3449
Fax (0151) 632 1224
E-mail: wkghs@liv.ac.uk
Internet: http://www.liv.ac.uk/~wkghs

- National ranking 106 (87, 77)
- GCSE 96% (97%)
- A-levels 39% (A/B); 93% (A/E)
- Higher education 85%

- Girls' grammar
- Pupils 1,248
- Boys *Not applicable*
- Girls (11–18) 1,248
- Sixth form 320 (26%)
- Education authority *Wirral*

Headteacher Joan Erskine, appointed in September 1984. Staff 84 (men 14, women 70).

Motto Ad metam contendo (I strive towards the goal).

Background Originally founded as an independent day school in 1913; situated in West Kirby on the Wirral peninsula, drawing pupils from the surrounding area. Oversubscribed, with three applications per place. The school 'strives to achieve excellence in all areas of the curriculum'. Competitors at national and international level in a range of sports, including hockey, netball, tennis and athletics. 'Within a caring ethos, the school strives to promote high standards of academic, personal and social life. Pupils are encouraged to develop their talents and interests through a broad and balanced curriculum in an environment which is intellectually stimulating but secure, enabling students to prepare for the challenges and opportunities of a rapidly-changing world.' Identified in 1996 Ofsted annual report as 'outstandingly successful school'.

Alumni Glenda Jackson, actress and Labour MP for Hampstead and Highgate; Shirley Hughes, children's book illustrator; Gillian Crawshaw, journalist.

Streaming Some setting in mathematics and French.

Approach to discipline 'The ethos is to promote positive attitudes and high standards of self-discipline.'

Uniform Years 7 to 11: plain navy skirt and jumper, blue blouse, navy coat. No uniform for sixth-formers. Strictly enforced.

Homework Average 11-year-old, four hours a week; 14-year-old, six hours; 16-year-old, nine to 10 hours.

Vocational qualifications *None*

Inspection May 1995: 'This is a very good

school. High achievement, a caring community, clear and supportive leadership and a committed staff are key features of the school.'; 'Results, whilst always good, have improved over the last five years.'; 'In English, standards are high. Pupils read and write fluently.'; 'Pupils are conscientious and make good progress. They have opportunities to carry out investigations, solve problems, apply knowledge to new situations in whole-class teaching, group work and individually. In all subjects more opportunities for individual research using library and information technology resources would further enhance the quality of learning. Teachers are highly competent in the subjects they teach.'; 'A clear set of values which are reflected in the high standards of achievement and care within the school.'

SIR HENRY FLOYD GRAMMAR SCHOOL

Oxford Road
Aylesbury
Buckinghamshire HP21 8PE
Tel (01296) 24781
Fax (01296) 24783

- National ranking 107 (121, 82, 87, 116)
- GCSE 96% (97%)
- A-levels 34% (A/B); 95% (A/E)
- Higher education 89%

- Mixed grammar
- Pupils 746
- Boys (12–18) 340
- Girls (12–18) 406
- Sixth form 257 (34%)
- Education authority *Buckinghamshire*

Headteacher Susan Margaret Powell, 51, appointed in September 1996. Staff 46 (men 21, women 25).

Motto *None*

Background Became mixed grammar school during 1960s, moving to its current site in 1962. Accommodation since improved for specialist teaching, including computer rooms, and science and technology facilities; new sixth-form block completed in 1991. Work on improved accommodation to start in 1997-98, with second phase partly funded from school's financial reserves built up since local management of schools. Original links with industry and commerce maintained and strengthened: the headteacher is the only secondary head on local action group of Thames Valley Enterprise. Regional and national success in Business Studies competitions; two flourishing Young Enterprise companies. Foreign Languages at Work schemes in French and German for sixth-formers; also Youth Award Scheme. Over-subscribed to varying degrees each year, especially in sixth form. All pupils in year 11 receive work-experience; sixth-formers undertake 'work-shadowing'; workplacement for teaching staff. Traditional academic education for able pupils: sixth-formers, including those who have transferred from independent schools, choose from 20 A-level courses. Established school exchange schemes with French and German schools; centenary exchange with Swiss school. Highlighted in 1995 annual Ofsted report as an 'outstandingly successful' school. Entry at 11 from 1998. 'We aim to help pupils to become self-confident but not arrogant, tolerant but not sub-servient, ambitious but not ruthless, and determined yet not self-centred.'

Streaming Some setting of GCSE pupils in years 10 and 11 where appropriate.

Approach to discipline Form-tutors and year-heads implement overall behaviour policy, overseen by deputy heads. Parents told of pupils' transgressions and sanctions imposed.

Uniform Boys: blazer with badge, grey worsted trousers, white shirt, school tie. Girls: grey skirt, white shirt, school tie, maroon sweatshirt/black sweater (lower and middle school). Dress code for sixth-formers. Regulations enforced 'strictly'.

Homework Average 14-year-old, eight hours 45 minutes a week; 16-year-old, 11 hours 15 minutes.

Vocational qualifications *None*

Inspection November 1993: 'Pupils are well-behaved, both in class and around the school. The overall quality of pupils' behaviour is very good. Attitudes in all age-groups are appropriately mature, pleasant, helpful and courteous. Pupils and parents are satisfied with the school's approach to the encouragement of good behaviour, where care for one another has a high priority. Pupils are happy at the school.'

Primary schools Wendover CE Middle; Bearbrook Combined; St Edward's RC Middle; Ashmead Combined; Haddenham Primary;

Haydon Abbey Combined. More than 50 feeder primary schools.

QUEEN ELIZABETH'S GRAMMAR SCHOOL, FAVERSHAM

Abbey Place
Faversham
Kent ME13 7PQ
Tel (01795) 533132
Fax (01795) 538474

- National ranking 108 (120, –, 119, 146)
- GCSE 96% (95%)
- A-levels 33% (A/B); 87% (A/E)
- Higher education 85%

- Grant-maintained
- Mixed grammar
- Pupils 787
- Boys (11–18) 401
- Girls (11–18) 386
- Sixth form 157 (20%)
- Education authority Kent

Headteacher Gino G. Carminati, appointed from September 1997. Staff 50 (men 22, women 28).

Motto None

Background Established in 1967 after amalgamation of William Gibbs School for Girls and Faversham Grammar School. Takes top 25% of ability range. 'Traditional grammar school with a positive response to change.' Marginally over-subscribed, with 126 applications for 120 places. Sporting achievements include notable national success in hockey. About 120 pupils learn musical instruments; two orchestras, two wind bands, two choirs; pupils in county orchestras. Three drama productions a year.

Alumni Mr Justice (Sir John) Vinelott, High Court, Chancery Division.

Streaming In mathematics from year 9; modern languages from year 10.

Approach to discipline 'We aim to create a well-ordered but friendly atmosphere in which pupils can both work and be happy. This is backed by a clear system of sanctions based on staff-supervised detentions. There is a system of appointed prefects from the upper-sixth.'

Uniform Boys: navy blazer with school crest, white/grey shirt, school tie, grey socks, black shoes. Girls: white blouse, school tie, navy cardigan (or blazer), navy skirt/tailored trousers, white/navy socks. Strictly enforced; guidelines for sixth-formers.

Homework Average 11-year-old, four hours a week; 14-year-old, seven hours; 16-year-old, 10 hours.

Vocational qualifications None

Inspection May 1995: 'This is a school that is well led, achieves high standards and provides a safe, secure and effective learning environment for its pupils.'; 'When ability is taken into account, in nearly all cases achievement was at the appropriate level, and often higher. There was very little evidence of under-achievement.'; 'Standards of reading are high in most subjects, but there is little reading for pleasure. Pupils write accurately and, in the great majority of cases, fluently and with confidence.'; 'Teaching throughout the school is well-informed and characterised by good preparation and clear exposition.'; 'There is insufficient accommodation of high quality, although what there is, is used well.'

Primary schools St Mary of Charity CE Primary, Faversham; Whitstable County Junior; Whitstable and Seasalter Endowed CE Junior; Ospringe CE Primary, Faversham; Swalecliffe County Primary. Total of 52 feeder schools.

DANE COURT GRAMMAR SCHOOL

Broadstairs Road
Broadstairs
Kent CT10 2RT
Tel (01843) 864941
Fax (01843) 602742
E-mail: dcpupil@aol.com
Internet: http://members.aol.com/
danecourt

- National ranking 109 (122, 120, 140, 139)
- GCSE 96% (95%)
- A-levels 30% (A/B); 90% (A/E)
- Higher education 86% (Cambridge 1)

- Grant-maintained
- Mixed grammar
- Pupils 1,050
- Boys (11–18) 436
- Girls (11–18) 614
- Sixth form 248 (24%)

• Education authority *Kent*

Headteacher Robin Henry Curtis, 50, appointed in September 1990. Staff 72 (men 35, women 37).

Motto *None*

Background Founded in 1957 as two single-sex technical high schools on the same site; amalgamated in 1970; modern buildings, 15-acre playing fields. Over-subscribed. Specialist teaching areas for all departments; 10 laboratories, three design and technology rooms; three computer rooms. Choice of 25 A-level courses. Music and drama among strengths, with 12 musical ensembles: two specialist music teachers, junior and senior wind bands, choirs and orchestras. Year 8 pupils attend annual week-long residential course in Cornwall.

Streaming Setting introduced early for mathematics; phased in later for other subjects.

Approach to discipline 'Clear expectations are set in terms of standards and behaviour. We try to ensure that a relaxed atmosphere exists within that framework.'

Uniform Black blazer with school crest, grey trousers/tartan kilt. Dress code for sixth-formers. Enforced 'with reasoned firmness'.

Homework Average 11-year-old, six hours a week; 14-year-old, nine hours; 16-year-old, 12 hours.

Vocational qualifications *None*

Inspection January 1997: 'A good school with many very good features. The standards of attainment and the quality of teaching and learning are high.'; 'It is a school committed to high achievement, good relationships and concern for the individual.'; 'Raising the attainment of students in terms of A-level results is a key issue for the school.'; 'Progress is consistently good in art, design and technology, mathematics, physical education and religious education, and seldom falls below satisfactory in other subjects.'; 'Teachers have a good knowledge of their subject and a clear understanding of the requirements of the National Curriculum.'; 'The behaviour of pupils is managed well and there are highly-effective procedures for encouraging good discipline.'

Primary schools Upton Junior, Broadstairs; St Saviour's CE Primary, Westgate; Garlinge Primary, Margate; Dame Janet Junior, Ramsgate; Haddon Dene School, Broadstairs.

SKEGNESS GRAMMAR SCHOOL

Vernon Road
Skegness
Lincolnshire PE25 2QS
Tel (01754) 610000
Fax (01754) 763947

• National ranking 110 (26, 28, 142, 90)
• GCSE 96% (100%)
• A-levels 29% (A/B); 92% (A/E)
• Higher education 95%

• Grant-maintained
• Mixed grammar
• Pupils 660
• Boys (11–18) 336
• Girls (11–18) 324
• Sixth form 175 (27%)
• Education authority *Lincolnshire*

Headteacher John Webster, 50, appointed in January 1981. Staff 43 (men 26, women 17).

Motto Murus aeneus conscientia sana (Strength comes through determination).

Background School traces its history to founding of Magdalen College School in Wainfleet in 15th century; in 1933, when the former site was abandoned, the headmaster, staff and pupils moved to new school in Skegness. The first grant-maintained school in Britain and the first to develop boarding for a quarter of a century; boarders live 'in some luxury' in Wainfleet Hall, close to old Tudor schoolroom that now serves as their library. Considerable development in past five years: 'superb' sports, information technology, music, modern languages, science and technology facilities. 'Open' sixth form; over-subscribed, with four applications for each place; competition for boarding places even more severe. Extra-curricular activities include fencing, archery, judo, water-skiing; county football champions. Proud of musical achievements; concert band and orchestra; cathedral organ in hall; weekend adventure activities for boarders. 'Old-fashioned approach, with a modern outlook.' Merited registration with the British Standards Institute in 1995.

Streaming Only in mathematics in middle school.

Approach to discipline 'Unashamedly traditional. The school believes that an ordered and structured environment is a purposeful and a happy one.' Only one school rule: 'Pupils must adopt a sensible and polite attitude and behave in a manner commensurate with their intelligence. Bad behaviour, rude or unsocial conduct or bad manners will not be tolerated.'

Uniform Traditional. Distinctive green blazer (with gold, in sixth form). 'Fiercely' enforced.

Homework Average 11-year-old, five hours a week; 14-year-old, seven hours 30 minutes; 16-year-old, 10 hours.

Vocational qualifications *None*

Inspection September 1994: 'Skegness Grammar School is a good school. The ethos of this selective grammar school is based upon sound academic traditions within an ordered environment that is also happy and caring.'; 'Pupils generally achieve high standards in relation to their abilities, both in the basic skills of literacy and numeracy and in nearly all subjects of the curriculum.'; 'The quality of education provided is high. Pupils at all stages are well-motivated, enthusiastic and have extremely positive attitudes to learning.'

Primary schools Burgh-le-Marsh CE Primary; Chapel St Leonards Primary; Friskney All Saints' CE Primary; Hogsthorpe County Primary; Ingoldmells Primary; Skegness County Junior; Skegness Richmond Primary; Skegness Seathorne Primary; Wainfleet Magdalen Primary; Viking Preparatory.

LAWRENCE SHERIFF SCHOOL

Clifton Road
Rugby
Warwickshire CV21 3AG
Tel (01788) 542074
Fax (01788) 567962
E-mail: lawrence@rmplc.co.uk
Internet: http://www.rmplc.co.uk/eduweb/
sites/lawrence/index.html

- National ranking 111 (100, 159, 114, 137)
- GCSE 96% (96%)
- A-levels 27% (A/B); 87% (A/E)
- Higher education 94% (Oxford 2, Cambridge 1)

- Boys' grammar

- Pupils 685
- Boys (11–18) 685
- Girls *Not applicable*
- Sixth form 235 (34%)
- Education authority *Warwickshire*

Headteacher Rex Hartley Pogson, 50, appointed in September 1985. Staff 39 (men 29, women 10).

Motto Orando laborando (By work and prayer).

Background Voluntary-aided school with tradition dating from Lawrence Sheriff, 16th-century member of Worshipful Company of Grocers whose bequest resulted in Rugby School. Grammar school founded in 1906 under governing body led by headmaster of Rugby. Mid-town site, with sufficient space for good-sized cricket field but with most of sports area a mile away. Seven-year £3 million building programme (laboratories, library refurbishment, technology block, computer networks) culminating in a programme of classrooms, music room and laboratories for the arrival of year 7 from September 1996. New sports hall built with lottery money to provide regional table tennis centre. New arts studio in response to success in community drama and music. Selects top 23% of ability range; more than three applications for each place; one in three sixth-form students from other schools. Close links, including 'parallel time-tabling' and shared classes, with Rugby High School. Rugby and cricket among sporting strengths, with players recently at national level. Foreign work-experience; art, drama, music, technology and debating awards. Average percentage of As and Bs at A-level is 43% over four years.

Streaming Some setting in mathematics.

Approach to discipline 'Firm line flexibly applied.' Close links between school and home; emphasis on care, self-discipline, compassion and respect for others.

Uniform Dark-blue blazer with badge in lower school. Sixth-formers wear suits or jacket and trousers that are 'smart, tidy, professional'. Reasonable flexibility allowed.

Homework Average 11-year-old, six hours a week; 14-year-old, 10 hours; 16-year-old, 12 to 15 hours. School emphasises parental support for set work as important as time taken over homework.

Vocational qualifications *None*

Inspection May 1994: 'The school is well led. The headteacher sets an excellent example. His knowledge of pupils and care for their welfare and academic progress is widely appreciated by the pupils themselves and their parents.'; 'Taken together, the teaching, resources for learning and accommodation make a positive contribution to the learning and the standards achieved, but the variety of teaching styles is unduly limited.'; 'The school deploys its financial resources effectively but does not give sufficient attention to monitoring and evaluation.'

GRAVESEND GRAMMAR SCHOOL FOR BOYS

Church Walk
Gravesend
Kent DA12 2PR
Tel (01474) 331893
Fax (01474) 331894

- National ranking 112 (95, 139, 129, 7)
- GCSE 96% (97%)
- A-levels 24% (A/B); 86% (A/E)
- Higher education 83% (Cambridge 2)

- Grant-maintained
- Boys' grammar
- Pupils 854
- Boys (11–18) 854
- Girls *Not applicable*
- Sixth form 218 (26%)
- Education authority *Kent*

Headteacher Peter John Read, 50, appointed in September 1985. Staff 52 (men 41, women 11).

Motto Consule cunctis (Take thou thought for everyone).

Background Founded in 1893, the school moved to its current site in 1938; took pupils aged 13 to 18 from 1964 to 1992, then reverted to 11-to-18 selective school. Total of £1.8m of building improvements in past two years; new sports hall; 'excellent' technology and information technology facilities. Staff are a mixture of experience and youth following recent expansion; all well-qualified. Over-subscribed, with two applications per place; increased from four-form entry to five-form entry in September 1993. Governors include Eric Hammond, former

general secretary of electricians' union, and John Hougham, ACAS chairman. Teaches Latin, French and German from year 7. Staying-on rate into sixth form is 95%; total of 48 Technology A-level students; other A-level strengths include English, mathematics and Theatre Studies, with 100% pass rates. Sporting strengths: rugby union, badminton, basketball, soccer, tennis and cricket; at least two international sporting representatives each year. Over half boys in school in one or more school teams.

Alumni Sir Richard Southwood, vice-chancellor of Oxford University; Jonathan Martin, head of BBC Sport.

Streaming None; top 25% of ability range selected for entrance.

Approach to discipline 'High expectations that are generally achieved, requiring low-profile discipline. The school is not frightened to take tough action to preserve standards where this is necessary.'

Uniform Years 7 to 11: navy/black blazer, grey trousers, white shirt, house tie. Sixth-formers dress 'appropriate for business environment', with sixth-form tie. High expectations met: 'Enforcement is not an issue.'

Homework Average 11-year-old, seven hours 30 minutes a week; 14-year-old, 10 hours; 16-year-old, 12 hours 30 minutes.

Vocational qualifications RSA, Information Technology.

Inspection November 1996: 'The school is a caring community in which all individuals are valued. Relationships and behaviour are good. Boys achieve well and make good progress.'; 'Pupils reach high levels of attainment and make good progress in all years.'; 'Teachers are conscientious, have an excellent knowledge of their subjects and, in most lessons, have high expectations.'; 'Pupil behaviour is good. Attitudes to learning are very positive and pupils work hard both in school and at their homework.'; 'In most lessons pupils benefit from teaching which challenges and interests them. In a relatively small number of lessons, however, pupils are too dependent on the teacher and are not provided with opportunities to use their own initiative and be responsible for their learning.'

Primary schools 'The pattern of primary school entrance varies significantly from year to year.'

OUR LADY'S GRAMMAR SCHOOL

Chequer Hill
Newry
County Down BT35 6DY
Tel (01693) 63552

- National ranking 113 (63 =, 64, 106, 50)
- GCSE 95% (98%)
- A-levels 48% (A/B); 95% (A/E)
- Higher education 75% (Cambridge 1)

- Girls' grammar
- Pupils 859
- Boys Not applicable
- Girls (11–18) 859
- Sixth form 229 (27%)
- Education authority Southern Education and Library Board

Headteacher Sister Mary Perpetua McArdle, appointed in September 1975. Staff 49 (men 7, women 42).

Motto Ora et labora (Pray and work).

Background Established in 1887 by the Sisters of Mercy in Newry. Site in Canal Street in a building in convent grounds until 1992 when school moved to new building on Chequer Hill five minutes' walk away: most up-to-date laboratories, computer rooms, art and design department, technology suite, specialist subject rooms, lecture theatre, sports facilities. Extensive tennis courts, use of playing fields. Local facilities: swimming pool, bowling alley, running track, arts centre, library. Two school orchestras, choirs, theatre visits, field work or visits for all subject disciplines; large number receive music tuition. Over-subscribed, with 173 applications for 121 places.

Streaming 'None, but within class groups differentiation is used as an integral part of the teaching/assessment method in all subjects.'

Approach to discipline 'The school does not experience many, if any, major discipline problems. Generally, pupils are well-behaved and courteous, and there is an atmosphere of calm in the school.' Formal policy insists 'high standards should be set and rules and sanctions applied firmly and fairly by all teachers'.

Uniform Junior school: navy blazer, navy tunic, navy jumper, white blouse, navy tie, white/navy socks or tights, black shoes.

Senior school: navy blazer, navy jumper with school crest, navy-and-white plaid pleated skirt, white blouse, navy tie, navy/white tights. 'Uniform is essential and regulations are very strictly enforced.'

Homework Average 11-year-old, seven hours a week; 14-year-old, 10 hours; 16-year-old, 12 hours 30 minutes to 15 hours.

Vocational qualifications None

DOWN HIGH SCHOOL

Mount Crescent
Downpatrick
County Down BT30 6EU
Tel (01396) 612103
Fax (01396) 616609

- National ranking 114 (143, 125, 143, 63)
- GCSE 95% (92%)
- A-levels 45% (A/B); 96% (A/E)
- Higher education 86%

- Mixed grammar
- Pupils 777
- Boys (11–18) 366
- Girls (11–18) 411
- Sixth form 209 (27%)
- Education authority South Eastern Education and Library Board

Headteacher Jack Ferris, 51, appointed in January 1989. Staff 46 (men 20, women 26).

Motto Floreat Dunum. Absque labore nihil (May Down flourish. Nothing achieved without effort).

Background Built on site of 19th-century gaol, overlooking ruins of Inch Abbey and the English Mound; walls surrounding school are part of original boundary walls. Founded in 1933 from amalgamation of technical and grammar school on same site. Close co-operation with Down Academy since 1990. Specialist rooms for practical subjects, computer room, music department, gymnasium, careers room, library, audiovisual aids recording room, assembly hall, dining room, sixth-form common room. Own playing fields and joint-use Down Leisure Centre. Three-house house system. School numbers rising substantially; over-subscribed, with 1.3 applications for each place. Strong commitment to sport: up to seven girls' hockey teams and five rugby teams play each Saturday morning; cricket, tennis and athletics. Duke of Edinburgh Award Scheme. More than 100 pupils receive specialist music tuition: choirs, orchestra. 'Typical Northern Ireland country grammar school.'

Streaming 'Light' streaming in mathematics, French and English.

Approach to discipline 'Firm but fair. Self-discipline encouraged and promoted, but a strong belief that without discipline learning cannot take place effectively.' Close liaison with parents; small pastoral units.

Uniform Green blazer with school crest, grey trousers/green skirt, green tie with house stripe and yellow stripe. Very strictly enforced.

Homework Average 11-year-old, six to eight hours a week; 14-year-old, eight to 10 hours; 16-year-old, 10 to 15 hours.

Vocational qualifications RSA, Computer Literacy and Information Technology, Word-processing; Young Enterprise Scheme; European Studies.

Primary schools Academy Primary, Saintfield; Ballynahinch Primary; Killinchy Primary; Newcastle Primary; Clough Primary.

SIR JOSEPH WILLIAMSON'S MATHEMATICAL SCHOOL

Maidstone Road
Rochester
Kent ME1 3EL
Tel (01634) 844008
Fax (01634) 818303

- National ranking 115 (156, 100, 158, 164)
- GCSE 95% (90%)
- A-levels 45% (A/B); 95% (A/E)
- Higher education 80% (Oxford 2, Cambridge 3)

- Boys' grammar
- Pupils 1,003
- Boys (11–18) 976
- Girls (16–18) 27
- Sixth form 250 (25%)
- Education authority *Kent*

Headteacher Keith Williams, 49, appointed in April 1989. Staff 58 (men 41, women 17).

Motto Sub umbra alarum tuarum (Under the shadow of thy wings).

Background School founded in 1701 in accordance with will of Sir Joseph Williamson, 1677 president of Royal Society and first editor of *London Gazette*. It is now voluntary-controlled and, after 260 years in Rochester High Street, moved to current premises outside town centre. Five-form entry; small number of girls admitted into sixth form from September 1993. New sixth-form centre opened in September 1996. Over-subscription in past three years has resulted in introduction of additional form of entry; two applications per place. Equipped with lift and ramps for disabled pupils. Heated indoor swimming pool, refurbished sports hall (1992) and tennis courts (1993). Five-year information technology development under way with £100,000 on new equipment.

Streaming Some streaming for mathematics and English.

Approach to discipline 'The school's emphasis is on the development of self-discipline, responsibility and courtesy within the context of an orderly but sympathetic school environment. Corporate pride is regarded as very important.'

Uniform Navy blazer, grey trousers, grey V-neck pullover edged in school colours, grey/white shirt, black shoes. Compulsory throughout.

Homework Average 11-year-old, four hours 30 minutes a week; 14-year-old, seven hours 30 minutes; 16-year-old, 10 hours.

Vocational qualifications *None*

Inspection May 1995: 'This is a good school. Achievement is high at Sir Joseph Williamson's Mathematical School. GCSE results are well above national average and A-level results are good. The quality of education is good, especially in the sixth form. Pupils are very well motivated and are effective learners. The school's reputation in the local community is justifiably very high.'

Primary schools The Delce Primary; Gordon Primary; Spinnens Acre Primary; St Andrew's Preparatory; Hilltop Primary.

DEVONPORT HIGH SCHOOL FOR BOYS

Paradise Road
Stoke
Plymouth
Devon PL1 5QP

Tel **(01752) 208787**
Fax **(01752) 208788**
E-mail: **school@dhsboys.prestel.co.uk**

- National ranking 116 (137, 58, 120, 132)
- GCSE 95% (93%)
- A-levels 45% (A/B); 94% (A/E)
- Higher education 90% (Oxford 2, Cambridge 3)

- Grant-maintained
- Boys' grammar
- Pupils 970
- Boys (11–18) 970
- Girls *Not applicable*
- Sixth form 200 (21%)
- Education authority *Devon*

Headteacher Dr Nicolas Michael Pettit, 46, appointed in September 1993. Staff 58 (men 41, women 17).

Motto Prorsum semper honeste (Always aim for the highest).

Background Founded in 1896 to provide for commissioned entry into Royal Navy Corps of Naval Contractors, and Customs and Excise. Moved to current site from Devonport at end of Second World War; building was former Stoke Military Hospital (opened 1797) overlooking extensive playing fields. The only boys' grammar school in Plymouth, serving wide rural area as well as the city. Eleven-plus selection test in early September; takes top 25% of ability range; roll is increasing, with introduction of sixth-form entry. The school has its own study centre in France, which is visited by 400 boys a year. Offers Classics, Latin, Greek and Sports Studies to A-level; modern languages and expressive arts 'are key elements of the curriculum'; sixth-formers can take up to five A-levels. Wide range of sports; local or national representation includes basketball, sailing, soccer, athletics and water-polo.

Alumni Sir Austin Pearce, former chairman of British Aerospace and BP; Lewis Hughes, assistant auditor-general; Rear-Admiral Gil Hitchens; Rt Rev Donald Snelgrove, former Bishop of Hull; Rt Rev Kenneth Pillar, former Bishop of Hereford.

Streaming In mathematics, English and modern languages in years 10 and 11.

Approach to discipline 'A civilised and reasoning approach within clear and firm boundaries.'

Uniform Bottle-green blazers. Sixth-formers wear black blazers with sixth-form or prefects' tie. 'All boys, including sixth form, wear uniform.'

Homework Average 11-year-old, five hours a week; 14-year-old, 10 hours; 16-year-old, 15 hours.

Vocational qualifications GNVQ Advanced is offered in combination with A-levels.

Inspection April 1994: 'Devonport High School for Boys is a good school providing an education with many notable features.'; 'The school has consistently high expectations which are realised in practice. Pupils work hard and demonstrate competence as learners; they are polite and well-behaved.'; 'Within a strong united ethos, social and moral values are well-developed; opportunities for cultural development are offered, but these are more limited in the field of spiritual and aesthetic development. The school is an orderly, caring community in which meaningful relationships flourish.' School action plan has addressed issues raised by inspectors' report.

Primary schools 'More than 100 feeder primary schools covering 750 square miles of Cornwall, Devon and Plymouth.'

LIMAVADY GRAMMAR SCHOOL

3 Ballyquin Road
Limavady
County Londonderry BT49 9ET
Tel **(015047) 62374**
Fax **(015047) 65183**
E-mail: **lg@schools.class-ni.org.uk**

- National ranking 117 (114, 129 = , 60, 103)
- GCSE 95% (95%)
- A-levels 43% (A/B); 96% (A/E)
- Higher education 65%

- Mixed grammar
- Pupils 891
- Boys (11–18) 412
- Girls (11–18) 479
- Sixth form 235 (26%)
- Education authority *Western Education and Library Board*

Headteacher Robert B. Matier, 61, appointed in September 1975. Staff 57 (men 29, women 28).

Motto Vita veritas victoria (Life, truth, triumph).

Background Origins in 1924; moved to current site in 1957 with about 250 pupils; substantial extension planned. Over-subscribed, with average of 1.25 applications for each place. Pupils from town of Limavady and extensive rural catchment area, from all religious and social backgrounds. Facilities include: 10 laboratories, two art rooms with pottery and photographic facilities, modern library, lecture theatre, assembly hall, sports hall and weight-training room. Spacious grounds: three rugby pitches, three cricket squares, two soccer pitches, two all-weather hockey pitches, four tennis courts, athletics facilities. Nearby recreation centre and country park. 1992 Schools Curriculum Award; recent winners of Northern Ireland Schools British Telecom Academic Decathlon. Duke of Edinburgh Award Scheme; orienteering. Musical and drama productions 'particularly strong'.

Alumni Derek McAleese, Ireland rugby international; Paula Reed, fashion director of *The Sunday Times*; Desmond Smyth, managing director of Ulster Television; Lady Norma Birley, pro-vice-chancellor of Coventry University.

Streaming From end of year 7 to year 9. In years 10 and 11, streaming in English, mathematics and French; in mathematics, physics and chemistry in sixth form.

Approach to discipline Rules distributed to pupils and parents at start of each year; enforced 'strictly but fairly'; well-developed personal and social education programme. 'Staff are encouraged to take a positive attitude in dealings with pupils and use is made of rewards as well as sanctions. Formal detentions are unnecessary and were abolished some years ago.'

Uniform Navy blazer for boys, navy pullover/cardigan for girls, white shirt/blouse, grey trousers/navy skirt, school tie, black shoes. Very strictly enforced.

Homework Average 11-year-old, 10 hours a week; 14-year-old, 10 hours; 16-year-old, 15 hours.

Vocational qualifications *None.*

Primary schools Limavady Central Primary; Drumachose Primary; Termoncanice Primary; Ballykelly Primary; Eglington Primary.

CHESHAM HIGH SCHOOL

Whitehill
Chesham
Buckinghamshire HP5 1BA
Tel (01494) 782854
Fax (01494) 775414
E-mail:chesham.ha@aol.com

- National ranking 118 (117, 105, 96, 26)
- GCSE 95% (95%)
- A-levels 41% (A/B); 87% (A/E)
- Higher education 80%

- Mixed grammar
- Pupils 903
- Boys (12–18) 408
- Girls (12–18) 495
- Sixth form 316 (35%)
- Education authority *Buckinghamshire*

Headteacher Tim Andrew, 50, appointed in September 1993. Staff 69 (men 27, women 42).

Motto *None*

Background One of 14 selective schools in Buckinghamshire; original foundation in 1947 when it was a boys' technical school; became co-educational grammar in late 1960s. Most of buildings, on edge of Chesham backing onto Chilterns farmland, have been constructed since 1970s; recently-built leisure centre. From July 1995 to December 1997, £1.5 million being spent on new buildings to improve facilities. School full, but not over-subscribed except in the sixth form; pupils from wide area of south Buckinghamshire and, increasingly, from Hertfordshire. Popular sixth form; wide curriculum; high standards in English, mathematics, science and traditional subjects, offered together with fashion, textiles, food, and craft, design and technology. Art 'outstanding'; county, regional and national success at sports. Pony club on site. Teachers are 'stable, well-qualified and experienced'. Proposal to become 11–18 school from September 1998.

Streaming In mathematics in years 10 and 11.

Approach to discipline No written rules, but strict code of conduct, well-known and adhered to. Rewards as well as punishments. 'Pupils are well-behaved most of the time, and the school has a very civilised and positive atmosphere.'

Uniform Girls: blue/black sweatshirt with school logo, straight black skirt, white shirt. Boys: black blazer with badge, black trousers, tie. Sixth-formers expected to wear 'appropriate dress'. Strictly enforced for years 8 to 11.

Homework Average 12-year-old, seven hours 30 minutes to 10 hours a week; 14-year-old, 10 hours to 12 hours 30 minutes; 16-year-old, 10 hours to 12 hours 30 minutes.

Vocational qualifications *None*

Inspection April 1995: 'A good school with some excellent features. It is an orderly and civilised community and much of its strength lies in its pupils. They behave responsibly, are courteous and friendly to others and relationships are generally good throughout the school. Pupils take a pride in their school, they are happy and secure.'; 'The quality of education which the school provides is good and, in many respects, it is very good.'; 'Pupils are well-motivated to learn and achieve, they are conscientious and persevering, responding well to opportunities to take responsibility for their own learning, sustaining their interest and concentration.'

Primary schools Brushwood Middle; Hawridge and Cholesbury CE Combined; Elangeni Middle; Chesham Preparatory; Our Lady's RC Combined.

CHRISTIAN BROTHERS GRAMMAR SCHOOL

Kevlin Road
Omagh
County Tyrone BT78 1LD
Tel (01662) 243567/247656
Fax (01662) 240656
E-mail: cbsomagh@schools.class-ni.org.uk

- National ranking 119 (145, 133, 159, 166)
- GCSE 95% (92%)
- A-levels 40% (A/B); 93% (A/E)
- Higher education 95% (Oxford 1, Cambridge 1)

- Boys' grammar
- Pupils 923
- Boys (11–18) 923
- Girls *Not applicable*
- Sixth form 236 (26%)

- Education authority *Western Education and Library Board*

Headteacher Roderick Tierney, 49, appointed in September 1993. Staff 60 (men 40, women 20).

Motto Facere et docere (To do and to teach).

Background Founded in 1861; moved to current site in centre of Omagh in 1967; substantial extension completed in 1994. Modern facilities: library, music suite, large sports hall, technology suite, information technology suite, A-level/social centre, drama suite and other specialist curricular facilities. Catholic voluntary grammar under trusteeship of the Irish Christian Brothers. Over-subscribed, with 1.3 applications for each place; takes top 33% of the ability range. 'Striving to live by the Gospel values, this school includes a religious dimension that permeates its whole schooling. We emphasise the uniqueness of each individual, promote the harmonious growth of the whole person and encourage a life-long willingness to sustain and develop this growth. We wish our pupils to be men for others, to acknowledge the dignity of each individual and to make decisions from the perspective of the poor and the underprivileged.' Full participation in Ulster Colleges Competitions. The school is a registered Young Enterprise Centre; received Health Promotion Award in 1995. Wide range of extra-curricular activities.

Streaming *None*

Approach to discipline 'The formation of a proper attitude that leads to self-discipline and proper behaviour – education of the full person.'

Uniform Black blazer with school crest, black/charcoal-grey trousers, blue shirt, blue jumper, blue tie with yellow-and-red stripe. 'Absolutely compulsory.'

Homework Average 11-year-old, 10 hours a week; 14-year-old, 14 hours; 16-year-old, 16 hours.

Vocational qualifications *None*

Primary schools St Colmcille's Primary, Omagh; St Conor's Primary, Omagh; St Mary's Primary, Killyclogher; Christ the King Primary, Omagh; Recarson Primary, Omagh.

ST MICHAEL'S COLLEGE

Chanterhill Road
Drumclay
Enniskillen
County Fermanagh BT74 6DE
Tel (01365) 322935
Fax (01365) 325128

- National ranking 120 (76, –, 78, 174)
- GCSE 95% (98%)
- A-levels 38% (A/B); 88% (A/E)
- Higher education 71%

- Boys' grammar
- Pupils 743
- Boys (11–18) 743
- Girls *Not applicable*
- Sixth form 237 (32%)
- Education authority *Western Education and Library Board*

Headteacher Rev Fr Patrick McEntee, 43, appointed in September 1994. Staff 47 (men 29, women 18).

Motto Orare studere agere (To pray, to study, to work).

Background Original school opened in 1903 and run by the Presentation Brothers; came under care of priests from Diocese of Clogher in 1957, initially with only 300 pupils; a Roman Catholic college under trusteeship of Bishop of Clogher and Fermanagh Roman Catholic Board of Education; staff has always included at least four priests. Elevated site about two miles from Enniskillen. Completion of £6m extension in 1993. Over-subscribed, with 1.3 applications for each place. Extensive sporting facilities: four playing fields, eight handball alleys, athletics facilities, sports hall and gymnasium; wide range of sports, including water sports; strong Gaelic football tradition. Also seven science rooms and IT suites, modernised in 1993. Cross-community programmes. Successful record in Gaelic games; 45-member brass band that has toured internationally, including appearance in St Patrick's Cathedral, New York. Two students gained five A-grades each at A-level in 1993. 'There is a very clear and distinct Catholic ethos in the school, designed to complement the Catholic ethos in the homes of the boys attending the school. The school is totally committed to the ideals of Catholic education and tries to create the atmosphere of a believing community committed to living out in its daily operation the Christian way of life.'

Alumni John Kelly, journalist and broadcaster; Fergal McKinney, journalist and broadcaster; Frank Ormsby, poet; Patrick Haren, Northern Ireland Electricity chief executive; Francis J. McManus, former MP.

Streaming Only in mathematics in years 11 and 12.

Approach to discipline 'The school believes that good discipline practices create the condition for effective learning and help to develop in pupils responsible attitudes and values for life. All staff are involved in building up good practices within the school and beyond in the interest of both the pupils and society. There is a hierarchy of discipline procedures and sanctions for dealing with all aspects of indiscipline and misconduct.'

Uniform Navy blazer with light-blue and maroon crest, mid-grey trousers, grey shirt, navy-and-sky-blue tie, 'solid' shoes; college scarf recommended. Very strictly enforced.

Homework Average 11-year-old, eight hours a week; 14-year-old, 10 hours; 16-year-old, 15 hours.

Vocational qualifications *None*

Inspection October 1993: 'Relationships throughout the school are good. There is a strong sense of loyalty to, and community within, the school: links with parents are good. The vast majority of pupils are well-motivated and take a pride in their work.'; 'The accommodation and resources are excellent; they are appreciated by pupils, teachers and parents; the buildings and grounds are well-maintained.'

Primary schools St Michael's Boy's Primary, Enniskillen; St Ronan's Primary, Lisnaskea; St Paul's Primary, Irvinestown; St Martin's Primary, Garrison; St Columban's Primary, Belcoo.

CARRE'S GRAMMAR SCHOOL

Northgate
Sleaford
Lincolnshire NG34 7DD
Tel (01529) 302181
Fax (01529) 413488
E-mail: carres@hotmail.com

- National ranking 121 (85, 104, 64, 38)

- GCSE 95% (97%)
- A-levels 35% (A/B); 91% (A/E)
- Higher education 90% (Cambridge 1)

- Grant-maintained
- Boys' grammar
- Pupils 570
- Boys (11–18) 570
- Girls *Not applicable*
- Sixth form 131 (23%)
- Education authority *Lincolnshire*

Headteacher Peter Freeman, 57, appointed in January 1983. Staff 36 (men 29, women 7).

Motto Por dysserver (In order to serve).

Background Founded by Robert Carre in 1604 and established on its current site in 1835. Some original buildings remain, although a new school was opened in 1904 by the Marquess of Bristol. In the early 1960s large teaching and science block added; new laboratories and technology centre opened in 1992, two years after the school became grant-maintained. On-site playing fields; sports hall completed in December 1996. Takes top 25% of ability range; over-subscribed, with average of 2.5 applications per place. Strong in sciences at A-level; Sleaford joint sixth form provides wide range of courses; more than eight in 10 pupils stay on into sixth form. Outstanding at soccer: county finalists in 10 of last 12 years, and champions seven times. Drama and music also strong. Duke of Edinburgh Award Scheme. Foreign trips have included France, Italy, Germany, United States and the former Soviet Union. Rugby team toured Australia in 1994.

Alumni Mark Wallington, former Leicester City goalkeeper; Ian Kelsall, CBI regional director for Wales.

Streaming *None*

Approach to discipline 'We expect good behaviour, good manners and politeness. Most boys live up to our standards. Friendly exhortation is preferred to fierce sanctions.'

Uniform Black blazer with badge and braid, grey trousers, white/grey shirt, school tie, grey socks, black shoes. Regulations enforced 'quite strongly, in a firm and friendly manner'.

Homework Average 11-year-old, five hours 30 minutes a week; 14-year-old, eight hours; 16-year-old, 11 hours.

Vocational qualifications *None*

Inspection October 1996: 'Carre's Grammar School provides a good standard of education in the context of a strongly academic, male social ethos. Management is supportive, friendly and based on good relationships and goodwill rather than systems and procedures.'; 'Progress is good in most lessons; it is very good in some. The best progress is supported by very good attitudes to learning, well-motivated pupils and good teaching.'; 'The variation in standards between, and occasionally within, subjects is directly related to teaching methods.'; 'The headteacher has provided clear leadership in establishing a distinctive ethos for the school, backed by the informed support of a governing body which provides a good range of appropriate professional expertise.'

Primary schools William Alvey Primary, Sleaford; Metheringham School; Rauceby CE Grant-maintained School; Kirkby-la-Thorpe CE Primary; St Andrew's CE Primary, Leasingham.

BEXLEY ERITH TECHNICAL HIGH SCHOOL

Hartford Road
Bexley
Kent DA5 1NE
Tel (01322) 556538
Fax (01322) 526224

- National ranking 122 (–, –, –, 161)
- GCSE 95%
- A-levels 34% (A/B); 94% (A/E)
- Higher education 90% (Oxford 1, Cambridge 2)

- Grant-maintained
- Boys' grammar
- Pupils 793
- Boys (11–18) 792
- Girls 1
- Sixth form 196 (25%)
- Education authority *Bexley*

Headteacher Jennifer Payne, 43, appointed from September 1997. Staff 49 (men 35, women 14).

Motto Learning for life.

Background Moved to current site in 1961, taking pupils from throughout the London borough of Bexley; top 25% of the ability range. Eight in 10 stay on into the sixth form. Technology background and proud of craft, design and engineering facilities; specialised music area; school hall used for drama productions. Strong sporting tradition. Sports field on site: rugby, soccer, cricket, athletics, tennis.

Alumni Steve Backley, Olympic javelin-thrower.

Streaming Pupils put in sets for mathematics and English in years 10 and 11.

Approach to discipline 'We encourage the development of self-discipline by making it clear to boys what they must do, and constantly encouraging them to do so: the best work; maximum consideration for others; maximum co-operation with others; the best behaviour.'

Uniform Blue blazer with Kent Invicta badge. Firmly enforced.

Homework Average 11-year-old, five hours a week; 14-year-old, 10 hours; 16-year-old, 15 hours.

Vocational qualifications *None*

Primary schools Hurst Junior; Bedonwell Junior; Upton Primary; St Paulinus CE Junior; Mayplace Primary.

BORDEN GRAMMAR SCHOOL

Avenue of Remembrance
Sittingbourne
Kent ME10 4DB
Tel (01795) 424192
Fax (01795) 424026
E-mail: bordengs@rmplc.co.uk
Internet: http://www.rmplc.co.uk/eduweb/
              sites/bordengs/index.html

- National ranking 123 (127, 59, 16, 41)
- GCSE 95% (94%)
- A-levels 34% (A/B); 91% (A/E)
- Higher education 80% (Oxford 1, Cambridge 1)

- Boys' grammar
- Pupils 740
- Boys (11–18) 740
- Girls *Not applicable*
- Sixth form 220 (30%)
- Education authority *Kent*

Headteacher Bryan Richard Short, 63, ap-

pointed in April 1968. Staff 45 (men 38, women 7).

Motto Nitere porro (Strive ever upward).

Background Founded by Barrow Trust in parish of Borden as an independent day and boarding school in 1878. Boarding was ended after the turn of the century and in 1929 the school moved to the centre of Sittingbourne. Voluntary-controlled; on-site playing fields. Recent developments include new hall and gymnasium; new block accommodating mathematics, computing, modern languages and geography; two technology rooms; extensive music suite. Work-experience. More than 90% of fifth-formers stay on into sixth form. Old Bordenian Association; Parents and Friends' Association. International representatives at soccer and hockey. Significant flow of candidates to engineering places in higher education reflect strengths in mathematics, physics and technology.

Alumni Sir Peter Kitkatt, Speaker's Secretary at House of Commons until April 1993; Sir Stanley Hooker, former group technical director of Rolls Royce; Admiral Sir Kenneth Eaton, controller of Royal Navy; Air Vice-Marshal Tony Stables, commandant of Royal Air Force College, Cranwell.

Streaming In mathematics.

Approach to discipline 'Firm framework but relaxed relationships within it. The school is run on the assumption that good order and discipline are essential to successful study.'

Uniform Navy blazer, charcoal-grey trousers, white shirt, school or sixth-form tie, grey socks, black shoes. Firmly enforced.

Homework Average 14-year-old, 10 hours a week; 16-year-old, 15 hours.

Vocational qualifications *None*

Primary schools Barrow Grove Primary; Grove Park Primary; Minterne Primary; Murston Primary; South Avenue Primary; Tunstall CE Primary.

BOSTON GRAMMAR SCHOOL

South End
Boston
Lincolnshire PE21 6JY
Tel (01205) 366444
Fax (01205) 310702

- National ranking 124 (171, 152, 147, 186)
- GCSE 95% (83%)
- A-levels 34% (A/B); 82% (A/E)
- Higher education 81% (Oxford 1)

- Grant-maintained
- Boys' grammar
- Pupils 626
- Boys (11–18) 624
- Girls (16–18) 2
- Sixth form 130 (21%)
- Education authority *Lincolnshire*

Headteacher John Ernest Neal, 45, appointed in January 1993. Staff 40 (men 30, women 10).

Motto Floreat Bostona (May Boston flourish)

Background The school's foundation dates from a charter of 1555; it has been on its current site since 1567; original school hall now its library and regarded as building of historical importance. Latest of several additions to the grant-maintained grammar is the Len Medlock Centre, a suite of rooms reserved for sixth-form use. Duke of Edinburgh Award Scheme. School proud of extra-curricular activities and rejects nine-till-four approach. Old Bostonians' Association thrives.

Alumni Barry Spikings, film producer (*The Deer Hunter*); Martin Middlebrook, author and military historian.

Streaming Some setting of pupils in mathematics.

Approach to discipline Self-discipline, tolerance and respect for others. 'Within the framework of a caring community, the school has, and demands, high standards of behaviour and courtesy. We believe that rewards and commendations are the most effective means of achieving the goals.' Sanctions applied if all else fails.

Uniform Black blazer with badge, school tie, white/grey shirt, dark-grey trousers, black/grey socks. Sixth-formers wear uniform, but with distinctive tie.

Homework Average 11-year-old, five hours a week; 14-year-old, seven hours 30 minutes; 16-year-old, 10 hours.

Vocational qualifications *None*

Primary schools Pupils drawn from large number of schools. 'Any pupil reaching the required standard on entry tests will be admitted irrespective of which primary school he attends.'

THE ROYAL BELFAST ACADEMICAL INSTITUTION

College Square East
Belfast BT1 6DL
Tel (01232) 240461
Fax (01232) 237464

- National ranking 125 (60, 86, 67, 120)
- GCSE 94% (98%)
- A-levels 47% (A/B); 97% (A/E)
- Higher education 85% (Oxford 2, Cambridge 1)

- Boys' grammar
- Pupils 1,040
- Boys (11–18) 1,040
- Girls *Not applicable*
- Sixth form 260 (25%)
- Education authority *Belfast Education and Library Board*

Headteacher Robert Michael Ridley, 50, appointed in August 1990. Staff 63 (men 53, women 10).

Motto Quaerere verum (Seek the truth).

Background Founded in 1810 to educate boys of all social classes and religious affiliations; pupils from city, suburbs and country; from almost 100 primary schools as well as from the preparatory school, Inchmarlo. Buildings on historic city-centre site include: 17 specialist laboratories; art, technology and design suite described by inspectors as best in Northern Ireland; music and career rooms; computer department; two gymnasia, indoor heated swimming pool; 50 classrooms, common hall with stage facilities, dining hall, library; new design and technology centre. Sixth-form centre with study and social accommodation. Playing fields in Malone Road area and boathouse at Stranmillis. Non-denominational; over-subscribed, with 1.3 applications for each place. Curriculum strengths include mathematics, science and geography; also music and drama. Wide range of sports: in 1995/6 40 boys played for Northern Ireland or Ireland; in the last 15 years school has provided 23 rugby schools' internationals; school has produced 10 British Lions, including two captains (more than any other school in the United Kingdom). Winners of Ulster Schools' Cup in tennis, cricket, rugby and hockey. Many school teams, including up to 16 rugby teams, seven hockey teams, six cricket teams and a rowing club. Community Service Group, Scouts and cadets. House system.

Alumni Baron Lowry of Crossgar, Appeal Court judge; Sir Robert Carswell, High Court judge; Sir Kenneth Bloomfield, BBC governor and former head of Northern Ireland Civil Service; Sir Peter Froggatt, director of TSB Bank (Northern Ireland) and former vice-chancellor of Queen's University, Belfast; Brian Mawhinney, Conservative MP for Peterborough and Conservative Party Chairman; Sir Ian Fraser, consulting surgeon; Kenneth Montgomery, artistic director of Opera Northern Ireland; Leonard Steinberg, chairman of Stanley Leisure; Dawson Stelfox, mountaineer; Keith Crossan, Ireland rugby player; Sammy Nelson, former Arsenal and Northern Ireland soccer player.

Streaming Pupils streamed in years 8 and 9. Years 10 and 11 in sets according to ability in each subject.

Approach to discipline 'Sensible. The focus is on intelligent good discipline with rules designed to provide a framework for all members of the school to have every opportunity to obtain the most from their education.' Traditional values.

Uniform School blazer, grey trousers, white shirt, school tie, black shoes.

Homework Average 11-year-old, seven hours 30 minutes a week; 14-year-old, 12 hours; 16-year-old, 15 hours.

Vocational qualifications None

Primary schools Inchmarlo, RBAI preparatory department; Strandtown Primary; Carryduff Primary; Dundonald Primary; Gilnakirk Primary; Cairnshill Primary.

WALLINGTON COUNTY GRAMMAR SCHOOL

Croydon Road
Wallington
Surrey SM6 7PH
Tel (0181) 647 2235
Fax (0181) 669 8190

- National ranking 126 (149, 99, 84, 114)
- GCSE 94% (92%)
- A-levels 47% (A/B); 95% (A/E)
- Higher education 96% (Oxford 3, Cambridge 1)

- Grant-maintained
- Boys' grammar
- Pupils 782
- Boys (11–18) 782
- Girls Not applicable
- Sixth form 184 (24%)
- Education authority Sutton

Headteacher Dr J. Martin Haworth, 47, appointed in September 1990. Staff 43 (men 31, women 12).

Motto None

Background Founded in 1927 as county school for scholarship boys in nine acres of landscaped grounds against background of Beddington Park. Traditional character that promotes academic values, personal qualities, sporting and cultural activities. Became grant-maintained in April 1993. Takes top 25% of the ability range; oversubscribed, with 600 applications for 120 places. Curriculum includes Latin, German, Spanish, Classical Studies, Economics and Information Technology. The only school-based art foundation course in the country. Pupils take up to 11 GCSEs; 23 subjects offered at A-level. Well-established industry links; work-experience for all in year 11 and sixth form. Orchestra, choir, wind band, debating, drama; regular concerts and theatrical events. Scout group; the many clubs include chess, Subbuteo, pottery, computing, Christian Union. Main competitive sports: rugby, hockey, cross-country, running, athletics, cricket; also soccer, tennis, swimming, fencing, badminton and squash. Parents', Teachers' and Friends' Association; Old Walcountians Association, with clubhouse and grounds in Woodmansterne.

Alumni Nick Ross, presenter of BBC Crimewatch; Baron Croham of Croydon, former head of Civil Service.

Streaming No streaming, but some setting to enable boys to enter GCSE mathematics in year 10.

Approach to discipline High standards of behaviour; prefects and senior boys take responsibility for junior boys. House system; anti-bullying policy. 'Boys are known individually and staff have established a style of caring which, while helping individual boys with problems, expects high standards of behaviour and work, together with a commitment and loyalty to the school.'

Uniform Navy blazer with school badge, grey trousers, black school tie with navy-and-gold stripe. 'Everyone wears the uniform and there is no need to labour the point.'

Homework Average 11-year-old, five to seven hours 30 minutes a week; 14-year-old, seven hours 30 minutes to 10 hours; 16-year-old, at least 10 hours.

Vocational qualifications *None*

Inspection May 1995.

Primary schools 'Two or three boys come from most local schools.'

OMAGH ACADEMY

21–23 Dublin Road
Omagh
County Tyrone BT78 1HF
Tel (01662) 242688
Fax (01662) 246737
E-mail: head.email@2410066/c.71961.
       dialnet

- National ranking 127 (73, 161 = , 102, –)
- GCSE 94% (98%)
- A-levels 46% (A/B); 95% (A/E)
- Higher education 91% (Oxford 1, Cambridge 1)

- Mixed grammar
- Pupils 664
- Boys (11–18) 263
- Girls (11–18) 401
- Sixth form 172 (26%)
- Education authority *Western Education and Library Board*

Headteacher James Benjamin McBain, 52, appointed in September 1984. Staff 40 (men 19, women 21).

Motto Veritas vincet (Truth will conquer).

Background Founded in 1903 as a small private school; in converted town house for first 30 years; taken over in 1935 by County Tyrone education authority, which developed small campus on edge of town for its newly-acquired grammar school. School completely refurbished, extended and equipped between 1989 and 1991. Oversubscribed, with average 1.2 applications for each place. Playing fields within easy walking distance. Wide range of extra-curricular activities: sporting, cultural, social and recreational. Inter-school competition encouraged; several pupils have achieved county, provincial and national honours in rugby, hockey and other sports. Charity fund-raising; community projects; Young Enterprise Group. 'The ethos is largely defined by the fact that Omagh Academy is a co-educational 11-to-18 grammar school. Against this backcloth, relationships among pupils and between staff and pupils are characterised by goodwill, good humour and a shared sense of purpose.'

Alumni Willie Anderson, Ireland and British Lions rugby international; Ian McLaren, president of Umbro International USA.

Streaming Annual intake of 100 pupils divided into four matched sets, in which they remain for most subjects. No banding or streaming.

Approach to discipline 'The school's approach to discipline is firm but fair. School rules are mostly to do with the well-being of pupils and consideration for others. Pupils understand why the rules exist and parents co-operate well with the school in their observance.'

Uniform Navy blazer with school crest, grey trousers/navy skirt, white shirt/blouse, school tie. School colours are navy and gold: 'Pupils are expected to wear the uniform and to be neat and tidy at all times.'

Homework Average 11-year-old, seven to 10 hours a week; 14-year-old, 10 to 12 hours; 16-year-old, 15 + hours.

Vocational qualifications Variety of enrichment courses offered in sixth form; some certificated, some vocational, e.g. Keyboard Skills, First Aid, Catering.

Inspection November 1993.

Primary schools Gibson Primary, Omagh; Omagh County Primary.

KING EDWARD VI SCHOOL

Edward Street
Louth
Lincolnshire LN11 9LL
Tel (01507) 600456
Fax (01507) 600316

- National ranking 128 (105 = , 154, 156, 160)
- GCSE 94% (96%)

- A-levels 42% (A/B); 92% (A/E)
- Higher education 89% (Oxford 4, Cambridge 5)

- Grant-maintained
- Mixed grammar
- Pupils 522
- Boys (14–18) 264
- Girls (14–18) 258
- Sixth form 255 (49%)
- Education authority *Lincolnshire*

Headteacher Arthur James Wheeldon, 49, appointed in September 1992. Staff 40 (men 24, women 16).

Motto *None*

Background Refounded in 1551 as Royal Free School of King Edward VI in Louth, with origins in 1278; attractive site on western edge of historic market town; accommodation for up to 80 boarders in two boarding houses (one for boys, one for girls). Teaching in rooms ranging from purpose-built to those of large 18th-century Grade 2 listed building. Over-subscribed, with 1.5 applications per place; open-access sixth form. 'Excellent' extra-curricular music tradition; exchanges and educational visits abroad, including bi-annual exchange with United States. Wide range of sports. Duke of Edinburgh Award Scheme.

Alumni Alfred Lord Tennyson; Captain John Smith, 16th-century founder of first permanent settlement in Virginia; Sir John Franklin, 18th-century Arctic explorer; Professor Philip Norton, leading academic on Parliament, Hull University; Christopher Wright, chairman of Chrysalis Group.

Streaming Only in mathematics.

Approach to discipline 'Firm but fair and appropriate to the individual situation.'

Uniform 'Simple, modern uniform in years 10 and 11; sixth-formers are expected to be clean and tidy, and must not be provocatively or aggressively dressed.'

Homework Average 14-year-old, 10 hours a week; 16-year-old, 15 hours.

Vocational qualifications RSA, Word-processing, Information Technology; Foreign Languages at Work.

WIRRAL GRAMMAR SCHOOL

Cross Lane
Bebington
Wirral L63 3AQ
Tel (0151) 644 0908
Fax (0151) 643 8317
Internet: http://www.wirrgram@liv.ac.uk

- National ranking 129 (17, 116, –, 103)
- GCSE 94% (100%)
- A-levels 38% (A/B); 94% (A/E)
- Higher education 80% (Oxford 2, Cambridge 1)

- Grant-maintained
- Boys' grammar
- Pupils 970
- Boys (11–18) 970
- Girls *Not applicable*
- Sixth form 236 (24%)
- Education authority *Wirral*

Headteacher Anthony Cooper, 52, appointed in April 1997. Staff 58 (men 42, women 16).

Motto Sapientia ianua vitae (Knowledge is the gateway to life).

Background In a semi-rural setting in mid-Wirral, the school, founded in 1931, is surrounded by 26 acres of playing fields. A sixth-form block in the early 1980s; new sports hall in May 1997; two new science laboratories planned for May 1998. It became grant-maintained in September 1993 and reports particular strengths in games and drama, with a national reputation for rugby; hockey, cross-country, athletics and cricket are other sports that the school is proud of. Over-subscribed. There are 17 visiting music tutors offering most instruments. Good performance in examinations has helped it establish firm links with universities.

Alumni Baron (Harold) Wilson of Rievaulx, former Labour prime minister.

Streaming Pupils in sets in mathematics and languages in year 8, and science in year 9.

Approach to discipline Sense of purpose and acclaim for achievements underpin the school's disciplinary policy. 'The ethos is one in which boys are encouraged to take a pride in themselves and the school. Where infringements take place they are dealt with promptly. Parents are kept informed.'

Uniform Black blazer with badge, white shirt,

house tie, grey trousers. Sixth-formers can wear own choice of clothes, provided they include jacket and tie; most wear suits. Regulations enforced strictly.

Homework Average 11-year-old, five hours a week; 14-year-old, up to 10 hours; 16-year-old, up to 12 hours 30 minutes.

Vocational qualifications *None*

Inspection February 1996: 'A highly successful grammar school which enjoys a well-deserved reputation for high standards of academic, cultural and athletic achievement. It is well-managed and provides a very good quality of education and excellent pastoral care.'; 'Pupils listen and speak well, and reading and written work are good in all year-groups. Numerical skills are very good and pupils apply them effectively in mathematics and in other subjects. Pupils use computers to good effect in lessons when given opportunities to do so.'; 'Teachers are very well-qualified and hard-working. The teaching is generally good and many lessons have outstanding qualities.'; 'Resources are generally good, but there are some shortages of textbooks, reference books, computers and of percussion instruments for music.'

Primary schools Poulton Lancelyn Primary; Brookhurst Primary; Brackenwood Junior; Higher Bebington Junior; Stanton Road Primary.

CALDAY GRANGE GRAMMAR SCHOOL

Grammar School Lane
West Kirby
Wirral L48 8AU
Tel (0151) 625 2727
Fax (0151) 625 9851
E-mail: caldaxgrange@campus.bt.com
Internet: http://www.liv.ac.uk/~caldyg

- National ranking 130 (92, 40, 57, 87)
- GCSE 94% (97%)
- A-levels 35% (A/B); 91% (A/E)
- Higher education 91% (Oxford 4)

- Grant-maintained
- Boys' grammar
- Pupils 1,307
- Boys (11–18) 1,255
- Girls (16–18) 52
- Sixth form 381 (29%)
- Education authority *Wirral*

Headteacher Nigel Briers, 53, appointed in April 1987. Staff 78 (men 54, women 24).

Motto Nisi dominus frustra (All is vain except the Lord).

Background The school was founded in 1636 and further endowed in 1676; became a grammar school in 1884. Set in residential area of the Wirral close to the Dee estuary and the east side of Caldy Hill. Old sandstone buildings demolished 30 years ago and replaced with modern laboratories, gymnasium and dining hall. Five-storey science block. The school was awarded over £1m for a new technology building which opened at Easter 1996; Technology College status. Over-subscribed, with more than 150 'out-of-area' applications and an average of three applications per place. Year 7 pupils choose two languages from French, German, Spanish, Russian and Latin; wide choice of A-levels includes Law, Russian, English Language, Sports Studies and Theatre Studies. Sporting strengths: hockey, rugby and cross-country. Combined Cadet Force. Exchange visits to schools in Virginia in the United States, Odessa in Ukraine, Germany and Spain. One play per term; three orchestral concerts per year.

Alumni Sir David Weatherall, haematologist, Regius Professor of Medicine, Oxford; Kenneth Fleet, executive editor of *The Times* (1983–1987); Michael Tait, British ambassador to Tunisia.

Streaming Setting only in mathematics from year 7.

Approach to discipline 'There is a firm approach to discipline that engenders a respect for all in the school society.' Parents involved; pastoral system aims to be 'proactive and not just reactive'.

Uniform Navy blazer with school badge, grey trousers, house tie. Sixth-formers wear smart business dress. 'The pupils conform to our expectations.'

Homework Average 11-year-old, six hours a week; 14-year-old, eight hours; 16-year-old, 12 hours.

Vocational qualifications *None*

Inspection October 1996: 'The school achieves high level of success in public examinations and is enabling pupils to develop into mature and responsible young people. The teaching is competent and well-informed. Staff and pupils cooperate in sustaining an extensive range of extra-curricular activities which contribute to open and friendly relationships.'; 'The strong emphases on sciences and languages create some imbalance in relation to the creative arts and religious education, though the many extra-curricular activities offer some compensation for many pupils.'; 'Class management is generally effective, although pupils are not always fully aware of the objectives of lessons. The few pupils with identified special needs are well catered for and make good progress.'; 'Pupils sustain excellent levels of attendance and tidy appearance. Despite some cramped conditions, movement around the premises is well-ordered and lessons start promptly.'

Primary schools St Peter's CE Primary, Heswall; St Bridget's CE Primary, West Kirby; Greasby Junior; Great Meols Primary, Meols; Barnston Primary, Heswall.

SALE GRAMMAR SCHOOL

Marsland Road
Sale
Cheshire M33 3NH
Tel (0161) 973 3217
Fax (0161) 976 4904

- National ranking 131 (159, 106, 139, 158)
- GCSE 94% (88%)
- A-levels 31% (A/B); 87% (A/E)
- Higher education 67% (Oxford 3, Cambridge 2)

- Mixed grammar
- Pupils 1,256
- Boys (11–18) 549
- Girls (11–18) 707
- Sixth form 330 (26%)
- Education authority *Trafford*

Headteacher Jennifer Emily Connelly, 50, appointed in September 1990. Staff 78 (men 25, women 53).

Motto *None*

Background Opened in 1991 as result of amalgamation of boys' and girls' grammar schools; situated in south Manchester commuter belt, buildings extended and refurbished on site of former girls' school: 10 science laboratories, language laboratory with satellite dish, video-conferencing facilities, library with computer annexe, gymna-sium and sports hall. Purpose-built blocks for technology, art and design. School attaches great importance to community links including feeder primary schools; and raises a lot of money for charity. Over-subscribed, with four applications per place; all pupils from Sale. School has expanded to include some off-site sixth-form provision. Wide range of A-level courses. Japanese introduced as extra-curricular subject in year 9 and leading to accreditation in sixth form. Regional and national success in sport. Well-established link with high school in Kentucky; many other activities at home and abroad. Two orchestras and various ensembles and choirs; music project with Halle Orchestra. 'Very high' standard in dance and performance. Pupils have regular success in local and national competitions. Prides itself on friendly and welcoming atmosphere. Investor in People Award in 1995.

Streaming Early setting in mathematics and some modern languages lessons. Form groups in lower school, with smaller groups for technology. Option groups in upper school.

Approach to discipline Encourage self-discipline; build on the positive; reward praise. 'To have a code of behaviour which has at its core respect of others and the environment, and behaviour that does not endanger the safety of others.'

Uniform Black and white, with purple and grey trim; may wear sweaters, sweatshirts, blazers. No uniform for sixth-formers, but required to dress in 'a professional manner'.

Homework Average 11-year-old, up to eight hours a week; 14-year-old, up to 14 hours; 16-year-old, up to eight hours per subject.

Vocational qualifications RSA, Information Technology, Word-processing.

Primary schools Brooklands Primary; Moorlands Primary; Park Road Primary; Wellfield Primary; St Anne's CE Primary; Springfield Primary; St Mary's CE Primary; Tyntesfield Primary; Woodheys Primary; Firs Primary.

URMSTON GRAMMAR SCHOOL

Newton Road
Urmston
Manchester M41 5UG
Tel (0161) 748 2875
Fax (0161) 747 2504

- National ranking 132 (142, 108, 157, 130)
- GCSE 94% (93%)
- A-levels 18% (A/B); 82% (A/E)
- Higher education 86% (Oxford 1)

- Mixed grammar
- Pupils 856
- Boys (11–18) 386
- Girls (11–18) 470
- Sixth form 211 (25%)
- Education authority *Trafford*

Headteacher Michael Holland, 53, appointed in January 1988. Staff 51 (men 22, women 29).

Motto Manners makyth man.

Background Near centre of Urmston in pleasant grounds next to cricket club. Original 1930s buildings added to by architect-designed classroom block and modern sports hall, with adjacent all-weather pitch. Original Urmston Grammar School was co-educational, replaced by single-sex grammar schools on separate sites in 1961; the two schools were replaced by new co-educational school on original site in 1988. Heavily over-subscribed. 'Excellent' computer rooms. Junior League of Friends providing voluntary service at Trafford General Hospital run exclusively by pupils and sixth-formers; also community service project one afternoon a week. Northwest regional winners of young Consumer of the Year Competition on three occasions; 1993 national finalists. In 1993, local authority inspectors described evident school aim as 'establishing good relations through tension-free but firm discipline'.

Streaming *None*

Approach to discipline 'We hope to achieve self-discipline by emphasising consideration for others and the importance of working together to achieve goals. We prefer general guidelines of a positive kind rather than many "do nots" and try to give reasons behind rules. Offenders are punished. We hope we operate a fair system.'

Uniform Navy blazer with school crest, white shirt/blouse, dark-grey trousers/skirt, school tie, navy V-neck jumper, navy/grey/white socks, black shoes. Firmly enforced.

Homework Average 11-year-old, seven hours 30 minutes a week; 14-year-old, nine hours 10 minutes; 16-year-old, 10 hours.

Vocational qualifications *None*

Inspection May 1996.

Primary schools Flixton Junior; Davyhulme Junior; Urmston Junior; Wellacre Junior, Barton Clowey; Kingsway Primary.

SLOUGH GRAMMAR SCHOOL

Lascelles Road
Slough
Berkshire SL3 7PR
Tel (01753) 522892
Fax (01753) 538618
E-mail: head@sloughgrammar.berks.sch.uk

- National ranking 133 (147, 177, –, 221)
- GCSE 93% (92%)
- A-levels 100% (A/B); 100% (A/E)
- Higher education 95% (Oxford 3)

- Grant-maintained
- Mixed grammar
- Pupils 781
- Boys (11—18) 367
- Girls (11—18) 414
- Sixth form 268 (34%)
- Education authority *Berkshire*

Headteacher Margaret Lenton, 53, appointed in September 1988. Staff 54 (men 19, women 35).

Motto Ad astra (To the stars).

Background Opened at the turn of the century, the main buildings date from the 1930s; oldest selective school in Slough, in residential area backing on to Lascelles Park and within sight of Windsor Castle. Additions include a gymnasium and science facilities; new technology area commissioned in 1994. Over-subscribed, with five applications per place. Over past three years, average of 70% of pupils gaining five or more GCSE grades A to C; popular and expanding. Faculty of Classical Studies and Civilisations; Latin and Classics offered throughout the school. 'At the end of their education at Slough, young people will have been prepared for citizenship in a democracy through working constructively with the local neighbourhood and the wider community.' Pupils admitted at 11 from September 1996, increasing school roll by 120.

Alumni Roger Thomas, chairman and managing director of Black and Decker; Philip Hinchcliffe, television producer; Philip Hubble, Olympic swimming silver-medallist; Baroness Platt of Writtle; Wills Morgan, baritone.

Streaming In mathematics, English and science.

Approach to discipline 'Firm but caring. Each pupil is allocated to a form on entry; the form tutor is essential to pastoral care in the school.'

Uniform Maroon blazer, black trousers/grey skirt. Sixth form: navy blazer, black trousers. Regulations strictly enforced.

Homework Average 11-year-old, five hours a week; 14-year-old, eight hours; 16-year-old, 12 hours.

Vocational qualifications BTEC First and National.

Inspection October 1993.

Primary schools Marish Middle; Montem Junior; Castleview; Ryvers Primary; St Mary's CE Middle. Sixty feeder schools over a wide area.

WESTCLIFF HIGH SCHOOL FOR BOYS

Kenilworth Gardens
Westcliff-on-Sea
Essex SS0 0BP
Tel (01702) 75443
Fax (01702) 470495

- National ranking 134 (136, –, 89, 126)
- GCSE 93% (93%)
- A-levels 52% (A/B); 96% (A/E)
- Higher education 93% (Oxford 13, Cambridge 1)

- Grant-maintained
- Boys' grammar
- Pupils 913
- Boys (11–18) 913
- Girls *Not applicable*
- Sixth form 233 (26%)
- Education authority *Essex*

Headteacher Andrew John Baker, 50, appointed in April 1990. Staff 56 (men 48, women 8).

Motto Fide et fortitudine (Faith and strength).

Background Six years after it was founded, Westcliff High moved to its current 12-acre site in 1926. Facilities include squash and tennis courts, a gymnasium, and a new technology block. Considerable refurbishment has been completed over past four years as part of a school development plan. Heavily over-subscribed, with an average of three applications per place. Aims at emphasising 'academic, personal and moral development' of pupils. Uses red and yellow cards to warn pupils about under-achievement.

Alumni Sir Graham Hills, former principal of Strathclyde University; Paul Bateman, chief executive of Save and Prosper Group; Edward Greenfield, music critic.

Streaming Pupils in sets in mathematics from year 8, and from year 9 in French.

Approach to discipline Rules and code of conduct known to all pupils, who are expected to show high level of responsibility and self-discipline. Graded system of sanctions, applied fairly and consistently.

Uniform Navy blazer and school badge, white/light blue shirt, school tie, dark-blue V-neck jumper, grey socks and black shoes. School attaches 'highest importance' to uniform; all pupils required to comply.

Homework Average 11-year-old, six hours a week; 14-year-old, eight hours; 16-year-old, 12 hours.

Vocational qualifications *None*

Inspection September 1994: 'Westcliff High School for Boys is a good school.'; 'Standards in reading, writing, listening and numeracy are good. There are wide variations in the standards of oracy. Investigation, problem-solving and the application of IT skills are under-developed.'; 'The quality of teaching and learning is variable, but lies above national averages. The positive attitudes of the boys have a significant effect in lessons and leads to progress. Diagnostic assessment is not having a sufficiently beneficial effect. Pupils have insufficient opportunities in many subjects to make choices and work independently.'; 'The school has excellent leadership. It is well run and provides good value for money.'; 'There is a strong work ethic which has a marked effect on achievements.'

ANTRIM GRAMMAR SCHOOL

Steeple Road
Antrim BT41 1AF
Tel (01849) 464091
Fax (01849) 428345
E-mail: antrimgrammar@btinternet.com
Internet: http://www.infm.ulst.ac.uk/
~neelb/antrim/agshtml.html

- National ranking 135 (111, 118, 113, 93)
- GCSE 93% (95%)
- A-levels 46% (A/B); 92% (A/E)
- Higher education 93% (Oxford 2)

- Mixed grammar
- Pupils 735
- Boys (11–18) 313
- Girls (11–18) 422
- Sixth form 183 (25%)
- Education authority *North Eastern Education and Library Board*

Headteacher James G. Hunniford, 57, appointed in September 1989. Staff 46 (men 23, women 23).

Motto Tolerance and development.

Background On 60-acre site near town centre; founded to cater for children from wider Antrim area; functional buildings are clean and well maintained; extensive playing fields include rugby and hockey pitches, cricket squares, tennis courts and 400m running track. Fully-subscribed. Video: Educational Television Association's Peter Turner Award winner 1992 and 1995, Sky TV Schools Project winner 1996, four awards at Co-operative Film Festival 1996, winner of TVU/Trotman National Video Award 1996. Video-conferencing facility. Northern Ireland winners of Mathematiques sans Frontieres Advanced section 1995 and 1996. Links with Lycee Jean Mermoz, Alsace. Music: two 100-voice choirs, 60-piece orchestra, 40-piece wind band. Squash: many representative honours. Charity fund-raising: over £3,000 annually. Traditional emphasis on academic excellence. Strong pastoral care programme. Enthusiastic parental involvement through Friends of Antrim Grammar School.

Alumni Jackie Burns, Great Britain hockey player and Olympic bronze-medallist.

Streaming Streamed in second year; adjusted in third year; pupils put in sets for core

subjects in fourth and fifth years.

Approach to discipline Sensible, well-publicised rules applied with firmness and understanding to encourage efficiency, self-discipline and consideration for others. 'High standards of behaviour are expected in and around the school, courtesy and respect being required in all interactions whether involving staff or pupils.'

Uniform French-blue blazer, mid-grey trousers/skirt, white shirt/blouse, school tie. Very strictly enforced.

Homework Average 11-year-old, seven hours 30 minutes a week; 14-year-old, 10 hours; 16-year-old, 12 hours 30 minutes.

Vocational qualifications BTEC Law, Typing, Word-processing; RSA Desktop Publishing, Accounting, Business Studies.

Primary schools Antrim Primary; Greystone Primary; Parkhall Primary; Randalstown Primary; Templepatrick Primary; Ballycraigy Primary.

QUEEN ELIZABETH'S HIGH SCHOOL

Morton Terrace
Gainsborough
Lincolnshire DN21 2ST
Tel (01427) 612354
Fax (01427) 612856

- National ranking 136 (90, 136, 76, 148)
- GCSE 93% (97%)
- A-levels 42% (A/B); 95% (A/E)
- Higher education 85% (Oxford 1, Cambridge 2)

- Mixed grammar
- Pupils 975
- Boys (11–18) 450
- Girls (11–18) 525
- Sixth form 161 (17%)
- Education authority *Lincolnshire*

Headteacher John Robert Child, 45, appointed in September 1995. Staff 64 (men 29, women 35).

Motto *None*

Background Formed from amalgamation in 1983 of 63-year-old Gainsborough Girls' High and much older Queen Elizabeth Grammar School for Boys, which was founded in 1589 under charter from Queen Elizabeth I to Robert Somerscales. Large site on a campus to north of town. Facilities include new sixth-form centre; strong in music and sport (athletics, cross-country and tennis). Also takes pupils from Nottinghamshire, South Yorkshire and Humberside; admits top 25% of ability range and has expanded from four-form entry to six-form entry since 1989; over-subscribed, with three applications per place. All-graduate teaching staff.

Alumni Sir Halford Mackinder, geographer (1861–1947).

Streaming Pupils put in sets in mathematics and languages from year 8.

Approach to discipline 'Students are generally very well-behaved. Staff are encouraged to be greatly insistent about basic good behaviour. This prevents more serious problems developing and allows good relationships with students.'

Uniform Navy blazer with badge (Viking ship), grey trousers/skirt. Strictly enforced in years 7 to 11, with sixth-formers wearing clothes 'suitable for office'.

Homework Average 11-year-old, eight hours a week; 14-year-old, ten hours; 16-year-old, 20 hours.

Vocational qualifications *Few*

Inspection September 1996: 'Behaviour in lessons and about the school is very good. Relationships are generally excellent both among pupils, and between pupils and staff.'; 'Teaching is satisfactory or better in nine out of 10 lessons, good or better in nearly two-thirds of lessons and very good in nearly a quarter of lessons.'; 'The best features of the teaching are teachers' subject knowledge and expertise and high expectations.'; 'Inappropriate methods and a lack of challenge are a feature of too many lessons in Latin, food technology and history.'; 'Reports to parents are too subjective and fail to give clear indication of pupils' progress in the National Curriculum.'; 'The headteacher provides strong leadership and a clear educational direction for the school.'

HIGHSTED SCHOOL

Highsted Road
Sittingbourne
Kent ME10 4PT
Tel (01795) 424223
Fax (01795) 429375

E-mail: highsted@rmplc.co.uk
Internet: http://www.rmplc.co.uk/eduweb/
           sites/highsted

- National ranking 137 (115, 142, 132, 106)
- GCSE 93% (95%)
- A-levels 42% (A/B); 89% (A/E)
- Higher education 80% (Cambridge 2)

- Girls' grammar
- Pupils 810
- Boys *Not applicable*
- Girls (11–18) 799
- Sixth form 249 (31%)
- Education authority *Kent*

Headteacher Jill E. H. Lambert, appointed in September 1979. Staff 52 (men 14, women 38).

Motto Esse quam videri (To be rather than seem to be).

Background Founded in 1904 as County School for Girls; became Sittingbourne Grammar School for Girls; moved to current site south of Sittingbourne in 1958, changing its name again 10 years later. Additions to 1960s-style buildings include new mathematics, computing and business studies block in 1990; new lower-school block in 1994. Changed from 13-to-18 school to 11-to-18 in September 1994. Over-subscribed, popular school which flourishes in drama, sport, music and achieves high academic standards. Eleven peripatetic music teachers visit school to give individual instrumental lessons; 'extremely high' standards of orchestra, wind band, recorder ensemble and choir. Sporting strengths include swimming, netball and indoor hockey, with teams performing at national level. 'Pupils are encouraged to use their initiative in planning and organising themselves in many of extra-curricular activities and cultural exchange visits.'

Streaming In sets in mathematics for years 8 to 11; in science for years 10 and 11.

Approach to discipline 'Great emphasis is placed on establishing an atmosphere where self-discipline can flourish.' Few sanctions needed.

Uniform Blue blazer, grey skirt, white blouse. Very strictly enforced.

Homework Average 11-year-old, introduced gently, increasing to five hours a week during the autumn term; 14-year-old, six hours; 16-year-old, eight hours.

Vocational qualifications *None*

Inspection January 1996: 'A good school, which offers a high quality of education to its pupils. It has many strong features. There are some areas which require further development.'; 'Literacy skills are good, most pupils read, speak and write well. There are relatively few errors of grammar or punctuation, although a few pupils have persistent problems with spelling. Skills in numeracy are also good, although techniques in mental arithmetic could be further reinforced.'; 'The quality of learning is outstanding and is enhanced by the pupils' positive attitudes and their high level of response.'

Primary schools Minterne County Junior; Grove Park County Primary; Barrow Grove County Junior; South Avenue County Junior; Tunstall CE Primary; Regis Manor County Primary.

THE GRAMMAR SCHOOL FOR GIRLS, WILMINGTON

Wilmington Grange
Parsons Lane
Wilmington
Kent DA2 7BB
Tel (01322) 226351
Fax (01322) 222607
E-mail: school1-wgl@ukc.ac.uk

- National ranking 138 (68, 16 =, 128, 70)
- GCSE 93% (98%)
- A-levels 40% (A/B); 92% (A/E)
- Higher education 66%

- Grant-maintained
- Girls' grammar
- Pupils 683
- Boys *Not applicable*
- Girls (11–18) 683
- Sixth form 101 (15%)
- Education authority *Kent*

Headteacher Dr Janette Viggers, appointed in April 1983. Staff 39 (men 12, women 27).

Motto The pursuit of excellence.

Background Grant-maintained since September 1989; three-form entry; grammar school since 1982; in semi-rural setting near Dart-

ford, 15 miles from central London. Variety of school buildings: The Manor, Victorian, but incorporates at least one 17th-century cottage; The Grange, completed in 1875, but main cellar dates from before 1680; main building opened in 1959; purpose-built music room in 1970s and a mathematics suite added in 1992. Over-subscribed, with four applications for each place. Twice nationally recognised for industry links; Neighbourhood Engineers Scheme; well-established work-shadowing and work-experience; Dartford Young Enterprise. Charity fund-raising. Extra-curricular strengths include drama, music and public performance; full range of sports. Three school holidays a year at home and abroad.

Alumni Nilgun Yusuf, fashion journalist.

Streaming Pupils are placed in sets for mathematics.

Approach to discipline 'Hard work, high ideals, commitment and capacity to care for and to value others are the essential principles of everything for which the school stands.'

Uniform Pale-blue blouse, maroon skirt/culottes, maroon V-neck pullover/cardigan, black/brown/maroon shoes. Very strictly enforced; sixth-formers required to dress 'appropriately'.

Homework Average 11-year-old, seven hours 30 minutes a week; 14-year-old, 14 hours; 16-year-old, 15 hours.

Vocational qualifications *None*

Inspection May 1995: 'A very good school which achieves high academic standards. The school environment is conducive to learning and recreation. It is treated responsibly by pupils and maintained in good condition.'; 'The school is well managed and purposefully led by a dedicated and compassionate headteacher, who possesses very competent management skills and has a clear vision for the school's future.'; 'The school has a sound and purposeful ethos and meets its aims to promote caring attitudes and sensitivity to the needs of others.'; 'Many pupils make good use of information technology but, in general, the skills of younger pupils are more developed than those of sixth-form students.'

Primary schools Crockenhill Primary; Hextable Primary; High Firs Primary; Joydens Wood Primary; Maypole Primary; Oakfield Primary; Our Lady's RC Primary, Dartford; St

Bartholomew's RC Primary, Swanley; Wilmington Primary.

MARLING SCHOOL

Stroud
Gloucestershire GL5 4HE
Tel (01453) 762251
Fax (01453) 756011

- National ranking 139 (–, 176)
- GCSE 93%
- A-levels 39% (A/B); 92% (A/E)
- Higher education 70%

- Grant-maintained
- Boys' grammar
- Pupils 796
- Boys (11–18) 796
- Girls Not applicable
- Sixth form 150 (19%)
- Education authority (Gloucestershire)

Headteacher Dr Graham Lowe, 42, appointed in September 1994. Staff 43 (men 27, women 16).

Motto Abeunt studia in mores (Through studies character is formed).

Background Founded in 1887 by Sir Samuel Marling and other local prominent people; original building in Cotswold stone, now a listed building; many additions since then on a site on edge of Cotswolds with extensive playing fields. Enlarged in 1965 by amalgamation with adjacent boys' technical school. New science block due to open. Over-subscribed, with two applications for each of its 120 places. Extra-curricular activities: foreign exchanges with France and Germany; regular foreign visits, ski trips, overseas watersports holidays, support for handicapped in Lourdes; adventure holidays, residential field courses. Sporting strengths include rugby, soccer, hockey and cricket; also athletics and cross-country; many musical concerts; much charity work. Parents' Society.

Alumni Professor Peter Hennessy, author, broadcaster and professor of Contemporary History, Queen Mary and Westfield College, London; Glyn Ford, Labour Euro-MP for Greater Manchester East; Sir Michael Angus, chairman of Whitbread and past president of CBI; Sir Anthony Reeve, British ambassador to South Africa.

Streaming Pupils in sets as they move up the school, particularly in mathematics, English, languages and science.

Approach to discipline Well-structured discipline within pastoral system: 'Processes are clearly understood and major problems are rare. The approach is firm but fair, with emphasis very much on self-discipline and mutual respect.'

Uniform Black blazer with blue badge, black trousers in years 7 to 11. Dress code for sixth-formers: to achieve 'tidiness without conformity'. Very strictly enforced, with more flexibility in sixth form.

Homework Average 11-year-old, five hours a week; 14-year-old, six hours; 16-year-old, six hours.

Vocational qualifications None

Inspection Autumn 1993.

HANDSWORTH GRAMMAR SCHOOL

Grove Lane
Birmingham
West Midlands B21 9ET
Tel (0121) 554 2794
Fax (0121) 554 5405

- National ranking 140= (123, 147, 123, 161)
- GCSE 93% (95%)
- A-levels 37% (A/B); 89% (A/E)
- Higher education 80% (Oxford 1, Cambridge 4)

- Grant-maintained
- Boys' grammar
- Pupils 836
- Boys (11–18) 836
- Girls Not applicable
- Sixth form 204 (24%)
- Education authority Birmingham

Headteacher Malcolm Cavendish, 61, appointed in September 1982. Staff 51 (men 40, women 11).

Motto Haec olim meminisse iuvabit (It will be a pleasure one day to remember these things).

Background Birmingham's oldest-surviving grammar school, founded on its current site in 1862 as The Bridge Trust School for Boys. An inner-city school drawing pupils from whole of Birmingham and beyond;

grant-maintained since January 1991. Over-subscribed, with seven applications for each place. Extensive playing fields in nearby Handsworth Wood. Recently-opened £1m science building. New dining facilities and classrooms for information technology. Strong in science and mathematics. Wide range of sports, particularly soccer; pupils represent Worcestershire and England at cricket. Sailing, camping and Duke of Edinburgh Award among outdoor activities. Parents' Association; Old Boys' Society, with own clubhouse and grounds.

Alumni Lord Howell of Aston Manor, former Labour MP and sports minister; Jack Payne, bandleader; Professor Sir David Cox, Warden of Nuffield College, Oxford; Terry Parks, the cartoonist 'Larry'.

Streaming Generally mixed-ability in a selective context, but some subjects in sets.

Approach to discipline 'Firm, fair, consistent, supportive.' Fully-developed pastoral system based on forms and year-groups. Supported by an eight-house system for sport and recreation; strong links with parents; prefects.

Uniform Black blazer with bridge-and-knot crest, dark-grey trousers, grey/white shirt, black-and-gold school tie, grey V-neck pullover, dark-grey/black socks, black shoes. All boys wear uniform.

Homework Average 11-year-old, five hours a week; 14-year-old, six hours 25 minutes; 16-year-old, eight hours 15 minutes.

Vocational qualifications *None*

Inspection October 1995: 'Learning at Handsworth Grammar School is supported by excellent relationships between teachers and boys, and between the boys themselves. There is a strong sense of purpose; positive teacher-pupil relationships are a central feature of this safe, caring, supportive and harmonious community which is characterised by equality of regard.'; 'The boys are very keen to learn. Sound progress is evident in most lessons, but it could be enhanced by higher teacher expectations and by recognition of the boys' appetite for learning and their ability to cope with more challenging tasks. Most teaching is competent and often good.'

Primary schools Grestone Primary; Cherry Orchard Primary; Moseley CE Primary; Welford Primary; West House Primary; Wilkes Green Primary.

ST BERNARD'S CONVENT SCHOOL

1 Langley Road
Slough
Berkshire SL3 7AF
Tel (01753) 527020
Fax (01753) 576919

- National ranking 140= (139, 156, 117, 153)
- GCSE 93% (93%)
- A-levels 37% (A/B); 89% (A/E)
- Higher education 79% (Oxford 5, Cambridge 2)

- Mixed grammar
- Pupils 903
- Boys (11–18) 359
- Girls (11–18) 544
- Sixth form 270 (30%)
- Education authority *Berkshire*

Headteacher Sister Mary Stephen, appointed in 1982. Staff 54 (men 13, women 41).

Motto Dieu mon abri (The Lord is my shelter).

Background Founded in 1897 by the Sisters of the Bernadine Cistercian Order, whose origins date from beginning of Benedictine monasticism in the 6th century. Original building built in middle of 19th century by Baroness Coutts, friend of Queen Victoria, and acquired by Charles Hawtrey, of the Hawtrey family, becoming a prep school for Eton, with pupils including Stanley Baldwin, the former prime minister. Chapel added to house; Jesuits bought building and added notable clock tower; also pseudo-Georgian extension. Voluntary-aided; over-subscribed, with three applications for each place. Increasing numbers in early 1960s resulted in addition of science block, gymnasium, art and home economics room and the New Hall; in 1989, when the school became co-educational, new facilities included design and technology block, music suite, drama studio, additional science laboratory, general classrooms, and improved cloakroom and changing facilities. Wide variety of languages taught: French, German, Spanish, Japanese and Latin to A-level; Russian and Greek to GCSE. All year 11 pupils continued with education after age of 16 in 1992. Voluntary-aided school that prides itself on family atmosphere, happy and supportive school community.

Streaming Pupils in sets in mathematics from year 9.

Approach to discipline 'Students are encouraged to be responsible for themselves and their own actions. They are encouraged to act with consideration for others within the school and wider community.'

Uniform Girls: blue blazer with badge, navy skirt, turquoise blouse, navy cardigan/jumper. Boys: blue blazer with badge, grey trousers, white shirt, school tie. Sixth form: black blazer for boys, white shirt, dark trousers or Black Watch tartan skirt, plain cardigan or jumper for girls, Black Watch tartan tie for boys. Regulations adhered to 'reasonably firmly'.

Homework Average 11-year-old, three hours a week; 14-year-old, six hours; 16-year-old, eight to 10 hours.

Vocational qualifications *None*

Inspection March 1996: 'A very good school with many excellent features.'; 'The school has a distinct community spirit, based firmly on its religious foundations and high expectations of its pupils. Parents are very supportive of the school and contribute effectively to its work.'; 'Governors and staff seek constantly to improve the accommodation but, in some areas, facilities remain limited and inhibit the range of experiences the school can offer.'; 'Standards are very high throughout the school.'; 'The education provided by the school is very effective in enabling pupils to achieve their potential.'; 'Pupils are confident and competent learners; their attitudes to work are excellent.'; 'The headteacher provides effective and purposeful leadership, based firmly on Christian values, a firmly-held educational philosophy and a concern for others.'

Primary schools Holy Family RC School, Slough; St Ethelbert's RC Combined, Slough; St Bernadette's Primary, Hillingdon; St Bernard's Preparatory, Slough; Our Lady of Peace RC Middle, Burnham; St Francis's RC Primary, Ascot; St Joseph's RC Primary, Bracknell; St Mary's Primary, Uxbridge.

BACUP AND RAWTENSTALL GRAMMAR SCHOOL

Glen Road
Waterfoot
Lancashire BB4 7BJ
Tel (01706) 217115
Fax (01706) 210960
E-mail 101377.2030@compuserve.com

- National ranking 142 (134, 135, 152, 40)
- GCSE 93% (94%)
- A-levels 29% (A/B); 89% (A/E)
- Higher education 82% (Cambridge 2)

- Grant-maintained
- Mixed grammar
- Pupils 1,040
- Boys (11–18) 489
- Girls (11–18) 551
- Sixth form 305 (29%)
- Education authority *Lancashire*

Headteacher Martyn Morris, 52, appointed in September 1988. Staff 56 (men 30, women 26).

Motto Fide et labore (Faith and work).

Background Endowment by John Kershaw in late 17th century is the origin of a school that opened in 1701 and later moved to Newchurch. Teachers from that school became nucleus of Bacup and Rawtenstall Secondary and Technical School, which opened on current site in 1913. Survived attempts to make it comprehensive; became grant-maintained in 1989 and became a technology college in 1994. Over-subscribed, with three applications per place. Four technology rooms completely refurbished and two new computer rooms equipped in 1994 so that information technology will be used in all subjects; four new sixth-form classrooms also built and library expanded to a resources centre. Additional extensive playing fields about half a mile away. National representatives in cricket, hockey, basketball, skiing and sailing. Strong music tradition. Sixth form has doubled in size in three years.

Alumni Sir John Egan, chairman of BAA (formerly British Airports Authority); Patty Coldwell, broadcaster; Betty Jackson, fashion designer; David Pickup, Sports Council director-general.

Streaming Groups divided in mathematics in

year 9; broad setting in English, mathematics, science, French and German in years 10 and 11.

Approach to discipline 'Firm, with total support of staff and parents.'

Uniform Navy blazer with badge, mid-grey trousers/navy skirt, white shirt, school tie, navy V-neck jumper, mid-grey socks for boys or white for girls, black shoes. Girls can wear trousers; no uniform for sixth-formers, but guidelines on appearance. Strictly enforced.

Homework Average 11-year-old, 10 hours a week; 14-year-old, 15 hours; 16-year-old, 20 hours.

Vocational qualifications *None*

Primary schools 'Numbers from each primary school vary annually. Places depend on entrance examination results, but admissions policy gives priority to pupils in Bacup and Rawtenstall if school is over-subscribed.'

STROUD HIGH SCHOOL

Beards Lane
Cainscross Road
Stroud
Gloucestershire GL4 5HF
Tel (01453) 764441
Fax (01453) 756304

- National ranking 143 (116, 138, 151, 182)
- GCSE 92% (95%)
- A-levels 58% (A/B); 93% (A/E)
- Higher education 72% (Oxford 2, Cambridge 1)

- Grant-maintained
- Girls' grammar
- Pupils 800
- Boys *Not applicable*
- Girls (11–18) 800
- Sixth form 180 (23%)
- Education authority *Gloucestershire*

Headteacher Jean Lord, 52, appointed in September 1984. Staff 43 (men 8, women 35).

Motto Trouthe and Honour, Fredom and Curteisye.

Background Founded in 1904 on edge of Stroud overlooking the Cotswolds, becoming a grammar school after the 1944 Education Act. Doubled in size in 1964 when almagamated with neighbouring technical school and then underwent period of uncertainty as Gloucestershire entered era of comprehensive schools. Became grant-maintained in 1990, giving the school stability and allowing it to make a start on 'rectifying the hotch-potch of temporary buildings acquired over the years'; four new science laboratories opened in 1993 and three new classrooms due to open in late 1997. The school also reverted to full selection. Over-subscribed, with more than two applications for each place. Extra-curricular activities: netball, table tennis, athletics at national level; all sports at county level; soccer and gymnastic clubs; musical activities include two orchestras, two choirs and many ensembles; at least one drama production and four concerts each year. Duke of Edinburgh Award Scheme; photography; Christian Union. Rag Week in Christmas term, run by sixth-form and raising £2,000 for charities. 'We aim to equip tomorrow's professional women with the education and skills needed for their future.'

Streaming Pupils put in sets for mathematics and modern languages from year 8.

Approach to discipline Emphasis on self-discipline, with persistent offenders given individual help. Support of parents sought and often crucial. 'We aim to reward as well as punish, and so there is a system of merit marks as well as penalty points and detention for both work and behaviour.'

Uniform Grey skirt/trousers, burgundy sweatshirt, pink-and-white striped blouse. Dress code for sixth-formers. No jeans. Enforced 'quite strictly' but with choice of styles.

Homework Average 11-year-old, five hours a week; 14-year-old, seven hours; 16-year-old, nine hours.

Vocational qualifications RSA, Word-processing (including French and German).

Primary schools Draws from more than 60 primary schools.

THE ROYAL SCHOOL, DUNGANNON

Northland Row
Dungannon
County Tyrone BT71 6AP

Tel (018687) 722710
Fax (018687) 752845/752506
Internet: http://www.ukschools.com/
        schools/dungannon
E-mail: headmaster.email@5422060/
        c71647.dialnet

- National ranking 144 (157, 145 =, 108, 45)
- GCSE 92% (90%)
- A-levels 48% (A/B); 95% (A/E)
- Higher education 85% (Oxford 1, Cambridge 1)

- Mixed grammar
- Pupils 703
- Boys (11–18) 345
- Girls (11–18) 358
- Sixth form 166 (24%)
- Education authority *Southern Education and Library Board*

Headteacher Paul D. Hewitt, 50, appointed in September 1984. Staff 42 (men 24, women 18).

Motto Perseverando (Through perseverance *or* Never say die).

Background Founded in 1608 and opened in 1614 by royal charter of James I, the oldest of all the royal schools of Ireland; became fully co-educational in 1986. On 48-acre rural site on edge of historic market town at geographical centre of Northern Ireland, 40 minutes from Belfast on the M1 motorway. Buildings a mixture of 18th-century and modern: new £6m science and technology building, sports hall, technology and computing laboratories, all-weather hockey pitches, four rugby pitches. Over-subscribed, with 1.5 applications per day place and two applications per boarding place. 'Very strong' music: symphonic band with more than 60 members, 100-member senior choir, 120-member junior choir; public and competitive performances. Art also a major curricular and extra-curricular activity. Computer networks. Many international sporting representatives, including several British Lions; Bisley success for shooting teams. 'A strongly academic school with a pleasant, relaxed yet respectful atmosphere.'

Alumni Ken Maginnis, Ulster Unionist MP for Fermanagh and South Tyrone; Paddy Johns and Alan Clark, Ireland rugby internationals; Rev Professor R. L. Marshall, critic, poet and theologian; Ed Curran, Editor of the *Belfast Telegraph*.

Streaming In second and third years; more loosely later, according to subject combinations.

Approach to discipline Traditional, orthodox approach, with strict rules on smoking, drinking, and drugs (automatic expulsion). 'However, such are the relationships between staff and pupils that the sanctions available are rarely needed. Prefects are "elected" by their sixth-form peers and appointed after a term's experience if suitable.'

Uniform Chocolate blazer with magenta braid, grey trousers/skirt, white shirt. Very strictly enforced.

Homework Average 11-year-old, seven hours 30 minutes a week; 14-year-old, 12 hours 30 minutes; 16-year-old, 15 hours.

Vocational qualifications RSA, Keyboarding; Computer Literacy and Information Technology.

Primary schools Dungannon Primary; Howard Primary; Killyman Primary; Bush Primary; Moy Regional Primary; Ballygawley Primary; Donaghmore Controlled Primary.

WILSON'S SCHOOL

Mollison Drive
Wallington
Surrey SM6 9JW
Tel (0181) 773 2931
Fax (0181) 773 4972

- National ranking 145 (61, 73, 116, 140)
- GCSE 92% (98%)
- A-levels 46% (A/B); 92% (A/E)
- Higher education 92% (Oxford 3, Cambridge 3)

- Grant-maintained
- Boys' grammar
- Pupils 813
- Boys (11–18) 813
- Girls *Not applicable*
- Sixth form 210 (26%)
- Education authority *Sutton*

Headteacher Christopher Tarrant, 45, appointed in January 1994. Staff 47 (men 32, women 15).

Motto Non sibi sed omnibus (Not for yourself but for all).

Background Founded in 1615 by Edward

Wilson, vicar of Camberwell; moved to London Borough of Sutton in 1975 as a voluntary-aided school. It became grant-maintained in September 1989. Although not a church school, Christian ethos pervasive and school has its own chaplain. Proud of record in sport, music, drama and Combined Cadet Force. Facilities include extensive playing fields, gymnasium, heated indoor swimming pool and squash courts; owns field study centre in Brecon Beacons National Park. Technology building opened in June 1991; also new art room and multi-purpose technology rooms opened in 1994. Regular skiing trips, sports tours, outdoor pursuits, exchanges to France and Germany. Recent trips to Paris, Moscow and St Petersburg. Substantially over-subscribed, with 826 applicants for 120 places; waiting list for occasional vacancies. Six pupils represented England in international academic and sporting competitions in 1994. Gained top score in 1995 British Mathematics Olympiad. National success in water-polo and soccer. Athletics and cross-country also strong.

Alumni Michael Caine, actor and film star; Brian Masters, author; John Galliano, fashion designer; Dr Roy Porter, historian and broadcaster; Harry Golombek, chess grand master.

Streaming Some setting in mathematics, science and modern languages.

Approach to discipline 'Firm, within a supportive and caring environment. The school sets high standards in all aspects of pupil development and expects the support of parents, staff and governors in achieving them.'

Uniform Black blazer, black-and-gold tie, dark-grey trousers. Strictly enforced.

Homework Average 11-year-old, five hours a week; 14-year-old, six hours 30 minutes; 16-year-old, seven hours 30 minutes. Recommended minimum of 15 hours for sixth-formers.

Vocational qualifications None

Inspection March 1993: 'Wilson's School is a very successful school. Its pupils achieve the high academic standards set in most areas of work. The quality of pupils' learning is generally good. The boys are interested in, and motivated by, the work. The achievements of some of the pupils, including some of the most able, are limited by the inadequate level of resources. The pupils' social

and cultural development is good. Responsible and mature behaviour is fostered by sound relationships which exist throughout the school.' *The School reports that it has addressed issue of inadequate level of resources, including a new network of 486 computers in three specialist rooms.*

Primary schools More than 100 feeder schools.

KESTEVEN AND SLEAFORD HIGH SCHOOL

Jermyn Street
Sleaford
Lincolnshire NG34 7RS
Tel (01529) 414044
Fax (01529) 414928

- National ranking 146 (125, 114, 34, 22)
- GCSE 92% (94%)
- A-levels 43% (A/B); 98% (A/E)
- Higher education 90%

- Girls' grammar
- Pupils 601
- Boys *Not applicable*
- Girls (11–18) 601
- Sixth form 123 (20%)
- Education authority *Lincolnshire*

Headteacher Alison Ross, 38, appointed in September 1996. Staff 32 (men 6, women 26).

Motto Must give else never can receive.

Background High school opened in 1902. Original 19th-century house and garden still part of school, although main buildings are of modern design. Major capital programme completed in spring 1996 provides new technology and classroom building and sports hall, together with remodelled science, art, geography, staff and administration areas. Investor in People Award 1996. Pupils come from wide area, including Lincoln and Newark, with admission based on Lincolnshire grammar schools' selection procedures. A-level pass rates in the past five years have always exceeded 90%. Fully subscribed, with admission governed by ability. Sporting strengths include hockey, archery, tennis, football, netball and basketball. Duke of Edinburgh Award Scheme. Field work includes European visits for history, geography and art; exchange schemes for modern language pupils. Broadly-based curriculum beyond requirements of national curriculum. Active parents' association.

Streaming Some setting in mathematics and French from year 9.

Approach to discipline 'Firm but fair. The school has a happy atmosphere and sanctions rarely need to be applied.'

Uniform Bottle-green skirt and jumper, white-and-green striped blouse in years 7 to 11. No uniform but dress code for sixth-formers. Ban on dyed hair, hair gel and wet-look sprays.

Homework Average 11-year-old, six hours a week; 14-year-old, nine hours; 16-year-old, 12 hours.

Vocational qualifications RSA, Computer Literacy and Information Technology; RSA, Typing; GNVQ, Health and Social Care.

Inspection October 1996: 'A sound school with many strengths. The standards which girls reach in class overall considerably exceed those expected nationally.'; 'In class and around the school, pupils demonstrate positive attitudes and behave well. They are courteous and friendly with each other, with staff and visitors.'; 'The quality of teaching is generally good, and only three per cent of the teaching observed during the inspection was of unsatisfactory quality.'; 'Teachers know their subjects well, and establish good relationships with pupils so classes are orderly.'; 'Low expectations are a feature of some lessons in English, mathematics, science, geography, religious education and modern languages.'

Primary schools William Alvery Primary, Sleaford; Sleaford RC Primary; St Andrew's CE Primary, Leasingham; Heckington CE Primary, Heckington; Metheringham County Primary, Metheringham.

THE KING'S SCHOOL

Park Road
Peterborough
Cambridgeshire PE1 2UE
Tel (01733) 751541
Fax (01733) 751542
E-mail: kings_school_peterboro@
        compuserve.com

- National ranking 147 (175, 151, 163, 175)

- GCSE 92% (81%)
- A-levels 41% (A/B); 94% (A/E)
- Higher education 78% (Oxford 1, Cambridge 6)

- Grant-maintained
- Mixed comprehensive
- Pupils 854
- Boys (11–18) 467
- Girls (11–18) 387
- Sixth form 231 (27%)
- Education authority *Cambridgeshire*

Headteacher Gary Leslie Longman, 43, appointed in September 1994. Staff 57 (men 32, women 25).

Motto *None*

Background Founded by Henry VIII in 1541 as the Cathedral Choir School; moved to current site in Victorian residential area in 1885, enabling it to expand as a grammar school. Playing fields are a mile from the school; significant building programme over past 20 years; new technology centre in 1993. Became grant-maintained in January 1993. New mathematics block in May 1996. Over-subscribed, with 1.6 applications for each place. Music is a particular strength, with many orchestras and choirs; 40 pupils have achieved Grade 6 or above in music examinations. Chess also strong: two British champions in school team in recent years; half the county sailing team are from the school; full fixture list at all ages in all main sports. Outdoor and residential education involves 500 pupils on trips each year, with many going abroad. Small boarding house; Church of England school; cathedral choristers attend the school.

Alumni General Sir John Archer, former Commander-in-Chief UK Land Forces; Sir Thomas Armstrong, former principal Royal Academy of Music; Peter Boizot, founder of Pizza Express; St Clair Thompson, personal physician to King Edward VII; John Fletcher, playwright and contemporary of Shakespeare; James Crowden, Lord Lieutenant for Cambridgeshire; Andy Bell, member of pop group Erasure; Brian Ford, scientist.

Streaming Pupils put in sets in mathematics and modern languages in years 7 to 9; setting in years 10 and 11 for core national curriculum subjects of mathematics, science, French and English. Years 7 to 11 are comprehensive; sixth form is academic, with all pupils taking at least three A-levels.

Approach to discipline 'Few rules and high expectations. The school staff supervise all stages of the school day carefully, with the help of prefects from the sixth form. There is a relaxed, friendly atmosphere, but lapses in behaviour are dealt with as soon as they occur.'

Uniform Maroon blazer and tie, grey trousers/skirt, black shoes. Prefects wear Oxford commoners' gowns. Very strictly enforced.

Homework Average 11-year-old, five hours a week; 14-year-old, seven hours 30 minutes; 16-year-old, 10 hours.

Vocational qualifications *None*

Inspection March 1994: 'The school provides learning of high quality. Pupils are in general very well-motivated. Teachers provide a variety of approaches to learning which stimulate their pupils' interest and assist their development into independent learners. Some teachers could do more to extend these aspects, without risk to standards, and indeed to promote more independent thought.'; 'The standards of pupils' work are high.'

Primary schools Pupils drawn from an average of 40–45 schools each year.

SIR THOMAS RICH'S SCHOOL

Oakleaze
Longlevens
Gloucester
Gloucestershire GL2 0LF
Tel (01452) 528467
Fax (01452) 382432

- National ranking 148 (105=, 127, 175, 88)
- GCSE 92% (96%)
- A-levels 38% (A/B); 90% (A/E)
- Higher education 100% (Oxford 5, Cambridge 1)

- Boys' grammar
- Pupils 723
- Boys (11–18) 683
- Girls (16–18) 40
- Sixth form 165 (23%)
- Education authority *Gloucestershire*

Headteacher Ian Kellie, 46, appointed in September 1994. Staff 42 (men 34, women 8).

Motto Garde ta foy (Keep the faith).

Background Founded in 1666 as a Blue Coat Hospital through the will of Sir Thomas Rich, which determined it should be run 'in the manner of Christ's hospital of London'; became grammar school in 1944, with support from United Charities. The school, which moved from old city-centre buildings in 1964 to purpose-built buildings on a greenfield site, has undergone a programme of expansion, with a £1.25m building plan completed in 1996; new sports hall, with additional changing facilities and multi-gym, due for completion by end of 1997. Recent refurbishment: redecorated, carpeted, modern furniture, new computer centre. Indoor swimming pool, library and sixth-form areas completed in 1994. Over-subscribed, with five applicants for each place. Clubs and activities include national chess success; well-developed industry links; campus shared with Old Richians Rugby Football Club, as well as bowling club; three pupils have national sports honours, with 65 city/county honours; Parents' Association; Old Richians' Association.

Alumni Barry Legg, Conservative MP for Milton Keynes South-West; Steve Boyle, England and British Lions rugby player; Ian Smith, Barbarians and Scotland rugby player.

Streaming In mathematics, years 9 to 11 (for early GCSE entry); English, French and science, years 10 and 11.

Approach to discipline 'Firm discipline within a warm, friendly and secure environment where self-discipline is encouraged.' System of awards and merit certificates; sanctions balanced by praise. Serious punishments such as exclusion rare: one pupil in 12 months.

Uniform Pale-blue blazer with arms of Sir Thomas Rich, white/grey shirt, school tie, V-neck pullover, dark-grey trousers and socks, black/dark-brown shoes. Total enforcement.

Homework Average 11-year-old, seven hours a week; 14-year-old, nine hours; 16-year-old, 11+ hours.

Vocational qualifications Young Enterprise Scheme; Young Engineers/Crest Awards.

Inspection September 1993: 'Standards of achievement are very good, with some evidence of excellence in the core subjects of

English, mathematics and science, in geography and in economics and business studies.'; 'There is a strong emphasis on science and languages. The social, cultural and moral development of pupils is a positive feature of the school.' October 1996: 'Sir Thomas Rich's School has three main aims, succinctly stated and easily understood. They are in brief: high academic standards; good behaviour and discipline; a wide range of extra-curricular activities. Its success in achieving them has led to a sharp rise in enrolment.'; 'Standards are high. The school's results are not only, as might be expected, well above national averages, but compare favourably with other selective schools, some of which have more exclusive criteria of admission.'; 'Teaching is particularly good in the sixth form. Teachers are well-qualified and very committed to their work in the classroom and outside. They have high expectations of pupils.'; 'A purposeful ethos that derives from school traditions, teachers' high expectations and pupils' desire to be successful, makes a strong impression.'

Primary schools Abbeymead Primary; Barnwood CE Primary; Dinglewell Junior; Elmbridge Junior; Innsworth County Junior; Longlevens Junior; Upton St Leonards Primary; Widden County Primary.

CHATHAM GRAMMAR SCHOOL FOR GIRLS

Rainham Road
Chatham
Kent ME5 7EH
Tel (01634) 851262
Fax (01634) 571928

- National ranking 149 (94, 121, 122, 167)
- GCSE 92% (97%)
- A-levels 32% (A/B); 93% (A/E)
- Higher education 76% (Cambridge 1)

- Grant-maintained
- Girls' grammar
- Pupils 849
- Boys (16–18) 47
- Girls (11–18) 802
- Sixth form 216 (25%)
- Education authority *Kent*

Headteacher Ingeborg Watson, 45, appointed in September 1991. Staff 54 (men 14, women 40).

Motto Honour before honours.

Background Entrance hidden between terrace houses on busy A2 road, but school in commanding position atop Chatham Hill overlooking countryside to south of Medway towns. Founded in 1907, the school was fee-paying before becoming a county grammar in 1944. It became grant-maintained in September 1992. Over-subscribed, with 1.5 applications per place. Main buildings old but sound; interior improved by double-glazing and modern decor. New technology block opened in May 1994; became first girls' grammar in the country to become Technology College (February 1994); local centre of excellence in music, developing Music Technology; one in four pupils play musical instruments. Strong tradition in public-speaking, to examination level. Bilingual headteacher generates enthusiasm for modern languages, with all girls in years 8 and 9 taking two foreign languages as well as Latin. Total of 21 A-level courses offered.

Streaming Setting according to ability in some subjects, principally mathematics.

Approach to discipline For pastoral and disciplinary purposes school divided into three, each under senior teacher: years 7 to 9; years 10 and 11; and sixth forms. 'High standards of behaviour and responsibility are expected, and parents are involved at earliest possible stage if problems arise.'

Uniform Navy blazer, navy skirt, navy V-neck jumpers with school badge, white blouse. Sixth-formers do not wear uniform. Regulations enforced 'very strictly'.

Homework Average 11-year-old, five hours a week; 14-year-old, seven hours 30 minutes; 16-year-old, 10 hours.

Vocational qualifications GNVQ Intermediate and Advanced, Business, Media and Communications, Health and Social Care, Technology.

Inspection October 1993: 'Pupils attending this school receive above-average academic and pastoral provision. Their educational experience is sound and should form the basis for good academic and personal development in later life.'; 'The quality of pupils' learning is impressive as is the quality of the teaching they receive. The staff are well-qualified, knowledgeable and enthusiastic about their subjects. The one area requiring attention is the need to match work within class more closely to the differing capabilities of the pupils in order to extend their learning. This is particularly important in the case of the most able pupils.'

Primary schools Fairview County Primary; Barnsole County Primary; Park Wood County Primary; Arden County Primary.

BOSTON HIGH SCHOOL

Spilsby Road
Boston
Lincolnshire PE21 9PF
Tel (01205) 310505
Fax (01205) 350235
E-mail: bostonhigh@aol.com

- National ranking 150 (151, 98, 103, 141)
- GCSE 92% (92%)
- A-levels 29% (A/B); 88% (A/E)
- Higher education 78% (Oxford 1, Cambridge 4)

- Girls' grammar
- Pupils 830
- Boys (16–18) 24
- Girls (11–18) 806
- Sixth form 226 (27%)
- Education authority *Lincolnshire*

Headteacher Barry David Searles, 44, appointed in September 1995. Staff 54 (men 30, women 24).

Motto Non nobis solum (Not for ourselves alone).

Background Moved to current site in 1938, 17 years after it was originally founded. Set in spacious grounds, with lawns and flowerbeds, on edge of Boston. Swimming pool behind main building. All applicants who pass entry test are accommodated in an area with several grammar schools. Recent building programme: two physics laboratories, economics room, business studies room, sports hall, French block, mathematics block, sixth-form centre, technology block, and refurbished chemistry laboratories and mathematics rooms, three art rooms and a dark room, two further computer rooms, 80 networked personal computers and 32 laptop computers, and an electronic music room. Athletics, swimming, netball and hockey teams and players compete at county and regional (occasionally national) level. Music: early music group, two choirs, ensembles, full and chamber orchestras. Dramatic production annually; 140 girls take part in Duke of Edinburgh Award Scheme. French, German and Spanish exchange every year; Classics trip to Italy/Greece and ski trip to Austria. Strong Classics department; Italian, Spanish, French and German taught. Total of 23 A-level subjects offered.

Streaming In mathematics, science and French in years 8 and 9.

Approach to discipline 'Firm but fair.' Teachers say good discipline is normal state of affairs, but 'if infringements occur, they are dealt with by detention and, in extreme cases, by suspension'.

Uniform Navy skirt/trousers, blazers, pullovers, white shirts.

Homework Average 11-year-old, five hours a week; 14-year-old, 10 hours; 16-year-old, 15 hours.

Vocational qualifications RSA, Computer Literacy and Information Technology.

Inspection November 1993: 'The pupils are well-motivated and work hard . . . The enthusiasm and commitment of the young people have created a climate in which much high-quality learning and achievement have taken place. In many lessons there was an authentic sense of intellectual excitement.'; 'Relationships between pupils, and between pupils and staff, are excellent.'; 'There is a happy, well-ordered atmosphere conducive to good learning throughout the school.'

Primary schools Tower Road Primary; Kirton Primary; Conway Primary; Butterwick Primary; Boston West; St Thomas' CE Primary.

ST PATRICK'S GRAMMAR SCHOOL

Cathedral Road
Armagh BT61 7QZ
Tel (01861) 522018
Fax (01861) 525930
E-mail: stpatsarma@ad.com
Internet: http://www.members.aol.com/
StPatsArma/home

- National ranking 151 (144, 160, 150, 169)
- GCSE 91% (92%)
- A-levels 50% (A/B); 97% (A/E)
- Higher education 95%

- Boys' grammar
- Pupils 800
- Boys (11–18) 800

- Girls *Not applicable*
- Sixth form 240 (30%)
- Education authority *Southern Education and Library Board*

Headteacher Rev Bro Leo S. Kelly, 54, appointed in August 1988. Staff 49 (men 32, women 17).

Motto Fratres in unum (Brothers in one).

Background Established in 1988 with amalgamation of Christian Brothers' Grammar School and St Patrick's College; occupies St Patrick's College site. Original buildings date from 1838, with many extensions; most recent was in 1974; Catholic boarding school, run by Archdiocese of Armagh and Congregation of Christian Brothers, situated beside St Patrick's Cathedral in own grounds with extensive playing fields. Over-subscribed, with two applications for each place; about 70 boarders. Prides itself on being in top four in Northern Ireland for football and basketball; music and drama strong, with regular school productions; winners of Ulster and All-Ireland debating honours. 'The school is a vital part of the life of Armagh (population 15,000).' Fine complex of outdoor and indoor sporting facilities; computerised library system; prominent in Ulster Colleges Gaelic football and basketball competitions.

Alumni Cardinal Tomas O'Fiaich, Primate of All-Ireland; Bishop G. Clifford, Auxiliary Bishop of Armagh; John Montague, poet; Paul Muldoon, poet; Tony McAuley, BBC producer.

Streaming Only in mathematics in year 10.

Approach to discipline 'The school has an excellent record of discipline. A caring and Christian approach is adopted by staff towards students, and students are encouraged to show a similar attitude towards fellow students.' System of class form teachers and year-heads to monitor discipline. 'In extreme cases, detention – and, as a last resort, suspension – is used.'

Uniform Dark-grey trousers, grey shirt, light-grey V-neck pullover with crest, black shoes. Compulsory for years 7 to 11; years 12 and 13 expected to dress in 'becoming fashion' with collar and tie. 'No eccentricities of dress or hairstyle are permitted.'

Homework Average 11-year-old, seven hours 30 minutes a week; 14-year-old, 10 hours; 16-year-old, 15 hours.

Vocational qualifications RSA; Computer Literacy and Information Technology.

Primary schools Christian Brothers' Primary, Greenpark; St Patrick's Primary, Armagh; St Malachy's Primary; St Jarlath's Primary, Blackwatertown; Tannaghmore Primary, Lurgan.

PLYMOUTH HIGH SCHOOL FOR GIRLS

St Lawrence Road
Plymouth
Devon PL4 6HT
Tel (01752) 208308
Fax (01752) 208309
E-mail 4155@911.4153.devon_cc.gov.uk

- National ranking 152 (77, 150, 144, 147)
- GCSE 91% (98%)
- A-levels 46% (A/B); 92% (A/E)
- Higher education 86% (Oxford 1)

- Girls' grammar
- Pupils 640
- Boys *Not applicable*
- Girls (11–18) 640
- Sixth form 128 (20%)
- Education authority *Devon*

Headteacher Rosemary Stoggall, appointed in April 1991. Staff 41 (men 12, women 29).

Motto Non scholae sed vitae discimus (For life not school we learn).

Background Established in 1874 to provide academic education for girls; one of oldest girls' schools in the country, it still occupies original purpose-built premises near centre of Plymouth and its university. Gradually expanded, combining Victorian elegance and modern facilities. Fully-subscribed; every girl qualifying for a place is guaranteed one. New science accommodation in 1993; facilities for technology extended in 1994. Sports facilities include gymnasium and netball/tennis courts; multi-purpose dance/drama area. Prides itself on looking after girls with physical handicap.

Alumni Michael Foot, former Labour Party leader (when school used to have a mixed preparatory department).

Streaming Only for mathematics from year 8.

Approach to discipline 'Firm and sensible.' Positive approach; caring community; simple school rules. 'Initially, poor behaviour is the subject of a simple reprimand. More serious problems with work and behaviour may result in a pupil being placed on report.' Discussion with parents welcomed.

Uniform Navy skirt and jumper, white shirt, school tie. Compulsory until end of year 11.

Homework Average 11-year-old, six to eight hours a week; 14-year-old, eight to 10 hours; 16-year-old, 10 to 12 hours.

Vocational qualifications *None*

Inspection March 1995: 'A friendly and orderly community in which the pupils are well-known as individuals and have excellent attitudes to their work. The standards of work are high and are comparable with other selective schools nationally.'; 'Work of particular merit is done in English, mathematics, science, German, geography and history.'; 'In the core subjects of English, mathematics and science achievements are good.'; 'The pupils are industrious and have very good attitudes to their work. They produce good quantities of written and other work. They are very well motivated and can concentrate for the full lesson-time.'; 'This is a friendly school and is recognised as such by parents.'

Primary schools Goosewell Primary; Kings School; Plymstock Primary; Elburton Primary, Stoke Damerel Primary; Lipson Vale Primary; Manadon Vale Primary; Plymouth College Prep; Widey Court Primary.

CHATHAM HOUSE GRAMMAR SCHOOL

Chatham Street
Ramsgate
Kent CT11 7PS
Tel (01843) 591075
Fax (01843) 591075

- National ranking 153 (158, 80, 149, 98)
- GCSE 91% (88%)
- A-levels 34% (A/B); 88% (A/E)
- Higher education 82% (Oxford 1, Cambridge 4)

- Grant-maintained
- Boys' grammar
- Pupils 720
- Boys (11–18) 705
- Girls (16–18) 15
- Sixth form 198 (28%)
- Education authority *Kent*

Headteacher John Donald Mathews, 49, appointed in April 1992. Staff 44 (men 35, women 9).

Motto Floreat domus Chathamensis (May Chatham House flourish).

Background Founded in 1797, Chatham House was originally an independent day and boarding school. Since 1921 it has been a county boys' grammar in central Ramsgate admitting only day pupils. Strong links with Clarendon House, its sister school, with which it shares a sixth-form timetable for up to 360 boys and girls. Pupils from Whitstable, 20 miles away, Herne Bay (16 miles), Margate, Broadstairs and Ramsgate; not as middle-class as some Kent grammar schools. Fully-subscribed. Strong house system. 'Sensible' level of competition. Notable for drama, sport, public speaking and design. Strong in hockey, with the 1993 England captain and several regional players; rugby and cricket also strong; musicians in county youth orchestra.

Alumni Sir Edward Heath, former Conservative prime minister; Air Vice-Marshal Sir William Wratten, British air command in Gulf War; Frank Muir, writer/humorist; Sean Kerly, England hockey player; Geoff Parsons, British high-jump champion.

Streaming Only for mathematics.

Approach to discipline 'Mature and not unnecessarily fussy.' Sensible partnership between school, pupil and home. 'There must be a shift from externally-imposed discipline towards self-discipline based ultimately upon mutual respect between boys and staff.'

Uniform Green blazer.

Homework Average 11-year-old, at least four hours 30 minutes a week; 14-year-old, at least seven hours; 16-year-old, at least 10 hours.

Vocational qualifications *None*

Inspection December 1993: 'The quality of education provided is generally good. Pupils are well-motivated and work hard. Teachers are knowledgeable in their subjects. They impart this knowledge to the pupils to encourage learning.'; 'The school has well-established values which are subscribed to by both pupils and parents. Behaviour is good, relationships are supportive and there are many opportunities for pupils to exercise responsibility and to develop leadership skills.'

Primary schools Total of 37 feeder schools.

CLARENDON HOUSE GRAMMAR SCHOOL

Clarendon Gardens
Ramsgate
Kent CT11 9BB
Tel (01843) 591074
Fax (01843) 851824

- National ranking 154 (75, 93, 145, 131)
- GCSE 91% (98%)
- A-levels 33% (A/B); 90% (A/E)
- Higher education 80% (Cambridge 1)

- Girls' grammar
- Pupils 785
- Boys (16–18) 12
- Girls (11–18) 773
- Sixth form 220 (28%)
- Education authority *Kent*

Headteacher Jane Bennett, 51, appointed in April 1991. Staff 45 (men 13, women 32).

Motto Ex humilibus excelsa (Success from small beginnings).

Background Founded in 1905 and still in pleasant original buildings, with additions and specialist science annexe, in centre of Ramsgate near to harbour. Two information technology networks; technology room; swimming pool; sixth-form study centre; fitness room. Over-subscribed, with expansion to four-form entry to satisfy demand in past four years; 110 applications for 90 places. Wide range of 25 A-level and eight AS-level courses; additional intake at 16+, including boys in the sixth form; on-site careers adviser. Extra-curricular activities: chess, drama, young engineers' club, Duke of Edinburgh Award Scheme, weight-training, trampolining, sports teams, orchestra, choir, wind band. Two music concerts a year and a major production with neighbouring boys' school. Increasing proportion of pupils entering higher education.

Streaming Pupils are put in sets in mathematics from year 8.

Approach to discipline 'High expectations of pupils' behaviour in a supportive environment.'

Uniform Bottle-green skirt, white blouse, school tie in house colours. Strictly enforced; no uniform for sixth-formers.

Homework Average 11-year-old, five to six hours a week; 14-year-old, eight hours 30 minutes; 16-year-old, nine to 10 hours.

Vocational qualifications *None*

Inspection March 1994: 'Pupils, parents staff and members of the community speak highly of the school's ethos. Pupils demonstrate they share these values by the way in which they co-operate in lessons, the respect and courtesy they show to staff and visitors to the school, and in their care for the school environment.' Standards of achievement satisfactory or better in 94% of lessons.

Primary schools The school draws from at least 30 primary schools in the Thanet, Herne Bay and Whitstable areas.

WATFORD GRAMMAR SCHOOL FOR GIRLS

Lady's Close
Watford
Hertfordshire WD1 8AE
Tel (01923) 223403
Fax (01923) 223403

- National ranking 155 (161, 164, 162, 172)
- GCSE 90% (87%)
- A-levels 50% (A/B); 97% (A/E)
- Higher education 90% (Oxford 1, Cambridge 3)

- Grant-maintained
- Girls' comprehensive
- Pupils 1,147
- Boys *Not applicable*
- Girls (11–18) 1,147
- Sixth form 250 (22%)
- Education authority *Hertfordshire*

Headteacher Helen Hyde, 50, appointed in September 1987. Staff 80 (men 16, women 64).

Motto Sperate parati (Go forward with preparation).

Background Founded by Dame Elizabeth Fuller in 1704 for 40 boys and 20 girls; the girls moved to their present site in 1907. Extensions were added and Lady's Close (year 7 base) purchased between 1914 and 1954.

After the 1944 Education Act the school became voluntary-controlled; further extensions were added after 1954; new technology suite, three new science laboratories. French, German, Latin and Italian among languages taught; school boasts strong science, music and religious studies departments; extended extra-curricular activities include three orchestras, two choirs, wide range of clubs; exchange visits to France, Germany and Italy. In 1991, the school became grant-maintained. Over-subscribed, with four applications per place. National Audit Office inspection in January 1996 found 'a reflective, thinking school . . . developing well, action-orientated. There is strong leadership.'

Streaming In mathematics, science and languages in years 9 to 11.

Approach to discipline Behaviour governed by school code drawn up by pupils and staff. Code intended to be positive guide rather than punitive list of rules. 'Pupils are expected to behave in a courteous, polite and caring manner.'

Uniform Navy blue skirt/smart trousers, gold blouses. Blazer and cardigan with embroidered crests. Sixth-formers wear navy trousers/skirt, with white blouses. Regulations strictly enforced.

Homework Average 11-year-old, six hours a week; 14-year-old, seven hours; 16-year-old, eight to nine hours.

Vocational qualifications *None*

Inspection September 1993: 'Pupils are almost always well-motivated and make good progress in lessons'; 'Expectations of pupils are high'; 'The school has clear and well-established values. The central elements are high achievement, good behaviour, and care and concern for others. Relationships between pupils and staff and amongst pupils are very good.'

SIR ROGER MANWOOD'S SCHOOL

Manwood Road
Sandwich
Kent CT13 9JX
Tel (01304) 613286
Fax (01304) 615336

- National ranking 156 (102, 91, 81, 25)
- GCSE 90% (96%)
- A-levels 45% (A/B); 90% (A/E)

- Higher education 97% (Oxford 2, Cambridge 2)

- Grant-maintained
- Mixed grammar
- Pupils 680
- Boys (11–18) 335
- Girls (11–18) 345
- Sixth form 170 (25%)
- Education authority *Kent*

Headteacher Christopher Morgan, 43, appointed in September 1996. Staff 47 (men 30, women 17).

Motto Sinite parvulos venire ad me (Suffer the little children to come unto me).

Background Founded in 1563, the school moved to its current 31-acre site in 1895; numbers have risen steadily; expansion to four-form entry from September 1997. Three boarding houses on site: Headmaster's House and The Lodge for boys; The Grange for girls. Boarding inquiries reported to be more numerous than ever; entry is by test and recommendation. Became grant-maintained in September 1992. Over-subscribed with 1.7 applications per place. New four-laboratory science block in September 1994; two new computer rooms recently added; new library, funded by appeal, opened in March 1995; computer network being further extended. Hockey among sporting strengths, with girls' team reaching national finals three times in four years, coming third in 1994. Music strong: individual music tuition, choirs, bands and orchestras. Combined Cadet Force. Public speaking; foreign exchanges to France and Germany. Academic success 'major priority' while also aiming to offer rounded education.

Alumni John Hougham, ACAS chairman; Johnny Beerling, former controller of BBC Radio One; Eugene Gilkes, decathlete; Richard Wells, chief constable of South Yorkshire; John Cavell, former Bishop of Southampton.

Streaming Pupils are in sets for mathematics; setting in French in years 10 and 11, when timetable permits; limited setting in science in years 10 and 11.

Approach to discipline Detailed rules governing behaviour. 'Firm but fair discipline underpins the school's approach to all its activities.'

Uniform Navy uniform worn by all except sixth-formers. Strictly enforced.

Homework Average 11-year-old, seven hours 30 minutes a week; 14-year-old, 10 hours; 16-year-old, 10 to 15 hours.

Vocational qualifications *None*

Inspection November 1994: 'This is a successful school.'; 'It is characterised by good motivation, concentration and hard work. Pupils co-operate well with each other and make good progress in subject knowledge, understanding and skills.'; 'The curriculum is sound, except that too low an emphasis is accorded to information technology.'; 'The ethos of the school is good; a hard-working and friendly atmosphere pervades, in which relationships are open and friendly.'

Primary schools Sandwich Junior; Eastry CE Primary; Wingham County Primary; Warden House Primary, Deal; Parochial CE Primary, Deal; St Faiths-at-Ash, Sholden; Cartwright & Kelsey CE Primary, Ash.

BARTON COURT GRAMMAR SCHOOL

Longport
Canterbury
Kent CT1 1PH
Tel (01227) 464600
Fax (01227) 781399

- National ranking 157 (154, 134, 154, 134)
- GCSE 90% (91%)
- A-levels 38% (A/B); 87% (A/E)
- Higher education 80%

- Grant-maintained
- Mixed grammar
- Pupils 723
- Boys (11–18) 253
- Girls (11–18) 470
- Sixth form 161 (22%)
- Education authority *Kent*

Headteacher Dr Stephen Charles Manning, 46, appointed in June 1992. Staff 40 (men 15, women 25).

Motto Enjoying high achievement.

Background Founded in the 1940s in a large Georgian house built in 1750 close to centre of cathedral city; school buildings arranged around ancient lake, the Abbot's fishpond for the adjacent St Augustine's Abbey since

the year 605. In 1990, the school changed from girls' school to become Canterbury's only mixed grammar school. Over-subscribed, with 1.2 applications per place. Prides itself on strength in all areas of national curriculum; A-level students able to study one or more elements of vocational courses in addition to A-levels. A £3m grant restored old house in May 1995 and to extend and develop science and technology accommodation completed Easter 1997. Identified by Ofsted in 1996 as 'outstandingly successful' school.

Streaming 'Sometimes for mathematics, English and science, but in a grammar school, selecting the top 25% of the ability range, this is not always necessary.'

Approach to discipline 'School rules are kept to a minimum, but transgressors are followed up immediately by form tutors and pastoral tutors who will involve parents if there is a serious problem.'

Uniform Navy blazer with school badge, grey/navy trousers or skirt, white shirt/blouse, navy tie with badge. Enforced 'as strictly as possible within the constraints of the present economic climate'.

Homework Average 11-year-old, five hours a week; 14-year-old, eight hours; 16-year-old, 10 to 12 hours.

Vocational qualifications Business French and German; Office Technology; RSA, Word-processing, Audio-typing etc; Computer Literacy and Information Technology; GNVQ Level 3, Business and Finance.

Inspection November 1994: 'A good school with many good features'; 'Good learning is characterised by high motivation, hard work and progress in subject knowledge, understanding and skills.'; 'Homework is regularly set and conscientiously completed.'; 'The ethos of the school is good; a hard-working atmosphere exists and relationships are open and friendly. Pupils are responsible, tolerant of each other and co-operative.'

Primary schools Barham CE Primary; Blean County Primary; Briary County Primary; Bridge and Patrixbourne CE Primary; Herne Bay Junior; Reculver CE Primary; St Philip Howard RC Primary; St Stephen's Primary; Whitstable County Junior.

BISHOP VESEY'S GRAMMAR SCHOOL 127

LADY MARGARET SCHOOL

Parson's Green
London SW6 4UN
Tel (0171) 736 7138
Fax (0171) 384 2553
E-mail: marg@rmplc.co.uk

- National ranking 158 (168, 196, 191, –)
- GCSE 90% (83%)
- A-levels 37% (A/B); 94% (A/E)
- Higher education 90% (Oxford 2)

- Girls' comprehensive
- Pupils 454
- Boys *Not applicable*
- Girls (11–18) 454
- Sixth form 105 (23%)
- Education authority *Hammersmith and Fulham*

Headteacher Joan Sheila Ross Olivier, 56, appointed in September 1984. Staff 27 (men 10, women 17).

Motto Yea, I have a goodly heritage.

Background Founded in 1917 by Enid Moberley Bell, acquiring new properties in 1937 and 1953 and having extensive building works done in the 1960s and 1970s: three listed Georgian houses fronting on Parson's Green, Fulham. Landscaped garden, and netball and tennis courts, to the rear of the buildings. New technology building in 1994. Over-subscribed, with six applications per place; school enlarged to three-form entry from September 1996 and another new building added. Inter-school sports fixtures. 'We pride ourselves on turning out extremely nice end-products. One of the strengths of the school is its small size, which allows us to give very personal service to pupils and parents.'

Alumni Janet Street-Porter, broadcaster and television executive.

Streaming Pupils are streamed after year 7 for English and mathematics.

Approach to discipline 'We think discipline is a good idea! Staff apply the rules consistently and fairly. All pupils acknowledge and respect the need for rules and they very rarely break them.'

Uniform Black blazer with red pin-stripe, black sweatshirt with school logo, red pin-striped shirt, black/brown shoes. Very strictly enforced.

Homework Average 11-year-old, seven hours 30 minutes a week; 14-year-old, 10 hours; 16-year-old, 15 hours.

Vocational qualifications *None*

Inspection October 1996: 'A very good school which has great strengths.'; 'Pupils' attitudes to learning are positive. They concentrate well on set tasks and are confident in posing and answering questions. Behaviour in lessons and around school is excellent.'; 'Teaching is kept at a brisk pace. Pupils' work is effectively assessed. In the very few unsatisfactory lessons, teachers direct pupils too closely, talk too much and do not encourage them to develop independent learning skills.'; 'The headteacher has a clear vision of how the school should develop, is highly committed to its success and leads by example.'

Primary schools More than 120 feeder schools.

BISHOP VESEY'S GRAMMAR SCHOOL

Lichfield Road
Sutton Coldfield
West Midlands B74 2NH
Tel (0121) 354 2552
Fax (0121) 321 1615
E-mail: veseysgs@rmplc.co.uk
Internet http://www.rmplc.co.uk/eduweb/sites/veseysgs

- National ranking 159 (141, 169, 134, 154)
- GCSE 90% (93%)
- A-levels 33% (A/B); 90% (A/E)
- Higher education 86% (Oxford 1, Cambridge 2)

- Boys' grammar
- Pupils 861
- Boys (11–18) 823
- Girls (16–18) 38
- Sixth form 262 (30%)
- Education authority *Birmingham*

Headteacher Marie Elaine Clarke, 49, appointed in January 1989. Staff 54 (men 35, women 19).

Motto Dextra dei exaltavit me (The right hand of God lifts me up).

Background John Harman, brought up by the Veseys, the family of his mother's distant relations, decided to improve his home town after he became Bishop of Exeter in 1519; established school in 1540. Extensive playing fields near centre of Sutton Coldfield on northern edge of Birmingham; oldest part of building dates from 1729, but many recent additions, the latest of which are a new £1m technology centre and a library. Over-subscribed, with 10 applications for each place. Sporting strengths: national representatives at rugby, chess, shooting and triathlon, while pupils have reached national finals in golf, swimming and athletics. Choir, band and orchestra; biennial opera. Community links and regular charity fund-raising.

Alumni Robert Burton, 17th-century author of *Anatomy of Melancholy*; Peter Robbins, England rugby player in 1950s; Peter Knight, vice-chancellor of University of Central England in Birmingham; Clive Richards, High Sheriff of Greater London 1992/3.

Streaming Some setting in mathematics and English.

Approach to discipline 'We believe in a firm but fair approach where the code of conduct has been laid out to emphasise consideration for other people and a need for self-discipline and self-esteem.' Detailed rules explained to pupils, who are expected to obey them.

Uniform Black blazer with bishop's mitre badge, grey trousers, white/grey shirt, house tie, grey/black socks, black shoes. Similar uniform worn by girls. Provision to help pupils with financial difficulties.

Homework Average 11-year-old, seven to eight hours a week; 14-year-old, eight to nine hours; 16-year-old, 10 to 12 hours.

Vocational qualifications *None*

Inspection October 1996: 'A good school. It helps its pupils to attain at higher levels than might be expected.'; 'The school has monitored its own performance and has used the results of external assessment well to work on some subjects and aspects that need to be improved.'; 'Teaching is satisfactory or good in most lessons, and most teachers prepare work, plan lessons and use their expertise conscientiously and in many cases with flair. Teachers are exceptionally committed to the school and provide excellent support for extra-curricular activities, including sport, often at weekends and after school. However, some of the teaching fails to ensure that pupils contibute fully to lessons.'; 'The school has a very pleasant and welcoming atmosphere and pupils are well-behaved,

articulate and extremely helpful.'

Primary schools 'There are 59 feeder schools this year and numbers coming from certain schools vary from year to year.'

LANGLEY GRAMMAR SCHOOL

Reddington Drive
Langley
Berkshire SL3 7QS
Tel (01753) 810850
Fax (01753) 810858
E-mail: langram@rossnet.co.uk

- National ranking 160 (133, 113, 164, 183)
- GCSE 89% (94%)
- A-levels 46% (A/B); 94% (A/E)
- Higher education 75% (Oxford 2)

- Grant-maintained
- Mixed grammar
- Pupils 781
- Boys (12–18) 399
- Girls (12–18) 382
- Sixth form 171 (22%)
- Education authority *Berkshire*

Headteacher Dr Alan George Robinson, 60, appointed in April 1976. Staff 47 (men 22, women 25).

Motto Sapientia Domine (Wisdom, O Lord).

Background Founded in 1956 and is the longest-established co-educational grammar school in the area; located on 20-acre site next to Kederminster Park within easy reach of M4 motorway. Over-subscribed, with four applications per place. Pupils attracted from wide area, including Slough, Colnbrook, Iver, Iver Heath, Denham, Hillingdon, Windsor, Datchet, Eton, Wraysbury, Staines and Ashford as well as Langley itself. Sporting strengths include boys' and girls' hockey, with players regularly representing county and region; several have gained national honours. Musical tradition, with large choir and orchestra; about 130 pupils learning musical instruments. Drama is strong, with contributions to county drama festival. Strong inter-house programme of events. 'The curriculum is modern and the traditional values of scholarship and hard work are upheld.'

Streaming In mathematics from year 9; in German and French in years 10 and 11.

Approach to discipline 'Discipline is firm but fair. Staff and pupils have joint responsibility in maintaining the school's high standard of behaviour. Pupils are required to behave courteously at all times.'

Uniform Years 8 to 11: girls, bottle-green skirt, white blouse; boys, bottle-green blazer, charcoal-grey trousers. Years 12 and 13: girls, beige/brown skirt, white/cream blouse; boys, black blazer, charcoal-grey trousers. The school insists on smart appearance and the wearing of uniform is compulsory.'

Homework Average 12-year-old, eight hours a week; 14-year-old, 10 hours; 16-year-old, 15 hours.

Vocational qualifications Pitman, Office Technology.

Primary schools Castleview Combined; Staines Preparatory; Wraysbury Combined; Long Close school; Marish Convent Junior.

QUEEN ELIZABETH ROYAL FREE GRAMMAR SCHOOL OF SPALDING

Priory Road
Spalding
Lincolnshire PE11 2XH
Tel (01775) 724646
Fax (01775) 713695

- National ranking 161 (67, 157, 73, 94)
- GCSE 89% (98%)
- A-levels 38% (A/B); 92% (A/E)
- Higher education 87% (Cambridge 1)

- Boys' grammar
- Pupils 774
- Boys (11–18) 724
- Girls (16–18) 50
- Sixth form 206 (27%)
- Education authority *Lincolnshire*

Headteacher Michael John Stewart, 52, appointed in September 1987. Staff 49 (men 31, women 18).

Motto *None*

Background Founded in 1588, commonly known as Spalding Grammar School, moved in 1881 to current site five minutes from the town centre. Numerous extensions added to Victorian buildings. Voluntary-aided: governors own land, buildings and 17 acres of surrounding playing fields.

Admission by examination at 11; about 375 pupils compete for 120 places; sixth form more or less at physical capacity. Rugby, hockey and cricket played to notable standard, with representatives at county level and above. Successful teams also in athletics, chess, cross-country, football, golf and swimming. In music, school band over 60-strong, concert band, dance band, string orchestra, brass ensemble, senior and junior choirs. Drama society responsible for up to three productions annually. Duke of Edinburgh Award Scheme.

Alumni Stuart Storey, athlete and BBC commentator.

Streaming In mathematics in year 8 and above.

Approach to discipline Discipline 'not a major issue'. Rules in interest of pupil safety and good maintenance of buildings; teachers report high standard of conduct, courtesy and self-discipline. 'Rules are based above all upon respect and consideration for the feelings, well-being and possessions of others.'

Uniform Blue blazer, dark trousers, white/light-blue shirt, school tie, dark shoes. Acceptable business dress in sixth form. Regulations enforced 'strictly but calmly'.

Homework Average 11-year-old, five hours a week; 14-year-old, eight hours; 16-year-old, 15 hours.

Vocational qualifications BTEC National, Business and Finance; GNVQ Advanced, Business Studies.

Inspection 'Spalding Grammar School provides pupils with a good education, which prepares them well for the next stages of education and for adult life. The teaching is good, the quality of pastoral care is high, and the range and quality of extra-curricular activities are a strength of the school.'

Primary schools Spalding Parish Church Day CE School; Spalding St John's Primary; The John Harrox Primary, Moulton; Pinchbeck East CE Primary; Holbeach County Primary; Holbeach William Stukeley Primary.

THE ROYAL SCHOOL, ARMAGH

College Hill
Armagh BT61 9DH
Tel (01861) 522807
Fax (01861) 525014

E-mail: admintd@rsathegap.com
Internet: http://www.gpl.net/customers/rsa

- National ranking 162 (170, 145 =, 127, 149)
- GCSE 89% (83%)
- A-levels 36% (A/B); 91% (A/E)
- Higher education 79%

- Mixed grammar
- Pupils 680
- Boys (11–18) 336
- Girls (11–18) 344
- Sixth form 144 (21%)
- Education authority *Southern Education and Library Board*

Headteacher Tom Duncan, 55, appointed in September 1988. Staff 47 (men 25, women 22).

Motto Honi soit qui mal y pense (Shame on him who thinks evil of it).

Background Founded in 1608 by James I; amalgamated in 1986 with Armagh Girls' High School to become co-educational. Prides itself on best facilities possible for GCSE and A-level teaching; £5.2m redevelopment programme recently completed. Boarding department for about 70 pupils, attracting pupils from around the world. Takes the top 35% of the ability range. Preparatory department for pupils aged four to 11. Over-subscribed, with average of 1.3 applications for each place. Wide range of extra-curricular activities. Sports include rugby, cricket and hockey. School orchestra, band and choir. Strong Combined Cadet Force. Regular visits to European cities; rugby tour to Canada in 1994.

Alumni Lord Castlereagh, 19th-century foreign secretary; Duke of Wellington (briefly).

Streaming Generally mixed-ability.

Approach to discipline 'The school has a positive attitude to discipline, with common-sense rules that are rigidly enforced. There is a system of suspension and a disciplinary policy outlined in the Code of Discipline.'

Uniform Navy blazer with red piping, charcoal-grey trousers or mid-grey skirt, white shirt/blouse, school tie, black shoes. Strictly enforced.

Homework Average 11-year-old, seven hours 30 minutes a week; 14-year-old, seven hours 30 minutes; 16-year-old, 10 to 12 hours.

Vocational qualifications RSA, Word-processing; Computer Literacy and Information Technology.

Inspection February 1994: 'The school's ethos, which is characterised by sound pupil-teacher relationships and mutual respect, contributes significantly to the all-round development of the pupils. Learning takes place in an orderly, purposeful atmosphere and lessons are enlivened by a shared sense of enjoyment and good humour. The pupils are attentive and diligent, responding positively. An exemplary standard of behaviour is maintained in class and about the school.'

Primary schools Armstrong Primary; Hardy Memorial Primary; Lisnadill Primary; Loughgall Primary; Royal School Preparatory.

RIBSTON HALL HIGH SCHOOL

Stroud Road
Gloucester
Gloucestershire GL1 5LE
Tel (01452) 528178
Fax (01452) 308833
E-mail: hkingham@ribstonhall.
demon.co.uk
Internet: http://www.ribstonhall.demon.co.
uk

- National ranking 163 (173, 183, 148, 118)
- GCSE 89% (82%)
- A-levels 29% (A/B); 87% (A/E)
- Higher education 60%

- Grant-maintained
- Girls' grammar
- Pupils 588
- Boys (16–18) 4
- Girls (11–18) 584
- Sixth form 90 (15%)
- Education authority *Gloucestershire*

Headteacher Hylary Kingham, 47, appointed from September 1996. Staff 33 (men 4, women 29).

Motto Fortior leone iustus (A just man is stronger than a lion).

Background Founded in 1921, school moved to purpose-built accommodation on open site on outskirts of Gloucester in 1962; expansion in 1980s resulted in temporary classrooms; technology block opened in 1992. Extensive sports area, with newly-resurfaced tennis/netball courts. Became grant-maintained in April 1990 to safeguard status as girls' grammar; popularity increased and is now over-subscribed, with four applications per place. 'Long tradition of excellence in music': peripatetic teachers, choirs, orchestras. Netball teams have been county champions and netball and volleyball teams have competed at national level.

Streaming Setting in mathematics and French for older pupils.

Approach to discipline 'The school expects considerate and sensible behaviour, emphasising self-discipline and independence. Detention after school acts as a deterrent and exclusion for serious offences is very rare.'

Uniform Green school blazer, skirt and jumper, yellow blouse, house tie. Sixth-formers have grey jumper and striped tie.

Homework Average 11-year-old, seven hours a week; 14-year-old, 10 hours; 16-year-old, 12 hours.

Vocational qualifications RSA, Typing, Word-processing, Computer Literacy and Information Technology; Associated Board Music Examinations; First Aid course (extra-curricular); Foreign Languages at Work.

Inspection Autumn 1994.

Primary schools Hempsted CE Primary; Heron Primary; Harewood Junior; Dinglewell Junior; Upton St Leonards CE Primary; Selwyn School; St Anthony's Convent School, Cinderford.

WILMINGTON GRAMMAR SCHOOL FOR BOYS

Common Lane
Wilmington
Dartford
Kent DA2 7DA
Tel (01322) 223090
Fax (01322) 289920

- National ranking 164 (164, 170, 186, 171)
- GCSE 89% (86%)
- A-levels 15% (A/B); 82% (A/E)
- Higher education 70%

- Grant-maintained
- Boys' grammar

- Pupils 693
- Boys (11–18) 693
- Girls *Not applicable*
- Sixth form 110 (16%)
- Education authority *Kent*

Headteacher Brian Titterington, 50, appointed in January 1992. Staff 40 (men 26, women 14).

Motto Non nobis sed communitati (Not only for ourselves but for the community).

Background The school is in the largely rural northwest corner of Kent, surrounded by green belt and ancient heathland. Also attracts pupils from Dartford and London boroughs of Bromley and Bexley. Purpose-built between 1956 and 1960; became boys' grammar in 1982; 35 acres of playing fields, tennis courts, running track and woods. Over-subscribed, with three applications for each place. Extensive computer network, fully refurbished science laboratories, well-equipped facilities for design, electronics and technology; stage lighting for drama and music; sports hall and gymnasium. Business and community links, regular links with continent. Soccer and rugby are notable among sporting successes.

Alumni Keith Richards, of the Rolling Stones.

Streaming Pupils are in sets from year 9.

Approach to discipline Emphasis on self-discipline, hard work and consideration for others. 'A disciplined framework supports the pupils so that they are able to learn without distraction or interference.'

Uniform Navy blazer, dark-grey trousers, white shirt, house tie, dark socks, black shoes. Sixth-formers wear suit or jacket and trousers, shirt and tie, and dark shoes. Uniform is 'daily requirement'.

Homework Average 11-year-old, five hours a week; 14-year-old, seven hours 30 minutes; 16-year-old, 10 hours.

Vocational qualifications *None*

Primary schools Hextable Junior; St Bartholomew's RC Primary; Harenc Preparatory; Old Bexley CE Junior; Joydens Wood Junior; West Hill Junior; York Road Junior; Sutton-at-Hone Junior.

DAME ALICE OWEN'S SCHOOL

Dugdale Hill Lane
Potters Bar
Hertfordshire EN6 2DU
Tel (01707) 643441
Fax (01707) 645011
E-mail: daosch@rmplc.co.uk
Internet: http://www.rmplc.co.uk/eduweb/
sites/daosch

- National ranking 165 (160, 158, 178, 190)
- GCSE 88% (87%)
- A-levels 51% (A/B); 95% (A/E)
- Higher education 90% (Oxford 3, Cambridge 4)

- Grant-maintained
- Mixed comprehensive
- Pupils 1,277
- Boys (11–18) 673
- Girls (11–18) 604
- Sixth form 289 (23%)
- Education authority *Hertfordshire*

Headteacher Aldon Williamson, 52, appointed in January 1995. Staff 81 (men 35, women 46).

Motto In God is all our trust.

Background Founded in 1613 by Dame Alice Owen; trustees of Dame Alice Owen Foundation are The Worshipful Company of Brewers; girls' school added in 1886. Moved from Islington to 34-acre green-belt site in Potters Bar in 1973; voluntary-aided until April 1993, when it became grant-maintained. Semi-selective Language College. Total of 22 acres of playing fields; small lake; up to seven acres of meadow, parkland and woods. Floodlit all-weather hockey/soccer pitch; sports hall and gymnasium; six tennis courts. New £1.8m high-technology Edinburgh Centre opened in November 1990, provided by Dame Alice Owen Foundation. Over-subscribed, with average of six applications per place. Sport and music among strengths: school symphony orchestra and concert band reached finals of 1995 National Festival of Music for Youth, for third successive year. Competition success for cricket, rugby and hockey teams, including national representation. 'The school is orderly, hard-working, traditional but innovative and happy.'

Alumni Dame Beryl Gray, ballerina; Gary and Martin Kemp, of Spandau Ballet pop group; Alan Parker, film director; Edmund Dell, former Labour MP for Birkenhead; Professor Sir Alan Harris, engineer and emeritus professor at Imperial College, London.

Streaming Pupils placed in two or three ability bands on entry. Also put in sets in English, mathematics, science and modern languages (French and German).

Approach to discipline Pupils expected to be punctual, tidily-dressed, polite, hard-working; friendly atmosphere. 'They are expected to show self-discipline, with respect for the well-being and property of others.'

Uniform Boys: black blazer, white shirt, dark-grey trousers, black shoes. Girls: white blouse, red V-neck pullover, kilts with black-and-white dog-tooth check.

Homework Average 11-year-old, five hours a week; 14-year-old, seven hours 30 minutes; 16-year-old, 10 to 15 hours.

Vocational qualifications GNVQ.

Primary Schools Accepts pupils from 82 primary schools.

FORT PITT GRAMMAR SCHOOL

Fort Pitt Hill
Chatham
Kent ME4 6TJ
Tel (01634) 842359
Fax (01634) 817386

- National ranking 166 (–, 155, 86, 97)
- GCSE 88%
- A-levels 50% (A/B); 94% (A/E)
- Higher education 74% (Cambridge 1)

- Girls' grammar
- Pupils 849
- Boys (16–18) 5
- Girls (11–18) 844
- Sixth form 160 (18%)
- Education authority *Kent*

Headteacher Marylyn Atkins, appointed in September 1984. Staff 51 (men 11, women 40).

Motto *None*

Background Opened in 1926 overlooking River Medway on historic site where there was once a fortress to defend approach up the river; military hospital later established on site during Crimean War; first Army

Medical School established by Florence Nightingale. Mixture of new buildings and old hospital wards; new science and computing block. Over-subscribed, but school expanding to accommodate extra numbers. New buildings planned by 1999. Sporting record for netball, cross-country and hockey, with several national players over the years. Art, mathematics, music and English among curriculum strengths.

Alumni Zandra Rhodes, fashion designer.

Streaming *None*

Approach to discipline 'The discipline is excellent and the ethos of the school is such that students behave in a courteous and well-ordered fashion.' Secure, well-defined framework; old-fashioned values and expectations; emphasis on self-discipline.

Uniform Blue skirt, blue jumper with school crest, pink checked blouse. Sixth-formers have a dress code.

Homework Average 11-year-old, seven hours 30 minutes a week; 14-year-old, 12 hours 30 minutes; 16-year-old, at least 18 hours.

Vocational qualifications GNVQ Advanced, Business.

Inspection March 1996: 'This is a good school which promotes effective learning. The headteacher provides strong leadership. The school is an orderly, caring and supportive community. Most pupils achieve standards that are high and appropriate to their ability.'; 'Overall, the quality of education in almost two-thirds of lessons is good or very good. In only a few lessons is it less than satisfactory. Pupils learn well and make good progress in all subjects and year-groups. They are generally well-motivated and work hard.'; 'Relationships are warm, friendly and secure.'

Primary schools Delce Primary; Gordon Primary; Luton Primary; Balfour Primary; Hilltop Primary.

OAKWOOD PARK GRAMMAR SCHOOL

Oakwood Park
Maidstone
Kent ME16 8AH
Tel (01622) 726683
Fax (01622) 721210
E-mail: oakwood@rmplc.co.uk
Internet: http://www.rmplc.co.uk/eduweb/sites/oakwood/

- National ranking 167 (132, 149, –, 10)
- GCSE 87% (94%)
- A-levels 38% (A/B); 94% (A/E)
- Higher education 73% (Oxford 1)

- Grant-maintained
- Boys' grammar
- Pupils 684
- Boys (11–18) 682
- Girls (16–18) 2
- Sixth form 179 (26%)
- Education authority *Kent*

Headteacher Michael John Newbould, 47, appointed April 1992. Staff 46 (men 30, women 16)

Motto Strive and Serve.

Background Founded in 1918, the school moved in 1959 to its current modern buildings in Oakwood Park, a private estate that has been developed as an educational campus on the outskirts of Maidstone. It became a grant-maintained 13–18 boys' grammar in April 1992; since September 1993, it has admitted boys aged 11. For the 120 places in each year group, it receives about 240 applications; it is a small school and intends to remain so. There are extensive playing fields for athletics, cricket, hockey, rugby and soccer. The school is one of the strongest soccer schools in Kent and is also represented at county level in cricket, rugby and athletics. There are also tennis courts and a large open-air heated swimming pool. About 15 pupils a year win Duke of Edinburgh Award Scheme gold awards.

Streaming Teaching groups based on 'friendship patterns'. No streaming.

Approach to discipline Framework of straightforward rules, but emphasis placed on self-discipline. 'Boys are encouraged to accept responsibility, and prefects work closely with year-heads in a well-developed pastoral system. A good indicator of success must be that we have almost no truancy.'

Uniform Years 7 to 11: standard uniform of black blazer with badge, grey trousers, black shoes, school tie. Dress code for sixth-formers includes sports jacket, blazer or suit, with school tie.

Homework Average 11-year-old, six hours a week; 14-year-old, 10 hours; 16-year-old, 15 hours.

Vocational qualifications *None*

Primary schools Draws from 44 primary schools throughout Mid-Kent.

STRABANE GRAMMAR SCHOOL

Milltown House
4 Liskey Road
Strabane
County Tyrone BT82 8NW
Tel (01504) 382319
Fax (01504) 383506

- National ranking 168 (96, 109, 104, –)
- GCSE 87% (97%)
- A-levels 36% (A/B); 92% (A/E)
- Higher education 74% (Oxford 1, Cambridge 1)

- Mixed grammar
- Pupils 358
- Boys (11–18) 172
- Girls (11–18) 186
- Sixth form 87 (24%)
- Education authority *Western Education and Library Board*

Headteacher Lewis John Lacey, 47, appointed in September 1996. Staff 23 (men 9, women 14).

Motto Concordia crescit (Let harmony flourish).

Background Founded in 1956 at Milltown House, formerly home of Cecil Frances Alexander, the hymn-writer; 23 acres of playing fields, gardens and woodland; mile from town centre, Cavanalee River forms southern boundary. Two extensions added in early 1960s, block of four laboratories in 1990, and technology suite in 1994. Also refurbishment of art studio and lower-sixth study under way. Over-subscribed, with 70+ applications for 54 places. Cricket and rugby strong compared with size of school: two boys played cricket for Ireland under-21s in 1994. Duke of Edinburgh Award Scheme; 40-member orchestra. 'The school works at providing a safe haven in the Northern Ireland situation. Pupils of both communities mix freely, socialise out of school and co-operate at all tasks. Of supreme importance are examination grades; on the way there, other aspects of education help produce students ready for the next stage.'

Streaming *None*

Approach to discipline 'Rules are upheld. Punishment is lunchtime detention, extra work or interview with parents.'

Uniform Royal-blue blazer with badge, grey trousers/skirt, black shoes. Sixth-formers wear blue shirt and red tie. Regulations enforced 'very firmly'.

Homework Average 11-year-old, seven hours 30 minutes to 10 hours a week; 14-year-old, 12 hours 30 minutes; 16-year-old, 15 hours.

Vocational qualifications A-levels include Business Studies, Computing, Home Economics, and Design and Technology.

Primary schools Strabane Primary; Sion Mills Primary; Artigarvan Primary; Bready Primary; Ardstraw Primary.

QUEEN ELIZABETH GRAMMAR SCHOOL

Ullswater Road
Penrith
Cumbria CA11 7EG
Tel (01768) 864621
Fax (01768) 890923

- National ranking 169 (–, 181, 146, 173)
- GCSE 87%
- A-levels 34% (A/B); 92% (A/E)
- Higher education 80+% (Oxford 2)

- Grant-maintained
- Mixed grammar
- Pupils 691
- Boys (11–18) 326
- Girls (11–18) 365
- Sixth form 188 (27%)
- Education authority *Cumbria*

Headteacher Colin Peter Birnie, 55, appointed in January 1994. Staff 44 (men 22, women 22).

Motto Semper eadem (Ever the same).

Background Queen Elizabeth Grammar School was founded by royal charter in 1564; since January 1992 it has been grant-maintained and in September 1993 the first intake at 11 was admitted according to selective criteria. Formerly in the centre of Penrith, the school moved to new buildings in 1915. It was extended in 1937 and 1958; new building for technology and information technology opened in 1995; additional classrooms and laboratories are in temporary buildings and the sixth form is accommodated in a neighbouring annexe; extensive playing fields adjacent to school, which serves large catchment area that extends 400 square miles and includes eastern Lake District. Over-subscribed, with 1.8 applications per place. Academic strengths evenly spread across curriculum. Drama and music are popular; orchestra has 40 players, drama productions have won county trophy twice in past five years. In sport, one boy is under 17/18 national champion in biathlon, triathlon and tetrathlon; two boys have played rugby for national sides.

Streaming Setting of pupils introduced in year 9.

Approach to discipline Indiscipline 'not a problem'. Self-discipline prevails; clear policy statement on what is expected and on 'unsocial behaviour', with list of sanctions. 'Pupils are in no doubt of their responsibilities. Close cooperation with parents is encouraged.'

Uniform Boys: black blazer, grey trousers, white shirt, tie. Girls: grey skirt/black trousers, grey jumper, white blouse. Sixth-form dress code emphasises respectability rather than uniformity. Regulations enforced 'as much as necessary, but with tact and sympathy'.

Homework Average 11-year-old, three hours a week; 14-year-old, four hours; 16-year-old, five to eight hours.

Vocational qualifications RSA, Computer Literacy and Information Technology in sixth form.

Inspection March 1996: 'Queen Elizabeth Grammar School provides a very good education for its pupils with some outstanding features. There is a very purposeful atmosphere in the school in which staff and pupils work hard to maximise achievement. The school enjoys the support and confidence of its parents.'; 'Standards in history, geography and physical education are consistently above national expectations, but in all subjects many pupils achieve standards which are above average for their ages.'; 'A very high proportion of teaching and learning is of high quality. Staff are hardworking, committed and well-qualified.'; 'Resources to support teaching and learning are often good, although in a few subjects materials are getting old. The library is well-stocked for English and for GCSE and A-level history, but for most other subjects its stock is insufficient to meet the needs of the National Curriculum and A-level courses. The recently-opened technology block is an asset to the school and is already helping to raise standards.'

Primary schools Beaconside CE Primary; Stainton CE Primary; Langwathby CE Primary; Penruddock Primary; Plumpton Primary. Total of 25 feeder schools in 400-square-mile catchment area.

THE CARDINAL VAUGHAN MEMORIAL SCHOOL

89 Addison Road
Kensington
London W14 8BZ
Tel (0171) 603 8478
Fax (0171) 602 3124

- National ranking 170 (247, –, 238, 214)
- GCSE 84% (67%)
- A-levels 53% (A/B); 98% (A/E)
- Higher education 90% (Oxford 4, Cambridge 1)

- Grant-maintained
- Boys' comprehensive
- Pupils 711
- Boys (11–18) 636
- Girls (16–18) 75
- Sixth form 173 (24%)
- Education authority *Kensington and Chelsea*

Headteacher Michael Anthony Gormally, 40, appointed from September 1997. Staff 50 (men 33, women 17).

Motto Amare et servire (To love and to serve).

Background Unique among Roman Catholic schools as national memorial to Herbert Vaughan, third Archbishop of Westminster. Started as private school in 1914; in 1944 became voluntary-aided grammar school; became comprehensive in 1977 and began to recruit girls into sixth form in 1980; grant-maintained since April 1990. Occupies pleasant site in leafy neighbourhood near Holland Park; original school existed in elegant Victorian terracotta building which now houses the Upper School. Pupils chiefly, but not exclusively, from inner London. One of first Catholic schools to appoint layman as headteacher, in 1976. School is 'absolutely unambiguous' in commitment to apostolic role of Catholic church; pupils encouraged to go on retreats and days of recollection. While holding excellence in esteem, it also caters for less able pupils. Over-subscribed, with 2.5 applications per place. One in 10 places for 11-year-olds are for pupils of marked musical aptitude; two orchestras, various ensembles, three choirs, with one travelling widely abroad; Vaughan Centre for young Musicians meets every Friday after school, for musical children aged seven to 11. 'The school also values the study of languages. Besides Latin and Greek, the most able linguists may study up to three modern languages.' New building for art, music, and design and technology; all laboratories refurbished in 1991; 'magnificent library and superbly-equipped common rooms for staff and sixth form'. Playing fields in Twickenham, where Rugby Football Union has built magnificent pavilion for the school. Wide range of sports, including fencing; soccer is main sport, but two former pupils have recently won Olympic gold medals in rowing. New three-storey building under construction to increase intake of pupils.

Alumni Bernard Joy, Arsenal and England footballer; Richard Greene, actor; Baron St John of Fawsley, Conservative politician; Martin Cross and Garry Herbert, Olympic rowing gold-medallists; Sir Allan Davies, Lord Mayor of London, 1985–86; Flying Officer D.E. Garland, first member of RAF to win Victoria Cross in World War II; Bishop Philip Harvey and Bishop Gerald Mahon, former RC Bishop in Archdiocese of Westminster; John Hilary Smith, Praelector of University College, Oxford, and former governor of Gilbert & Ellis Islands.

Streaming Pupils divided into sets in all subjects.

Approach to discipline 'The Vaughan is particularly concerned with civilised standards of behaviour, on the way to and from school as well as in school. Its discipline is strict, even old-fashioned, but not repressive.' Sanctions range from detentions, attendance on Saturdays, an exclusion room, and exclusion from the school. 'The school believes in praise and encouragement as indispensable to motivation.'

Uniform Black blazer with badge, black trousers, white shirt, school tie, grey V-neck pullover, grey/black socks, school scarf (optional). School bag compulsory in first three years; years 10 and 11 can bring other bags which must be plain dark-blue/black/ grey without inscriptions other than maker's name. Sixth-formers expected to wear distinctive grey suit, white shirt and school tie (for boys) or maroon blazer, cream blouse and grey skirt (for girls).

Homework Average 11-year-old, at least seven hours 30 minutes a week; 14-year-old, at least 10 hours; 16-year-old, at least 15 hours.

Vocational qualifications BTEC National, Business and Finance; GNVQ Intermediate, Business.

Inspection Summer 1997.

Primary schools St Charles RC Primary; St Francis of Assisi RC Primary; Sacred Heart of Brook Green RC Primary; Mount Carmel RC Primary; St Mary RC Primary.

SEXEY'S SCHOOL

Cole Road
Bruton
Somerset BA10 0DF
Tel (01749) 813393/812236
Fax (01749) 812870
E-mail: sexeys@mail.zynet.co.uk
Internet: http://www.zynet.co.uk/sexeys

- National ranking 171 (78, 172, 169, 151)
- GCSE 84% (98%)
- A-levels 32% (A/B); 95% (A/E)
- Higher education 91% (Oxford 2, Cambridge 1)

- Grant-maintained
- Mixed comprehensive
- Pupils 407
- Boys (11–18) 222
- Girls (11–18) 185
- Sixth form 199 (49%)
- Education authority Somerset

Headteacher Stephen Gerald Burgoyne, 49, appointed in January 1996. Staff 37 (men 18, women 19).

Motto None

Background Takes its name from Hugh Sexey, auditor to Queen Elizabeth I and James I, who set up a foundation in Bruton in 1638; current school, in rural setting overlooking valley of River Brue, celebrated centenary in 1991. Formerly a boys' grammar, now mixed school where all pupils up to 16 are boarders; an 'open' sixth form. Anglican foundation but all faiths (and those with none) are welcomed. Core of Victorian buildings with additions: purpose-built classrooms, new laboratories and art complex, sports hall, indoor swimming pool. Over-subscribed, with about 60 applications for 40 boarding places. International links with France, Germany, Russia and Australia; one of first schools to have full exchange with Russia. Clubs and societies: fell-walking, canoeing, computing, astronomy. Duke of Edinburgh Award Scheme. Regular and frequent assessment; pioneers of 'value added' statistics to measure pupils' progress. 'Sexey's School has boarding without snobbery, academic success without elitism, and manners without moulding.'

Alumni Ned Sherrin, broadcaster and journalist; Hubert Phillips, author; Harold Scott, former Metropolitan Police commissioner; John Bryant, deputy editor of *The Times*.

Streaming Pupils in sets for some subjects in year 8; setting in years 9 to 11.

Approach to discipline 'Clearly-defined and agreed set of rules and expectations. Pupils develop within a secure and caring framework, knowing that they will be dealt with fairly and appropriately.'

Uniform Black blazer with crest, grey trousers/maroon skirt, white shirt and tie. Sixth-formers have choice within agreed guidelines.

Homework Average 11-year-old, six to seven hours a week; 14-year-old, 10 hours; 16-year-old, 11 to 12 hours.

Vocational qualifications RSA, Word-processing.

Inspection October 1996: 'A good school which gives a very effective education to its pupils. Achievements are high at GCSE and are satisfactory and improving at A-level. Standards of behaviour and courtesy are very high: pupils are a credit to themselves and their school. Boarding contributes well to the social development of pupils. Most accommodation is satisfactory and some is good; however, the provision for music, the library and study space for sixth-formers is inadequate.'; 'Teachers mostly have very good knowledge of their subjects and plan work effectively. Their skills in class management are very good.'

STRETFORD GRAMMAR SCHOOL

Edge Lane
Stretford
Manchester M32 8JB
Tel (0161) 865 2293
Fax (0161) 866 9938

- National ranking 172 (165, 137, 105, 209)
- GCSE 84% (85%)
- A-levels 29% (A/B); 84% (A/E)
- Higher education 80% (Cambridge 1)

- Mixed grammar
- Pupils 642
- Boys (11–18) 307
- Girls (11–18) 335
- Sixth form 130 (20%)
- Education authority *Trafford*

Headteacher Philippa Revill, 63, appointed in September 1971. Staff 39 (men 18, women 21).

Motto *None*

Background Formed in 1986 when girls' and boys' grammar schools amalgamated; in extensive grounds in residential area of Trafford; well-located for ease of access from many parts of Greater Manchester and Cheshire; many pupils from outside Stretford and borough of Trafford. Over-subscribed, with four applications per place. New purpose-built block for technology, art and design, modern languages, and sixth-form common room. Set in 18 acres of playing fields with pitches and courts for hockey, rugby, soccer, cricket, netball, tennis and athletics; specialist coaching for golf, lacrosse, rugby, soccer and cricket; area, county and national representatives. Strong links with industry; sixth-form industry education; winners of Trafford prize for best preparation for work-experience.

Alumni Professor Arnold Wolfendale, the Astronomer Royal and professor of physics at Durham University; Ian McShane, actor; Tony Lloyd, Labour MP for Stretford; John Tomlinson, professor of education at Warwick University; Ernest Marples, former transport minister; Kay Adshead, actress and writer; Paula Cohen, athlete; Debbie Moore, of Pineapple Dance Studios; June Ritchie, actress; Brenda Dean, former deputy general secretary of Graphical, Paper and Media Union.

Streaming In mathematics, French and English from year 8.

Approach to discipline Pupils required to behave in polite, friendly and considerate manner. 'The school will not accept any form of intolerant behaviour on grounds of gender, race or disability. Where it is felt necessary to go beyond counselling and verbal reproof there is a range of sanctions that are strictly enforced.'

Uniform Black with red trim and school badge. Firmly enforced.

Homework Average 11-year-old, eight hours a week; 14-year-old, 10 hours; 16-year-old, 13 hours.

Vocational qualifications None

Primary schools Moss Park Junior; Seymour Park Primary; Chorlton-cum-Hardy CE Primary; Oswald Road Primary; Gorse Hill Primary. Total of 52 other feeder schools.

ARDEN SCHOOL

Station Road
Knowle
Solihull
West Midlands B93 0PT
Tel (01564) 773348
Fax (01564) 771784

- National ranking 173 (183, 167)
- GCSE 83% (77%)
- A-levels *Not applicable*
- Higher education *Not applicable*

- Mixed comprehensive
- Pupils 1,059
- Boys (11–16) 521
- Girls (11–16) 538
- Sixth form *Not applicable*
- Education authority *Solihull*

Headteacher David Chamberlain, 51, appointed in January 1988. Staff 60 (men 25, women 35).

Motto None

Background About 30 years old, set in 'beautiful' catchment area of privately-owned houses in leafy lanes on the edge of countryside. Extensive playing fields and 'excellent' facilities, including new gymnasium to complement sports hall. 'A lovely place to live, work and play.' Substantially over-subscribed, with 240 applications for 200 places. All-round curriculum and sporting strengths. 'Our facilities are very good, but our real assets are our people.' Chess team regularly reaches last stages of national finals.

Streaming None

Approach to discipline 'Firm but fair. We encourage pupils to take responsibility for their behaviour and appreciate the importance of self-discipline.'

Uniform Green blazer, tie, white shirt, grey trousers/skirt, black socks for boys/white or black socks for girls, black leather shoes, black coat, school scarf. 'No pupil is tolerated without the uniform.'

Homework Average 11-year-old, eight hours a week; 14-year-old, 10 hours; 16-year-old, 12 to 15 hours.

Vocational qualifications Diploma of Vocational Education; City and Guilds.

Inspection November 1993: 'Arden is a very good school with some outstanding features.'; 'Staff are well-qualified and highly-committed. Teaching is competent and sound. Praise and encouragement are used frequently with pupils to promote high expectations of work and behaviour. Pupils respond enthusiastically to these high expectations; they are well-motivated and relationships are excellent. Pupils feel happy and privileged to belong to the school. Attendance is good and punctuality excellent.'

Primary schools Dorridge Primary; Bentley Heath Primary; Knowle Primary.

WATFORD GRAMMAR SCHOOL FOR BOYS

Rickmansworth Road
Watford
Hertfordshire WD1 7JF
Tel (01923) 224950
Fax (01923) 256131
E-mail: wbgs@rmplc.co.uk

- National ranking 174 (163, 184, 168, 162)
- GCSE 82% (86%)
- A-levels 53% (A/B); 97% (A/E)
- Higher education 90% (Oxford 4, Cambridge 4)

- Grant-maintained

- Boys' comprehensive
- Pupils 1,118
- Boys (11–18) 1,118
- Girls *Not applicable*
- Sixth form 308 (28%)
- Education authority *Hertfordshire*

Headteacher John Holman, 50, appointed in September 1994. Staff 66 (men 52, women 14).

Motto Sperate parati (Hope – being well-prepared).

Background Founded by Dame Elizabeth Fuller in 1703; the old Free School building remains, next to St Mary's Parish Church. In 1884 the school was split into separate boys' and girls' schools. The boys' school moved to its current site in 1912; original building Grade 2 listed building. Later additions: science block, technology block, sports hall, theatre and canteen. Adjoining playing fields include two cricket squares and hockey pitch; the 'new field' is half a mile away, mainly for rugby but also has one cricket square. Over-subscribed, with four applications per place. School theatre helps drama remain a strength, as is music: 15 different groups, orchestras, bands and choirs. Rugby, hockey and cricket among sporting achievements; most fixtures against independent schools. Finalists in national hockey championships. Traditional 'grammar school' ethos and achievements, even though mixed-ability intake.

Alumni Andrew Davis, conductor; Terry Scott, comedian; Rt Rev John Taylor, Bishop of St Albans; Michael Rosen, poet.

Streaming Pupils in sets in mathematics from halfway through year 7; in French and German from year 8; and in English and science from year 10.

Approach to discipline 'Firm but friendly and caring disciplinary structure.'

Uniform Black blazer, dark-grey trousers, white shirt, school tie. Jackets, shirt and tie in sixth form. No jeans. Regulations enforced 'to the letter'.

Homework Average 11-year-old, five to six hours a week; 14-year-old, at least eight hours; 16-year-old, eight to 10 hours.

Vocational qualifications *None*

Inspection May 1996: 'Watford Grammar School for Boys promotes effective learning and high standards of achievement. In this very good school, high standards are achieved across the curriculum and are only rarely below average.'; 'The school is an orderly and civilised community with high standards of behaviour. There is a positive learning culture within which high achievement is valued. Pupils are skilled and enthusiastic learners who come to lessons prepared and eager to work, and make rapid progress.'; 'The ethos and direction of the school strongly promote high expectations, hard work and intellectual rigour, which support high attainment.'

Primary schools Cassiobury Junior; Eastbury Farm Primary; Nascot Wood Junior; Rickmansworth Park Primary; Little Green Primary; St Mary's Primary. Total of 162 boys from 57 schools.

HASMONEAN HIGH SCHOOL

Holders Hill Crescent	2-4 Page Street
London NW4 1NA	London NW7 2EU

Tel (0181) 203 1411/4294
Fax (0181) 202 4526/4527

- National ranking 175 (179, 163, 166, 152)
- GCSE 82% (78%)
- A-levels 51% (A/B); 94% (A/E)
- Higher education 98% (Cambridge 3)

- Grant-maintained
- Mixed comprehensive
- Pupils 953
- Boys (11–18) 490
- Girls (11–18) 463
- Sixth form 206 (22%)
- Education authority *Barnet*

Headteacher Dr Dena Coleman, 44, appointed in September 1993. Staff 58 (men 27, women 31).

Motto Torah im derech eretz (Hebrew quotation from 'Ethics': Religion and the world is one).

Background Established in 1944 as part of the Jewish Secondary Schools movement; boys and girls taught separately on sites 1.5 miles apart. Boys' school granted voluntary-aided status in 1959; girls' school remained independent until 1984, when the two schools amalgamated. Became grant-maintained in 1994. In Hendon, near M1. Girls' site modern and purpose-built. Boys' site newly-rebuilt: facilities for science, technology, information technology, art, music, business studies, modern languages, English and mathematics; also library and hall. Over-subscribed, with 1.5 applications per place. Duke of Edinburgh Award Scheme; annual winners of chess awards; regular finalists in mathematics Olympiad and chemistry competitions. Aim is 'thoroughly sound Jewish and general education'.

Alumni Edward Mirzoeff, television producer and royal documentary maker (producer and director of BBC's *Elizabeth R*).

Streaming Pupils in sets in mathematics, modern languages, religious studies and sciences.

Approach to discipline Traditional. 'School rules are such that all pupils can understand them fully. Parents and pupils co-operate.'

Uniform Boys: black blazer, grey trousers, grey jumper, white shirt, school tie. Girls: grey skirt, grey-and-white striped blouse, grey jumper. Regulations enforced strictly: pupils sent home if they persistently neglect them. Rarely necessary.

Homework Average 11-year-old, seven hours 30 minutes a week; 14-year-old, 10 hours; 16-year-old, 12 hours.

Vocational qualifications GNVQ.

Inspection November 1994: 'The school provides a demanding and rigorous education for its pupils.'; 'Pupils are articulate and expressive, and develop ideas through discussion. They apply sound numeracy skills in several curriculum areas, but their skills of problem-solving, investigation and the application of information technology are less well developed.'; 'Teachers' subject expertise is strong and most have high expectations of pupils' achievement, and plan and prepare for lessons carefully. Some teachers and pupils have a casual attitude to the beginning and end of lessons'; 'Leadership at senior level is good and provides a firm direction for the future.'

Primary schools Menorah Primary; Menorah Foundation; Hasmonean Primary; Rosh Pinah Primary; Independent Jewish Day School.

RANELAGH SCHOOL

Ranelagh Drive
Bracknell
Berkshire RG12 3DA

Tel **(01344) 421233**
Fax **(01344) 301811**
E-mail: **er71@dial.pipex.com**

- National ranking 176 (169, 174, 174, 168)
- GCSE 82% (83%)
- A-levels 36% (A/B); 89% (A/E)
- Higher education 90% (Oxford 6, Cambridge 2)

- Mixed comprehensive
- Pupils 821
- Boys (11–18) 373
- Girls (11–18) 448
- Sixth form 183 (22%)
- Education authority *Berkshire*

Headteacher Kathryn M. Winrow, 46, appointed in April 1993. Staff 51 (men 19, women 32).

Motto Coelitus mihi vires (From heaven my strength).

Background Founded in 1709 by Lord Ranelagh at Cranbourne, the school moved to its current site, in a secluded six acres close to the centre of Bracknell, in 1908 and has been a voluntary-aided Church of England school in the Diocese of Oxford since 1953. It was a two-form entry mixed grammar school until 1981 when it became a four-form all-ability comprehensive with a catchment area in the deaneries of Bracknell and Sonning. School over-subscribed and operates waiting list: 1.5 applications per place. Although the original building dates from 1908, substantial additions were made in 1980; first phase of a new building open in 1997. Among its strengths are drama, dance, performing arts and music (choral works, senior choir, chamber choir and senior orchestra). Latin taught from year 9. 'The school aims to provide a supportive, stimulating and secure environment where high standards of learning and personal responsibility are expected and achieved, and where every member of the school community is respected and valued.'

Alumni Sheila Browne, former HMI senior chief inspector and principal of Newnham College, Cambridge.

Streaming Pupils set according to ability in languages and mathematics from year 8, and in science and English from year 9.

Approach to discipline 'Firm but sensitive. A

strong supportive ethos has been established within the school and this is valued by students and parents.'

Uniform Boys: grey suits, blue-and-gold striped tie, blue jackets in sixth form. Girls: grey skirt and sweater, blue blouse with blue-gold tie in winter, blue-white check blouse in summer. Strictly enforced (uniform available from one outfitter).

Homework Average 11-year-old, six hours 15 minutes a week; 14-year-old, eight hours; 16-year-old, eight hours.

Vocational qualifications GNVQ.

Inspection Spring 1995.

Primary schools Pupils drawn from more than 40 schools.

ST ANDREW'S SCHOOL

Warrington Road
Croydon
Surrey CR0 4BJ
Tel (0181) 686 8306
Fax (0181) 681 6320

- National ranking 177 (191 = , 334 = , 279 = , 260 =)
- GCSE 81% (75%)
- A-levels *Not applicable*
- Higher education *Not applicable*

- Mixed comprehensive
- Pupils 400
- Boys (11–16) 196
- Girls (11–16) 204
- Sixth form *Not applicable*
- Education authority *Croydon*

Headteacher John A. Coatman, appointed in January 1985. Staff 22 (men 10, women 12).

Motto Per crucem ad coronam (Through the cross to the crown).

Background Established by St Andrew's Church in 1857; in 1964, moved to current site on a hill to west of town centre surrounded by parkland and residential areas; playing fields on site. Most recent developments: two new laboratories, art room, music centre with four practice rooms; also new art rotunda. Joint sixth form established in 1978 with Archbishop Tenison's School. Voluntary-aided Church of England school; over-subscribed by three to one of those with church affiliation.

Streaming Years 7 and 8: the two intake forms divided into three mixed-ability groups except technologies, taught in four groups, and mathematics, taught in three ability groups. Year 9: ability groups for mathematics and modern languages.

Approach to discipline Great reliance on traditional standards of behaviour and discipline. 'The development of good citizenship, combined with a sound moral code based on Christian principles, is one of the primary aims of the school.'

Uniform Black-and-grey uniform with school tie for both boys and girls. Strictly enforced.

Homework Average 11-year-old, five hours a week; 14-year-old, seven hours 30 minutes; 16-year-old, 10 hours.

Vocational qualifications *Under review*

Inspection March 1994: 'The school provides a good education for its pupils. They show good levels of achievement, particularly in GCSE examinations, although the proportion of grade As varies from subject to subject in comparison with national averages. Girls achieve noticeably better than boys in examinations.'; 'Pupils are given opportunities to take responsibility and they respond positively, exhibiting maturity and good behaviour. Space is cramped, but good use is made of what is available, although the lack of a library is having an effect on pupils' learning.'; 'The pupils' social attitudes and approaches to issues of morality are good throughout the school.'

Primary schools Pupils drawn from about 50 schools.

BISHOP LUFFA SCHOOL

Bishop Luffa Close
Chichester
West Sussex PO19 3LT
Tel (01243) 787741
Fax (01243) 531807

- National ranking 178 (185, 189, 194, 188)
- GCSE 79% (76%)
- A-levels 48% (A/B); 95% (A/E)
- Higher education 84% (Oxford 5, Cambridge 1)

- Mixed comprehensive
- Pupils 1,289
- Boys (11–18) 641

- Girls (11–18) 648
- Sixth form 244 (19%)
- Education authority *West Sussex*

Headteacher John Basil Ashwin, 59, appointed in September 1981. Staff 77 (men 41, women 36).

Motto Nothing but the best; everyone matters.

Background Opened in 1963 as two-form entry secondary modern church school; expanded with substantial building programme in 1969; in 1971, with more building, it became a six-form entry Church of England comprehensive to the west of Chichester. Buildings divided into subject blocks: large design and technology area, seven laboratories with three prep rooms; new technology centre opened in 1990; re-equipped business studies room; gymnasium, multi-gym. Sports hall in autumn 1995; two new classrooms and two new laboratories in autumn 1996. Hours are from 8am until 2.30pm. Voluntary-aided; over-subscribed, with 307 applicants for 210 places. Pupils also drawn from Bognor, Felpham, Lavant, Southbourne, Selsey, the Witterings, and Yapton. Eight-house house system. School boasts better A-level results than two of the county's three sixth-form colleges. Music and drama among strengths; community service. Duke of Edinburgh Award Scheme. Parents' and Friends' Association.

Streaming Mixed-ability house groups. Pupils in sets for mathematics and languages from year 8; in all subjects for GCSE classes.

Approach to discipline Clear rules; strong parental support; range of sanctions from house detention (30 minutes) to school detention (one hour), to up to 10 days' exclusion for serious offences. Permanent exclusion possible. Usual approach is to see parents before problems develop. Firm but fair.

Uniform Maroon-and-gold blazer, white or grey shirt/gold blouse, grey trousers/medium-grey skirt, school tie (optional for girls). All pupils wear uniform, except sixth-formers.

Homework Average 11-year-old, five to six hours a week; 14-year-old, 10 to 12 hours; 16-year-old, 15 to 20 hours.

Vocational qualifications GNVQs.

Inspection March 1996: 'The quality of teaching and learning is frequently good in both key stages and in the sixth form. Pupils' attitudes to learning are a particular strength. Their commitment to work, both in class and at home, is a key factor in their achievement. Pupils at all stages benefit from the specialist knowledge of their teachers. Teachers have appropriately high expectations of pupils and students, and many are skilled in matching work to their different needs and abilities.'; 'The purposeful leadership of the headteacher and senior and middle managers sets high expectations and pursues continuing improvements'.

Primary schools Central CE Junior; Southbourne County Junior; Jessie Younghusband Primary; St James CE Primary, Emsworth; Fishbourne CE Primary.

HARROGATE GRAMMAR SCHOOL

Arthurs Avenue
Harrogate
North Yorkshire HG2 0DZ
Tel (01423) 531127
Fax (01423) 521325
E-mail: harrogag@rmplc.co.uk

- National ranking 179 (174, 166, 167, 180)
- GCSE 79% (82%)
- A-levels 41% (A/B); 91% (A/E)
- Higher education 85% (Oxford 4, Cambridge 9)

- Mixed comprehensive
- Pupils 1,614
- Boys (11–18) 803
- Girls (11–18) 811
- Sixth form 390 (24%)
- Education authority *North Yorkshire*

Headteacher Kevin McAleese, 50, appointed in January 1992. Staff 97 (men 53, women 44).

Motto Arx celebris fontibus (Town with the celebrated water).

Background The school, founded in 1903, moved to its current 13-acre site south of Harrogate, close to the Stray, as a grammar school in 1933. It expanded as a comprehensive in 1973, since when its buildings and quadrangles have been supplemented by a sports hall, gymnasium, music centre and sixth-form centres (a second was opened in

1992). Over-subscribed, with 1.5 first-choice applications per place. Emphasis on modern languages; sciences taught separately; strong debating and public-speaking record; winner of 1994 Observer Silver Mace. More than one in five pupils play musical instruments; gold-medallists for concert bands at 1996 National Festival of Music for Youth. Weekly fixtures for hockey, netball and rugby teams; other sports include athletics, cricket and tennis. Duke of Edinburgh Award Scheme; five Gold Awards in 1995.

Streaming Mixed-ability in intake year. Banded by ability in year 8, followed by a review at end of year 9 and subject-setting in years 10 and 11.

Approach to discipline School code of conduct emphasises importance of good behaviour, care, consideration and courtesy. 'Staff maintain high expectations and place great emphasis on the positive: for example, letters of commendation to parents for good work or effort.' Sanctions include detentions and pupils being put 'on report'. Exclusions are rare.

Uniform Blazer, school tie, grey trousers/skirt for years 7 to 9. Black senior school jumper makes blazers optional in years 10 and 11. Dress code but no uniform in sixth form. Jeans banned and smart appearance required.

Homework Average 11-year-old, five hours a week; 14-year-old, eight hours; 16-year-old, 10 to 11 hours.

Vocational qualifications GNVQ Level 3, Business and Finance.

Inspection October 1994: 'This is an excellent comprehensive school which provides a high quality of education.'; 'There is a high degree of concern for the spiritual, moral, social and cultural development of the pupils.'; 'The staff is well-qualified and highly-committed.'; 'Pupils display high levels of motivation and positive attitudes to learning. The majority of pupils are highly articulate and demonstrate above average levels of reading ability. These abilities are not always fully exploited in class.'; 'The school operates a well-ordered community in which pupils' behaviour is of a consistently high standard.'

Primary schools Oatlands Primary; Pannal Primary; Rossett Acre Primary; St Peter's CE Primary; Western County Primary. Total of 45 feeder schools.

BENNETT MEMORIAL DIOCESAN SCHOOL

Culverden Down
Tunbridge Wells
Kent TN4 9SH
Tel (01892) 521595
Fax (01892) 514424

- National ranking 180 (227, 238, 173, 215)
- GCSE 79% (70%)
- A-levels 34% (A/B); 86% (A/E)
- Higher education 70%

- Grant-maintained
- Mixed comprehensive
- Pupils 1,119
- Boys (11–18) 320
- Girls (11–18) 799
- Sixth form 232 (21%)
- Education authority Kent

Headteacher Rev John Caperon, 52, appointed in September 1992. Staff 71 (men 28, women 43).

Motto Semper tenax (Ever bold).

Background One of the few genuine comprehensives in Kent. Founded by Lady Elena Bennett in memory of Sir Thomas Bennett, her husband, and opened as Church of England secondary school for girls in 1953. Became comprehensive in 1976, with catchment area widened to include much of Diocese of Rochester as well as parts of Diocese of Chichester. Boys admitted since September 1993, increasing admission limit from 150 to 180. Over-subscribed, with average of 1.7 applications per place. Substantial recent building programme. Early 20th-century Mansion Block houses administrative and sixth-form areas; surrounded by 1970s accommodation on 40-acre site bordered by woodland. 'The completion of new buildings, and the recent refurbishment of part of the Mansion Block has left school adequately and attractively housed.' Distinctive emphasis on religious education as core subject up to year 11. Pupils organised into six Guilds or houses. Christian ethos.

Streaming Pupils in sets for English and mathematics in year 7; setting in other subjects from year 8.

Approach to discipline 'We encourage high

standards of personal behaviour, and emphasise the shared role of school and parents if there are individual problems. We aim for a well-disciplined and purposeful atmosphere based on mutual respect.'

Uniform Bottle-green jumper/sweatshirt, mid-grey trousers/skirt. Dress code for sixth-formers. Strictly enforced, with parental support.

Homework Average 11-year-old, six hours a week; 14-year-old, 10 hours; 16-year-old, 12 hours.

Vocational qualifications GNVQ Intermediate and Advanced, Health and Social Care; Pitman, Typing, Keyboarding, Word-processing.

Primary schools Draws pupils from between 60 and 80 schools in Kent and Sussex. Numbers vary according to the effect of religious criteria for admissions.

HAYBRIDGE HIGH SCHOOL

Brake Lane
Hagley
Worcestershire DY8 2XS
Tel (01562) 886213
Fax (01562) 887002

- National ranking 181 (237, 168, 171, 212)
- GCSE 78% (69%)
- A-levels 46% (A/B); 97% (A/E)
- Higher education 90% (Oxford 5)

- Mixed comprehensive
- Pupils 692
- Boys (13–18) 347
- Girls (13–18) 345
- Sixth form 239 (34%)
- Education authority *Hereford and Worcester*

Headteacher Melvyn James Kershaw, 49, appointed in September 1988. Staff 45 (men 19, women 26).

Motto *None*

Background The school was purpose-built in 1976 as a result of parental pressure for a school to serve the local area of Hagley, Belbroughton, Romsley and Clent. Set on spacious campus below Clent Hills in village of Hagley. Substantial building programme in progress: new sports hall and modern foreign languages suite. Average of

1.1 applications per place. Music and drama among strong points: one in seven pupils in school orchestra, which in past four years has toured France, Austria, Venice and Norway; also chamber orchestra, swing bands, choirs and brass. Sixth-formers receive management and leadership training before helping younger pupils in personal tutoring, organising clubs and societies. Week-long work-experience in Caen, Normandy, for sixth-formers. Strong in boys' and girls' team sports; Duke of Edinburgh Award Scheme. Successful Parents' Association.

Streaming Mathematics set from year 9. Otherwise, two broad bands in year 9; within subject sets in years 10 and 11.

Approach to discipline 'Praise, encouragement and respect within a clear and firm code of conduct and an expectation of high standards engenders a purposeful and hardworking attitude and the development of self-discipline.'

Uniform Years 9 to 11: honey-gold shirt/blouse, brown skirt/trousers, sweater, brown-and-gold tie. Years 12 and 13: sensible dress. No denims. Regulations enforced 'fully'.

Homework Average 14-year-old, eight hours a week; 16-year-old, 12 hours.

Vocational qualifications GNVQ, Health and Care, Business Studies, Science.

Inspection April 1996: 'An outstanding school which achieves very high standards of teaching and learning for its pupils.'; 'Links with parents, a strong pastoral system, very good provision for special educational needs, very good teaching, a wide range of extra-curricular activities, and a well-developed involvement with industry combine to produce a well-ordered school which provides an excellent all-round education at reasonable cost'.; 'The quality of teaching and learning is very high. Teachers are well-qualified and knowledgeable subject specialists; lessons are very well organised and conducted at a suitable pace.'

Primary schools Hagley Middle; Comberton Middle.

KING DAVID HIGH SCHOOL

Childwall Road
Childwall
Liverpool L15 6UZ

Tel (0151) 722 7496
Fax (0151) 738 0259

- National ranking 182 (231, 210, 172, 165)
- GCSE 78% (69%)
- A-levels 42% (A/B); 93% (A/E)
- Higher education 95% (Oxford 1)

- Mixed comprehensive
- Pupils 565
- Boys (11–18) 265
- Girls (11–18) 300
- Sixth form 113 (20%)
- Education authority *Liverpool*

Headteacher John Smartt, appointed in April 1994. Staff 39 (men 19, women 20).

Motto Let there be light by faith and work.

Background Built in 1957, a two-storey building in residential suburb in south of the city with its own attached playing fields. Indoor swimming pool, recently-built sixth-form centre and music and drama suites; newly-refurbished science laboratories and technology room. Over-subscribed, with three applications per place. Proud of regional reputation for music and 'distinguished' record in drama. 'The school provides a stimulating and enriching Jewish and secular education for all Jewish children in the city of Liverpool and its environs, and provides an education of similar quality and relevance to non-Jewish pupils admitted to the school. It demonstrates the finest standards of multicultural education by cultivating the distinctive qualities of the cultures within the school rather than by blurring their distinctions.'

Alumni Simon Fischel, scientific director of Reproduction Research Unit, Nottingham University; Malandra Burrows, actress.

Streaming Initially only in English and mathematics. Setting in years 10 and 11.

Approach to discipline 'Caring and formative through a recognition of their responsibilities towards the community to which they belong.'

Uniform White polo shirt with school crest, navy sweatshirt with crest, mid-grey trousers/skirt, black shoes. Very strictly enforced.

Homework Average 11-year-old, three hours a week; 14-year-old, five hours; 16-year-old, seven hours 30 minutes.

Vocational qualifications GNVQ Level 3, Business and Finance.

Inspection February 1996: 'King David High School is a popular school, well-supported by parents and governors, which gains good examinations results and provides an effective education for its pupils. It is a harmonious school and has developed a strong ethos which successfully takes full account of the cultures it represents.'; 'Written, speaking, listening and numeracy skills are well developed. Learning is particularly impressive in modern Hebrew and history and aesthetic achievements in music, art and drama. Less well developed at present are investigative and independent learning skills, and creative and expressive skills through drama and dance in the curriculum.'

Primary schools King David Primary (provides two-thirds of year 7 intake; remaining 30 places filled by pupils from more than 20 other feeder schools).

ST AUGUSTINE'S

Wingfield Road
Trowbridge
Wiltshire BA14 9EN
Tel (01225) 350001
Fax (01225) 350002
E-mail: staugschl@aol.com

- National ranking 183 (195=)
- GCSE 78% (74%)
- A-levels *Not yet applicable*
- Higher education *Not yet applicable*

- Grant-maintained
- Mixed comprehensive
- Pupils 691
- Boys (11–16) 335
- Girls (13–18) 356
- Sixth form *Not yet applicable*
- Education authority *Wiltshire*

Headteacher Robert Graham Cook, 47, appointed September 1987. Staff 45 (men 20, women 25).

Motto Striving for excellence

Background Established 30 years ago, providing Catholic education for all pupils in west Wiltshire and part of Somerset. Wiltshire's first grant-maintained school; sixth form from September 1996, with first A-level results in August 1998; more than £1 million spent on new buildings in last three years, including 'superb' technology facilities and new sixth-form block; newly-furbished science laboratories, new library, 'excellent' specialist accommodation and spacious grounds 'illustrate an environment for learning of the highest order'. Caring Christian environment. Over-subscribed, with two applications per place. 'The school stretches able pupils, supports those with learning difficulties, but is highly regarded for ensuring that students of average ability realise their potential. The school holds on to the best of the traditional, while also being regarded as a school at the forefront of educational thinking.'

Alumni Jilly Mack, actress and wife of actor Tom Selleck; Dr Tony Gardiner, medical practitioner and comedian (part of double act 'Struck off and Die').

Streaming Departmental autonomy. Streaming is rigid in mathematics, banding used in modern languages and English; mixed-ability in other curriculum areas.

Approach to discipline 'The school is uncompromising on the standards of discipline it expects from its pupils. The golden rule is that each student has only one opportunity to be educated at any given age and nobody has the right to disrupt this.' Parents notified immediately of any concerns, 'as they are of praiseworthy aspects'. Homework diaries used widely.

Uniform Years 7 to 11: maroon blazer with crest, short-sleeved crested school shirt/blouse, grey trousers for boys/official skirt for girls, black (non-fashion) shoes. Sixth-form: black jacket with designer crest, black pin-tuck trousers for boys/Douglas tweed skirt for girls, pin-stripe shirt/white blouse, crested tie for boys. Regulations enforced 'rigidly'.

Homework Average 11-year-old, five hours a week; 14-year-old, seven hours 30 minutes; 16-year-old, 12 hours.

Vocational qualifications *None*

Inspection May 1996: 'St Augustine's is an excellent school. Its mission statement is clear and unequivocal and the school sets high standards of behaviour, attendance, attainment and relationships. These targets are achieved. In a few years, St Augustine's has developed from an 11–16 school with modest achievements to one which has greatly raised the academic attainment of

its pupils, undertaken substantial building improvements and extensions, and has been given authority to start a sixth form which will be housed in a new block in September 1996.'; 'Pupils come from a very wide range of backgrounds, socially and economically.'; 'Teaching is predominantly good to very good and excellent on occasion. Teachers make considerable demands on pupils, but always on the understanding that there is help, support and guidance in the lesson so that those who find the work difficult are not left to struggle.'

Primary schools St John's RC Primary, Trowbridge; St Joseph's RC Primary, Devizes; St George's RC Primary, Warminster; St Louis RC Primary, Frome; St Patrick's RC Primary, Corsham.

ARCHBISHOP TENISON'S CHURCH OF ENGLAND HIGH SCHOOL

Selborne Road
Croydon
Surrey CR0 5JQ
Tel (0181) 688 4014
Fax (0181) 681 6336
Internet: http://www.rmplc.co.uk/eduweb/
sites/archten

- National ranking 184 (176, 345, 183, 157)
- GCSE 77% (81%)
- A-levels 46% (A/B); 94% (A/E)
- Higher education 70% (Oxford 2, Cambridge 1)

- Mixed comprehensive
- Pupils 531
- Boys (11–18) 227
- Girls (11–18) 304
- Sixth form 203 (38%)
- Education authority *Croydon*

Headteacher Richard T. Ford, 50, appointed in January 1988. Staff 34 (men 16, women 18).

Motto Tenaciter (Tenaciously).

Background Archbishop Thomas Tenison founded the school in 1714 for the education of poor boys and girls. Originally in centre of what is now Croydon's main shopping area and after latest of two moves in 1959, school in residential area of Park Hill, 15 minutes from East Croydon rail station. Enlarged by addition of sixth-form centre, art centre and recent design and technology centre. Became grammar school in 1952, then comprehensive from 1978. Up to three applications per place. School takes pride in exam success, particularly in English, history, art, religious studies, mathematics, French and geography. Senior girls' netball team in 1992 national finals. Music is strong, both instrumental and choral; nearly one in three (30%) pupils have instrumental lessons. Anglican voluntary-aided comprehensive with Christian ethos pervasive.

Streaming Pupils in sets in years 7 to 9 for mathematics, science, French and German; in years 10 and 11, mathematics, science and French.

Approach to discipline Orderliness, consideration for others, high standards of behaviour and courtesy expected. Parents involved at every stage. 'Parents are sent a copy of the school rules for them to sign on behalf of their children. Extra work, detention, and placing pupils "on report", when work and behaviour are monitored daily, are the principal sanctions.'

Uniform Boys: blue blazer with badge, grey trousers, blue V-neck pullover with school crest, white/grey shirt, house tie, black shoes. Girls: blue blazer, grey skirt/trousers, blue V-neck pullover with school crest, blue blouse, house tie, white/black socks, black/brown shoes. Sixth-formers expected to wear clothes 'appropriate for a place of work'. Regulations compulsory and strictly enforced.

Homework Average 11-year-old, five to seven hours a week; 14-year-old, 12 to 15 hours; 16-year-old, 16+ hours.

Vocational qualifications GNVQ, Business Studies.

Inspection March 1995: 'The quality of education provided by the school is good. Pupils enjoy their work and have good attitudes to learning; they are co-operative and diligent and make good progress. The opportunity to use learning skills varies across the curriculum, some weaknesses emerge when pupils have to work independently, solve problems or demonstrate their critical skills.'; 'Pupils' spiritual, moral, social and cultural development is good. The headteacher plays a key leadership role in promoting the spiritual life of the school.'

Primary schools Christ Church CE Primary; Coulsdon CE Primary; Parish Church CE Primary; St John's CE Primary; Park Hill Primary. Admission criteria based on family involvement in the life of the church; school serves the whole of the Archdeaconry of Croydon, covering Croydon, West Wickham and Sutton.

THE ECCLESBOURNE SCHOOL

Wirksworth Road
Duffield
Belper
Derbyshire DE56 4GS
Tel (01332) 840645
Fax (01332) 841871

- National ranking 185 (–, 175, 200, 222)
- GCSE 77%
- A-levels 45% (A/B); 91% (A/E)
- Higher education 96% (Oxford 5, Cambridge 2)

- Grant-maintained
- Mixed comprehensive
- Pupils 1,342
- Boys (11–18) 728
- Girls (11–18) 614
- Sixth form 271 (20%)
- Education authority *Derbyshire*

Headteacher Dr Robert Dupey, 56, appointed in 1976. Staff 69 (men 28, women 41).

Motto Integrity, tenacity, service.

Background Opened in 1957 as a two-form entry co-educational grammar; grew in popularity and size before becoming comprehensive in 1976 under current headteacher; in grounds of Duffield Hall in dormitory village of Duffield on the A6 four miles north of Derby. Over-subscribed, with 1.75 applications per place; buildings have previously failed to keep pace with increased size of school. Newly-built technology centre eased the problem after opening in September 1993; library extended in September 1994. County and national representatives in sport and music, described as 'very strong and successful'. Extra-curricular activities include writers' club, debating society, inter-house drama and spoken English. Well-staffed special needs department; 'unusually strong' religious studies department, well-established music tradition, growing drama department, and significant increases in information technology facilities; committed to Cognitive Acceleration through Science Education scheme developed by King's College, London. Links with France, Spain, Germany, Denmark and United States. Staff handbook: 'We owe it to our pupils to have high expectations of them and it is ultimately contemptuous of young people for us not to make demands on them.' Identified as 'outstandingly successful' in 1996 annual Ofsted report.

Alumni Dr Stefan Buczacki, of BBC Radio Four *Gardeners' Question Time*; Barrie Douce, 1993 BBC *Mastermind* runner-up.

Streaming Variety of setting and mixed ability in different subjects and years 'where not to do so would have a detrimental effect on pupil progress'.

Approach to discipline Rational and humane, balancing needs of individual and needs of the community. 'We have high expectations of behaviour and the sky must fall if these are seriously infringed. Minor misbehaviours incur "fines": major problems require a great deal of hard work to get at the root of the problem.'

Uniform Years 7 to 11: burgundy blazer, grey trousers/skirt. Sixth form: grey suits for boys and agreed range of dress for girls. Enforced 'strictly enough to avoid argument over interpretation'.

Homework Average 11-year-old, four hours a week; 14-year-old, five hours; 16-year-old, at least six hours (varies with coursework).

Vocational qualifications GNVQ Intermediate and Advanced, Business and Finance.

Inspection March 1995: 'Standards in the school are good overall.'; 'In English, standards are very high. Pupils can speak, write and read very well for their age. Examination results are considerably above the national average and most pupils are doing well for their ability.'; 'Pupils are exceptionally well-motivated. Learning skills are good and pupils work hard and with enthusiasm.'; 'Teachers have a good command of their subjects, prepare and plan well, and manage classes skilfully.'; 'The school is strongly led and very well managed.'

Primary schools Duffield Meadows Primary; William Gilbert Primary; Little Eaton Primary; Walter Evans CE Primary; Muggington CE Primary; Curzon CE Primary; Kirk Langley CE Primary.

GOFFS SCHOOL

Goffs Lane
Cheshunt
Hertfordshire EN7 5QW
Tel (01992) 627432
Fax (01992) 640891
E-mail: goffs_edu@msn.com

- National ranking 186 = (224, 332, 330, 237)
- GCSE 77% (70%)
- A-levels 34% (A/B); 88% (A/E)
- Higher education 85% (Oxford 1)

- Grant-maintained
- Mixed comprehensive
- Pupils 1,056
- Boys (11–18) 563
- Girls (11–18) 493
- Sixth form 256 (24%)
- Education authority *Hertfordshire*

Headteacher Dr John M. B. Versey, 50, appointed in September 1994. Staff 71 (men 33, women 38).

Motto Sola virtus invicta (Only strength of character prevails).

Background The school, in a suburban setting on the fringe of the green belt north of London, was founded in 1964 as a three-form entry co-educational grammar school. It became a five-form entry comprehensive between 1976 and 1978. Ample playing fields include artificial cricket pitches and an open-air swimming pool; there is also a sports hall, with fitness studio and gymnasium. Consistently over-subscribed, with two applications per place. The school has 14 visiting musical instrument teachers and many ensembles. Foreign languages emphasised: French, German and Spanish to A-level, Italian to GCSE; some pupils taught some subjects in French; exchanges with France, Belgium, Germany, Spain and Russia. Language College status. Strong house system and active parents' association. Sport, music and drama are 'flourishing'; many trips and visits both home and abroad, including sports tours.

Streaming Pupils are placed in sets for most subjects from year 7.

Approach to discipline Clear system of rewards and punishments: credits, merit marks leading to grade commendations and governors' commendations; weekly reports, prefects' detentions, departmental detentions, and school detentions.

Uniform Full dark-blue and grey uniform worn by years 7 to 11. Sixth-formers wear 'business dress'. Regulations enforced 'completely'.

Homework Average 11-year-old, eight hours a week; 14-year-old, 10 hours; 16-year-old, 15 hours.

Vocational qualifications GNVQ Levels 2 and 3, Business Studies module.

Inspection November 1993: 'The standards achieved by pupils are generally high . . . The proportion of pupils obtaining the highest grade at GCSE in some subjects, including core subjects, is, however, below the national averages.'; 'Standards of work in basic skills are good overall. Pupils make significant progress throughout the school in oral and written work. They develop good study skills and habits.'; 'The school is an orderly community, with high expectations from pupils who for the most part fulfil those expectations.'

Primary schools Flamstead End Primary; Cuffley Primary; Woodside Primary; St Paul's RC Primary; Goff's Oak Primary; Bonney Grove Primary; Fairfields Primary.

TRINITY CATHOLIC HIGH SCHOOL

Mornington Road
Woodford Green
Essex IG8 0TP
Tel (0181) 504 3419
Fax (0181) 505 7546

- National ranking 186= (241, 239, 332, 310)
- GCSE 77% (68%)
- A-levels 34% (A/B); 88% (A/E)
- Higher education 67% (Oxford 3)

- Mixed comprehensive
- Pupils 1,576
- Boys (11–18) 757
- Girls (11–18) 819
- Sixth form 436 (28%)
- Education authority *Redbridge*

Headteacher Dr Paul Doherty, 50, appointed in September 1981. Staff 88 (men 40, women 48).

Motto *None*

Background Situated in north of London borough of Redbridge on the fringe of Epping Forest. Based on two sites about quarter of a mile apart: years 7 to 9 on lower site in Sydney Road and years 10 to 13 on upper site in Mornington Road. Voluntary-aided Catholic school under Diocese of Brentwood. Formed in 1976 by amalgamation of St Paul's Catholic Secondary School (now lower site) and the Holy Family School (now upper site). Over-subscribed, with two applications per place. Throughout the year, enhancement classes in English, word-processing, mathematics science and religious education, incorporating special GCSE revision programmes. Extra-curricular successes: individual and team champions in swimming, cross-country and football. County and district champions in netball, runners-up in All-England under-14 netball championships. Centre of excellence for art. Music and drama productions throughout the year. Champions of East London Rotary Club 'Youth Speaks Out' senior section; 1997 finalists in junior, intermediate and senior sections. Purpose-built Natural History Unit in its own conservation and nature study area; specially-designed drama suite with state-of-the-art technical and production equipment; purpose-built sixth-form centre, with common room, reference and conference rooms. Commended for the development of information technology with a ratio of one computer for every eight pupils. Identified as 'outstandingly successful' in 1997 annual Ofsted report.

Alumni Louise Lombard, actress; Natasha Gelston, lead singer of National Jazz Orchestra; Orla Bermingham, triple gold medallist in European Junior Club Championships.

Streaming Only in mathematics; pupils divided into eight ability sets that are reviewed twice a year.

Approach to discipline High standards expected and maintained inside and outside the school. 'Discipline is firm yet compassionate with the emphasis on rewards. Pupils are encouraged to respect themselves, others, their school environment and local community.'

Uniform Boys: navy blazer with school crest, white shirt, school tie (navy with red-and-white stripe), charcoal-grey trousers. Girls:

navy blazer with crest, blue shirt and school tie, navy box-pleated skirt. Very strictly enforced.

Homework Average 11-year-old, 10 hours a week; 14-year-old, 10 to 15 hours; 16-year-old, at least 15 hours.

Vocational qualifications RSA, Pitman, Office Studies, Word-processing, Typing, Teeline shorthand, Keyboarding Applications.

Inspection December 1995: 'A very good school which has many strengths. It offers a high quality of education to its pupils.'; 'With the exception of music, where standards are below expectations, overall standards in all subjects of the curriculum are at least sound and often they are good. In art and drama, standards are particularly high.'; 'The quality of education provided by the school is good. Most pupils progress well. In the great majority of lessons they are confident and respond with interest.'; The headteacher has a very clear vision for the school and provides outstanding leadership.'

Primary schools St Antony's RC Primary, Woodford Green; St Augustine's RC Primary, Barkingside; St John Fisher RC Primary, Loughton; St Mary's RC Primary, Chingford; Our Lady of Lourdes RC Primary, Wanstead.

WYMONDHAM COLLEGE

Golf Links Road
Morley
Wymondham
Norfolk NR18 9SZ
Tel (01953) 605566
Fax (01953) 603313

- National ranking 188 (212, 195, 263, 229)
- GCSE 76% (72%)
- A-levels 15% (A/B); 92% (A/E)
- Higher education 76% (Oxford 1, Cambridge 1)

- Grant-maintained
- Mixed comprehensive
- Pupils 885
- Boys (11–18) 459
- Girls (11–18) 426
- Sixth form 290 (33%)
- Education authority *Norfolk*

Headteacher John Haden, 54, appointed in

September 1992. Staff 72 (men 38, women 34).

Motto Floreat sapientia (Let wisdom flourish).

Background Europe's biggest state boarding school. Founded on site of former wartime United States Air Force hospital, originally to provide boarding accommodation for pupils from Norfolk's more remote areas. The school has more than 500 boarders, most paying fees that are about one-third of equivalent independent schools. All day-pupils and day-boarders are local. Some boarders are on Ministry of Defence grants or from expatriate families; increasing number from European union families. Buildings are a mixture of wartime and modern, on 82-acre site southwest of Norwich; new £1.4m design and technology centre opened in 1994, with £200,000-worth of equipment: 10 science laboratories, seven workshops, two computer rooms, sports hall, gymnasium, swimming pool, fitness rooms. Oversubscribed for day school, with average of 2.5 applications per place. House system. County and national representatives in variety of sports, which include rugby, soccer, hockey, cricket, tennis, canoeing, judo and squash. Duke of Edinburgh Award Scheme; Combined Cadet Force.

Alumni Mark Brayne, former BBC Far East correspondent.

Streaming Pupils placed in sets according to ability for English, mathematics and modern languages from year 7; science from year 10.

Approach to discipline 'Acceptable behaviour expected of all pupils at all times, with breaches being dealt with. The aim is to encourage and instil in pupils a sense of self-discipline.'

Uniform Blue blazer, grey trousers/skirt for years 7 to 11. Dress code for sixth-formers. Regulations applied fully in school hours.

Homework Average 11-year-old, five hours a week; 14-year-old, seven hours 30 minutes; 16-year-old, 10 hours.

Vocational qualifications GNVQ Advanced, Business and Finance, Manufacturing and Leisure and Tourism, Health and Social Care, Community Sports Leadership Award.

Inspection January 1994: 'The standard of achievement is satisfactory or better at all levels throughout the school.'; 'The college is an orderly community where the routines of day and boarding are well-established, are understood by pupils and teachers, and function efficiently. The pupils are courteous and polite: discipline and behaviour is good.'

Primary schools As the United Kingdom's largest maintained boarding school, pupils come from 285 different schools, including 45 independent schools and 40 overseas schools. Only UK and European Union citizens admitted, with pupils from a total of 20 countries.

NEWLANDS SCHOOL

Farm Road
Maidenhead
Berkshire SL6 5JB
Tel (01628) 25068
Fax (01628) 75352

- National ranking 189 (187, 199, 214, 211)
- GCSE 75% (75%)
- A-levels 46% (A/B); 96% (A/E)
- Higher education 93%

- Girls' comprehensive
- Pupils 1,068
- Boys Not applicable
- Girls (11–18) 1,068
- Sixth form 159 (15%)
- Education authority Berkshire

Headteacher Susan Mary Benton, 54, appointed in September 1990. Staff 64 (men 8, women 56).

Motto Vincit veritas (Truth conquers).

Background Founded as Maidenhead Girls' High School in 1905, the school moved from the town centre in 1958 to accommodate greater numbers and became comprehensive in 1973, when it was renamed. Buildings added as numbers continued to expand on site on northwest edge of Maidenhead, close to National Trust areas of Pinkney's Green and Maidenhead Thicket. Most recently, three blocks to replace 'terrapin' classrooms for modern languages department, science, mathematics and music classrooms and an extension to the Senior Library. Over-subscribed, with 1.5 applications per place. Languages among best examination results; drama and public speaking also strong; orchestral and choral music throughout school; senior choir re-

cords for BBC. Hockey teams compete at national level; also notable performance at netball, athletics and badminton. Public service encouraged; sixth-formers involved in education of younger pupils.

Streaming Mathematics, from year 7; French, from year 8; from year 9 a lower group is taken out for English, although other groups remain mixed-ability.

Approach to discipline Clear expectations of work, behaviour and attendance; increasing self-discipline is the aim. 'There is a strong emphasis on celebrating success, rewarding good work and behaviour, and fostering a sense of responsibility.'

Uniform Grey skirt, white shirt, pale-blue sweater. Sixth-formers do not have uniform, but expected 'to dress appropriately for working environment'. Jewellery restrictions. Daily monitoring.

Homework Average 11-year-old, six to seven hours a week; 14-year-old, seven hours 30 minutes; 16-year-old, 12 hours.

Vocational qualifications GNVQ, Business; A-level and AS-level, Business Studies.

Inspection January 1994: 'Newlands is a good school with some excellent features. The school provides good value for money and makes a very positive contribution to the development of its pupils.'; 'The staff are experienced, well-qualified and highly-committed. Teaching is competent and sound. Pupils are well-motivated and keen to learn; they would benefit from greater opportunities to become independent learners.'

Primary schools Courthouse Junior; Ellington Primary; Oldfield Primary; St Luke's CE Primary; Holyport CE Primary.

SILVERDALE SCHOOL

Bents Crescent
Sheffield S11 9RT
Tel (0114) 236 9991
Fax (0114) 262 0627
E-mail: silverdale.sheffield.se@campus.
bt.com
Internet: http://www.campus.bt.com/CampusWorld/orgs/org2869/index.html

- National ranking 190 (201, 219, 179, 194)
- GCSE 75% (73%)
- A-levels 43% (A/B); 91% (A/E)

- Higher education 93% (Oxford 2, Cambridge 4)

- Mixed comprehensive
- Pupils 1,106
- Boys (11–18) 529
- Girls (11–18) 577
- Sixth form 247 (22%)
- Education authority *Sheffield*

Headteacher Enid Fitzgeorge-Butler, 46, appointed in January 1995. Staff 64 (men 27, women 37).

Motto Excellence in Education.

Background Silverdale School opened in 1956 as an 11–16 school; sixth form added in 1977. On a single site in 17 acres of grounds in southwestern area of city with extensive views over Sheffield and surrounding countryside. Over-subscribed, with 210 applications for 180 places. More than three in four year 11 pupils (80%) stay on into sixth form. Unit for profoundly-deaf children, staffed by teachers from Maud Maxfield service. Work-experience for all pupils; records of achievement; work-shadowing for pupils in year 12; 10-week Enterprise Scheme for pupils in year 10, supported by 16 local industrialists. At least one foreign language to GCSE: French, German, Spanish; intensive language courses in each country. Work-experience in Europe for A-level linguists. Latin also offered. Separate courses for physics, chemistry and biology as well as Coordinated Science course. Year 7 camp and year 9 summer-term curriculum enrichment. Two ski trips annually. Competitive inter-school and inter-form sport. Regular drama and music productions: choir, orchestra, wind band, brass group. Parent-Teacher Association.

Streaming Pupils in sets from year 8, according to the policy of each department.

Approach to discipline Punctuality and homework records of all pupils checked weekly. Parents contacted immediately if there are social, academic, behaviour or homework problems. Pupil-report system to monitor pupils. Headteacher's detention available each week for any serious indiscipline. Merit system to support achievement.

Uniform Years 7 to 11 wear 'standard dress': sweater with school logo in choice of four colours, black/blue/grey trousers/skirt, dark shoes.

Homework Average 11-year-old, six hours 30 minutes a week; 14-year-old, seven hours 30 minutes; 16-year-old, seven hours 30 minutes.

Vocational qualifications RSA, French for Business and Desktop Publishing.

Inspection February 1996: 'A school of high academic standards with well-motivated and confident pupils. Examination results are excellent in relation to both local and national standards. The school includes a unit for the profoundly deaf which is also of high quality.'; 'Standards are high in the core subjects of English, mathematics and science.'; 'The majority of lessons are characterised by well-motivated and attentive pupils with good levels of concentration. They have very positive attitudes to their work and are confident and articulate.'; 'The behaviour of pupils is excellent and they acquire a range of study skills which enables them to make good progress in their lessons. The quality of learning within lessons is usually good or very good. Pupils are supported by hard-working and well-qualified teachers who provide lessons of at least sound quality and more often of good quality.'

Primary schools Dobcroft Junior; Ecclesall CE Junior; Springfield Junior; St Wilfrid's RC Primary; Carter Knowle Junior; Nether Green Junior; Dore Junior; Porter Croft CE Primary

BULLERS WOOD SCHOOL

St Nicolas Lane
Logs Hill
Chislehurst
Kent BR7 5LJ
Tel (0181) 467 2280
Fax (0181) 295 1425
E-mail: bullersuk@aol.com

- National ranking 191 (288, 240, 208, 184)
- GCSE 75% (64%)
- A-levels 39% (A/B); 97% (A/E)
- Higher education 70%

- Grant-maintained
- Girls' comprehensive
- Pupils 1,100
- Boys (16–18) 1
- Girls (11–18) 1,099
- Sixth form 164 (15%)

- Education authority *Bromley*

Headteacher Thomas McGeough, 50, acting from April 1997. Staff 67 (men 16, women 51).

Motto Quod potes tenta (Strive to your utmost).

Background Appearance of traditional girls' school in Victorian landscaped gardens and woodlands; original William Morris decoration. Totally refurbished since 1991; also has a house in Normandy, visited by all year 9 and 10 pupils as well as A-level and vocational groups. House to be extended to take in international groups of students and hold international conferences. Modern teaching blocks, refurbished pavilion (1992), new technology block and language centre (1993), science laboratories (1994), classroom block (1996), sports hall (1997) and good facilities for music and drama. Over-subscribed, with three applications per place. Lively International Dimension programme; Language College from April 1996; additional languages are Spanish, Italian and Japanese. Numerous links with schools throughout Europe and Asia. Works closely with Ravensbourne College of Communication and Design on productions and sixth-form courses.

Alumni Susan Marling, journalist; Ruthie Henshall, lead actress in musical *Crazy for You* and *Oliver!*; Judy Oakes, shot-putter; Claire Perry, chief executive of Bromley Health Authority.

Streaming Pupils set in ability groups from year 7. Movement between sets as appropriate.

Approach to discipline 'Pupils are expected to take responsibility for their behaviour, acting courteously and thoughtfully in all their dealings with others in the community. Strict adherence to rules concerning punctuality, attendance and remaining on the school site at all times is expected.'

Uniform Cream blouse, Black Watch tartan kilt, navy jumper with school badge, black/navy shoes, coat. No jewellery. Very strictly enforced; sixth-formers wear own choice of clothes.

Homework Average 11-year-old, nine to 12 hours a week; 14-year-old, 15 hours; 16-year-old, 18 hours.

Vocational qualifications GNVQ Level 3, Business and Finance; GNVQ Level 2 and 3, Hotel and Catering; GNVQ Level 3, Leisure and Tourism; CACHE Diploma and Certificate in Child Care Education; City and Guilds, Photography, Sports Leadership Award; Foreign Languages at Work (French and German); Institute of Linguists (Japanese, Italian, Spanish).

Inspection September 1994: 'This is a good school. Most pupils are achieving at least the national expectation and many beyond it. Half the pupils are attaining at high levels and almost all are achieving appropriately for their ability.'; 'Basic communication skills are very well developed, especially accuracy and clarity of writing. Pupils are less confident in their numerical skills, but graphs and statistics are used competently when required. Information technology skills are under-developed, but there are some examples of good practice within the school.'; 'The quality of learning is good in a majority of classes and sound throughout the school.'

Primary schools Crofton Junior; Scotts Park Primary; Southborough Primary; St George's Bickley CE Primary; Raglan Primary; Burnt Ash Primary.

THE HOLT SCHOOL

Holt Lane
Wokingham
Berkshire RG41 1EE
Tel (01734) 780165
Fax (01734) 890831

- National ranking 192 (200, 204, 237, 210)
- GCSE 75% (73%)
- A-levels 34% (A/B); 90% (A/E)
- Higher education 90% (Oxford 1)

- Girls' comprehensive
- Pupils 1,185
- Boys *Not applicable*
- Girls (11–18) 1,185
- Sixth form 185 (16%)
- Education authority *Berkshire*

Headteacher Lorna Roberts, appointed in September 1989. Staff 68 (men 12, women 56).

Motto Honor quam honores (Prefer self-respect to accolades).

Background The Holt School was founded as

Wokingham Girls' Grammar School on edge of the market town in 1931; original school was in the Dower House of the Holt Estate, dating from 1648; became comprehensive in 1972. Facilities include eight laboratories, drama studio, two workshops, two computer rooms; specialist blocks for English, music, mathematics, humanities and languages, and drama. School's grounds extend to 13 acres, including shrubbery and gardens from original estate; two hockey pitches, six netball courts. Over-subscribed, with 270 applications for 200 places. Prides itself on strength in modern languages, mathematics, technology, music and art. South East Berkshire under-12 netball champions; Berkshire cross-country champions at under-12, under-13, under-14 and under-15. Two pupils are in the under-15 county hockey team; a sixth-former is a reserve in under-21 English netball team. Karen Roberts, a world champion, represents Great Britain in judo, with Kelly Roberts and Holly Cameron. Three pupils in TSB English Schools' track and field finals.

Alumni Dianne Nelmes, Granada Television head of factual programmes.

Streaming Individual subjects set according to ability of each girl in each subject: mathematics, from October in year 7; modern languages, from January in year 7; everything else from year 8. Mixed-ability forms.

Approach to discipline Keynote is orderly atmosphere and consideration for others. 'Staff encourage and insist on a good working environment, providing a firm framework for good behaviour and the development of self-discipline.' Sanctions used within framework of discussion 'so that what has gone wrong is absolutely clear'.

Uniform Navy/scarlet sweater, navy skirt, blue-and-white striped blouse, black shoes. Correct uniform is 'absolute requirement'; no uniform in sixth form.

Homework Average 11-year-old, seven hours 30 minutes a week; 14-year-old, seven hours 30 minutes; 16-year-old, 10 hours.

Vocational qualifications *None*

Inspection May 1995: 'The Holt is a very good school with many excellent features. It is a well-ordered community, which is purposeful and hard-working. Relationships are good. There are high expectations of pupils and they respond well to opportunities to take responsibilities, to help in the organisation and management of their affairs and to provide service to the school and the wider community. They are courteous, well-behaved and they respect others.'

Primary schools St Paul's CE Junior, Wokingham; The Hawthorns, Woosehill; Winnersh Primary, Winnersh; Bearwood Primary, Winnersh; Arborfield CE Junior, Arborfield.

THORNDEN SCHOOL

Winchester Road
Chandlers Ford
Eastleigh
Hampshire SO53 2DW
Tel (01703) 269722
Fax (01703) 268393

- National ranking 193= (186, 187=, 209=, 202)
- GCSE 75% (76%)
- A-levels *Not applicable*
- Higher education *Not applicable*

- Mixed comprehensive
- Pupils 1,255
- Boys (11–16) 654
- Girls (11–16) 601
- Sixth form *Not applicable*
- Education authority *Hampshire*

Headteacher Dr Robert Sykes, 45, appointed in April 1993. Staff 73 (men 33, women 40).

Motto Fight for the truth.

Background Purpose-built comprehensive opened in 1973; buildings on two levels overlooking extensive playing fields and open land. Specialist blocks for art and technology as well as fully-equipped science laboratories. Two main information technology rooms, with newly installed network. Gymnasium, large sports hall, nine tennis courts. More than nine in 10 pupils (91%) continue their education after 16. Over-subscribed. Year system; School Council. Sporting achievements: county and regional success at tennis and badminton.

Alumni Julia Snell, England freestyle skier.

Streaming Setting as appropriate, particularly in mathematics, science and modern languages.

Approach to discipline 'There are clear rules known to all pupils and procedures adopted by all staff. There is a high-status pastoral system and the headteacher and deputy heads are actively involved with disciplinary issues. A firm system is generated with sensitivity and genuine regard for pastoral concerns.'

Uniform Navy pullover, black trousers or navy skirt/trousers, tie. Firmly enforced.

Homework Average 11-year-old, six hours a week; 14-year-old, eight hours; 16-year-old, 11 hours.

Vocational qualifications *None*

Primary schools Hiltingbury Junior; Otterbourne CE Primary; Merdon Junior; Scanatabout Primary; Shakespeare County Junior.

TUDOR GRANGE SCHOOL

Dingle Lane
Solihull
West Midlands B93 8RB
Tel **(0121) 705 5100**
Fax **(0121) 709 0455**

- National ranking 193= (191=, 227=, 295=, 275=)
- GCSE 75% (75%)
- A-levels *Not applicable*
- Higher education *Not applicable*

- Mixed comprehensive
- Pupils 1,247
- Boys (11–16) 649
- Girls (11–16) 598
- Sixth form *Not applicable*
- Education authority *Solihull*

Headteacher John Gwynne Evans, 50, appointed in September 1990. Staff 71 (men 31, women 40).

Motto Omnibus prodesse (Succeed in all things).

Background Established in 1956 as two grammar schools, which amalgamated in 1974 to form mixed comprehensive on 20-acre site in suburban parkland to south of Solihull town centre. Application to establish sixth-form supported by local education authority and being considered by Education Secretary. Draws pupils from villages as well as prosperous suburbs. Regularly and increasingly over-subscribed, with two applications per place. Pupils take up to 10 GCSEs; Latin and Russian among options; most able mathematicians take GCSE in year 10 and

AS-level mathematics in year 11. High level of participation in sport, with national success: gymnastics, tennis, swimming, athletics, hockey and cricket. Facilities include well-equipped Learning Resource Centre (Information Technology centre and library) and new technology suite; relocation and refurbishment of science facilities in September 1995. Nine in 10 pupils go on to further education. Extra-curricular activities: Duke of Edinburgh Award Scheme, Scout group, foreign exchange visits, drama and music, and residential activities. 'Open-door' policy at lunchtimes. Parents' Association. Foreign exchanges to Germany, France and Russia; planned sporting exchange visit to Mexico City; foreign visits to France and Switzerland, for skiing, and Italy, for Latin and Classical Studies; also the Mediterranean and Holy Land for religious education and south of France for sailing and other water sports. Technology College status from September 1995; new business studies area; substantial investment in personal computers and industry-standard software. Chosen to trial Part One GNVQ courses from September 1997. Identified for praise in 1996 annual Ofsted report.

Alumni Jeremy Bates, tennis player.

Streaming Gradually introduced. Extension courses built into curriculum in years 8 to 11, catering for pupils' individual abilities, interests and needs.

Approach to discipline High standards embodied in code of conduct, emphasising collaboration, respect for oneself, others and the environment, good manners and need for pupils to take responsibility for their own learning.

Uniform Green blazer, dark-grey trousers/skirt, white shirt and school tie (for boys), green blouse (for girls). 'Compulsory and strictly enforced.'

Homework Average 11-year-old, five hours a week; 14-year-old, seven hours 30 minutes; 16-year-old, 11 hours.

Vocational qualifications GCSE, Travel and Tourism; Keyboarding. Part One GNVQ, Business Studies, Information Technology.

Inspection November 1995: 'A good school with very many strengths. It provides a caring environment with a clear focus upon the achievement of high academic standards. Pupils are confident and articulate and, with very few exceptions, are highly motivated.

The leadership, organisation and teaching in the school strongly promote the development of a good work ethic which capitalises upon the pupils' commitment to learning.'

Primary schools Hockley Heath Primary; Monkspath Primary; St Alphege CE Junior; St James's CE Junior; Sharmans Cross Junior; Widney Junior.

HOWARD OF EFFINGHAM SCHOOL

Lower Road
Effingham
Surrey KT24 5JR
Tel (01372) 453694
Fax (01372) 456952
E-mail: howard@mailbox.rmplc.co.uk
Internet: http://rmplc.co.uk/eduweb/sites/
howard

- National ranking 195 (257, 305, 201, 203)
- GCSE 74% (66%)
- A-levels 42% (A/B); 90% (A/E)
- Higher education 85% (Oxford 2, Cambridge 2)

- Mixed comprehensive
- Pupils 1,510
- Boys (11–18) 788
- Girls (11–18) 722
- Sixth form 300 (20%)
- Education authority *Surrey*

Headteacher Michael Marchant, 46, appointed in April 1989. Staff 89 (men 39, women 50).

Motto *None*

Background 'The Howard' was opened in 1940 in pleasant countryside in central Surrey, midway between Guildford and Leatherhead. It developed into a comprehensive with good examination results, with buildings extended in several phases. In the past four years, it has been Surrey's fastest-growing comprehensive. Recent extensions include a £1.3m humanities block; new sixth-form centre in September 1996; sports hall, science and teaching extensions under construction. Teachers say they resist temptation to require pupils to specialise too early; school teams in wide range of sports, from soccer to squash; also inter-house competitions. Arts, drama and music well catered for; parents involved in Friends' Association. Extensive playing fields surrounded by trees and fields. Over-sub-

scribed, with 1.3 applications per place.

Streaming Pupils are put in sets for mathematics and languages in year 7. From year 8, there is separate setting in mathematics, languages, science, English, and humanities. Mixed-ability groups for technology, art, music, physical education and drama.

Approach to discipline 'Discipline rules are clear and simple, and are applied firmly and fairly.' Sanctions include conduct marks, detentions, report sheets, and privilege bans. Encouragement includes house points, merit certificates, effort and achievement prizes.

Uniform Black blazer with school crest, house tie, black sweater with crest (optional), grey trousers/skirts. Uniform does not apply in sixth form, but is strictly applied otherwise.

Homework Average 11-year-old, eight hours a week; 14-year-old, 10 hours; 16-year-old, 12 hours.

Vocational qualifications GNVQ Intermediate, Business and Finance, Leisure and Tourism, Health and Social Care; GNVQ Advanced, Business and Finance; Leisure and Tourism.

Inspection January 1995: 'Howard of Effingham is a good school.'; 'All students receive a broad and balanced curriculum enhanced by opportunities for extra-curricular activities, especially in music, drama productions and physical education.'; 'Staff expertise and good classroom relationships contribute greatly to the quality of the education.'; 'Many students with special educational needs and the few whose first language is not English make slow progress and are not always given suitable work or appropriately targeted support.'; 'The school benefits from the strong and effective leadership of the headteacher, who is well supported by the senior management and an excellent governing body.'; 'Relationships across the school are good. Students receive a sound moral education as well as opportunities to display initiative.'

Primary schools Eastwick County Junior; The Raleigh County Primary; The Dawnay County Primary; St Lawrence County Primary; Royal Kent CE Primary; Oakfield County Junior.

ST AIDAN'S CHURCH OF ENGLAND HIGH SCHOOL

Oatlands Drive
Harrogate
North Yorkshire HG2 8JR
Tel (01423) 885814
Fax (01423) 884327
E-mail: staidanshgt@aol.com

- National ranking 196 (184, 190, 207, 244)
- GCSE 74% (76%)
- A-levels 41% (A/B); 94% (A/E)
- Higher education 83% (Oxford 1, Cambridge 2)

- Mixed comprehensive
- Pupils 1,547
- Boys (11–18) 706
- Girls (11–18) 841
- Sixth form 379 (24%)
- Education authority *North Yorkshire*

Headteacher Dennis Richards, 51, appointed in January 1989. Staff 100 (men 39, women 61).

Motto *None*

Background St Aidan's was opened in September 1968 in its own grounds on 'superb' site close to centre of Harrogate, near its famous Stray. Buildings include Bede House, a listed Edwardian building, where the sixth form is largely housed. A 'magnificent' £1.1m suite of six science laboratories, four classrooms and information technology centre opened by Princess Royal in October 1994. New Chapel Hall in summer 1997. Other facilities include 'superbly-equipped' sports hall used as centre of excellence for cricket and basketball. Over-subscribed, with 340 applications for 216 places. Music: wide range of ensembles; concert band has toured United States, Canada and Europe; 85 players at Grade Five or above; pupils in National Youth Orchestra, National Youth Band and National Youth Choir; School Chamber Choir; concert band and chamber choir both reached finals of 1994 National Festival of Music for Youth. Sports: basketball, soccer, cricket, tennis, hockey, netball, athletics; rugby introduced in 1994. Flourishing links with Europe, including work-experience in Geneva and Dusseldorf area. School noted for charitable fund-raising of £10,000 a year. Many staff, including headteacher, have their own children educated in the school.

Streaming Setting in mathematics, science and modern languages at early stage. Later, humanities and English.

Approach to discipline Strong pastoral team. Each year-group of 220 pupils has a year-head who is virtually a head of school; noted for 'non-confrontational' atmosphere, cooperation, friendliness. 'The children are valued individuals in their own right and treated as such. Behaviour is of the highest standard.'

Uniform Simple and straightforward: navy sweater with white shirt, school tie. No trainers or boots. Regulations enforced 'totally'.

Homework Average 11-year-old, five hours a week; 14-year-old, eight hours; 16-year-old, 10 hours.

Vocational qualifications GNVQ, Business and Finance, Health and Social Care; Youth Award Scheme, RSA courses.

Inspection November 1996: 'An outstanding school which provides an extremely high quality education for its pupils. Educational standards are very high.'; 'Pupils are very good speakers and listeners; most are good readers; their writing is of very high quality; and they are very numerate.'; 'Pupils' attitudes to their studies are extremely positive and are a strength of the school. There is a clear learning culture and caring ethos in the school.'; 'Staff are very caring, extremely hardworking and committed; many are very talented, showing flair and enthusiasm, and inspire pupils. Teaching is of consistently high quality across the school.'

Primary schools St Peter's CE Primary; Richard Taylor CE Primary; Oatlands Junior; Woodlands Junior; Coppice Valley Primary. Total of more than 70 feeder schools.

BACKWELL SCHOOL

Station Road
Backwell
Bristol BS19 3PB
Tel (01275) 463371
Fax (01275) 463077
E-mail: 100567.2670@compuserve.com

- National ranking 197 (205, 185, 239, 238)

- GCSE 74% (73%)
- A-levels 40% (A/B); 92% (A/E)
- Higher education 80% (Oxford 2, Cambridge 1)

- Mixed comprehensive
- Pupils 1,544
- Boys (11–18) 784
- Girls (11–18) 760
- Sixth form 305 (20%)
- Education authority *North Somerset*

Headteacher Richard John Nosowski, 53, appointed in September 1988. Staff 93 (men 44, women 49).

Motto *None*

Background Opened in 1954 as a secondary modern school for 300 pupils; became fully comprehensive by 1976 and now has large academic sixth form. Located in semi-rural setting, seven miles southwest of Bristol. Primarily serves commuter villages; takes some children from Bristol and Weston-super-Mare when space allows. Over-subscribed, with two applications per place. School has large playing fields and district council leisure centre on campus: swimming pool, squash courts, sports hall and gymnasium. Music, art, drama and sports among strengths: art facilities notable; three computer networks; library plays key role. Pupils take active role in setting targets; all reports include pupil self-assessment. Identified by Ofsted as a 'good and improving' school in 1996.

Alumni Mervyn Kitchen, test umpire and former Somerset cricketer; Andrew Sherborne, golfer.

Streaming Pupils grouped differently according to subject; setting 'so that children's specific abilities are met'.

Approach to discipline Necessary minimum of rules. 'The main sanctions are an "on report" system to a senior member of staff after every two lessons and a formal detention system. Suspension is rarely used.'

Uniform Basic navy-and-grey uniform with school tie. No blazer. Sixth-formers follow dress code. 'There is wide consensus in favour of uniform. It is broad enough to allow for some individuality and enforcement is not a difficulty.'

Homework Average 11-year-old, five to eight hours a week; 14-year-old, eight to 10 hours; 16-year-old, 10 to 15 hours.

Vocational qualifications GNVQ Advanced, Business Studies; RSA and Pitmans, Staged examinations in typing, word-processing and information systems; all 16-year-olds can take a GCSE Information Technology endorsement.

Inspection April 1995: 'This is a very good school. Overall standards of achievement are high across the curriculum, and GCSE results in recent years have been outstanding. Good quality teaching contributes to effective learning, and the school's high reputation in the community is fully justified.'; 'Teachers are well-qualified and experienced. They have high expectations and establish good relationships with the pupils.'; 'The school's ethos and sense of purpose promotes a committed and mature approach to learning. Its commitment to the comprehensive ideal is well established, although the school's overall aims are less clearly presented.'

Primary schools Backwell St Andrew's Primary; Yatton CE Junior; Court de Wyck CE Primary, Claverham; Flax Bourton CE Primary.

ST PETER'S ROMAN CATHOLIC HIGH SCHOOL

Howards Lane
Orrell
Wigan WN5 8NU
Tel (01942) 747693
Fax (01942) 747694

- National ranking 198 (302 = , 314 = , 182, 218)
- GCSE 74% (63%)
- A-levels *Not applicable*
- Higher education *Not applicable*

- Mixed comprehensive
- Pupils 920
- Boys (11–16) 450
- Girls (11–16) 470
- Sixth form *Not applicable*
- Education authority *Wigan*

Headteacher Alan Edwards, 48, appointed in April 1992. Staff 54 (men 15, women 39).

Motto *None*

Background Started on current 18-acre site, just off the M6, in 1962 after two years occupying nearby grammar school. Accommodation includes six science laboratories, information technology rooms, sports hall, gymnasium, 13 acres of playing fields, all-weather games pitch, lecture theatre, craft, design, technology suite, pottery room. New library and music suite in 1997. Over-subscribed, with 220 applications for 170 places. Strongly Catholic. Curriculum strengths include art, drama, music, English, science, second and third modern languages. 'The school is characterised by high expectations, firm but fair discipline, friendly, caring relationships and an atmosphere of trust.' About 85% of pupils go on to further education.

Streaming Pupils put progressively into sets; by end of year 9, setting in virtually all subjects.

Approach to discipline 'We insist on high standards in discipline as in every other aspect of life.' Aim to create atmosphere of mutual respect and collective responsibility. Sanctions: additional work, conduct sheet, restrictions of liberty at breaks or lunchtimes; detention after school for older pupils; regular contact with parents.

Uniform Brown blazer with badge, dark-brown trousers/brown skirt, cream or white shirt/blouse, brown tie with red/yellow stripe, optional brown pullover with red/yellow stripe, dark-brown socks (white for girls), dark-brown shoes. All year 11 pupils are prefects with distinctive uniform. Very strictly enforced; high priority given to standards of uniform.

Homework Detailed monitoring and documenting of minimum amount of homework required in years 7 to 9. Average 16-year-old, 12 to 18 hours a week, with coursework deadlines strictly enforced.

Vocational qualifications Range of RSA courses.

Inspection March 1994: 'St Peter's Roman Catholic High School, Orrell, is a successful and flourishing school.'; 'It is a happy, orderly school. Pupils are well-behaved, confident and have a high level of self-esteem. They are highly-motivated; the quality of their learning is very good.'

Primary schools St James' RC Primary, Orrell; St Mary's RC Primary, Billinge; St Teresa's RC Primary, Upholland; St Joseph's RC Primary, Wrightington; St Marie's RC Primary, Standish; St Bernadette's RC Primary, Shevington.

MAIDEN ERLEGH SCHOOL

Silverdale Road
Earley
Reading
Berkshire RG6 2HS
Tel (01734) 262467
Fax (01734) 266111

- National ranking 199 (221, 284, 241, –)
- GCSE 73% (70%)
- A-levels 49% (A/B); 93% (A/E)
- Higher education 76% (Oxford 2)

- Mixed comprehensive
- Pupils 1,536
- Boys (11–18) 797
- Girls (11–18) 739
- Sixth form 295 (19%)
- Education authority *Berkshire*

Headteacher Wilton Wills, 56, appointed in September 1983. Staff 93 (men 33, women 60).

Motto Qui veut peut (He who strives will succeed).

Background Opened in 1962 as a small secondary modern; re-organised and expanded into comprehensive in early 1970s; eight-form entry school in residential suburbs of Reading, near the university. Buildings are mainly of recent design and purpose-built for teaching a wide range of academic, creative and technical subjects, including fine drama studio fully equipped with stage lighting. Over-subscribed, with 350 applications for 248 places. Flourishing house system regularly involves large numbers of pupils competing in sporting and cultural activities. Extra-curricular activities include musical groups (bands, orchestras, choirs, instrumental tuition), drama groups, Christian Union, sailing, Young Enterprise Award Scheme, subject-based clubs, fund-raising for charity. Several school trips each year, including exchange visits to France and Germany. School is one of three which jointly own educational residential centre at Tirabad in Mid-Wales, offering adventure courses and range of outdoor pursuits.

Streaming Mixed-ability groups in year 7; pupils in sets for mathematics after one term, for French after one year. English and science banded in year 10. Pupils with special needs receive help from support unit in accordance with national code of practice.

Approach to discipline 'Pupils are required to show consideration and courtesy to others at all times, and a high standard of personal behaviour is expected. Anti-social behaviour such as use of foul language, bullying and smoking is not tolerated and severely dealt with. There is close liaison with parents at all times.'

Uniform Navy blazer, grey trousers for boys; white blouses, navy jumpers and skirts for girls. Sixth-formers wear grey suits. Strictly enforced.

Homework Average 11-year-old, seven hours a week; 14-year-old, nine hours; 16-year-old, 11 hours.

Vocational qualifications GNVQ.

Inspection April 1993: 'The school is a well-ordered community. Pupils are polite and courteous. They are highly-motivated and vigorously challenged. Learning takes place in a cooperative and mutually respectful environment and there is a committed teaching staff of high quality.'

ST MARY'S ROMAN CATHOLIC HIGH SCHOOL

Newbold Road
Upper Newbold
Chesterfield
Derbyshire S41 8AG
Tel (01246) 201191
Fax (01246) 279205
E-mail: stmarys.highschool@campus.bt.com

- National ranking 200 (225, 197, 199, 267)
- GCSE 73% (70%)
- A-levels 45% (A/B); 96% (A/E)
- Higher education 93% (Oxford 1, Cambridge 1)

- Grant-maintained
- Mixed comprehensive
- Pupils 1,168
- Boys (11–18) 552
- Girls (11–18) 616
- Sixth form 212 (18%)
- Education authority *Derbyshire*

Headteacher Tom Moore, 49, appointed in September 1992. Staff 63 (men 27, women 36).

Motto *None*

Background Founded in 1865 but moved to new buildings, designed on a village principle with separate blocks for different subjects, in 1981. A Catholic comprehensive on western edge of Chesterfield overlooking countryside; landscaped grounds. Serves wide catchment area in northeast Derbyshire. Over-subscribed, with two applications for each place. Local industry support for new and re-equipped technology area; in music: large orchestra, concert band, choirs, ensembles. Public speaking and debates also a strength, reaching national competition finals for fourth successive year. Sports include soccer, hockey, athletics, rugby, netball. Winners of county area group tennis and cross-country competitions and town basketball league. Annual art and textiles exhibition. Ethos based on 'gospel values'.

Streaming Banded according to ability.

Approach to discipline 'Good behaviour is encouraged, rewarded and reinforced.' Clear guide about what is unacceptable; misdemeanours followed up swiftly by pastoral team; 'well-ordered, courteous and disciplined regime'.

Uniform Navy-blue blazer with school badge, grey trousers/navy box-pleated skirt, white shirt/blouse, school tie. Regulation summer dress for girls from May to September. 'There is no compromise in respect of uniform.'

Homework Average 11-year-old, at least five hours a week; 14-year-old, seven to eight hours; 16-year-old, at least 10 hours.

Vocational qualifications RSA, Typing, Word-processing.

Inspection February 1994: 'The school has a strong Catholic Christian ethos which permeates all aspects of the life of the school.'; 'There is a powerful sense of community within the school which contributes to the quality of learning and pastoral support experienced by pupils.'; 'The quality of learning in the school is generally high. Teaching is of good quality and the staff have a very high commitment to the school; a large number of teachers give time to supporting the wide range of extra-curricular activities.'; 'Pupils are well-motivated, well-behaved and committed to their learning.'; 'In some lessons the learning is tightly-controlled by the teacher and pupils are less involved in their learning than could be the case.'; 'The 12-year-old building is in an excellent state of repair with no evidence of vandalism or graffiti.'

Primary schools St Mary's RC Primary, Chesterfield; St Joseph's RC Primary, Langwith Junction; Christ the King RC Primary, Alfreton; St Joseph's RC Primary, Staveley; Immaculate Conception RC Primary, Spinkhill; St Joseph's RC Primary, Matlock.

PRESDALES SCHOOL

Presdales School
Hoe Lane
Ware
Hertfordshire SG12 9NX
Tel (01920) 462210
Fax (01920) 461187

- National ranking 201 (194, 176, 278, 294)
- GCSE 73% (74%)
- A-levels 40% (A/B); 94% (A/E)
- Higher education 80% (Oxford 1, Cambridge 1)

- Girls' comprehensive
- Pupils 975
- Boys *Not applicable*
- Girls (11–18) 975
- Sixth form 164 (17%)
- Education authority *Hertfordshire*

Headteacher Janine Robinson, 49, appointed in April 1988. Staff 65 (men 10, women 55).

Motto Bold in God.

Background Original foundation as Ware Grammar School for Girls in 1906 on Amwell House site; moved to current site in 1964. Became comprehensive in 1975, accepts girls from wide area of Hertfordshire and neighbouring counties. School building comprises mansion house, which accommodates new sixth-form centre and library; attached is the majority of the accommodation, which has been built since 1960s: music suite, dance/drama studio, eight science laboratories, eight language rooms, five technology rooms, two art rooms, assembly hall, dining rooms, gymnasium. All classrooms in modern buildings surrounded by 22 acres of grounds, including 11.5 acres of lawn and playing fields; open-air heated swimming pool. Over-subscribed, with 200 applications for 165 places. Awarded Language College status from April 1996. Languages taught: French, German, Spanish, Latin, Russian and Italian to A-level; Portuguese, Japanese and Ancient Greek to GCSE in sixth form. Further Mathematics a permanent feature at A-level. Separate sciences as well as double-science GCSE. Extra-curricular music: orchestra, senior and junior choirs, wind band, junior string ensemble, recorder group, composing/performing group and various chamber groups. 'Modest' fee for tuition in instrumental music, and singing; regular concerts. Sporting activities: netball, hockey, cross-country, gymnastics, dance, athletics, swimming, tennis, rounders. Two school plays annually. Parent-Teacher Association. Identified by Ofsted as 'outstandingly successful' in 1996.

Alumni Baroness Blackstone of Stoke Newington, Master of Birkbeck College; Kim Wilde, pop singer; Nicola Fibbens, international swimmer.

Streaming Broad banding of pupils in year 7, with careful monitoring and setting in mathematics and science after one term. Pupils set according to subject in years 8 and 9 in mathematics, science, English and French. Setting extended in years 10 and 11.

Approach to discipline 'Firm but fair and not repressive. The school rules are the minimum required for the orderly running of a large community. The girls are expected to show consideration for others and to behave in a seemly manner at all times. Clear sanctions exist, but in practice very few girls contravene the code of conduct.'

Uniform Navy blazer with badge, navy school jumper edged in school colours, white blouse, navy skirt, white socks/navy tights, black/brown/navy shoes. No uniform for sixth-formers, but smart dress required; no jeans. Strictly enforced.

Homework Average 11-year-old, six hours 30 minutes a week; 14-year-old, eight hours; 16-year-old, 11 hours 30 minutes.

Vocational qualifications GNVQ Advanced, Business.

Inspection October 1994: 'The quality of learning has many good features, some outstanding aspects and very few shortcomings. The range of learning methods is often restricted and this is not only a consequence of some very large teaching groups. Teaching also has good features, some outstanding. Pupils of high ability are not always challenged to excel and expectations of pupils placed in lower-ability groups are not high enough. The school is favoured with an excellent site with much good accommodation.'; 'The school is caring and staff commitment is high. Parents value the school's ethos and the pupils are proud of their school.' *The school reports it has successfully addressed the issues raised by the 1994 inspection.*

Primary schools St Mary's Junior; Christ Church Primary; Bengeo Primary, Hertford; Roselands Primary, Hoddesdon; Duncombe School, Hertford.

BISHOP STOPFORD SCHOOL

Headlands
Kettering
Northamptonshire NN15 6BJ
Tel (01536) 514204
Fax (01536) 416058
E-mail: bishop@rmplc.co.uk

- National ranking 202 (211, 234, 242, –)
- GCSE 73% (72%)
- A-levels 36% (A/B); 88% (A/E)
- Higher education 87% (Cambridge 3)

- Mixed comprehensive
- Pupils 1,342
- Boys (11–18) 641
- Girls (11–18) 701
- Sixth form 342 (25%)
- Education authority *Northamptonshire*

Headteacher Dr John Trevor Hopkins, 63, appointed in September 1974. Staff 75 (men 38, women 37).

Motto *None*

Background Diocesan school taking pupils from 1,000 square miles of Northamptonshire, Leicestershire and Cambridgeshire; school population reflects 'socio-economic balance of the diocese rather than the school's immediate residential environment'. From 1535 to 1965, the foundation was a parochial school; in 1965, moved to new site on edge of Kettering and broadened its remit. 'Pupils come from families that accept a common Christian ethic, although as an ecumenical school we take pupils from many denominations.' Over-subscribed, with 360+ applications for 180 places. Extensive £2m building programme completed in 1996: new library, sixth-form centre, technology and language blocks, upgrading of other facilities. Affiliated to Technology Colleges Trust. Total of 15 sports and wide range of athletics offered. Representative honours: district cross-country champions (six teams); three individual county champions; international cross-country representation; district athletics champions (five teams); seven individual county champions in various disciplines; Midlands under-17 champion, county AAA champion and English champion are all sixth-formers at the school; further success in hockey, netball, football, cricket, and basketball. Reputation for music: orchestra, band, ensemble. School praised in 1995 annual Ofsted report. Headteacher awarded OBE in 1997 New Year Honours.

Streaming Two mixed-ability bands in each year. Year 7: setting within bands in English from autumn term. Year 8: similar setting in English, mathematics and modern languages. Year 9: setting in science; continues in years 10 and 11. 'Movement between sets can take place according to a child's needs.'

Approach to discipline 'Rules are important to the school. Discipline, however, usually comes from the child and reflects the individual's self-discipline, self-respect and respect for others. There is an excellent relationship between child, sixth-form student and teacher. Suspension has been used, but only as a last resort. The "friendly" approach works wonders.'

Uniform Royal-blue jumper with school crest, white shirt/blouse, grey trousers/skirt, house tie, plain white/grey/black socks or neutral/grey/black tights, plain grey/navy/black shoes. Strictly enforced.

Homework Average 11-year-old, five hours a week; 14-year-old, seven hours 30 minutes; 16-year-old, 12 hours 30 minutes.

Vocational qualifications Diploma of Vocational Education; GNVQ Levels 1 and 2; GNVQ Advanced, Science, Health and Community Care; City and Guilds, 14–16 Foundation Programme.

Inspection May 1994: 'The overall quality of pupils' learning and standards of achievement is very good.'; 'Development of school facilities is taking place, but this will not fully meet the needs of pupils when completed.'; 'Pupils show good respect for people and property. There is a strong work ethic which permeates the whole school and encourages pupils to value their learning experiences. This is a very orderly school. Pupils are polite and friendly and are aware of the needs of others.'

Primary schools Barton Seagrave Primary; Hawthorn Primary. Pupils drawn from more than 64 schools throughout the Anglican Diocese of Peterborough.

THE CAMPION ROMAN CATHOLIC SCHOOL FOR BOYS

Wingletye Lane
Hornchurch
Essex RM11 3BX
Tel (01708) 452332
Fax (01708) 456995

- National ranking 203 (250, 220, 218, 245)
- GCSE 73% (67%)
- A-levels 32% (A/B); 88% (A/E)
- Higher education 68% (Cambridge 1)

- Boys' comprehensive
- Pupils 800
- Boys (11–18) 794
- Girls (16–18) 6
- Sixth form 190 (24%)
- Education authority *Havering*

Headteacher John A. Johnson, 46, appointed in September 1993. Staff 47 (men 29, women 18).

Motto Auctore deo (The enterprise is of God).

Background Jesuits established the voluntary-aided school in 1962 and named it after Edmund Campion, the Jesuit martyred in 1581. However, it is now run entirely by lay staff and serves the Catholic community of Havering and the surrounding area. Oversubscribed, with 1.6 applications for every place. Purpose-built buildings; parents have built swimming pool and sports hall on a site that has extensive grounds and playing fields on the edge of the green belt. All pupils in year 7 study Russian and French; Latin for all in year 8; Greek offered from year 9. Business Studies reported to be popular and successful. Sporting reputation, particularly as one of leading rugby schools in the country. Describes itself as 'traditional'.

Alumni David Alton, Liberal Democrat MP for Mossley Hill; Damien Cronin, Scotland and

British Lions rugby player.

Streaming Limited banding by ability in mathematics and science.

Approach to discipline 'Well-disciplined and caring. We put great stress on relationships, between pupils, and between staff and pupils. We expect our pupils to have the highest standards of courtesy, behaviour and appearance.'

Uniform Black blazer, white shirt, school tie, dark-grey trousers. Regulations strictly enforced and obeyed.

Homework Average 11-year-old, five hours a week; 14-year-old, seven hours 30 minutes; 16-year-old, 10 hours.

Vocational qualifications GNVQ Intermediate and GNVQ Levels 2 and 3, Business Studies.

Primary schools St Joseph's CE Primary, Upminster; St Mary's CE Primary, Hornchurch; St Helen's CE Primary, Brentwood; St Peter's Primary, Romford; St Patrick's CE Primary, Collier Row; St Alban's CE Primary, Elm Park; St Thomas of Canterbury, Grays; La Salette CE Primary, Rainham; St Ursula's CE Primary, Harold Hill; Holy Cross CE Primary, Ockenden.

BRENTWOOD URSULINE CONVENT HIGH SCHOOL

Queen's Road
Brentwood
Essex CM14 4EX
Tel (01277) 227156
Fax (01277) 229454
E-mail: bursuline@aol.com

- National ranking 204 (172, 171, 203, 193)
- GCSE 73% (82%)
- A-levels 31% (A/B); 87% (A/E)
- Higher education 57%

- Grant-maintained
- Girls' comprehensive
- Pupils 821
- Boys *Not applicable*
- Girls (11–18) 821
- Sixth form 135 (16%)
- Education authority *Essex*

Headteacher Helen Penny, 52, appointed in January 1996. Staff 52 (men 10, women 42).

Motto Duty.

Background Founded in 1900 by Ursuline nuns from Forest Gate originally for 60 girls, day and boarding; boarding facility closed 1993. Buildings dating from late 19th century to 1960s surround a hilly site overlooking lake and trees, with distant views of Canary Wharf; survived heavy bombing in Second World War. Originally direct-grant; became voluntary-aided in 1979; became grant-maintained in 1994. Still over-subscribed even though expanded intake: two applications per place. All pupils learn French and German, or Spanish, in years 7 to 11; offer of other languages in years 12 and 13; Latin taught in year 7 and is an option in years 8 and 9. Work-experience for all in year 10; work-experience abroad in year 12; work-shadowing in year 13. Exchanges, visits and joint projects with two French schools, two German, Spain and Kenya. Indoor heated swimming pool among sporting facilities; county and national players in netball, athletics, tennis and fencing; league players in soccer. Catholic ethos pervasive; emphasis on European view of life; tradition in textiles, stemming from the Ursuline's origins in Belgium, is preserved in lacemaking and other activities. Proud of musical achievements: school provides about half of town's philharmonic and cathedral's orchestra.

Alumni Princess Marie José of Belgium, later Queen of Italy (currently president of Old Girls' Association).

Streaming Pupils are in sets for mathematics in years 7 to 11; in English, modern languages and sciences in years 8 to 11.

Approach to discipline Rules mainly relate to safety and security. 'Punishments are more practical than ritualistic: sanding defaced tables, cleaning off chewing gum, picking up litter etc. Incentive scheme for the more serious problems include "paid" work and privileges that can be withdrawn.'

Uniform Blue-brown-and-gold striped blazer, gold blouse, brown skirt, brown shoes and brown coat. White blouse replaces gold blouse in sixth form. Regulations enforced strictly 'with good supply of nearly-new uniforms to aid those who need it'.

Homework Average 11-year-old, seven hours 30 minutes a week; 14-year-old, 10 hours; 16-year-old, more than 10 hours.

Vocational qualifications City and Guilds, Catering, Textiles, Embroidery and Lacemaking; RSA, Typing, Shorthand and Word-processing; GNVQ, Art and Design.

LANGLEY PARK SCHOOL FOR GIRLS

Hawksbrook Lane
South Eden Park Road
Beckenham
Kent BR3 3BE
Tel (0181) 650 7207/8082
Fax (0181) 663 6578
E-mail: lpgs@rmplc.co.uk

- National ranking 205 (263, 241, 246, –)
- GCSE 73% (66%)
- A-levels 29% (A/B); 84% (A/E)
- Higher education 56%

- Grant-maintained
- Girls' comprehensive
- Pupils 1,336
- Boys (11–18) *Not applicable*
- Girls (11–18) 1,336
- Sixth form 232 (17%)
- Education authority *Bromley*

Headteacher Jan Sage, 50, appointed in January 1993. Staff 69 (men 20, women 49).

Motto Ad rem mox nox (Hasten to the task, night is coming).

Background Founded as Beckenham Grammar School for Girls in 1919; moved to current site in 1959; became six-form entry comprehensive in 1976, increasing to seven-form in 1992. Buildings concentrated in a cluster on site surrounded by open space and playing fields; well-served by public transport. 'Excellent' facilities: well-stocked library, 10 science laboratories, five technology workshops, four information systems rooms, drama and ceramics studios, suites of subject rooms, floodlit all-weather pitch and courts. Outside areas recently landscaped. Over-subscribed, with three applications per place. School regularly participates in United Kingdom Mathematics Challenge, with high level of success; well-established sporting reputation, with teams successfully competing in regional and national competitions. Music and drama 'very strong': orchestra, bands and large choir perform two concerts annually. 'The ethos is very positive. The school is welcoming and friendly, and our many visitors invariably comment on its quiet, orderly and business-like atmosphere. An adherence to traditional values is combined with an appreciation of the requirements of an international and technological culture, and a progressive pace.'

Streaming Pupils put in sets according to ability in mathematics, science and modern languages. Otherwise, they are taught in tutor-groups in years 7 to 9.

Approach to discipline 'The school has high expectations of behaviour and attitude to learning. Relationships between staff and pupils and between school and home are of a high quality. Systems of reward and sanction are operated consistently and fairly.'

Uniform Navy skirt, navy blazer, pale blue shirt, navy jacket or coat. Dress code for sixth-formers. 'Requirements are consistent.'

Homework Average 11-year-old, at least two hours 15 minutes a week; 14-year old, at least seven hours 30 minutes; 16-year-old, at least 10 hours.

Vocational qualifications GNVQ, Leisure and Tourism, Health and Social Care, Business and Administration; Business Administration; Foreign Languages at Work; Computer Literacy and Information Technology.

Inspection February 1995: 'This is a good school.'; 'Pupils display excellent attitudes towards learning and make sound or good progress in the large majority of lessons. In some subjects, greater demands should be made of the most able pupils. The quality of teaching is consistently sound or good, with teachers displaying considerable subject expertise, enthusiasm and commitment.'; 'The leadership of the school is strong and effective; the governing body is very committed to the school.'; 'The school is an orderly community and standards of behaviour are very good.'

Primary schools Oak Lodge Primary; Highfield Junior; Marian Vian Primary; Pickhurst Junior; Balgowan Primary; Hawes Down Junior.

HERSCHEL GRAMMAR SCHOOL

Northampton Avenue
Slough
Berkshire SL1 3BW
Tel **(01753) 520950**
Fax **(01753) 530984**
E-mail: **mail@herschel.berks.sch.uk**

- National ranking 206 (177, 165, 160, –)
- GCSE 73% (81%)
- A-levels 26% (A/B); 90% (A/E)
- Higher education 64%

- Grant-maintained
- Mixed grammar
- Pupils 667
- Boys (11–18) 304
- Girls (11–18) 363
- Sixth form 207 (31%)
- Education authority *Berkshire*

Headteacher Julian King-Harris, 41, appointed in January 1996. Staff 43 (men 17, women 26).

Motto Achievement, challenge, excellence.

Background Sited on west of Slough town centre, within easy travelling distance of Slough as well as M4 and M40 motorways. Strong tradition of science and technology in a school that developed from former Slough Technical School, originally founded in 1943; moved to current site in 1957; adopted name from Sir William Herschel, the astronomer, who came from Slough; became Herschel Grammar School in 1984; grant-maintained since April 1992; Technology College from 1994. The school has undergone substantial refurbishment and boasts 'excellent resources and learning environment, particularly in technology and information technology which is spread throughout the school'. Facilities include open-learning centre with chartered librarian, CD-Rom and interactive video; also four fully-equipped computer rooms with multimedia Pentium technology; network of more than 85 486 computers provides a ratio of one for every five pupils; refurbished classrooms and technology block. Sporting success at rugby, rounders, netball and athletics; choir, band, instrumental lessons; strong tradition in drama and public performances; participants in Maths Challenge. Links to industry and commerce 'very strong', in particular with Slough Estates and The DataBase, principal sponsors of the Technology College.

Streaming Pupils put in sets in mathematics and English from year 9.

Approach to discipline School places great emphasis on 'positive and pro-active approach': 'Responsibility and respect for others is encouraged as the school is committed to helping the pupils develop as confident, caring, responsible and well-qualified adults. We demand high personal standards. The school has a highly supportive pastoral team and achievement is celebrated. There is a strict but fair discipline code which includes after-school detentions.'

Uniform Black blazer with school badge, white shirt, school tie (green and blue), grey trousers/skirt, grey V-neck jumper. Sixth-formers expected to wear 'smart business-like attire'.

Homework Average 12-year-old, seven hours 30 minutes a week; 14-year-old, 10 hours; 16-year-old, 10 to 12 hours 30 minutes.

Vocational qualifications GNVQ Intermediate and Advanced, Business and Finance.

Inspection March 1996.

Primary schools William Penn Primary; Claycots Middle; Godolphin Junior; James Elliman Middle; Montem Junior.

BISHOP CHALLONER RC SCHOOL

St Michael's Road
Basingstoke
Hampshire RG22 6SR
Tel (01256) 462661
Fax (01256) 810359
E-mail: 4602nezz@hants.gov.uk

- National ranking 207 (244 = , 448 = , 177, –)
- GCSE 73% (68%)
- A-levels *Not applicable*
- Higher education *Not applicable*

- Mixed comprehensive
- Pupils 589
- Boys (11–16) 290
- Girls (11–16) 299
- Sixth form *Not applicable*
- Education authority *Hampshire*

Headteacher Michael Whitty, 47, appointed in April 1995. Staff 34 (men 12, women 22).

Motto 'Sanctity . . . consists in doing ordinary things extraordinarily well' (Richard Challoner, 1691–1781).

Background Founded in 1975 as the first Roman Catholic secondary school in the area; although within the town of Basingstoke, the school draws pupils from as far as Andover, 23 miles away to the south, Tadley

and Mortimer to the north, and Hook and Odiham to the east; 'very good cross-section of socio-economic groups'; strong parental network and links with feeder parishes and schools. Over-subscribed, with 1.2 applications per place. More than nine in 10 pupils continue in full-time education at 16. New buildings in 1994: four classrooms, business studies room, information technology room, special educational needs suite, departmental office and workroom. Challoner Association of parents, pupils, staff, governors and friends of the school. Catholic faith central to life of school. Identified for praise in 1996 annual Ofsted report.

Streaming *None*

Approach to discipline 'All discipline is self-discipline based on self-respect. Pupils encouraged to value themselves and each other. Staff treat pupils with dignity and support. A few, simple regulations: deviation dealt with early, before chronic problems arise; thoroughgoing pastoral structure which subsumes academic structures.'

Uniform French-blue blazer with school badge, plain blue tie for boys, pale-blue shirt/blouse, mid-grey trousers/navy skirt. Optional pullover with school crest in colder weather. Firmly enforced.

Homework Average 11-year-old, five hours a week; 14-year-old, eight hours; 16-year-old, 12 hours.

Vocational qualifications RSA.

Inspection October 1995: 'This is a very good school with an immensely positive ethos in which pupils expect to do well and where standards are high.'; 'Pupils and staff bring commitment and enthusiasm to their work and have high expectations of themselves. Pupils meet challenge eagerly and complete work at a good pace. At times, a delayed start to some lessons detracts from the learning experience. The quality of teaching is very high. Teachers' subject expertise and their respect and care for pupils contribute significantly to progress and achievement.'; 'In assessment and reports, it is not made sufficiently clear to pupils what they have achieved and how to progress.'; 'Effective leadership at all levels is supported by the goodwill and responsiveness of staff.' *The school reports that the issues raised by the inspection have been successfully addressed.*

Primary schools St Anne's RC Primary; St

Bede's RC Primary; St John the Baptist RC Primary, Andover.

RADYR COMPREHENSIVE SCHOOL

Heol Isaf
Radyr
Cardiff CF4 8XG
Tel (01222) 842059
Fax (01222) 842139

- National ranking 208 (209, 203, 365, 227)
- GCSE 72% (72%)
- A-levels 49% (A/B); 96% (A/E)
- Higher education 91%

- Mixed comprehensive
- Pupils 1,224
- Boys (11–18) 646
- Girls (11–18) 578
- Sixth form 275 (22%)
- Education authority *Cardiff*

Headteacher Steven Michael Fowler, 47, appointed in September 1995. Staff 70 (men 28, women 42).

Motto *None*

Background Purpose-built comprehensive school opened in 1972 to serve an area to north of Cardiff and out into the Vale of Glamorgan; elevated site overlooking city and up the Taff Valley. School built around multi-level quadrangle and surrounded by extensive playing fields, including all-weather pitch and 10 tennis courts. Over-subscribed, with 1.2 applications per place. Facilities include indoor heated swimming pool and drama studio. Most teaching in departmental rooms; each year-group has its own area equipped with individual lockers for pupils. 'Great success' in wide competitive sports programme and 'excellent' performance in dance, music and drama; annual Eisteddfod a major feature of Easter term; wide-ranging Project Week in summer term. Links with schools in France and Germany include geography and science departments as well as languages; developing links with schools in Spain and elsewhere in Europe. Opportunities to learn Japanese in sixth form. The school seeks to work in close partnership with parents to help every student fulfil their potential in academic and other spheres.

Streaming Setting in modern languages and mathematics from year 8; science from year 9. Setting in most subjects in years 10 and 11.

Approach to discipline Fostering sense of self-discipline and community responsibility is central; close home–school relationship, particularly between home and form tutor, who progresses with form throughout years 7–13. Parents involved early if problem occurs.

Uniform Years 7 to 9: grey skirt/trousers, pale-blue blouse/shirt, grey V-neck pullover. Years 10 and 11: navy skirt/grey trousers, pale-blue blouse/shirt, navy V-neck pullover. Dress code for sixth-formers; no jeans. 'Full compliance is expected.'

Homework Average 11-year-old, seven hours 30 minutes a week; 14-year-old, 9 hours; 16-year-old, 15 hours.

Vocational qualifications GNVQ Intermediate, Manufacturing (years 10 and 11); GNVQ Intermediate, Art and Design, Health and Social Care (sixth form), GNVQ Advanced, Art and Design.

Inspection November 1992: 'Overall, the standards achieved range from satisfactory to good, with several instances of excellent work.'; 'The quality of education provided is generally good, spanning an appropriate range of scholastic, sporting and community experiences. Good efforts are made in various school pursuits to develop the natural talents possessed by many pupils.'

Primary schools Radyr Primary; Bryn Deri Primary; Creigiau Primary; Pen–tyrch Primary; Tongwynlais Primary; Gwaelod–y–Garth Primary.

ST NICHOLAS ROMAN CATHOLIC HIGH SCHOOL

Greenbank Lane
Hartford
Northwich
Cheshire CW8 1JW
Tel (01606) 75420
Fax (01606) 784586

- National ranking 209 (198, 233, 211, 283)
- GCSE 72% (73%)
- A-levels 39% (A/B); 88% (A/E)
- Higher education 97% (Oxford 2)

- Mixed comprehensive
- Pupils 1,068
- Boys (11–18) 539
- Girls (11–18) 529
- Sixth form 158 (15%)
- Education authority *Cheshire*

Headteacher Gerard Boyle, 48, appointed from September 1995. Staff 60 (men 25, women 35).

Motto In omnibus labora (Work in all things).

Background Catholic comprehensive in mid-Cheshire with wide catchment area. Facilities include new science wing and music suite, with another substantial extension completed in September 1994 for English, mathematics, technology, religious education and library. Extensive playing fields with athletics track shared with neighbouring school. Latin available from year 8, with classical studies in the sixth form. School noted for music; choir competes nationally and has toured United States, Holland and Austria. Over-subscribed, with 265 applications for 180 places.

Streaming All pupils in sets for English, mathematics, sciences and modern languages.

Approach to discipline Pupils expected to measure up to highest standards. 'There are clear guidelines and openly-shared values with a firm, positive and rewarding emphasis on courtesy and good behaviour.'

Uniform Years 7 to 11: brown blazer, brown sweater, grey skirt/trousers, white shirt, school tie. Sixth-formers wear black sweater, grey skirt/trousers, white shirt, school tie. Uniform is 'obligatory' throughout the school.

Homework Average 11-year-old, 10 hours a week; 14-year-old, 12 hours; 16-year-old, 14 hours.

Vocational qualifications *None*

Inspection November 1993: 'The school is efficient in creating an education that is of high quality and of benefit to all pupils. It is equally efficient in maintaining the Christian ethos of the school. All pupils of whatever level of ability are encouraged to achieve excellence in all they do. The school has created a situation in which success and achievement are valued by all.'; 'The behaviour of pupils in lessons and around the school is excellent.'

Primary schools St Wilfrid's CE Primary, Northwich; St Bede's RC Primary, Weaverham; St Mary's RC Primary, Middlewich; St Vincent's RC Primary, Knutsford; St Joseph's RC Primary, Winsford.

CHARTERS SCHOOL

Charters Road
Sunningdale
Ascot
Berkshire SL5 9QY
Tel (01344) 24826
Fax (01344) 875182

- National ranking 210 (248, 198, 265, –)
- GCSE 72% (67%)
- A-levels 37% (A/B); 92% (A/E)
- Higher education 88% (Oxford 1, Cambridge 2)

- Mixed comprehensive
- Pupils 1,361
- Boys (11–18) 715
- Girls (11–18) 646
- Sixth form 224 (16%)
- Education authority *Berkshire*

Headteacher J. Barry Mitchell, 55, appointed in April 1988. Staff 79 (men 41, women 38).

Motto Unity, respect, excellence.

Background Considerable building since school opened on 30-acre site in 1958, particularly since 1970; 'excellent' specialist accommodation for art, science, home economics, craft design technology and music; additional suites of rooms for all major departments. Other accommodation: sixth-form common room, sports hall, gymnasium, tennis courts, computer-aided design room, drama hall, careers room and school shop. New library and resource centre completed in 1992; three fully-operational information technology rooms. Sports facilities extended and open for community use. Over-subscribed, with 1.6 applications per place. School adapted to give access to physically-impaired pupils and is supported by additional teaching and non-teaching staff; physically-handicapped pupils fully integrated since 1984; wheelchair ramps and lifts; well-equipped medical suite, welfare assistant, specialist help to provide physiotherapy when needed. More than three in four pupils take part in extra-curricular activities; several sports teams at county or national level. Residential centre in Wales; Duke of Edinburgh Award Scheme.

Streaming Extensive liaison with feeder primary schools before placing year 7 pupils in mixed-ability tutor-groups that form the teaching groups. A common curriculum for the first three years. Pupils are put in sets in some subjects from year 8.

Approach to discipline 'Charters has a strong commitment to achieving the highest possible standards. The school adopts a firm and consistent but nonetheless fair approach to discipline. School discipline is supported by a comprehensive rewards system and pupils are encouraged to accept responsibility.'

Uniform Boys: black blazer with school badge, dark-grey trousers, school tie. Girls: grey skirt, white blouse, V-neck pullover with badge, school tie. Sixth-formers required to dress in 'formal manner appropriate to study and to life in a school where other students are wearing uniform'. Extremes of fashion in dress or hairstyle not permitted.

Homework Average 11-year-old, at least six hours 30 minutes a week; 14-year-old, at least 10 hours; 16-year-old, at least 13 hours.

Vocational qualifications GCSE, Business Education; GNVQ Intermediate and Advanced.

Inspection September 1996: 'A very good school with some outstanding features, which include its excellent atmosphere and very good examination results. The school has worked hard to achieve its deserved success.'; 'English skills are good in all subjects. Pupils have some strong skills in mathematics, though some basic weaknesses persist in number work.'; 'Teaching is a strength of the school. It is assured and professional in most lessons, and is of good quality in over half the lessons.' 'Though most teaching is satisfactory or good in the lower years, it is here that some shortcomings appear. These are often concerned with lack of pace, lessons which are too dominated by the teacher, and a lack of materials suitable for pupils in classes of mixed ability.'; 'Teaching is characterised by the careful setting and marking of homework. The marking of work is regular and thorough.'

Primary schools Ascot Heath CE Junior; Cheapside CE Primary; Crownwood Primary; Holy Trinity CE Primary; St Francis RC Primary; Cranbourne Primary; Harmans Water Primary; St Michael's CE Primary; Swinley Primary.

YSGOL GYFUN BRO MYRDDIN

Wellfield Road
Croesyceiliog
Carmarthen SA32 8DN
Tel (01267) 234829
Fax (01267) 221838
E-mail: myrddin@satproj.org.uk

- National ranking 211 (240, 237, 185, 205)
- GCSE 72% (68%)
- A-levels 37% (A/B); 90% (A/E)
- Higher education 82% (Oxford 1, Cambridge 1)

- Mixed comprehensive
- Pupils 773
- Boys (11–18) 413
- Girls (11–18) 360
- Sixth form 139 (18%)
- Education authority *Carmarthenshire*

Headteacher Gareth Huw Evans, 58, appointed in January 1978. Staff 44 (men 19, women 25).

Motto *None*

Background Bilingual comprehensive on town-centre site of former boys' grammar school after reorganisation of secondary education in 1978. New buildings on greenfield site in 1997. Catchment area covers rural area of Twyi Valley and extends to south Pembrokeshire. School accepts all pupils opting for a bilingual education; not over-subscribed. Up to 80% of curriculum taught in Welsh.

Alumni Emyr Lewis, Welsh rugby international.

Streaming Setting according to departmental requirements from year 8.

Approach to discipline School aims at clear, positive and consistent approach. 'A code of acceptable behaviour based on self-discipline and mutual respect is set out for pupils and discussed with them in personal and social education lessons.' Indiscipline dealt with 'fairly and objectively'; parents involved according to circumstances.

Uniform Lilac shirt, black skirt/trousers.

White shirt for sixth-formers. Rigidly enforced.

Homework Average 11-year-old, five hours a week; 14-year-old, seven hours 30 minutes; 16-year-old, 10 hours.

Vocational qualifications GNVQ Intermediate and Advanced.

Primary schools Ysgol–y–Dderwen, Carmarthen; Ysgol Nantgaredig; Ysgol Cynwyl; Ysgol Teilo Sant, Llandeilo; Ysgol Gruffydd Jones, St Clears.

BISHOPSTON COMPREHENSIVE SCHOOL

The Glebe
Bishopston
Swansea SA3 3JP
Tel (01792) 234121/234197
Fax (01792) 234808

- National ranking 212= (206=, 227=, 209=, 247=)
- GCSE 72% (73%)
- A-levels *Not applicable*
- Higher education *Not applicable*

- Mixed comprehensive
- Pupils 1,026
- Boys (11–16) 513
- Girls (11–16) 513
- Sixth form *Not applicable*
- Education authority *Swansea*

Headteacher Jacqueline Williams, 50, appointed in 1989. Staff 58 (men 27, women 31).

Motto Egni a lwydd (Effort leads to success).

Background Bishopston is set on a 20-acre site on the Gower Peninsula, designated area of outstanding natural beauty. Opened in 1976 with purpose-built facilities: well-equipped faculty rooms, two gymnasia, tennis courts, extensive playing fields. New Learning Resource Centre includes library, five computer networks, audio-visual equipment. Popular school that attempts to accept all who wish to attend; not over-subscribed. Broad curriculum strength. Sporting achievements include local and national titles in rugby, cricket, hockey, netball, tennis and swimming. Creative arts: two school productions annually; successes in local debating and writing competitions. Overseas trips include skiing, sporting exchange with Canada, and cultural exchange with France.

Streaming Various pupil-groupings used, according to the needs of pupils and subjects. Setting by ability used in mathematics and languages.

Approach to discipline High standards set. 'Pupils are required to be courteous, co-operative and contributing members of the school community. Indiscipline is penalised immediately.'

Uniform White shirt, navy V-neck sweater with school badge, grey trousers or navy skirt, school tie, white socks/navy tights, black shoes. Rigidly enforced.

Homework Average 11-year-old, nine to 10 hours a week; 14-year-old, 10 to 12 hours; 16-year-old, 10 to 15 hours.

Vocational qualifications *None*

Inspection October 1995: 'The quality of pupils' learning is generally at least satisfactory and is often good. Pupils display responsible attitudes to their work, co-operate well together and respond positively to challenges. In most cases, they work at a good pace, with a good degree of independence and with confidence. In a small minority of cases, pupils are more passive and contribute less. The teaching provided is also at least satisfactory in the great majority of cases, with a significant proportion being good.'; 'The school has a positive ethos which emphasises high academic standards and is generally well-regarded by parents. Attendance is high. The school is an orderly community in which good standards of behaviour are both expected and evident in practice. Pupils are generally courteous and considerate, and exercise self-discipline.'

Primary schools Bishopston Primary; Crwys Primary; Knelston Primary; Mayals Primary; Newton Primary; Pennard Primary.

DEBENHAM CHURCH OF ENGLAND HIGH SCHOOL

Gracechurch Street
Debenham
Stowmarket
Suffolk IP14 6BL
Tel (01728) 860213
Fax (01728) 860998

- National ranking 212 = (302 =, 494 =, 279 =, 230 =)
- GCSE 72% (63%)
- A-levels *Not applicable*
- Higher education *Not applicable*

- Mixed comprehensive
- Pupils 380
- Boys (11–16) 185
- Girls (11–16) 195
- Sixth form *Not applicable*
- Education authority *Suffolk*

Headteacher Michael Crawshaw, 45, appointed in April 1989. Staff 27 (men 13, women 14).

Motto *None*

Background School built in 1964, with new science, music and languages block added in 1980. Set on rural western edge of picturesque village of Debenham. Continuous programme of redecoration and refurbishment. School roll has risen considerably to record level; entry limit increase in 1993 to satisfy demand for places; over-subscribed, with waiting list for several year-groups. Nearly three in four school-leavers go on to post-16 education. School has won several awards for poetry; published school anthology in 1993; received special award in 1993 W. H. Smith Young Writers' competition; one pupil won national competition to design postcard for Amnesty International; school pop group; annual arts festival; scientific links with industry, particularly British Telecom Research plc. 'We are a small school but we have big ideas and aim high!'

Streaming Some ability sets for English, mathematics, science and languages.

Approach to discipline Discipline reported to be very good; few rules but teachers expect them to be obeyed. 'Pupils are trusted and given responsibility (open classrooms at lunchtimes, for example), and respond positively.' Pupils learn responsibility as school councillors, prefects and librarians.

Uniform White shirt, black/dark-grey trousers or skirt, black V-neck sweater, black shoes. Boys wear house tie.

Homework Average 11-year-old, five to six hours a week; 14-year-old, eight to 10 hours; 16-year-old, 10 to 12 hours.

Vocational qualifications *None*

Inspection November 1996: 'Debenham High School offers a happy and caring learning environment in which pupils are encouraged to develop a sense of reponsibility and concern for others and are challenged to achieve to their full potential.'; 'Pupils' attitudes and behaviour are major strengths of the school and have a significantly positive impact upon pupils' attainment and progress. The academic, cultural and sporting success of pupils are evidence of their positive attitudes to school.'; 'Pupils' behaviour in lessons and around the school is excellent.'; 'The quality of teaching at the school is high and is a major contributory factor to the progress and attainment of pupils. Teachers generally have a good command of their subject and a detailed knowledge of their pupils. Many have taught their subject for some years to the same pupils and are able to give them careful individual assistance.'; 'Lessons move forward urgently with a variety of activities to motivate pupils.'

Primary schools Sir Robert Hitcham CE Primary; Stonham Aspal CE Primary; Wetheringsett CE Primary.

ST THOMAS MORE CATHOLIC HIGH SCHOOL

Dane Bank Avenue
Crewe
Cheshire CW2 8AE
Tel (01270) 68014
Fax (01270) 650860

- National ranking 212 = (279 =, 242 =, –, 368 =)
- GCSE 72% (65%)
- A-levels *Not applicable*
- Higher education *Not applicable*

- Mixed comprehensive
- Pupils 520
- Boys (11–16) 250
- Girls (11–16) 270
- Sixth form *Not applicable*
- Education authority *Cheshire*

Headteacher George Redmond Pollard, 60, appointed in September 1977. Staff 32 (men 11, women 21).

Motto *None*

Background Located on outskirts of Crewe on

Dane Bank campus in buildings dating from 1965, when school was established as a secondary modern. Additions in 1975 and 1980; some recent internal remodelling. Reorganised in 1978 as a comprehensive serving Catholics in south Cheshire; pupils from Crewe, Alsager, Sandbach and Nantwich. Not over-subscribed; seven in 10 (70%) continue with education. Voluntary-aided; Christian ethos; 'creative approach' to religious education; day retreats and residential visits in all five year-groups.

Streaming Mixture of setting and mixed-ability teaching in year 7. Extended in year 8 on basis of faster and slower set in each half-year group. 'Pupils are extracted for extra help in mathematics and English, and supported by extra staff in some other subjects.'

Approach to discipline Insistence on orderly environment. 'It is fair and firm, but there is a relaxed and friendly atmosphere. Sanctions are few, but after-school detention is one.'

Uniform Blue blazer with school emblem, pale-blue shirt/blouse, school tie, grey trousers/skirt, grey V-neck sweater with blue trim, grey/white socks. 'All pupils always in full uniform.'

Homework Average 11-year-old, 10 hours a week; 14-year-old, 12 hours 30 minutes; 16-year-old, 15 hours.

Vocational qualifications *None*

Inspection December 1993: 'This is a good school providing education of a high standard fully in accord with its stated aims. It has the strong support of parents and is respected by the community it serves. Its lively Catholic ethos pervades all aspects of school life.'; 'The quality of pupils' learning is good or very good in well over half of all lessons, despite the limitations on learning resources in some areas and the pressure on accommodation.'; 'The quality of teaching is high. Staff work hard to compensate for any constraints related to time or resources and to fulfil the potential of pupils.'; 'The school is an orderly, safe and caring community.'

Primary schools St Mary's RC Primary, Crewe; St Anne's RC Primary, Nantwich; St Gabriel's RC Primary, Alsager.

ST ANNE'S CONVENT SCHOOL

Rockstone Place
Southampton
Hampshire SO15 2WZ

Tel (01703) 328200
Fax (01703) 331767

- National ranking 215 (213, 212, 228, 223)
- GCSE 71% (72%)
- A-levels 65% (A/B); 91% (A/E)
- Higher education 73% (Oxford 2, Cambridge 1)

- Grant-maintained
- Girls' comprehensive
- Pupils 1,117
- Boys *Not applicable*
- Girls (11–18) 1,117
- Sixth form 150 (13%)
- Education authority *Hampshire*

Headteacher Catherine Hargaden, 51, appointed in January 1989. Staff 66 (men 10, women 56).

Motto Semper fidelis (Ever faithful).

Background Established in 1906 by the Sisters of the La Sainte Union congregation. Has grown with addition of three new blocks. The school, which receives 1.4 applications for each place, is close to the city centre in a business and residential area. Pupils come from all of south Hampshire to attend. Became grant-maintained in April 1994. In music, its choir has reached national finals as well as touring various countries. Pupils have also appeared nationally for public speaking and science. Careers programme includes opportunities for work experience and work-shadowing. Prides itself on all-round curriculum strength, but mathematics and science departments regarded as particularly strong, enabling girls to go on to careers in medicine, engineering and veterinary science.

Streaming Pupils taught in broad ability groups in early years. Placed in sets for individual subjects in years 9 to 11.

Approach to discipline 'Firm but kind.' Emphasis on personal responsibility; discipline 'viewed in the context of relationships and pastoral care'.

Uniform Navy blazer, skirt and jumper, pale-blue blouse, navy tie with diagonal stripe. No uniform for sixth-formers; regulations applied 'rigorously and sensitively'.

Homework Average 11-year-old, four hours a week; 14-year-old, six hours; 16-year-old, 10 hours.

Vocational qualifications GNVQ Levels 2 and 3, Health and Social Care; GNVQ Levels 2 and 3, Business Studies; Certificate of Childcare Education; RSA, Word-processing.

Primary schools Springhill Catholic Primary; Holy Family RC Primary; St Patrick's RC Primary; St Jude's Catholic Primary; St Swithun Wells RC Primary.

SANDBACH HIGH SCHOOL

Middlewich Road
Sandbach
Cheshire CW11 3NT
Tel (01270) 765031
Fax (01270) 768544
E-mail: sandhigh@rmplc.co.uk

- National ranking 216 (182, 371, 366, 213)
- GCSE 71% (77%)
- A-levels 41% (A/B); 97% (A/E)
- Higher education 75% (Oxford 1, Cambridge 1)

- Girls' comprehensive
- Pupils 1,095
- Boys *Not applicable*
- Girls (11–18) 1,095
- Sixth form 176 (16%)
- Education authority *Cheshire*

Headteacher John Leigh, 38, appointed in September 1993. Staff 67 (men 25, women 42).

Motto *None*

Background Developed in 1979 from a mixed secondary modern; six-form entry school, built in 1960 in pleasant residential area; substantial extensions opened in 1975; further additions in 1995. Facilities include: assembly hall, dining room, seven science laboratories, two computing rooms, technology suite, art suite and gallery, music suite, drama studio, library. Sixth-form centre, including common room and new classroom/study block, opened in spring 1997. Playing fields next to school; all-weather pitch, hard tennis courts; joint-use swimming pool, sports hall, squash courts. Fully-subscribed, taking 45 'out-of-zone' pupils annually. International acclaim for music; 150 girls take instrumental tuition in school time; orchestra, various school choirs, folk group, concert band, string groups. Festival choir won international competition in Switzerland, and acclaim for performances in Maastricht, Cologne, Barcelona and Strasburg. Sporting strengths include athletics, hockey, netball, volleyball, cross-country, and tennis. Junior athletics team came third in 1993 TSB National Athletics Cup. French exchange with school near Paris; Spanish exchange with school near Madrid. Parents' and Friends' Association.

Streaming Flexible setting or groupings in years 7 to 9; setting in most subjects from year 10.

Approach to discipline 'Pupils are expected to conform to an established standard of behaviour both in and out of school and, in particular, to observe matters of courtesy and consideration at all times.'

Uniform Years 7 to 11: black blazer with school badge, black skirt, white shirt, school tie. Strictly enforced.

Homework Average 11-year-old, seven hours at week; 14-year-old, 10 hours; 16-year-old, 10 hours.

Vocational qualifications GNVQ Intermediate and Advanced, Business, Health and Social Care; NVQs; RSA; Pitman.

Inspection November 1995: 'This is a high-achieving, successful and flourishing school community which enables girls to become mature and articulate young people. The school provides a calm working environment in which girls learn effectively.'; 'Pupils generally enjoy their lessons and are highly-motivated. They co-operate well with their teachers and with each other. They display excellent attitudes to work, are well-behaved and work hard to succeed in a climate of endeavour successfully created by well-qualified and hard-working staff.'

Primary schools Offley County Junior; Elworth CE Primary; Elworth Hall County Primary; Sandbach County Primary; St John's CE Primary; Wheelock County Primary; Haslington County Primary; The Dingle County Primary, Haslington.

STOKESLEY SCHOOL

Station Road
Stokesley
North Yorkshire TS9 5AL
Tel (01642) 710050
Fax (01642) 710836

E-mail: stoke@campus.bt.com
Internet: http://www.campus.bt.com/
campusWorld/orgs/org1733/
index.html

- National ranking 217 (219, 410 = , 196, 197)
- GCSE 71% (70%)
- A-levels 41% (A/B); 91% (A/E)
- Higher education 97% (Cambridge 4)

- Mixed comprehensive
- Pupils 1,232
- Boys (11–18) 587
- Girls (11–18) 645
- Sixth form 235 (19%)
- Education authority *North Yorkshire*

Headteacher Brian Owen, 46, appointed in September 1994. Staff 72 (men 31, women 41).

Motto Labor omnia vincit (Toil conquers all).

Background Main building dates from 1958 and commended by Pevsner in guide to local architecture; subsequent additions; extensive playing fields with views of nearby hills of North Yorkshire Moors to the south. Became comprehensive in 1972. Pupils travel up to 18 miles, from villages or small towns between Castleton and Danby in the east and the A19 (Ingleby Arncliffe) in the west; some parents from Cleveland opt to send children to the school. School community is mixture of urban and rural pupils, with many parents commuting to Teesside. Over-subscribed, with 246 applications for 231 places. Sporting facilities described as excellent; reputation in sport, music and drama; series of clubs and activities; wide opportunities for educational visits; school's sixth-form college has established strong reputation. Both individuals and teams 'achieve highly' in all areas of extra-curricular activity. 'The school's great strength is that it neither pursues trendiness nor fails to respond to initiatives.' Identified as 'highly successful' following Ofsted inspection.

Streaming Pupils put in sets in mathematics and modern languages from early stage; several subjects create upper and lower group from among two forms in year 9; examination pupils grouped according to their targets. 'The policy is to be flexible and to keep the doors of opportunity open as long as possible.'

Approach to discipline Friendly but firm; pupils

know where they stand and are supportive of rules that are recognised to be sensible and for the good of everyone. 'Visitors comment frequently on the politeness and openness of pupils, the lack of graffiti and the warm welcome extended at the reception office, and from staff and pupils.'

Uniform Navy school sweatshirt, white shirt, black/navy trousers or skirt, plain grey/white/navy/black socks or tights, black shoes. 'There is no discrimination between boys and girls, and the wearing of uniform is compulsory at all times. The rules are enforced firmly, but the school makes clear that the priorities are important matters such as work, effort and commitment.'

Homework Average 11-year-old, five hours a week; 14-year-old, eight to 10 hours; 16-year-old, 12 to 13 hours.

Vocational qualifications GNVQ Advanced, Business Studies, Health and Social Care; Diploma of Vocational Education.

Inspection December 1996.

Primary schools Stokesley Primary; Roseberry Primary; Hutton Rudby Primary; Kirby and Broughton CE Primary; Swainby Primary.

COTHAM GRAMMAR SCHOOL

Cotham Lawn Road
Bristol BS6 6DS
Tel (0117) 908 2200
Fax (0117) 908 2209

- National ranking 218 (287, 179, 231, 224)
- GCSE 71% (64%)
- A-levels 37% (A/B); 85% (A/E)
- Higher education 90% (Oxford 1)

- Mixed grammar
- Pupils 1,060
- Boys (11–18) 540
- Girls (11–18) 520
- Sixth form 224 (21%)
- Education authority *Bristol*

Headteacher James Wetz, 49, appointed in April 1997. Staff 67 (men 28, women 39).

Motto Mens bona regnum possidet (The good mind possesses the kingdom).

Background Occupied site within a mile of Bristol city centre since 1920; main school built in 1931, with substantial additions in

1960s and 1970s. Tradition goes back 150 years and is linked to education provided by the Merchant Venturers. Originally a boys' school, it became co-educational in 1973. Over-subscribed, with three applications per place. Aim in Mission Statement: 'A caring, challenging community built on tradition, open to change.' Proud of 'exceptional ability' of pupils in performing and creative arts.

Alumni John James, former radio retailer and philanthropist; Paul Dirac, Nobel prizewinner for theoretical physics; Derek Robinson, playwright and broadcaster; Gary Mabbutt, Tottenham Hotspur and England soccer player; Arthur Milton, David Allen, John Mortimore, the only three England cricketers from one school to play tests in one year.

Streaming Pupils in sets in mathematics and modern languages from year 8; broad ability bands in science from year 10.

Approach to discipline 'Our approach aims to foster self-discipline and create an atmosphere in which achievements can be celebrated, valued and enjoyed.' Carefully-documented rewards and discipline procedures; close partnership with parents.

Uniform Dress code incorporates sweatshirts and sports kit with school's 'tower' emblem, the traditional badge of the school. All pupils in years 7 to 11 expected to adhere to dress code.

Homework Average 11-year-old, five hours a week; 14-year-old, eight hours; 16-year-old, 10 hours.

Vocational qualifications GNVQ Intermediate and Advanced, Business.

Primary schools Colston's Primary; Westbury Park Primary; Sefton Park Primary; Bishop Road Primary; St John's CE Primary.

CORFE HILLS SCHOOL

Higher Blandford Road
Broadstone
Dorset BH18 9BG
Tel (01202) 697541
Fax (01202) 658974

- National ranking 219 (359, 344, 311, 329)
- GCSE 71% (60%)
- A-levels 34% (A/B); 90% (A/E)
- Higher education 75% (Oxford 4)

- Mixed comprehensive
- Pupils 1,616
- Boys (13–18) 802
- Girls (13–18) 814
- Sixth form 470 (29%)
- Education authority *Dorset*

Headteacher Andrew Huw Williams, 46, appointed in September 1990. Staff 100 (men 46, women 54).

Motto Comprehensive Excellence.

Background School founded in 1976 as upper school for a pyramid now comprising six first schools and three middle schools. Takes name from low hills north of Poole Harbour where it has heathland site, serving mix of rural and suburban catchment area. Over-subscribed, with 1.2 applications per place and more than 50 'out-of-area' applicants annually. Specialist suites for business studies, art and design, drama, music and technology; large sports hall and 14-laboratory science area. All year 9 pupils study two languages; distance-learning of Latin available to older pupils. Most pupils enter 10 GCSEs from a choice of 26 subjects; 28 A-level subjects offered; annual musical productions feature among professional companies at Poole Arts Centre's Towngate Theatre. High parental involvement: 98% attendance at 'report evenings'.

Streaming Opposed to streaming. But pupils are set by ability in separate subjects. Mixed-ability in religious, personal and social education, physical education, creative arts.

Approach to discipline 'Open, firm, fair but, wherever possible, friendly.' Stress on close liaison with home and importance of self-discipline; well-defined rewards structure; clearly escalating sanctions.

Uniform Distinctive camel and dark-brown uniform with school logo. Dress code for sixth-formers within brown/cream colour range. Enforced strictly.

Homework Average 14-year-old, 10 hours a week; 16-year-old, 12 hours.

Vocational qualifications NVQ Level 2 and 3, Business Administration; GNVQ Level 2 and 3, Leisure, Health and Social Care.

Inspection October 1993: 'The school provides an education of the highest quality.'; 'Students, parents, staff and governors share the school's ideals in a consistent, powerful and pervasive way. Relationships between staff and students, and between students and students, are excellent. Student behaviour in and out of the classroom, supervised and unsupervised, is excellent. There is an attitude of mutual respect and a sense of relaxed good humour and purposefulness. The quality of learning is enhanced by self-discipline.'

Primary schools Broadstone Middle; Lockyers Middle; Allenbourn Middle.

RANGE HIGH SCHOOL

Stapleton Road
Formby
Liverpool
Merseyside L37 2YN
Tel (01704) 879315
Fax (01704) 833470

- National ranking 220 (262, 224, 198, 185)
- GCSE 71% (66%)
- A-levels 33% (A/B); 92% (A/E)
- Higher education 84% (Oxford 1, Cambridge 2)

- Mixed comprehensive
- Pupils 1,108
- Boys (11–18) 573
- Girls (11–18) 535
- Sixth form 164 (15%)
- Education authority Sefton

Headteacher Michael J. Dixon, 45, appointed in September 1992. Staff 67 (men 25, women 42).

Motto None

Background Opened in 1975 in new buildings on 20-acre site close to sea near pine woods and sand dunes on National Trust Reserve. Catchment area mainly from private housing developments to west and south of Formby (population 27,000); increasing number of pupils from Southport, seven miles away, and northern suburbs of Liverpool, 14 miles away. Over-subscribed, with 285 applications for 195 places. 'Excellent' pastoral care system; Duke of Edinburgh Award Scheme; community service and charitable work. School designated to accommodate pupils with physical disabilities, with total integration into mainstream education. Innovative careers programme. Identified in 1996 Ofsted annual report as 'providing good quality education and achieving high standards'.

Streaming Pupils put in sets for English and mathematics in year 7, with extra help for those with special needs. Increased setting as pupils progress through school. All pupils entered for external examinations.

Approach to discipline 'The approach to discipline is based on firmness balanced by fairness, the two broad principles being respect for people and respect for property. The school's approach is to provide a caring environment in which all pupils have the right to learn and all teachers have the right to teach.'

Uniform Black blazer with school badge, grey skirt/trousers, blue shirt/blouse, magenta-and-blue tie. 'Our emphasis is on smartness and all pupils are expected to wear full uniform.'

Homework Average 11-year-old, six hours a week; 14-year-old, nine hours; 16-year-old, 15 hours.

Vocational qualifications GNVQ Intermediate and Advanced, Health and Social Care, Business and Finance.

Inspection October 1995: 'A good school with a deservedly high reputation for academic success. The pupils respond well to the wide range of educational experience provided within a positive and supportive ethos.'; 'Pupils are well-motivated and responsive and generally make good progress, although in some cases the nature of the task prevents the ablest pupils from achieving the levels of which they are capable.'; 'Attitudes to work are very positive and most pupils are able to sustain concentration over long periods. There is a culture in the school that values learning highly and this contributes significantly to attainment.'

Primary schools Woodlands Primary; St Luke's CE Primary; St Jerome's RC Primary; Redgate Primary; St Peter's CE Primary; Our Lady's RC Primary.

ST BEDE'S SCHOOL

Carlton Road
Redhill
Surrey RH1 2DD
Tel (01737) 212108
Fax (01737) 212118
E-mail: stbedes@tcns.co.uk

- National ranking 221 (222, 390, 215, 199)

- GCSE 71% (70%)
- A-levels 25% (A/B); 93% (A/E)
- Higher education 75% (Cambridge 1)

- Mixed comprehensive
- Pupils 1,486
- Boys (11–18) 664
- Girls (11–18) 822
- Sixth form 290 (20%)
- Education authority *Surrey*

Headteacher Julian D. Marcus, 53, appointed in January 1985. Staff 81 (men 33, women 48).

Motto *None*

Background Sited in residential area of Redhill and Reigate under southern slope of the North Downs, used by the school for field work and Duke of Edinburgh Award Scheme. St Bede's was founded in 1976 as Britain's first voluntary-aided mixed, ecumenical comprehensive. It was the result of the amalgamation of two smaller Church of England and Roman Catholic schools. More than £4m spent since 1988 on improvements: technology centre, drama studio, connected suites of rooms for most departments; new £1.84 million science centre in 1998. There are four computer networks, a fitness room with 'computerised treadmill' and an all-weather Astroturf pitch. Oversubscribed, with average of 1.3 applications per place. Five partner schools in France, Germany, Spain, New York and Tanzania. Creative arts has included resident artist and project with Royal Opera House. Creative arts include 'exceptional' drama performances, art exhibition annually in town and two orchestras. Voluntary Church of England Eucharists, Roman Catholic Masses and Free Church services organised weekly by chaplains.

Streaming Mixed-ability in first year. Setting in national curriculum core subjects and modern languages from year 8. Learning Support Department provides special help, in class and by withdrawal, for pupils with special needs; enhancement and extra tutorial system for gifted pupils.

Approach to discipline Heads of year and form-tutors responsible for welfare and discipline within the year; normally move up with the year to maintain continuity. 'We seek a civilised, hard-working and well-ordered school in which students' growing maturity is encouraged and reinforced. We regard praise as far more important than punishment, and incidents of indiscipline are few.'

Uniform In years 7 to 11. Girls: navy skirt, school blouse. Boys: dark trousers, white/blue shirt, school tie. Both wear school pullover with logo. 'Uniform is enforced firmly, but not obsessively.'

Homework Average 11-year-old, two hours 30 minutes to three hours 30 minutes a week; 14-year-old, five to six hours; 16-year-old, six to eight hours.

Vocational qualifications RSA, Information Technology; GNVQ Intermediate and Advanced, Health and Care, Business.

Primary schools St Joseph's RC Primary; St Francis's RC Primary; Reigate Priory Primary; Brambletye Junior; St John's CE Junior.

ROBERT MAY'S SCHOOL

West Street
Odiham
Hook
Hampshire RG25 1NA
Tel (01256) 702700
Fax (01256) 703012
E-mail: 4511Nezz@hants.gov.uk

- National ranking 222
- GCSE 71%
- A-levels *Not applicable*
- Higher education *Not applicable*

- Mixed comprehensive
- Pupils 1,110
- Boys (11–16) 530
- Girls (11–16) 580
- Sixth form *Not applicable*
- Education authority *Hampshire*

Headteacher Will Sarell, 46, appointed in April 1987. Staff 65 (men 38, women 27).

Motto *None.*

Background Founded in 1694; became comprehensive in 1975 and moved to new buildings; located in rural setting overlooking the Whitewater Valley in north Hampshire, with its own extensive grounds and playing fields. Over-subscribed, with 1.2 applications per place. High standards in music, drama and sport; purpose-built facilities for music, also orchestra, steel band, swing band, various instrumental groups, choir. The school has teams in all year-groups for: athletics, hockey, netball, football, badminton, cricket, basketball; competes at local, county and national level. The school aims to be a friendly, caring community where all pupils will feel valued and in which all pupils will be encouraged to aim for excellence in all that they do.' Investors in People Award 1997; identified as 'outstandingly successful' in 1997 annual Ofsted report.

Streaming Setting in various subjects.

Approach to discipline 'Firm but fair. Parents always involved if serious problems arise.'

Uniform Jumper with school logo for boys and girls, white shirt, dark-grey trousers/ grey skirt, tie for boys.

Homework Average 11-year-old, seven hours a week; 14-year-old, 10 hours; 16-year-old, 12 to 15 hours.

Vocational qualifications City and Guilds, Diploma in Vocational Education.

Primary schools Hook Junior; Mayhill Junior; Greenfields Junior; Long Sutton CE Primary; Whitewater CE Primary; St Mary's CE Primary.

ALSAGER SCHOOL

Hassall Road
Alsager
Cheshire ST7 2HR
Tel (01270) 873221
Fax (01270) 884335
E-mail: 9064121.depot@dialnet.co.uk
Internet: http://www.alsager-school.demon.co.uk/alsager/als.html

- National ranking 223 (396, 211, 193, 287)
- GCSE 70% (58%)
- A-levels 42% (A/B); 96% (A/E)
- Higher education 90% (Oxford 1, Cambridge 3)

- Mixed comprehensive
- Pupils 1,497
- Boys (11–18) 760
- Girls (11–18) 737
- Sixth form 269 (18%)
- Education authority *Cheshire*

Headteacher David Black, 45, appointed in September 1993. Staff 88 (men 46, women 42).

Motto Educating and preparing for life so that all achieve their highest potential. Serving the community in the widest possible way.

Background The school became a comprehensive in 1971 on a site previously occupied by Alsager County Secondary School. Five-year building programme: classroom block, science laboratories, canteen, design block, joint-use leisure centre with floodlit all-weather Astro-turf pitch. Campus neighbours Grig Woodland, a conservation area. Increasing proportion of 'out-of-area' pupils (25%), particularly from north Staffordshire. Over-subscribed, with 290 applications for 245 places. Only secondary school in the town; many staff have their own children at the school. Enterprise Week; continental work-experience in Brittany and Bavaria; charity fund-raising; soccer, rugby, swimming, athletics, gymnastics and archery among sporting strengths; a total of 20 pupils represented county in 1995; 1994 national archery champions; two pupils in English gymnastics team; Cheshire sailing champions; 1995 national under-14 swimming champions in freestyle and medley relay; eight pupils in Cheshire Youth Orchestra and two in National Youth Orchestra.

Streaming Mixed-ability in year 7; in all other years, setting according to ability in mathematics, English, science, humanities, modern languages, technology, music and art. Drama and physical education taught in mixed groups.

Approach to discipline Emphasis on co-operation rather than confrontation; code of behaviour. 'The code is intended to encourage self-discipline while laying down a framework within which the school can operate in the best interests of all pupils.' Staff have received 'assertive discipline' training.

Uniform Black blazer with badge, grey skirt/ trousers, white shirt, blue-white-and-black striped tie, mid-grey V-neck jumper, grey/ white socks or black/neutral tights, black shoes. Sixth-formers wear 'office dress'. No denim. Strictly enforced.

Homework Average 11-year-old, five to six hours a week; 14-year-old, seven hours 30 minutes to eight hours; 16-year-old, 10 hours.

Vocational qualifications Foreign Languages at Work; RSA, Computer Literacy and Information Technology; GNVQs being considered.

Inspection November 1996: 'A very good school. The quality of teaching is markedly good and pupils achieve well and make good progress within a caring and secure framework.'; 'Internal accommodation is sufficient but not extensive. However, the school benefits from the leisure centre which is located on its premises.'; 'Standards of literacy are generally good in both key stages and in the sixth form. Pupils present their ideas in a confident and informed manner and they are good listeners.'; 'Throughout the school, the quality of teaching is mainly good and better.'; 'Quality of teaching is a strength in the school; an unusually high proportion of good teaching reports were awarded. There are instances of outstanding teaching in a range of subjects, including English, design and technology, mathematics, modern foreign languages and religious education. However, pupils need further opportunities to develop independent learning in some subjects, including some in the sixth form.'; 'Homework is given regularly throughout the school and well used to extend and reinforce learning.'

Primary schools Pikemere County Primary; Cranberry County Junior; Excalibur County Primary; Alsager Highfields County Primary; Church Lawton Gate County Primary; Rode Heath County Primary; St Gabriel's RC Primary.

THE PIGGOTT SCHOOL

Twyford Road
Wargrave
Reading
Berkshire RG10 8DS
Tel (0118) 9402357
Fax (0118) 9404892

- National ranking 224 (–, 428, 351 =)
- GCSE 58%
- A-levels 41% (A/B); 94% (A/E)
- Higher education 88% (Cambridge 1)

- Mixed comprehensive
- Pupils 813
- Boys (11–18) 405
- Girls (11–18) 408
- Sixth form 125 (15%)
- Education authority *Berkshire*

Headteacher Dr Keith Atton, 50, appointed in September 1989. Staff 49 (men 20, women 29).

Motto Sursum corda (Lift up your hearts).

Background Founded as co-educational Church Foundation School in 1796 by Robert Piggott; moved to current rural site in commuter belt in 1940; became voluntary-controlled in 1965, and comprehensive in 1973. Not over-subscribed; local population declining; increasing proportion of intake (30%) choose the school from outside the catchment area. Successful at sport, particularly cross-country. 'Outstanding' choral tradition. Christian ethos. Quality of sixth-form teaching commended in inspectors' report and follow-up visit.

Streaming Mixed-ability in year 7; pupils in sets in modern languages from year 8, and in mathematics, English, science and humanities from year 9.

Approach to discipline Firm discipline. Monitored by heads of year and departments, with reference to pastoral deputy head and headteacher. Punishments include extra work, break-time or afterschool detention, 'on report', working in isolation and exclusion as last resort. Code of conduct 'encourages the development of self-discipline'.

Uniform White shirt, royal-blue jumper, grey trousers/skirt, tie for boys. Strictly enforced.

Homework Average 11-year-old, four to five hours a week; 14-year-old, five to six hours; 16-year-old, five to 10 hours.

Vocational qualifications GNVQ, Intermediate and Advanced, Business, Health and Social Care.

Inspection January 1994: 'The Piggott School is a good school with some very good features. The school provides an effective education and good value for money.'; 'Staff are well-qualified and hard-working. Teaching is competent and sound. Teachers use praise and encouragement frequently with pupils to promote high expectations of work and behaviour. Most pupils respond well to these high expectations; they are well-motivated and relationships are good. Most pupils feel happy and cared for in the school.'

Primary schools Polehampton Junior; Robert Piggott CE Junior; Colleton Primary; Sonning CE Primary; Waltham St Lawrence Primary.

HIGHCLIFFE SCHOOL

Parkside
Highcliffe
Christchurch
Dorset BH23 4QD
Tel (01425) 273381
Fax (01425) 271405
E-mail: highclif@rmplc.co.uk

- National ranking 225= (382=, 378=, 337=, 260=)
- GCSE 70% (59%)
- A-levels *Not applicable*
- Higher education *Not applicable*

- Grant-maintained
- Mixed comprehensive
- Pupils 918
- Boys (11–16) 482
- Girls (11–16) 436
- Sixth form *Not applicable*
- Education authority *Dorset*

Headteacher Frederick Shepherd, 49, appointed in September 1987. Staff 58 (men 23, women 35).

Motto *None*

Background Originally established upon re-organisation of former Christchurch Grammar School. Original buildings completed in 1962, with additional laboratories and classrooms added later; single site, with six acres of playing fields. Over-subscribed, with small catchment area and many 'out-of-area' pupils; 1.5 applications per place. More than 300 pupils learn musical instruments. Regional and national competition for sports teams. Winner of Queen's Anniversary Trust Silver Award for long-term project on access for the disabled; also winner of Southern England in Bloom Chairman's Prize. Healthy Schools Award for 1995–7 for its wide-ranging attention to health-related issues. 'We expect to work hard and achieve a great deal in academic, sporting and musical achievements within an atmosphere that is friendly yet firm.'

Alumni Stacey Hillyard, 1984 women's world snooker champion.

Streaming In mathematics and French.

Approach to discipline Principles based on consideration for others, and respect for them and their property. 'Staff at the school work hard to assist the pupils to behave well,

and this emphasis has fostered excellent pupil behaviour and discipline.' New discipline code developed by staff and pupils in 1996.

Uniform Purple pullover/cardigan, grey trousers/skirt, school tie, black/brown/grey shoes.

Homework Average 11-year-old, six to seven hours a week; 14-year-old, seven hours 30 minutes; 16-year-old, 10 hours.

Vocational qualifications *None*

Inspection October 1993: 'This is a good school. The standards achieved by pupils are good in both key stages, except for information technology capability, which is more variable.'; 'Pupils are competent learners and are well organised and motivated.'; 'The school is well-organised and managed. Although spending on educational resources has increased this year, limited resources is affecting learning in some areas. There is a strong sense of community and shared values.'

Primary schools Highcliffe Junior; Mudeford Junior; Burton CE Primary; Sway St Luke's CE Primary; Tiptoe Primary.

MILLAIS SCHOOL

Depot Road
Horsham
West Sussex RH13 5HR
Tel (01403) 254932
Fax (01403) 211729

- National ranking 225= (195=, 205=, 188=, 190)
- GCSE 70% (74%)
- A-levels *Not applicable*
- Higher education *Not applicable*

- Girls' comprehensive
- Pupils 1,210
- Boys *Not applicable*
- Girls (11–16) 1,210
- Sixth form *Not applicable*
- Education authority *West Sussex*

Headteacher Leon Nettley, 44, appointed in January 1997. Staff 65 (men 10, women 55).

Motto There are no limits.

Background School has existed since 1973 on east side of Horsham; serves town and surrounding villages, with many girls choosing to come to the school from a very wide area. Main school building, with lower school building, separate music block and mathematics block. Each department has own suite of rooms. Waiting lists for all year-groups with 1.1 applications per place. Nine in 10 pupils (90%) continue education after 16. All pupils take 10 subjects at GCSE. A *seccion bilingue* runs in years 10 and 11 in which girls study GCSE Business Studies entirely in Spanish. 'The school promotes a positive ethos of courtesy, co-operation, caring, and commitment. Students are expected to exercise personal responsibility, to be well-motivated and involved. The school encourages girls not only to achieve their potential, but also to set their sights high and to explore career paths that are not traditionally female.' Wide range of off-site visits and other extra-curricular activities.

Streaming Pupils set according to ability in mathematics, English, science, modern languages and humanities.

Approach to discipline 'Very high standards of behaviour, dress and attitude are set, expected and enforced. Rewards are offered in preference to sanctions.'

Uniform Bottle-green skirt, tights and sweater/sweatshirt, cream blouse, school tie. 'Full and correct uniform is worn by all girls.'

Homework Average 11-year-old, five hours a week; 14-year-old, seven hours 30 minutes to 10 hours; 16-year-old, 10 to 15 hours.

Vocational qualifications *None*

Inspection May 1996: 'A very good school with some outstanding features. It serves its community well. Its effective monitoring of performance enables it to identify potential or actual weaknesses.'; 'Its achievements are significant given its size, the above-average teaching load and well-below average funding.'; 'There is continuous improvement as pupils of differing abilities move through the school. They respond well to the individual target-setting, whatever their levels of attainment or subject studied. The few instances of limited progress occur where there are severely-limited resources and expertise in, for example, information technology which affects most departments.'; 'In lessons, pupils are achieving well in their overall attainment and progress. Their positive attitudes contribute much to the warm ambience and good ethos of the school.'; 'Pupils are per-

forming equally well in their many extra-curricular activities. They do so with considerable flair and enthusiasm.'; 'A few pupils require and receive considerable support if their behaviour falls below expectations. The sanctions are few and clearly understood.'; 'Leadership is of the highest quality. It is closely in touch with all aspects of school life and leads reform and review across the school.'

Primary schools 'We have a large number of feeder schools, all within the Horsham community designated area.'

THE BISHOP OF HEREFORD'S BLUECOAT SCHOOL

Hampton Dene Road
Tupsley
Hereford HR1 1UU
Tel (01432) 357481
Fax (01432) 278220
E-mail: bluecoatschool@campus.bt.com

- National ranking 225= (279=, 314=, 295=, 275=)
- GCSE 70% (65%)
- A-levels *Not applicable*
- Higher education *Not applicable*

- Mixed comprehensive
- Pupils 1,158
- Boys (11–16) 599
- Girls (11–16) 559
- Sixth form *Not applicable*
- Education authority *Hereford and Worcester*

Headteacher Andrew James Marson, 49, appointed in September 1986. Staff 64 (men 31, women 33).

Motto Semper Christo fidelis (Always faithful to Christ).

Background The school was formed in 1973 from the union of two former church secondary schools: the ancient Bluecoat (founded 1710) and the Bishop's School (1958). Sited in a prosperous, leafy suburb of eastern Hereford, it serves the local community and the Hereford Diocese. The original building is red-brick, below which spread flat-roofed buildings dating from 1973. Facilities include nine laboratories, craft workshops, a music suite, two-storey sports hall and an outdoor heated swimming pool. Christian principles determine the way the voluntary-aided school is run. It has a special education centre for pupils with moderate learning difficulties and physical disabilities, of whom there are 40; a new centre was opened in 1994. About 1.35 applications for every place. Strengths include: dance and drama; rugby; music, with two main orchestras and choirs; Duke of Edinburgh Award Scheme.

Alumni Gilbert Harding, former pupil of Bluecoat School; Susan and Angela Tooby, international cross-country athletes.

Streaming All pupils in ability-groups for all subjects by end of year 7, allowing them 'to work at the pace best suited to their ability in a particular subject'.

Approach to discipline The school looks to parents for support in its effort to create and maintain an ordered society. 'Consistency and firmness are sought so that learning can take place effectively where education is set in the framework of warm, trustful relationships.'

Uniform Navy skirt or grey trousers, with blue shirt, blue blazer and maroon-and-yellow striped tie. 'Full uniform strictly enforced.'

Homework Average 11-year-old, five hours; 14-year-old, seven hours 30 minutes; 16-year-old, 10 hours.

Vocational qualifications BTEC/City and Guilds; NVQs.

Inspection February 1995: 'The Bishop of Hereford's Bluecoat School provides a good education for its pupils. The standards the school achieves are good. Pupils are well-motivated and willing learners and teachers have appropriately high expectations of them. The school has a strong Christian ethos and there is a high level of commitment to the school from pupils, parents, staff and governors. Pupils enjoy a wide range of extra-curricular activities which are a major strength of the school.'; 'Relative to their ability, pupils do particularly well in geography, modern foreign languages and in the arts: art, music and drama.'

Primary schools St Paul's CE Primary; Hampton Dene Primary; Mordford CE Primary; St Mary's CE Primary, Fownhope; Lugwardine Primary.

THE GREENSWARD SCHOOL

Greensward Lane
Hockley
Essex SS5 5HG
Tel (01702) 202571
Fax (01702) 200083
E-mail: d.a.triggs@rmplc.co.uk

- National ranking 225 = (−, 374 = , −)
- GCSE 70%
- A-levels *Applicable from August 1997*
- Higher education *Applicable from August 1997*

- Grant-maintained
- Mixed comprehensive
- Pupils 1,279
- Boys (11–16) 671
- Girls (11–16) 608
- Sixth form 123 (10%)
- Education authority *Essex*

Headteacher David A. Triggs, 44, appointed in April 1994. Staff 76 (men 40, women 36).

Motto To make our best better.

Background Set on greenfield site in centre of large village near Southend; built in 1960 and extended in 1967; buildings refurbished September 1994: technology in one building; upgraded science department. Became grant-maintained in April 1993; sixth form from September 1995; Technology College status 1995. Sports facilities supplemented by pitches and changing rooms on neighbouring site; heated indoor swimming pool, two gyms. School houses Centre for Community Education. Over-subscribed and school roll rising. Senior orchestra with 90 members; thriving drama department puts on four productions a year; juggling troupe; new purpose-built drama studio in September 1994. Sporting achievement in 1994: athletics, runners-up in national finals of TSB athletics competition; basketball, six county titles and national and district successes. Visits and exchanges with Georgia in United States, Germany, France; annual skiing and outward bound holidays, cultural visits abroad and fieldwork activities around England.

Streaming School bands and sets in all areas possible.

Approach to discipline 'We believe in and insist upon high standards of courtesy and consideration for others. School rules exist to ensure pupil safety and to maintain our high standards in all areas of school life. They are enforced firmly but fairly. Pupils are involved in the formulation of rules and the code of conduct via the School Council.'

Uniform Girls: white blouse, mid-grey skirt/blue trousers, blue jumper with school logo, school tie, black shoes. Boys: white shirt, mid-grey trousers, blue jumper with school logo, school tie, black shoes. Very strictly enforced.

Homework Average 11-year-old, eight hours a week; 14-year-old, 10 hours; 16-year-old, 15 hours.

Vocational qualifications RSA, Practical Skills Profile.

Inspection February 1994: 'The school is a well-ordered and civilised community with a clear code of conduct about respect for individuals and for property.'; 'Standards of behaviour, discipline and attendance are high.'; 'The school has established an ethos where good behaviour is expected, both in class and the public areas of the school. This is recognised and valued by pupils and their parents.'; 'The quality of relationships contributes significantly to pupils' motivation to learn and be responsible members of the school.'

Primary schools Ashingdon County Primary; Hockley Primary; Plumberow Primary; The Westerings Primary.

YSGOL GYFUN GŴYR

Stryd Talbot
Gowerton
Swansea SA4 3DB
Tel (01792) 872403
Fax (01792) 874197
E-mail: yggwyr@aol.com

- National ranking 225= (238=, 194, 233=, 295=)
- GCSE 70% (69%)
- A-levels *Not applicable*
- Higher education *Not applicable*

- Mixed comprehensive
- Pupils 744
- Boys (11–16) 328
- Girls (11–16) 416
- Sixth form *Not applicable*
- Education authority Swansea

Headteacher Dr Neville Daniel, 53, appointed in September 1985. Staff 48 (men 19, women 29).

Motto *None*

Background Established in 1984 as an additional Welsh-medium secondary school in West Glamorgan. Sited on the edge of the Gower Peninsula, the school serves a wide catchment area incorporating the Llwchwr, Afan and Lower Tawe Valleys as well as Swansea. About nine in 10 go on to post-16 education or training. Annual intake increasing; over-subscribed, with 180 applications for 150 places. Apart from English and some science in senior school, all lessons in Welsh; three in four pupils, however, come from non-Welsh-speaking homes. Schools Curriculum Award in 1990. Sporting and cultural visits and exchanges: Canada, Czechoslovakia, France, Germany, Holland, Finland and Turkey. Pupils have won places in National Youth Theatre, Choir and Orchestra; national honours in rugby, cricket, hockey, athletics, netball, gymnastics, swimming, karate and chess. National success for teams in sporting, cultural and public-speaking competitions.

Alumni Gwyn Jones and Lori Morgan, Wales rugby internationals; John Hartson, West Ham United and Wales footballer.

Streaming Principle to maintain mixed-ability teaching 'with emphasis on differentiated learning and teaching strategies'. Degree of setting from year 9 in core subjects.

Approach to discipline Emphasis on respect for the individual. 'We strive to develop the principle of self-discipline, emphasising individual responsibility through courtesy, kindness, sensitivity, and a sense of fair play.'

Uniform Boys: black trousers, white shirt and school tie, or white polo shirt. Girls: black skirt/trousers, white blouse/polo shirt. 'Pupils accept the guidelines and the flexibility.'

Homework Average 11-year-old, five hours a week; 14-year-old, six hours; 16-year-old, 10 hours.

Vocational qualifications GNVQ Intermediate, Manufacturing, Health and Social Care.

Inspection May 1994: 'The school is a civilised, orderly and effectively managed community.'; 'The governors, head and staff have a clear and positive vision of its aims and philosophy. Emphasis is constantly given to the value and importance of the individual within the school community and this message permeates all aspects of its life.'; 'The school site is basically rather untidy in terms of buildings and many of the teaching rooms are confined. In some subject areas there is a shortage of specialised accommodation.'; 'Pupils are offered a wide and rich range of extra-curricular activities.'

Primary schools Ysgol Gynradd Gymraeg Bryniago; YGG Ponty Brenin; YGG Bryn-Y-Mor; YGG Lonlas; YGG Login Fach.

COWBRIDGE SCHOOL

Aberthin Road
Cowbridge
Vale of Glamorgan CF7 7EN
Tel (01446) 772311
Fax (01446) 775357
Internet: http://www.rmplc.co.uk/eduweb/sites/cowbdg/index.html

- National ranking 230 (208, 232, 266, 266)
- GCSE 69% (72%)
- A-levels 69% (A/B); 100% (A/E)
- Higher education 95% (Cambridge 4)

- Mixed comprehensive
- Pupils 1,210
- Boys (11–18) 627
- Girls (11–18) 583
- Sixth form 228 (19%)
- Education authority *Vale of Glamorgan*

Headteacher Joan Dawson, 43, appointed in September 1995. Staff 68 (men 30, women 38).

Motto *None*

Background The split-site school, in a rural environment in a market town in the Vale of Glamorgan, can trace its origins to the 17th century: formed in 1974 as a comprehensive from a secondary modern and two grammar schools (boys' grammar founded 1608; girls' grammar, 1896). The lower school accommodates pupils in years 7 and 8 in the centre of the town, while the middle school and sixth form are on its edge. The school possesses extensive playing fields, while the buildings range from those which are over 100 years old to a large number of temporary classrooms. Over-subscribed, taking pupils from 43 primary schools; 'very strong' emphasis on academic achieve-

ments; numbers entering the sixth form have increased significantly in recent years; more than two in three Year 11 pupils go on to the sixth form. In the past three years, pupils have received national awards in physics, biology and geology. Vigorous links with industry; annual week-long Enterprise programmes for pupils in years 9 and 12. Pupils excel in wide range of sporting activities: national individual honours in rugby, soccer, hockey, judo, tai-kwan-do and badminton. Strong musical tradition, with thriving orchestras and choirs; many pupils perform with outside orchestras, ensembles and choirs.

Alumni Anthony Hopkins, Oscar-winning actor; Alun Lewis, Second World War poet and Welsh teacher who died in Burma; Patrick Hannan, columnist and broadcaster; Sir Idwal Pugh, first Ombudsman for Wales.

Streaming Mixed-ability in years 7 and 8, with setting in English and mathematics in years 8 and in all core subjects in year 9.

Approach to discipline 'A strong pastoral care system which involves form- and year-tutors and heads of lower and middle schools and the sixth form. Pupils are involved in drawing up codes of behaviour through participation in Year Councils. Emphasis is placed on high standards, courtesy and respect for all members of the school community.'

Uniform Black blazer, blue tie with motif. Uniform throughout the school, with distinct variation for years 12 and 13. Strictly enforced.

Homework Average 11-year-old, four hours a week; 14-year-old, six hours; 16-year-old, 10 hours.

Vocational qualifications RSA and Pitman, Key-boarding.

Inspection March 1996.

Primary schools Y Bont Faen; St David's Church-in-Wales Primary, Colwinston; Llangan Primary; Pendoylan CIW Primary; Llansannor CIW Primary; Llancarfan Primary; St Bride's Major CIW Primary; St Nicholas CIW Primary; Peterston-super-Ely CIW Primary.

ANGLO EUROPEAN SCHOOL

Willow Green
Ingatestone
Essex CM4 0DJ
Tel (01277) 354018
Fax (01277) 355623
E-mail: aes1@rmplc.co.uk

- National ranking 231 (284, 218, 184, –)
- GCSE 69% (64%)
- A-levels 45% (A/B); 98% (A/E)
- Higher education 98% (Oxford 1, Cambridge 2)

- Grant-maintained
- Mixed comprehensive
- Pupils 1,141
- Boys (11–18) 537
- Girls (11–18) 604
- Sixth form 218 (19%)
- Education authority Essex

Headteacher Robert James Reed, 49, appointed in September 1990. Staff 84 (men 43, women 41).

Motto *None*

Background Originally conceived in February 1967, the school opened in Ingatestone in September 1973 to provide comprehensive education, informed by strong European and international dimension, for wide area of Essex. 'At this school, Jean Monnet's concept of a peace-promoting Europe which shares its wealth with the world lies at the heart of much of what we do. Our aim is to provide the highest-quality national education enriched by a European ethos.' Oversubscribed, with more than two applications per place; many pupils travel up to 50 miles to school including from Central London; 30 partner schools. International Baccalaureate (IB) offered as alternative to A-levels for 19 years; about one half of sixth-formers follow IB course. Sixteen language teachers; more than 30 languages represented in the school. Six languages taught: German, French, Russian, Spanish, Japanese and English as a foreign language; other languages supported and examined; minimum of two languages for all pupils. Work-experience elsewhere in Europe; range of visits to, and exchanges with, Belgium, France, Germany, Austria, Russia and Denmark. One of the first two schools to be designated a specialist Language College in 1995;

awarded DTI National Languages for Export Award in 1996.

Streaming Students are put in sets according to performance; setting arrangements reflect each student's needs.

Approach to discipline 'The student population is well-motivated and extremely self-disciplined, requiring little management by the staff. This allows what few breaches there are to be dealt with quickly and effectively.'

Uniform Full uniform of traditional nature in years 7 to 11. Dress code for sixth-formers. 'Regulations are meaningless unless they are enforced.'

Homework Average 11-year-old, seven hours 30 minutes a week; 14-year-old, 10 + hours; 16-year-old, 15 hours plus private study.

Vocational qualifications *None*

Inspection October 1994: 'A good school in a number of important respects. The pupils are articulate, literate and positive in their attitudes towards both the school and their own learning. The leadership is strong and positive and the teachers are able, hardworking and dedicated to the success and well-being of their pupils and of the school as a whole. Relationships are good and are based upon mutual respect and a pride in the distinctive nature of the school and of its achievements. This pride is shared by parents who support the school strongly.'; 'Lessons are characterised by well-prepared, sound and thorough teaching.'; 'The headteacher and senior management team provide strong and energetic leadership and are ably supported by the governing body and the staff of the school as a whole.'

Primary schools Ingatestone CE Junior; Mountnessing CE Primary; Margaretting CE Primary. Average of 80 feeder schools.

LADY MANNERS SCHOOL

Shutts Lane
Bakewell
Derbyshire
DE45 1JA
Tel (01629) 812671
Fax (01629) 814984

- National ranking 232 (322, 306, 262, 291)
- GCSE 69% (62%)
- A-levels 40% (A/B); 95% (A/E)

- Higher education 92% (Oxford 1, Cambridge 2)

- Grant-maintained
- Mixed comprehensive
- Pupils 1,480
- Boys (11–18) 744
- Girls (11–18) 736
- Sixth form 328 (22%)
- Education authority *Derbyshire*

Headteacher Mary Patricia Sellers, 45, appointed from September 1996. Staff 88 (men 43, women 45).

Motto Pour y parvenir (Strive to attain).

Background In the heart of the Peak District, the school was founded in 1636 by Grace, Lady Manners. Site was gift of Duke of Rutland, the Manners family. Extensive playing fields, tennis courts, all-weather hockey pitch, floodlit games area. Current buildings date from 1938; additions and modifications completed in 1959 and 1972, when school became comprehensive. Extensive new library and resources centre facilities, science laboratories, special needs centre and additional information technology centres completed in 1995. Facilities include sports hall, gymnasium, assembly hall, stage, drama hall, language centre, computer rooms, 10 science laboratories. Speech Day and Commemoration Services retained; house system strong. The school's Castle Hill boarding house is for girls and boys aged 11 to 19; each has personal academic tutor; boarding available full-time or weekly, annual fees of £4,725 and £4,290 respectively. Campbell Blair Endowment trust fund gives financial help to pupils who have lost one or both parents. Over-subscribed for both day and boarding places, with 1.25 applications per place.

Alumni Alison Uttley (1892–1903), children's writer; Professor John W. Purseglove (1924–1931), scientist and expert on tropical biology; Sir Maurice Oldfield (1926–1934), former head of MI6; Phillip Whitehead (1948–1955), chairman of Consumers' Association, former Labour MP, Euro-MP and writer.

Streaming Setting from year 8 onwards.

Approach to discipline Disciplined environment is essential; as are respect for others and for fabric of buildings. The school seeks to promote self-discipline resulting from wanting to learn and wanting to participate. Anti-social behaviour is not tolerated.'

Uniform Navy blazer with badge (braid added for sixth-formers), white shirt/blouse, school tie, V-neck navy pullover/cardigan, dark-grey trousers/navy skirt, black shoes. All pupils required to conform.

Homework Average 11-year-old, five to seven hours a week; 14-year-old, seven to nine hours; 16-year-old, 14+ hours.

Vocational qualifications *None*

Primary schools Bakewell Methodist Junior; Curbar Primary; Great Rowsley CE Primary; St Anne's Primary; Great Hucklow Primary; Litton CE Primary; Longstone CE Primary; Monyash CE Primary; Stanton-in-Peak CE Primary; Bishop Purseglove CE Primary; Cressbrook Primary; Pilsley CE Primary; Stoney Middleton Primary; Youlgreave All Saints CE Primary.

JOHN TAYLOR HIGH SCHOOL

Barton-under-Needwood
Burton-on-Trent
Staffordshire DE13 8AZ
Tel (01283) 712476
Fax (01283) 716971

- National ranking 233 (347, 346)
- GCSE 69% (61%)
- A-levels 40% (A/B); 93% (A/E)
- Higher education 79% (Cambridge 4)

- Mixed comprehensive
- Pupils 1,312
- Boys (11–18) 683
- Girls (11–18) 629
- Sixth form 270 (21%)
- Education authority *Staffordshire*

Headteacher Geoffrey Peter Gallie, 55, appointed in September 1988. Staff 72 (men 36, women 36).

Motto *None*

Background Established in 1957; became comprehensive in 1971, with major extensions and a sports hall. Pupils come from attractive area of large commuter villages and smaller rural settlements. Sixth form has expanded significantly in recent years; three in four (75%) pupils stay to study A-levels or BTEC courses; new buildings planned. The school is strongly supported by the community as well as local businesses and organisations. Over-subscribed. Well-equipped resources centre with information technology used in and out of school time. Strong in a variety of sports, with considerable programme of fixtures and pupils competing at county and national level. Growth in arts, music and drama; regular performances. 'We encourage pupils to establish high expectations. Whatever their ability or interests, we give them time and support, deliberately fostering friendly relationships and a sense of orderly behaviour. Parental support and involvement is strongly encouraged.'

Streaming Initially in mixed-ability groups; setting in mathematics, languages and science from year 8; further setting for GCSE.

Approach to discipline 'We establish an atmosphere in which good order is assumed. Where discipline is applied, it is part of longer-term monitoring and support for individuals.'

Uniform Black pullover, black trousers/skirt, white shirt, school tie for boys. 'Smartness and tidiness are expected at all times in school. Conformity is required, with the main emphasis on smartness. Parents are contacted when uniform is not worn.'

Homework Average 11-year-old, five hours a week; 14-year-old, seven hours; 16-year-old, 10 hours.

Vocational qualifications BTEC National, Business and Finance, Health and Caring, Science; BTEC Advanced, Business and Finance, Health and Caring.

Inspection November 1996: 'A very good school with outstanding features.'; 'There is an excellent record of individual and team success in a wide range of sporting and other activities at all representative levels, including national.'; 'Many courses are well planned to meet the statutory requirements and those of the examination boards. There is, however, a significant weakness in the provision for information technology for all pupils across the curriculum.'; 'Generally, teachers have high expectations, particularly of older pupils and students, and demand from them significant quantities of work.'; 'Teachers have very good subject knowledge. Highly-effective teaching is widespread, but some pupils have experiences of less than satisfactory

teaching, particularly in Key Stage 3.'; 'The headteacher and governors are clearly focused on maintaining the breadth and quality of curriculum provision whilst improving standards of achievement. They achieve this within an income-per-pupil which is very low by national standards.'

Primary schools Thomas Russell Junior; All Saints' CE Primary, Alrewas; St Peter's CE Primary, Yoxall; Shobnall County Primary, Shobnall; Mosley Primary, Anslow.

THE BISHOP'S STORTFORD HIGH SCHOOL

London Road
Bishop's Stortford
Hertfordshire CM23 3LU
Tel (01279) 757515
Fax (01279) 501630

- National ranking 234 (289, 247, 387, 216)
- GCSE 69% (64%)
- A-levels 39% (A/B); 91% (A/E)
- Higher education 72% (Oxford 3, Cambridge 2)

- Grant-maintained
- Boys' comprehensive
- Pupils 1,073
- Boys (11–18) 992
- Girls (16–18) 81
- Sixth form 301 (28%)
- Education authority *Hertfordshire*

Headteacher Ian Shaw, 62, appointed in September 1980. Staff 77 (men 54, women 23).

Motto *None*

Background Originally established at the turn of the century, the school's buildings, a mile south of the town centre, date from 1957. More recent developments include a sports hall and sixth-form centre; a new science and mathematics block; and a school pavilion rebuilt for rugby, soccer and cricket. School proud of extra-curricular activities, clubs, rugby, soccer, cricket teams and societies; music strong point as well as drama, with three full plays each year; public speaking popular. Duke of Edinburgh Award Scheme. Over-subscribed, with 1.5 applications per place. Distinct Christian ethos.

Streaming Mixed-ability in year 7. Setting begins in year 8.

Approach to discipline 'We prize courtesy and regard for others, both in and out of school.' Sixth-form prefects lead by example; teachers praise good conduct, reinforced by merit marks; boys encouraged to express themselves within restraints; detention, at lunchtime or after school, is main punishment.

Uniform Black blazer with badge, white/grey shirt, school tie, charcoal-grey trousers, grey socks, black shoes, grey V-neck pullover, navy/black coat. No motifs other than school's mitre to be worn. Fully enforced.

Homework Average 11-year-old, five hours a week; 14-year-old, six hours; 16-year-old, seven hours.

Vocational qualifications GNVQ Intermediate and Advanced, Business.

Inspection May 1994: 'An effective school, setting and achieving high standards in many subjects. Standards have risen consistently.'; 'Staff are dedicated and well-qualified.'; 'The school has a positive ethos characterised by a clear identity, a work ethic, high academic achievement, and maintenance of values which develop pride and worth for all pupils.'; 'Parents are very supportive. Links with the local community are well developed.'

THE BISHOP OF LLANDAFF CHURCH-IN-WALES HIGH SCHOOL

Rookwood Close
Llandaff
Cardiff CF5 2NR
Tel (01222) 562485
Fax (01222) 578862

- National ranking 235 (232, 182, 213, 226)
- GCSE 69% (69%)
- A-levels 37% (A/B); 90% (A/E)
- Higher education 70% (Oxford 1, Cambridge 1)

- Mixed comprehensive
- Pupils 1,158
- Boys (11–18) 590
- Girls (11–18) 568
- Sixth form 236 (20%)
- Education authority *Cardiff*

Headteacher Leonard Parfitt, 55, appointed in September 1983. Staff 65 (men 28, women 37).

Motto Faith in education.

Background Within walking distance of Llandaff Cathedral in own grounds. Buildings completed in 1963: main classroom block, laboratories, gymnasium, workshops, hall. Doubled in size in 1971 to include sixth-form centre and suite of laboratories within second classroom block; extended technology facilities, sports hall. Demand for places resulted 10 years later in four temporary classrooms; governors plan to replace them soon with eight-room humanities building. Voluntary-aided; over-subscribed, with 1.4 applications per place. All pupils entered for GCSEs; 100% achieved grades A to G in 1993 and 1994. County representatives in most sports; national representatives in rugby, soccer and athletics. Pupils are members of county orchestras, bands and choirs; school concerts, drama productions, church services. Debating team helped represent Wales in World Debating competition in Canada in 1992 and New Zealand in 1993. Raises up to £5,000 annually for charity. Most pupils Christian and school is a Church-in-Wales (Anglican) Foundation: 'There is no attempt at "indoctrination" as we believe faith is learned by example.'

Alumni Sarah Loosemore, tennis player.

Streaming Timetable allows pupils to be put in sets in all national curriculum subjects except art and music; teaching groups decided by subject heads. Currently pupils set in mathematics during year 7, English from year 8, modern languages and Welsh from year 9, and science from year 10.

Approach to discipline 'Pupils are expected to show self-discipline, and are encouraged and motivated in the early years by the award of house points in weekly competition. Lack of effort or unacceptable behaviour leads to increasingly severe sanctions.' Parents involved early in disciplinary process.

Uniform Years 7 and 8: black blazer with school badge, black trousers/skirt, white shirt/blouse, school tie. Years 9–11: black sweater with school badge.

Homework Average 11-year-old, five to seven hours a week; 14-year-old, six to 10 hours; 16-year-old, seven to 14 hours.

Vocational qualifications *None*

Inspection March 1994: 'The quality of learning reflects the demands made upon pupils. When the work is challenging, the response is positive and the majority of pupils produce work of high quality demonstrating sound knowledge well applied. Basic skills are generally sound. Frequently, however, the pace of lessons is too slow and, because the work is insufficiently demanding, pupils respond less positively.'; 'The school is well-ordered and there are good inter-personal relationships between pupil and teacher, and pupil and pupil.'; 'Teachers promote Christian values through their concern for the welfare of individuals.'

Primary schools Llandaff City Church-in-Wales Primary, Cardiff; All Saints' CIW Primary, Barry; St Fagan's CIW Primary, Cardiff; Danescourt Primary, Llandaff. Total of 54 feeder schools.

THOMAS MILLS HIGH SCHOOL

Saxtead Road
Framlingham
Woodbridge
Suffolk IP13 9HE
Tel (01728) 723493
Fax (01728) 621098
E-mail: thomasmills.framlingham@
campus.bt.com

- National ranking 236 (202, 392)
- GCSE 69% (73%)
- A-levels 34% (A/B); 89% (A/E)
- Higher education 72% (Oxford 1, Cambridge 4)

- Mixed comprehensive
- Pupils 1,005
- Boys (11–18) 460
- Girls (11–18) 545
- Sixth form 320 (32%)
- Education authority *Suffolk*

Headteacher David Graham Floyd, 49, appointed from September 1995. Staff 62 (men 30, women 32).

Motto Temporis filia veritas (Truth is the daughter of time).

Background Established in 1979 by the amalgamation of Mills Grammar School and Framlingham Modern School; serves wide rural catchment area; more than four in 10 pupils come from outside catchment area; pupils from neighbouring schools transfer at 16. Set on a pleasant site on outskirts of historic small town of Framlingham, within easy reach of the coast. Named after 17th-century benefactor of the town; school still receives money from his foundation. Oldest school buildings date from 1937; latest of several building phases was in 1990. Special mention of 'very high quality' art, music and drama. All pupils study both French and German initially, with option to continue both at GCSE. A-level students have a free choice of subject combinations. 'Good discipline and the maintenance of a calm, productive atmosphere are regarded as of the highest importance.'

Streaming 'Different systems are used in subjects in line with the teaching and learning strategies which need to be used.' Pupils grouped by ability in French, German, mathematics, science and English after their work has been assessed by staff.

Approach to discipline 'School rules are designed to ensure safety of pupils and their property and to teach consideration for others.' Agreed code of behaviour; disciplinary sanctions include detention, impositions, 'on report' and exclusion in 'very rare' serious cases.

Uniform Years 7 to 11: White blouse/shirt, school tie, grey skirt/trousers, navy V-neck pullover. Sixth-formers 'expected to conform to a dress code'. Regulations 'actively' enforced. 'We are rightly proud of the generally high standard of school dress.'

Homework Average 11-year-old, three hours 30 minutes a week; 14-year-old, five hours; 16-year-old, 10 hours.

Vocational qualifications GNVQ Advanced, Business, Science; GNVQ Intermediate, Business, Health and Social Care, Leisure and Tourism, Manufacturing; Part 1 GNVQ, Business and Manufacturing.

Primary schools Wickham Market Primary; Sir Robert Hitcham's CE Primary, Framlingham; Charsfield CE Primary; Dennington CE Primary; Easton Primary.

HIGH STORRS SCHOOL

High Storrs Road
Sheffield
South Yorkshire S11 7LH
Tel (0114) 267 0000
Fax (0114) 266 3624
E-mail: hghstorrs@campus.bt.com

- National ranking 237 (326, 271, 292, 307)

- GCSE 69% (62%)
- A-levels 32% (A/B); 85% (A/E)
- Higher education 88% (Oxford 2, Cambridge 3)

- Mixed comprehensive
- Pupils 1,760
- Boys (11–18) 900
- Girls (11–18) 860
- Sixth form 420 (24%)
- Education authority *Sheffield*

Headteacher Dr Cheryle Berry, 48, appointed in January 1989. Staff 106 (men 50, women 56).

Motto Deo adiuvante labor proficit (With God's help hard work gets its reward).

Background Established in 1880 as the Central School in the middle of Sheffield; the school moved to current site in southwest of the city in 1933 as two separate grammar schools for boys and girls, and renamed High Storrs. Grade 2 listed building recently restored to original art-deco splendour; 26 acres of grounds on edge of Peak District. Well provided with specialist rooms, large library, drama and music facilities. Schools Curriculum Award 1992; Technology Schools Initiative Award 1993; second in national competition for top sporting school in 1992; notable achievement in art. Total of 370 applications for 240 places. Great Britain under-16 Scrabble champions in 1994 and 1995. Investors in People Award. Largest orchestras in South Yorkshire. All pupils learn Latin and classics in lower school.

Alumni Baron Dainton of Hallam Moors, chancellor of Sheffield University; Joe Ashton, Labour MP for Bassetlaw; Sir Thomas Lodge, consultant radiologist; Sir Thomas Padmore, senior civil servant.

Streaming Pupils in sets for mathematics and modern languages from year 8; some setting in science from year 9.

Approach to discipline Code of conduct developed through consultation with parents, students, staff and governors; based on respect for others, environment, property and themselves. 'There are relevant sanctions and rewards to reinforce this policy. Parents are always fully involved.'

Uniform No uniform. Optional sweatshirt with school logo.

Homework Average 11-year-old, seven hours a week; 14-year-old, 10 hours; 16-year-old, 15+ hours.

Vocational qualifications GNVQ Foundation; GNVQ Intermediate, Health and Social Care, Leisure and Tourism, Hospitality and Catering, Engineering; GNVQ Advanced, Business, Science, Manufacturing. NVQ, Outdoor Education.

Inspection November 1994: 'This is a successful school with many good features, some of them very good.'; 'Behaviour and discipline in the school are excellent. The school has well-established values and a well-developed code of conduct.'; 'The quality of teaching clearly results in successful learning by the majority of pupils and the attainment of good standards. The teachers are well-qualified, experienced and committed to the pupils.'

Primary schools Eccleshall CE Junior; Greystones Primary; Hunter's Bar Junior; Porter Croft CE Junior; Carter Knowle Junior.

THE JOHN FISHER SCHOOL

Peaks Hill
Purley
Surrey CR8 3YP
Tel (0181) 660 4555
Fax (0181) 763 1837

- National ranking 238 (301, 357, 293, –)
- GCSE 69% (63%)
- A-levels 31% (A/B); 90% (A/E)
- Higher education 90% (Oxford 1, Cambridge 1)

- Grant-maintained
- Boys' comprehensive
- Pupils 858
- Boys (11–18) 858
- Girls *Not applicable*
- Sixth form 159 (19%)
- Education authority *Sutton*

Headteacher Robin Peter Monamy Gregory, 55, appointed in January 1993. Staff 51 (men 40, women 11).

Motto *None*

Background Founded in 1927 by Archbishop Amico of Southwark; became comprehensive in 1977; set in fine grounds in pleasant part of Purley, with 25-acre sports field nearby; attracts Roman Catholic boys from

Sutton, Croydon, and adjacent parts of south London and Surrey; became grant-maintained in 1992. Over-subscribed, with two applications per place. 'Outstanding' reputation for sporting achievements; regularly produces county rugby players, cricketers and athletes; also international honours in rugby and athletics. 'High level competitive sport is an integral part of school life, widely supported by boys, staff and parents.' Christian education; strong Catholic faith.

Alumni Lord (Barney) Hayhoe, former government minister and Conservative MP for Brentford and Isleworth; Professor Jack Scarisbrick.

Streaming Pupils put in sets rather than streamed.

Approach to discipline 'A very traditional approach to discipline; the pastoral system is based on year-heads who meet regularly with the headmaster and deputy head.'

Uniform 'Full details of uniform are made available to families on acceptance and are printed in the school prospectus.'

Homework Average 11-year-old, eight hours a week; 14-year-old, 10 hours; 16-year-old, 'as required'.

Vocational qualifications GNVQ Level 3, Business and Finance.

Inspection October 1993.

Primary schools Margaret Roper Primary; St Mary's RC Primary; Regina Coeli Primary; St Elphege's RC Primary; St Aidan's RC Primary.

LANGLEY PARK SCHOOL FOR BOYS

South Eden Park Road
Beckenham
Kent BR3 3BP
Tel (0181) 650 9253
Fax (0181) 650 5823

- National ranking 239
- GCSE 69%
- A-levels 25% (A/B); 89% (A/E)
- Higher education 71%

- Grant-maintained
- Boys' comprehensive
- Pupils 1,177
- Boys (11–18) 1,177
- Girls *Not applicable*
- Sixth form 240 (20%)

- Education authority *Bromley*

Headteacher Roger Sheffield, appointed in January 1990. Staff 83 (men 65, women 18).

Motto Mores et studia (Good character and learning).

Background Parkland setting among own playing fields. Specialist rooms for all subjects: nine science laboratories, design department with four workshops, technology studio, three art rooms, games hall, gymnasium, multi-gym, library and resources centre, fully-equipped drama studio, two computer laboratories with 30 computers. Over-subscribed, with 3.5 applications for each place. Full range of computing, television and audio-visual equipment, printing machinery and three minibuses. Sports grounds include nine tennis courts, athletics facilities, rugby, hockey and cricket pitches, cricket pavilion, all-weather sports pitch. The school has its own outdoor pursuits and study centre, a converted chapel in the Peak District given by parents. Admissions policy makes allowance for a proportion of pupils to be selected according to academic ability. 'The school's traditions, resources and timetable allocation make it possible to enhance the curriculum and development of musicians and sportsmen.'

Alumni Bill Wyman, member of Rolling Stones; Henry Mee, portrait painter; Derek Underwood, former Kent and England cricketer.

Streaming 'On entry pupils immediately placed in sets according to ability in subject, or small clusters of subjects. Little, if any, mixed-ability teaching.'

Approach to discipline 'This school is seen first and foremost as a place of work, and a structured, well-ordered environment is created in the belief that effective learning takes place best in such an atmosphere. Teachers are corporately encouraged to adopt a firm, fair and friendly line with the pupils.'

Uniform Maroon blazer (black for year 11), school tie. Formal dress for sixth-formers. Very strictly enforced.

Homework Average 11-year-old, five hours a week; 14-year-old, seven hours 30 minutes; 16-year-old, 10 hours.

Vocational qualifications Foreign Languages at Work; Intermediate and Advanced GNVQs; Computer Literacy and Information Technology.

Inspection March 1997: 'A good school with several outstanding features. Pupils reach very good standards in public examinations at the ages of 14, 16 and 18. In sport, individual pupils and teams reach very high standards. Boys perform well in a wide range of musical activities. The school provides an excellent range of extra-curricular opportunities in which many pupils participate. Parents and pupils show a strong sense of loyalty towards the school.'

Primary schools Oak Lodge Primary; Highfield Junior; Marian Vian Primary; Balgowan Primary; Worsley Bridge Primary; Hawes Down Junior.

OATHALL COMMUNITY COLLEGE

Appledore Gardens
Haywards Heath
West Sussex RH16 2AQ
Tel (01444) 414001
Fax (01444) 417027
E-mail: oathall2@pavilion.co.uk

- National ranking 240= (266=, 293=, 374=, 356=)
- GCSE 69% (66%)
- A-levels *Not applicable*
- Higher education *Not applicable*

- Mixed comprehensive
- Pupils 1,279
- Boys (11–16) 639
- Girls (11–16) 640
- Sixth form *Not applicable*
- Education authority *West Sussex*

Headteacher John Rimmer, 54, appointed in April 1981. Staff 88 (men 34, women 54).

Motto *None*

Background The school is 15 miles north of Brighton, between Haywards Heath and the historic village of Lindfield. Catchment area includes Ardingly, Horsted Keynes, Lindfield, Scaynes Hill and most of Haywards Heath. Sporting facilities include heated swimming pool, large sports hall and assembly hall. Specialist accommodation includes five-acre farm, resources centre, drama studio, information technology centre, community suite and a youth wing. A new building with specialist facilities for modern languages and a new music centre have recently been completed. Further technology accommodation, new drama studio and physical education facilities planned. Small waiting list for 'out-of-area' applicants, result of reluctance to allow overcrowding and large classes; average class size is 23. All pupils study two forgeign languages and information technology. The school is proud of how it caters for highly-able pupils, while least able also receive special help with basic skills. Emphasis on 'the quality of learning'. Investor in People Award. Wide range of extra-curricular activities: concerts, sports, productions and travel. 'Oathall is committed to the development of potential into excellence within a caring and challenging environment.'

Streaming From year 8, pupils taught in sets according to ability in each subject.

Approach to discipline 'There are few problems, evidence of a highly-effective pastoral system that is founded on self-assessment, encouragement, support, praise and reward as the surest means to foster in pupils a sense of responsibility for their own behaviour.'

Uniform Maroon and grey are uniform colours for years 7 to 10. Pupils in year 11 vote to agree their uniform.

Homework Average 11-year-old, six hours a week; 14-year-old, nine hours; 16-year-old, 13 hours.

Vocational qualifications NVQ, Agriculture and Horticulture.

Inspection January 1994: 'Oathall is outstandingly effective and highly regarded by the community it serves. The standards achieved by pupils in lessons are good and sometimes very good.'; 'There is a high degree of motivation and application amongst pupils. The standards achieved are good and sometimes very good.'; 'There is a good range of opportunities to develop personal responsibilities, moral, social and cultural understanding. The college needs to place more emphasis on spiritual development.' *The school reports it has since placed more emphasis on spiritual development.*

Primary schools Lindfield Junior; Blackthorns Primary; Heyworth Primary; Northlands Wood Primary; St Wilfred's CE Primary; Scaynes Hill CE Primary; St Giles CE Primary; St Peter's CE Primary.

ST HILDA'S ROMAN CATHOLIC GIRLS' HIGH SCHOOL

Coal Clough Lane
Burnley
Lancashire BB11 5BT
Tel (01282) 36314
Fax (01282) 832198

- National ranking 240= (354=, 401=, 248=, 241=)
- GCSE 69% (61%)
- A-levels *Not applicable*
- Higher education *Not applicable*

- Girls' comprehensive
- Pupils 664
- Boys *Not applicable*
- Girls (11–16) 664
- Sixth form *Not applicable*
- Education authority *Lancashire*

Headteacher Bernadette Bleasdale, 41, appointed in September 1992. Staff 39 (men 10, women 29).

Motto *None*

Background Opened in 1954 as a secondary modern for Catholic girls from Burnley and Todmorden; became a comprehensive in 1966. Extensive site surrounded by playing fields. New £1 million technology area, art area, second gymnasium with latest climbing wall, and three upgraded science laboratories. Over-subscribed, with 185 applications for 150 places. School proud of extra-curricular life: more than 100 pupils play a musical instrument, contributing to junior and senior orchestras; more than 200 are in two choirs. Successful teams in netball, hockey, football, tennis, cross-country, trampoline. Ski trip. 'The religious life of the school can be clearly seen not only in our daily activities, but also in the many extra-curricular activities which take place.' Parent-Teacher Association since 1968. Identified by Ofsted in 1996 as a 'good and improving school'.

Streaming Pupils in ability sets for most subjects.

Approach to discipline School principle that every individual should be regarded with consideration and respect, courtesy and politeness. Detailed school rules. 'Girls are expected to keep the school rules conscientiously.'

Uniform Navy skirt, white shirt, navy-and-red school tie, school sweater (navy with school name embroidered). 'Very strictly enforced. We are proud of our appearance!'

Homework Average 11-year-old, five to seven hours 30 minutes a week; 14-year-old, seven hours 30 minutes to 10 hours; 16-year-old, 10 to 12 hours.

Vocational qualifications Pilot NVQ in year 10, Business Administration.

Inspection May 1995. 'A challenging and flourishing school community which enables girls to become mature and articulate young people.'; The good standard of literacy contributes significantly to high levels of achievement across the curriculum, notably in history and geography.'; 'Teachers successfully create a climate of endeavour in which most girls are highly-motivated, eager to learn and prepared to work hard.'; 'Classroom resources are deployed effectively to promote learning, but the library, although well used, has many books which are out of date or inappropriate.'; 'Girls behave well and are happy within a secure and orderly community.'

Primary schools St Mary's RC Primary; St John's RC Primary; St Mary Magdalene's RC Primary; Christ the King RC Primary; St Augustine's RC Primary.

J F S (JEWS' FREE SCHOOL)

175 Camden Road
London NW1 9HD
Tel (0171) 485 9416
Fax (0171) 284 3948
E-mail: 101701.3250@compuserve.com

- National ranking 242 (339, 264, 220, 219)
- GCSE 68% (61%)
- A-levels 47% (A/B); 97% (A/E)
- Higher education 90% (Oxford 1)

- Grant-maintained
- Mixed comprehensive
- Pupils 1,445
- Boys (11–18) 698
- Girls (11–18) 747
- Sixth form 308 (21%)
- Education authority *Camden*

Headteacher Ruth Robins, 49, appointed in September 1993. Staff 101 (men 46, women 55).

Motto Ora vikar (Light and honour).

Background Origins go back to 1732 when school opened as Talmud Torah of the Great Synagogue; became Jews' Free School in 1817 on model of Lancastrian schools; by end of 19th century there were 3,500 boys and girls at the biggest school in the world. New site after war. Became grant-maintained in September 1993. Housed in modern linked buildings: specialist teaching accommodation, 'excellent' facilities for information technology. Science laboratories; three prep rooms, laboratory workshop, photographic dark room; design and technology accommodation; separate provision for fine art, pottery, home economics. Two gymnasia and a swimming pool. Heavily over-subscribed, with 1.6 applications per place. Strong links with Israel: five-month residential stay for 13-year-old pupils. Charity work. A-level strengths include mathematics, politics and economics. 'School activities reflect the Jewish and Zionist commitment of the school.'

Alumni Barbara Roche, Labour MP for Hornsey and Wood Green; Charles Golding, former deputy editor of the *Sunday Express*; Dr Sassoon Levi, Research Fellow in Gastroenterology, Hammersmith Hospital, London.

Streaming Two or three accelerated groups in year 7. Learning support department for pupils in need of help. Pupils put in sets for modern languages and mathematics from year 8, and in other subjects in subsequent years.

Approach to discipline Firm. 'Clear standards of what is and is not acceptable are known to pupils, parents and teachers. We believe everyone has a right to work in a pleasant environment, and to courtesy from everyone else.'

Uniform Girls: grey skirt, pale-blue blouse and royal-blue sweatshirt or sweater. Boys: royal-blue blazer, grey trousers and sweater, white shirt, school tie, Kipah. Very strictly enforced: 'Pupils not in uniform may be sent home.' Not applicable to sixth form.

Homework Average 11-year-old, seven hours 30 minutes a week; 14-year-old, 10 to 15 hours; 16-year-old, about 20 hours.

Vocational qualifications GNVQ Intermediate and Advanced.

Inspection March 1995: 'This is a good school which provides a sound and effective education for its pupils.'; 'Across the age range, pupils speak clearly, read with expression and understanding, write effectively in a range of forms, use number competently and present their work carefully. However, many pupils have less skill in identifying and solving problems independently, and their creativity and aesthetic sensitivity are limited in some subjects.'; 'Pupils have positive attitudes to their education and are highly-motivated.'; 'Staff are energetic, committed and generous in the time that they give for the benefit of the pupils.'

Primary schools Rosh Pinah Jewish Primary; Michael Sobell Sinai School; Simon Monks Jewish Day School; Mathilda Marks Jewish Primary; Broadfields Primary.

ST LAURENCE SCHOOL

Ashley Road
Bradford-on-Avon
Wiltshire BA15 1DZ
Tel (01225) 867691
Fax (01225) 867694
E-mail: admin.st.laurence@bath.ac.uk

- National ranking 243 (218, 213, 314, 255)
- GCSE 68% (71%)
- A-levels 44% (A/B); 91% (A/E)
- Higher education 87% (Oxford 1, Cambridge 2)

- Mixed comprehensive
- Pupils 1,167
- Boys (11–18) 545
- Girls (11–18) 622
- Sixth form 231 (20%)
- Education authority *Wiltshire*

Headteacher Nicholas Sorensen, 42, appointed from September 1997. Staff 77 (men 28, women 49).

Motto Working with and for the community.

Background Derived from Fitzmaurice Grammar School (1897) and Trinity School, a church school with more than 250 years of history. Voluntary-controlled with governors appointed by Salisbury Diocesan Council of Education and Fitzmaurice Foundation along with Wiltshire education authority. Opened in 1980 on site of former Trinity School; pupils drawn also from Atworth, Monkton Farleigh, Winsley, South Wraxall and parts of Limpley Stoke and Freshford. Over-subscribed. Support for information technology, design and technology, expansion of 16–19 education, provision for exceptionally-able pupils, Wiltshire music centre (£2.8m specialist music centre). Art, dance and music among strengths: one in five pupils receives weekly instrumental tuition; orchestra, jazz group, choir. Science and modern languages also strong; support for pupils with learning difficulties; emphasis on personal tutoring and small teaching groups (average of 23 for pupils aged 11 to 16). Support staff include chartered librarian, school nurse, careers adviser and school counsellor. Outward Bound/Challenge programmes for all year-groups.

Streaming Setting introduced progressively from year 8.

Approach to discipline Positive approach; seeks to be full of praise and marginalise poor behaviour by affirming good behaviour. 'Seeks to punish behaviour and not the child; has clear policy of rewards and sanctions shared with all.' Anti-bullying campaign.

Uniform Boys: navy/dark-grey trousers or navy skirt/trousers/culottes for girls, tailored navy cotton shorts (summer term only), pale-blue shirt/blouse, navy polo shirt, navy sweatshirt with school logo, grey/black/navy/white socks, brown/black/navy/grey shoes. 'Strong emphasis' on uniform.

Homework Average 11-year-old, maximum three hours 30 minutes a week; 14-year-old, at least seven hours 30 minutes; 16-year-old, at least five hours per subject.

Vocational qualifications GNVQ Level 3, Business and Finance.

Primary schools Christ Church Primary; Fitzmaurice Primary; Winsley CE Primary; Atworth Primary; Monkton Farleigh CE Primary.

ILKLEY GRAMMAR SCHOOL

Cowpasture Road
Ilkley
West Yorkshire LS29 8TR
Tel (01943) 608424
Fax (01943) 601285
E-mail:staff@ilkleygs.demon.co.uk

- National ranking 244 (320, 248, 212, 301)

- GCSE 68% (62%)
- A-levels 40% (A/B); 93% (A/E)
- Higher education 70% (Oxford 1, Cambridge 2)

- Mixed comprehensive
- Pupils 1,059
- Boys (13–18) 526
- Girls (13–18) 533
- Sixth form 286 (27%)
- Education authority Bradford

Headteacher Peter Wood, 55, appointed in 1979. Staff 59 (men 32, women 27).

Motto Sapientia et statura proficiamus (Going in wisdom and stature).

Background Founded in 1607 and has occupied current site since 1893; selective boys' school until 1939 when it became co-educational; became comprehensive in 1970. Close to Ilkley Moor with impressive views of Wharfe valley and serving Addingham, Ilkley and Burley. Specialist accommodation includes sports hall and swimming pool. Older parts of building date from 1893, with substantial additions in late 1960s and early 1970s. Over-subscribed. Full programme of out-of-school activities, visits, residential trips and foreign travel. 'Sound discipline and a caring atmosphere are the basis of the school's work. We seek to provide opportunities for each pupil to develop a lively, flexible and enquiring attitude and to make the most of his or her talents.'

Streaming Pupils placed in teaching groups for most subjects on basis of their ability. Some subjects taught in tutor groups.

Approach to discipline 'Pupils are expected to conduct themselves in a sensible and considerate manner, both within the school and within the local community. Good discipline, including self-discipline, is seen as vital in establishing the orderly purposeful atmosphere that is the basis of a successful school.'

Uniform Navy pullover with school badge, dark-grey trousers/navy skirt. Strictly enforced, but with greater latitude for sixth-formers.

Homework Average 14-year-old, seven hours a week; 16-year-old, nine hours.

Vocational qualifications GNVQ Intermediate and Advanced, Business and Finance; BTEC National Diploma, Science (Health).

Inspection March 1993: 'This is a very good school.'; 'Across all age-groups, standards of achievement are good and at times outstanding. Achievement was satisfactory or better in 90% of lessons and good in over 60%.'; 'When opportunities are provided for the pupils to extend, refine and consolidate their understanding by means of talk they respond well.'; 'The behaviour of pupils is excellent.' February 1997: 'A very good school. It provides a high quality of education which enables pupils to reach high standards of attainment and to develop their personal skills and qualities. Pupils benefit from a positive ethos, a good quality of support and guidance and from the strong partnership the school enjoys with parents and the community.'; 'The rate of progress is better at Key Stage 3 and in the sixth form than at Key Stage 4.'; 'Curriculum-related policies, including those for sex and health education, are in place. That for homework is not fully implemented in practice. When homework is given, the quality of the tasks set vary in their relevance and usefulness.'; 'The headteacher offers strong and decisive leadership, which is delivered with conviction and integrity.'; 'The school succeeds in providing a well-ordered and supportive community in which all pupils and staff are valued in an atmosphere of mutual respect.'

Primary schools Burley Middle; Ilkley Middle; Addingham Middle.

TOLWORTH GIRLS' SCHOOL

Fullers Way North
Surbiton
Surrey KT6 7LQ
Tel (0181) 397 3854
Fax (0181) 974 2600

- National ranking 245 (454, 353, 404, –)
- GCSE 68% (53%)
- A-levels 33% (A/B); 84% (A/E)
- Higher education 65%

- Girls' comprehensive
- Pupils 1,078
- Boys (16–18) 10
- Girls (11–18) 1,068
- Sixth form 185 (17%)
- Education authority *Kingston upon Thames*

Headteacher Clarissa C. Williams, 50, appointed in September 1985. Staff 76 (men 16, women 60).

Motto Sic luceat lux (Let your light so shine).

Background Built in 1932 close to A3 near Tolworth; well-maintained buildings extended over the years; new mathematics and light-technology block in July 1995. Well-stocked library with open access at all times; two learning resource centres, two computer rooms. School shares site with recreation centre; well-resourced art, ceramics and textiles studios, drama and dance workshop, music suite. Well-furnished Senior Student Common Room; science and technology faculty has benefited from recent government funding. Anti-bullying policy has achieved national recognition. Over-subscribed, with 500+ applications for 180 places. All pupils learn two foreign languages and full range of humanities subjects; technology, information technology and business studies facilities 'considered to be of excellent standard'; nationally-recognised arts department; high participation rate in sports and leisure activities; competitive sports include basketball, tennis, athletics, hockey, football, trampolining and netball. Identified by Ofsted as 'a very good school'.

Streaming Flexible approach: 'Girls with aptitude in mathematics and science are taught in the same groups. The school refuses to label pupils, preferring not to set a ceiling on levels of expectation.'

Approach to discipline 'Discipline is underpinned by a School Community Code, which is accepted by all pupils and their parents on entry to the school. There is an emphasis on courtesy, care and respect for others.' High expectations; sanctions used 'fairly and consistently'. Relies upon 'and expects' parental support.

Uniform Navy pleated skirt, navy jumper with embroidered school logo, white blouse, school tie with house-colour stripe, navy/black jacket/coat. Details contained in code of conduct: 'Pupils are encouraged to wear the uniform with pride.'

Homework Average 11-year-old, six hours a week; 14-year-old, 10 hours; 16-year-old, 15 hours. Pupils are encouraged to take greater responsibility for independent learning.

Vocational qualifications GNVQ Level 2 and 3, Business, Social Care; variety of Business Studies qualifications with additional modules, eg. Languages, Travel and Tourism, Food and Hospitality, Art and Design.

Primary schools Tolworth Junior; St Paul's CE Primary, Hook; St Matthew's CE Primary; Knollmead Primary; Our Lady Immaculate RC Primary.

POYNTON COUNTY HIGH SCHOOL

Yew Tree Lane
Poynton
Stockport
Cheshire SK12 1PU
Tel (01625) 871811
Fax (01625) 874541

- National ranking 246 (249, 180, 181, 207)
- GCSE 68% (67%)
- A-levels 32% (A/B); 84% (A/E)
- Higher education 90% (Oxford 2, Cambridge 1)

- Mixed comprehensive
- Pupils 1,721
- Boys (11–18) 845
- Girls (11–18) 876
- Sixth form 302 (18%)
- Education authority *Cheshire*

Headteacher John Anthony Parry Jones, 52, appointed in May 1979. Staff 102 (men 43, women 59).

Motto *None*

Background Between Stockport and Macclesfield in the village of Poynton, the school also takes children from relatively prosperous rural areas of Disley, Adlington and Pott Shrigley. It was opened in 1965, began building programme in 1968, designated county high school in 1972, and became fully comprehensive in 1976. Over-subscribed, with about 320 applications for 270 places. Recent additions include extra laboratories and a music suite; joint-use leisure centre on site, with sports hall and swimming pool; about 12 acres of land attached to school. New sixth-form centre in autumn 1994. Library includes flexible learning base and is run by qualified manager; special needs children well catered for; technology workshops and 10 science laboratories; music, dance and drama productions; four art studios with ceramic processing. Sporting success up to national level: all-weather pitch, gymnasium, tennis and netball courts, rugby and soccer pitches. Public speaking and debating. Languages include French, German and Spanish (all offered from year 7) as well as Russian and Italian; annual exchange visits to France, Germany and Spain; cultural exchanges with two schools in Germany. Parent-Teacher Association.

Streaming Policy decided within curriculum teams and year-groups. Setting policy varies: modern languages set in year 8, whereas English is taught in mixed-ability classes throughout.

Approach to discipline Formal policy statement based on honesty, respect, self-discipline, courtesy and understanding, both within and outside school. 'Where the expected standards are not met, correction and punishment may be necessary. More severe sanctions include suspensions, although these are used sparingly under the formula agreed by Cheshire County Council.' Parents informed immediately of serious breaches.

Uniform Navy jumper with badge, charcoal-grey trousers/navy pleated or A-line skirt, white shirt, school tie. Sixth-formers may wear 'sensible dress'. High standards set and maintained.

Homework Average 11-year-old, five hours a week; 14-year-old, seven hours; 16-year-old, nine to 12 hours (according to subject choice).

Vocational qualifications GNVQ Advanced, Leisure and Tourism, Health and Social Care.

Inspection September 1993: 'A very good school with excellent results.'; 'Standards in the day-to-day work of the school are equally high. The quality of pupils' work fully meets expectations of the various age and ability groups, and often exceeds them.'; 'Teaching methods are generally lively and varied, and well fitted to the purposes of lessons.'; 'The school is sensitively but firmly led.'; 'The school successfully creates a climate of endeavour which is not confined to academic success and, as a result, pupils are strongly motivated, willing to learn and prepared to work hard.'

Primary schools Vernon County Junior; Lower Park County Primary; Lostock Hall County Primary; Worth County Primary; Disley County Primary; Adlington County Primary, Adlington.

LINTON VILLAGE COLLEGE

Cambridge Road
Linton
Cambridge
Cambridgeshire CB1 6JB
Tel (01223) 891233
Fax (01223) 894476

- National ranking 247= (266=, 448=, 318=, –)
- GCSE 68% (66%)
- A-levels *Not applicable*
- Higher education *Not applicable*

- Mixed comprehensive
- Pupils 665
- Boys (11–16) 354
- Girls (11–16) 311
- Sixth form *Not applicable*
- Education authority *Cambridgeshire*

Headteacher Clive Robert James Bush, 46, appointed in September 1993. Staff 31 (men 17, women 14).

Motto Home, school, community – Education for the future.

Background One of the original village colleges designed by Henry Morris in 1937; set in large well-planted and maintained grounds, including lawns, borders and 'superb' sporting facilities; serves large rural catchment area of pleasant villages in rolling countryside; two miles from new A11–M11 link road and nine miles from Cambridge; 'particularly good facilities in technology and information technology'; strong tradition of visual and performing arts. Examination results particularly notable in English, mathematics and languages. Over-subscribed, with 1.1 applications per place, but more to be considered because of expansion. Community facilities and activities in evenings and at weekends; adult education and leisure pursuits; fully-equipped sports centre; Sports Council Award for Community Sport. 'Linton Village College is a calm, organised and well-disciplined environment where the individual student is encouraged to realise his or her potential. The stress is on individual responsibility, and a wide range of resources and facilities are made available to assist this.'

Streaming Mixed-ability in year 7; setting from year 8.

Approach to discipline 'The college believes that a strong discipline framework is essential to learning and the happiness of students. Therefore, this is maintained by all staff and students, and sanctions are clearly understood.'

Uniform Years 7 to 10: blue jumper with crest, charcoal-grey trousers/skirt, school tie for boys. Alternative jumper, of agreed alternative colour, for year 11 pupils. Regulations enforced 'strictly'.

Homework Average 11-year-old, six hours a week; 14-year-old, eight hours; 16-year-old, 10 hours.

Vocational qualifications *None*

Inspection October 1993.

Primary schools Linton Heights Junior; Burrough Green Endowed CE Primary; Castle Camps CE Primary; Great Abington Primary; Meadow Primary, Balsham.

WARDEN PARK SCHOOL

Broad Street
Cuckfield
Haywards Heath
West Sussex RH17 5DP
Tel (01444) 457881
Fax (01444) 417024

- National ranking 247= (215, 205=, 205=, 225)
- GCSE 68% (72%)
- A-levels *Not applicable*
- Higher education *Not applicable*

- Mixed comprehensive
- Pupils 1,467
- Boys (11–16) 786
- Girls (11–16) 681
- Sixth form *Not applicable*
- Education authority *West Sussex*

Headteacher Brian David Webb, 55, appointed in September 1988. Staff 85 (men 34, women 51).

Motto The best from all.

Background Opened in 1956 with seven teaching staff and 297 students, rising to 520 by 1960. Buildings have been continually added since it opened; a £1.7m investment programme completed in 1996. Oversubscribed each year; a waiting list of eight for each of the first three years is the norm.

Significant sporting achievements: national finalists for past 11 years in English Schools' Track and Field Athletics Cup; area athletics champions 1981 to 1996; national finalists in cross-country cup; Sussex dry-ski champions; county representatives in soccer; also successes in basketball, rugby, and cricket. More than £7,500 raised for charity in 1996.

Streaming Pupils in sets in English, mathematics and modern languages in years 8 and 9. Setting in almost all subjects in years 10 and 11.

Approach to discipline High standard owing 'almost entirely to the support given by parents and the excellent self-discipline which exists'. School rules, including possible deterrents, given to all parents; suspension and expulsion among deterrents, but rarely required.

Uniform Years 7 to 9: dark-grey/black trousers or grey skirt, blue shirt/blouse, lower school tie (optional for girls), light-grey V-neck jumper 'preferably with school crest', dark socks for boys and white/grey for girls, black shoes. Years 10 and 11: navy trousers/skirt, upper- school tie, navy V-neck jumper, black/navy shoes.

Homework Average 11-year-old, five hours 30 minutes a week; 14-year-old, seven hours 30 minutes; 16-year-old, 11 hours 30 minutes.

Vocational qualifications *None*

Primary schools Harlands County Primary, Haywards Heath; Cuckfield Holy Trinity CE Primary; Twineham CE Primary; Southway County Junior, Burgess Hill; St Peter's CE Primary, Henfield. Total of 68 feeder schools.

CHRISTLETON HIGH SCHOOL

Village Road
Christleton
Chester
Cheshire CH3 7AD
Tel (01244) 335843
Fax (01244) 332173

- National ranking 249 (417, 410 = , 195, 306)
- GCSE 67% (56%)
- A-levels 42% (A/B); 88% (A/E)
- Higher education 72% (Oxford 1, Cambridge 4)

- Mixed comprehensive
- Pupils 1,257
- Boys (11–18) 637
- Girls (11–18) 6205
- Sixth form 257 (20%)
- Education authority *Cheshire*

Headteacher Geoffrey Lawson, 53, appointed in January 1990. Staff 73 (men 31, women 42).

Motto Learn, to serve.

Background On seven-acre site in Cheshire village of Christleton, three miles from Chester city centre; draws pupils from immediate neighbourhood, although four in 10 come from outside catchment area. Oversubscribed, with up 1.1 applications per place. Up-to-date facilities include new science laboratories, drama and music suite, sports hall and swimming pool. Reputation for performing arts; biennial musical productions; creative writing; public-speaking competitions. 'Happy, hard-working and courteous.'

Alumni Erroll Pickford, ballet dancer; Keith Harris, 'Orville' puppeteer; Ben Johnston, artist.

Streaming Pupils put in sets in science, English, mathematics and modern languages in years 8 to 11; mixed-ability groupings in humanities and creative subjects throughout the school.

Approach to discipline 'Firm but fair. The school is well-ordered as a result. Form-tutors and year-heads remain with pupil groups throughout their schooling and so know them and their parents well. Staff continuity makes for positive pupil-teacher relationships.'

Uniform Navy and white, with option of school badge, school tie or school jumper with emblem. Colour is strictly enforced, with opportunity for personal style. 'We prefer to describe it as school dress rather than uniform, but each person wears a school identifier.'

Homework Average 11-year-old, eight hours a week; 14-year-old, 12 hours; 16-year-old, 20 hours.

Vocational qualifications GNVQ Level 3, Health and Social Care.

Inspection November 1994: 'Christleton High School is a very good school. Standards of achievement are very high.'; 'Pupils are confident, capable and enthusiastic learners.'; 'The governors, with the headteacher and the senior management team, provide strong leadership, which has a positive impact on the quality of pupils' learning and the standards they achieve.'; 'Pupils' behaviour and discipline, and the quality of relationships within the school, are very good. The positive ethos of the school is further enhanced by the extent of the school community's participation in a wide range of extra-curricular activities.'

Primary schools Barrow Primary; Christleton Primary; Cherry Grove Primary; Oldfield Primary; Waverton Primary.

ROSEBERY

White Horse Drive
Epsom
Surrey KT18 7NQ
Tel (01372) 720439
Fax (01372) 749219
E-mail: roseberyschool@tens.co.uk

- National ranking 250 (340, 320, 254, 247 =)
- GCSE 67% (61%)
- A-levels 36% (A/B); 94% (A/E)
- Higher education 92% (Cambridge 3)

- Grant-maintained
- Girls' comprehensive
- Pupils 1,200
- Boys *Not applicable*
- Girls (11–18) 1,200
- Sixth form 220 (18%)
- Education authority *Surrey*

Headteacher Heather Saunders, 49, appointed in September 1991. Staff 72 (men 9, women 63).

Motto *None*

Background Founded on current site in 1927, the school was named after the 5th Earl of Rosebery whose family name is Primrose. (A primrose is still used as the school emblem.) In 1977, Rosebery Grammar School was merged with Epsom County Girls' School to become a comprehensive, the only all-girls state school in Surrey. Spacious site with conservation area, ponds, sports field, but close to Epsom centre and its theatres, galleries and museums. Buildings added over the years with no common architectur-

al design. Known for musical achievement; also strong in mathematics and technology; new music suite and technology suite; open-air swimming pool. Over-subscribed, with two applications per place.

Alumni Jackie Ashley, ITN political correspondent; Lynn Barton, first woman to fly long-haul jumbo jets for British Airways.

Streaming Ability sets for English, mathematics, science, modern languages and music from entry to school. Broad bands for humanities in GCSE years.

Approach to discipline Strong links with pupils' families. 'High standards of behaviour are expected and achieved. Parents supportive of ethos, which includes code of conduct for pupils.'

Uniform Navy sweater with school emblem, white shirt, Mackenzie tartan skirt. Strictly enforced.

Homework Average 12-year-old, eight hours a week; 14-year-old, nine hours; 16-year-old, 10+ hours.

Vocational qualifications GNVQ Intermediate and Advanced, Business and Finance.

Primary schools St Martin's CE Primary; Wallace Fields Primary; Stamford Green Primary; St Anne's RC Primary, Banstead; West Ashtead Primary. Total of more than 30 feeder schools.

THE MINSTER SCHOOL

Nottingham Road
Southwell
Nottinghamshire NG25 0HG
Tel (01636) 814000
Fax (01636) 814788

- National ranking 251
- GCSE 67%
- A-levels 35% (A/B); 90% (A/E)
- Higher education 85% (Oxford 1, Cambridge 2)

- Mixed comprehensive
- Pupils 1,510
- Boys (8–18) 800
- Girls (8–18) 710
- Sixth form 310 (21%)
- Education authority *Nottinghamshire*

Headteacher Philip John Blinston, 42, appointed in April 1994. Staff 87 (men 48, women 39)

Motto *None.*

Background The Minster School, in rural cathedral village, lays claim to be one of the oldest educational establishments in the country, as old as Southwell Minster, which dates to AD 956. Remains member of Choir Schools' Association. Small Church of England grammar until 1976, it now has eight-form entry, with a junior department (aged 8–11) for cathedral choristers and musically-gifted pupils; choir school for Southwell Minster. Over-subscribed for Governors Foundation places (20% of total); two applications per place. Voluntary-aided; maintains link with St John's College, Cambridge, which appoints one of its governors. Strong county representation in athletics, cross-country and swimming; also strong in rugby and hockey; Duke of Edinburgh Award Scheme. Particular strength in music; many assemblies and choirs. Major building programme from autumn 1997: improved accommodation for technology, art and design, information technology, library and English.

Streaming Mainly mixed-ability classes in years 7 and 8; setting by ability in years 9 to 11.

Approach to discipline 'Relaxed and open'. Pupils expected to be self-disciplined; sanctions include detentions and exclusion.

Uniform Boys: navy blazer, grey flannels, white shirt, school tie. Girls: navy blazer and skirt, white shirt, school tie. For sixth-formers, regulations are relaxed but formal dress is required.

Homework Average 11-year-old, five hours a week; 14-year-old, seven hours 30 minutes; 16-year-old, 10 hours.

Vocational qualifications GNVQ Intermediate, Business.

Inspection November 1995: 'The Minster School is a good school.'; 'Overall, the quality of learning is good. Pupils generally show interest in their work, concentrate well and make good progress through the school.'; 'Teachers have good command of their subjects, lessons are well planned and relationships are positive. Good work is done with pupils with special educational needs.'; 'The headteacher provides purposeful leadership and is supported by an effective team of senior staff.'

Primary schools Lowes Wong Junior; Bleasby Primary; Farnsfield CE Primary; Walter D'Ayncourt Primary, Farnsfield; Kirkington Primary; Dean Hole CE Primary, Caunton.

COPTHALL SCHOOL

Pursley Road
Mill Hill
London NW7 2EP
Tel (0181) 959 1937
Fax (0181) 959 8736
E-mail: copthall@rmplc.co.uk

- National ranking 252 (180, 173, 197, 228)
- GCSE 67% (78%)
- A-levels 32% (A/B); 99% (A/E)
- Higher education 85% (Oxford 2, Cambridge 2)

- Girls' comprehensive
- Pupils 1,127
- Boys *Not applicable*
- Girls (11–18) 1,127
- Sixth form 228 (20%)
- Education authority *Barnet*

Headteacher Lynn Gadd, 43, appointed in January 1997. Staff 70 (men 19, women 51).

Motto Copthall celebrates excellence.

Background 'Happy, over-subscribed, multi-ethnic and multi-faith comprehensive.' Formed in 1973 by amalgamation of Copthall County Grammar School and Woodcroft Secondary Modern; six-form entry, with more than three applications for each place. Original 1930s grammar school building now joined to new wing of equal size on one site, in leafy part of Mill Hill. Playing fields and tennis courts in attractive grounds. Facilities: new building open in October 1996 houses all specialist rooms, including three 'superbly well-equipped' computer rooms, five technology workshops, nine laboratories suited for GCSE and A-level teaching; four art rooms, ceramics workshop, modern dark-room. Large sports hall with viewing gallery, multi-gym, multi-purpose space with sprung floor ideal for dance performances, theatre and music. Integrated learning computer system, CD-ROMs, language laboratory. Local success for hockey, netball and athletics teams. Identified by Ofsted in 1996 as 'outstandingly successful'.

Streaming Pupils put in sets in mathematics

and modern languages from year 7; in science in years 7 to 11, with broad bands for English and humanities.

Approach to discipline 'Firm and fair. Pupil behaviour is expected to be courteous and cooperative.' Heads of year and departments deal with minor infringements; parents kept informed. Head and deputies follow up any major acts of indiscipline. Exclusion rare.

Uniform From September 1996: Blackwatch tartan kilt, mint-green blouse, navy V-neck jumper with mint-green stripe, plain black shoes, plain navy coat. Very strictly enforced, with year-heads and deputies following up infringements as they occur.

Homework Average 11-year-old, six hours 30 minutes a week; 14-year-old, seven hours 30 minutes; 16-year-old, 10 hours.

Vocational qualifications GNVQ.

Inspection October 1993: 'The school provides very good education.'; 'Relationships are good throughout the school, as is communication at all levels. Behaviour is exemplary and there is an effective ethos of work and success. The school is efficient and well managed; it uses its resources well and provides value for money. This is particularly commendable given the difficulties experienced in operating on two sites. The personal, social and religious education programme is a particular strength of the school.'

Primary schools Dollis Junior; Woodcroft Primary; St Mary's CE Primary, N3; St Mary's CE Primary, NW4; St Paul's CE Primary; Grahame Park Primary; Deansbrook Junior; Sunnyfields Primary; Frith Manor Primary; Edgware Junior; Garden Suburb Junior.

CONYERS SCHOOL

Green Lane
Yarm
Stockton-on-Tees TS15 9ET
Tel (01642) 783253
Fax (01642) 783834

- National ranking 253 (350, 192, 273, 196)
- GCSE 67% (61%)
- A-levels 32% (A/B); 92% (A/E)
- Higher education 87% (Oxford 1)

- Mixed comprehensive

- Pupils 1,204
- Boys (11–18) 630
- Girls (11–18) 574
- Sixth form 203 (17%)
- Education authority *Stockton-on-Tees*

Headteacher John Morgan, 43, appointed in April 1995. Staff 73 (men 38, women 35).

Motto Perseverando (Persevere).

Background Founded as Yarm Grammar School in 1590 by Thomas Conyers; became a comprehensive in 1975; moved to current site two years later. 'Standard, undistinguished accommodation that is overcrowded. No assembly hall.' Nine mobile classrooms; new music suite in 1996. Originally new buildings were on a greenfield site, but extensive developments mean the school is now bordered by estates on two sides. Over-subscribed, with average of 1.5 applications per place. High participation rate in wide range of extra-curricular activities: rugby, soccer, netball, orienteering, tennis. 'Success rate high, but more concerned with pupils taking part.' Duke of Edinburgh Award Scheme. 'Though teaching styles may vary, the easy informality between staff and pupils not only brings out the best in able and less able pupils, but also aims to encourage them all to treat each other with a more tolerant respect.'

Streaming To a limited extent in mathematics and modern languages.

Approach to discipline Co-operation rather than coercion. 'Firm framework within which the majority of pupils can be trusted to impose self-discipline.'

Uniform White/pale-blue shirt/blouse, school tie, black/dark-grey trousers or navy skirt/trousers, navy V-neck pullover with crest (optional), dark shoes. Co-operation means uniform rarely has to be enforced strictly.

Homework Average 11-year-old, five hours 30 minutes a week; 14-year-old, six hours 30 minutes; 16-year-old, 10 hours 30 minutes.

Vocational qualifications GNVQ Advanced, Business, Health and Social Care.

Inspection March 1993: 'Standards of pupils' homework and coursework are often high. Levels of achievement in lessons are more varied across the curriculum and the age range. Good standards are achieved by pupils with special educational needs. Standards of pupils' behaviour in classrooms and throughout the school are excellent.'; 'In some lessons the teaching lacks challenge and pace, in others the approach is too narrow and does not adequately cater for pupils of all abilities. By their industry, motivation and positive attitudes to work, pupils make a significant contribution to their own learning; however, pupils' progress in lessons is frequently limited by the teaching approach.'; 'The school succeeds in creating a very positive ethos.'

Primary schools Layfield Primary; Levendale Primary; Kirklevington Primary; Yarm Primary; Ingleby Mill Primary; Whinstone Primary.

CLEEVE SCHOOL

Two Hedges Road
Bishops Cleeve
Cheltenham
Gloucestershire GL52 4AE
Tel (01242) 672546
Fax (01242) 678604
E-mail: bdgcleeve@aol.com

- National ranking 254 (251, 288, 325, –)
- GCSE 67% (67%)
- A-levels 29% (A/B); 92% (A/E)
- Higher education 86% (Cambridge 2)

- Mixed comprehensive
- Pupils 1,500
- Boys (11–18) 780
- Girls (11–18) 720
- Sixth form 297 (20%)
- Education authority *Gloucestershire*

Headteacher Brian David Gardiner, 53, appointed in September 1987. Staff 82 (men 37, women 45).

Motto Working together in search of success.

Background Well-established comprehensive with large catchment area; on large, compact site on edge of Bishops Cleeve, with 'excellent' facilities. Over-subscribed, with 1.3 applications per place. 'The school has rightly gained an excellent reputation for its work. Academic, sporting and musical achievements are celebrated. Pupils are expected to reach their potential in a caring, supportive environment. Most staff who have children of secondary school age send their children to the school.'

Streaming Pupils taught in ability sets for all subjects from year 8.

Approach to discipline 'The ethos of the school is that of a well-controlled, friendly institution. Children are given responsibility and are expected to exercise responsibility in a mature manner.'

Uniform Blazer, grey trousers/skirt, school tie. Strictly enforced.

Homework Average 11-year-old, five to eight hours a week; 14-year-old, 12 to 14 hours; 16-year-old, 14 + hours.

Vocational qualifications *None*

Inspection November 1996: 'This is a good school. It has particular strengths in teaching and in analysing and using assessment information.'; 'Most pupils make good progress, at a rate faster than is usually expected.'; 'Results in the sixth form for A-level are broadly average and, given the good performance in the earlier key stages, not as high as the school might expect.'; 'The quality of teaching is a good feature of the school. Teaching is at least sound in over nine out of 10 lessons.'; 'Most teachers have high expectations of pupils, plan lessons well and provide pupils with opportunities to develop independence in their learning. Some higher-attaining pupils at all stages are not always sufficiently challenged.'; 'Most classes are managed well: in a few lessons, most of them at Key Stage 4, disruptive pupils spoil lessons and are not properly dealt with. Pupils' responses in lessons are often good, they are well-motivated, rise well to challenges when these are presented and work effectively, independently and with each other.'; 'The school is well led and managed.'

Primary schools Woodmancote Primary; Bishops Cleeve Primary; Gotherington Primary; St Mary's CE Junior; Swindon Village Primary.

ST PHILOMENA'S CATHOLIC HIGH SCHOOL FOR GIRLS

Pound Street
Carshalton
Surrey SM5 3PS
Tel (0181) 642 2025
Fax (0181) 643 7925
E-mail: st.carshalton.se@connect.bt.com

- National ranking 255 (328, 191)
- GCSE 67% (62%)
- A-levels 23% (A/B); 79% (A/E)
- Higher education 79% (Oxford 1)

- Grant-maintained
- Girls' comprehensive
- Pupils 980
- Boys (11–18) *Not applicable*
- Girls (11–18) 980
- Sixth form 162 (17%)
- Education authority *Sutton*

Headteacher Moira Kilkenny, 52, appointed in February 1992. Staff 62 (men 9, women 53).

Motto Nisi dominus aedific vanum (Unless the Lord build the house, they labour in vain that build it).

Background Founded in 1894 by the Daughters of the Cross; housed in 18th-century Carshalton House, which provides the sixth-form accommodation, and turn-of-the-century buildings. Listed chapel in 25 acres of grounds, with water tower and hermitage of antiquarian interest. Science and technology accommodated in recent buildings. Oversubscribed, with four applications per place. Indoor swimming pool, gymnasium, new science laboratories. Developing vocational courses in business; centre for BTEC qualifications. Aims 'to give every girl the opportunity to develop intellectually, morally and spiritually in a Catholic community, and to recognise and value the uniqueness of every individual.'

Alumni Mary Wilkinson, television producer; Michelle Martin, actress.

Streaming For mathematics only in year 7; in other subjects from year 8.

Approach to discipline 'Supportive rather than punitive. Girls are encouraged to exercise self-discipline and to relate to staff and other students with consideration.'

Uniform Years 7 to 11: Brown blazer with crest, brown-and-cream kilt, cream blouse, brown sweater. 'Very strictly' enforced: 'Girls are encouraged to take pride in their uniform.'

Homework Average 11-year-old, seven hours 30 minutes a week; 14-year-old, 10 hours; 16-year-old, 12 hours 30 minutes.

Vocational qualifications GNVQ Intermediate and Advanced, Business.

Inspection February 1995: 'St Philomena's is a successful comprehensive school. It provides a good-quality education for all its pupils, within a well-ordered community founded on strong Christian principles and beliefs. The ethos of the school, which encourages pupils to work hard to achieve their potential and to be considerate to others, is a considerable strength. Relationships throughout the school are very good. Pupils take a pride in their school; they are happy and secure. Their behaviour is exemplary.'; 'In some subjects, there is insufficient variety of activities to challenge and stimulate pupils' thinking and enable them to express their ideas.'

Primary schools Regina Coeli RC Primary, South Croydon; St Mary's RC Primary; St Cecilia's RC Primary; st Elphege's RC Primary; St Anne's RC Primary, Banstead; Margaret Roper RC Primary, South Croydon; St Thomas of Canterbury RC Primary, Mitcham.

BRINE LEAS HIGH SCHOOL

Audlem Road
Nantwich
Cheshire CW5 7DY
Tel (01270) 625663
Fax (01270) 610373
E-mail: 9064220.depot@dialnet.co.uk

- National ranking 256= (302=, 293=)
- GCSE 67% (63%)
- A-levels *Not applicable*
- Higher education *Not applicable*

- Mixed comprehensive
- Pupils 945
- Boys (11–16) 490
- Girls (11–16) 455
- Sixth form *Not applicable*
- Education authority *Cheshire*

Headteacher Michael Butler, 49, appointed in September 1986. Staff 53 (men 24, women 29).

Motto *None*

Background Set in open countryside on southern edge of Nantwich; well-maintained buildings surrounded by extensive playing fields; large, well-equipped sports hall contains cricket coaching centre. Three main buildings: six laboratories, three computer suites, technology block, music centre, drama studio, full range of well-resourced classrooms. The school is over-subscribed, exceeding its formal limit of 900 pupils; it has a policy of admitting all local children who apply. More than one in three pupils come from normal catchment area. All pupils normally study two foreign languages; able pupils may sit GCSE Mathematics a year early; many study three separate sciences. 'In the Upper School, students normally study a broader range and number of subjects than is generally available.' Wide range of pre-vocational courses; strong tradition of extra-curricular activities; wide range of competitive sports; orchestra and brass band. Governors plan to introduce sixth form 'as soon as practicable'. School supported by 'enthusiastic' Parent-Teacher Association and The Brine Leas Trust. Strong links with local business and professional community. 'The school has a distinctive philosophy and curriculum which promotes individual success and self-responsibility. It places excellent teaching at the heart of its work, supported by a House system that provides a structured programme of competitions and opportunities ranging from sport and music to drama and public-speaking.'

Streaming 'The school believes that students are entitled to equal access to resources, curriculum and facilities. We believe that academic needs vary according to attainment and, after an induction period in year 7, students are set in mathematics, foreign languages, science and English.'

Approach to discipline Based on school's own 'positive schooling' programme to promote self-discipline and reward individual effort. House system 'encourages loyalty and personal development'.

Uniform Black blazer with badge, House tie, blue shirt/blouse, grey trousers/skirt. 'Uniform applies to all students in school and is fully enforced.'

Homework Average 11-year-old, two hours 30 minutes to five hours a week; 14-year-old, five to 10 hours; 16-year-old, 10+ hours.

Vocational qualifications City and Guilds, Diploma of Vocational Education (Foundation level).

Inspection 'Brine Leas High School is a good, caring and efficient school.'; 'Within an atmosphere conducive to learning, the general quality of education provided by the school is good, with some excellent attributes.'; 'Many examples of good teaching were observed, characterised by a high degree of commitment, good planning and hard work.'; 'Lessons are well-ordered and staff-pupil relationships are excellent.'; 'The school benefits from strong leadership, an effective and well-organised governing body and skilful management and administration at all levels.'; 'There is an outstanding range of extra-curricular activities, well-developed music and other cultural provision, and the curriculum is further enhanced by visits, foreign exchanges and other enrichment activities.'

Primary schools The Weaver County Primary; St James' CE Primary, Audlem; The Wyche County Primary, Nantwich; Wrenbury County Primary; Sound County Primary.

COMBERTON VILLAGE COLLEGE

West Street
Comberton
Cambridge
Cambridgeshire CB3 7DU
Tel (01223) 262503
Fax (01223) 264116

- National ranking 256= (244=, 293=, 374=, –)
- GCSE 67% (68%)
- A-levels *Not applicable*
- Higher education *Not applicable*

- Grant-maintained
- Mixed comprehensive
- Pupils 920
- Boys (11–16) 483
- Girls (11–16) 437
- Sixth form *Not applicable*
- Education authority *Cambridgeshire*

Headteacher Rosalie Clayton, 48, appointed in January 1987. Staff 56 (men 17, women 39).

Motto *None*

Background Built in 1960 with pupil roll of 300 as one of Cambridgeshire's unique group of village colleges; located on 26-acre site on edge of one of 15 villages that it serves. Squash courts, sports hall, tennis courts, swimming pool, fitness centre. Pupils can take up to 10 GCSEs. 'Strong academic environment along with an extensive programme of extracurricular activities.' Over-subscribed with 245 applications for

180 places in year 7; other years are full and have small waiting lists. School day starts at 8.30am and ends at 2.50pm, with short lunch break; after-school programme 3pm to 4pm. Music: orchestra, jazz band, instrumental groups, rock groups, choir, music, technology group, three concerts per year, Summer Arts Festival, 10 instrumental teachers for percussion, guitar, wind, brass, strings and piano. Sports: soccer, rugby, hockey, netball, basketball, badminton, volleyball, tennis, cricket, rounders, athletics, swimming, squash, cross-country; interschool, district and county competitions; several representatives at district/county, national level. Duke of Edinburgh Award Scheme. Pupils study two languages in years 7 to 9; two exchange programmes a year with schools in Germany and France; provides continuing education and leisure activities for local community, including more than 2,000 adults and young people.

Alumni Keith Fletcher and Suzie Kitson, England cricketers; Amanda Caine, England athlete.

Streaming 'Pupils are set in most subjects according to their ability. Setting takes place from year 7 and remains flexible until well into the upper school when examination entry demands impose limitations on this flexibility.'

Approach to discipline 'Discipline is good and based on an ethos of strong values, mutual respect, shared responsibility and collective purpose.' Code of conduct; if transgressed, range of sanctions. 'Teaching staff try wherever appropriate to involve parents in resolving problems and to work in partnership with them.'

Uniform White shirt, grey pullover (with school motif), school tie, black trousers for boys, grey skirt/trousers for girls. Strictly enforced.

Homework Average 11-year-old, five to six hours a week; 14-year-old, six to eight hours; 16-year-old, nine to 12 hours.

Vocational qualifications *None*

Inspection January 1995: 'Pupils are overwhelmingly well-motivated and have positive attitudes to their work.'; 'Relationships between pupils and teachers are positive and supportive.'; 'Accommodation is well-maintained, but the availability and quality of learning resources is variable.'; 'The college provides most effectively for the development of the whole pupil. Behaviour is good and relationships are warm, friendly and trusting. Pupils frequently demonstrate concern and support for others. Punctuality and attendance are very good. There is extensive provision of curricular and extra-curricular activity to give pupils a rich experience of their own culture.'

Primary schools Bourn Parochial CE Primary; Coton Community CE Primary; Hardwick Community Primary; Haslingfield Endowed Primary; Meridian Primary.

CROFTON SCHOOL

Marks Road
Stubbington
Fareham
Hampshire PO14 2AT
Tel (01329) 664251
Fax (01329) 668525
E-mail: croftonsh@aol.com

- National ranking 256= (266=, 205=, 295=, 247=)
- GCSE 67% (66%)
- A-levels *Not applicable*
- Higher education *Not applicable*

- Grant-maintained
- Mixed comprehensive
- Pupils 989
- Boys (11–16) 490
- Girls (11–16) 499
- Sixth form *Not applicable*
- Education authority *Hampshire*

Headteacher Spencer James Horner, 48, appointed in September 1987. Staff 58 (men 20, women 38).

Motto *None*

Background Opened in 1974 as purpose-built comprehensive on spacious site, partly wooded; seven tutor-groups in each of the five years. Became grant-maintained in April 1992. Specialist music block; arts, design, home economics and technology block; also school hall, weights room, gymnasium, sports hall and drama studios; inter-connecting series of blocks containing science laboratories and other facilities. Building programme completed in September 1994 included eight-laboratory science block; also hall extension, including extra music recital room and three practice rooms; newly-refurbished language suite. More than eight in

10 (85%) go on to further education. Over-subscribed, with average of 1.5 applications per place. School employs 15 music teachers, with instrumental tuition to about one in four pupils. Sporting tradition marked by under-19 girls' squash team being runners-up in national championship. Proposals for sixth form submitted to Education Secretary in 1996.

Streaming Pupils placed in mixed-ability tutor groups in year 7; setting in year 7 for mathematics and languages; in science from year 8; and in English from year 9.

Approach to discipline 'Positive reinforcement of appropriate types of behaviour rather than on a rigid system of disciplinary sanctions.' Students expected to learn responsibility for own actions, consideration for others and environment. School expects high standards of pupils, and recognises pupils entitled to same from school.

Uniform Boys: charcoal-grey/black trousers, white/light-blue shirt, school tie, navy V-neck sweater/cardigan, dark/white socks. Girls: navy skirt, white/pale-blue shirt/blouse, navy V-neck/round-neck jumper/cardigan, white/navy socks, black shoes, school tie optional. Regulations enforced 'firmly but compassionately'.

Homework Average 11-year-old, five hours a week; 14-year-old, seven hours 30 minutes; 16-year-old, students encouraged to organise their own work programmes.

Vocational qualifications *None*

Inspection April 1994: 'Crofton is a good school.'; 'The quality of education provided is good and the curriculum planning is detailed and thorough. Staff are committed and give generously of their time. Departments are well-resourced. All pupils in the school are receiving a broad and balanced curriculum enriched by extra-curricular activities.'; 'The school is well led through an effective partnership of the headteacher, governors and senior staff.' 'Pupils have a clear view of what is expected of them and respond accordingly.'; 'Behaviour is of a high standard.'

Primary schools Crofton Anne Dale Junior; Crofton Hammond Junior; Peel Common Junior; Solent Junior.

ST GREGORY'S ROMAN CATHOLIC HIGH SCHOOL

Cromwell Avenue
Westbrook
Warrington
Cheshire WA5 1HG
Tel (01925) 574888
Fax (01925) 574888
E-mail: 9064622.depot@dialnet.co.uk

- National ranking 256= (290=, 214=, 337=, 230=)
- GCSE 67% (64%)
- A-levels *Not applicable*
- Higher education *Not applicable*

- Mixed comprehensive
- Pupils 960
- Boys (11–16) 520
- Girls (11–16) 440
- Sixth form *Not applicable*
- Education authority *Cheshire*

Headteacher Thomas John Brophy, 55, appointed in September 1980. Staff 53 (men 23, women 30).

Motto *None*

Background Purpose-built voluntary-aided comprehensive, opened in 1981 on west side of Warrington in new-town development of Westbrook. The school has recently completed a substantial building development, giving capacity of 850 pupils. Oversubscribed by the equivalent of three forms of entry each year. Three in four (75%) of school-leavers go on to further education. 'What animates us, fires and fuels our curriculum, must be the spirit, values and norms of the gospel.' Inspectors recently praised it as 'outstandingly effective' school. Extra-curricular activities have included calligraphy, justice and peace group, sweet-making, theatre technology and sculpture. Duke of Edinburgh Award Scheme.

Streaming Mainly mixed-ability groups in years 7 to 9; setting in mathematics from Christmas of year 7; setting, banding and mixed-ability all used in years 10 and 11.

Approach to discipline 'While staff are quick to react against anti-social behaviour or negative attitudes, they are equally rapid in praise and encouragement.' Merit awards in years 7 to 9; individual and form awards; gold awards for excellence. Firm discipline but no persecution. Sanctions: reprimand, note of apology, breaktime detention, evening detention, daily report.

Uniform Boys: royal-blue blazer with badge, school tie, white/pale-blue shirt/blouse, grey trousers/skirt, grey pullover, grey socks for boys or navy/white for girls. Agreed in consultation with Parents' Association Committee. Jewellery and make-up not allowed.

Homework Average 11-year-old, five to seven hours 30 minutes a week; 14-year-old, 10 hours; 16-year-old, 10 to 15 hours.

Vocational qualifications BTEC Foundation.

Inspection March 1993: 'The school is outstandingly effective and highly regarded by the community it serves.'; 'The quality of teaching is satisfactory in all subjects and often very good. It is matched by an extremely high degree of motivation, application and attention amongst pupils, whose behaviour in classes and around the school is excellent and who show a high degree of confidence in their capacities and a marked determination to improve their standards. This reflects the heavy concentration in the school of well-qualified, specialist teachers and their high expectations of pupils.' November 1996: 'A high-achieving school with many excellent features. It is well-managed.'; 'Pupils' behaviour is exceptionally good and parents are exceptionally supportive of the school.'; 'During Key Stage 3 pupils acquire a good range of computer skills, but there is little application of these skills across the work of the whole school. There is, however, some excellent computer work in several subjects.'; 'Some teachers give pupils responsibility for aspects of their own learning. Pupils readily accept it. This growth in self-responsibility, however, is an area for further development. Pupils are too frequently given prepared handouts or told exactly how to complete a task. This makes them too reliant on their teachers.'

Primary schools St Joseph's RC Primary; St Vincent's RC Primary; Sacred Heart RC Primary; St Alban's RC Primary; St Benedict's RC Primary.

ST MONICA'S ROMAN CATHOLIC HIGH SCHOOL

Bury Old Road
Prestwich
Manchester M25 1JH
Tel (0161) 773 6436
Fax (0161) 773 6650

- National ranking 256= (382=, 359=, 233=, –)
- GCSE 67% (59%)
- A-levels *Not applicable*
- Higher education *Not applicable*

- Mixed comprehensive
- Pupils 1,113
- Boys (11–16) 554
- Girls (11–16) 559
- Sixth form *Not applicable*
- Education authority *Bury*

Headteacher William Austin Campbell, 59, appointed in May 1987. Staff 63 (men 27, women 36).

Motto Prayer and service.

Background Founded in 1987 north of Manchester city centre after amalgamation of St Peter's and St Joseph's RC High Schools; continues tradition of serving Catholic community south of Bury; draws pupils equally from urban and residential areas of Manchester and Salford. Over-subscribed, with average of 1.25 applications per place. New classroom block is part of extensive building and refurbishment programme. 'Very strong' in public music performance, especially choir and orchestra; up to five drama productions a year. Emphasis on breadth and choice in curriculum: 27 different subjects studied in years 10 and 11; attention to children with special needs, including particularly able pupils. Policy on environmental education. Competitive sports include soccer, rugby, netball and hockey; inter-house competitions; success also at table tennis athletics and cross-country. Public speaking among extra-curricular strengths. 'Jesus Christ is central to our school. Our vocation is the cultivation of human values originating in Christ, so that pupils may grow in faith through prayer and service.'

Alumni Dave Roberts, England cricket team physiotherapist.

Streaming Pupils taught in mixed-ability

roups in year 7. In years 8 to 11, pupils
aught mainly in sets according to ability in
particular subjects.

approach to discipline All members of staff
nvolved in pastoral system based on form
groups and year groups. 'School discipline is
einforced by reprimand, the monitoring of
ehaviour by means of a report card, deten-
on, conduct contracts and, if necessary,
xclusion from school. Pupils may be
harged an appropriate sum for repair or
eplacement of materials, equipment and
chool fabric damaged as a result of their
ehaviour.'

niform Bottle-green blazer with school
adge, grey skirt/trousers, white blouse/
hirt, bottle-green pullover with gold
ands, green tie with white-and-gold
tripes, black/brown 'sensible' shoes. Pre-
cts have distinctive tie. '100% enforce-
ent.'

omework Average 11-year-old, seven hours
0 minutes a week; 14-year-old, eight hours;
6-year-old, 16 hours.

ocational qualifications RSA, Word-proces-
ng.

ispection November 1994: 'A successful
chool.'; 'The school provides a broad cur-
culum to match its aim and reflect the
haracter and ethos of a Roman Catholic
chool.'; 'The excellent range of extra-curri-
ular activities is well-supported by pupils.';
'upils respond well to teachers' high ex-
ectations demonstrating their keenness to
ake progress and engaging enthusiastically
learning activities.'; 'The headteacher
rovides the school with strong and coher-
nt leadership.'; 'There is a strong moral
nse throughout the school, which offers
ecurity and safety for all and provides the
asis on which sound and caring relation-
ips are formed.'

rimary schools Our Lady of Grace RC Pri-
ary; St Bernadette's RC Primary; St Mi-
ael's RC Primary; St Mary's RC Primary;
Philip's RC Primary, Salford.

WAVESEY VILLAGE COLLEGE

ibraltar Lane
wavesey
ambridge
ambridgeshire CB4 5RS
el (01954) 230366

Fax (01954) 230437
E-mail: swaveseyvc@dial.pipex.com

- National ranking 256= (290=, 259=, 374=, 275=)
- GCSE 67% (64%)
- A-levels *Not applicable*
- Higher education *Not applicable*

- Mixed comprehensive
- Pupils 822
- Boys (11–16) 430
- Girls (11–16) 392
- Sixth form *Not applicable*
- Education authority *Cambridgeshire*

Headteacher Patrick Talbott, 52, appointed in
September 1985. Staff 44 (men 21, women
23).

Motto I lead.

Background One of the group of village
colleges rooted in the Cambridgeshire
tradition of community education that
form a 'necklace' of education, training
and leisure provision around the city of
Cambridge. Campus-style accommodation
in extensive grounds; original 1958 buildings remodelled and extended in 1990/1.
Dual-use sports centre opened in 1993:
large sports hall, fitness room, three
squash courts, indoor swimming pool,
floodlit hard tennis courts. Purpose-built
performing arts facilities, including music
suite, drama and recording studios. Teaching accommodation described as 'good
and generous' by independent inspectors, who commented on quality and
range of specialist teaching and facilities.
Further building programme to be completed summer 1998. Accepts pupils above
planned admission limit, with 15% of
applications from outside traditional catchment area; over-subscribed, with 200 applications for 180 places. Nine in 10
pupils continue education after 16. Strong
links with business through Neighbourhood Partnership scheme. Annual musical
and drama productions; school magazine;
Christian Union; Duke of Edinburgh
Award Scheme; Young Engineers Club.

Streaming Mixed-ability on entry; progressively banded or setted by ability, depending on departmental policy.

Approach to discipline Firm but fair and based
on mutual respect; clear code of conduct;
high expectations and supportive parents.

Only three exclusions (temporary) in past three years.

Uniform Contrasting maroon and pale-blue uniform. Year 11 prefects wear distinctive tie as badge of office. Compulsory; regular formal checks.

Homework Average 11-year-old, five hours a week; 14-year-old, seven hours 30 minutes; 16-year-old, 10 hours.

Vocational qualifications *None*

Inspection April 1993: 'A good college with many excellent features.'; 'Pupils' achievements are good; sound progress is made in the core and foundation subjects of the national curriculum.'; 'Pupils are well-motivated and make significant progress as they move through the college. The quality of teaching is good and often very good. However, the tasks set do not always match the abilities of all pupils. Provision for pupils with special educational needs is inadequate. The marking of pupils' work lacks consistency.'; 'The college has a strong, positive ethos and provides a secure, supportive and caring environment. Standards of behaviour and of relationships between pupils and staff and amongst pupils are very good.' The school reports that provision for pupils with special educational needs has undergone significant development and is now recognised throughout the county as an example of best practice.

Primary schools Bar Hill Primary; Over Primary; Elsworth CE Primary; Papworth Primary; Fen Drayton Primary; Swavesey Primary; Hatton Park Primary; Longstanton.

THE ARNEWOOD SCHOOL

Gore Road
New Milton
Hampshire BH25 6RS
Tel (01425) 610186
Fax (01425) 612036
E-mail: arniesch@campus.bt.com

- National ranking 256 = (331 = , 278 = , 248 = , 275 =)
- GCSE 67% (62%)
- A-levels *Not applicable*
- Higher education *Not applicable*

- Grant-maintained
- Mixed comprehensive
- Pupils 1,531

- Boys (11–18) 768
- Girls (11–18) 763
- Sixth form 220 (14%)
- Education authority *Hampshire*

Headteacher Gordon Roger Skirton, 53, appointed in September 1982. Staff 101 (men 50, women 51).

Motto *None*

Background Created as a comprehensive in the early 1970s, Arnewood School became grant-maintained in 1991. It is proud of its 'excellent accommodation' and up-to-date specialist facilities: swimming pool, squash courts and sports hall jointly provided with New Forest District Council. The school is in the southwestern corner of Hampshire, between the New Forest and the sea, serving a 'compact' catchment area that includes Bransgore, New Milton, Barton-on-Sea, Ashley, Hordle and Tiptoe. It is becoming increasingly over-subscribed, although priority is given to children who attend designated schools in the catchment area. Christian ethos. Pupils have opportunity to study up to 14 subjects at GCSE; strengths include music, drama, sport. More than eight in 10 school-leavers (85%) go on to further education; one to Cambridge in 1993. The school became an 11-to-18 school when the first sixth-form year began in September 1995.

Streaming All pupils are put in sets according to ability in all subjects.

Approach to discipline Traditional approach that the school marries with its 'excellent' pastoral care system. Firm but fair.

Uniform Grey trousers/knee-length skirt, black blazer with burgundy trim and school badge, burgundy jumper with silver trim, white shirt, burgundy school tie. Uniform is compulsory throughout. 'Pupils would not be accepted unless parents accepted this school rule.'

Homework Average 11-year-old, six hours a week; 14-year-old, 10 hours; 16-year-old about 12 hours, at discretion of subject teachers.

Vocational qualifications *None*

Inspection October 1995: 'A very good school with many outstanding features in which children learn well and achieve good standards for their ability. The school provides a positive and orderly environment in which children develop academically and socially.'; 'The school's reputation in the local community is justifiably high.'; 'The ethos of the school is supportive to pupils, but also purposeful. Pupils are well-mannered and feel a strong sense of identification and commitment to the school.'

Primary schools Bransgore CE Primary; Ashley GM Junior; Hordle CE Primary; New Milton County Junior; Tiptoe County Primary.

THE CASTLE SCHOOL

Wellington Road
Taunton
Somerset TA1 5AU
Tel (01823) 283551
Fax (01823) 336211

- National ranking 256= (366=, 259=)
- GCSE 67% (60%)
- A-levels *Not applicable*
- Higher education *Not applicable*

- Mixed comprehensive
- Pupils 982
- Boys (11–16) 479
- Girls (11–16) 503
- Sixth form *Not applicable*
- Education authority *Somerset*

Headteacher Kevin John Freedman, 45, appointed in January 1996. Staff 55 (men 28, women 27).

Motto Working together; developing potential; aiming for quality; recognising success.

Background Opened in 1966; became 11–16 co-educational comprehensive in 1978. Occupies large site with extensive playing fields next to Somerset College of Arts and Technology. 'Good quality' buildings: classrooms arranged in faculty blocks; new six-room teaching block opened in 1992 to replace temporary accommodation and containing English, mathematics and learning support rooms. Floodlighting installed on tennis and netball courts in 1994; the courts are used extensively by the community at night. Over-subscribed, with 1.3 applications per place. 'Longstanding traditions of excellence' in music, drama and sport: annual drama production, several concerts in and out of school; orchestra, choir, jazz and concert bands. Winners of six county championships in soccer and cricket in the last 10

years. House system, with six Houses 'which encourage loyalty and competition in a wide range of sporting and other competitions for each year-group. Pupils from the same family are always placed in the same House.' Committed to raising individual attainment, parental involvement in each pupil's education and links with the local community, including businesses and industry. Identified by Ofsted in 1996 as 'good and improving' school.

Streaming 'The school philosophy is to achieve ability-setting by subject. This achieves maximum flexibility of ability groupings.'

Approach to discipline 'High standards of conduct, discipline and manners are expected. The house system plays a significant part in achieving standards.'

Uniform Green tops for boys and girls. Boys wear House ties and white shirts; girls wear distinctive green-striped blouses. Uniform is compulsory 'and is achieved because the requirements are based on realistic expectations of pupils and parents'.

Homework Average 11-year-old, five hours a week; 14-year-old, seven hours 30 minutes; 16-year-old, 10 hours.

Vocational qualifications *None*

Inspection February 1995: 'The school provides a high quality of education and achieves high standards.'; 'Standards of reading and speaking and listening are high; standards in writing and number are good, and in information technology they vary.'; 'The aims of the school are evident in practice. Pupils are well-motivated with a positive attitude to learning.'; 'Teaching is successful and often very good. The vast majority of the teachers have high expectations of the pupils and almost all lessons are well-planned and stimulating.'; 'The school is well led and the leadership is open, consultative, participative and committed to high standards.'; 'The ethos of the school is friendly and relationships are excellent.'

Primary schools Bishop Henderson CE Primary; Bishops Hull Primary; Parkfield Primary; Trull CE Primary; Churchstanton Primary.

THE HENRY BEAUFORT SCHOOL

East Woodhay Road
Harestock
Winchester
Hampshire SO22 6JJ
Tel (01962) 880073
Fax (01962) 883667

- National ranking 256= (252=, 293=, 374=, 337=)
- GCSE 67% (67%)
- A-levels *Not applicable*
- Higher education *Not applicable*

- Mixed comprehensive
- Pupils 971
- Boys (11–16) 503
- Girls (11–16) 468
- Sixth form *Not applicable*
- Education authority *Hampshire*

Headteacher David John Dickinson, 47, appointed in September 1990. Staff 52 (men 20, women 32).

Motto Nobody made a greater mistake than they who did nothing because they could only do a little.

Background Bears name of former Bishop of Winchester, three times chancellor and buried in Winchester Cathedral. Opened in 1972 as city's first purpose-built co-educational comprehensive on northern outskirts. Draws pupils from suburbs of Weeke, Harestock, Teg Down, Kings Worthy as well as villages of Littleton, Wonston, South Wonston, Sutton Scotney, Itchen Abbas, Easton and Micheldever. Central administration block surrounded by separate buildings with specialist teaching accommodation; sports hall and health education suite. More than eight in 10 (85%) pupils continue their education after 16. Over-subscribed. Compressed school day from 8.45am to 2.25pm. 'Well-known' for excellence in expressive arts: art, drama, music and dance; specialist course for talented musicians. Sporting achievements: county under-15 rugby champions, district under-16 hockey champions; district and county representatives in soccer (boys and girls), netball, cross-country, athletics and tennis; gymnastics club. Language exchanges to France and Germany; normal timetable suspended for one week in summer term, when whole school takes part in residential trips at home or abroad.

Streaming Variety of mixed-ability and setting, with full range of teaching methods and styles whatever the type of grouping.

Approach to discipline Aim to provide secure, caring environment; courtesy, co-operation and consideration are the watchwords. 'We believe rewards are as important as punishments, praise as important as criticism. We tell parents when good positive behaviour occurs as well as when bad behaviour and poor work happens.'

Uniform Royal-blue school sweatshirts, white shirt/blouse, dark-grey trousers/royal-blue skirt, school tie (obligatory with trousers), white/royal-blue/black/grey socks, black shoes. Alternative summer Aertex shirt.

Homework Set regularly according to timetable; rely on parents' cooperation; each student given handbook in which homework recorded daily. 'Homework will require a measure of self-discipline from each student, but it is not intended that it should make unreasonable demands on leisure time.'

Vocational qualifications *None*

Inspection September 1996: 'A very good school, offering education of great quality. Pupils respond very well, achieve high standards and make very good progress.'; 'Pupils show very positive attitudes to learning and to other aspects of school life. They respond enthusiastically to the many opportunities offered, including after school. They are mature, talking sensibly and appreciatively about the school. Behaviour is excellent. Pupils display confidence without arrogance.'; 'Teachers have good subject expertise and a constant commitment to sharing and refining ideas.'; 'Time is not always given for pupils to reflect and explore what they are learning. Learning objectives are not always clear for pupils and books and information technology are not always used to the full.'; 'The headteacher leads the school well, ably supported by the strength of his senior management team and confidently endorsed by governors.'

Primary schools Harestock Primary; King's Worthy Primary; Micheldever Primary; South Wonston Primary; Weeke Primary.

THE PHILIP MORANT SCHOOL

Rembrandt Way
Gainsborough Road
Colchester
Essex CO3 4QS
Tel (01206) 545222
Fax (01206) 577563

- National ranking 256= (244=, 205=, 188=, 230=)
- GCSE 67% (68%)
- A-levels *Not applicable*
- Higher education *Not applicable*

- Grant-maintained
- Mixed comprehensive
- Pupils 1,464
- Boys (11–18) 735
- Girls (11–18) 729
- Sixth form 82 (New sixth form)
- Education authority *Essex*

Headteacher David Edward Jones, 56, appointed in January 1984. Staff 88 (men 39, women 49).

Motto Hold fast to that which is good.

Background Opened in 1963 as three-form entry secondary school; became seven-form entry comprehensive in 1971; a second substantial building programme was completed in 1974; became grant-maintained in April 1992; new technology college status has resulted in enhanced facilities, particularly in science; another building programme under way. Over-subscribed, with 450 applications for 280 places. Proud of community links. Work-experience and cultural exchanges as a result of close relationship with other schools in Europe, particularly Germany. Biennial study cruise to Mediterranean. Up to nine in 10 continue education after 16. 'We place the highest levels of expectation on pupils and staff, create a celebratory atmosphere with regard to all pupil achievements and provide the strongest possible support for the development of every individual pupil.' Duke of Edinburgh Award Scheme. Tradition of musical productions; choir, recorder ensemble, junior orchestra, junior band and jazz-rock orchestra. Clubs: chess, Christian Union, running, drama, amateur radio. Sixth form from September 1996.

Alumni Neil Foster, Essex and England cricketer.

Streaming Two broad ability bands in lower school; ability setting from year 9.

Approach to discipline 'Pupils are very much encouraged to make a positive contribution to school life and discipline is very much encouraged.' Supportive pastoral system works with pupils and parents.

Uniform Bottle-green blazer, grey trousers/skirt, white shirt/blouse, house tie. 'Uniform is strictly adhered to.'

Homework Average 11-year-old, seven hours 30 minutes a week; 14-year-old, 10 hours; 16-year-old, 15 hours.

Vocational qualifications City and Guilds Foundation; Cambridge Certificate in Information Technology; GNVQ.

Inspection April 1996: 'An outstanding school with many excellent features.'; 'Most pupils, regardless of ability and including those with special educational needs, make strong and appropriate progress in all subjects. Some minor weaknesses do exist, however, in the year 10 and 11 modular courses, where progress is sometimes less than satisfactory.'; 'The very good attitudes to work displayed by pupils are a significant strength of the school. Throughout the school, and in all subjects, pupils show enthusiasm for their work and are seen to enjoy school. Behaviour in class is almost always good and generally classrooms are full of purposeful activity with pupils concentrating hard.'

Primary schools Hamilton County Primary; Home Farm County Primary; Gosbecks County Primary; Lexden County Primary; Prettygate County Junior.

THE WESTGATE SCHOOL

Cheriton Road
Winchester
Hampshire SO22 5AZ
Tel (01962) 854757
Fax (01962) 840080
E-mail: 4012cezz@hants.gov.uk

- National ranking 256= (266=, 416=, 279=, 315=)
- GCSE 67% (66%)
- A-levels *Not applicable*
- Higher education *Not applicable*

- Mixed comprehensive
- Pupils 906

- Boys (11–16) 470
- Girls (11–16) 436
- Sixth form *Not applicable*
- Education authority *Hampshire*

Headteacher Peter David Jenner, 52, appointed in 1983. Staff 54 (men 22, women 32).

Motto *None*

Background Created in 1973 out of former Winchester County High School for Girls; name chosen because it is the nearest gate into the historic city. About 6% of pupils are boarders in Rotherly, attractive house on edge of school site. About one in three pupils (35%) from outside official catchment area; school has grown 40% in recent years because of parental demand; not oversubscribed. Six new buildings on site have provided extra facilities for mathematics, science, technology, music, drama and physical education. Annual exchange visits with France, Germany and United States.

Streaming Setting from year 8 according to ability in each subject. Regularly reviewed.

Approach to discipline 'Minor matters are dealt with internally, the form-tutor and head-of-year being key figures; more serious misbehaviour is dealt with in such a way that parents are immediately involved. Indiscipline is only a small feature of life at the school.' Good performance is readily rewarded.

Uniform Blazer, grey trousers/skirt, white shirt/blouse, school tie. Has to be smartly worn by all.

Homework Average 11-year-old, eight hours a week; 14-year-old, 14 hours; 16-year-old, 18 hours.

Vocational qualifications *None*

Inspection February 1994: 'The Westgate School provides an education of very good quality for its pupils.'; 'Teaching quality is good and expectations high. The great majority of pupils are highly-motivated and developing the knowledge and understanding necessary to achieve success.'; 'The school is an orderly environment marked by the consideration staff and pupils show one another.'; 'The level of challenge is high.'

Primary schools Western CE Primary; St Bede CE Primary; Twyford CE Primary; All Saints' CE Primary; Winnall Primary.

WELLSWAY SCHOOL

Chandag Road
Keynsham
Bristol BS18 1PH
Tel (0117) 986 4751
Fax (0117) 986 1504

- National ranking 267 (–, 307, 351, 327)
- GCSE 66%
- A-levels 48% (A/B); 98% (A/E)
- Higher education 86% (Oxford 1, Cambridge 1)

- Mixed comprehensive
- Pupils 1,286
- Boys (11–18) 729
- Girls (11–18) 557
- Sixth form 228 (18%)
- Education authority *Bristol and North-East Somerset*

Headteacher Paul Kent, 47, appointed from September 1995. Staff 74 (men 32, women 42).

Motto *Futura aedificamus* (We build for the future).

Background On the eastern side of Keynsham on a spacious campus site, housed in three buildings: lower school for pupils in years 7 to 9, dates from 1956; middle school for years 10 and 11, dates from similar period; sixth-form centre built in 1973. Library, eight science laboratories, four home economics rooms, four design and technology rooms, three art rooms, pottery room, school garden, two computer rooms, business studies suite, music studio. For sport: two gymnasia, four rugby pitches, four soccer pitches, two hockey pitches, two cricket squares, six cricket nets, all-weather cricket pitch, 10 tennis courts, six netball courts and covered swimming pool. Building programme provided extra accommodation from September 1996: purpose-built art block, drama studio and additional laboratory. Over-subscribed, 1.6 applications per place. Links with three sixth-form colleges in southern Norway; also partner schools in France and Germany; Education Business Partnership. Sporting reputation for soccer, rugby, netball, hockey and athletics.

Streaming Variety of mixed-ability, broad banding and fine setting after year 7, according to subject requirements.

Approach to discipline 'When punishment has to be imposed, the particular sanction used is decided in the light of the seriousness of the offence, the pupil's behaviour, and his or her response to acceptable standards.' Parents involved as much as feasible; parents supportive, with few pupils giving cause for serious concern.

Uniform Black blazer, grey trousers/green skirt, white/grey shirt or white blouse for girls, school tie for boys, green jumper. No uniform in sixth form.

Homework Average 11-year-old, five to seven hours a week; 14-year-old, 10 hours; 16-year-old, 15 hours.

Vocational qualifications GNVQ Intermediate, Business and Finance, Design; GNVQ Advanced, Business.

Inspection May 1997.

Primary schools Chandag Junior; Saltford CE Primary; St John's CE Primary; Castle Primary; Longwell Green Primary.

QUEEN ELIZABETH SCHOOL

**Kirkby Lonsdale
Carnforth
Lancashire LA6 2HJ
Tel (015242) 71275
Fax (015242) 72863
E-mail: qes@qeskl.demon.co.uk**

- National ranking 268 (214, 267, 190, 201)
- GCSE 66% (72%)
- A-levels 42% (A/B); 92% (A/E)
- Higher education 77% (Oxford 1)

- Grant-maintained
- Mixed comprehensive
- Pupils 950
- Boys (11–18) 470
- Girls (11–18) 480
- Sixth form 159 (17%)
- Education authority *Cumbria*

Headteacher Christopher Clarke, 43, appointed in September 1992. Staff 56 (men 31, women 25).

Motto *None*

Background On 23 July 1991, Queen Elizabeth School celebrated the 400th anniversary of the signing of a royal charter by Queen Elizabeth I. The buildings, some dating from the 1840s, are recently refurbished and some just completed on a 'beautiful' site that is near both the Lake District and the Yorkshire Dales. A former grammar school, it is now a co-educational 11–18 grant-maintained comprehensive school with a large and expanding sixth form. Over-subscribed, with 220 applications for 150 places. While most pupils are drawn from towns and villages around Kirkby Lonsdale, some travel considerable distances to school each day. The admissions limit was recently raised to accommodate demand and new building has ensued. Over half the pupils are from North Lancashire and North Yorkshire and, with two-thirds coming through parental preference, are 'unsurprisingly well-motivated and from supportive backgrounds'. The school prides itself on a relaxed but purposeful atmosphere.

Streaming Year 7 is taught in mixed-ability classes. Pupils are then put in sets or bands according to subject.

Approach to discipline 'A belief in the highest standards of behaviour, politeness, co-operation and friendliness with clearly-defined parameters promoting a secure and happy atmosphere.'

Uniform Years 7 to 11: bottle-green sweater with school crest, grey trousers/skirts, tie striped green, red and silver. Sixth form: navy sweater, grey trousers/navy skirts, green tie emblazoned with crest. 'Sensible enforcement' of regulations.

Homework Average 11-year-old, eight hours a week; 14-year-old, 12 hours; 16-year-old, 16 to 18 hours.

Vocational qualifications GNVQs, Leisure and Tourism, Business.

Primary schools St Mary's CE Primary, Kirkby Lonsdale; Holme Primary; St Paul's CE Primary, Caton; Burton Morewood Primary, Burton-in-Kendal; St Wilfred's Primary, Halton.

GUMLEY HOUSE CONVENT SCHOOL

**St John's Road
Isleworth
Middlesex TW7 6DN
Tel (0181) 568 8692
Fax (0181) 758 2674**

- National ranking 269 (381, 292, 333, 240)
- GCSE 66% (59%)
- A-levels 39% (A/B); 93% (A/E)
- Higher education 86% (Oxford 2, Cambridge 1)

- Grant-maintained
- Girls' comprehensive
- Pupils 1,080
- Boys *Not applicable*
- Girls (11–18) 1,080
- Sixth form 170 (16%)
- Education authority *Hounslow*

Headteacher Sister Brenda Wallace, appointed in September 1988. Staff 68 (men 11, women 57).

Motto Vive ut vivas (Live that you may have life).

Background Gumley House was built by – and named after – John Gumley in about 1700. The Faithful Companions of Jesus established a convent in the house and opened a school in 1841; still own building and grounds, and appoint head-teacher and Foundation Governors. Buildings added in 1863, 1921, 1969, 1971 and 1975; 11-acre site at Isleworth Cross, close to Syon Park and the Thames. Octagonal assembly hall, with adjacent music suite, sports hall includes four badminton courts, specialist technology block, science block, two general teaching blocks, library and learning resources centre refurbished in 1993 at cost of £1.5m. Over-subscribed, with two applications for each place. Strong in sport, with pupils in British rowing, canoeing and gymnastics teams; county representatives at hockey and netball. Duke of Edinburgh Award Scheme. Annual drama and music productions; satellite reception used for languages, science and geography. Industrial links. Access for wheelchair users. 'There is a sense of unbroken tradition, of gospel values explicitly stated and encouraged, of excellence pursued and witnessed to, of purpose-filled learning that takes place within.'

Alumni Sarah Smith, producer of BBC Radio Four's *Just A Minute* programme; Terry Marsh, television executive.

Streaming Setting in mathematics and English.

Approach to discipline 'The disciplinary system in the school is based primarily upon the development of a sense of responsibility in the pupil. A set of school rules is given to the parents and the pupils. For those who transgress the rules, a system of sanctions operates. It is not a repressive system but firm.'

Uniform, Brown blazer with blue-and-gold stripe, dark-brown skirt, cream blouse, dark-brown pullover, school tie in house colours. Strictly enforced.

Homework Average 11-year-old, seven hours 30 minutes a week; 14-year-old, 10 hours to 12 hours 30 minutes; 16-year-old, 15 hours.

Vocational qualifications GNVQ Level 2, Health and Social Care, Business; GNVQ Level 3, Leisure and Tourism.

Inspection February 1996: 'Gumley House Convent School is a highly successful school with many strong features.'; 'The school's strong commitment to promoting pupils' wider personal development is fully apparent in its daily life and ethos.'; 'Standards of behaviour are good and pupils behave well in most lessons. The school emphasises the need for high levels of attendance and punctuality, generally with good results.'; 'The school curriculum is generally satisfactory. There are, however, certain weaknesses, particularly in Key Stage 3, where insufficent time is allocated to art, geography, history and music, and the National Curriculum requirements are not fully met in music and information technology.'; 'The standards of pupils' work are raised by the strong emphasis given to homework. Pupils' experience is further extended by the exceptional range and quality of the extra-curricular activities.' *The school reports that the issues raised by the inspection have been addressed, with the use of extra time and resources.*

Primary schools Total of 39 feeder schools.

KING EDWARD VI SCHOOL, LICHFIELD

Upper St John Street
Lichfield
Staffordshire WS14 9EE
Tel (01543) 255714
Fax (01543) 418118
E-mail: keslich1@rmplc.co.uk

- National ranking 270 (226, 309)
- GCSE 66% (70%)

- A-levels 39% (A/B); 92% (A/E)
- Higher education 89% (Oxford 4, Cambridge 2)

- Mixed comprehensive
- Pupils 1,341
- Boys (11–18) 632
- Girls (11–18) 709
- Sixth form 293 (22%)
- Education authority *Staffordshire*

Headteacher Alastair Duncan Meikle, 39, appointed in April 1997. Staff 76 (men 32, women 44).

Motto Pro deo, patriae, scholae (For God, country and school).

Background The school's 500th anniversary in 1995. In 1903, the then grammar school moved to current site; subsequent building in 1950s and 1960s. In 1973, the grammar school was merged with secondary modern school on adjacent site to become one of three comprehensives serving the city of Lichfield and the surrounding rural area. Major building programme provided a £2.2 million dual-use sports and leisure centre, incorporating an all-weather pitch; with existing swimming pool and gymnasium, the school has 'probably the best sporting facilities in the county'. New teaching block, with eight new classrooms and three science laboratories; more than £50,000 raised for computer and technology equipment. Over-subscribed, with 270 applications for 210 places. Wide range of sporting activities. 'The school seeks to provide a caring structured environment where high expectations are held of teachers and pupils, and where all are given positive encouragement to develop to the maximum of their capabilities.' List of school aims displayed in all classrooms. Investors in People Award in 1995.

Alumni Dr Samuel Johnson; Professor Edward Hitchcock, late professor of neuro-surgery at Birmingham University; Helen Baxendale, actress; Simon Smith, former England rugby player.

Streaming Broad bands in year 7; in subsequent years, pupils are placed in one of four sets according to achievement in particular subjects.

Approach to discipline 'The pastoral care system embraces both welfare and discipline. Self-discipline is encouraged within a firm and clearly-understood framework of order based upon the recognition of the rights of all. Parents are much involved in the process which is operated through a deputy head (pastoral) and year-heads.'

Uniform Black blazer and tie in years 7 to 11. Uniform slightly modifed in sixth form. 'Maintained in consequence of a democratic vote involving students, parents and staff.' Achieved 'through appeals to parents and persistence'.

Homework Average 11-year-old, five to seven hours a week; 14-year-old, 10 to 12 hours 30 minutes; 16-year-old, 10 to 15 hours.

Vocational qualifications GNVQ Intermediate; GNVQ Advanced, Art and Design, Health and Social Care, Business Studies.

Primary schools Whittington County Primary; Greysbrooke County Primary; St Michael's CE Primary; Little Aston Primary.

THE BLUE COAT CHURCH OF ENGLAND COMPREHENSIVE SCHOOL

Egerton Street
Oldham OL1 3SQ
Tel (0161) 624 1484
Fax (0161) 628 4997
E-mail: 100546.1531@compuserve.com

- National ranking 271 (189, 250, 216, 239)
- GCSE 66% (75%)
- A-levels 38% (A/B); 94% (A/E)
- Higher education 91%

- Mixed comprehensive
- Pupils 1,259
- Boys (11–18) 536
- Girls (11–18) 723
- Sixth form 184 (16%)
- Education authority *Oldham*

Headteacher Kenneth William Pleasant, 52, appointed in September 1988. Staff 78 (men 37, women 41).

Motto Semper virtutem quaeramus (Let us always seek virtue).

Background Thomas Henshaw, who died in 1810, left £40,000 to found the school; boys' boarding school opened in 1834; converted to co-educational secondary modern in 1952, converting to comprehensive in 1966. Imposing listed central building dates from foundation of the school. Accommodation recently enhanced by new science building with 10 laboratories, a new library and five new classrooms. Two gymnasia, technology and creative arts building; new business studies/information technology suite. Strong house system, with special building known as the House Block. Kirkman House building for sixth-formers. Oversubscribed, with just over two applications per place. Voluntary-aided; strong Christian ethos; 'academically strong but with active special needs programme.' More than 300 pupils receive musical tuition; 'well-known' for musical excellence. Sport emphasises breadth of participation 'rather than personal glory'. In recent years, pupils have represented England at soccer, running and fencing. Duke of Edinburgh Award Scheme; Christian Union.

Streaming Pupils placed in sets according to ability within subject areas.

Approach to discipline New behaviour policy after consulting pupils and parents: detailed list of do's and don'ts. Reward for success strongly promoted.

Uniform Boys: navy blazer with school badge, mid-grey trousers, white/grey/blue shirt with school tie, grey/navy V-neck pullover, grey/navy/black socks, dark shoes. Girls: navy blazer with badge, mid-grey skirt/pinafore dress, white blouse with tie, grey/navy V-neck pullover, white/grey socks, dark shoes. Enforced 'thoroughly but positively'.

Homework Average 11-year-old, seven hours 30 minutes a week; 14-year-old, 10 hours; 16-year-old, 15 hours.

Vocational qualifications GNVQ.

Inspection March 1994: 'The Blue Coat School is offering an excellent education to its pupils.'; 'The pupils' standards of oracy, literacy and numeracy are well-developed at all key stages. There are, however, small numbers of pupils, at both ends of the ability range, who underachieve in some subjects.'; 'The school staff is well-qualified, competent, committed and caring and they have high expectations of their pupils. The school ethos encourages co-operation and the pupils respond well demonstrating high levels of motivation and very good behaviour. In a number of curriculum areas, however, the work is not matched to the abilities of some of the pupils.' *The*

school reports that since the inspection it has 'continued to develop its strategies for extending and differentiating the curriculum in order to make it more accessible to children of all abilities'.

FINHAM PARK SCHOOL

Green Lane
Coventry
West Midlands CV3 6EA
Tel (01203) 418135
Fax (01203) 840803
E-mail: cjhunt@finhampark.demon.co.uk
Internet: http://www.finhampark.demon.co.uk/home.html

- National ranking 272 (273, 351, 258, –)
- GCSE 66% (65%)
- A-levels 34% (A/B); 90% (A/E)
- Higher education 80%

- Mixed comprehensive
- Pupils 1,474
- Boys (11–18) 714
- Girls (11–18) 760
- Sixth form 317 (22%)
- Education authority *Coventry*

Headteacher Christopher John Hunt, 50, appointed in April 1989. Staff 85 (men 34, women 51).

Motto *None*

Background A purpose-built school in the southwest of Coventry, Finham Park opened in 1971 and serves a residential area. Over-subscribed with about 1.4 applications for each place. Mathematics, business studies and science among academic strengths. Music, art, drama and outdoor education are strong as extra-curricular activities; national reputation for gymnastics.

Alumni Vicki Howe, president of Oxford Union; Andrew Moles, Warwickshire cricketer.

Streaming Flexible approach. Mixed-ability groups in year 7; some subjects set by ability soon afterwards, others not set at all.

Approach to discipline Courtesy, common sense and respect for others are the goal. 'Breaches of this code are firmly dealt with and parents are involved in all instances of serious concern.'

Uniform Grey/black trousers/skirt, white

shirt/blouse, school tie (optional), black/ grey sweater. Black blazer with badge (optional). School motif must be worn on shirt or sweater if tie not worn.

Homework Average 11-year-old, eight hours a week; 14-year-old, 11 hours; 16-year-old, 13 hours.

Vocational qualifications GNVQ.

Inspection March 1995: 'A good school. On the whole, the pupils are sociable and hard-working, and they are helped to thrive in an atmosphere of security and steady endeavour.'; 'The strong team spirit of many departments greatly helps individual teachers to work confidently and effectively. Relationships in the classroom are generally good and teachers often encourage pupils to think and work independently, though more might be expected of the most able, and more support might be given to those of lesser ability who do not qualify for special help.' *The school reports that key issues raised by the inspection have been successfully addressed.*

Primary schools Finham Primary; St Michael Primary; Grange Farm Primary; Earlsdon Primary; Manor Park Primary.

ORMSKIRK GRAMMAR SCHOOL

Ruff Lane
Ormskirk
Lancashire L39 4QY
Tel (01695) 572405
Fax (01695) 571910
E-mail: ogs-net.demon.co.uk

- National ranking 273 (204, 223, 204, 271)
- GCSE 66% (73%)
- A-levels 34% (A/B); 85% (A/E)
- Higher education 74%

- Mixed comprehensive
- Pupils 1,278
- Boys (11–18) 646
- Girls (11–18) 632
- Sixth form 251 (20%)
- Education authority *Lancashire*

Headteacher Anthony Crompton Richardson, 55, appointed in January 1987. Staff 74 (men 21, women 53).

Motto Abeunt studia mores (Through studies character is formed).

Background Founded in 1612; buildings, some dating from 1850, in residential district close to centre of Ormskirk on the West Lancashire plain; playing fields about quarter of a mile away. Considerable improvements over recent years: all classrooms in main part of school have been refurnished and carpeted; total re-decoration; part of building re-roofed, heating system upgraded, playing areas re-surfaced, assembly hall improved. Fully-equipped drama studio, new music room, two new information technology rooms, two new science laboratories, improved accommodation for home economics, new art room and extra classrooms as a result of conversions. Over-subscribed, with 250 applications for 192 places. Wide range of sports teams: hockey, netball, rugby, cricket, tennis, rounders and athletics. Major games backed by Parent Support Groups. Orienteering club. Annual music/arts festival. Orchestra, choirs, ensembles and regular concerts. Drama productions and show with cast of 200 pupils. National finalists in debating and Bar Mock Trial competitions. Foreign visits: Germany, France and Spain; rugby tours to France and Isle of Man, skiing in Austria, study trips to United States and Italy. Charity week raises £3,000. Active Parents' Society.

Alumni Vicky Dixon, England and Great Britain hockey player (1982–1992).

Streaming Year 7: pupils taught for most subjects in groups of similar ability, with separate group for small number of children needing additional support. Increasingly differentiated setting in mathematics, in year 7; French and science, from year 8; and English, from year 9. All subjects in years 10 and 11.

Approach to discipline 'Discipline is clear and firm, based on the principle of mutual respect. The support of parents in maintenance of good standards is actively sought.'

Uniform Boys: navy blazer with badge, dark-grey trousers, grey/white shirt, school tie. Girls: navy skirt, school blouse and tie, navy jumper. All pupils expected to wear uniform.

Homework Average 11-year-old, five to six hours a week; 14-year-old, eight to 10 hours; 16-year-old, 10 to 12 hours.

Vocational qualifications GNVQ Advanced, Health and Social Care.

Inspection April 1993: 'This is a good school where learning is effective. Pupils' willingness to learn and their good behaviour is reflected in the standards achieved. The school provides an orderly environment with clear values. Pupils relate well to one another and teacher-pupil relationships are warm.' April 1997: 'Ormskirk Grammar School is a popular and highly-successful comprehensive school which provides a very good education for all its pupils. It is an orderly community which is well managed and purposeful, and which deserves its good reputation.'

Primary schools Ormskirk CE Primary; Town Green County Primary; Christ Church CE Primary; St Michael's CE Primary; West End County Primary.

ST HILDA'S CHURCH OF ENGLAND HIGH SCHOOL

Croxteth Drive
Sefton Park
Liverpool L17 3AL
Tel (051) 733 2709
Fax (051) 735 0530

- National ranking 274 (–, 315, 351 =)
- GCSE 66%
- A-levels 32% (A/B); 77% (A/E)
- Higher education 70% (Oxford 1)

- Grant maintained
- Girls' comprehensive
- Pupils 820
- Boys (16–18) 2
- Girls (11–18) 818
- Sixth form 151 (18%)
- Education authority *Liverpool*

Headteacher John Christopher Yates, 43, appointed in 1997. Staff 46 (men 10, women 36).

Motto Laborare est orare (To work is to pray).

Background Founded in 1894 by the Community of the Sisters of the Church, an Anglican order of nuns; modern buildings on edge of Sefton Park, four miles from Liverpool city centre. Over-subscribed, with 238 applications for 128 places. School proud of rate of A-level success, and 'high-quality' business studies and vocational training course for sixth-formers; recently-renovated and extended sixth-form centre. Sporting success: international repre-

sentatives in swimming, swimmers in Olympic squad; city champions in hockey, netball and swimming; English Schools' intermediate cross-country champions for third consecutive year; represented England in China at International School Games. Prizewinners in regional Young Enterprise examinations. Winners of senior section of BBC TV Carol Competition; prize-winning entries in art competitions and choral section of Merseyside Music and Drama Festival. 'Unmistakably' Anglican atmosphere, weekly communion services, school chaplain, three choral communions each term.

Streaming Streamed in mathematics and French; pupils in sets for other subjects.

Approach to discipline 'The Christian ethos of the school encourages pupils to develop self-discipline, and respect for themselves and for others is held to be paramount.'

Uniform Purple blazer, purple/white checked blouse, navy skirt. Senior school: white blouse, navy skirt. Strictly enforced.

Homework Average 11-year-old, eight hours a week; 14-year-old, 12 hours; 16-year-old, 15 hours.

Vocational qualifications NVQ, Business Administration; RSA, Young Enterprise; Pitman.

NEWPORT FREE GRAMMAR SCHOOL

Newport
Saffron Walden
Essex CB11 3TR
Tel (01799) 540237
Fax (01799) 542189

- National ranking 275 (265 , 358, 336, –)
- GCSE 66% (66%)
- A-levels 31% (A/B); 81% (A/E)
- Higher education 75% (Oxford 1, Cambridge 1)

- Grant-maintained
- Mixed comprehensive
- Pupils 741
- Boys (11–18) 499
- Girls (11–18) 242
- Sixth form 112 (15%)
- Education authority (*Essex*)

Headteacher Richard John Priestley, 49, appointed in January 1991. Staff 45 (men 26, women 19).

Motto Suffer and serve.

Background Founded in 1588 by Dame Joyce Frankland under trusteeship of Gonville and Caius College, Cambridge; set in undulating countryside in northwest Essex on 34-acre site two miles west of Saffron Walden, 17 miles south of Cambridge and eight miles north of Bishop's Stortford. Buildings range from original listed Victorian building to modern arts centre opened in 1992, financed by the school and including drama studio and music suite; about to build new technology facilities and all-weather pitch with floodlighting, for hockey and soccer. Over-subscribed, with two applications per place. 'Music, drama and sport are very strong and the school enjoys high reputation for all three.' Links with schools in Czech Republic, Holland, Italy, Israel, India, Poland and Sweden. Maximum class size is 25 pupils. 'The school is a friendly and caring community. Pupils are recognised as individuals. We have high expectations of all pupils.'

Alumni Robert Knopwood, original settler in Tasmania in 1804; Salter Jehosophat Mountain, original settler in Canada and Rector of Quebec in 1797; Kurt Nicol, world moto-cross champion.

Streaming In languages from year 7; in mathematics from year 8; in science from year 9.

Approach to discipline 'Firm but fair. There is a structured approach to discipline which accords with the clearly-defined guidelines laid down by the governing body.'

Uniform Navy blazer, white shirt/blouse, grey trousers or tartan kilt/grey slacks, house tie, black socks or flesh tights/white socks, black shoes. Separate dress code for sixth-formers. Rigidly enforced.

Homework Average 11-year-old, six hours 30 minutes a week; 14-year-old, nine hours; 16-year-old, 12 hours.

Vocational qualifications University of Cambridge Certificate of Information Technology; GNVQ Intermediate and Advanced, Business.

Inspection March 1995: 'Much has been achieved in recent years, not least the transition to grant-maintained status and the successful introduction of co-education.'; 'Pupils are well-motivated and work hard.'; 'Pupils are courteous, and their attendance, punctuality and behaviour are good.'; 'The headteacher, senior staff and governors together offer clear leadership.'; 'Staff show considerable care and concern for pupils.'; 'The philosophy and aims are mainly concerned with the achievements of high standards, pupils' personal and social development and the creation of a distinctive school ethos.'

Primary schools Newport County Primary; Clavering County Primary; Henham and Ugley County Primary; Bentfield County Primary, Stansted; St Thomas More RC Primary.

CANON SLADE SCHOOL

Bradshaw Brow
Bolton
Greater Manchester BL2 3BP
Tel (01204) 401555
Fax (01204) 401556
E-mail: canonslad.ss@connect.bt.com

- National ranking 276 (190, 311, 391, 208)
- GCSE 66% (75%)
- A-levels 29% (A/B); 88% (A/E)
- Higher education 85% (Cambridge 2)

- Grant-maintained
- Mixed comprehensive
- Pupils 1,500
- Boys (11–18) 720
- Girls (11–18) 780
- Sixth form 280 (19%)
- Education authority *Bolton*

Headteacher Rev Peter Shepherd, 48, appointed in January 1989. Staff 97 (men 42, women 55).

Motto Ora et labora (Pray and work).

Background Founded in 1855 by Canon James Slade, vicar of Bolton; became direct-grant grammar in 1946; moved to current 57-acre site on northern edge of town in 1956; became voluntary-aided in 1976; comprehensive in 1978; grant-maintained in April 1993. The site was developed in the late 1970s and a sports hall, paid for with £250,000 by parents and supporters, was added in 1990. Science laboratories and library block planned; professional librarian. Basketball, soccer, hockey, cross-country, athletics and swimming all pursued to national level. Pupils admitted on basis of church affiliation, serving Bolton, Darwen to Manchester, and Bury to Atherton. Heavily-subscribed sixth form offering more than 30 A-level subjects. Latin taught. Total of about 400 applications for 240 places; taking 270 a year from 1998. Individual music tuition for brass, strings and woodwind; drama and arts also strong. Many school clubs: chess, model railway, computer, dance, poetry, learn-to-drive.

Alumni Viscount Leverhulme; Sir Gordon Booth, former diplomat and adviser to Hanson PLC; Alyn Ainsworth, conductor.

Streaming Setting as appropriate. Some mixed-ability groups in lower school.

Approach to discipline Stress on self-discipline within supportive Christian community. 'We are not afraid to use the word "love".'

Uniform Boys: bottle-green blazer, white shirt, school tie. Girls: bottle-green cardigan, skirt, white blouse. Special year 11 uniform. No uniform for sixth-formers. Regulations enforced 'absolutely'.

Homework Average 11-year-old, five or six hours a week; 14-year-old, 10 to 12 hours; 16-year-old, 15+ hours.

Vocational qualifications *None*

Inspection February 1994: 'This is a high-achieving and successful school.'; 'Pupils of all ages and abilities achieve well in a wide range of subjects. They are confident and articulate, and have a good competence in reading and writing. Numerical skills are above average, but information technology skills are underdeveloped.'; 'The teachers are well-qualified and teaching is careful and thorough, although there is under-expectation and lack of challenge in a small number of lessons.'

Primary schools St Peter's CE Primary, Smithills Dean; St Thomas CE Primary, Chequerbent; Church Road Primary; Christ's Church CE Primary, Harwood; St James' CE Primary, Daisy Hill. Up to 90 feeder schools; admission based on church attendance.

CAMS HILL SCHOOL

Shearwater Avenue
Fareham
Hampshire PO16 8AH
Tel (01329) 231641
Fax (01329) 283996
E-mail: camstaf@rmplc.co.uk
/camspupl@rmplc.co.uk

- National ranking 277= (290=, 227=, 355=, 315)
- GCSE 66% (64%)
- A-levels *Not applicable*
- Higher education *Not applicable*

- Grant-maintained
- Mixed comprehensive
- Pupils 879
- Boys (11–16) 452
- Girls (11–16) 427
- Sixth form *Not applicable*
- Education authority *Hampshire*

Headteacher Joy Hayward, 46, appointed in September 1989. Staff 55 (men 25, women 30).

Motto Quality and achievement.

Background Greenfield and wooded site next to the renovated Cams Hall and golf course on upper reaches of Portsmouth Harbour with views across Fareham Creek and the Solent. Main building was formerly girls' grammar school; new blocks added in late 1960s and early 1970s to accommodate comprehensive intake. More than nine in 10 pupils continue education after 16, with estimated 40% later entering higher education. Over-subscribed, with more than 200 applications for 166 places (180 admitted). Stable staff; regularly involved in pilot curriculum schemes; Latin taught. Extra-curricular activities: foreign visits include skiing in Italy and Austria; summer activities and exchanges to Germany, Spain, Cherbourg and Rouen in France; one in three pupils go abroad each year. Isle of Wight Activities Centre for year 9 pupils; school radio station; school orchestra, band and choir. Clubs: flute and guitar, chess, art, photography. School Council. Community Council established. Duke of Edinburgh Award Scheme.

Streaming Pupils in sets for science, mathematics and modern languages from year 8.

Approach to discipline Basic rules 'not repressive but reflect a consideration for others and the environment in which we all work'. Recognises value of praise and positive rewards. Sanctions include extra work, variety of detentions, senior prefects' detention at lunchtime, 'on report', withdrawal from lessons. Rarely exclusion for short periods and very rarely permanent exclusion.

Uniform Years 7 to 10: mid-blue shirt/blouse,

mid-grey skirt/trousers, school jumper with badge, school tie. Year 11: navy-and-white prefect dress. Enforced very firmly.

Homework 'Homework time and a pupil's motivation to extend work will vary, but there is an increase in what we expect as a (daily) minimum, from one hour in year 7 to three hours in years 10 and 11, plus weekend study.' Homework diaries monitored.

Vocational qualifications *None*

Primary schools Harrison Primary, Fareham; Uplands Primary, Fareham; Wicor Primary, Portchester.

CHEADLE HULME HIGH SCHOOL

Woods Lane
Cheadle Hulme
Cheadle
Cheshire SK8 7JY
Tel (0161) 485 7201
Fax (0161) 486 6301
E-mail: chhs@rmplc.co.uk

- National ranking 277 = (422 = , 386, 328, –)
- GCSE 66% (56%)
- A-levels *Not applicable*
- Higher education *Not applicable*

- Mixed comprehensive
- Pupils 1,350
- Boys (11–16) 652
- Girls (11–16) 698
- Sixth form *Not applicable*
- Education authority *Stockport*

Headteacher Ronald Dixon, 53, appointed in September 1989 Staff 80 (men 35, women 45).

Motto Excellence through achievement.

Background Originally built in 1930s; became secondary modern after Second World War; became comprehensive in 1972, more than doubling in size and acquiring sixth-form; further re-organisation in 1991 resulted in increasing year 7 admissions to 270 and sixth-form being phased out. Situated in suburban area of south Manchester; three-year building programme has resulted in improvements; adapted to cater for disabled pupils. Over-subscribed, with 280 applications for 270 places. Five modern languages: French, German, Italian, Spanish, Russian; Language College from September 1997. Strong in music and art; consistently outstanding English examination results. Winners of 1993 Times Education Supplement Award for governors' report to parents. Investor in People Award in October 1996. 'The school has a supportive, friendly, hard-working atmosphere, where all students are equally valued (as well as having equal opportunities). Increasingly, students are being involved in areas of school life through year and school councils.'

Streaming Mixed-ability in year 7. Setting by ability in year 8 in English, science and modern languages; also in mathematics, from year 9.

Approach to discipline 'Firm but fair. The school has developed an anti-bullying policy, with student involvement, and has both a school charter and a whole-school behaviour policy. Parents are involved early in disciplinary concerns.'

Uniform Grey V-neck jumper, grey skirt/trousers, white shirt/blouse, school tie. Optional school sweatshirt for years 10 and 11. 'Strictly enforced, but with understanding where family circumstances create temporary problems.'

Homework Average 11-year-old, 11 hours a week; 14-year-old, 13 hours; 16-year-old, 15 hours.

Vocational qualifications Diploma of Vocational Education; RSA, Information Technology, Office Skills.

Inspection January 1997: 'A good school with some very good features. Standards of attainment are consistently high and teaching often good or very good.'; 'Progress in lessons is generally sound and in over half of them it is good. The higher attainers are doing very well and those with special educational needs make sound to good progress when work is appropriately targeted to their needs, but this does not happen in every lesson. The average-ability pupils in a few subjects mark time and make limited progress.'; 'A major strength of the school is the high quality of the teaching, which always shows commitment and thoroughness of preparation.'; 'There is little evidence of bullying and pupils express a sense of confidence in their school. They attend well and are punctual to lessons, but in some classes they do not work as hard as they should.'

Primary schools Hursthead Junior; Thorn Grove Primary; Bruntwood Primary; Bradshaw Hall Junior; Lane End Primary; Ladybrook Primary; Orrishmere Primary; Queens Road Primary.

CLAVERHAM COMMUNITY COLLEGE

North Trade Road
Battle
East Sussex TN33 0HT
Tel (01424) 772155
Fax (01424) 774106
E-mail: info@claverham.cablenet.co.uk
Internet: http://cablenet.net/local/
educate/secondry/clavindx.htm

- National ranking 277= (366=, 448=, 432=, –)
- GCSE 66% (60%)
- A-levels *Not applicable*
- Higher education *Not applicable*

- Mixed comprehensive
- Pupils 1,001
- Boys (11–16) 537
- Girls (11–16) 464
- Sixth form *Not applicable*
- Education authority *East Sussex*

Headteacher Richard Pitts, 47, appointed in September 1992. Staff 57 (men 30, women 27).

Motto Numquam certo scire potest (One can never tell for sure).

Background Rural comprehensive in extensive grounds to west of market town of Battle; centre for adult and community education, responsible for youth club, sports centre and day nursery. Recent additions include two laboratories and purpose-built music centre. New humanities classroom block, opened in January 1997, and extension of technology facilities, by autumn 1996. Over-subscribed, with 1.2 applications per place. Established academic strengths: English, mathematics, science, IT, art and drama; one of a few secondary schools to win Sainsbury's Arts Education Award in 1993. 'Exceptional' sporting facilities: outdoor heated swimming pool, 80-metre sports hall, squash court, weight-training rooms, climbing wall. Sports representatives in local, county and national competitions. 'Claverham has a formal approach to education in a well-disciplined environment. The college has high expectations of all students and takes its role as a community college very seriously indeed.'

Streaming Separate setting from year 7 for English, mathematics, science, languages and humanities.

Approach to discipline 'We have high expectations of our pupils and this is reflected in the priority we give to our disciplinary system. Our approach to discipline is formal, with pupils being required to observe courteous and quiet behaviour at all times.'

Uniform Navy blazer, shirt, tie, sweater, skirt. 'We attach a great deal of importance to the personal appearance of each pupil and expect school uniform to be strictly adhered to and correctly worn. This is an essential part of Claverham's ethos.'

Homework Average 11-year-old, five hours a week; 14-year-old, nine hours; 16-year-old, 10 to 15 hours.

Vocational qualifications BTEC; City and Guilds.

Inspection September 1994: 'Claverham Community College promotes positive attitudes to achievement and enables many pupils to attain high standards.'; 'Excellent classroom relationships, the dedication of the staff and the good behaviour of the pupils form the basis for an effective learning environment.'; 'In some lessons there is insufficient account taken of the varying abilities of pupils and their different learning needs.'; 'Behaviour and dress are of a high standard.'

Primary schools Battle and Langton CE Primary; Ninfield Primary; Westfield Primary; Catsfield CE Primary; Netherfield CE Primary; St Peter and St Paul Primary, Bexhill.

EAST BERGHOLT HIGH SCHOOL

Heath Road
East Bergholt
Colchester
Essex CO7 6RJ
Tel (01206) 298200
Fax (01206) 298162
E-mail: ebhs@rmplc.co.uk
Internet: http://www.giraffe.rmplc.co.uk/
eduweb/sites/sitec/bergholt

- National ranking 277= (302=, 334=)
- GCSE 66% (63%)

- A-levels *Not applicable*
- Higher education *Not applicable*

- Mixed comprehensive
- Pupils 814
- Boys (11–16) 408
- Girls (11–18) 406
- Sixth form *Not applicable*
- Education authority *Suffolk*

Headteacher Moira Anne Humphreys, 45, appointed in January 1990. Staff 45 (men 25, women 20).

Motto *None*

Background Rural school on northern edge of the village of East Bergholt, on a 20-acre site surrounded by fields and greenery. Buildings erected in three stages: 1957, 1971 and 1981. The older buildings have been modernised and refurbished in recent years. Extensive facilities include sports hall and swimming pool. The school, a few minutes from the A12, is located between Ipswich and Colchester in the Dedham Vale. Oversubscribed, with 1.2 applications per place. Information technology 'well-established across the curriculum, with pioneering work in mathematics and science'. Registered as a Young Enterprise School; links with local business community. 'Education Extra' award for extra-curricular activities, including conservation and Duke of Edinburgh Award Scheme. Pastoral scheme strong: long books used to monitor achievement and progress. 'The school is a lively and purposeful community, with high standards and expectations. We are committed to celebrating the achievements of young people and fostering a positive ethos which is based on equality of opportunity, self-discipline and consideration for others.'

Streaming After year 7, pupils taught in different types of groups (mixed-ability, banded or setting) depending on subject requirements and individual needs.

Approach to discipline 'Working with parents, we want to maintain a firm but fair policy of caring discipline. Our aim is to foster a sense of community and, therefore, pupils are expected to behave in an orderly, courteous and caring way.' Rules to encourage responsibility, tolerance and respect; school promotes 'a positive approach to pupil behaviour'.

Uniform Navy sweater/cardigan, white shirt, tie, dark-grey trousers for boys and girls/navy skirt for girls.

Homework Average 11-year-old, five hours a week; 14-year-old, seven hours 30 minutes; 16-year-old, 10 hours.

Vocational qualifications *None*

Primary schools East Bergholt CE Primary; Brooklands Primary, Brantham; Capel St Mary Primary; Bentley CE Primary; Stratford St Mary Primary.

PAINSLEY ROMAN CATHOLIC HIGH SCHOOL

Station Road
Cheadle
Stoke-on-Trent
Staffordshire ST10 1LH
Tel (01538) 752341
Fax (01538) 750956

- National ranking 277= (382=, 378=)
- GCSE 66% (59%)
- A-levels *Not applicable*
- Higher education *Not applicable*

- Mixed comprehensive
- Pupils 833
- Boys (11–16) 416
- Girls (11–16) 417
- Sixth form *Not applicable*
- Education authority *Staffordshire*

Headteacher Francis Raymond Tunney, 47, appointed in September 1990. Staff 44 (men 20, women 24).

Motto Nosce te ipsum (Know thyself).

Background Founded in 1964 and named after Painsley Hall, which was a Catholic centre. 'The building is light and spacious, but classroom accommodation is currently difficult: new music suite and religious education area under construction. All specialist areas are provided, in extensive grounds. Wide catchment area serving the whole of the Staffordshire Moorlands and the outskirts of Stoke-on-Trent. Pupil numbers have risen from 300 in 1990. Over-subscribed, with two applications per place. Applied to become 11–18 school. 'Very strong' in religious education, English, mathematics, German, technology, science, history, music and physical education. Also noted for drama productions, musical concerts, gymnastics festivals and sporting achievements. National reputation for hockey: second in the country at under-16 and fourth at under-13; county and Midlands champions. 'Painsley provides a Christian ethos and climate in which faith may grow and develop. This brings individuals to a deeper knowledge of Jesus and to an understanding of themselves.'

Alumni Katie O'Riley, England under-16 and under-18 hockey player; Louise Carnwell, England 100m butterfly swimming champion.

Streaming Pupils placed in teaching groups according to ability. Year 7 pupils banded according to ability.

Approach to discipline 'Form teachers are immediately responsible for the pastoral care of those within their form. Heads of year have overall responsibility for each year-group and they, in turn, are supported by assistant heads of year and senior staff. Every member of staff is expected to promote the Christian ethos which is the *raison d'être* of the school.'

Uniform Black blazer with badge, dark-grey trousers/skirt, white shirt, tie with red-and-silver-grey stripe on navy background, grey socks/tights (white for girls in summer), black shoes. 'No modification of uniform is accepted.'

Homework Average 11-year-old, five hours a week; 14-year-old, five to seven hours 30 minutes; 16-year-old, seven hours 30 minutes to 10 hours.

Vocational qualifications *None*

Primary schools St Giles RC Primary, Cheadle; St Mary's RC Primary, Leek; St Thomas's RC Primary, Upper Tean; St Filumena's RC Primary, Caverswall; St Joseph's RC Primary, Uttoxeter; The Faber RC Primary, Cotton; St John's RC Primary, Alton; Bishop Rawle CE Primary, Cheadle; St Augustine's RC Primary, Meir.

THE BURGATE SCHOOL

Salisbury Road
Fordingbridge
Hampshire SP6 1EZ
Tel (01425) 652039
Fax (01425) 656625

- National ranking 277= (228=, 359=, 205, 315=)

- GCSE 66% (70%)
- A-levels *Not applicable*
- Higher education *Not applicable*

- Grant-maintained
- Mixed comprehensive
- Pupils 729
- Boys (11–18) 366
- Girls (11–18) 363
- Sixth form 124 (17%)
- Education authority *Hampshire*

Headteacher Celia Judith Nicholls, 43, appointed in April 1988. Staff 51 (men 18, women 33).

Motto Learning for life.

Background Main building dates from 1957 on a site in rural area on edge of New Forest; expanded in 1972; also science block (1976), sports hall (1984), music block and other extensions (1988); drama studio and science laboratories completed in 1994; sixth-form block also added in 1994. Became grant-maintained in September 1991; sixth form started in September 1995. Seven in 10 school-leavers (70%) continue their education after 16. Over-subscribed, with 210 applications for 120 places; waiting lists open to year 2013. Extra-curricular activities: inter-house chess competition, with some pupils playing at county level; residential trips to Cornwall, Normandy and Paris; skiing in France or Germany. Proud of community service and charity fund-raising. 'Quality Assurance' statement promises full information to parents and rigorous internal, and independent, monitoring of standards. School Association.

Streaming Setting begins in year 7 and introduced for all academic subjects from year 8. Accelerated classes to GCSE and above.

Approach to discipline 'As we are firm, fair, friendly (in that order), we have very few problems. No permanent exclusions have taken place in the last five years.' School rules kept to a minimum: courtesy, consideration for others and their property. Merit marks and commendations for good work; sanctions include detentions, daily report, and withdrawal from class lessons.

Uniform Years 7 to 10: black blazer (optional), charcoal-grey trousers/dark-grey skirt, white or light-blue shirt/blouse, school tie (optional for girls), royal-blue V-neck jumper with school crest, grey/

white socks (also navy/black for boys), grey/black shoes. Alternative colours for year 11. Regulations strictly enforced.

Homework Average 11-year-old, up to five hours a week; 14-year-old, up to seven hours 30 minutes; 16-year-old, up to 12 hours.

Vocational qualifications *None*

Primary schools Fordingbridge Junior; Western Downland CE Primary; Hyde CE Primary; Breamore CE Primary; Hale Primary.

TWYNHAM SCHOOL

Soper's Lane
Christchurch
Dorset BH23 1JF
Tel (01202) 486237
Fax (01202) 486230
E-mail: twynham@rmplc.co.uk

- National ranking 277= (401=, 278=, 295=, 356=)
- GCSE 66% (58%)
- A-levels *Not applicable*
- Higher education *Not applicable*

- Mixed comprehensive
- Pupils 1,025
- Boys (11–16) 546
- Girls (11–16) 479
- Sixth form *Not applicable*
- Education authority *Dorset*

Headteacher Brian Driver, 44, appointed in September 1989. Staff 56 (men 23, women 33).

Motto Ut prosim (To be of service).

Background Established in 1932 when Christchurch was part of Hampshire, Twynham School became a comprehensive in 1970, four years before it was incorporated into Dorset. Site close to centre of Christchurch, with substantial playing fields close to River Avon. School roll has risen from 790 since 1990, during which time £1m spent on re-cladding buildings and creating new science laboratories; swimming pool re-clad in 1994. Intake increased to 235 from September 1996; 300-plus applications. Creative and Recreational Arts Faculty has reputation for public performances and work in sport, art, music, drama and dance. Committed to teacher training, with links to Bath University for postgraduate training. Technology College status; sixth-form application pending.

Alumni Kevin Reeves, former Manchester City and England soccer player; Jamie Redknapp, Liverpool and England soccer player.

Streaming Pupils streamed in mathematics in years 7 to 11; in French, German and science, in years 8 to 11.

Approach to discipline High expectations; provides opportunities to display responsibility, with would-be prefects required to submit formal letters of application and attend interviews. 'We believe in the value of placing most emphasis upon rewarding and encouraging good behaviour. Consequently sanctions such as suspension or exclusion are rarely necessary. However, if students do break our code of behaviour they jeopardise their place at the school.'

Uniform Navy pullover with crest and motto, grey trousers/navy skirt, white shirt, blue striped tie, black/brown shoes. Regulation navy sportswear.

Homework Average 11-year-old, five hours a week; 14-year-old, seven hours 30 minutes; 16-year-old, 10 hours.

Vocational qualifications *None*

Inspection May 1995: 'Twynham is an outstanding school which has achieved very good standards of work and examination results. It is a happy, confident community which provides a good all-round education for its pupils.'; 'The quality of teaching and learning is high. The teachers are suitably qualified and knowledgeable subject specialists. Their lessons are well-organised and are conducted at suitable pace.'; 'The present framework for the timetable is causing some strains in time allocations and distribution of lessons, and in the allocation of non-teaching time.'; 'There is no standardised testing of all pupils on entry to the school, as a basis for grouping the teaching groups and assessing the incremental attainments of pupils in subsequent years.'; 'The pupils are highly-motivated and are engaged by the teaching. They have very good attitudes to their work and make good progress.'

Primary schools Christchurch Junior; The Priory CE Primary; Stourfield Primary; St Katherine's CE Primary.

WEAVERHAM HIGH SCHOOL

Lime Avenue
Weaverham
Cheshire CW8 3HT
Tel (01606) 852120
Fax (01606) 854033
E-mail: 9064132.depot@dialnet.co.uk

- National ranking 277= (252=, 259=, 295=, −)
- GCSE 66% (67%)
- A-levels Not applicable
- Higher education Not applicable

- Mixed comprehensive
- Pupils 1,080
- Boys (11–18) 566
- Girls (11–18) 514
- Sixth form Not applicable
- Education authority Cheshire

Headteacher Edward George Studd, 62, appointed in January 1977. Staff 58 (men 26, women 32).

Motto Honesty, industry, courtesy.

Background Opened in semi-rural location in 1956 as three-form entry secondary modern; re-organised as comprehensive in 1978, with up to seven forms of entry. Substantial additions to buildings; significant building programme recently completed to provide new music and science accommodation. New all-weather pitch recently enhanced school's sporting facilities. Over-subscribed, with 1.5 applications per place. Prides itself on excellence of achievement in all subjects, particularly English, science and technology. 'Unparalleled' evening and weekend activities in Enrichment and Enhancement Programme. Sporting fixtures; notable performance in hockey, rugby, cross-country and athletics. 'Our aim is to develop young people who are confident and well-equipped for the next stage of their lives. We believe this can best be achieved by working in partnership with parents, and by providing a happy, caring and well-ordered environment.'

Streaming Increased use of setting according to ability, beginning with mathematics from spring of year 7.

Approach to discipline 'Our codes of conduct are clearly defined and expectations are high. The school encourages a warm, happy and caring environment. We look to change behaviour rather than automatically applying punitive measures. Discipline must be seen to be firm but fair.'

Uniform 'There is an agreed form of dress that allows a small measure of flexibility. The emphasis is on it being smart, functional and a reasonable price.' Navy V-neck sweater with embroidered school badge, pale-blue blouse/shirt, navy skirt or charcoal grey trousers, navy tie with gold motif, brown/black shoes.

Homework Average 11-year-old, six hours a week; 14-year-old, nine to 10 hours; 16-year-old, 12 hours.

Vocational qualifications City and Guilds; Diploma of Vocational Education.

Inspection September 1994: 'A good school in which pupils of all abilities achieve well.'; 'Pupils are generally eager to learn and develop productive habits of study that help to create purposeful lessons and positive attitudes towards learning.'; 'Resources are well-managed in most departments despite the inconvenience of the main building. Firm leadership and judicious management of daily routines help to ensure that the physical drawbacks do not inhibit learning or standards of achievement.'; 'Open and harmonious relationships are a prominent feature of the ethos of the school.'

Primary schools Forest County Primary; Cuddington County Primary; Wallerscote County Primary; Sandiway County Primary; Comberbach County Primary.

FALLIBROOME HIGH SCHOOL

Priory Lane
Macclesfield
Cheshire SK10 4AF
Tel (01625) 827898
Fax (01625) 820051
E-mail: info@fallibroome.cheshire.sch.uk
Internet: http://www.fallibroome.cheshire.sch.uk

- National ranking 285 (259, 252, 229, 304)
- GCSE 65% (66%)
- A-levels 48% (A/B); 90% (A/E)
- Higher education 90% (Oxford 1, Cambridge 2)

- Grant-maintained

- Mixed comprehensive
- Pupils 1,100
- Boys (11–18) 554
- Girls (11–18) 546
- Sixth form 166 (15%)
- Education authority *Cheshire*

Headteacher Michael Wakeham Batson, 55, appointed in January 1986. Staff 66 (men 29, women 37).

Motto Prospice (Look forward).

Background Opened in 1978, the school, which became grant-maintained in April 1993, is on the edge of Macclesfield with easy access to Peak District, Chester and Manchester. Looking out on open farmland; next to leisure centre. Over-subscribed, with up to 51% of applications from 'out-of-area' pupils; 286 applications for 210 places. Substantial building programme completed to meet growing demand; 'excellent' facilities for information technology. Became technology college in April 1995. Numerous industrial links; full range of work-experience for years 10 and 12. Won 1990 Schools Curriculum Award and one of only eight in the country to receive Queen's Anniversary Award. Investor in People Award in January 1995. Fallibroome Leisure Club runs evening clubs for local residents as well as annual summer school.

Streaming Setting begins in mathematics in year 8; in English, mathematics, science, geography, history, French and German in year 9; continues in English. Mathematics and science in years 10 and 11.

Approach to discipline Well-organised pastoral structure aims at close overview of pupils' lives; strong emphasis on disciplined, ordered atmosphere; small number of rules. 'The partnership between home and school is considered essential.' Operates policy of 'positive pupil management'.

Uniform Bottle-green blazer, mid-grey trousers/skirt, white shirt/blouse, school tie (green with red-and-white stripes), mid-grey V-neck pullover/cardigan, white/black/grey/green socks, black shoes. Strictly enforced to high standard.

Homework Average 11-year-old, eight hours a week; 14-year-old, 12 hours; 16-year-old, 18 hours.

Vocational qualifications Diploma of Vocational Education; Foreign Languages at Work.

Inspection April 1994: 'Fallibroome High School is a good school which serves its pupils well.'; 'Pupils communicate effectively orally. Written work is usually of a high standard and reading is fluent and purposeful. The staff are committed, well-qualified and hard-working.'; 'Because of its prudent stewardship, the high levels of achievement, the good quality teaching and learning, and its strong and appropriate ethos, the school provides very good value for money.'

Primary schools Bollinbrook CE Primary; Prestbury CE Primary; Upton Priory County Junior; Mottram St Andrew Primary; Nether Alderley County Primary.

TURTON HIGH SCHOOL

Bromley Cross Road
Bromley Cross
Bolton BL7 9LT
Tel (01204) 595888
Fax (01204) 306712

- National ranking 286
- GCSE 65%
- A-levels 44% (A/B); 89% (A/E)
- Higher education 84% (Cambridge 2)

- Mixed comprehensive
- Pupils 1,505
- Boys (11–18) 707
- Girls (11–18) 798
- Sixth form 302 (20%)
- Education authority *Bolton*

Headteacher Frank Vigon, 51, appointed in September 1988. Staff 93 (men 45, women 48).

Motto Integrity and honour.

Background Situated in northern extremity of Bolton in suburban commuter area; re-organised as a comprehensive in 1971. Original 1954 buildings extensively modified and extended. Community swimming pool; sports hall. Over-subscribed, with 432 applications for 240 places. Sporting success: hockey, netball, soccer, rugby, basketball, tennis, cricket, rounders, badminton, table tennis, volleyball, softball. Also dance, gymnastics, swimming, aerobics, outdoor pursuits, canoeing, sailing and rock-climbing. Music: junior and senior choirs, training orchestra, senior orchestra, wind band, brass band, string quartet, wind quartet. Other extra-curricular activities range from chess, technology, computers, drama, writing groups that produce school magazine and newsletter, discos. Industrial Awareness Conference; Young Enterprise; sixth-form debating. Various charity events.

Streaming Pupils put in sets from year 8.

Approach to discipline 'Our code of conduct emphasises life values, personal growth, responsibility and accountability, initiative, mature judgment and reflection on mistakes made rather than punishment. Whenever possible, we will endeavour to modify undesirable behaviour rather than punish a pupil merely to inhibit such behaviour.' Rewards as well as sanctions; pupils generally given chance to redeem themselves.

Uniform Boys: navy blazer with school badge, white shirt, grey trousers, school tie, navy V-neck pullover/cardigan with school logo (optional). Girls: navy blazer or navy pullover/cardigan, white blouse, navy skirt, school tie. Black/brown/navy shoes. 'Pupils are expected to conform with regulations.'

Homework Average 11-year-old, six hours a week; 14-year-old, nine hours; 16-year-old, 12 hours.

Vocational qualifications *None*

Inspection January 1997: 'Steady progress is maintained in all but a tiny minority of lessons and in almost 50 per cent it is good or better.'; 'Attainment in English is good overall. Speaking and listening are marked by confidence and a willingness to ask questions and discuss issues. Reading skills are well-developed, but independently pupils do not generally read widely enough. Written work is more variable in quality.'; 'Teaching is very effective in the school.'; 'While some lessons are satisfactory in that they reach the objective of examination success, they have become a routine process which too often fails to stimulate interest for a sizeable minority of pupils in the class.'; 'Homework plays an important part in pupils' success. It is regularly set, as the homework diaries show, but it is often not sufficiently demanding.'

Primary schools Eagley Junior; St Maxentius CE Primary; Walmsley CE Primary; Longsight Primary; Edgworth CE/Methodist Primary.

PARMITER'S SCHOOL

High Elms Lane
Garston
Watford
Hertfordshire WD2 7JU
Tel (01923) 671424
Fax (01923) 894195
E-mail: pmiter@rmplc.co.uk

- National ranking 287 (203, –, –, 183=)
- GCSE 65% (73%)
- A-levels 42% (A/B); 91% (A/E)
- Higher education 74% (Oxford 2, Cambridge 2)

- Grant-maintained
- Mixed comprehensive
- Pupils 1,145
- Boys (11–18) 601
- Girls (11–18) 544
- Sixth form 223 (19%)
- Education authority *Hertfordshire*

Headteacher Brian Coulshed, 47, appointed in January 1993. Staff 73 (men 32, women 41).

Motto Nemo sibi nascitur (No man is born unto himself alone).

Background The school has its origins in the will in 1681 of Thomas Parmiter, a silk merchant. Founded in Bethnal Green, east London, it has been a charity school, public school, endowed grammar and voluntary-aided grammar. In 1977, when it moved from London to a rural site in Garston, just north of Watford, it became a comprehensive. It became grant-maintained in September 1991. Buildings dating from 1967 are surrounded by playing fields, with all-weather facilities for some games. The school owns a field centre near Aberystwyth. Significantly over-subscribed, with four applications per place. Parmiter's Foundation credited for well-kept buildings and grounds. New building, Withersfield House, accommodating geography and history departments opened in October 1994; administration block extension (1995); allocated National Lottery grant for new sports centre in 1996; also acquired additional 17 acres for development into further adjacent playing fields. 'A family atmosphere is encouraged and Parmiter's receives very strong support from its wide-ranging community, which includes board of governors, trustees, parents' association.'

Alumni Emrys Davies, diplomat, High Commissioner to Barbados; John Crow, Bank of Canada governor-general; Robert Addis, founder of Addis Brushes and Domestic Utensils; Graham Stillwell, international tennis player.

Streaming Pupils streamed on entry into 'upper' or 'mixed' band. Banding and setting exists in years 7 to 9; setting by ability in some subjects in years 10 and 11.

Approach to discipline High standard of behaviour and personal appearance expected from all Parmiterians. 'School rules are kept to a minimum but must be obeyed. Punishments include detention, set work or various tasks within the school.'

Uniform Traditional navy blazers for pupils in years 7 to 11. Sixth-formers wear smart 'business' dress according to defined code. Strict adherence required.

Homework Average 11-year-old, eight hours a week; 14-year-old, 10 hours; 16-year-old, 15 hours.

Vocational qualifications RSA, Computer Literacy and Information Technology.

Inspection January 1997.

Primary schools Cassiobury Primary; Nascot Wood Primary; Mount Pleasant Lane Primary; Killigrew Primary; Knutsford Primary.

OXTED COUNTY SCHOOL

Bluehouse Lane
Oxted
Surrey RH8 0AB
Tel (01883) 712425
Fax (01883) 723973
E-mail: oxted@tcns.co.uk
Internet: http://www.surreycmc.gov.uk/iproject/schools/oxted

- National ranking 288 (297, 349, 368, 349)
- GCSE 65% (63%)
- A-levels 40% (A/B); 92% (A/E)
- Higher education 93% (Oxford 4)

- Mixed comprehensive
- Pupils 1,940
- Boys (11–18) 950
- Girls (11–18) 990
- Sixth form 340 (18%)
- Education authority Surrey

Headteacher Roger Coles, 56, appointed in April 1981. Staff 112 (men 48, women 64).

Motto Fortiter fideliter (Bravely and faithfully).

Background Founded as Surrey's first co-educational grammar school in 1929; set in 30 acres on edge of North Downs. The school has had only four headteachers in 66 years, reflecting the traditional stability that is a school trademark. Range of architectural styles from original colonnaded buildings to state-of-art science block with 16 laboratories, purpose-built drama studio, new learning resource centre, technology block, open-air heated swimming pool. New technology block under construction and floodlit Astroturf pitch planned. Regularly over-subscribed with 410 applications for 330 places. Healthy competition between five houses. Drama, music and art are strengths: school troupe performed at Edinburgh Fringe Festival in 1992. Cross-country, basketball and netball among sporting achievements. School has its own unit for visually-impaired pupils, run by specialist staff. Duke of Edinburgh Award Scheme. Identified as 'outstandingly successful' in 1997 annual Ofsted report.

Alumni Karen Brown, Great Britain Olympic hockey international; John Jones, Dean of Balliol College, Oxford; Alison Streeter, 20-times cross-channel swimmer; Ian Pearce, Blackburn Rovers Premiership medallist and England Under-21 international; Nicky Forster, England Under-21 footballer.

Streaming Mixed-ability groups on entry in year 7. All National Curriculum subjects setted by start of year 8.

Approach to discipline 'For the minority, early warning signs dealt with through counselling by house staff. Thereafter sanctions progressively applied up to permanent exclusion (about five a year).'

Uniform Black blazer with school crest, black trousers for boys, navy sweater with school crest, navy skirt/trousers for girls. White shirt/blouse to take school tie with house colour band. Dress code for sixth-formers. 'High standard of smartness required.'

Homework Average 11-year-old, five hours a week; 14-year-old, 10 hours; 16-year-old, 10 to 15 hours.

Vocational qualifications Information Technology Certificate of Competency (ULEAC).

GNVQ Intermediate (from September 1997), Art and Design, Business Studies.

Inspection March 1994: 'A good school with many very good features.'; 'There are many good teachers who employ a range of approaches and display high levels of specialist expertise. The quality of teaching in most subjects is good and it contributes to the standards achieved in the school. However, attention needs to be given to sixth-form teaching in order to provide greater challenge.'; 'The headteacher provides strong and effective leadership.'; 'The school has high expectations of its pupils both in relation to achievement and behaviour.'; 'The ethos of the school and the standards of behaviour are very good.' The school reports: 'The School Action Plan has addressed the issues raised concerning sixth-form teaching and is moving ahead well in this area.'

Primary schools St Mary's CE Junior; Lingfield Primary; Holland Junior; St John's CE Junior, Caterham; St Stephen's CE Primary, South Godstone.

BEVERLEY HIGH SCHOOL

Norwood
Beverley
East Yorkshire HU17 9EX
Tel (01482) 881658
Fax (01482) 870935
E-mail: beverleyhi@aol.com
Internet: http://www.curdev.hull.ac.uk/bhigh

- National ranking 289 (285 = , 310, 269, –)
- GCSE 65% (64%)
- A-levels 40% (A/B); 91% (A/E)
- Higher education 82% (Cambridge 1)

- Girls' comprehensive
- Pupils 758
- Boys *Not applicable*
- Girls (11–18) 758
- Sixth form 109 (14%)
- Education authority *East Yorkshire*

Headteacher Ruth Vincent, 45, appointed in September 1989. Staff 46 (men 7, women 39).

Motto Pietas (Piety).

Background Founded in 1908 in centre of market town of Beverley; shares joint sixth form with Beverley Grammar School; long-established tradition of 'excellent' achievement in academic work, music, drama, art, sport and work-experience. 'It enjoys a high reputation within the community, both at local and county levels.' Subject departments housed in purpose-built rooms; library and sixth-form in Grade 1 Georgian house within grounds. New technology block opened in 1991; new art suite in 1995; additional science facilities. Over-subscribed, with average of 1.25 applications per place. Catchment area is 'socially mixed' and provides full range of ability, taking pupils from Beverley and surrounding villages of Tickton, Walkington and Wawne. Total of 100 computers available to pupils. Wide range of sports and clubs. More than 20 teams represented in inter-school competitions: netball, hockey, athletics, rounders and badminton. Sport, music and drama notable among extra-curricular activities: choirs, orchestras; school productions and concerts; lunchtime clubs include gym, trampolining, wind band, Scripture Union, judo, dance, weekly charity fund-raising events, hockey, netball and athletics. More than 20 clubs and societies also include European Society and Crime Prevention Panel.

Streaming Ability-groups used only in mathematics.

Approach to discipline 'Cooperation between school and parents is regarded as fundamental to good home–school relationships, which underpin the school's approach to discipline. Pupils are given a clear understanding of the school's high expectations and emphasis is based on self-discipline and respect for others, both in the school and the community at large.'

Uniform 'The school has a dress code of navy and white with school tie, which is enforced and supported by parents and pupils.'

Homework Average 11-year-old, five hours a week; 14-year-old, seven hours; 16-year-old, 10 hours.

Vocational qualifications GNVQ Advanced, Art and Business; GNVQ Foundation, Business.

Inspection February 1996: 'This is a very good school which provides good and, in several respects, outstanding quality of education. It makes an important contribution to the life of the local community and deserves its high reputation.'; 'The difficulties over capital funding for accommodation, which lie outside the school's responsibility, are a significant constraint which the school manages skilfully.'; 'When assessed against the measures of ability on entry, there is clear evidence that the school is developing the potential of its pupils across the full range of ability to a very commendable extent.'; 'The quality of extra-curricular provision makes an important contribution to the achievement of high standards. This is evident in music, especially in choral singing and in the instrumental work strongly supported by the local authority, and in sport and games.'

Primary schools Beverley Minster CE Primary; St Nicholas County Primary; Swinemoor Primary; St Mary's CE Primary; Walkington. Plus another 18 feeder schools.

ALL HALLOWS CATHOLIC HIGH SCHOOL

**Brooklands Avenue
Macclesfield
Cheshire SK11 8LB
Tel (01625) 426138
Fax (01625) 500315**

- National ranking 290 (256, 485, 288, 331)
- GCSE 65% (66%)
- A-levels 39% (A/B); 89% (A/E)
- Higher education 89%

- Mixed comprehensive
- Pupils 1,065
- Boys (11–18) 564
- Girls (11–18) 501
- Sixth form 185 (17%)
- Education authority *Cheshire*

Headteacher Richard K. Weremczyk, 48, appointed in September 1986. Staff 61 (men 21, women 40).

Motto Christi crux est mea lux (The cross of Christ is my light).

Background The school, in a residential area of Macclesfield, is jointly maintained by Cheshire and the Roman Catholic Diocese of Shrewsbury. Original buildings opened in 1962; further additions in the mid-1970s. Facilities include: workrooms for design and technology, home economics, assembly hall and stage, drama studio, recently-opened business studies suite; four fully-equipped information technology rooms; information technology used in all departments; extensive playing fields, sports hall, all-weather pitch. Over-subscribed, with 1.3 applications per place; after all Catholic applicants accepted, there are about three applications for each of the remaining places. School sets great store by religious education and practice; reputation for music and drama, with pupils going on to university or repertory companies. International links, with paired schools in France, Germany, Spain and Poland. National sporting success in badminton, athletics, cross-country, netball and swimming. Centre of Excellence for music; regular invitation to finals of choral singing at Royal Festival Hall and studio recordings; joint productions with schools in Wissembourg, Bad Bergzabern and Erfurt.

Streaming Gradually put in sets from year 8; GCSE sets in all subjects from year 10.

Approach to discipline 'We believe in building on the innate goodness in our pupils. We are a community built on love, trust, respect and personal dignity where each student is valued highly.' Breaches of good behaviour addressed in partnership with parents.

Uniform Black blazer with school badge, grey trousers/skirt, white shirt/blouse, grey pullover, school tie, black shoes. Black tights for girls. Strictly enforced, except for sixth-formers.

Homework Average 11-year-old, minimum of five hours a week; 14-year-old, minimum of six hours 30 minutes; 16-year-old, minimum of 12 hours.

Vocational qualifications Northern Partnership for Records of Achievement; GNVQ BTEC Level 3, Business and Finance Level; GNVQ Level 2, Manufacturing, Business, Art and Design.

Inspection Autumn 1994: 'A good school providing a very effective education for its pupils.'; 'Pupils have very good attitudes to learning, are well-motivated and cooperative. The needs of all learners are appropriately catered for and pupils make significant progress.'; 'The school is well led and effectively managed.'; 'Pupil behaviour, discipline and attendance are very good. The school is a pleasant, orderly and civilised community with a strong ethical code. In it, individuals are valued for what they are and what they may become. Pupils respond accordingly and with enthusiasm.'

Primary schools St Alban's RC Primary; St

Edward's RC Primary; Ivy Bank County Primary; Park Royal County Primary; Gawsworth County Primary; St Benedict's RC Primary, Handforth; St Gregory's RC Primary, Bollington; St Mary's RC Primary, Poynton; St Mary's RC Primary, Congleton; St Peter's RC Primary, Hazel Grove; All Saints Primary, Glossop; St Mary's Primary, New Mills; St John's CE Primary, Macclesfield; St Barnabas CE Primary, Macclesfield.

CAERLEON COMPREHENSIVE SCHOOL

Cold Bath Road
Caerleon
Newport
Gwent NP6 1NF
Tel (01633) 420106
Fax (01633) 430048

- National ranking 291 (357, 370, 308, –)
- GCSE 65% (60%)
- A-levels 37% (A/B); 89% (A/E)
- Higher education 74% (Oxford 3, Cambridge 1)

- Mixed comprehensive
- Pupils 1,421
- Boys (11–18) 722
- Girls (11–18) 699
- Sixth form 252 (18%)
- Education authority *Newport*

Headteacher Adrian Griffiths Davies, 48, appointed in June 1995. Staff 77 (men 30, women 47).

Motto Perseverance.

Background Origins traced to 1587 and to 'free school erected in Caerleon'; Charles Williams Endowed School was built in 1724; on current site for 30 years; became comprehensive for pupils aged 11 to 18 in 1976. Greenfield site in lower Usk valley next to important Roman sites, including barracks and amphitheatre. Over-subscribed, with 260 applications for 230 places. 'Academic success is the fundamental aim and the school culture is one of constant high expectations.' Musical achievements: three major concerts each year; two orchestras and a big band; two members of National Youth Orchestra. Also members in 1996 of Welsh Jazz Youth Orchestra (2), National Youth Theatre (2), National Youth Ballet (2) and Welsh Youth Brass Band (1). More than 200 pupils receive specialist instrumental teaching, most of whom are members of county ensembles. One major dramatic or musical production each year. Sporting achievements: six rugby teams, four soccer teams, six netball teams, five girls' hockey teams and boys' hockey team, four cricket teams. Also athletics, basketball, tennis, golf, trampolining and outdoor pursuits. In 1996, the school had several international representatives: Wales girls' hockey team (3), swimming (1), badminton (1), athletics (1), showjumping (2), archery (1), boys' hockey (1), cricket (1), grass-skiing (1), squash (1).

Alumni Nigel Vaughan, Wales soccer player; Stuart Watkins, David Waters and Rhys Morgan, Wales rugby internationals; Nicola Donald and Rachel Bradford, Welsh hockey internationals; Kevin Helps, Welsh international weight-lifter.

Streaming In mathematics in year 7, remaining subjects in mixed-ability classes. Flexible setting arrangements for all subjects from year 8.

Approach to discipline Code of practice signed by all pupils and parents. 'We insist on punctuality, regular attendance, respect for others, courtesy and hard work at all times. The aim is for pupils to enjoy their schooling in a structured and secure environment. Sanctions include detention and community service. Exclusions are rare.'

Uniform Girls: maroon skirt, V-neck jumper and tights, blue blouse, distinctive tie; black tailored trousers optional during winter. Boys: black V-neck jumper, black trousers, blue shirt, distinctive tie. Years 12 and 13: white shirt-blouse, sixth-form tie. Plain dark top coat. 'Strictly enforced. all must wear jumpers in formal situations and restaurant. No trainers and, for safety reasons, no earrings for boys.'

Homework Average 11-year-old, five hours a week; 14-year-old, six to seven hours; 16-year-old, at least 10 to 14 hours.

Vocational qualifications Plans for GNVQ.

Inspection March 1994: 'Caerleon School aims for high standards of achievement for its pupils and succeeds to a notable degree.'; 'Pupils are challenged and extended whatever their ability. The school has recently changed its policy in regard to pupils with special educational needs in order to incorporate them into the mainstream of the school, and in so doing has enriched their experience and increased their self-esteem.'; 'The atmosphere is conducive to learning. Relationships between pupils and teachers are good. Pupils are interested and involved.'; 'The school has no serious weaknesses. It does suffer, however, from ill-drained and muddy surroundings, the effects of which the best efforts of the caretaking and cleaning staff can do little to counteract in poor weather.'

Primary schools Caerleon Endowed Junior; Caerleon Lodge Hill Junior; Goytre Primary; Langstone Primary; Ponthir Primary; Usk Primary.

NAILSEA SCHOOL

Mizzymead Road
Nailsea
Bristol BS19 2HN
Tel (01275) 852251
Fax (01275) 854512

- National ranking 292 (260, 324, 382, 302)
- GCSE 65% (66%)
- A-levels 37% (A/B); 88% (A/E)
- Higher education 75% (Oxford 3, Cambridge 1)

- Mixed comprehensive
- Pupils 1,291
- Boys (11–18) 650
- Girls (11–18) 641
- Sixth form 239 (19%)
- Education authority *North Somerset*

Headteacher Dr Trevor White, 59, appointed in September 1976. Staff 78 (men 40, women 38).

Motto Opportunity for all.

Background Opened as Nailsea Grammar School in 1959, serving north Somerset; became comprehensive in 1966 and new buildings added to accommodate 1,200 pupils. Design on school badge based on life of Sir Richard Perceval, celebrated Elizabethan who lived at Nailsea Court. Fully-subscribed. Avon under-16 soccer champions for four successive years; national school croquet champions. Many pupils in county orchestra and Symphonic Wind Band; representatives in National Youth Orchestra. 'A place to try things out, to take risks in a safe environment, to discover whatever talents one has, and develop individuality as well as teamwork.'

Alumni Sue Slocombe, Great Britain women's hockey coach.

Streaming Setting operates in most subjects as pupils move through school.

Approach to discipline Defining acceptable standard of behaviour; high expectations of pupils; praising good behaviour, being consistent; dealing promptly and appropriately with misbehaviour; using acceptable sanctions; involving parents as appropriate.

Uniform White shirt, navy skirt/trousers for girls and grey trousers for boys. School colours are dark-blue and yellow. Enforced 'with firmness and common sense'.

Homework Average 11-year-old, five hours a week; 14-year-old, seven hours 30 minutes: 16-year-old, 10 + hours.

Vocational qualifications GNVQ; RSA.

Inspection March 1996.

Primary schools Golden Valley Primary; Grove Junior; Tickenham CE Primary; Nailsea Christ Church CE Primary; Wraxall CE Primary.

DESBOROUGH SCHOOL

Shoppenhangers Road
Maidenhead
Berkshire SL6 2QB
Tel (01628) 34505
Fax (01628) 39263
E-mail: headmaster@desborough.org.uk
Internet: http://www.desborough.org.uk

- National ranking 293 (440, 372, 369, –)
- GCSE 65% (54%)
- A-levels 32% (A/B); 88% (A/E)
- Higher education 85% (Oxford 2)

- Grant-maintained
- Boys' comprehensive
- Pupils 912
- Boys (11–18) 912
- Girls (11–18) *Not applicable*
- Sixth form 160 (18%)
- Education authority *Berkshire*

Headteacher David William Eyre, 44, appointed in April 1996. Staff 55 (men 32, women 23).

Motto Strenuis ardua cedunt (Difficulties yield to those who persevere).

Background Founded in 1894 within easy walking distance of town centre; moved to current site in 1910, having previously occupied site in centre of Maidenhead; formerly Maidenhead County Boys' Grammar School; became comprehensive in 1973, and grant-maintained in January 1992. Original buildings, including the Headmaster's House (now the music centre) have been extended, with new blocks in 1960, 1971 and 1972; £500,000 Reynolds Technology Centre opened in 1993. Sports facilities: gymnasium, sports hall, all-weather pitch, tennis courts, ample playing field and well-maintained cricket square. Notable GCSE success in mathematics, science, modern languages, English, science and technology; also history, English, modern languages, mathematics and art at A-level. Language exchange programme with schools in Duisburg and Villeneuve-sur-Lot. Established sporting reputation: regular rugby tours (Canada, United States and Ireland in recent years); hockey developing under international player Mike Williamson (Wales and Hounslow); winners of county indoor hockey tournament for 1993 and 1994. Saturday and weekday fixtures in all main sports, often against independent schools: hockey, rugby and cricket; also basketball, badminton and tennis. Proud of music and drama; school choir sings at Royal Festival Hall each year. Annual arts festival; more than one in 10 pupils receive instrumental tuition. Expeditions to Morocco (1995) and Borneo (1997). Recently established Student Council with delegated budget to improve facilities for benefit of pupils. 'Desborough School prepares pupils for life in society by providing a wide range of challenging, high-quality educational activities, in a caring, well-ordered community committed to the achievement of excellence, and the academic, personal and social development of each boy.'

Alumni Dick Francis, novelist and former jockey; Roy and John Boulting, film-makers; Charles Hart, lyricist; Toby Anstis, television presenter; Nick Hornby, writer; Mark Richardson, athlete; Robert Hayward, former Conservative MP for Bristol Kingswood.

Streaming Extensive setting from year 7 in most academic subjects. German introduced for most able linguists in year 8.

Approach to discipline Simple code of conduct that pupils and parents are asked to sign on admission; formal anti-bullying policy. Rewards for academic achievement: badges (year 7); pens (year 8); gift vouchers (year 9); funded by Parents' Association. School colours for sporting achievement; lapel badges for music or drama contribution.

Uniform Navy blazer with school badge, grey trousers, white/grey shirt, school tie, grey/navy/yellow pullover, grey socks, black shoes. Sixth-formers can wear dark suit as alternative to blazer and grey trousers; distinctive tie for prefects and sixth-formers.

Homework Average 11-year-old, five hours a week; 14-year-old, seven hours 30 minutes; 16-year-old, 10 hours.

Vocational qualifications GNVQ Level 3, Business and Finance; Foreign Languages at Work (French).

Primary schools Courthouse Junior; Ellington Primary; Holyport CE Primary; Cookham Primary; Oldfield Primary; St Edmund Campion RC Primary.

THE GREEN SCHOOL FOR GIRLS

Busch Corner
London Road
Isleworth
Middlesex TW7 5BB
Tel (0181) 568 3137
Fax (0181) 568 2523

- National ranking 294 (278, 330, –, 202)
- GCSE 65% (65%)
- A-levels 26% (A/B); 80% (A/E)
- Higher education 94%

- Girls' comprehensive
- Pupils 756
- Boys *Not applicable*
- Girls (11–18) 756
- Sixth form 124 (16%)
- Education authority *Hounslow*

Headteacher Janet Anne Bartlett, 60, appointed in September 1978. Staff 46 (men 9, women 37).

Motto Serve with gladness.

Background Founded as a Sunday school about 200 years ago; on current site, in centre of Hounslow on land provided by

Duke of Northumberland, since 1906; became comprehensive in 1978 and expanded from two-form to four-form entry. Extra building in 1978 for science, design technology, business studies, library and extra classrooms. Two applications for each place. Strong sporting tradition, with girls representing Middlesex in hockey and athletics; international representatives in rhythmic gymnastics. Strong links with schools in France and Germany: language exchanges, overseas work-experience available. Sixth form run as part of consortium to offer wide range of subjects. Church of England voluntary-aided comprehensive where Christian values are 'most important fact about school'.

Alumni Vanessa Latarche, concert pianist; Monica Huggett, violinist; Margaret Edwards, Olympic swimmer.

Streaming In mathematics, modern languages and science.

Approach to discipline Sound discipline based on good personal relationships; close contact with parents. 'Our aim is to develop self-discipline within a set school procedure that is explained to parents and pupils when they enter the school.'

Uniform Bottle-green skirt and jumper, white blouse, bottle-green or black coat. Sixth form do not wear uniform; enforced strictly in other years.

Homework Average 11-year-old, six hours 30 minutes a week; 14-year-old, eight hours 30 minutes; 16-year-old, 11 hours.

Vocational qualifications GNVQ Intermediate.

Inspection September 1996: 'The Green School for Girls maintains high academic standards, enables pupils to make good progress and provides equally well for their personal development. It is heavily oversubscribed and deservedly so.'; 'Overall, A-level results are not as good as might be expected from the school's National Curriculum test or GCSE results.'; 'Pupils have highly positive attitudes to learning. Most are strongly-motivated and actively enjoy their work. Parents rightly regard pupils' behaviour as one of the major strengths of the school. The impressive standards of classroom behaviour create ideal conditions for successful learning. Pupils demonstrate high levels of courtesy and relationships between different ethnic groups are harmonious.'; 'Teaching is a strength of the school in

almost all subjects and makes a major contribution to good standards of attainment and progress.'

Primary schools Marlborough Primary; The Blue School, Isleworth; Heston Junior; St Lawrence and St Paul's Primary, Brentford; Alexandra Junior.

FROGMORE COMMUNITY SCHOOL

Potley Hill Road
Yateley
Camberley
Surrey GU46 6AG
Tel (01252) 870563
Fax (01252) 890459
E-mail: 4183nexx@hants.gov.uk

- National ranking 295 (471, 525, 324, –)
- GCSE 65% (52%)
- A-levels 26% (A/B); 78% (A/E)
- Higher education 58%

- Mixed comprehensive
- Pupils 647
- Boys (11–18) 324
- Girls (11–18) 323
- Sixth form 147 (23%)
- Education authority *Hampshire*

Headteacher Paul Charles Harwood, 45, appointed in September 1989. Staff 44 (men 18, women 26).

Motto *None*

Background Opened in 1979 on 50-acre rural site, largest community campus in Hampshire; well-designed low-level buildings; attracts pupils from Hampshire, Surrey and Berkshire; separate sixth-form accommodation at Blackwater Valley Centre. New purpose-built library, resource centre, recently refurbished drama studio, four squash courts, music suite, three information technology suites, specialist art provision; £1.8m improvement to sporting facilities, including floodlit all-weather pitch. Purpose-built recording studio; also extensive new technology facilities. Playing fields: four football pitches, rugby pitch, running track. Fully-subscribed. Headteacher's daughter attended school; son in year 12. Recognised by 1991 inspectors' report for 'excellence in the physical and creative arts' as well as 'outstanding pastoral care'; identified for praise in annual Ofsted report; offers 10 GCSEs at end of year 11, and 99% of year 11 students got at least one pass in 1994. Extensive extra-curricular programme; large number of school journeys and foreign exchanges. Investors in People Award.

Alumni Darren Barnard, Chelsea and England Under-18 soccer player.

Streaming Mixed-ability in year 7; in sets in most subjects from year 8. Setting becomes more refined in years 10 and 11.

Approach to discipline 'The school has a rigorous and consistent approach to discipline. We expect high standards from all students and will not tolerate bad manners or poor behaviour. Self-discipline and courtesy towards others are an integral part of an excellent working atmosphere at Frogmore. It is a caring school where individuals matter and personal qualities are valued.'

Uniform Blazer, white shirt/blouse, grey skirt/trousers, school tie (for both girls and boys), plain socks, shoes; no trainers. Very strictly enforced: 'Students are removed from lessons if they breach the uniform code.'

Homework Average 11-year-old, seven hours 30 minutes a week; 14-year-old, nine hours; 16-year-old, 12 hours.

Vocational qualifications GNVQ Intermediate and Advanced, Art and Design, Leisure and Tourism, Business and Administration; NNEB Nursery Nursing Diploma; Nursery Nursing Certificate.

Inspection March 1996: 'This is a good school in which pupils' achievements are valued and which has set clear targets for continued improvement.'; 'The school is strongly led and well managed by senior managers and governors.'; 'The excellent attitude of pupils is encouraged and enhanced by the good support and guidance they receive.'; 'The spiritual, moral, social and cultural development of the pupils is a strength of the school.'; 'The ethos of the community contributed positively to raising pupils' achievements and to the good quality of the education provided.'

Primary schools Potley Hill Primary; Frogmore Junior; Hawley County Primary; College Town Junior.

BEAL HIGH SCHOOL

Woodford Bridge Road
Ilford
Essex IG4 5LP

Tel (0181) 551 4954
Fax (0181) 551 4421

- National ranking 296 (–, 399, 317, –)
- GCSE 65%
- A-levels 25% (A/B); 84% (A/E)
- Higher education 60%

- Mixed comprehensive
- Pupils 1,121
- Boys (11–18) 550
- Girls (11–18) 571
- Sixth form 209 (19%)
- Education authority Redbridge

Headteacher Sue Snowdon, 40, appointed in September 1996. Staff 77 (men 32, women 45).

Motto Faire sans dire (Deeds without words).

Background Origins of school date back to founding Beal Modern School in 1931; named after Alderman John Beal, local dignitary; became grammar school in 1948; became fully comprehensive in 1983. Rich heritage of playing fields covering 28 acres, between Ilford and Woodford, next to North Circular and close to M11. Over-subscribed, with waiting lists in all years. Wide range of competitive games; many county representatives. Longstanding reputation for music; annual musicals. Duke of Edinburgh Award Scheme. 'In a multi-cultural school, pupils and staff are committed to a policy of equal regard for all. The school enjoys a reputation for academic excellence in Redbridge and beyond. The number of pupils wishing to stay on into the sixth-form has ensured the A-level traditions of the former grammar school have continued.'

Alumni Victor Maddern, actor; Barry Hearn, boxing promoter; Barry Kyle, theatre director; Kevin Tillett, singer.

Streaming Placed in three ability bands on entry. Head of year studies junior school records and consults with primary schools teachers before placements made.

Approach to discipline 'The school has a firm but friendly atmosphere. Heads of year work closely with form teachers to ensure that pupils' behaviour is of a high order. When problems arise, parents are approached immediately to ensure there is full co-operation between school and home.'

Uniform Brown blazer, brown skirt or grey/black trousers, white/cream shirt or blouse, brown-and-yellow tie for boys. Sixth-formers: Navy blazer, navy skirt or grey/black trousers, white/pale-blue blouse or shirt, navy-and-yellow tie for boys. 'Pupils not conforming to school uniform regulations are sent home to change. Weekly inspections made by headmaster and senior staff to ensure high standards of dress/appearance are maintained.'

Homework Average 11-year-old, five hours a week; 14-year-old, seven hours 30 minutes; 16-year-old, 12 hours.

Vocational qualifications *None*

Inspection September 1996: 'A good school, which is in the process of setting up structures to enable it to become a very good school. It provides its pupils with a caring, supportive environment in which to develop their academic and social skills. Levels of attainment achieved by pupils are mostly in line with, or higher than, national standards. Bilingual pupils achieve significantly better than other groups of pupils.'; 'Attainment in drama is under-developed.'; 'Pupils are able to read fluently, write with interest and speak confidently, with enthusiasm.'; 'Although there is not a consistent pattern throughout the school, the higher- and lower-attaining pupils generally do not achieve as well as their potential indicates.'; 'The school provides a good quality of education. Generally, pupils are motivated and work with enthusiasm.'; 'The headteacher is providing a clear sense of direction and purpose, and this is having a significant impact on the school's development.'

Primary schools Redbridge Junior; Parkhill Junior; Gearies Junior.

COTTENHAM VILLAGE COLLEGE

High Street
Cottenham
Cambridge
Cambridgeshire CB4 4UA
Tel (01954) 288944
Fax (01954) 288949
E-mail: cottenham.college@a4038.
camcnty.gov.uk

- National ranking 297= (460=, 437=, 482=, –)
- GCSE 65% (53%)
- A-levels *Not applicable*
- Higher education *Not applicable*

- Mixed comprehensive
- Pupils 850
- Boys (11–16) 418
- Girls (11–16) 432
- Sixth form *Not applicable*
- Education authority *Cambridgeshire*

Headteacher Tony Cooper, 44, appointed in September 1989. Staff 45 (men 19, women 26).

Motto *None*

Background Serves villages of Cottenham, Landbeach, Rampton, Waterbeach and Willingham; in pleasant, spacious grounds; provides part-time education, leisure and recreation for more than 2,000 adults. Over-subscribed. Original teaching block for mathematics, English, modern languages; new block has six science laboratories, close to well-stocked library, careers centre, information technology base and suite of rooms for humanities. Modern expressive arts block: three art studios, drama studio, two main music rooms and several practice rooms. Sports facilities: sports hall, gymnasium, outdoor swimming pool, tennis courts, floodlit all-weather playing surface. 'The principal aim of the college is to serve the community by providing facilities and opportunities for education and leisure for people of all ages. We believe that such provision must enable individuals and groups of individuals to develop their talents and interests, allowing them to contribute to the organisation and development of their community.' Able students are offered accelerated courses through mathematics and science at GCSE, with separate sciences in addition to integrated science and A-level mathematics. Schools Curriculum Award in 1997.

Streaming 'Students are not streamed, but are set according to ability for many subjects at different stages.'

Approach to discipline Eight-point Statement of Values; also Code of Conduct: 'Good order in school is the responsibility of everybody. Good order does not just happen; it has to be worked for. High standards of work and behaviour depend on the example of all of us.'

Uniform Black blazer with badge, white shirt/blouse, medium-grey trousers/skirt, grey V-neck jumper (optional), school tie (optional for girls), black shoes.

Homework Average 11-year-old, four hours a week; 14-year-old, six hours; 16-year-old, 10 hours.

Vocational qualifications Under consideration.

Inspection February 1996: 'Cottenham Village College is a well-run school and community college, justifiably popular with parents and the community it serves. The college caters fully for students of all abilities and backgrounds, promoting an ethos in which high standards are valued and achieved.'; 'The college provides a high quality of education for all students in a pleasant and welcoming environment.'; 'There is an excellent range of extra-curricular activities which many students enjoy and which adds greatly to their lives at the college. Relationships in the college are generally excellent. Behaviour is good, within an orderly and civilised community.'

Primary schools Cottenham Primary; Waterbeach Community Primary; Willingham Primary; Milton CE Primary.

GRAYS CONVENT HIGH SCHOOL

College Avenue
Grays
Essex RM17 5UX
Tel (0375) 376173
Fax (0375) 394724

- National ranking 297= (–, –, –, 315=)
- GCSE 65%
- A-levels *Not applicable*
- Higher education *Not applicable*

- Girls' comprehensive
- Pupils 600
- Boys *Not applicable*
- Girls (11–16) 600
- Sixth form *Not applicable*
- Education authority *Essex*

Headteacher Philip John Charles Kynds, 46, appointed in September 1995. Staff 37 (men 11, women 26).

Motto None

Background School founded in 1906 by Sisters of La Sainte Union; changed from grammar school to voluntary-aided comprehensive for pupils aged 11 to 18 in 1969; local sixth-form college established in 1972. Set in quiet cul-de-sac on outskirts of Grays town centre. Extensive building between 1969 and 1972: new gymnasium, laboratories, a practical block as well as general teaching space and new assembly hall/chapel. Over-subscribed, with 175 applications for 124 places. Strong sporting activities: district athletics champions in 1992. Long music tradition.

Streaming In mathematics, English and French throughout the school. Regular reviews.

Approach to discipline Based upon Christian courtesy and respect; promotes self-control, high standards of conduct and character-building. 'This form of caring discipline depends on close co-operation between home and school.'

Uniform Navy blazer with badge, navy skirt, white blouse, navy V-neck jumper, black shoes. Regulations strictly enforced.

Homework Average 11-year-old, seven hours 30 minutes a week; 14-year-old, ten hours; 16-year-old, 15 hours.

Vocational qualifications *None*

Primary schools St Thomas of Canterbury RC Primary; St Joseph's RC Primary, Stanford-le-Hope; St Mary's RC Primary, Tilbury; Holy Cross RC Primary, Aveley; Little Thurrock Primary.

HARTISMERE HIGH SCHOOL

Castleton Way
Eye
Suffolk IP23 7BL
Tel (01379) 870315
Fax (01379) 870554

- National ranking 297= (331=, 437=)
- GCSE 65% (62%)
- A-levels *Not applicable*
- Higher education *Not applicable*

- Mixed comprehensive
- Pupils 636
- Boys (11–16) 325
- Girls (11–16) 311
- Sixth form 81 (since September 1996)
- Education authority *Suffolk*

Headteacher Richard John Hewitt, 50, appointed in April 1987. Staff 42 (men 20, women 22).

Motto Discamus ut serviamus (Let us learn that we may serve).

Background Serves catchment area previously catered for by Eye grammar and secondary moderns. Purpose-built accommodation on campus in beautiful countryside on outskirts of market town of Eye. Purpose-built sixth-form centre in September 1996, for pupils from Hartismere and Debenham High Schools. 'Excellent' sporting facilities; House and inter-school team games, with many pupils gaining national representative honours. Drama and music notable in 'strong and broad' curriculum. Extra-curricular activities. 'All individuals are valued, and students are respected and approached firmly and fairly. We aim to develop self-discipline and the highest levels of personal achievement. Students respond with trust.'

Streaming Setting occurs increasingly through the school from year 7 to years 10 and 11, where most subjects are set by ability.

Approach to discipline 'Students have the right to learn, the right to be treated with respect and the right to feel safe. Any behaviour that prevents these goes against our code of conduct and there is a clear and firm discipline policy that is followed. Close contact with parents is maintained in any discipline matters and students are supported as well as sanctioned.'

Uniform Grey trousers, skirt/culottes/tailored knee-length shorts in summer, white shirt, school tie, navy jumper. No trainers, denim or leather jackets. 'The uniform is flexible, reasonable and affordable. We thus expect all parents and students to support it, and students dressed incorrectly for an unacceptable reason are disciplined.'

Homework Average 11-year-old, five hours a week; 14-year-old, 10 hours; 16-year-old, 15 hours.

Vocational qualifications Pre-16 GNVQ units in Art and Design, Leisure and Tourism.

Inspection April 1992: 'The school is successful in providing a good education for its pupils.'; 'The quality of learning is very good. Pupils concentrate well in lessons, co-operate productively and make good progress in their learning. The overall quality of teaching is a major strength. The curriculum is generally sound and balanced.'; 'Many aspects of management are good and people, both teachers and pupils, are valued for the contributions they make to the life of the school.'; 'Behaviour and discipline are very good and relationships are excellent.'

Primary schools St Botolph's CE Primary, Botesdale; St Peter and Paul CE Primary, Eye; Gislingham CE Primary; St Edmund's County Primary, Hoxne; Mellis CE Primary; Occold County Primary; Palgrave CE Primary; Thorndon CE Primary; Stoke Ash County Primary; Wortham Long Green County Primary.

ST GREGORY'S CATHOLIC COMPREHENSIVE SCHOOL

Combe Hay Lane
Odd Down
Bath BA2 8PA
Tel (01225) 832873
Fax (01225) 835848

- National ranking 297 = (302 =, 187 =, 192, –)
- GCSE 65% (63%)
- A-levels *Not applicable*
- Higher education *Not applicable*

- Mixed comprehensive
- Pupils 729
- Boys (11–18) 371
- Girls (11–18) 358
- Sixth form *Not applicable*
- Education authority *Bath and North-east Somerset*

Headteacher David William Byrne, 50, appointed in September 1986. Staff 40 (men 14, women 26).

Motto Ad deum per discendum (To God through learning).

Background Established in 1979 as a result of reorganisation of Catholic education in Bath area; formed from amalgamation of small secondary school and small convent grammar (Sisters of La Sainte Union); set in own grounds overlooking attractive Englishcombe Valley on southern tip of Bath. The school serves a wide catchment area, which includes parts of Somerset and Wiltshire. Buildings that date from 1960s have been substantially improved and developed; new suite of six classrooms recently completed to accommodate rising numbers. Over-subscribed, with two applications per place. National reputation for performing arts: winner of 1993 Sainsbury's Award, which funded collaborative dance/drama project with Northern Ballet Theatre; recently took part in Barclays Music Theatre Awards; also success in public-speaking and creative writing; winner of Barclays 'New Futures' Award in 1996. 'As a Christian school, we see the care and development of the individual within the framework of a community as paramount.'

Alumni Ann Widdecombe (former pupil of Sisters of La Sainte Union Convent), Conservative MP for Maidstone and former Home Office minister.

Streaming After one term taught in tutor groups, year 7 pupils placed in streamed groups for a number of academic subjects; in mathematics and modern languages they are set separately. In years 10 and 11, all subjects are taught in sets.

Approach to discipline 'The school insists on high standards of appearance, behaviour and work.' Agreed policy stresses need for high expectations, respect and consideration for others, an atmosphere of mutual co-operation, and for a system of rewards and sanctions founded on justice and reconciliation. 'The school code is rooted in the attitudes and values expressed in the Gospels.'

Uniform Dark-brown blazer with school badge (optional), gold blouse/shirt, school tie, dark-brown skirt/trousers, dark-brown jumper with school crest, 'sensible' brown/black shoes. No trainers. 'All pupils wear school uniform.'

Homework Average 11-year-old, five hours a week; 14-year-old, seven hours 30 minutes; 16-year-old, 10 hours.

Vocational qualifications *None*

Inspection November 1995: 'An excellent school in which pupils are given the support they need to develop their individual talents and abilities. Standards of achievement are well above national and county averages. The headteacher provides visionary leadership and is well supported by managers of good quality.'; 'The quality of teaching is excellent. Expert teachers, many of whom have an infectious enthusiasm for their subject, provide lessons which are enjoyable experiences for the pupils; pupils and teachers work together in an atmosphere of pleasurable scholarship.'

Primary schools St Benedict's RC Primary, Midsomer Norton; St Joseph and St Teresa RC Primary, Wells; St John's RC Primary, Bath; St Mary's RC Primary, Bath; St Mary's RC Primary, Chippenham; St Patrick's RC Primary, Corsham.

WALDEGRAVE SCHOOL FOR GIRLS

Fifth Cross Road
Twickenham
Richmond-upon-Thames TW2 5LH
Tel (0181) 894 3244
Fax (0181) 893 3670
E-mail: wald@mail.rmplc.co.uk

- National ranking 297= (238=, 471=, 248=, 241=)
- GCSE 65% (69%)
- A-levels *Not applicable*
- Higher education *Not applicable*

- Girls' comprehensive
- Pupils 1,008
- Boys *Not applicable*
- Girls (11–16) 1,008
- Sixth form *Not applicable*
- Education authority *Richmond-upon-Thames*

Headteacher Heather Flint, 47, appointed in January 1992. Staff 57 (men 4, women 53).

Motto *None*

Background The only single-sex school among eight secondary schools in London borough of Richmond-upon-Thames. Formed in 1981 from amalgamation of Twickenham Girls' and Kneller Girls' on the 14.5-acre Kneller site; original building on site occupied by Thames Valley Grammar School. Entry increased to 200 places to cater for demand in 1995: up to 400 applications for September 1997. Girls also from neighbouring boroughs of Hounslow and Kingston-upon-Thames. Special educational needs policy includes the most able. Extra-curricular activities include orchestras, choirs, debating society, environment club, and a wide range of sporting activities. All girls in upper school undertake two weeks' work-experience. French and German taught to all girls in year 7. New wing of school has library resource centre, reprographics room, technology and science rooms. Parents' Association.

Streaming Pupils in sets for mathematics throughout; in years 8 and 9, setting for other subjects.

Approach to discipline 'We are convinced that

rewarding achievements is the best way to reinforce success and create a positive ethos in the school.' Merit system for work of high standard, improvement, hard work and helpfulness. Sanctions include detentions, daily report, and exclusion 'in extraordinary circumstances'. Parents kept informed.

Uniform Royal blue jumper with school logo, white blouse, black skirt/trousers. All pupils expected to wear full uniform.

Homework Average 11-year-old, seven hours a week; 14-year-old, 10 hours; 16-year-old, 10 hours.

Vocational qualifications *None*

Inspection May 1993: 'Standards of achievement are satisfactory or better in most areas of the curriculum. In some subjects they are consistently high and supported by good teaching. Standards are less satisfactory in a small minority of cases where the teaching makes insufficient demands on pupils. Examination results are very good across the curriculum.'; 'Waldegrave is a good, well-managed and justifiably popular school. It creates a secure environment for its pupils and at the same time encourages their independence of mind. The school's concern to develop pupils' spiritual and moral development is reflected in good relationships and standards of behaviour.'

Primary schools Stanley Junior School; Sheen Mount Primary; Trafalgar Primary; Chase Bridge Primary; Archdeacon Cambridge's CE Primary.

YSGOL-Y-PRESELI

Crymych
Pembrokeshire SA41 3QH
Tel (01239) 831406
Fax (01239) 831416

- National ranking 302 (–, –, –, 247 =)
- GCSE 64%
- A-levels 57% (A/B); 96% (A/E)
- Higher education 90%

- Mixed comprehensive
- Pupils 444
- Boys (11–18) 221
- Girls (11–18) 223
- Sixth form 68 (15%)
- Education authority *Pembrokeshire*

Headteacher Martin Lloyd, 46, appointed in April 1991. Staff 29 (men 12, women 17).

Motto Cofia ddysgu byw (Remember to learn to live a good life).

Background Established in 1958 in village of Crymych on the A478 Cardigan-to-Tenby road; has almost exclusively rural catchment area; officially designated bilingual comprehensive, with a number of subjects taught in Welsh to all pupils. Not over-subscribed. Strong sporting tradition, with many former pupils having played for their country at rugby or hockey. Musical strengths include school choir, which is proud of national recognition; prides itself on being a community school, with full-time warden employed by the local authority to oversee community education. 'Equal opportunity for all pupils, whatever their ability, sex or ethnic origin is very important.'

Alumni Brian Williams, Kevin Phillips and John Davies, Wales rugby players; Eirian James, opera singer.

Streaming *None*

Approach to discipline 'We believe that discipline is based upon self-discipline and ensuring that pupils themselves realise when they have done wrong and feel sorry for their misdeeds. Various sanctions are used for misdemeanours.'

Uniform Boys: black blazer with school badge, grey/white/light-blue shirt, black/dark-grey trousers. Girls: white blouse, maroon jumper with school badge, maroon skirt. Very strictly enforced.

Homework Average 11-year-old, 10 hours a week; 14-year-old, 12 hours; 16-year-old, 15 hours.

Vocational qualifications Diploma of Vocational Education; GNVQs.

CARDIFF HIGH SCHOOL

Llandennis Road
Cardiff CF2 6EG
Tel (01222) 757741
Fax (01222) 763001

- National ranking 303 (178, 245, 180, 192)
- GCSE 64% (80%)
- A-levels 53% (A/B); 95% (A/E)
- Higher education 94% (Oxford 5, Cambridge 4)

- Mixed comprehensive
- Pupils 1,227
- Boys (11–18) 662
- Girls (11–18) 565
- Sixth form 285 (23%)
- Education authority *Cardiff*

Headteacher Griff O. Roberts, 61, appointed in 1988. Staff 69 (men 29, women 40).

Motto Tua'r goleuni (Towards the light).

Background Set in attractive grounds two miles from Cardiff city centre in residential Cyncoed/Lakeside district. The school was established in 1970 following merger of two single-sex grammar schools and Ty Celyn secondary. Unified on single site in 1973: two halls, gymnasium, sports hall, nine science laboratories, recording studio, catering kitchen and restaurant, dance/drama studio, technology and information technology rooms. Sixth-form teaching concentrated in one part of school, with study area and seminar rooms. Grass hockey pitch, two rugby pitches, netball and tennis courts. Over-subscribed, with two applications per place; most unsuccessful applicants appeal. Prides itself on all-round curriculum strength.

Alumni Jeremy Bowen, BBC foreign correspondent; Craig Thomas, author; Ann Leach, actress; John Humphrys, presenter of BBC Radio Four's *Today* programme.

Streaming Pupils in sets for mathematics in year 8; in most subjects (if numbers allow) in year 9; all pupils normally in sets for years 10 and 11.

Approach to discipline Listed among school objectives: encourage self-discipline; create suitable structure for effective discipline; range of sanctions.

Uniform Girls: black/black and red-striped blazer; black A-line skirt/trousers, scarlet V-neck jumper, red blouse, black coat. Boys: black blazer, school tie, grey trousers, white shirt, black pullover, black coat. No uniform in sixth form; strict enforcement.

Homework Average 11-year-old, five hours a week; 14-year-old, seven hours 30 minutes; 16-year-old, 10 hours.

Vocational qualifications GNVQ.

Inspection February 1995: 'Knowledge is secure and investigative skills are well-developed. Literacy and numeracy skills range from good to very good. Information technology skills are generally satisfactory.'; 'The quality of learning is predominantly good. The majority of pupils show high levels of concentration, commitment and motivation. Overall, very good progress is made across the majority of subjects.'; 'In general, the school is an orderly community. Some areas of the school become congested, but pupils are patient and movement around the site is not a source of concern.'

Primary schools Lakeside Primary; Rhydypenau Primary; Roath Park Primary.

HUNTINGTON SCHOOL

Huntington Road
York
North Yorkshire YO3 9PX
Tel (01904) 752100
Fax (01904) 752101
E-mail: mail@huntington-ed.org.uk

- National ranking 304 (296, 427, 364, 235)
- GCSE 64% (63%)
- A-levels 49% (A/B); 97% (A/E)
- Higher education 75% (Oxford 1, Cambridge 1)

- Mixed comprehensive
- Pupils 1,483
- Boys (11–18) 753
- Girls (11–18) 730
- Sixth form 220 (15%)
- Education authority *York*

Headteacher Dr Keith Wragg, 55, appointed in September 1982. Staff 92 (men 42, women 50).

Motto *None*

Background Opened in 1966, Huntington School became a comprehensive seven years later. On the northern outskirts of York, it draws pupils from a wide area in and around the city; half of them from outside 'normal' catchment area. Over-subscribed, with 270 applications for 240 places in September 1997. A single-site school, with specialist accommodation in all subjects and particularly in technology and science. It has had a sixth form only since 1979. Duke of Edinburgh Award Scheme. Extensive links with schools in France, Germany, Denmark and Austria. Between

60 and 70 extra-curricular activities at lunchtime each week; more than 120 out-of-school visits, many residential, in past year.

Streaming Pupils in sets according to ability in different subjects from year 8.

Approach to discipline Well-established framework of discipline. 'Young people are expected and encouraged to follow the guidelines. They are also encouraged to develop self-discipline. Steps are taken to ensure that no individual is allowed to disrupt the work of others.'

Uniform Grey for years 7 to 9; navy for years 10 and 11.

Homework Average 11-year-old, seven hours a week; 14-year-old, 11 hours; 16-year-old, 15 hours.

Vocational qualifications City and Guilds Foundation; BTEC First and National; GNVQ Intermediate and Advanced.

Inspection December 1995: 'An exceptionally good school which provides an excellent education for its students. It provides a secure and happy environment. Academic standards are consistently amongst the highest in the country and are much higher than expectations based on objective measures of ability of the students on entry would indicate.'; 'The school enjoys exemplary leadership and fully deserves its very high reputation.'

Primary schools Huntington County Primary; Robert Wilkinson County Primary; Yearsley Grove Junior; Hempland Junior; Haxby Road County Primary.

FORTISMERE SCHOOL

Tetherdown
Muswell Hill
London N10 1NE
Tel (0181) 444 5124
Fax (0181) 444 7822

- National ranking 305 (–, 301, 290, 273)
- GCSE 64%
- A-levels 46% (A/B); 88% (A/E)
- Higher education 86% (Oxford 1, Cambridge 2)

- Mixed comprehensive
- Pupils 1,445
- Boys (11–18) 788

- Girls (11–18) 657
- Sixth form 340 (24%)
- Education authority *Haringey*

Headteacher Andrew M. Nixon, 54, appointed in March 1982. Staff 89 (men 36, women 53).

Motto *None*

Background Opened in 1983 as result of amalgamation of Alexandra Park School and Creighton School. Since 1986, the school has been on single-site Muswell Hill campus; sixth-formers in Tetherdown Centre and Strathlene House. Modern buildings with ample teaching accommodation; has own playing fields, all-weather sports area and heated swimming pool. Since 1989 the school has also provided the base for the secondary department of Blanch Nevile School for the hearing impaired. Over-subscribed, with 1.7 applications per place. Some 20 sports available at representative and school level; music includes orchestra, instrumental groups and choirs that perform in concerts and festivals. Drama and dance performances; regular workshops for science, mathematics and information technology; School Council and year committees help formulate school policy.

Streaming No streaming or banding by ability. Pupils are put into subject sets by ability in some subjects from year 10.

Approach to discipline 'Pupils are expected to work in a friendly and relaxed atmosphere for learning. Guidelines are kept to a common-sense minimum, but are effectively enforced. Great stress is laid upon the importance of self-discipline, consideration for others and care of the school environment.' Although emphasis is on cure rather than punishment, sanctions include detentions, extra work, 'daily report'. Threatening or violent behaviour results in exclusion. Code of behaviour displayed prominently around the school.

Uniform *None*

Homework Average 11-year-old, five hours a week; 14-year-old, seven hours 30 minutes; 16-year-old, 10 hours.

Vocational qualifications GNVQ Intermediate in all vocational areas through local consortium; GNVQ, Art and Design, Leisure and Tourism taught at Fortismere; some GNVQ studies in Business, Health and Social Care,

Leisure and Tourism on offer in years 10 and 11.

Inspection September 1996: 'The pupils at Fortismere School receive a good quality education. The standards achieved in all subjects are at least sound and good in the majority. The school has a positive ethos in which respect for the individual is encouraged and independence and self-discipline are developed.'; 'Attainment in English, science and mathematics, and in most other subjects, is in line with or above the national expectation. In art, attainment is well above average, whilst in information technology it is below the national expectation.'; 'Pupils with special educational needs and those who have English as a second language make good progress when they are set clearly-focused targets and receive appropriate support.'; 'Pupils speak confidently and articulately and have good listening skills. Standards in reading are mostly sound and often good. However, the progress of the lowest-attaining pupils in reading is unsatisfactory.'; 'The school works diligently to maintain good attendance.'; 'The school enjoys a good partnership with parents and there is an active Fortismere School Association, which is constructively engaged in educational, social and fund-raising activities.'; 'There is sufficient accommodation in the school. However, the quality of much of the accommodation is very poor and shows signs of lack of sufficient maintenance and refurbishment over a long period of time.'

Primary schools Coldfall Primary; Muswell Hill Junior; Rhodes Avenue Primary; St James CE Primary; Tetherdown Primary.

COLLINGWOOD COLLEGE

Kingston Road
Camberley
Surrey GU15 4AE
Tel (01276) 64048
Fax (01276) 676151
E-mail: collingwood@dial.pipex.com

- National ranking 306 (343, 303, 398 = , 256)
- GCSE 64% (61%)
- A-levels 44% (A/B); 92% (A/E)
- Higher education 58% (Oxford 1, Cambridge 3)

- Grant-maintained
- Mixed comprehensive
- Pupils 2,105
- Boys (12–18) 1,026
- Girls (12–18) 1,079
- Sixth form 373 (18%)
- Education authority *Surrey*

Headteacher Malcolm Jeremy Oddie, 46, appointed in January 1996. Staff 125 (men 50, women 75).

Motto *None*

Background Four substantial buildings on 34-acre wooded campus about a mile from Camberley and two miles from Bagshot. Sixth-form centre dates from late 19th century; others from 1963 to 1970. School formed in 1971 following amalgamation of Frimley and Camberley Grammar School with two secondary moderns; became grant-maintained in September 1991; became one of first 12 technology colleges in September 1994. New humanities building. Learning Resource Centre open after school every evening, with facilities for individual study. Intake reduced to 315 in 1994; not over-subscribed. Facilities include 'extremely good' laboratories and computer rooms. More than 400 pupils involved in Duke of Edinburgh Award Scheme; more than 200 learning musical instruments. National under-16 girls' and under-13 mixed badminton champions in 1995; under-19 girls' trampolining champions; swimming team ranked fourth in the country. National finalists in 1994 Young Enterprise competition. Inspectors commented on politeness of pupils in 1991 HMI report, which also noted that pupils of average and below-average ability were producing better-than-expected results.

Alumni Karen Kennedy, British women's gymnastics champion; Richard Neat, chef and joint owner of Pied à Terre restaurant in London.

Streaming Initially in forms according to friendship patterns; for academic subjects, pupils in sets according to ability in individual subject or group of subjects; sets within six months of entry; promotion more common than demotion. Special needs department offers extra support.

Approach to discipline Firm but fair. Anti-social behaviour, particularly bullying, severely dealt with; range of sanctions includes permanent exclusion (rarely).

Uniform Years 7 to 11: sweater with school logo, mid-grey trousers/skirt. Different colours differentiate lower and senior school pupils. Sweaters sold by School Association; 'smart' dress is requirement for sixth-formers.

Homework Average 11-year-old, 10 to 12 hours a week; 14-year-old, 15 to 18 hours; 16-year-old, 20+ hours.

Vocational qualifications GNVQ Intermediate and Advanced, Business, Health and Social Care, Art and Design, Science, Leisure and Tourism, Media: Communication and Production.

Inspection October 1996: 'Collingwood College provides a good education for its students. There is a strong commitment to enable students to do well and to raise attainment. A notable strength lies in the exceptional range of extra-curricular activities offered to students of all ages.'; 'Standards of literacy are good throughout the college. Reading is of a high standard. Students speak confidently and listen attentively.'; 'Students are generally well-motivated and keen to do well. They have a good attitude towards homework. Behaviour is mostly good, but there are instances of unsatisfactory behaviour, particularly in Key Stage 3. Attendance is good.'; 'Examples of good teaching occur in all subjects. It is consistently good in art, English and drama in the upper years.'; 'The recently-appointed principal provides very strong professional leadership and a clear sense of direction for the college.'

Primary schools Hammond Junior; Crawley Ridge Junior; Cordwalles Junior; Connaught Junior; Holy Trinity Junior; Ravenscote Junior.

ST GREGORY'S CATHOLIC COMPREHENSIVE SCHOOL

Reynolds Lane
Tunbridge Wells
Kent TN4 9XL
Tel (01892) 527444
Fax (01892) 546621
E-mail: stgregs@rmplc.co.uk
Internet: http://www.rmplc.co.uk/eduweb/
sites/stgregs

- National ranking 307 (364, 275, 294, 200)
- GCSE 64% (60%)
- A-levels 44% (A/B); 90% (A/E)
- Higher education 98%

- Grant-maintained
- Mixed comprehensive
- Pupils 952
- Boys (11–18) 543
- Girls (11–18) 409
- Sixth form 174 (18%)
- Education authority *Kent*

Headteacher Rosemary Olivier, 49, appointed in April 1994. Staff 66 (men 31, women 35).

Motto Gospel values at work.

Background Proudly comprehensive, St Gregory's, on the outskirts of Tunbridge Wells, takes pupils from a wide catchment area, from Otford in the north to Uckfield in the south, and Cranbrook in the east to Edenbridge in the west. Most come from Tunbridge Wells, Tonbridge, Sevenoaks and Crowborough. Although a Roman Catholic school, the governors do accept some children of parents from other Christian denominations in response to specific requests. Over-subscribed with 1.5 applications per place. Extensive grounds include seven tennis courts; neighbouring town sports centre; 300-seat school chapel; purpose-built technology building and suite of four computer rooms; sixth-form centre in 1997.

Streaming Year 7: mixed-ability classes of 25 or 26 pupils. Years 8 and 9: sets for mathematics; banding in broad ability bands, but mixed-ability for technology, science and art. Years 10 and 11: individual sets for subjects.

Approach to discipline High standard of courtesy, discipline, self-control expected at all times; based on mutual respect between student and teacher, high self-esteem. 'Forgiveness is identified as essential ingredient in the school discipline routine.' 'Excellent' communication with parents.

Uniform Girls: mid-grey worsted skirt, white blouse, navy V-neck pullover with school logo. Boys: grey trousers, white shirt, school tie, V-neck pullover with school logo. Sensitive implementation of uniform agreed with pupils, parents and governors.

Homework Average 11-year-old, five to 10 hours a week; 14-year-old, seven hours 30 minutes to 15 hours; 16-year-old, up to 15 hours.

Vocational qualifications GNVQ Foundation, Hospitality and Catering; GNVQ Advanced, Business.

Inspection September 1994: 'A very good school which provides an education of high quality.'; 'Pupils can work autonomously and independently when given the opportunity, but this is still an area for development as pupils are not always given chances to develop these skills.'; 'Teaching is skilful in all departments.'; 'The ethos of the school is caring but also rigorous and purposeful.'; 'Behaviour and relationships are excellent and there is a high level of order and courtesy.'

Primary schools St Augustine's RC Primary, Tunbridge Wells; St Margaret Clitherow RC Primary, Tonbridge; St Thomas' RC Primary, Sevenoaks; St Mary's RC Primary, Crowborough; St John's CE Primary, Tunbridge Wells; Southborough CE Primary.

THE JOSEPH ROWNTREE SCHOOL

Haxby Road
New Earswick
York
North Yorkshire YO3 4BZ
Tel (01904) 768107
Fax (01904) 750458

- National ranking 308 (285 = , 321, 268, –)
- GCSE 64% (64%)
- A-levels 41% (A/B); 96% (A/E)
- Higher education 83% (Oxford 1, Cambridge 1)

- Mixed comprehensive
- Pupils 1,168
- Boys (11–18) 602
- Girls (11–18) 566
- Sixth form 140 (12%)
- Education authority York

Headteacher Hugh Porter, 45, from September 1997. Staff 73 (men 30, women 43).

Motto Mente manuque (By brain and hand). *Also*: Strive and succeed.

Background Opened in 1942 as a result of initiative by Joseph Rowntree Village Trust, product of Quaker family's concern for its workforce. Situated in more than 15 acres on northern outskirts of York; buildings are mixture of styles, reflecting growth of population the school serves; well-supplied with specialist rooms for all subjects: science laboratories, language laboratory, information technology rooms, new library/resource centre with its own information technology facilities. Sports provision is 'excellent': large sports hall, gymnasium, multi-gym, on-site pitches; grounds have been professionally mapped for orienteering on site. Not oversubscribed. The school has its own study centre on North Yorkshire moors. Design technology department has record of success in local, regional and national competitions: 1993 Young Engineer for Britain. In girls' sport, netball is particularly strong with teams in three age-groups in 1995 English Schools' Netball Finals. Links with industry and commerce; 1992 Schools Curriculum Award; praised by name in 1995 national Ofsted report; won first prize in 1995 in science competition organised by Ministry of Agriculture, Fisheries and Food. 'The school's values and approaches at all levels are based upon a caring philosophy, the legacy of its foundation. It is not a school that relies on an over-rigid formal discipline, but instead succeeds as a consequence of the excellent relationships that teachers work hard to create and maintain.'

Alumni Norman Marlborough, shadow minister in Western Australian parliament; Steve Webster, former world sidecar champion; Andy Smith, British speedway champion; Stephen Tutill, York City FC captain.

Streaming Pupils are placed in bands and sets whenever the timetable permits.

Approach to discipline 'The school expects pupils to show self-discipline. Expectations are high and are founded upon excellent teacher–pupil relationships.' System of rewards; parents involved at early stage if work or behaviour causes concern; heads of school in contact with parents by letter when praise is due.

Uniform Navy skirt/trousers for girls, midgrey trousers for boys, white polo shirt with school insignia, navy sweatshirt with school name. Regulations enforced 'as strictly as possible'.

Homework Average 11-year-old, four to five hours a week; 14-year-old, seven hours 30 minutes; 16-year-old, seven hours 30 minutes to 11 hours 15 minutes.

Vocational qualifications GNVQ Intermediate, Health and Social Care, Science, Business Studies.

Inspection October 1993: 'A good school with a number of very positive features.'; 'Teaching quality is good and an appropriate variety of teaching methods is adopted. Pupils are well-motivated and they show a positive attitude to their learning. Behaviour and discipline are of a high standard.'; 'It is a well-ordered school and the financial management is sound.'

Primary schools Wiggington Primary; New Earswick Undenominational Primary; Oaken Grove Primary, Haxby; Headlands Primary, Haxby; Ralph Butterfield Primary, Haxby; Robert Wilkinson Primary, Strensall.

QUEEN ELIZABETH HIGH SCHOOL

**Whetstone Bridge Road
Hexham
Northumberland NE46 3JB
Tel (01434) 605211
Fax (01434) 601068**

- National ranking 309 (317, 304, 243, 286)
- GCSE 64% (62%)
- A-levels 40% (A/B); 87% (A/E)
- Higher education 73% (Oxford 1, Cambridge 3)

- Mixed comprehensive
- Pupils 1,400
- Boys (13–18) 687
- Girls (13–18) 713
- Sixth form 470 (34%)
- Education authority *Northumberland*

Headteacher Tony Webster, 48, appointed from September 1997. Staff 80 (men 37, women 43).

Motto Spes avorum durat (Hopes of ancestors endure).

Background Created in 1599 by Elizabethan charter (which is still in the school), a grammar school until 1976 when it was transformed into a community comprehensive; half the school in impressive Victorian building, half in 1964 building. In grounds originally set out in 1852, the school is on a hillside to the west of Hexham with views across the Tyne valley. Pupils from Hexham (population 10,000), Corbridge and neighbouring villages or hamlets within 25-mile radius. Over-subscribed, with 320 applications for 300 places. Competitive teams in main sports in all year groups; outstanding at rowing and successful at rugby. Youth theatre; orchestra, wind band, stage band, choir and madrigal group. Caters for adult and youth courses, with 1,400 on roll. Emphasis on extra-curricular activities.

Streaming Pupils in sets in mathematics and science in year 9; pupils set according to ability in almost all subjects in years 10 and 11.

Approach to discipline School prides itself on pupils' behaviour. Offences result in minor chores or detention; serious cases result in suspension (very rare).

Uniform Only in years 9 to 11. Boys: black pullover, black/grey trousers, white shirt, tie. Girls: dark-green pullover and skirt/trousers, no tie. Liberally enforced.

Homework Average 14-year-old, 10 hours a week; 16-year-old, 15 hours.

Vocational qualifications BTEC GNVQ Level 2, Business, Health and Social Care, Leisure and Tourism; BTEC GNVQ Level 3, Business; City and Guilds NVQ Levels 1 and 2, Food and Beverage Service, Food, Preparation and Cooking.

Inspection March 1996: 'Queen Elizabeth High School serves its community well and its reputation is justifiably high. It provides for its students an effective education with many outstanding features which results in high academic standards of achievement.'; 'In all subjects, standards are consistently high in the main school and in the sixth form.'; 'The wide range of activities in vocational subjects challenges students to work at a good level resulting in sound achievements.'; 'Opportunities for extra-curricular activities are excellent. These are significantly enhanced by the community and youth programmes. Teachers have a secure knowledge of their subject and the quality of teaching is one of the school's main strengths.'; 'The school's ethos is friendly and courteous, with a high regard for mutual respect.'

Primary schools Hexham Middle; St Joseph's RC Middle; Corbridge Middle.

EGGLESCLIFFE SCHOOL

Urlay Nook Road
Eaglescliffe
Stockton-on-Tees TS16 0LA
Tel (01642) 783686
Fax (01642) 785566

- National ranking 310 (374, 221, 475, –)
- GCSE 64% (59%)
- A-levels 38% (A/B); 94% (A/E)
- Higher education 90%

- Mixed comprehensive
- Pupils 1,320
- Boys (11–18) 654
- Girls (11–18) 666
- Sixth form 247 (19%)
- Education authority *Stockton-on-Tees*

Headteacher Angela Darnell, 44, appointed in September 1994. Staff 79 (men 39, women 40).

Motto Forward together.

Background Comprehensive school since 1969 in rural setting near attractive town of Yarm on River Tees; buildings added in early 1970s to accommodate growing school; extensive facilities for technology, information technology, science, art, sports; electron microscope, recording studio, library. Purpose-built house accommodation enhances strong pastoral system. Sixth-form has its own block. Over-subscribed; with 109 applications for 65 places. Winners of 1992 Schools Curriculum Award; school orchestra won National Festival of Music for Youth finals at Royal Festival Hall in 1993, 1994, 1995 and 1996, played in Schools Proms at Royal Albert Hall concert. Chamber orchestra, brass band, flute choir, brass quartet, choir: all in 1994 and 1995 national festival finals. Extensive extra-curricular programme: Duke of Edinburgh Award Scheme; many educational visits; languages, mathematics, sciences and pastoral system also notable. GNVQ Business courses 'thriving'; success in Young Enterprise scheme; northern regional finalists in 1994 and 1995. 'Friendly, busy school enjoying good local reputations in its community. High standards of achievement and behaviour aimed for. Mutual respect between pupils and adults in school community produces very good working atmosphere. Creative, dynamic and posi-

tive.' Identified for praise in 1997 annual Ofsted report.

Streaming Mixed-ability in years 7 to 9, except in mathematics and languages from year 7 and science from year 9.

Approach to discipline 'Clearly-defined code of conduct for pupils and behaviour policy implemented. Close home contacts involve parents in merit and sanctions system.'

Uniform Navy V-neck jumper, black trousers for boys or navy skirt/trousers, white shirt/blouse, school tie, black shoes. Strictly enforced.

Homework Average 11-year-old, six hours a week; 14-year-old, 10 hours; 16-year-old, 14 hours.

Vocational qualifications GNVQ Intermediate and Advanced, Business.

Inspection January 1996: 'Egglescliffe School provides a very good education for its pupils. In many areas of the curriculum, there is work of real excellence. The school has the enthusiastic support of parents and has forged strong links with the various communities that it serves.'; 'The curriculum emphasises understanding as well as knowledge. Pupils are encouraged to debate issues and ideas, and they are able to think for themselves.'; 'Relationships are good. In many classrooms, enthusiasm and good humour are the norm.'

Primary schools Egglescliffe CE Primary; The Links Primary; Durham Lane Primary; Junction Farm Primary.

SHARNBROOK UPPER SCHOOL AND COMMUNITY COLLEGE

Odell Road
Sharnbrook
Bedford
Bedfordshire MK44 1JX
Tel (01234) 782211
Fax (01234) 782431
E-mail: sharnbrookupper@campus.bt.com

- National ranking 311 (–, 325, 271, –)
- GCSE 64%
- A-levels 37% (A/B); 92% (A/E)
- Higher education 85% (Oxford 2, Cambridge 4)

- Grant-maintained
- Mixed comprehensive

- Pupils 1,417
- Boys (13–18) 686
- Girls (13–18) 731
- Sixth form 486 (34%)
- Education authority *Bedfordshire*

Headteacher David S. Jackson, 48, appointed in 1987. Staff 97 (men 43, women 54).

Motto Ad serviendum (To serve).

Background Semi-rural school opened in 1975 on 30-acre site overlooking Ouse Valley in north Bedfordshire; final phase of original building programme completed in 1981; designated a community college in 1984, it has up to 3,000 adult students a year enrolling for daytime, evening and weekend classes. Became grant-maintained in January 1993; new mathematics, languages and art block in November 1995; also remodelling and expansion for expressive arts, science, technology and English areas. Over-subscribed, with 1.1 applications per place. School has own farm unit and 2.5-acre copse. More than one in three year 10 pupils in Duke of Edinburgh Award Scheme; all pupils in Youth Award Scheme. Expressive Arts is a core subject for years 9 to 11, resulting in significant number of county and national arts performers. International sports representatives.

Streaming Pupils put in sets for mathematics, modern languages and science; broader ability groups for English and humanities.

Approach to discipline 'We aim for discipline to be friendly but firm, with the emphasis upon respect for others and upon taking responsibility for oneself. It is the responsibility of all staff and students to maintain a caring, industrious working environment. The normal range of sanctions are used and the partnership with parents is a key factor in remedying any problems that do arise.'

Uniform Bottle-green pullover with school insignia, golden-yellow shirt, black/dark-grey trousers or skirt; dark-grey school tie with golden-yellow and green, with school crest. High expectations for appearance.

Homework Average 14-year-old, up to seven hours 30 minutes a week; 16-year-old, up to 10 hours.

Vocational qualifications GNVQ Intermediate, Health and Social Care, Leisure and Tourism, Business, Science; BTEC First Diploma, Land-based Industries; GNVQ Advanced,

Health and Social Care, Business, Media; modular programme of word-processing, keyboarding, office skills, business studies in business technology.

Inspection April 1996: 'An outstandingly good school. It serves its community well and fulfils its aim to provide quality education for all its pupils. The head provides excellent leadership and has attracted staff of high calibre. The quality of teaching is exceptional and pupils of all abilities attain well.'; 'People are respected for what they have to contribute and this sets the tone for an orderly but lively community. The maturity of pupils and their willingness to take responsibility is a strength.'; 'The school is very well led by a headteacher who enjoys the wholehearted support of his staff, governors and parents.'

BISHOP WALSH SCHOOL

Wylde Green Road
Sutton Coldfield
Birmingham
West Midlands B76 1QT
Tel (0121) 351 3215
Fax (0121) 313 3142

- National ranking 312 (–, –, 316, –)
- GCSE 64%
- A-levels 34% (A/B); 92% (A/E)
- Higher education 90%

- Mixed comprehensive
- Pupils 914
- Boys (11–18) 463
- Girls (11–18) 451
- Sixth form 161 (18%)
- Education authority *Birmingham*

Headteacher John Upton, 59, appointed in September 1985. Staff 57 (men 28, women 29).

Motto Caring to learn; learning to care.

Background Founded in 1966, serving northernmost suburb of Birmingham; set in middle of fields. Facilities include seven science laboratories, two computer rooms, extensive playing fields, two specialist music rooms, pottery room, new library with two professional librarians and computer facilities for pupils. Over-subscribed, with two applications for each place. Total of 160 pupils receive instrumental lessons from six visiting music teachers; performing arts a feature, including A-level subject; Royal Shakespeare company actors have visited the school; school orchestra on video with ELO. Hockey is major sport for boys and girls; under-18 netball team has been West Midlands champions for three years. 'We hope to nurture Christian practice and belief whilst encouraging respect for all. We celebrate achievement in all spheres: social, sporting, religious and academic.'

Alumni Jane Sixsmith, Great Britain hockey player; David Black, Olympic athlete; Richard Donnelly, Professor of Medicine, Nottingham University.

Streaming Special needs group in years 7 and 8; setting in three ability bands; separate setting for arts subjects, science and mathematics, modern languages.

Approach to discipline Courtesy code: 'Pupils are expected to behave well at all times, being polite to staff and friendly to each other. Although sanctions exist, we put the stress on positive behaviour and have a merit system and prizes.'

Uniform Boys: navy blazer with badge, grey trousers, white shirt, school tie, black shoes. Girls: navy blazer with badge, Cambridge-blue jumper and blouse, navy skirt, black shoes. Sixth-formers wear 'business-like dress, including tie for boys'. No exceptions made.

Homework Average 11-year-old, seven hours 30 minutes a week; 14-year-old, 10 hours; 16-year-old, 12 hours.

Vocational qualifications GNVQ, Leisure and Tourism, Finance; RSA, Typing, Keyboarding Skills.

Primary schools St Joseph's RC Primary; Holy Cross RC Primary; St Nicholas RC Primary; Abbey RC Primary; St Peter and St Paul RC Primary.

ST PETER'S CATHOLIC SCHOOL

Whitefields Road
Solihull
West Midlands B91 3NZ
Tel (0121) 705 3988
Fax (0121) 705 9803

- National ranking 313 (411 =, 293 =)
- GCSE 64% (57%)
- A-levels 34% (A/B); 90% (A/E)
- Higher education 76%

- Mixed comprehensive
- Pupils 1,087
- Boys (11–18) 544
- Girls (11–18) 543
- Sixth form 176 (16%)
- Education authority *Solihull*

Headteacher Henry Keith Mercer, appointed in September 1973. Staff 64 (men 28, women 36).

Motto Fides petra nostra (Faith is our foundation).

Background Opened in 1974 as an all-ability 11–16 school with 650 pupils following the merger of a small secondary modern and an independent convent school. Original buildings set in parkland date from 1965; substantial extensions added in 1975, 1978 and 1988, as the school expanded to 900 pupils. Building programme costing £1.5m completed in September 1994: self-contained sixth-form centre, sixth-form library, sports hall. The school raised £100,000 towards the cost of the sports hall. The first sixth-form intake was in September 1994; grew to 170 pupils in two years. Regularly oversubscribed, with 250+ applications for 185 places. Good accommodation: eight science laboratories, language laboratories, 36 486-SX networked computers, sixth-form and main school libraries, drama room, art and craft facilities. Playing fields surround the school; sports hall plus gymnasium. Four languages offered: French, German, Spanish and Italian. 'English and mathematics obtain excellent results at GCSE and are popular choices at A-level.' Education is 'firmly rooted in the Catholic tradition and attempts to relate the Gospel message to everyday work and life. The purpose of the school is the Christian education of the children, not simply a growth in their own faith, but an increasing awareness of the world as a mature Christian.' Flourishing extra-curricular sporting programme; regular entrant in local competitive events; five pupils are national representatives in a variety of sports; boys' under-13 badminton team ranked second in England.

Streaming Used on entry in year 7; setting in all major areas from year 8. Headteacher does not support mixed-ability teaching.

Approach to discipline School divided into upper school (years 10 and 11) and lower school (years 7 to 9) for pastoral purposes.

'Heads of school, assisted by year and form tutors, work closely with parents to develop a firm but fair disciplinary policy. The aim is the gradual growth of individuals to self-discipline and responsible behaviour. The governors are actively involved in the overall process.'

Uniform Drawn up after consultation with Parents' Association. Boys: black blazer with school badge, grey trousers, grey V-neck pullover, white/grey shirt, school tie, grey/black socks, grey or blue coat/anorak, black shoes (no boots or trainers). Girls: black blazer with school badge, grey A-line/pleated skirt, grey V-neck pullover/cardigan, white/grey blouse, school tie, plain white/grey/black ankle socks (heavy white/grey/black tights in winter), black low-heeled shoes. No uniform for sixth-formers.

Homework Average 11-year-old, seven hours 30 minutes a week; 14-year-old, 10 hours; 16-year-old, 12 to 15 hours.

Vocational qualifications GNVQ Intermediate and Advanced; Business.

Inspection December 1996: 'A well-led school with high standards of academic attainment and behaviour. Its aims are successfully achieved within a Christian community.'; 'Information technology skills are not widely used across the curriculum. Pupils across the ability range make good progress. The behaviour of pupils, their attitudes to work, their attendance and their relationships with others promote high standards of work.'; 'Teaching is good, despite some being affected by timetable and accommodation problems.'; 'The headteacher, senior staff and governors give a very clear educational direction to the school. Aims and values are being realised in all aspects of school life.'

Primary schools Our Lady of the Wayside RC Primary; Our Lady of Compassion RC Primary; St George and St Teresa RC Primary; St Andrew's RC Primary; St Augustine's RC Primary.

LORD WILLIAMS'S SCHOOL

Oxford Road
Thame
Oxfordshire OX9 2AQ
Tel (01844) 213681
Fax (01844) 261382
E-mail: lordwill@rmplc.co.uk

- National ranking 314 (258, 225)
- GCSE 64% (66%)
- A-levels 34% (A/B); 89% (A/E)
- Higher education 70% (Oxford 1, Cambridge 3)

- Mixed comprehensive
- Pupils 1,954
- Boys (11–18) 955
- Girls (11–18) 999
- Sixth form 384 (20%)
- Education authority *Oxfordshire*

Headteacher Patricia O'Shea, 48, appointed in April 1997. Staff 102 (men 42, women 60).

Motto A tous venants (To all-comers); Sic itur ad astra (Thus the way to the stars).

Background Founded 1559; modern comprehensive opened in 1971. Two large sites: one for 11–14, another for 14–18; extensive playing fields. Newly-completed £3m development of lower school 'provides some of the best and most up-to-date facilities in Oxfordshire'. Two sports halls. Business support for sixth form and Business Studies facilities in Foundation Building. 'Genuine community comprehensive', with most pupils from local area. Consistently over-subscribed, with 1.1 applications per place. Teams at all levels in all major sports. 'Outstanding' extra-curricular opportunities in music, drama and dance. Outdoor education experience for all. Strong links with business. Strong learning support. 'Equal concern for all pupils, whatever their needs and aptitudes.'

Alumni John Hampden.

Streaming 'Initially only in mathematics, but sets for higher-attaining pupils gradually introduced in other subjects as they move up the school.'

Approach to discipline Clear expectations communicated to all pupils. Orderly behaviour and consideration of others 'required and obtained'. Positive reinforcement of good behaviour. 'Main sanction is detention, but not needed for most pupils.'

Uniform White shirt, black trousers/skirt/culottes, school tie (optional for middle-school pupils), black jumper or school sweatshirt, black/white socks or tights, plain black shoes. 'There is no uniform for sixth-form students, but they should wear appropriate clothes.'

Homework Average 11-year-old, four hours a week; 14-year-old, six hours; 16-year-old, 12 + hours.

Vocational qualifications GNVQ Foundation, Intermediate and Advanced.

Inspection January 1993: 'A good school with a friendly, hard-working and civilised atmosphere. Most of its pupils achieve consistently well in relation to their ages and abilities.'; 'The school provides a well-planned, broad and largely balanced curriculum, enriched by an impressive array of extra-curricular activities, which contribute much to the cultural and social development of the pupils.'; 'The good qualities of the school are due in no small measure to the presence of a well-qualified and dedicated teaching staff, well-supported by capable and committed support staff, and led with intelligence, efficiency and enterprise.'; 'Standards and quality in humanities and technology in Key Stage 3 are in some respects disappointing.' *School reports that this latest finding is now out of date following enhancements introduced with new building.* December 1996: 'A good school with some very good features. Its strengths lie in the support and guidance of pupils, very good GCSE performance, consistently good quality of teaching, well-established and effective links with parents, the community and local industry, and the provision for the incorporation of pupils with special educational needs into the life of the school.'; 'Pupils' attitudes and behaviour are good. They are keen to learn and participate well in lessons. Only on rare occasions is their response to work less than satisfactory. They work well together and are sensitive to the needs of others. Attendance is good.'

Primary schools Barley Hill Primary; John Hampden Primary; St Joseph's RC Primary; St Andrew's CE Primary, Chinnor; Mill Lane Primary, Chinnor; Long Crendon Primary; Brill Primary.

HEART OF ENGLAND SCHOOL

Gipsy Lane
Balsall Common
Coventry CV7 7FW
Tel (01676) 535222
Fax (01676) 534282
E-mail: heartofenglandsch@campus.bt.com

- National ranking 315 (236, 374, 431, 313)
- GCSE 64% (69%)
- A-levels 27% (A/B); 81% (A/E)
- Higher education 62%

- Mixed comprehensive
- Pupils 1,251
- Boys (11–18) 629
- Girls (11–18) 622
- Sixth form 199 (16%)
- Education authority Solihull

Headteacher Dr David Snoswell, 52, appointed in April 1990. Staff 82 (men 33, women 49).

Motto Non sine deo (Not without God).

Background Opened in 1957 in what was then Warwickshire; became part of Solihull in 1970s, when further buildings added; in pleasant, large commuter village between Solihull and Coventry, with most pupils coming from surrounding villages and fringes of Birmingham and Coventry. Buildings refurbished in last 12 months; indoor and outdoor recreation and sports facilities continuously used by school and community. Recent additions include third computer information technology room, fitness room, sixth-form flexible learning centre; also geography and technology rooms. Over-subscribed, with 345 applications for 210 places. District, regional and national sporting success: cross-country, athletics, swimming, basketball and soccer. Vocational courses taken by all pupils in years 10 and 11; accredited courses based at school and Solihull College of Technology.

Streaming Pupils put in sets in mathematics and French in year 7; broad banding used in history, geography and science.

Approach to discipline 'Our approach to discipline is to promote respect for oneself and each other, both the person and their property. A partnership with parents, pupils and staff is pursued to ensure high standards of communication, relationship and achievement. We endeavour to maintain discipline that is both fair and firm.'

Uniform Boys: black blazer with badge, grey trousers, white shirt, red-and-black striped school tie, black socks, black shoes. Girls: black blazer with badge, grey skirt, grey-and-white/red-and-white striped blouse, black/white/grey socks or tights, black shoes. 'Governors, staff, parents and pupils lay great emphasis on all aspects of school uniform.'

Homework Average 11-year-old, nine hours a week; 14-year-old, 12 hours; 16-year-old, 12 hours.

Vocational qualifications NVQ Levels 1 and 2, Administration; RSA, Initial Awards, Information Technology (Levels 1 to 3); Pitman, Secretarial Skills, Typing, Shorthand; GNVQ Intermediate, Business, Leisure and Tourism; GNVQ Advanced, Business, Health and Social Care.

Inspection November 1994: 'This is a good school with a strong and positive ethos. It provides an effective education of high quality for pupils and gives good value for money.'; 'The quality of teaching and learning is sound or good in almost all lessons. Expectations are high. Teachers are well-qualified and experienced, with a good command of their subjects.'; 'There is an impressive programme of extra-curricular activities. Pupils have excellent attitudes to learning and are articulate, literate and numerate.'; 'Accommodation is well-maintained, but cramped in some departments.'; 'Behaviour and attendance are excellent.'

Primary schools Balsall Common Primary; Meriden CE Primary; Berkswell CE Primary; George Fentham Primary; Park Hill Primary.

ST MARK'S CATHOLIC SCHOOL

106 Bath Road
Hounslow
Middlesex TW3 3EJ
Tel (0181) 577 3600
Fax (0181) 577 0559

- National ranking 316 (–, –, 430, –)
- GCSE 64%
- A-levels 26% (A/B); 88% (A/E)
- Higher education 73% (Oxford 2)

- Mixed comprehensive
- Pupils 1,148
- Boys (11–18) 600
- Girls (11–18) 548
- Sixth form 231 (20%)
- Education authority *Hounslow*

Headteacher David John Sheath, 52, appointed in December 1986. Staff 64 (men 26, women 38).

Motto Veritas (Truth).

Background Successor school to Archbishop Myers School, which opened in 1960 on same compact site west of Hounslow town centre, before changing name in 1973 when it became comprehensive. Has expanded significantly in recent years; modern facilities enhanced since 1993 by £2m 10-laboratory science centre, new learning resource centre and chapel; also specially-designed sixth-form area; GNVQ centre opened in September 1994; GNVQ courses have led to 50% increase in sixth-form numbers. Over-subscribed, with average of 1.8 applications per place. Curriculum enrichment classes after school for most able pupils. Duke of Edinburgh Award Scheme. Highly-acclaimed performing arts faculty, including computer/keyboard laboratory and theatre workshop. Sports reputation: soccer, netball, cross-country, athletics and basketball. 'Our Christian beliefs and values are very central to the life and heart of the school.'

Alumni Elvis Costello, rock musician.

Streaming 'Where departments find it necessary for effective subject delivery, students are put into different ability sets (mathematics and modern languages, for example). The main thrust of curriculum delivery, though, is mixed-ability.'

Approach to discipline 'Discipline can be truly seen within the context of the totally caring relationship between teacher and student. Rules exist as guidelines to sensible behaviour.' Sanctions are 'varied and flexible'. Only one permanent exclusion in past 10 years.

Uniform Navy blazer with badge, light-blue shirt, school tie, navy pullover, dark-grey trousers or navy skirt. 'No variations or fashionable changes are allowed. Uniform policy is strictly enforced, even down to the colour of shoelaces.'

Homework Average 11-year-old, at least eight hours a week; 14-year-old, at least 12 hours; 16-year-old, at least 14 hours.

Vocational qualifications BTEC Intermediate, Engineering; BTEC Advanced, Business and Finance; GNVQ Intermediate, Business and Finance, Leisure and Tourism, Health and Social Care.

Inspection November 1994: 'A successful Catholic school in which pupils achieve good academic standards.'; 'The quality of education provided by the school, with very few exceptions, is extremely high. Pupils make a considerable contribution to this feature, by their commitment to hard work and their varied contributions to all aspects of school life.'; 'The school offers a caring and purposeful environment for learning.'

Primary schools St Michael's and St Martin's RC Primary; Rosary RC Junior; Botwell RC Primary, Hayes; St Edmund's RC Primary, Whitton; St James RC Primary, Twickenham.

NOADSWOOD SCHOOL

North Road
Dibden Purlieu
Southampton
Hampshire SO45 4ZF
Tel (01703) 840025
Fax (01703) 843532
E-mail: noadswood@interalpha.co.uk
Internet: http://www.rmplc.co.uk/eduweb/sites/noads

- National ranking 317= (191=, 488=, 355=, 275=)
- GCSE 64% (75%)
- A-levels *Not applicable*
- Higher education *Not applicable*

- Mixed comprehensive
- Pupils 905
- Boys (11–16) 434
- Girls (11–16) 471
- Sixth form *Not applicable*
- Education authority *Hampshire*

Headteacher John Frederick Samuels, 47, appointed in September 1988. Staff 48 (men 21, women 27).

Motto *None*

Background Sited on 15-acre site on edge of New Forest; in its 35 years, it has had only four headteachers. Three main teaching blocks and large sports hall; new music block, library and gymnasium. An average of 1.3 applications per place; eight in 10 school-leavers (80%) continue their education. Pupils have won two of the six scholarships to Atlantic College that Hampshire has awarded in the past three years. Winner of 1992 Schools Curriculum Award. County representatives in sports; music and drama listed among strengths: workshops with Bournemouth Symphony Orchestra; choir

and orchestra toured Belgium and Germany in 1992. 'Traditional but not old-fashioned school.' Extra-curricular activities include sailing, engineering, enterprise groups and drama.

Streaming Pupils in sets for all subjects, according to ability in each subject.

Approach to discipline Pupils expected to treat others with respect and courtesy: 'No pupil has the right to disrupt the education of others.' Merit awards for achievement and effort; pupils encouraged to take on responsibility as prefects, library monitors or members of school council.

Uniform Black blazer, black trousers/skirt, white shirt/blouse, tie, black/brown shoes. Rigidly enforced.

Homework Average 11-year-old, five hours a week; 14-year-old, seven hours; 16-year-old, 10 hours.

Vocational qualifications *None*

Inspection May 1995: 'A very good learning environment in which pupils have access to a wide range of subjects and extra-curricular activities. The school provides a good education for its pupils and is rightly well-regarded in the local community. Some outstanding work was seen in modern languages. The school is very well led and efficiently managed.'; 'There is some under-achievement at Key Stage 3 in mathematics, science and religious education.'; 'Pupils make good progress in their first three years, sometimes starting from a low base line. Motivation and concentration are very good, with pupils showing an eagerness to learn and enthusiasm for their work. Behaviour is good and pupils are able to work productively and well together. In the few lessons where learning is less effective, pupils are over-dependent on the teacher and a little passive.'; 'The site and buildings are exceptionally well-maintained.'

Primary schools Holbury Junior; Hythe Junior; Langdown Junior; Orchard Junior; Wildground Junior.

TANBRIDGE HOUSE SCHOOL

Farthings Hill
Guildford Road
Horsham
West Sussex RH12 1SR

Tel **(01403) 263628**
Fax **(01403) 211830**

- National ranking 317= (446=, 488=, 455=, 295=)
- GCSE 64% (54%)
- A-levels *Not applicable*
- Higher education *Not applicable*

- Mixed comprehensive
- Pupils 1,200
- Boys (11–16) 760
- Girls (11–16) 440
- Sixth form *Not applicable*
- Education authority *West Sussex*

Headteacher Dr Peter Thomas, 44, appointed in September 1995. Staff 68 (men 29, women 39).

Motto Quality and equality.

Background Created in 1976, developing from the former Horsham High School for Girls. The school takes its name from a large Victorian house that Thomas Oliver, a wealthy railway contractor, built for his wife and family in 1887. School moved in 1994 to completely new buildings, specially designed to meet needs of national curriculum, on site to the west of Horsham. Campus designed as village community around a central square: science and technology centres, interlinked suites of classrooms, drama studio, music school, outdoor heated swimming pool, sports hall with spectator accommodation. The school has been oversubscribed with 70 applications more than its admission number. Notable music, drama and dance. Basketball and cross-country teams have won county championships. 'Flourishing' Duke of Edinburgh Award Scheme.

Streaming Pupils grouped into two ability bands in year 7 for all subjects except mathematics, which is in sets; setting increases as pupils get older.

Approach to discipline 'The school has a code of conduct setting out clear expectations for pupils. When a student's conduct falls short of expectations, action is taken, ranging from a brief reprimand to a helpful task, through to detention or a letter to parents.' Serious breaches may lead to exclusion.

Uniform Girls: grey skirt, school blouse with navy-and-white stripes, navy V-neck jumper with gold logo, natural/navy tights or white/navy socks. Boys: grey trousers, school striped shirt, navy V-neck pullover with logo, school tie.

Homework Average 11-year-old, five hours a week; 14-year-old, seven hours 30 minutes; 16-year-old, 10 hours.

Vocational qualifications *None*

Primary schools Southwater Primary; Greenway Primary; Arunside Primary; Shelley Primary; Warnham CE Primary.

WARDLE HIGH SCHOOL

Birch Road
Wardle
Rochdale
Lancashire OL12 9RD
Tel **(01706) 373911**
Fax **(01706) 377980**

- National ranking 317=
- GCSE 64%
- A-levels *Not yet applicable*
- Higher education *Not yet applicable*

- Grant-maintained
- Mixed comprehensive
- Pupils 1,219
- Boys 583
- Girls 636
- Sixth form *Not yet applicable*
- Education authority *Rochdale*

Headteacher Christopher John Giblin, 49, appointed in April 1997. Staff 77 (men 33, women 44).

Motto Excellence for all.

Background Opened in 1977 in rural surroundings with a first year of 110 pupils; attracts pupils from throughout Rochdale; pupils include 38 physically disabled and two visually-impaired children. Over-subscribed, with two applications per place. Avowedly non-political governing body; same chairman of governors for 20 years. Insists it became grant-maintained for greater independence rather than financial gain. Total of 260 clubs meet each week; teams for all main sports; members of Rochdale schools' soccer team are pupils. Music 'an outstanding feature': performers at National Festival of Music for Youth nine times with brass and woodwind bands; also four School Proms performances and royal command performance in front of Princess Margaret.

National Junior Brass Band champions four times. Sixth form opened in September 1996.

Streaming Pupils put in sets from year 8 according to ability in separate subjects.

Approach to discipline Pupils entitled to strive for excellence in caring and stimulating environment. 'No form of bullying is tolerated. Governors, staff and parents work in partnership to ensure each individual takes responsibility for actions and for quality of life of others.'

Uniform Bottle-green jersey/cardigan, charcoal-grey or dark-grey trousers/skirt, white shirt, red/green tie.

Homework Average 11-year-old, at least five hours a week; 14-year-old, at least six hours; 16-year-old, at least 10 hours.

Vocational qualifications NVQS.

Inspection Autumn 1993.

Primary schools St John's CE Primary, Smallbridge; St James CE Primary, Wardle; St Andrew's CE Primary, Dearnley; Smithy Bridge County Primary; Littleborough Primary; Stansfield Hall CE/Free Church Primary.

JOHN HENRY NEWMAN SCHOOL

Hitchin Road
Stevenage
Hertfordshire SG1 4AE
Tel (01438) 314643
Fax (01438) 747882
E-mail: johnhenr@mail.rmplc.co.uk

- National ranking 320 (–)
- GCSE 54%
- A-levels 29% (A/B); 78% (A/E)
- Higher education 58% (Cambridge 2)

- Grant-maintained
- Mixed comprehensive
- Pupils 935
- Boys (11–18) 465
- Girls (11–18) 470
- Sixth form 165 (18%)
- Education authority *Hertfordshire*

Headteacher Michael Kelly, 41, appointed in September 1993. Staff 75 (men 32, women 43).

Motto Cor ad cor loquitur (Heart speaks to heart).

Background Established in September 1987 upon amalgamation of St Michael's (Boys) and St Angela's (Girls) Schools; situated on site of former St Angela's School in buildings dating from mid-1960s. Set in pleasant surroundings on edge of Stevenage, with easy road access (A1 motorway) and public transport, serving Stevenage, north Hertfordshire and east Bedfordshire: modern purpose-built science/technology block (1987) and dual-use sports facilities, with sports hall and all-weather pitch (1988); refurbished drama studio (1995) and art/home economics facilities (1996). 'Excellent' teaching facilities; four specialist computer rooms; class, group and individual music teaching and practice rooms, with extensive instrumental tuition; 'strong and vibrant' sporting, music and cultural traditions. All baptised and communicant Roman Catholic applicants interviewed with parents; remaining places heavily over-subscribed and allocated by the governors, after interview, according to published admissions policy. Ethos described by school as 'caring, Catholic and comprehensive'; emphasis placed on 'a whole education' where all may strive to attain individual excellence within the context of Catholic moral and religious teachings. 'High standards of achievement, conduct, dress and behaviour are expected of all.'

Streaming Pupils are setted by ability in all subjects of the National Curriculum at the start of year 7.

Approach to discipline 'The school seeks to provide an orderly and supportive environment where sound learning may take place and where all may develop their several talents to the full. Indiscipline, where it occurs, is fairly and firmly handled by form tutor, year-head and, in the most serious cases, by the headteacher.'

Uniform French-navy blazer, white blouse/shirt, school tie for boys, grey trousers or Holyrood Tartan kilt for girls, black shoes. Sixth-formers expected to dress 'as young professionals'.

Homework Average 11-year-old, 10 hours a week; 14-year-old, 12 hours 30 minutes; 16-year-old, 15 hours. 'Homework is set and checked on a regular basis.'

Vocational qualifications GNVQ Advanced, Business, Art and Design, Science.

Primary schools St Vincent de Paul RC Primary; St Margaret Clitherow RC Primary; Our Lady's RC Primary; St Thomas More RC Primary; St John's RC Primary; St Mary's RC Primary; Holy Family RC Primary.

CHICHESTER HIGH SCHOOL FOR GIRLS

Stockbridge Road
Chichester
West Sussex PO19 2EB
Tel (01243) 787014
Fax (01243) 786543
E-mail: chichester_girls@dialnet.co.uk

- National ranking 321 (298, 388)
- GCSE 63% (63%)
- A-levels 52% (A/B); 96% (A/E)
- Higher education 90% (Oxford 1, Cambridge 2)

- Girls' comprehensive
- Pupils 1,455
- Boys *Not applicable*
- Girls (11–18) 1,455
- Sixth form 200 (14%)
- Education authority *West Sussex*

Headteacher Llyn Parkin, appointed in September 1980. Staff 83 (men 30, women 53).

Motto *None*

Background In central position next to bus and train stations in the county town of West Sussex. Formed in 1972 following the amalgamation of the Girls' High School and the Lancastrian Secondary School; High School building dates from the turn of the century and currently houses the Upper School. Lower School shares the Kingsham Campus, including all-weather Astroturf pitch, with the High School for Boys. The Lancastrian Building opened in 1958 on the Kingsham site. New premises for humanities (1989) and music (1993). Plans to locate the whole school on the single site. Oversubscribed, with 1.5 applications per place. Well-placed to foster strong links with Chichester Cathedral and Festival Theatre. Strong competitive sport with representation at national and local level. Traditional strength in modern languages, English and humanities balanced by 'excellence in mathematics, science and technology'. Open access to sixth-form courses at the boys' school. Links with industry and commerce. School boasts 'high academic standards, good discipline and courtesy in an atmosphere of care for each girl's individual needs'.

Alumni Ruth Tomalin, author; Jane Chambers, member of Dr Christiaan Barnard's first heart-transplant team; Kate Mosse, author and television presenter; Amanda Denise Ursell, television food presenter.

Streaming Pupils divided on entry into two parallel ability bands and setting by ability begins from the start of year 7. Cognitive ability tests used to ensure pupils achieve their potential in all subjects.

Approach to discipline 'The policies of the school are based on the acceptance of the fact that thoughtful behaviour, determination to fulfil one's potential, courtesy and good manners are the norm for every pupil.' Sanctions include detention.

Uniform Navy blazer with school badge, regulation pattern navy skirt, white blouse, navy pullover with red stripe on V-neck, plain black shoes, flesh/navy/black tights or white/black/navy socks.

Homework Average 11-year-old, eight hours a week; 14-year-old, 16 hours; 16-year-old, 20 hours.

Vocational qualifications GNVQ Advanced, Business Studies, Leisure and Tourism; GNVQ Intermediate, Health and Social Care, Science; BTEC National Nursery Nursing.

Inspection March 1994: 'The quality of learning across the school is good. Pupils are highly-motivated, listen well, participate enthusiastically in lessons and maintain good levels of concentration. They show responsibility and maturity when set challenging open-ended research tasks.'; 'The teachers are committed and hard-working professionals. Lessons are well-planned with clear objectives which are communicated effectively to pupils.'; 'High expectations of pupils' achievement and behaviour are evident in lessons and the everyday life of the school.'

Primary schools Chichester Central CE Primary; Kingsham County Primary; Parklands County Primary; St James's County Primary; Jessie Younghusband Primary.

BEWDLEY HIGH SCHOOL

Stourport Road
Bewdley
Worcestershire DY12 1BL
Tel (01299) 403277
Fax (01299) 405480

- National ranking 322 (217)
- GCSE 63% (71%)
- A-levels 50% (A/B); 97% (A/E)
- Higher education 92% (Oxford 1, Cambridge 1)

- Mixed comprehensive
- Pupils 700
- Boys (13–18) 360
- Girls (13–18) 340
- Sixth form 150 (21%)
- Education authority *Hereford and Worcester*

Headteacher Margaret Griffiths, appointed in July 1987. Staff 42 (men 21, women 21).

Motto *None*

Background Situated in spacious and attractively landscaped setting, leading down to River Severn; in the 40 years since it opened, the school has developed into a modern comprehensive serving historic town of Bewdley and the surrounding area. Specialist accommodation includes laboratories, art, pottery and textile studios, design technology suite, gymnasium, sports hall, music room, library, and full-size sports pitches; separate purpose-built sixth-form block; £1 million building programme to provide improved mathematics, science, humanities and modern languages accommodation; lottery bid made to help fund new drama and music suite. Over-subscribed, with 200 applications for 180 places. Aim is 'to create an environment that enables all pupils to fulfil their potential, based on reward and encouragement. The school actively fosters equal opportunities and is the designated school in the area for visually-impaired pupils.'

Streaming Mixed-ability, with some setting in year 9; setting in years 10 and 11.

Approach to discipline 'The arrangements for the smooth running of the school are clearly defined for pupils. The requirement for good behaviour and high standards is absolutely fundamental. It is vital that each pupil considers the welfare of others. The school encourages the development of self-discipline, but will instigate procedures to modify unacceptable behaviour.'

Uniform All pupils in years 9 to 11 wear smart, practical and economical uniform based on school's colours of blue, white and yellow. Dress code for sixth-formers. Enforcement 'based on consensus and with co-operation of parents and pupils'.

Homework Average 14-year-old, seven to eight hours a week; 16-year-old, nine to 10 hours.

Vocational qualifications GNVQ Foundation, Intermediate and Advanced.

Inspection March 1995: 'Bewdley High School is a good school; it provides a very supportive and caring environment within which pupils derive great benefit from a good quality of education. There are no serious weaknesses other than the accommodation, which is inadequate for the number and needs of pupils currently on roll. The school's reputation in the local community is justifiably high.'; 'Pupils are hard-working and eager to learn. They show maturity and responsibility in their approach to work. Teaching is good in a number of subjects and is rarely less than sound. Lessons are well-ordered and teacher-pupil relationships are generally good. Teachers have good levels of specialist subject knowledge.'

Primary schools St John's CE Middle, Kidderminster; Lickhill Middle, Stourport-upon-Severn; Burlish Middle, Stourport-upon-Severn; St Anne's CE Middle, Bewdley; Wribben Hall Middle, Bewdley.

OLCHFA SCHOOL

Gower Road
Sketty
Swansea SA2 7AB
Tel (01792) 201222
Fax (01792) 297174
E-mail: cburden@enterprise.net

- National ranking 323 (230, 245, 267, 268)
- GCSE 63% (69%)
- A-levels 50% (A/B); 96% (A/E)
- Higher education 97% (Oxford 4, Cambridge 3)

- Mixed comprehensive
- Pupils 1,890
- Boys (11–18) 985

- Girls (11–18) 905
- Sixth form 454 (24%)
- Education authority *Swansea*

Headteacher Trevor Church, 44, appointed in January 1996. Staff 110 (men 54, women 56).

Motto Dysg, dawn, daioni (Learning, talent, goodness).

Background The school, which opened in 1969, is a two-storey building in extensive grounds and playing fields in a residential area on western edge of Swansea, next to Mumbles and the Gower Peninsula; open landscaped site, with much tree-planting. Resources centre, swimming pool, two gymnasia, three halls. Over-subscribed, with 340 applications for 289 places. Total of 31 A-level courses include theatre studies, psychology, sociology, politics and physical education. Music a strength, with productions in Brangwyn Hall and Taliesin. Duke of Edinburgh Award Scheme. Strong record of international sporting representation; currently has 28 internationals in various sports. Winners of British Isles schools' debating competition. Exchanges with France, Germany and Holland. 'The predominant emphasis is upon endeavour, achievement and excellence.'

Streaming Setting in mathematics in year 7; also special education form. Ability groups for most subjects from year 8.

Approach to discipline 'There is an emphasis upon positive reinforcement and self-discipline within a set of clear and shared expectations and responsibilities. The guidelines are clear and expectations are high, with sanctions imposed if the agreed rules are challenged. A caring and orderly culture with positive encouragement of achievement.'

Uniform Boys: dark/grey/black trousers, white shirt, school tie, royal-blue V-neck pullover (navy is optional for sixth-formers), grey/navy/black socks, black shoes. Hair no longer than collar-length. Girls: medium or dark-grey skirt, white blouse, school tie, royal-blue V-neck sweater, grey/white/black socks, black shoes. Regulations enforced 'strictly'.

Homework Average 11-year-old, six hours 15 minutes a week; 14-year-old, eight hours 45 minutes; 16-year-old, 10 hours.

Vocational qualifications GNVQ Intermediate and Foundation, Business and Finance, Leisure and Tourism; GNVQ Intermediate, Engineering; GNVQ Advanced, Business Education; RSA; Pitman.

Inspection March 1994: 'The quality of learning and the quality of teaching in lessons are generally satisfactory to good throughout the school and pupils demonstrate positive attitudes to learning and show commitment to their work. Teachers' specialist knowledge is good. Most lessons are well planned and prepared, and learning objectives are clear. Care is usually taken to match work to the needs of individual pupils and this is most effective with the more able.'; 'A very good variety of extra-curricular activities is provided, covering a wide range of interests. The high participation of pupils confirms their value as a worthwhile educational experience.'; 'The quality of relationships is generally good, with pupils displaying supportive attitudes to others and being friendly and helpful.'

Primary schools Parkland Junior; Sketty Primary; Dunvant Junior; Hendrefoilan Junior; Cila Primary.

FARMOR'S SCHOOL

The Park
Fairford
Gloucestershire GL7 4JQ
Tel (01285) 712302
Fax (01285) 713504
E-mail: farmors@mail.rmplc.co.uk

- National ranking 324 (321, 347, 245, 258)
- GCSE 63% (62%)
- A-levels 47% (A/B); 97% (A/E)
- Higher education 76%

- Mixed comprehensive
- Pupils 802
- Boys (11–18) 412
- Girls (11–18) 390
- Sixth form 141 (18%)
- Education authority *Gloucestershire*

Headteacher Edmund Wickins, 39, appointed in September 1995. Staff 43 (men 21, women 22).

Motto Pare ut vincas (Prepare that you may conquer).

Background Founded in 1738, the school is in a parkland setting on edge of Cotswold market town of Fairford; 18 acres of playing fields. Substantial extensions and alterations in 1972. School has grown to meet increasing demand for places. Specialist teaching areas for all national curriculum subjects, including seven science laboratories, music rooms, art, pottery and textiles suite, sports hall, gymnasium and library. New technology suite in 1993; new sixth form in 1996. New creative arts facility in 1995. Proud of 'energetic' variety of activities: sporting competition, work-experience, music, charity and community work, special curriculum days and visits. Duke of Edinburgh Award Scheme. Mission statement: 'We provide quality teaching and learning, set high expectations and offer broad opporunities so that every student is encouraged to acquire the skills and values to become a successful person in society.'

Streaming Gradual introduction of setting: mathematics and French/Spanish from year 8; sciences from year 9.

Approach to discipline Form tutor has immediate responsibility for pastoral care and discipline. Serious breaches referred to heads of year, deputy head and headteacher, as appropriate. Sanctions include detention, withdrawal of privileges, extra work, formal reprimand. 'In serious cases, an attempt is made to reflect the sanctions used in society and to make pupils aware of, and fully accountable for, consequences of their actions.'

Uniform Girls: navy skirt/trousers, white polo shirt with crest, blue sweatshirt with crest, white/navy/plain tights, black/brown/navy flat shoes. Boys: dark-grey/black trousers, white polo shirt with crest, blue sweatshirt with crest, dark/black/brown shoes. Dress code for sixth-formers.

Homework Years 7 to 9: homework timetable issued annually, with one or two subjects a day and tasks taking about 30 minutes each. Years 10 and 11: purpose and scope varies. Some subjects requiring regular short tasks and immediate deadlines; others more complex over longer period.

Vocational qualifications Post-16 GNVQ Intermediate and Advanced.

Primary schools Fairford CE Primary; St Lawrence CE Primary, Lechlade; Kempsford CE Primary; Bibury CE Primary; Meysey Hampton CE Primary; Down Ampney CE Primary; Hatherop CE Primary; Southrop CE Primary; St Sampsons CE Primary; Cricklade Primary.

LYMM HIGH SCHOOL

Oughtrington Lane
Lymm
Cheshire WA13 0RB
Tel (01925) 755458
Fax (01925) 758439
E-mail: lhsit@enterprise.net

- National ranking 325 (351, 222, 326, 303)
- GCSE 63% (61%)
- A-levels 42% (A/B); 92% (A/E)
- Higher education 95% (Oxford 2)

- Mixed comprehensive
- Pupils 1,490
- Boys (11–18) 770
- Girls (11–18) 720
- Sixth form 265 (18%)
- Education authority *Cheshire*

Headteacher Sidney Michael Slater, 50, appointed in May 1992. Staff 89 (men 46, women 43).

Motto Olim meminisse iuvabit (One day it will be a joy to remember).

Background Origins in later days of Queen Elizabeth I, receiving main endowments in second half of 17th century. In 1885 school moved to new premises in Grammar School Road; lower school based on Oughtrington site, which first came into use in 1957; two schools until 1985 when Lymm High School and Lymm Oughtrington High School amalgamated. Voluntary-controlled; over-subscribed, with two applications per place. Completion in summer 1994 of £6m building programme to provide eight-form entry single-site school with sixth form; new building in keeping with Oughtrington Hall (a listed building) with purpose-built accommodation for each subject, new sports hall, new sixth-form block. Fifty-bed, 3-acre Ty'n-y-Felin Outdoor Pursuits Centre in Anglesey; German and French language exchanges and other continental visits: Belgium, France, skiing and European work experience in Holland, Spain, Germany and Belgium. Sporting success in rugby, soccer, hockey and netball; other sports include cross-country, athletics, tennis, basketball trampolining, badminton, and swimming in school's own indoor pool. Musical activities: Big Band, junior wind band, choir, string ensemble, wind groups, orchestra, annual musical drama production. Christian Union; Duke of Edinburgh Award Scheme; Young Enterprise. Clubs include sport, music, drama, computing, sailing. Parent-Teacher Association; Old Students' Association. Schools Curriculum Award in 1990; Investor in People certification in 1996; Language College status.

Alumni Neil Fairbrother, Lancashire and England cricketer; Ruth Lea, CBI policy unit head; Horace Banner, author and missionary in Brazilian forests.

Streaming All taught in mixed-ability groups in year 7; progressively set in subjects as they move through the school.

Approach to discipline Guidelines for pupils; seek to help develop self-discipline with help of parents; system of rewards and sanctions; some lower school pupils given chance of exercising responsibility as prefects, as well as sixth-formers. 'Most importantly we firmly believe in praise and rewards. Achievement Awards and Certificates are presented regularly to deserving pupils throughout the school.'

Uniform Boys: navy blazer with badge, medium-grey trousers, white/grey shirt, school tie, grey V-neck pullover, plain socks, black/grey/brown shoes. Girls: navy blazer with badge, medium-grey skirt, navy cardigan/V-neck pullover, white/pale-blue blouse, school tie, grey/black/navy/white socks, black/grey/brown shoes.

Homework Average 11-year-old, five to eight hours a week; 14-year-old, eight to 10 hours; 16-year-old, 15+ hours.

Vocational qualifications Range of vocational and GNVQ courses: Business, Manufacturing, Health and Social Care.

Inspection November 1994: 'Lymm High School commands the respect and confidence of pupils and parents. It provides education of a very good quality to its pupils. It is a popular school which has grown considerably in pupil population, particularly in the sixth form, over recent years.'; 'Staff respond well to the clear, sensitive and purposeful leadership provided by the headteacher and undertake their responsibilities with enthusiasm and effectiveness.'; 'Library provision is sound, although the stock in some respects is underdeveloped. Information technology is unevenly used across the school.'; 'Relationships are very good; pupils are well-mannered and courteous towards adults and each other. The quality of accommodation is generally outstanding.'

Primary schools Lymm Ravenbank County Primary; Lymm Oughtrington County Primary; Lymm Statham County Primary; Lymm Cherry Tree County Primary; High Legh County Primary; Thelwall County Primary; Grappenhall Bradshaw County Primary; Little Bollington County Primary; Grappenhall St Wilfrid's CE Primary.

CROMPTON HOUSE SCHOOL

Rochdale Road
Shaw
Oldham
Greater Manchester OL2 7HS
Tel (01706) 847451/845936
Fax (01706) 291454

- National ranking 326= (365, 400, 408, –)
- GCSE 63% (60%)
- A-levels 38% (A/B); 91% (A/E)
- Higher education 99% (Oxford 1, Cambridge 1)

- Mixed comprehensive
- Pupils 1,105
- Boys (11–18) 528
- Girls (11–18) 577
- Sixth form 150 (14%)
- Education authority Oldham

Headteacher Malcolm Taylor, 58, appointed in September 1985. Staff 69 (men 38, women 31).

Motto Sapere aude (Dare to be wise).

Background School of Anglican foundation opened in 1926, gift of Crompton family to church commissioners; now voluntary-aided and maintained by Oldham Borough Council; set in residential area on boundary of Oldham. Facilities include hall, gymnasium, dining areas, library, music and practice rooms, technology areas, rooms for home economics, textiles, art, business studies, information technology and modern languages. Many modern buildings: purpose-built science block, fifth-form block, sixth-form centre; new £1m block of classrooms and four science laboratories completed in 1994. Extensive playing fields, including two all-weather pitches and a grass pitch. Over-subscribed, with two applications per place; also attracts pupils from Rochdale, Middleton, Alkrington, Bamford and Littleborough; sharp increase in numbers since 1985. 'Very strong' musically: band, wind band, swing band, orchestra, boys' and girls' choirs, many concerts, National Festival of Youth Music. Strong drama tradition. Sporting success: Oldham school champions at athletics and cross-country, both boys and girls. 'The corporate life of the school is based on clear principles and values. Pupils know what is expected of them and what the school stands for.'

Streaming Pupils are put in sets according to ability in each academic subject.

Approach to discipline 'The school is run on traditional lines with a firm but fair approach to discipline.'

Uniform Black blazer with school badge, school tie, dark-grey trousers/grey skirt, grey/white shirt or gold-and-white check blouse, black shoes, grey V-neck pullover (optional).

Homework Average 11-year-old, five hours a week; 14-year-old, eight hours; 16-year-old, 10 to 12 hours.

Vocational qualifications *None*

Inspection October 1996: 'A very good school with many outstanding features. The school is served by a dedicated and hardworking teaching and non-teaching staff. The quality of the curriculum is enhanced by the wide range of extra-curricular activities provided for pupils. The school's ethos is excellent. Standards of behaviour around the school are very good and pupils' attitudes to learning are very positive.'; 'The quality of teaching is a major strength in the school.'; 'Homework is used very effectively and homework diaries are carefully monitored.'

Primary schools Total of 70 feeder schools.

MALMESBURY SCHOOL

Upper School
Corn Gastons
Malmesbury
Wiltshire SN16 0DF
Tel (01666) 822296
Fax (01666) 825773

E-mail: malmbury@rmplc.co.uk
Internet: http://www.rmplc.co.uk/eduweb/sites/malmbury/index.html

- National ranking 326 = (276, 290, 473, 334)
- GCSE 63% (65%)
- A-levels 38% (A/B); 91% (A/E)
- Higher education 76% (Oxford 3)

- Mixed comprehensive
- Pupils 961
- Boys (11–18) 487
- Girls (11–18) 474
- Sixth form 153 (16%)
- Education authority *Wiltshire*

Headteacher Malcolm James Trobe, 49, appointed in January 1992. Staff 56 (men 29, women 27).

Motto *None*

Background Formed in 1971 as a mixed comprehensive on two sites: lower and upper schools. Rural environment; serves Malmesbury and large number of surrounding villages covering 100 square miles, including Minety, Oaksey, Brinkworth, Dauntsey, Luckington and Sherston. Lower school, built in 1964 on outskirts of town, accommodates about 330 pupils in years 7 and 8; no requirement for travel to other site. Upper school built in 1952 in one of town's housing estates, just over a mile from lower school. Most staff work at both sites. Not over-subscribed; intake governed by availability of transport rather than parental choice. Notable for drama and music; teams and individuals have competed both at county and national level. Home and School Association raises more than £5,000 a year. School emphasises importance of in-service training and staff development.

Streaming Mixed-ability in year 7; setting by ability in mathematics in year 8; some setting in half-year groups in year 9; setting by ability in nearly all subjects in years 10 and 11.

Approach to discipline 'Children need a disciplinary structure that makes them secure, happy and able to work to their potential, not by producing lengthy list of rules but by expecting behaviour that reflects common sense and consideration for others.' Sanctions: 'on report'; detention; parents always informed of serious breaches.

Uniform Grey or black trousers/skirt, white shirt/blouse, grey/black sweatshirt or pullover. 'The dress code is enforced.'

Homework Average 11-year-old, five hours a week; 14-year-old, up to nine hours; 16-year-old, 10 to 12 hours.

Vocational qualifications GNVQ Advanced, Business, Art and Design; RSA Initial Awards; some GCSEs available in sixth-form are vocational, including Print Workshop and Photography.

Primary schools Malmesbury CE Primary; Crudwell CE Primary; Hullavington Primary; Lea and Garsdon CE Primary; Brinkworth Earl Danby's CE Primary; Luckington Primary; St Joseph's RC Primary; Minety CE Primary; Walter Powell Primary; Sherston CE Primary; Oaksey CE Primary; Seagry CE Primary.

DAVENANT FOUNDATION SCHOOL

Chester Road
Loughton
Essex IG10 2LD
Tel (0181) 508 0404
Fax (0181) 508 930
E-mail: davenant@rmplc.co.uk
Internet: http://www.rmplc.co.uk/eduweb/sites/davenant

- National ranking 328 (319, 272, –, 246=)
- GCSE 63% (62%)
- A-levels 37% (A/B); 94% (A/E)
- Higher education 85% (Oxford 1, Cambridge 2)

- Grant-maintained
- Mixed comprehensive
- Pupils 970
- Boys (11–18) 500
- Girls (11–18) 470
- Sixth form 205 (21%)
- Education authority *Essex*

Headteacher Andrew James Puttock, 36, appointed in April 1997. Staff 66 (men 32, women 34).

Motto Tel gran, vel pain (As is the grain, so is the bread).

Background Founded in 1860, a pioneering church school. Moved to current site next to deer sanctuary in Epping Forest in 1965; extensive building programme before it became a Christian comprehensive in 1980. It is supported by a trust fund and stands in its own grounds; sports facilities include swimming pool. Significantly over-subscribed,with two applications per place. Operates own music and drama tuition, employing 18 peripatetic music and dance teachers; four in 10 pupils involved. Duke of Edinburgh Award Scheme and community service are strong features.

Streaming Pupils in broad ability bands on entry. Setting introduced in year 8, particularly in mathematics and modern languages. Mixed-ability teaching is not seen as way forward.

Approach to discipline Work hard, live cheerfully and allow others to do the same. Firm but friendly, with praise and reward given pride of place. Credits system in years 7 to 9. 'A report system caters for the daily monitoring of those few pupils failing to fulfil their potential.'

Uniform Black blazer with badge, white shirt/blouse, school tie, black trousers/skirt, black shoes. Sixth-form boys wear 'sober suit'; girls dress 'in the spirit of that regulation'. Firmly stated; all pupils follow regulations.

Homework Average 11-year-old, seven hours 30 minutes a week; 14-year-old, 10 hours; 16-year-old, 15 hours.

Vocational qualifications BTEC GNVQ Level 2, Business; Pitman, Word-processing, Spreadsheets, Secretarial Duties; RSA, Business Communications; Teeline Shorthand.

Inspection 'A good school in which the extremely responsive and highly-motivated pupils achieve well in their formal studies and most benefit greatly from the excellent range and quality of extra-curricular activities provided by the committed and able staff. Parents were notably fulsome in their praise of the school and the effect of the school's Christian ethos.'; 'Numeracy standards are generally sound, but further attention needs to be given to approximation and measurement. Speaking and listening skills are highly developed; reading and writing skills are satisfactory, but not as generally high.'; 'Teachers use the whole range of strategies available to them and pupils respond with great enthusiasm, even when pace or delivery could be sharper. Classes are very well managed by the well-qualified teaching staff who are secure and confident in their knowledge and expertise.'; 'Teachers contribute widely to the outstanding range of extra-curricular activities, often linked to the taught curriculum, and these activities enhance markedly the quality of education provided.'

Primary schools Theydon Bois County Primary; St John Fisher RC Primary; St John's CE Primary; Staples Road County Primary.

ST BARTHOLOMEW'S SCHOOL

Andover Road
Newbury
Berkshire RG14 6JP
Tel (01635) 521255
Fax (01635) 516420
E-mail: stbartad@rmplc.co.uk

- National ranking 329 (233, 323, 272, 288)
- GCSE 63% (69%)
- A-levels 37% (A/B); 86% (A/E)
- Higher education 80% (Oxford 7, Cambridge 6)

- Grant-maintained
- Mixed comprehensive
- Pupils 1,664
- Boys (11–18) 808
- Girls (11–18) 856
- Sixth form 663 (40%)
- Education authority *Berkshire*

Headteacher Stuart Jackson Robinson, 49, appointed in September 1994. Staff 103 (men 46, women 57).

Motto Ad lucem (Towards the light).

Background Result of amalgamation of St Bartholomew's Grammar School (founded 1466) and Newbury County Girls' School (founded 1904); two sites about 300 yards apart on southwest side of Newbury; lower school on Luker site; on Wormestall site school provides sixth-form education for much of West Berkshire and Hampshire/ Wiltshire borders. Over-subscribed, with 1.3 applications per place. Music: junior and senior choir, chamber groups, junior and intermediate bands, dance band; annual drama production. House plays, House evenings, House music competition. Sport: rugby, soccer, hockey, cricket, lacrosse, netball, rounders, tennis, athletics, swimming, table tennis, cross-country. Strong house system; senior pupils provide much of leadership and organisation. Parents' Association.

Streaming Pupils put in sets subject to subject, according to ability.

Approach to discipline 'Firm. Pupils are expected to behave in a courteous manner at all times and to do their best to make the school a place of which they and everyone else can be proud.' Rules and Customs booklet for all new pupils; commendations and termly Good Work prizes; formal detentions thrice weekly, with Headmaster's detention on Saturday morning for serious offences.

Uniform Years 7 to 11: black trousers/skirt, white shirts, black jacket for boys/grey jumper for girls. Strictly enforced.

Homework Average 11-year-old, eight hours a week; 14-year-old, 10 hours; 16-year-old, 12 hours.

Vocational qualifications Business Skills courses.

Primary schools John Rankin Junior; St Nicolas CE Junior; Speenhamland Primary; Wooden Hill County Junior; St Joseph's RC Primary; Burghclere County Primary; Kingsclere Primary.

GLYN ADT TECHNOLOGY SCHOOL

The Kingsway
Ewell
Epsom
Surrey KT17 1NB
Tel (0181) 394 2955
Fax (0181) 786 7668
E-mail: 106477.1370@compuserve.com

- National ranking 330 (445, 466, 289, 269)
- GCSE 63% (54%)
- A-levels 36% (A/B); 87% (A/E)
- Higher education 65% (Oxford 3, Cambridge 1)

- Grant-maintained
- Boys' comprehensive
- Pupils 1,231
- Boys (12–18) 1,231
- Girls *Not applicable*
- Sixth form 232 (19%)
- Education authority *Surrey*

Headteacher Stuart Turner, 50, appointed in September 1988. Staff 79 (men 56, women 23).

Motto Tenax propositi ulteriora peto (Holding fast to what I have gained, I reach forward to further achievements).

Background Main building dates from 1938; set in own grounds. Recent developments include 10-laboratory science block (1991), technology suite and five-badminton-court sports hall (1993), and second technology suite (1995). Games field is a short walk away and comprises 17 pitches for soccer and rugby, as well as three cricket squares. The school is always over-subscribed, with 1.6 applications per place. Traditional standards and values. Strong House system, with competitions including debating, drama, music, chess and variety of sports. Every Saturday in winter there are up to 12 soccer teams and 10 rugby teams and three cross-country teams in action; six cricket teams in summer. Frequent representatives in county, Southeast England and national competition.

Alumni David Hemmings, actor and film star; Barry Wordsworth, conductor of BBC Concert Orchestra and musical director of Royal Ballet, Covent Garden; Tony Jarvis, Olympic swimmer; Paul Stimpson, captain of Great Britain Olympic basketball team; Dario Gradi, manager of Crewe Football Club; Andrew Longhurst, chief executive of Cheltenham and Gloucester Building Society; Douglas French, Conservative MP for Gloucester; John Austin-Walker, Labour MP for Woolwich; Ed Crooks, BBC economics correspondent.

Streaming Mixed-ability groupings in lower year-groups with some setting, with increasing use of setting in Key Stage 4.

Approach to discipline 'Firm, safe environment to maximise each boy's learning opportunities.' Hierarchical pastoral system: form tutor, head of faculty, head of year, deputy head.

Uniform Blue blazer and House tie for years 7 to 11; black blazer and sixth-form tie for sixth-formers. Strictly enforced; no jewellery.

Homework Average 11-year-old, seven hours 30 minutes a week; 14-year-old, 10 hours; 16-year-old, at least 10 hours.

Vocational qualifications BTEC Intermediate and Advanced, Business and Finance.

Primary schools Wallace Fields Junior; St Martin's CE Junior; Sparrow Farm Junior; Cuddington Croft Primary; Auriol Junior.

ST EDWARD'S CHURCH OF ENGLAND COMPREHENSIVE SCHOOL

London Road
Romford
Essex RM7 9NX
Tel (01708) 730462
Fax (01708) 731485

- National ranking 331 (468, 291, 370, –)
- GCSE 63% (52%)
- A-levels 27% (A/B); 93% (A/E)
- Higher education 57% (Cambridge 1)

- Mixed comprehensive
- Pupils 1,078
- Boys (11–18) 552
- Girls (11–18) 526
- Sixth form 184 (17%)
- Education authority *Havering*

Headteacher Giles Christian Summers Drew, 49, appointed in January 1992. Staff 67 (men 31, women 36).

Motto *None*

Background Founded as charity school in 1710; now the only Church of England secondary school in Chelmsford diocese; foremost among entry criteria is parental commitment to, and involvement in, Christian work and worship. Facilities include extensive playing fields next to school, gymnasium, multi-gym, sports hall, indoor heated swimming pool. Over-subscribed, with average of 1.8 applications for each place. 'Excellent' physical education, music and sporting facilities. Full range of extra-curricular activities. Strong drama tradition, including four productions at Edinburgh Fringe, and full programme of foreign exchanges.

Alumni Tony Copsey, Welsh rugby international.

Streaming Pupils put in ability sets in mathematics and languages.

Approach to discipline Strictly enforced code of conduct. 'We work closely with parents, believing partnership is essential to success in resolving pupil problems. Detentions and community service are used as sanctions, as well as report cards to monitor academic progress and behaviour. Merit points, commendations, sports colours, lapel badges are all used to celebrate success, which is reinforced through the school newsletter and presentation to governors.'

Uniform Navy blazer with badge, grey trousers/navy skirt, white shirt/blouse, school tie, black shoes. Sixth-formers wear same uniform except that shirt/blouse may be coloured.

Homework Average 11-year-old, five hours a week; 14-year-old, seven to eight hours; 16-year-old, 10+ hours.

Vocational qualifications RSA, Computer Literacy and Information Technology; GNVQ, Business and Finance.

Inspection May 1994: 'The school provides a good education.'; 'The competence of the pupils at speaking and listening is particularly good.'; 'For pupils with identified special educational needs, the organisation of learning and the teaching methods used are often inappropriate.'; 'The leadership provided by the headteacher is positive and clear, and the governing body and senior staff fully support the direction he sets.'; 'The school has a strong, clear Christian ethos which underpins its day-to-day working. Behaviour is of a high standard and relationships are characterised by respect.'

Primary schools St Edward's CE Primary (part of the same foundation and accounting for about 40 per cent of intake); St Margaret's CE Primary, Barking.

QUEEN ELIZABETH'S GIRLS' SCHOOL

High Street
Barnet
Hertfordshire EN5 5RR
Tel (0181) 449 2984
Fax (0181) 441 2322

- National ranking 332 (234, 273)
- GCSE 63% (69%)
- A-levels 22% (A/B); 85% (A/E)
- Higher education 76%

- Girls' comprehensive
- Pupils 1,050
- Boys *Not applicable*
- Girls (11–18) 1,050
- Sixth form 155 (15%)
- Education authority *Barnet*

Headteacher Anne Hilary Shinwell, 45, appointed in January 1995. Staff 66 (men 16, women 50).

Motto Forward thinking.

Background Situated centrally within High Barnet, on the edge of the green belt. Original buildings date from 1891, but all the earlier blocks have been modernised. 'Excellent, well-equipped facilities' include drama studio, lecture room, multi-gym, swimming pool, technology suite, computer rooms and adjacent sports centre. Opening of new building in autumn 1995 provided school hall, new main library with a central resources area, music suite with attached practice rooms and additional teaching space. Over-subscribed, with two applications per place. Particular strength in expressive arts. 'We wish all our girls to achieve their full potential and to develop a sense of self-confidence and self-esteem. They should be able to value and recognise the worth in other people and we would wish them to be people who make a positive contribution to their immediate environment and the wider community. We aim to provide for all who share in the life of the school a quality of experience which respects them as individuals and gives fulfilment and reward.'

Alumni Stephanie Beacham, actress; Elaine Paige, singer and actress.

Streaming Pupils are set in mathematics and modern languages.

Approach to discipline 'We aim to establish an ethos of high expectations in terms of both work and standards of behaviour. The school has an agreed code of conduct which has been designed to ensure the smooth running of the whole school and the main emphasis is on preventing hurtful actions and behaviour.'

Uniform Blue kilt (checked for years 7 to 9; navy for years 10 and 11), pale-blue blouse, navy sweater/sweatshirt. Introduction of navy trousers as optional part of uniform in September 1997. 'Girls are expected to be in appropriate school uniform at all times.'

Homework Average 11-year-old, seven hours 30 minutes a week; 14-year-old, eight to 10 hours; 16-year-old, 10 to 15 hours.

Vocational qualifications In sixth form, NVQ Business Studies and Child Care.

Primary schools Underhill Primary; Foulds Primary; Christchurch CE Primary; St Catherine's RC Primary; Queenswell Primary.

BOTTISHAM VILLAGE COLLEGE

Lode Road
Bottisham
Cambridge
Cambridgeshire CB5 9DL
Tel (01223) 811250
Fax (01223) 813123

- National ranking 333= (446=, 471=, 279=, 260=)
- GCSE 63% (54%)
- A-levels *Not applicable*
- Higher education *Not applicable*

- Mixed comprehensive
- Pupils 950
- Boys (11-16) 487
- Girls (11-16) 463
- Sixth form *Not applicable*
- Education authority *Cambridgeshire*

Headteacher Peter Banks Hains, 44, appointed in June 1997. Staff 52 (men 21, women 31).

Motto *None*

Background Second of Cambridgeshire Village Colleges founded in 1937; continues to reflect vision of Henry Morris. Mixture of attractive buildings, sculpture, ponds and gardens. Serves 22 villages in open countryside between Cambridge and Newmarket. Not over-subscribed; admission limit raised to meet demand. Two-thirds of pupils participate in Duke of Edinburgh Award Scheme; community service and outdoor adventure education are regarded as important elements. 'Exceptional' facilities extensively used by local community: large sports hall, indoor heated swimming pool, 35 acres of playing fields; new community library in 1995. 'Twilight classes' for young people; all year 7 pupils go camping during annual whole-school Activities Week; most year 10 and 11 pupils in Duke of Edinburgh Award Scheme.

Streaming Balanced groups in year 7. Pupils put in sets according to aptitude in particular subjects from year 8.

Approach to discipline Bottisham Code promotes responsibility and mutual tolerance; calm, purposeful atmosphere; school works closely with parents and has well-developed year-group organisation. 'The whole pastoral team aims to overcome the many day-to-day difficulties of children with sensitivity and the minimum of fuss.'

Uniform Navy sweater, white shirt, navy skirt/trousers for girls or dark trousers, tie for boys. 'Appropriate uniform required, and enforced with co-operation of parents.'

Homework Average 11-year-old, five hours a week; 14-year-old, seven hours; 16-year-old, nine hours.

Vocational qualifications *None*

Inspection February 1994: 'Bottisham Village College is successful in meeting its aims, which emphasise the all-round development of its pupils. It is valued by the community it serves. Pupils of all abilities achieve high standards in a range of subject areas.'; 'The college provides a positive learning culture through a broad and balanced curriculum taught by well-qualified and committed teachers. The curriculum is planned and delivered with vision and imagination. Pupils respond with enthusiasm; the college is purposeful and orderly, and pupils are motivated to succeed. Pupils' progress is partly restricted in some subjects where their prior learning is not fully acknowledged and is not best served by the teaching arrangements in year 10.'; 'Relationships between pupils and with teachers are very good. The college promotes the aesthetic and imaginative experience of its pupils, reinforcing success and emphasising moral development and equality of opportunity.' *School reports that comments relating to year 10 no longer apply.*

Primary schools Fulbourn Primary; Bottisham County Primary; Burwell Village College; Cheveley CE Primary; Kettlefields Primary; Teversham Primary; Swaffham Prior CE Primary; Swaffham Bulbeck CE Primary; Great Wilbraham Primary; Fen Ditton Primary.

CAPE CORNWALL SCHOOL

Cape Cornwall Road
St Just
Penzance
Cornwall TR19 7JX
Tel (01736) 788501
Fax (01736) 787100

- National ranking 333= (302=, 334=, 414=, –)
- GCSE 63% (63%)
- A-levels *Not applicable*
- Higher education *Not applicable*

- Mixed comprehensive
- Pupils 642
- Boys (11–16) 348
- Girls (11–16) 294
- Sixth form *Not applicable*
- Education authority *Cornwall*

Headteacher Robin Francis Gough Kneebone, 46, appointed in September 1996. Staff 36 (men 19, women 17).

Motto *None*

Background Established at end of last century for children of St Just. New buildings on existing site in former mining town in 1966; has since been enlarged by purpose-built accommodation; now serves whole of Land's End peninsula, with more than one in five pupils travelling from outside traditional catchment area. Over-subscribed, with 140 applications for 120 places. Excellent views towards Cape Cornwall and Isles of Scilly. Playing fields next to the school, with cricket club field sharing boundary on one side. New art and science accommodation in 1997. Over-subscribed. Reputation for mathematics, science, and performing and creative arts; also for staff–pupil relationships. Sporting strengths: netball, county champions and national under-14 finalists in 1993; county under-14 and under-16 champions in 1995; cricket, third in national under-15 knockout in 1993. Community activities include active recycling and environmental group, steel band, Christmas hamper distribution to elderly. 'The school offers a small-school family atmosphere. It prides itself on setting high standards and a friendly, supportive atmosphere.' Identified by Ofsted in 1996 as an 'outstandingly successful' school.

Streaming 'Pupils are placed in sets for those subjects where sequential learning is important: mathematics, languages, sciences, and so on. Otherwise, they are taught in mixed-ability groups.'

Approach to discipline 'The school believes in a "firm but friendly" approach. Pupils are encouraged to follow a code of conduct.' Sanctions clearly identified.

Uniform Black V-neck sweater with school logo, white shirt, dark-grey/black trousers/skirt, school tie, black shoes. Strictly enforced.

Homework Average 11-year-old, about five hours a week; 14-year-old, about six hours

30 minutes; 16-year-old, about eight or nine hours.

Vocational qualifications Preliminary certificate for Foreign Languages at Work.

Inspection October 1994: 'Cape Cornwall School provides a high quality of education for all its pupils. The school has high expectations, good relationships and a hard-working, civilised ethos in which all members of the community are valued. The high standards of work seen in many classrooms are further enhanced by the richness of the extra-curricular provision.'; 'There are some inadequacies in specialist accommodation which impair the quality of work, particularly in art and music.'

Primary schools Cape Cornwall County Primary, St Just; Sennen County Primary; St Bunyan County Primary; St Levan County Primary; Pendeen County Primary.

FAIRFIELD HIGH SCHOOL

Peterchurch
Hereford HR2 0SG
Tel (01981) 550231
Fax (01981) 550171
E-mail: fhsadmin@freemail.tacin.co.uk

- National ranking 333= (290=, 259=, 337=, 315=)
- GCSE 63% (64%)
- A-levels *Not applicable*
- Higher education *Not applicable*

- Mixed comprehensive
- Pupils 259
- Boys (11–16) 132
- Girls (11–16) 127
- Sixth form *Not applicable*
- Education authority *Hereford and Worcester*

Headteacher Peter C. Fieldhouse, 47, appointed in September 1983. Staff 16 (men 10, women 6).

Motto Together we strive.

Background In the heart of the Golden Valley close to the Black Mountains on the edge of the village of Peterchurch, 12 miles west of Hereford and nine miles from Hay-on-Wye. The main building was originally a Victorian gentleman's residence in fine gardens. Over-subscribed, with 1.8 applications per place. Most pupils go on to Hereford Sixth-Form College, but school claims that no pa pupils wanting work immediately after leaving school have found themselves unemployed.

Streaming Sets for each curriculum area as well as mixed-ability groups.

Approach to discipline Friendly but firm, open and orderly. 'There is a sense of discipline and purpose about the school as the community goes about its daily work.'

Uniform Bottle-green sweater, bottle-green skirt/grey trousers, white shirt, green-and-gold tie.

Homework Average 11-year-old, five hours a week; 14-year-old, six hours; 16-year-old, 10 hours.

Vocational qualifications *None*

Inspection November 1995: 'A good school with many outstanding features. High standards are achieved in many areas of the curriculum, and the school has established an important role in the life of the local community of the Golden Valley.'; 'Teaching and learning is of high quality.'; 'Pupils are highly-motivated and engaged learners, and are lively and attentive listeners.'; 'The limitations of accommodation restrict achievement in some areas, most notably in physical education, which is also affected by insufficient time.'

Primary schools Peterchurch County Primary; Clifford County Primary; Longtown County Primary; Michaelchurch Escley County Primary; Ewyas Harold County Primary; Madley County Primary.

HIGHWORTH WARNEFORD SCHOOL

Shrivenham Road
Highworth
Swindon
Wiltshire SN6 7BZ
Tel (01793) 762426
Fax (01793) 861865
E-mail: warneford@ccp.net

- National ranking 333= (366=, 314=, 295=, 275=)
- GCSE 63% (60%)
- A-levels *Not applicable*
- Higher education *Not applicable*

- Mixed comprehensive
- Pupils 861
- Boys (11–16) 444
- Girls (11–16) 417
- Sixth form *Not applicable*
- Education authority *Swindon*

Headteacher John Saunders, 42, appointed in September 1995. Staff 48 (men 23, women 25).

Motto *None*

Background Established in 1975 to replace a secondary modern that had served area since 1957; set on edge of high ground, looking across Vale of the White Horse to the Ridgeway and Berkshire Downs. Substantial additions to buildings made in 1970s; proud of facilities for design technology, science, information technology, music; large purpose-built library. Popular school that is 'very full'; slightly over-subscribed, with 185 applications for 180 places. Modern languages and information technology among strengths. Duke of Edinburgh Award Scheme. Parent-Teacher Association; consultation meetings with parents, with topics such as format of school reports, sex education policy, and programmes for social and personal education.

Streaming Pupils in sets according to ability in each subject from year 8.

Approach to discipline High value placed on good behaviour and hard work; rules, sanctions and positive rewards. Works closely with parents. 'The importance of developing responsibility and initiative is recognised through a prefect system involving a large number of older pupils.'

Uniform 'Simple, practical, affordable and smart.' Blue sweater, shirt/blouse, dark-grey trousers/skirt, shoes (not trainers), tie for boys. Enforced strictly: 'It is not an open invitation to conform to a vague code of dress.'

Homework Average 11-year-old, four hours a week; 14-year-old, seven hours 30 minutes; 16-year-old, 10 hours.

Vocational qualifications Pitman/RSA, Information Technology, Word-processing.

Primary schools Southfield Junior; Northview Primary; Westrop Primary; Blunsdon Primary.

HOLBROOK HIGH SCHOOL

Ipswich Road
Holbrook
Ipswich
Suffolk IP9 2QX
Tel (01473) 328317
Fax (01473) 327362
E-mail: 106175.3130@compuserve.com

- National ranking 333= (195=)
- GCSE 63% (74%)
- A-levels *Not applicable*
- Higher education *Not applicable*

- Mixed comprehensive
- Pupils 387
- Boys (11–16) 196
- Girls (11–16) 191
- Sixth form *Not applicable*
- Education authority *Suffolk*

Headteacher Anthony Allen Green, 55, appointed in January 1982. Staff 27 (men 16, women 11).

Motto *None.*

Background Opened in 1935 as Holbrook Area School; renamed Holbrook County High School in 1977, when it became a mixed 11–16 comprehensive; serves rural community on Shotley Peninsula, an area of outstanding natural beauty, on 10-acre site on outskirts of village of Holbrook. Oversubscribed. Successful teams in most sports, particularly basketball. Several girls chosen for England basketball team each year; under-15 team were national champions in 1995. Music flourishes, with school invited to perform at Snape Maltings Concert Hall. 'We pride ourselves on having a friendly and welcoming atmosphere which stresses the value of individuals and the importance of maintaining good relationships. The approach to learning is business-like and well-controlled. Well-qualified and committed teachers and support staff working within a low pupil-teacher ratio mean pupils feel valued and levels of achievement are exceptionally high.'

Streaming Mixed-ability in year 7; thereafter, pupils in sets in most subjects.

Approach to discipline 'Firm discipline based on clear Behaviour Policy. Expectations and standards of behaviour are high.'

Uniform Navy school sweatshirt, navy skirt/

black trousers, white shirt. Year 11 may wear black school sweatshirt. 'Pupils are expected to be smartly dressed, avoiding all extremes of fashion. Any deviations from the requirements are challenged and rectified, with parental support.'

Homework Average 11-year-old, five hours a week; 14-year-old, eight hours; 16-year-old, 10 hours.

Vocational qualifications *None*

Inspection November 1995.

Primary schools Shotley Primary; Holbrook Primary; Chelmondiston CE Primary; Stutton CE Primary; Tattingstone CE Primary.

HUMMERSKNOTT COMPREHENSIVE SCHOOL

Edinburgh Drive
Darlington DL3 8AR
Tel (01325) 461191
Fax (01325) 462159
E-mail: hummersknottcompsch@campus.
    bt.com

- National ranking 333= (422=, 437=, 482=, –)
- GCSE 63% (56%)
- A-levels *Not applicable*
- Higher education *Not applicable*

- Mixed comprehensive
- Pupils 1,199
- Boys (11–16) 595
- Girls (11–16) 604
- Sixth form *Not applicable*
- Education authority *Darlington*

Headteacher David Henderson, 52, appointed in January 1984. Staff 66 (men 37, women 29).

Motto *None*

Background Originally Darlington Girls' High School, the school moved to current building in 1955. Reorganisation in 1968 resulted in it becoming comprehensive taking boys for first time and losing its sixth form. On edge of Darlington with 'excellent' facilities: three computer suites, resource centre, sports hall, swimming pool and six sports fields. Over-subscribed, with 285 applications for 245 places. House system and inter-house competition: sport, music, reading, speaking and quizzes. Sporting strengths include athletics, swimming and badminton; annual fun run. New special needs suite. 'We try not to allow the changes of the last few years to affect us too much, and try to keep a sense of humour.'

Streaming All pupils taught for each subject in half-year blocks, of which there are five groups or more; each faculty able to set pupils by subject ability where appropriate.

Approach to discipline Relaxed atmosphere: 'Virtually all pupils behave sensibly.' Pastoral programme, but also 'on report', detention and exclusion if required. 'Serious breaches of discipline lead to indefinite exclusion, which is supported by the governing body.'

Uniform Grey or black trousers/skirt, white shirt/blouse, school tie, burgundy sweater. Enforced very strictly 'but the local education authority would not support exclusion'.

Homework Average 11-year-old, 10 hours a week; 14-year-old, 14 hours; 16-year-old, 15+ hours.

Vocational qualifications GNVQ, Art and Design, Leisure and Tourism.

Primary schools Abbey Primary; Mowden Junior; Skerne Park Junior; Reid Street Primary; Cockerton CE Primary.

PENAIR SCHOOL

St Clement
Truro
Cornwall TR1 1TN
Tel (01872) 274737
Fax (01872) 42465

- National ranking 333= (331=, 314=, 337=, –)
- GCSE 63% (62%)
- A-levels *Not applicable*
- Higher education *Not applicable*

- Mixed comprehensive
- Pupils 1,091
- Boys (11–16) 565
- Girls (11–16) 526
- Sixth form *Not applicable*
- Education authority *Cornwall*

Headteacher Barbara Vann, appointed in April 1997. Staff 60 (men 27, women 33).

Motto Disce ut vivas (Learn to live).

Background Opened in 1978 as purpose-built comprehensive serving eastern part of city. Buildings set in more than 53 acres of grounds and overlook cathedral. Has grown steadily over the years; pupils transfer at 16 to newly-established Truro College. Oversubscribed. 'Excellent' sporting reputation, regularly winning county and national competitions in major sports; 'greatest achievement' in cross-country running, for which school has provided national squad. Two orchestras, stage band, numerous ensembles; two drama productions a year. 'The school seeks to create a caring, learning community where everyone is valued for who they are and for what they might become.'

Streaming 'Pupils are grouped in whatever way is appropriate for the subject they are studying. A variety of strategies, including ability setting, are employed.'

Approach to discipline 'The school has a well-developed behaviour management policy which covers both rewards and sanctions. Staff have a high expectation of pupils and insist on good manners at all times. Inconsiderate behaviour, in whatever form, is not acceptable.'

Uniform Blue shirt, school tie, grey pullover, grey trousers/navy skirt. Very strictly enforced.

Homework Average 11-year-old, five hours a week; 14-year-old, seven hours 30 minutes; 16-year-old, 10 hours.

Vocational qualifications Welsh Board Certificate of Education; BTEC; RSA; Pitman.

Primary schools Kea Primary; Archbishop Benson CE Primary; Tregolls Primary; St Erme with Trispen County Primary; Devoran Primary; St Mary's Primary.

ST THOMAS MORE SCHOOL

Croftdale Road
Blaydon-on-Tyne
Gateshead
Tyne and Wear NE21 4BQ
Tel (0191) 499 0111
Fax (0191) 414 1116
E-mail: zarrag@rmplc.co.uk
Internet: http://www.campus.bt.com/CampusWorld/orgs/org417

- National ranking 340 (315, 265, 260, 274)
- GCSE 62% (62%)

- A-levels 52% (A/B); 100% (A/E)
- Higher education 75% (Oxford 2)

- Mixed comprehensive
- Pupils 1,200
- Boys (11–18) 600
- Girls (11–18) 600
- Sixth form 250 (21%)
- Education authority *Gateshead*

Headteacher Michael Zarraga, 55, appointed in September 1980. Staff 72 (men 38, women 34).

Motto Regis servus dei prius (The King's servant but God's first).

Background Opened as secondary modern in 1967; reorganised as comprehensive in 1987. The school serves the Roman Catholic community in western part of Gateshead; also non-Catholics who enrol under open-admissions policy. Number of pupils grown from about 500 in 1987. Three building phases completed on site with extensive playing fields overlooking River Tyne near border of Northumberland. Strong sporting tradition: has reached national finals in netball and cross-country. National leader in introducing BTEC vocational courses in sixth form. European exchanges and visits; outward bound weekends; won through to finals of Lloyds Bank National Theatre Challenge, performing at the National Theatre in London; pupils have also performed at the Edinburgh Fringe Festival. More than nine in 10 pupils (94%) studying GNVQ Advanced courses achieve the award.

Streaming Pupils in sets within each subject.

Approach to discipline High standards seen as prerequisite for success; students in no doubt of what expected from them. Christian ethos pervasive; firm framework. 'Pupils are motivated to live up to these standards by encouragement, praise and example. There is an atmosphere of mutual respect between staff and pupils that is constantly encouraged.'

Uniform Sky-blue shirt/blouse, grey skirt or black trousers, navy jumper with house crest, school tie, grey/navy socks, black shoes. Enforced 'absolutely'.

Homework Average 11-year-old, eight hours a week; 14-year-old, 10 hours; 16-year-old, 15 to 18 hours.

Vocational qualifications GNVQ Intermediate, Health and Social Care, Business, Engineering; GNVQ Advanced, Health and Social Care, Business, Engineering, Science, Art and Design.

Primary schools St Joseph's RC Primary, Blaydon; St Mary's Primary, Whickham; St Mary and St Thomas Aquinas, Stella; Corpus Christi RC Primary, Gateshead; Rowlands Gill Junior.

CAEREINION HIGH SCHOOL

Llanfair Caereinion
Welshpool
Powys SY21 0HW
Tel (01938) 810888
Fax (01938) 810544
E-mail: caerhigh@mail.rmplc.co.uk

- National ranking 341 (199, 508, 444, –)
- GCSE 62% (73%)
- A-levels 45% (A/B); 95% (A/E)
- Higher education 95%

- Mixed comprehensive
- Pupils 500
- Boys (11–18) 253
- Girls (11–18) 247
- Sixth form 87 (17%)
- Education authority *Powys*

Headteacher David Charles, 50, appointed in September 1993. Staff 37 (men 14, women 23).

Motto Golud pawb ei ymgais (One's effort is one's wealth).

Background Small rural comprehensive school in own grounds overlooking the town of Llanfair Caereinion and River Banwy in north Powys. Original school established in 1894 as a result of Welsh Intermediate Education Act and local pressure. Over-subscribed, with average of 1.1 applications for each place. Adjoining leisure centre: sports hall, squash courts, fitness room. Bilingual curriculum (Welsh and English).

Alumni Gwyn Erfyl, broadcaster; Ieuan Jones, international harpist; Nerys Jones, opera singer.

Streaming *None*

Approach to discipline 'Conduct and discipline revolves around relationships and permeates every aspect of the school. As teachers and adults we quite rightly expect consideration and courtesy. It is our intention to treat children with respect, courtesy, and with more consideration than many of them are able to give us.' Year-tutors and department heads deal with repeated acts of indiscipline, with deputy head, senior mistress and head-teacher if necessary. Minor punishments, lunch-hour detentions, after-school deten-tions, suspension or expulsion.

Uniform Boys: navy jumper with school motif, light-blue shirt, navy tie with sky-blue stripes, charcoal-grey trousers, black/brown shoes, socks. Girls: navy skirt, roy-al-blue and white-candy-stripe blouse, navy tie, navy jumper with school motif, white socks or white/navy stockings, black/brown/navy shoes.

Homework Average 11-year-old, five hours a week; 14-year-old, eight hours; 16-year-old, 10 hours.

Vocational qualifications GNVQ Intermediate and Advanced, Leisure and Tourism, Busi-ness Studies.

Inspection May 1996: 'Examination results are a particularly strong feature of the school.'; 'Both boys and girls consistently show a good attitude towards learning and good rates of progression are secured be-tween all key stages.'; 'The quality of teach-ing is satisfactory or better in nearly all classes and good or very good in 77 per cent. Teaching is always well-planned and purposeful, and lessons proceed at a good pace. The quality relationships between teachers and pupils is very good and there is a good level of interaction in lessons.'; 'Pupils' behaviour in lessons is consistently good and the school is an orderly commu-nity. Bullying is not a significant problem and staff deal with any cases effectively.'; 'The headteacher provides effective leader-ship which is well-matched to the culture of the school.'

Primary schools Llanfair Caereinion Primary; Ysgol Rhiw-Bechan; Hafren Junior; Castle Caereinion Church-in-Wales Primary; Mei-fod Primary; Ysgol Y Banw Primary; Llanerfyl Church-in-Wales Primary; Maes-Y-Dre Pri-mary.

RAINFORD HIGH SCHOOL

Higher Lane
Rainford
St Helens
Merseyside WA11 8NY
Tel (01744) 885914
Fax (01744) 884642
E-mail: headteacher@rainhs.demon.co.uk

- National ranking 342= (358, 394, 421, 354)
- GCSE 62% (60%)
- A-levels 44% (A/B); 90% (A/E)
- Higher education 91% (Oxford 5, Cam-bridge 3)

- Mixed comprehensive
- Pupils 1,709
- Boys (11–18) 849
- Girls (11–18) 860
- Sixth form 296 (17%)
- Education authority St Helens

Headteacher Brian Arnold, 54, appointed in September 1994. Staff 108 (men 54, women 54).

Motto None

Background Opened in 1940 taking 127 pupils aged 11 to 15 from Rainford Village and suburbs of St Helens; sixth form dates from 1961; by 1971 the school had 1,000 pupils. Now self-contained school buildings on 30-acre site. Over-subscribed, with 1.25 applications per place. Facilities include: sixth-form block, 16 science laboratories, five information technology suites, eight technology rooms, two language labora-tories, arts theatre, sports hall, gymnasium, music and art suites. European Curriculum Award 1993: links and exchanges with Den-mark, Holland, France, Germany, Norway, Spain. International representatives in cross-country, rugby, basketball, rhythmic gym-nastics, athletics; national finalists in rugby and basketball; many county players. Inter-house competitions, including public speak-ing. Competitive spirit encouraged; weekly magazine for parents. Strong pastoral care based on House system.

Alumni Willy Russell, playwright; Nigel He-slop, England rugby union player, Oldham rugby league.

Streaming Pupils in sets in most subjects within two half-year groups of equal ability; pupils in sets across whole year for mathematics and English in years 10 and 11.

Approach to discipline Firm but caring; clear and detailed code of conduct with high expectations, recently revised. 'Every student and member of staff has the right to enjoy learning, enjoy leisure and enjoy safety. There are clear rules to ensure this happens.'

Uniform Maroon blazer with school badge, white shirt, House tie, grey trousers/skirt, white/grey/black socks, plain black shoes. No jewellery, make-up or earrings. Strictly enforced.

Homework Average 11-year-old, five hours a week; 14-year-old, 10 to 15 hours; 16-year-old, 15 hours or more.

Vocational qualifications GNVQ Advanced.

Inspection December 1993: 'A good school. Pupils achieve high standards which accurately reflect the expectations of teachers, parents and the wider community.'; 'The level of pupil motivation is high across all subject areas. Pupils arrive at lessons well-prepared and ready to work, concentrate willingly, and show commitment and industry towards the tasks with which they are challenged. Lessons are generally well-prepared with interesting content and varied activities by teaching staff who have a very good command of their subject.'; 'The quality of pupils' behaviour in lessons is good and has a positive impact on standards of achievement and the quality of learning.'

Primary schools Rainford CE Primary; Eccleston Mere Primary; Chapel End Primary; Brook Lodge Primary; St Aidan's CE Primary; Bleak Hill Primary.

ST JOHN FISHER ROMAN CATHOLIC HIGH SCHOOL

Hookstone Drive
Harrogate
North Yorkshire HG2 8PT
Tel (01423) 887254
Fax (01423) 881056
E-mail: sjfrchs@aol.com

- National ranking 343 (316, –, 308)
- GCSE 62% (62%)
- A-levels 41% (A/B); 94% (A/E)
- Higher education 95% (Cambridge 2)

- Mixed comprehensive
- Pupils 999
- Boys (11–18) 501
- Girls (11–18) 498
- Sixth form 167 (17%)
- Education authority *North Yorkshire*

Headteacher Terry Thomas Keelan, 54, appointed in January 1989. Staff 60 (men 31, women 29).

Motto Truth and Justice.

Background Voluntary-aided school set in 22 acres of parkland south of Harrogate and skirted by Hookstone Wood and a golf course; provides a Catholic education for pupils from a 400-square-mile catchment area. With a history going back almost a century, buildings have been updated with a modern science, art and technology wing. Reputation for musicals, 'excellent' swing band, choir, string orchestra. Sporting strengths include soccer, netball, hockey and athletics. Sixth-formers in Joint Ecumenical Organisation with pupils at nearby Church of England school. Over-subscribed; admission limit raised by 10% in 1990 to meet increased demand for places.

Streaming Pupils are in sets from year 8 in mathematics, science, modern languages. In English, from year 9.

Approach to discipline Praise-oriented, with few discipline problems reported. Pupils apparently respond well to high expectations and trust placed in them. 'Children who misbehave may be placed on a school report; parents are fully involved at an early stage.'

Uniform Navy blazer with school crest, blue shirt/blouse, school tie. Girls wear navy skirt, navy V-neck jumper/cardigan; boys wear grey trousers, navy V-neck jumper, dark shoes. No trainers. 'Uniform is checked by tutors daily and strictly enforced.'

Homework Average 11-year-old, five hours a week; 14-year-old, nine hours; 16-year-old, 15 hours.

Vocational qualifications BTEC National Diploma, Business and Finance.

Primary schools St Robert's RC Primary, Harrogate; St Joseph's RC Primary, Wetherby; St Joseph's RC Primary, Harrogate; St Mary's RC Primary, Knaresborough; St Wilfrid's RC Primary, Ripon.

THE KINGS OF WESSEX COMMUNITY SCHOOL

Station Road
Cheddar
Somerset BS27 3AQ
Tel (01934) 742608
Fax (01934) 742757
E-mail: kowessex@rmplc.co.uk

- National ranking 344 (–, –, –, 350)
- GCSE 62%
- A-levels 37% (A/B); 89% (A/E)
- Higher education 66% (Oxford 2, Cambridge 1)

- Mixed comprehensive
- Pupils 1,010
- Boys (13–18) 512
- Girls (13–18) 498
- Sixth form 258 (26%)
- Education authority *Somerset*

Headteacher Chris Richards, 37, appointed in September 1995. Staff 58 (men 27, women 31).

Motto To get the best out of everyone.

Background The school opened in 1964 as a secondary modern, becoming a comprehensive in 1976. In 1963, while excavating the site within a mile of Cheddar gorge, the foundations of a 10th-century Saxon palace were found; hence the name the Kings of Wessex. In addition to full-time pupils, the community school also accommodates more than 1,000 part-time students. Only marginally over-subscribed, although 150 'out-of-area' pupils admitted. New joint-use leisure centre in September 1993; new library. Strengths include team sports, drama and music: 460 pupils in Cheddar Valley have instrumental lessons. Exchange links with Gesamtschule in Felsberg, Germany, for past 10 years; and Bungoma High School for Boys and Cardinal Otunga High School for Girls in Kenya for past three years. Identified for praise in 1996 Ofsted annual report.

Streaming 'The school has a strong policy of setting on ability in every individual subject. This enables each student to be stretched according to their ability.'

Approach to discipline High expectations; no form of physical or mental bullying is tolerated. 'It is key to the school's operation that all students are secure and happy, and able to flourish in the school.'

Uniform Black trousers/skirt, white shirt/blouse, bottle-green jumper with embroidered crown logo, black-and-green tie, black/brown shoes. No denim. Regulations enforced 'with concern for standards'.

Homework Each department specifies policy on setting homework and project work, which is monitored by deputy headteacher. Homework diaries issued to years 9 to 11.

Vocational qualifications GNVQ Intermediate, Business, Health and Social Care; GNVQ Advanced, Business, Science.

Inspection March 1996: 'The Kings of Wessex School provides an education of good quality and has many strengths. Throughout the school standards of achievement are good.'; 'Standards of reading, writing, speaking, listening and numeracy are high. Standards in information technology are satisfactory and sometimes good.'; 'A good range of A-level subjects is provided and the school is extending its provision to meet the needs of a broader range of ability in the sixth form. The vast majority of the students are well-motivated with positive attitudes to learning. Teaching was good in a very high proportion of the lessons seen, especially in year 9 and the sixth form. Most teachers have appropriately high expectations of the performance of students. Sometimes, the content, level and methods used do not sufficiently stimulate and challenge the students, especially the most able. Small classrooms restrict the range of teaching and learning methods that can be used in some subjects.'; 'Leadership of the school is effective. The new headteacher has made many positive changes which the school now needs to evaluate.'

Primary schools Fairlands Middle, Cheddar; Hugh Sexey Middle, Blackford.

BRENTWOOD COUNTY HIGH SCHOOL

Seven Arches Road
Shenfield Common
Brentwood
Essex CM14 4JF
Tel (01277) 226482
Fax (01277) 200853

- National ranking 345 (–, 514, 463, –)
- GCSE 62%

- A-levels 36% (A/B); 89% (A/E)
- Higher education 75% (Cambridge 1)

- Grant-maintained
- Mixed comprehensive
- Pupils 1,256
- Boys (11–18) 649
- Girls (11–18) 607
- Sixth form 164 (13%)
- Education authority (*Essex*)

Headteacher Michael Robert James Trett, 56, appointed in September 1979. Staff 74 (men 29, women 45).

Motto Keep trust.

Background Situated in pleasant Shenfield Common area of Brentwood; founded in 1913 as a girls' grammar school; became mixed comprehensive in 1972; achieved grant-maintained status in January 1994. 'Charming' 1926 red-brick building, with adjoining modern block built in the early 1970s; substantial building in 1995 to provide more science laboratories and general classrooms. Over-subscribed, with average of two applications per place. Art department listed in study of 15 best art departments in England and Wales. Three languages to A-level: French, German and Spanish. All students study two languages to the end of year 9 at least. 'Hard-working, caring environment, particularly strong and flourishing sixth-form involved in all activities of the school community.'

Alumni Paul Prichard, Essex cricketer; Gary Webster, actor.

Streaming Pupils in sets for mathematics, English, science, modern languages.

Approach to discipline 'System of rewards (commendations and merit marks) and punishment (hierarchy of detentions), based on emphasis of positive rewards.'

Uniform Navy blazer with school badge, navy-and-light-blue tie, white/grey shirt, charcoal-grey trousers/navy skirt. Enforced 'very strictly'.

Homework Average 11-year-old, three hours 10 minutes a week; 14-year-old, seven hours 30 minutes; 16-year-old, seven hours 30 minutes.

Vocational qualifications *None*

Primary schools Hogarth County Primary; The Holly Trees County Primary; Harold Court Primary; Harold Wood Primary; West Horn-don County Primary; St Thomas of Canterbury RC Primary.

HABERDASHERS' ASKE'S HATCHAM COLLEGE

Pepys Road
New Cross
London SE14 5SF
Tel (0171) 652 9500
Fax (0171) 277 9680
E-mail: hahc@rmplc.co.uk

- National ranking 346 (510, 467, –)
- GCSE 62% (44%)
- A-levels 34% (A/B); 85% (A/E)
- Higher education 29% (Oxford 2, Cambridge 2)

- City Technology College
- Pupils 1,212
- Boys (11–18) 583
- Girls (11–18) 629
- Sixth form 277 (23%)
- Education authority Lewisham

Headteacher Dr Elizabeth Sidwell, 47, appointed in April 1991. Staff 119 (men 63, women 56).

Motto Promoting excellence.

Background One of the first city technology colleges, opened in September 1991, aiming to be 'centre of excellence' through technological, artistic, physical and vocational pursuits. Incorporated Haberdashers' Aske' Hatcham Girls' and Boys' Schools, which served this part of southeast London for more than a century. Voluntary-controlled grammar schools in 1944 before becoming comprehensives in 1979. College sponsored by Robert Aske Foundation, charity administered by Haberdashers' Company; single sex education up to age of 16; co-educational sixth form. Catchment area: Greenwich Lewisham and Southwark. Follows national curriculum, but particular emphasis on mathematics, science and technology. Heavily over-subscribed, with six applications per place. £4.8m upgrading and refurbishment of buildings: technology block including specialist facilities for art and design, business education and information technology; more than 200 computer work-stations; also music rooms, science and library facilities. Longer-than-average school day; wide range of 'enrichment' activities. Large and varied

A- and AS-level programme. Music, sport and drama 'particularly strong'.

Alumni Baron (Donald) Soper, former president of Methodist Conference; Rowland Hilder, painter.

Streaming Mixed-ability in year 7; taught in sets according to ability in separate or grouped subjects from year 8.

Approach to discipline 'The college's approach to discipline is firm and fair.'

Uniform Traditional uniform. Very strictly enforced.

Homework Average 11-year-old, seven hours a week; 14-year-old, 10 hours; 16-year-old, 15 hours.

Vocational qualifications GNVQ Intermediate and Advanced, Business, Manufacturing, Science, Health and Social Care.

Inspection March 1997.

Primary schools Total of 88 feeder schools in Lewisham, Greenwich and Southwark.

THE BROXBOURNE SCHOOL

High Road
Broxbourne
Hertfordshire EN10 7DD
Tel (01992) 464639
Fax (01992) 470173
E-mail: broxschool@aol.com
Internet: http//www.members.aol.com/
    broxschool

- National ranking 347 (243, 350, 226, 220)
- GCSE 62% (68%)
- A-levels 31% (A/B); 91% (A/E)
- Higher education 83% (Oxford 1)

- Mixed comprehensive
- Pupils 1,242
- Boys (11–18) 670
- Girls (11–18) 572
- Sixth form 207 (17%)
- Education authority *Hertfordshire*

Headteacher Dr Alan Horner Baines, 58, appointed in September 1978. Staff 75 (men 28, women 47).

Motto Learn and serve.

Background The school, set in 25-acre landscaped site, dates from 1968 when adjoining Broxbourne Grammar School amalgamated with Baas Hill Secondary School. Most of buildings date from 1959. Recent additions include sixth-form block, computer rooms, technology room, suite of rooms for special educational needs, and soundproof instrumental music rooms. Two libraries, indoor swimming pool, two gymnasiums, two artificial cricket wickets. Over-subscribed, with 290 applications for 206 places. High participation in Duke of Edinburgh Award Scheme (pupils achieved 14 golds, 79 bronzes in 1997); girls' netball team national champions in 1996 and 1997 after being national runners-up or semifinalists for previous six seasons; regular sporting tours abroad, including rugby and hockey visit to Canada every three years; art, music, dance and drama also notable. School raises more than £10,000 annually for charities. Parental support 'excellent'.

Streaming Two broad ability bands for years 7 to 9; upper band of four parallel forms and the lower band of three parallel forms have identical curriculum to facilitate movement between bands.

Approach to discipline Excellence is the aim: good behaviour and smart appearance are highly regarded. 'Good behaviour is not only expected, it is very positively encouraged by a "firm but fair" regime. Children and parents are fully aware of what is expected.'

Uniform Girls: pale-blue blouse, cherry-coloured V-neck jumper and kilt. Boys: cherry blazer (black from year 10), grey trousers, white shirt, cherry tie. Very strictly enforced: 'no aberrations permitted'.

Homework Average 11-year-old, six hours a week; 14-year-old, seven hours 30 minutes; 16-year-old, 10 hours.

Vocational qualifications GNVQ Advanced, Business.

Inspection September 1993: 'The school provides education of a high quality.'; 'Teaching is satisfactory or better in a high proportion of lessons. Pupils are well motivated. The school's approach and the overall ability of the staff encourage learning.'; 'The values promoted by the school, although not always explicitly stated, are evident in the approaches of teachers, other staff and pupils. The school combines academic rigour with a caring approach.'

Primary schools Broxbourne CE Primary; Wormley Primary; Sheredes Primary; Ley Park Primary; St Cross RC Primary; St Augustine's RC Primary.

BENTON PARK SCHOOL

Harrogate Road
Rawdon
Leeds LS19 6LX
Tel (0113) 250 2330
Fax (0113) 250 9177
E-mail: j.smith@bpark.demon.co.uk

- National ranking 348 (469, 433, 384, –)
- GCSE 62% (52%)
- A-levels 30% (A/B); 91% (A/E)
- Higher education 78% (Oxford 1, Cambridge 2)

- Mixed comprehensive
- Pupils 1,371
- Boys (11–18) 692
- Girls (11–18) 679
- Sixth form 225 (16%)
- Education authority *Leeds*

Headteacher Jeffrey R.G. Smith, 61, appointed in January 1975. Staff 82 (men 46, women 36).

Motto *None*

Background Set in attractive parkland with panoramic views of Airedale, Wharfedale and Yorkshire Moors beyond; opened in 1960 on site earlier occupied by Benton Park, which opened in 1838 as a place 'where young gentlemen are boarded and educated', buildings later became Benton Park Hall (now demolished); part of walled garden remains. Three computer rooms, with £30,000-worth of personal computers, with Internet access; library with computer, video and CD-ROM facilities. Oversubscribed, with average of 1.3 applications per place. Languages taught: French, Spanish, German, also Latin; exchanges to France, Germany and Spain. Offers 24 A-level subjects, including Music, Further Mathematics, Theatre Studies and Latin. Music: senior orchestra with more than 80 members, concert tour of Italy in 1995, two concerts at Bolton Abbey; 30-member training orchestra; several pupils in Leeds Youth Orchestra; senior and junior choirs, concert band, early-music group, ensembles; house competitions. Drama; national finalists in public speaking; Young Enterprise, with seven companies. Economics and Business Studies trips to Barcelona, Prague and Heidelberg in past three years. Success in sports: 1994 West Yorkshire rugby cup-winners;

1st XV, under-15s and under-14s were West Yorkshire Merit Champions in 1995; five players selected for Yorkshire. National netball finalists; local hockey cup-winners; cricket and athletics. Success in sport 'almost too much to report': two international swimmers; one pupil is member of under-16 Yorkshire rugby union team.'The school has been compared to an old-fashioned grammar school, but with the facilities of a progressive school. Pupils behave in a very responsible manner and are committed to the school and its success.'

Streaming Pupils are banded on entry to the school in broad ability bands in two half-year groups; all intake subject to comprehensive testing to establish academic potential, levels of ability and where individual mentoring needed. Setting in mathematics and science in years 7 and 8, in English in year 9, in all subjects in years 10 and 11.

Approach to discipline 'One of the principal aims of the school is a concern for law and order, without which we believe effective teaching cannot take place. There are few discipline problems, and when they do arise are dealt with immediately and effectively. Staff–pupil relationships are excellent.'

Uniform Navy blazer or grey pullover with school badge, grey trousers/skirt, white/grey shirt or pale-blue blouse, school tie, brown/black shoes. Very strictly enforced.

Homework Average 11-year-old, five hours a week; 14-year-old, 10 + hours; 16-year old, up to 15 hours.

Vocational qualifications GNVQ, Business.

Inspection November 1994: 'A good school.'; 'The development of information technology skills across the curriculum is weak.'; 'The school has a positive ethos and sense of purpose.'; 'Working relationships amongst the staff are very good.'; 'The school is a well-ordered community and is supported by parents. The behaviour of pupils is excellent. Relationships amongst pupils and between staff and pupils are also excellent.'; 'The ethos of the school encourages achievement for all pupils, but school planning takes insufficient account of equality of opportunity.' *The school reports opening of a third purpose-built computer room to meet IT requirements, plus further equipping of individual departments. Equal opportunities policy adopted as part of school development plan.*

Primary schools Rawdon CE Primary; Littlemoor Primary; Calverley CE Primary; Calverley Parkside Primary; Westfield Junior; Yeadon South View Primary; Horsforth Newlaithes Junior.

THE DEANERY CHURCH OF ENGLAND HIGH SCHOOL

Frog Lane
Wigan
Lancashire WN1 1HQ
Tel (01942) 768801
Fax (01942) 202293
E-mail: enquiries@deanery.wigan.sch.uk
Internet: http://www.rmplc.co.uk/eduweb/sites/deanery

- National ranking 349 (325, 236, 354, 332)
- GCSE 62% (62%)
- A-levels 30% (A/B); 86% (A/E)
- Higher education 80%

- Mixed comprehensive
- Pupils 1,636
- Boys (11–18) 761
- Girls (11–18) 875
- Sixth form 237 (14%)
- Education authority Wigan

Headteacher Roger Howard Mallows, 47, appointed in January 1997. Staff 111 (men 43, women 68).

Motto Valuing the past, improving the present, founding the future.

Background Founded in 1970 close to Wigan town centre, the school's facilities include a new classroom block, sports hall, media centre, large library, 11 laboratories, technology and computer rooms; technology college status approved by Department of Education. An average of 1.5 pupils apply for each of the 260 places. Anglican tradition; students sit on elected school council, which reports to headteacher and directs school's 'lively' charitable work; Parent-Teacher Association; house system monitors discipline, academic progress and family links. Champion sports teams in rugby league, athletics and netball, with national representatives; Duke of Edinburgh Award Scheme; 'open admissions' policy for sixth form, and courses include 26 A-level subjects. Strong industrial and international links; Education Business Partnership. Partner schools in Germany, France, Ukraine and Nigeria.

Alumni Andrew Gregory, Great Britain and Wigan rugby league player; Gaynor Stanley, Olympic swimmer; Alex Childs, fashion model.

Streaming Setting begins towards end of year 7. By end of year 8, all pupils in sets in mathematics, modern languages, science, English, history and geography.

Approach to discipline Bullying and intimidation are not tolerated; aim is to encourage self-discipline through concern for others. Formal system of merits to reward effort and achievement; detention and special report system where necessary. 'Safety of pupils is paramount, so 'imposition sheets' are set instead of detentions during dark evenings between November and February.'

Uniform Royal-blue blazer with badge, grey trousers/navy pleated skirt. But sixth-formers 'wear clothes suitable for student business'.

Homework Average 11-year-old, five hours a week; 14-year-old, seven hours 30 minutes; 16-year-old, 12 hours.

Vocational qualifications BTEC; GNVQ; NVQ.

Inspection October 1996: 'A most effective school with many very good features in which high academic standards are achieved within a caring Christian ethos.'; 'Standards of reading and writing are good. Pupils have very good listening skills and are articulate speakers. Standards of numeracy are good and competence in the use of information technology is above average. Standards of behaviour, dress and attendance are very good.'; 'The quality of teaching is good or better in nearly two thirds of lessons and satisfactory in all but a handful – in one in eight it is very good. In some lessons a restricted range of teaching methods does not always foster higher order learning skills, such as the development of problem-solving techniques.'; 'Pupils conduct themselves well around the school and accept responsibility sensibly.'

Primary schools St Andrew's CE Primary; St Paul's CE Primary; Mab's Cross County Primary; Woodfield County Primary; St Matthew's CE Primary.

ANSFORD COMMUNITY SCHOOL

Castle Cary
Somerset BA7 7JJ
Tel (01963) 350895
Fax (01963) 351357
E-mail: jhardy7105@aol.com

- National ranking 350 = (302 =, 334 =)
- GCSE 62% (63%)
- A-levels *Not applicable*
- Higher education *Not applicable*

- Mixed comprehensive
- Pupils 553
- Boys (11–16) 288
- Girls (11–16) 265
- Sixth form *Not applicable*
- Education authority *Somerset*

Headteacher Denise Strutt, 40, appointed in September 1997. Staff 31 (men 12, women 19).

Motto Achieving in a caring society.

Background Opened in 1940 with a mixture of local children and wartime evacuees from Southampton and East London; became comprehensive in 1979; Somerset's first community school in 1986; adapted for physically-disabled pupils in 1987; the county's smallest secondary school, with facilities recently modernised with a grant from the Foundation for Sports and Arts. Situated on a hill above the small market town of Castle Cary, with views across the Polden Hills and surrounded by extensive playing fields. Serves rural area of south Somerset between Shepton Mallet and Yeovil; seven local primary schools comprise the Ansford Foundation. Local and national reputation for multi-cultural work and European links; Enterprise work. Won awards from Somerset's Education and Business Curriculum Centre, Central Bureau and the Commonwealth Institute. Work-experience for pupils in Holland; exchange link with Mufulira School in Zambia. The school 'places emphasis on self-discipline and responsibility'. Code of conduct established by pupils and staff. School Council; older pupils have responsibility as year-leaders and bullying counsellors.

Streaming In sets after year 7 in mathematics, French, science and English. Changes and developments from year 8 to 10.

Approach to discipline 'It expects respect from the pupils who are rewarded for hard work and achievements. There is a clear punishment system, but the emphasis is on working with the individual pupil to make him or her a positive member of the school community.'

Uniform Black trousers/skirt, white shirt, school tie, school sweatshirt with badge.

Homework Average 11-year-old, six hours 30 minutes a week; 14-year-old, nine hours; 16-year-old, nine hours 30 minutes.

Vocational qualifications RSA Initial Awards.

Inspection October 1995: 'A good school which provides its pupils with a supportive working environment where they learn effectively and feel valued.'; 'Parents value highly the school's academic achievements, the care and welfare of the pupils and the opportunities for social interaction through its extra-curricular and community provision.'; 'In physical education, standards are low in a range of games and gymnastics.' *The school reports that the issue of physical education has since been addressed, with new staff and a local education authority report on the provision of PE.*

Primary schools Castle Cary Primary; Evercreech CE Primary; Ditcheat Primary; Lovington Primary; Keinton Mandeville Primary; North Cadbury Primary; Queen Camel Countess Gwytha Primary; Bruton Primary.

BENTLEY WOOD HIGH SCHOOL

Bridges Road
Stanmore
Middlesex HA7 3NA
Tel (0181) 954 3623
Fax (0181) 954 0427

- National ranking 350 = (446 =, 494 =, 337 =, –)
- GCSE 62% (54%)
- A-levels *Not applicable*
- Higher education *Not applicable*

- Girls' comprehensive
- Pupils 720
- Boys *Not applicable*
- Girls (12–16) 720
- Sixth form *Not applicable*
- Education authority *Harrow*

Headteacher Annette Ford, 41, appointed in April 1992. Staff 44 (men 10, women 34).

Motto *None*

Background Built originally as Heriots Wood Grammar School in 1955 on site of old house, with 27 acres of woodland, parkland and extensive games areas; came into being as Bentley Wood High School in 1975 with borough re-organisation. New buildings created drama studio, music and art suite, humanities area, and large well-stocked library. Fully-subscribed, with about 180 applications for 180 places. Sports facilities 'excellent' because of advantages of the school site, which is also used for science and art. All faculty areas have specialist rooms, which are updated to provide information technology support. 'Bentley Wood is a friendly, hard-working community. Opportunities are provided for all girls to maximise their potential, participate fully in all areas of school life and attain their highest level of achievement in an atmosphere that is safe, well-ordered, supportive and stimulating.'

Streaming *None*

Approach to discipline 'Pupils are encouraged to behave with courtesy and respect towards all members of the school community. High standards of work and behaviour are expected from all pupils. Relationships between staff and pupils are based on mutual respect and co-operation.'

Uniform Bottle-green blazer, jumper and skirt or tailored slacks, white blouse (or polo-neck jumper in winter), black shoes. 'Girls are encouraged to look smart, allowing a little choice in types of skirt.'

Homework Average 12-year-old, six hours 30 minutes a week; 14-year-old, eight hours 30 minutes; 16-year-old, 10 hours, 'to encompass coursework demands'.

Vocational qualifications *None*

Inspection October 1996: 'A good school, with many significant strengths and a few areas for development. A cooperative and stimulating environment is provided in which a climate of courtesy enables staff and pupils to learn happily and well. The extent of racial harmony is exceptional.'; 'Standards of literacy across all subjects of the curriculum are good. Pupils' numeracy skills are adequate for the demands of other subjects, though there is some weakness in mental arithmetic. Pupils' information technology skills are good.'; 'Nearly all pupils show enthusiasm for and interest in their work. The development of their capacity for personal study is a particular strength and contributes significantly to the standards achieved. Behaviour is very good indeed, often excellent. Pupils show respect for people and for property. A good rapport exists between most pupils and their teachers, and relationships are harmonious. Pupils show unusual willingness to volunteer help and to take responsibility in school and in the wide community. The school is a happy place and many lessons are characterised by good humour.'

Primary schools Up to 38 feeder schools.

FERNWOOD COMPREHENSIVE SCHOOL

Goodwood Road
Wollaton
Nottingham
Nottinghamshire NG8 2FT
Tel **(0115) 928 6326**
Fax **(0115) 985 4250**

- National ranking 350= (331=, 401=, 392=, −)
- GCSE 62% (62%)
- A-levels *Not applicable*
- Higher education *Not applicable*

- Mixed comprehensive
- Pupils 823
- Boys (11–16) 396
- Girls (11–16) 427
- Sixth form *Not applicable*
- Education authority *Nottinghamshire*

Headteacher Jean Evelyn Amy Gemmell, 56, appointed in January 1983. Staff 44 (men 23, women 21).

Motto Vincit qui conatur (Who tries, conquers).

Background Opened in 1960 as 'bilateral' school; became 11-to-16 comprehensive in 1973; compact buildings 'incorporating an appropriate range of specialist facilities' on 'spacious and pleasantly appointed' campus shared with infant and junior schools. Over-subscribed, with 1.5 applications per place. Regular exchange visits with schools in France or Germany. Proud of sporting achievements, also strong tradition in music and drama. 'Good relationships with local industry and neighbourhood community, based on trust and mutual respect, have been built up over many years. The school strives to uphold the best ideals of comprehensive education with a rich mixture of cultures working together harmoniously and a commitment to good academic standards and a willingness to adapt to change without compromising the school's philosophy.'

Streaming Some setting in languages and mathematics.

Approach to discipline 'Firm, consistent, fair and, as far as possible, friendly. Self-discipline and co-operation are extolled at all times.'

Uniform Dark-grey/black trousers or skirt/culottes, white shirt/blouse, school tie, grey/black V-neck/cardigan, black/grey shoes. 'Pupils are expected to adhere to the agreed uniform.'

Homework Average 11-year-old, three to five hours a week; 14-year-old, five to seven hours; 16-year-old, more than seven hours, as needed.

Vocational qualifications City and Guilds, Diploma of Vocational Education.

Inspection September 1994: 'This is a good school.'; 'Pupils write well and have good listening skills. Oral skills are of high quality and are a strength of the school.'; 'Pupils' behaviour is excellent. They have positive attitudes to their work and good learning skills. Teachers are appropriately qualified, plan lessons carefully and have a competent grasp of subject matter. They show a high level of commitment and motivate pupils with praise and encouragement; in some areas of the curriculum teaching lacks pace and challenge, particularly for the more able pupils.'; 'The school has clear, moral, social and cultural values which promote an orderly and caring learning environment.'

Primary schools Fernwood Junior; Middleton Junior; Beeston Fields Primary; Firbeck Primary; Portland Primary.

NOWER HILL HIGH SCHOOL

George V Avenue
Pinner
Middlesex HA5 5RP
Tel (0181) 863 0877/8
Fax (0181) 424 0762

E-mail: nowerhil@rmplc.co.uk
Internet: http://www.rmplc.co.uk/eduweb/sites/nowerhil

- National ranking 350 = (290 =, 378 =, 392 =, 241 =)
- GCSE 62% (64%)
- A-levels Not applicable
- Higher education Not applicable

- Mixed comprehensive
- Pupils 1,200
- Boys (12–16) 603
- Girls (12–16) 597
- Sixth form Not applicable
- Education authority Harrow

Headteacher Simon Peter Hensby, 58, appointed in September 1983. Staff 73 (men 31, women 42).

Motto Service not self.

Background Nower Hill High was founded in 1974 when Harrow changed to a system of high schools for pupils 12–16; previously, Headstone Secondary School, which opened in 1929, on same site in Pinner, with farmland and open spaces nearby. Buildings comprise linked blocks built in 1929, 1950 and 1970s. Additional buildings and alterations under way to accommodate extra 240 pupils in 1996. Expansion includes laboratories, technical and information technology facilities, sports hall, music and drama suites. Among sports played on extensive grounds are netball, hockey, tennis, athletics, rugby, soccer and cricket; gymnastics, weight-lifting and badminton also popular. All pupils take 10 GCSEs; oversubscribed with 390 applications for 300 places; 92% of pupils continue with their education. Prides itself on reputation for music, drama and sport; Duke of Edinburgh Award Scheme.

Streaming Mixed approach, with departments making own judgment. 'Differentiated learning provides for all abilities, particularly the very able.'

Approach to discipline 'Firm and friendly, with strong emphasis on responsibilities as well as rights.' Supervision organised by head of pastoral care with four year-heads, each with team of form tutors. Head holds surgery on Monday evenings for parents without an appointment.

Uniform Navy-and-silver uniform 'based on

the idea of smart business wear'.

Homework Average 12-year-old, seven hours 30 minutes; 14-year-old, 10 hours; 16-year-old, 12 hours.

Vocational qualifications *None*

Inspection January 1993: 'In many respects, this is a good school.'; 'The school is very successful at helping pupils gain good results at GCSE. It is now in a position to complete the implementation of the school's aims and provide a broader range of educational experiences.'; 'Teachers are hard-working and the teaching is sound. The majority of the lessons are well planned. Pupils are confident and generally happy, applying themselves well to the tasks they are asked to perform.' October 1996: 'This is a good school with many very strong features. It provides a well-balanced education for most pupils. It has a hard-working and committed staff and enjoys a positive relationship with its pupils and their parents.'; 'Though boys and girls make good progress overall, girls' progress is particularly good. The school is aware of this and is seeking to further improve boys' progress.'; 'Teachers' expectations of their pupils are generally appropriate. The quality of teaching varies widely, however, and in some departments ranges from poor to very good. More consistency is needed.'; 'The school is well-managed and efficiently administered.'

Primary schools Cannon Lane Middle; Longfield Middle; Pinner Park Middle; Pinner Wood Middle; West Lodge Middle.

THE ROMSEY SCHOOL

Greatbridge
Romsey
Hampshire SO51 8ZB
Tel (01794) 512334
Fax (01794) 511497
E-mail: drskinner@romseyschool.org.uk
Internet: http://www.romseyschool.org.uk

- National ranking 350 = (331 =, 448 =, 355 =, 337 =)
- GCSE 62% (62%)
- A-levels *Not applicable*
- Higher education *Not applicable*

- Mixed comprehensive
- Pupils 1,025
- Boys (11–16) 543

- Girls (11–16) 482
- Sixth form *Not applicable*
- Education authority *Hampshire*

Headteacher Dr Richard Adams Skinner, 58, appointed in January 1981. Staff 66 (men 26, women 40).

Motto Siege perilous (Seat without parallel).

Background Originally a secondary modern, the school moved to current site in 1958; became comprehensive in 1973; designated community school in 1985. Extensive community programme 'a major strength', with wide range of links with outside organisations. 'Facilities are good and, although not enjoying favourable resources in the past and not being a purpose-built comprehensive, new facilities recently added have enhanced the school's provision.' New performing arts building opened in 1996; developments include science laboratory, fourth IT network suite, new library centre. Set in 19 acres, the school enjoys fine views of Romsey Abbey. Over-subscribed, with three applications per place; official intake is 185, but takes 210 pupils per year with education authority approval; 35% from outside catchment area. More than eight in 10 (85%) of school-leavers continue in further education, with 40% going on to higher education. Extensive Business Project 'a notable feature' for years 9–11. Notable for performing arts, large orchestra and choir, with brass, wind and string ensembles. National success in public-speaking competitions. 'Sporting facilities are excellent and the competitive spirit unashamedly encouraged, with considerable emphasis on team games.' Pupils gaining local and national recognition. Two Schools Curriculum Awards, including 1997. Investor in People Award 1996. Charity fundraising 'part of the school's moral and community responsibility': £80,000 in 10 years. 'Excellence, endeavour and enterprise are the school's guiding principles.' School hosts local ATC squadron; permanent HQ on site opened in 1997.

Alumni Todd Bennett, Olympic athlete.

Streaming Setting by ability in most subjects. 'A pupil's specific abilities should be recognised and met.'

Approach to discipline Strict but fair and consistent. 'The focus is on common-sense rules clearly understood by everyone, designed to provide a framework for all to act in a responsible way.' Clear policy on bullying; strict code with sanctions for any verbal abuse or violent behaviour. Strong pastoral system with good support from parents.

Uniform Boys: black blazer with school badge, white/grey shirt, black/dark-grey trousers, school tie, grey/black socks, grey pullover with badge, black shoes. Girls: maroon blazer with badge, white blouse, grey skirt, school tie, maroon socks, black shoes. Enforced 'absolutely 100%'; agreed after consulting Romsey School Association.

Homework Average 11-year-old, five hours a week; 14-year-old, 10 hours; 16-year-old, 15 hours.

Vocational qualifications *None*

Inspection 'The school is adequately accommodated and the grounds are well kept and litter-free. Internal and external decoration is good and well maintained with no evidence of vandalism or graffiti.'; 'The school is a well-ordered and purposeful community. Considerable value is placed on personal achievement and excellence. Clear expectations about behaviour and discipline, including matters of dress are laid down in the code of conduct and are met.'; 'The stress on excellence, endeavour and enterprise is evident in all aspects of school life and contributes to the ethos and high expectations apparent in lessons and other activities.'

Primary schools Cupernham Junior; Romsey Abbey CE Primary; Awbridge Primary; Romsey Junior; Braishfield Primary; Ampfield CE Primary.

WOODLANDS COMMUNITY SCHOOL

Blenheim Drive
Allestree
Derby
Derbyshire DE22 2LW
Tel (01332) 551921
Fax (01332) 553869

- National ranking 350= (366=, 359=, 337=, 337=)
- GCSE 62% (60%)
- A-levels *Not applicable*
- Higher education *Not applicable*

- Grant maintained
- Mixed comprehensive
- Pupils 989

- Boys (11–16) 488
- Girls (11–16) 501
- Sixth form 89 (Year 12 only)
- Education authority *Derbyshire*

Headteacher Alan Wayment, 49, appointed in July 1985. Staff 58 (men 37, women 21).

Motto Committed to excellence within a caring environment.

Background Set in northern suburbs of Derby, overlooking fields and, across Vicar Wood valley, Kedleston Hall and its expansive estates. Good maintenance of school and its site is a priority. Facilities include library and information centre, language bases, information technology and computer suites, purpose-built technology block, science laboratory suite, art and design studios, humanities base, creative and performing arts suite, music suite and media studio; also swimming pool. Special teaching facility for hearing-impaired children. Oversubscribed by up to 45%. Strong art, music and drama tradition: annual art exhibition and drama production; school boasts own music school that is supported outside normal school hours. Adult community programme, youth provision and extensive sports programmes. City, county and national success at sport. 'Woodlands is a place of hard work and high academic achievement, and equally importantly, a place where people matter and learn respect for each other.'

Alumni Nigel Clough, England and Nottingham Forest soccer player; Philip Harries, Olympic hurdler; Paula Bishop, 1991 BBC Choirgirl of the Year; Janet Haslam, author.

Streaming Limited setting in years 10 and 11.

Approach to discipline 'High standards of behaviour are demanded and the school is proud of being well ordered and a centre of excellence. There is a strong and consistently-applied behaviour policy, which also supports students who may be experiencing difficulties.'

Uniform 'The school is committed to a school dress policy and students are required to wear navy-blue as a key school colour.' High standard maintained.

Homework Average 11-year-old, two hours 30 minutes a week; 14-year-old, three hours 20 minutes; 16-year-old, five hours.

Vocational qualifications RSA.

Inspection November 1996: 'A successful school that has good features in a significant number of important areas.'; 'Students with special educational needs attain appropriately; some with specific learning difficulties, especially those with hearing impairment, make very good progress as a result of the high-quality support given by the school.'; 'At present, some of the most able students make less progress than expected because some of the work is insufficiently challenging.'; 'Most students have very positive attitudes to their work. The majority are well-behaved in lessons, listen attentively and respond willingly to their teachers. In only a very few lessons and with a small group of students is there a tendency towards misbehaviour. The school functions as a very orderly community.'; 'Strong leadership by the headteacher, supported by the senior management team and the governing body, has had an increasingly beneficial effect on the management of the school.'

Primary schools Lawn Primary; Markeaton Primary; Portway Primary; Ashgate Primary. Total of 27 feeder schools.

GORDANO SCHOOL

St Mary's Road
Portishead
Bristol BS20 9QR
Tel (01275) 842606
Fax (01275) 817420
E-mail: gordano@rmplc.co.uk

- National ranking 356 (487, 286, 386, 333)
- GCSE 61% (50%)
- A-levels 44% (A/B); 96% (A/E)
- Higher education 63% (Cambridge 1)

- Mixed comprehensive
- Pupils 1,239
- Boys (11–18) 643
- Girls (11–18) 596
- Sixth form 210 (17%)
- Education authority *North Somerset*

Headteacher Robert Sommers, 54, appointed in September 1991. Staff 73 (men 30, women 43).

Motto *None*

Background Purpose-built school with extensive grounds on semi-rural site in the Gor-

dano Valley on the outskirts of Portishead, nine miles from Bristol. Opened in 1956 and became the first full comprehensive in the area in 1964. Additional buildings since then include: specialist art, music and drama complex; sports hall; science faculty; all-weather pitch opened in 1994. Over-subscribed. Hockey outstanding among school's sporting success: girls' team winners of both indoor and outdoor national championships in 1995 and 1997; winners of indoor championships (1995); under-16 mixed hockey champions (1995 and 1996); under-16 soccer county finalists (1996); under-15 county cricket league champions (1995); county golf champions (1996); regional 3-v-3 basketball champions (1997). Orienteering also strong: two members of England under-16 squad. Well-established work-experience; finalists in Woodspring Schools Debating Competition 1993–96; commended in national schools' newspaper competition in 1995 and 1997. English and drama links with local theatre; Shakespeare taught to all pupils; public speaking competition. Eleven gold certificate winners in National Schools Mathematics competition. Visits to France and Germany; outdoor activities residential week; Duke of Edinburgh Award Scheme; annual musical, plays, concerts.

Alumni Ian Manners, international cross-country runner; Suzie Garland and Robert Dawes, ice-skaters; Simon Sheppard, England Youth soccer player; Rob McElwee, BBC weather forecaster; Denise Marston-Smith, England indoor hockey team.

Streaming Pupils in sets according to ability in French, mathematics and German from year 8. Setting for science and ability bands for English from year 10.

Approach to discipline High expectations, courtesy and self-discipline; strong house system helps monitoring; pupils' achievements recognised through merits, certificates, cups, awards and praise. 'Discipline and relationships are very good.'

Uniform Black sweatshirt with school crest in house colours, white shirt/blouse, dark-grey/black trousers/skirt/culottes. Agreed following working group of parents, governors and staff; sixth-formers are not required to wear uniform.

Homework Average 11-year-old, four to six hours a week; 14-year-old, five to eight hours; 16-year-old, six to 10 hours.

Vocational qualifications Accounts; GNVQ Advanced, Business; GNVQ Intermediate, Leisure and Tourism; Information Technology Certificate of Competence.

Inspection January 1994: 'Teachers and non-teaching staff are committed to providing high-quality education.'; 'Pupils are courteous and self-confident.'; 'The school has a friendly, supportive and caring ethos, characterised by good relationships between staff, pupils, parents and the local community.'; 'Pupils are consistently challenged at their own level.'

Primary schools St Peter's RC Primary; Highdown Primary; Portishead Primary; St Joseph's RC Primary; St Barnabas CE Primary.

WHICKHAM SCHOOL

Burnthouse Lane
Whickham
Newcastle upon Tyne NE16 5AR
Tel (0191) 496 0026
Fax (0191) 488 0968

- National ranking 357 (408, 443, 291, –)
- GCSE 61% (57%)
- A-levels 43% (A/B); 96% (A/E)
- Higher education 87% (Oxford 1)

- Mixed comprehensive
- Pupils 1,615
- Boys (11–18) 838
- Girls (11–18) 777
- Sixth form 304 (19%)
- Education authority *Gateshead*

Headteacher John William Lea, 56, appointed in September 1992. Staff 94 (men 49, women 45).

Motto *None*

Background Started life as new secondary modern in 1962; re-organised as 11–18 comprehensive in 1970; on large site on southwest edge of Tyneside conurbation; extensive playing fields; sports hall, gymnasium, 10 laboratories, modern resource centre, purpose-built pastoral accommodation. Over-subscribed, with average of 1.2 applications per place. Strong sporting tradition. Recent international honours in athletics, cricket (England under-14 captain), and swimming. Music is 'strong' with large school band performing at a number of concerts and public events. Regular dance and drama productions. Pupils are expected to behave with courtesy and consideration towards others. School rules are kept to a minimum consistent with maintaining an orderly well-disciplined atmosphere. The working environment should be friendly and purposeful. The development of character and good citizenship is considered to be of great importance.'

Streaming Pupils placed in ability sets according to their strength in particular subject: from year 7 in English, mathematics and languages; from year 8 in science, history and geography.

Approach to discipline 'Emphasis must be given to praise and reward. Pupils are encouraged to develop the habits of self-discipline. The school has a strong, supportive house system to ensure the achievement of these objectives.'

Uniform Burgundy sweater, white shirt, house tie, grey skirt/trousers, black shoes. 'All pupils are expected to conform to the school uniform requirements.'

Homework Average 11-year-old, five hours a week; 14-year-old, seven hours; 16 year-old, nine hours, plus coursework.

Vocational qualifications GNVQ Intermediate and Advanced, Business and Finance; GNVQ Intermediate, Community Care; GNVQ Advanced, Art and Design.

Inspection November 1996: 'A very good school.'; 'Pupils attain educational standards in most subjects which are high in relation to their ability and overall standards of attainment are above the national average.'; 'The pupils are well-behaved and very attentive in their lessons.'; 'The teaching is good, and frequently very good or excellent, and this makes a major contribution to the standards achieved.'; 'The attainment in lessons of pupils in the sixth form is significantly better than might be expected for pupils of that age and following similar courses. Attainment is particularly high in design technology, English, geography, history, physical education, religious education and the sciences.'; 'The vast majority of pupils have a very good attitude to learning. They exhibit an ability to concentrate in lessons and show a level of participation and enthusiasm which enhances their learning. Their behaviour is generally very good, both in lessons and around the school.'; 'The overall quality of teaching is good, with a significant proportion being very good or excellent.'; 'The school is very well staffed with suitably-qualified and experienced teachers.'

Primary schools Clover Hill Primary; Fellside Primary; Front Street Primary; Marley Hill Primary; Parochial CE Primary; Washingwell Primary.

WHEATLEY PARK SCHOOL

Holton
Oxford
Oxfordshire OX33 1QH
Tel (01865) 872441
Fax (01865) 874712
E-mail: wpschool@rmplc.co.uk
Internet: http://www.rmplc.co.uk/eduweb/
sites/wpschool

- National ranking 358 (464, 227, 305)
- GCSE 61% (54%)
- A-levels 39% (A/B); 87% (A/E)
- Higher education 90% (Oxford 1, Cambridge 2)

- Mixed comprehensive
- Pupils 1,382
- Boys (11–18) 709
- Girls (11–18) 673
- Sixth form 239 (17%)
- Education authority *Oxfordshire*

Headteacher Nicholas Young, 49, appointed in September 1993. Staff 74 (men 35, women 39).

Motto *None*

Background Wheatley Park occupies fine site of Holton Park, with Georgian mansion and extensive parklands. It draws pupils from a wide and largely rural area immediately to the east of Oxford and from a small part of Buckinghamshire. Until 1983, it was on two sites, but over the past 11 years nearly £3m has been spent, including a sports centre that is shared with the community. Georgian mansion converted into arts centre for school and community use from September 1995. Over-subscribed, with 180 of 230 entrants coming from immediate catchment area; average of 1.2 applications per place. Reputation for high-quality provision for children with special needs, including the most able. Latin available in year 9. Musical tours to Canada, France, Czechoslovakia, Georgia, Germany and Italy. Strong industry links. Duke of Edinburgh Award Scheme.

Alumni Baroness Mallalieu of Studdridge.

Streaming Setting from year 8 in English, mathematics, science and modern languages. Individual programmes in years 10 and 11.

Approach to discipline 'All pupils and parents are aware of high standards of behaviour expected at Wheatley Park and pupils meet these demands. Courtesy, honesty, good relationships and care of the school environment are priorities. We work as a partnership – pupil, parent, teacher – when problems arise.'

Uniform White shirt/blouse, turquoise-and-grey tie, grey sweatshirt, grey trousers/skirt, black shoes. For sixth-formers, blue is 'offered' colour. 'Uniform is an important matter in years 7 to 11.

Homework Average 11-year-old, seven hours a week; 14-year-old, nine hours; 16-year-old, 12 + hours.

Vocational qualifications RSA; City and Guilds; GNVQ Intermediate and Advanced.

Primary school Wheatley CE Primary; Sandhills Primary; Garsington CE Primary; Oakley Primary; Great Milton CE Primary; Chalgrove Primary; Ickford Primary; Beckley CE Primary.

WHITLEY BAY HIGH SCHOOL

Deneholm
Whitley Bay
Tyne and Wear NE25 9AS
Tel (0191) 200 8800
Fax (0191) 200 8803
E-mail: wbhs@rmplc.co.uk

- National ranking 359 (345, 329, 425, –)
- GCSE 61% (61%)
- A-levels 38% (A/B); 91% (A/E)
- Higher education 90% (Cambridge 2)

- Mixed comprehensive
- Pupils 1,178
- Boys (13–18) 556
- Girls (13–18) 622
- Sixth form 332 (28%)
- Education authority *North Tyneside*

Headteacher Adam Chedburn, 43, appointed in April 1994. Staff 73 (men 37, women 36).

Motto *None*

Background Opened in 1973 in buildings dating from 1962 and previously occupied by Whitley Bay Grammar School; school surrounded by substantial playing fields and shares use of 'excellent' council leisure facilities nearby; about a quarter of a mile from the sea and has impressive views from top-floor classrooms. New sports hall in April 1996; extensive recent development of sixth-form information technology facilities. Over-subscribed; staying-on rate into sixth-form is 70%. Strong musical and drama tradition; recent productions of *Amadeus, Dancing at Lughnasa, Cabaret,* and *The Plough and the Stars;* regular summer production at Whitley Bay Playhouse. Wide range of sport played at all levels; regular national success in basketball and athletics; sports clubs start at 7.30am. Foreign exchanges to Pau and Münchengladbach, and sixth-form work-experience in Berlin. 'A neighbourhood comprehensive, widely-respected in the area; it has a strong academic tradition that has been retained while curriculum provision has been broadened and taken more account of vocational issues.'

Streaming 'Pupils are setted flexibly across national curriculum subjects, but there is no rigid streaming.'

Approach to discipline Clear expectations and guidelines concerning behaviour, discipline and referral systems: 'Pupils are courteous, have a clear understanding of what constitutes acceptable behaviour and show a good deal of self-discipline.'

Uniform Girls: navy skirt/trousers, white blouse, year tie, black shoes. Boys: dark-grey trousers, white shirt, year tie, black shoes. Sixth-formers 'dress appropriate to place of work'.

Homework Average 14-year-old, 12 to 15 hours a week; 16-year-old, 15 hours.

Vocational qualifications GNVQ Intermediate and Advanced, Health and Social Care, Leisure and Tourism, Business.

Primary schools Valley Gardens Middle; Marden Bridge Middle; Wellfield Middle; Monkseaton Middle.

WETHERBY HIGH SCHOOL

Hallfield Lane
Wetherby
West Yorkshire LS22 6JS

Tel **(01937) 520500**
Fax **(01937) 520501**

- National ranking 360 (379, 327, –, 380)
- GCSE 61% (59%)
- A-levels 38% (A/B); 90% (A/E)
- Higher education 92% (Cambridge 1)

- Mixed comprehensive
- Pupils 781
- Boys (11–18) 394
- Girls (11–18) 387
- Sixth form 117 (15%)
- Education authority *Leeds*

Headteacher Adrian White, 52, appointed in September 1985. Staff 49 (men 22, women 27).

Motto *None*

Background Founded in 1966 on pleasant site in market town on River Wharfe, close to the A1 and centres such as Harrogate, York and Leeds; buildings vary in age, with newest less than 10 years old. Not over-subscribed. Sport is strong and all main team or individual games are offered. Duke of Edinburgh Award Scheme. Music includes concert band, orchestra and wide range of instrumental teaching. 'The school has a quiet, purposeful atmosphere, but one that is happy and quite relaxed. Bullying is rare.' Parent-Teacher Association.

Alumni Jon Craig, *Daily Express* deputy political editor; Michael Makin, triple-jumper; Graham Bradley, jockey; John Heaton, television producer; Stuart Naylor, West Bromwich Albion soccer player.

Streaming Pupils put in sets, especially in mathematics, modern languages, English and science.

Approach to discipline 'The approach attempts to blend firmness, fairness and a caring approach. Parents are involved at an early stage of any problem. There is a well-established pattern of sanctions.'

Uniform Grey pullover with school badge, grey trousers/skirt, pale-blue shirt/blouse, school tie, white/grey socks, dark shoes. Strictly enforced with parental agreement and offer of financial support where needed.

Homework Average 11-year-old, four hours a week; 14-year-old, six hours; 16-year-old, seven hours. Homework planners issued to all pupils.

Vocational qualifications BTEC National, Business and Finance; BTEC First, Business Studies.

Inspection October 1996: 'A successful school with a strong commitment to high standards of personal and academic attainment.'; 'Very good attendance and the positive attitudes of the great majority of pupils contribute to good attainment.'; 'The school is a friendly place and pupils readily give support and consideration to each other.'; 'Lessons are very well planned and classroom management and discipline is very good. In almost all cases there are high expectations of pupils and the content of lessons and methods of teaching are appropriate to their levels of knowledge and understanding.'

Primary schools Deighton Gates Primary; Crossley Street Primary; St James CE Primary, Wetherby; St John's Primary, Roundhay. Total of 26 feeder schools.

BOHUNT COMMUNITY SCHOOL

Longmoor Road
Liphook
Hampshire GU30 7NY
Tel (01428) 724324
Fax (01428) 725120
E-mail: aleech@bohunt.demon.co.uk

- National ranking 361= (428=, 416=, 295=, 315=)
- GCSE 61% (55%)
- A-levels *Not applicable*
- Higher education *Not applicable*

- Grant-maintained
- Mixed comprehensive
- Pupils 1,115
- Boys (11–16) 592
- Girls (11–16) 523
- Sixth form *Not applicable*
- Education authority *Hampshire*

Headteacher Dr Alan Leech, 53, appointed in April 1978. Staff 75 (men 27, women 48).

Motto *None*

Background Established in 1978 as a new community comprehensive in 25 acres of parkland on the western edge of Liphook: extensive playing fields, playcourt area, floodlit area, large sports hall, squash courts and fitness room. Area centre of musical excellence with three orchestras. Over-sub-

scribed. Vigorous able child policy; annual art and design exhibition; integrated approach to special needs. Annula European exchanges with Le Havre, Chartres and Nürnberg.

Streaming In languages in years 8 and 9; various setting arrangements by subject in years 10 and 11.

Approach to discipline Code of conduct gives examples of basic good standards of behaviour, politeness and manners: 'in queuing, receiving a marked book, listening to the comments or contribution of another'. Procedures include in-school discussions, letters to, or meetings with, parents, community service, internal and eventual external suspension.

Uniform Green blazer, mid-grey trousers/skirt, white shirt/blouse, school tie. Enforced 'very firmly'.

Homework Average 11-year-old, five hours a week; 14-year-old, seven hours; 16-year-old, 10 hours.

Vocational qualifications RSA, Information Technology.

Inspection December 1993: 'Bohunt provides a good education for all its pupils.'; 'Pupils are well-motivated, ready to learn and they are able to apply what they have learnt. They cooperate well with teachers and with each other. The teachers are hard working and committed. Their planning is thorough and provides an exceptionally clear framework for staff and pupils. The teaching is effective, and at its best when questioning is used skilfully.'

Primary schools Liphook CE Junior; Liss County Junior; Grayshott CE Primary; Greatham County Primary; Shottermill Junior.

BRAMHALL HIGH SCHOOL

Seal Road
Bramhall
Stockport
Cheshire SK7 2JT
Tel (0161) 439 8045
Fax (0161) 439 8951
E-mail: jpeckham@campus.bt.com
Internet: http://www.doc.mmu.ac.uk/schools/bramhall

- National ranking 361= (266=, 214=, 248=, 204)

- GCSE 61% (66%)
- A-levels Not applicable
- Higher education Not applicable

- Mixed comprehensive
- Pupils 1,450
- Boys (11–16) 741
- Girls (11–16) 709
- Sixth form Not applicable
- Education authority Stockport

Headteacher John Peckham, 41, appointed in January 1996. Staff 85 (men 35, women 50).

Motto None

Background Opened as co-educational grammar school in 1967; became comprehensive in 1971; over-subscribed, with 1.4 applications per place. Re-organisation in 1991 resulted in school becoming 11–16; opt-out considered annually, and rejected 'unanimously'; more than nine in 10 pupils stay in full-time education, mostly to take A-levels. Single site in residential area south-west of Stockport, with good facilities and extensive playing fields including all-weather pitch. More than 53 different sporting teams in competitive matches each year. High level of parental involvement: each year-group has its own parents' discussion group; Parents' Association thrives.

Streaming Setting increases as students move up the school. Begins in year 8 for mathematics, French and German, and in science from year 9.

Approach to discipline 'Firm and fair; high expectations and clear code of behaviour. Positive reward system for good work and behaviour; clearly-spelled-out sanctions for misbehaviour. Elected Student Council and student charities committee.'

Uniform Black sweatshirt with embroidered school badge, black trousers/skirt, white shirt/blouse, school tie for boys, grey/black/white socks. High expectations for smart appearance.

Homework Average 11-year-old, seven hours a week; 14-year-old, eight hours; 16-year-old, 12 hours.

Vocational qualifications GNVQ, Business and Manufacturing.

Inspection January 1993: 'This is a very good school. Standards are high and pupils' achievements are good in almost all respects. There is some under-achievement, however, by the most able pupils.'; 'Pupils are cooperative and keen to learn. They respond well to realistic challenges and generally apply themselves well to their work. The quality of teaching is consistently sound with few weaknesses.'; 'Behaviour is good and relationships between pupils and teachers are respectful.' May 1996: 'A successful school that maintains high standards of achievement in both academic and extra-curricular activities. The school has a well-deserved good reputation and is supported by both parents and students in its aim of providing a stimulating environment in which students can develop their knowledge and learning skills.'; 'The great majority of students make good progress, and most work diligently and with enthusiasm.'; 'Students have very positive attitudes to learning, are enthusiastic and energetic learners and often show initiative in selecting their own learning activities and resources.'; 'Standards of behaviour in school are generally high and relationships are good. Students are friendly, relaxed and usually show mutual respect to each other and teaching staff. The few reported incidents of bullying are dealt with quickly when brought to the attention of staff.'

Primary schools Queensgate Primary; Nevill Road Primary; Ladybrook Primary; Pownall Green Primary; Moss Hey Primary.

BROUGHTON HIGH SCHOOL

Woodplumpton Lane
Broughton
Preston
Lancashire PR3 5JJ
Tel (01772) 863849
Fax (01772) 864712

- National ranking 361 = (–, –, –, 295 =)
- GCSE 61%
- A-levels Not applicable
- Higher education Not applicable

- Mixed comprehensive
- Pupils 880
- Boys (11–16) 425
- Girls (11–16) 455
- Sixth form Not applicable
- Education authority Lancashire

Headteacher Robert Davies, 43, appointed in January 1997. Staff 48 (men 20, women 28).

Motto None

Background Opened in modern buildings in 18-acre landscaped grounds in 1975. The school serves a large suburban and widespread rural community in the Wyre and Fylde areas. Three in four pupils (75%) enter full-time further education, of whom about half enter higher education. The school has close involvement with pupils with special needs. Consistently over-subscribed, with 260 applications for 176 places. Art, drama and music listed among strengths. In sport, tennis, table tennis, rugby, soccer and athletics noted for competition at county level with county representatives.

Streaming Pupils placed in ability sets; composition varies according to subject. Criteria include national curriculum assessments, ability tests and teacher reports.

Approach to discipline High expectations; self-discipline. 'Emphasis is placed on good attendance, commitment to high behaviour and work standards, and pride in achievement.'

Uniform Black blazer with badge, dark-grey skirt/trousers, white shirt/blouse, green-and-gold tie. 'Conformity is a condition of admission but recognition given to clothing requirements in respect of specific religious observances.'

Homework Average 11-year-old, seven hours a week; 14-year-old, eight hours; 16-year-old, 12 hours.

Vocational qualifications GNVQ, Tourism and Leisure, Art and Design, Business Studies, Health and Social Care.

Inspection January 1997: 'A very successful school which achieves high standards for its pupils; it has a talented, enthusiastic staff who consistently demonstrate professional commitment and initiative.'; 'Most pupils achieve above-average standards for their age in all subjects of the curriculum and the majority of pupils make good and often very good progress. Pupils with special educational needs also do well. a small minority of pupils make insufficient progress.'; 'Teachers are extremely hard-working and their high-quality teaching is a strength of the school.'; 'Most pupils have very positive attitudes to lessons and are keen to learn; they listen attentively and work productively. Outside lessons they are generally mature and well-behaved. A very small minority find it more difficult to maintain interest in their work and on occasion these pupils are disruptive; behaviour on some of the school buses has been of concern recently and the school has taken steps to improve it.'; 'The school makes generally good use of resources available to it, but there is limited funding for, and insufficient use of, the library.'

Primary schools Harris County Primary; Queen's Drive County Primary; Oliverson's CE Primary, Goosnargh; St Peter's CE Primary; Broughton CE Primary.

HADLEIGH HIGH SCHOOL

High Lands Road
Hadleigh
Ipswich
Suffolk IP7 5HU
Tel (01473) 823496
Fax (01473) 824720
E-mail: hadhigh@rmplc.co.uk

- National ranking 361 = (382 =, 416 =, 392 =, 356 =)
- GCSE 61% (59%)
- A-levels *Not applicable*
- Higher education *Not applicable*

- Mixed comprehensive
- Pupils 669
- Boys (11–16) 331
- Girls (11–16) 338
- Sixth form *Not applicable*
- Education authority *Suffolk*

Headteacher Roger Davies, 47, appointed in September 1987. Staff 41 (men 18, women 23).

Motto *None*

Background Built in the early 1970s on outskirts of Suffolk market town of Hadleigh, eight miles from Ipswich and 10 miles from Colchester and Sudbury; single-storey buildings; all classrooms carpeted. New community sports centre includes fitness room. Spacious grounds include conservation area, four soccer pitches, two hockey pitches and one rugby pitch. Not over-subscribed. School colours awarded for achievement in sport or school activities. Form captains appointed from year 10 pupils; two school captains act as head boy or girl at public functions. Under-16 netball team are Suffolk champions, reached national finals in 1993; music includes swing band; termly music and/or drama productions. Up to four visits a year to continent, including exchanges with France and Germany. Eight in 10 pupils remain in full-time education after 16; sixth-form partnership arrangement with neighbouring 13–18 school.

Streaming Pupils in sets in mathematics, French, science from year 8.

Approach to discipline 'Firm but caring.' High expectations; self-discipline emphasised to produce orderly, disciplined, courteous school. Merit system for academic work or community service.

Uniform Boys: navy V-neck pullover, pale-blue shirt, gold tie, dark-grey/navy trousers, black/dark-brown shoes. Girls: navy cardigan/V-neck jumper, navy skirt/culottes/trousers; pale-blue shirt/blouse, black/dark-brown shoes. 'Strict enforcement, very positively supported by parents.'

Homework Average 11-year-old, five hours a week; 14-year-old, seven hours 30 minutes to 10 hours; 16-year-old, 10 to 15 hours.

Vocational qualifications Diploma of Vocational Education; part of national pilot scheme for GNVQ.

Inspection February 1996: 'A good and successful school. It is a purposeful and caring community with many strengths.'; 'Pupils' attitudes to learning are good. They are self-motivated and keen to learn.'; 'The quality of teaching is sound and often good. Good or outstanding teaching was seen in all subjects. Teachers have a good command of their subjects and employ a good balance and variety of teaching methods. They have high expectations of pupils.'; 'A relative weakness is the use of different tasks and resources matched to the needs of pupils of different abilities.'; 'Marking is regular and is generally good. There is good feedback to pupils either through written comments or verbally.'; 'The school's provision for extra-curricular sport is a strength.'

Primary schools Hadleigh County Primary; Hadleigh St Mary's CE Primary; Bildeston County Primary; Elmsett CE Primary; Hintlesham CE Primary.

HARTFORD HIGH SCHOOL

Hartford Campus
Chester Road
Northwich
Cheshire CW8 1LH
Tel (01606) 79233
Fax (01606) 783941

- National ranking 361= (428=, 448=)
- GCSE 61% (55%)
- A-levels *Not applicable*
- Higher education *Not applicable*

- Mixed comprehensive
- Pupils 1,170
- Boys (11–16) 542
- Girls (11–16) 628
- Sixth form *Not applicable*
- Education authority *Cheshire*

Headteacher Dr Peter John Llewellyn, 54, appointed in September 1989. Staff 61 (men 22, women 39).

Motto *None*

Background Formed from Hartford Secondary Moderns for Boys and Girls in 1978; serves Hartford, Winnington and Barnton, with about three in 10 pupils from outside catchment area. Split-site on 123-acre campus shared with other schools. Running track, several full-size soccer pitches, hockey/rugby pitches, tennis courts, two libraries, halls, canteens, gymnasiums, eight laboratories, drama studio, workshops, three computer rooms. Not over-subscribed: 237 applications for 240 places. Regular sporting successes in competitive sports: soccer, rugby union, hockey, netball, basketball, cricket. Facilities for the most able: early exam entry, promotion to next year-group, advanced lessons for some able pupils. Facilities for least able: withdrawal, in-lesson support, regular testing and reporting to parents. Complete primary education in English and mathematics available for appropriate pupils. 'We accept pupils with physical disabilities, although there are no special facilities for them.' Three networked computer suites; school builds computers to parents' or pupils' specification for private use. CD-Rom available on all networks. Ten-subject GCSE course for all in years 10 and 11, with wide choice; combined and separate sciences; three modern languages taught in all years. Two weeks' work-experience in year 10; full careers' education in years 9 to 11. Wide range of out-of-school activities: music and sport in particular; trips abroad, including work-experience in France. Full programme of concert, drama, dance, art and fashion events. 'In an ordered atmosphere of disciplined study, high expectation and strong pastoral support, pupils seek and achieve academic success regardless of personal disadvantage, physical disability, or prior achievement.'

Streaming Pupils put in ability sets in different subjects at different ages: mathematics from year 7; modern languages and science from year 8. All others except history and single classes are in ability sets from year 10.

Approach to discipline Code of behaviour negotiated with all pupils. Socially-acceptable behaviour and teamwork taught in Personal and Social Education; parental involvement in early problems; behaviour modifications by rewards and sanctions; strongest sanctions – exclusion or expulsion – used if necessary. Major formal rewards ceremonies with prizes at the end of year, with more informal ones during daily assemblies.

Uniform Navy jumper/blazer, blue shirt/blouse, navy tie, dark shoes. 'If pupils arrive without items of uniform, they are loaned them from a store. Pupils may not take part in school activities or lessons, or start school in the new year, without uniform. Those without the means to buy full uniform can receive some subsidy from school fund.'

Homework Average 11-year-old, eight hours a week; 14-year-old, 12 hours; 16-year-old, 15 hours.

Vocational qualifications *None*

Inspection March 1993: 'Hartford High School provides education of high quality. The pursuit of all-round excellence is central to its aims.'; 'The school also fulfils its commitment to give equal value to each child and to each child's education. Careful consideration is given to moral, social and cultural education.'; 'Good relationships between staff and pupils contribute to an environment in which effective teaching and learning take place. In most lessons, pupils are well-motivated and make good progress.'; 'The school is firmly led. The headteacher's flexible, pragmatic style of leadership enables the school to accommodate change.'; 'The school provides a harmonious and civilised environment for staff and pupils alike. Pupils are well-behaved and are courteous to one another and to adults.'

Primary schools Barnton County Junior; Riddings Hartford County Primary; Hartford Manor County Primary; Winnington Park County Primary; Darwin Street County Primary.

ST BEDE'S ROMAN CATHOLIC HIGH SCHOOL

St Anne's Road
Ormskirk
Lancashire L39 4TA
Tel (01695) 570335/577320
Fax (01695) 571686

- National ranking 361= (206=, 416=, 279=, 260=)
- GCSE 61% (73%)
- A-levels *Not applicable*
- Higher education *Not applicable*

- Mixed comprehensive
- Pupils 560
- Boys (11–16) 295
- Girls (11–16) 265
- Sixth form *Not applicable*
- Education authority *Lancashire*

Headteacher Philip Entwistle, 56 appointed in September 1983. Staff 31 (men 14, women 17).

Motto Lex tua lux (The law is your light).

Background Opened in 1956 in semi-rural residential area to the south of Ormskirk; re-organised in 1970, when school received its first fully-comprehensive intake. Voluntary-aided school, with parish priests of contributory parishes on governing body; school chaplain appointed by archbishop. Over-subscribed, with wide catchment area resulting from parental choice; 25 'feeder' primary schools; 165 applications for 110 places. More than nine in 10 pupils (91%) continue education after 16; most go to St John Rigby Roman Catholic Sixth-form College at Orrell, near Wigan. Sporting success includes winning 18 soccer trophies in past five years. Music: orchestra, choir, musical productions. Support for pupils with special needs. 'Our overall aim is to provide a caring Catholic environment within which every pupil is enabled to develop his/her personality and abilities as fully as possible and to live a rich and satisfying personal life in accordance with the principles and teachings of the Catholic Church.'

Streaming For all subjects. Pupils are put in sets for mathematics and English from year 7.

Approach to discipline 'Sanctions such as "lines", additional work and detention are used. Pupils who are late twice in one week are usually placed in the late detention on the following Tuesday evening. Pupils not in full uniform can expect to be excluded for disciplinary reasons. Temporary and permanent exclusion are further options available for dealing with extreme cases of persistent indiscipline.'

Uniform Black blazer with badge, white/pale-blue/grey shirt or blouse, black/dark grey trousers or medium-grey skirt, school pullover, dark-grey/navy/black socks, black/dark-brown/navy shoes. 'We are persistently insistent.'

Homework 'It is the policy that homework will be given on a regular basis to all pupils in most subjects. The amount set and the form the homework takes will be influenced by the pupil's age and ability and by the needs of the course.' Parents informed when pupils not completing homework on regular basis.

Vocational qualifications Commercial courses leading to RSA examinations; technology and information technology.

Inspection November 1994: 'A good school with many outstanding features. The life and work of the school is set within a strong and supportive Catholic ethos.'; 'Pupils have positive attitudes to learning. They approach their work with interest and commitment, and in the great majority of lessons pupils make worthwhile progress.'; 'Pupils' work is marked regularly and parents are kept informed of their children's progress by the annual record of achievement and meetings with teachers.'; 'The quality of education provided by the school is high.'; 'The leadership of the school is strong and has a clear sense of purpose. The school runs with quiet efficiency on a day-to-day basis.'; 'Behaviour is excellent and pupils show care and concern for each other.'

Primary schools St Anne's RC Primary, Ormskirk; Burscough RC Primary, Burscough; St Mary's Primary, Scarisbrick; Our Lady and All Saints' RC Primary, Parbold.

ST GABRIEL'S ROMAN CATHOLIC HIGH SCHOOL

Bridge Road
Bury
Greater Manchester BL9 0TZ
Tel (0161) 764 3186
Fax (0161) 761 3469

- National ranking 361 = (411 =, 278 =, 337 =, –)
- GCSE 61% (57%)
- A-levels *Not applicable*
- Higher education *Not applicable*

- Mixed comprehensive
- Pupils 1,009
- Boys (11–16) 522
- Girls (11–16) 487
- Sixth form *Not applicable*
- Education authority *Bury*

Headteacher Paul Hopkins, appointed in September 1980. Staff 55 (men 25, women 30).

Motto Fortitudo mea dominus (The Lord is my strength).

Background Opened in 1954; serves six parishes of northern half of Bury; buildings provide 'good facilities'; extensive playing fields; part of educational complex with four other neighbouring secondary schools. 'The school has excellent relations with a good and responsive local education authority.' Strong and supportive parent-teacher association. Over-subscribed, with average of 1.5 applications for each place. Many staff have children at the school. New resource centre to update learning and research facilities. 'The school's philosophy is one of wholeness in developing all aspects of each pupil. The school expects high standards across the whole curriculum; it does not see the need to set one pupil against another in competition to achieve this.' Emphasises Gospel values.

Streaming Pupils placed in structured pastoral groups on entry; put in sets for English, mathematics, science, French, history and geography. 'The school is concerned to ensure that it meets the needs and abilities of each individual pupil and therefore reviews progress on a regular basis throughout the year.'

Approach to discipline Based upon trust and self-respect; pupils taught to respect other people and their property. 'Every member of the community is responsible for its well-being. Hence, the school does not have a prefect system. Courtesy, consideration and common sense are the watchwords of a community which has close links with its parents, and which aspires to live the gospel values.'

Uniform Navy blazer, navy sweater, navy skirt/trousers, school tie. 'All pupils are expected to wear uniform and to take a pride in it. The regulations are enforced with common sense.'

Homework Average 11-year-old, five hours a week; 14-year-old, six hours 30 minutes; 16-year-old, 10 hours.

Vocational qualifications Computer Literacy and Information Technology.

Inspection April 1995: 'An outstandingly effective school.'; 'Among several features of excellence which the inspection identified, one of particular importance, underpinning the whole of the school's work, is its attitude to pupils and the response which this elicits.'; 'Pupils are treated in ways which build self-esteem and confidence, and this is seen as the basis for concern and love for others.'; 'Throughout the school, standards of reading and writing are good, pupils can express themselves clearly and confidently in speech in both less and more formal contexts, and many display a concern for accurate expression and an enjoyment in the use of words.'; 'The substantial majority of pupils are positively motivated to learn and work with a sense of purpose and commitment.'

Primary schools Guardian Angels' RC Primary; Hollymount RC Primary; Our Lady of Lourdes RC Primary; St Joseph's and St Bede's RC Primary; St Joseph's RC Primary, Ramsbottom; St Marie's RC Primary, Bury.

ST JAMES' ROMAN CATHOLIC HIGH SCHOOL

St James' Way
Cheadle Hulme
Stockport
Cheshire SK8 6PZ
Tel (0161) 486 9211
Fax (0161) 486 6607
E-mail: 3564600.c_33423@dialnet.co.uk

- National ranking 361= (509, 511=, 482=, -)
- GCSE 61% (45%)
- A-levels Not applicable
- Higher education Not applicable

- Mixed comprehensive
- Pupils 732
- Boys (11–16) 375
- Girls (11–16) 357
- Sixth form Not applicable
- Education authority Stockport

Headteacher Paul Anthony Doherty, 50, appointed in May 1989. Staff 45 (men 21, women 24).

Motto Religio eruditionis radix (Religion is the foundation of learning).

Background One of the newest Roman Catholic High Schools in the United Kingdom; purpose-built, single-storey buildings in 'delightful surroundings' south of Cheadle Hulme; relatively small, 'a factor which is perceived as one of its strengths'. First-class facilities include fine sports hall. Heavily over-subscribed, with 180 applications for 151 places. Notable sporting success; 'thriving' art, music and drama: regular pupil exhibitions and performances; fine choir; programme of visits, trips and educational excursions and holidays, including skiing, and German and Italian exchanges. 'St James' Roman Catholic High School is involved in the pursuit of excellence in a Christian community in which we aim to create a happy, hard-working and successful atmosphere in which all members are supported in developing their abilities to the fullest possible extent.'

Streaming Year 8, banded according to ability in English and mathematics; year 9, setted/streamed in English and mathematics.

Approach to discipline 'A caring and very well-ordered school. Emphasis is upon positive reward and encouragement of achievement, reflecting the ethos of the school's Mission Statement.'

Uniform Navy blazer with school badge, navy skirt or charcoal-grey/black trousers, white blouse/shirt, school tie, navy/grey pullover white/navy socks, dark-brown/black shoes. Very strictly enforced.

Homework Average 11-year-old, five hours a week; 14-year-old, seven hours 30 minutes; 16-year-old, 10 hours.

Vocational qualifications *None*

Inspection September 1996: 'St James' Roman Catholic High School succeeds in its aim of promoting within a Christian community, a happy, hard-working and successful atmosphere in which all members are supported in developing their abilities to the fullest possible extent. The school provides a supportive working environment in which enthusiastic pupils learn effectively both in the subjects studied and in the wider concerns of the school.'; 'The school is popular. It has a well-deserved, good reputation for the care, support and educational development which it promotes.'; 'Pupils have very positive attitudes to their school work, take pride in their achievements, are enthusiastic and enjoy their lessons.'; 'Most concentrate in lessons and cooperate with staff. However, in a few lessons there is some distraction either when pupils are not interested in the work or when work is poorly matched to their abilities. Standards of behaviour are very high and relationships are good.'

Primary schools Cheadle Catholic Junior; St Peter's RC Primary; Our Lady's RC Primary; St Ambrose RC Primary.

THE DOWNS SCHOOL

Manor Crescent
Compton
Newbury
Berkshire RG20 6NU
Tel **(01635) 578213**
Fax **(01635) 578913**
E-mail: thedownssch@campus.bt.com

- National ranking 361 = (228 = , 359 =)
- GCSE 61% (70%)
- A-levels *Not applicable*
- Higher education *Not applicable*

- Grant-maintained
- Mixed comprehensive
- Pupils 631
- Boys (11–16) 310
- Girls (11–18) 321
- Sixth form *Not applicable*
- Education authority *Berkshire*

Headteacher Graham Taylor, 52, appointed in January 1984. Staff 41 (men 12, women 29).

Motto None

Background Opened in 1960; became grant-maintained in 1992. Five-form entry school serving scattered communities of the Berkshire Downs. Significant proportion of the intake is from outside the immediate catchment area. Praised in 1995 annual Ofsted report; over half of all GCSE grades were grade A in 1994. Over-subscribed, with 180 applications for 150 places. Substantial investment in information technology. New buildings have provided 'excellent' facilities for geography, religious education, information technology and music. Strong European links, particularly in France and Germany. 'We aim to provide a caring community and an effective learning environment. The relatively small size of the school, generous staffing levels and purpose-built teaching spaces all contribute to the success we have achieved.'

Streaming Pupils in sets according to ability in particular subjects; mixed-ability in technology, physical education, music, drama, religious education.

Approach to discipline 'Effective system of rewards and punishments.' Code of conduct issued to all parents and forms a contract between them and the school. 'We believe that parents should be fully informed and involved in pastoral matters. Good discipline leads to effective learning.'

Uniform Formal uniform is expected, with blazer and ties for both boys and girls. 'High standards of dress and behaviour are enforced. No exceptions are allowed.'

Homework Average 11-year-old, five hours a week; 14-year-old, seven hours 30 minutes; 16-year-old, 12 hours 30 minutes.

Vocational qualifications RSA Information Systems.

Primary schools Compton CE Primary; Hermitage Primary; Chieveley Primary; St Marks CE Primary, Cold Ash. Ten feeder schools in the catchment area, but pupils from another 25 schools are admitted each year.

PRINCE HENRY'S HIGH SCHOOL

Victoria Avenue
Evesham
Worcestershire WR11 4QH
Tel **(01386) 765588**
Fax **(01386) 40760**

- National ranking 370 (499, 463, 402, –)
- GCSE 60% (48%)

- A-levels 48% (A/B); 96% (A/E)
- Higher education 85%

- Grant-maintained
- Mixed comprehensive
- Pupils 1,023
- Boys (13–18) 507
- Girls (13–18) 516
- Sixth form 259 (25%)
- Education authority *Hereford and Worcester*

Headteacher Bernard Roberts, 45, appointed in September 1993. Staff 63 (men 28, women 35).

Motto Parva magna crescunt (Great things develop from small beginnings).

Background History goes back 600 years and its beginnings in Abbey of Evesham; refounded by James I, the school was renamed after eldest son, Henry. Set on 18-acre site in north of Evesham, with excellent views over river Avon to Cotswolds; mix of building styles, well-sited garden and recreational space, 'excellent' sports facilities; attracts pupils from many parts of town and surrounding villages. All-round curriculum strength; 'exceptional' range of extra-curricular activities on offer; leadership course for sixth-formers. 'We create an ordered society based on sensible rules and high expectations. Appearance, behaviour, achievement and common courtesies all matter. Pupils are encouraged to accept responsibility. We believe and expect that learning should take place without disruption. Pupils are industrious, creative and expressive.'

Streaming Setting in most subject areas from year 9.

Approach to discipline 'Clear guidelines based on traditional standards of behaviour and good manners. The guidelines are consistently reinforced. Positive reinforcement of pupil achievement is paramount. Expectations of pupils are high. Sanctions, when needed, are firm, fair and consistently applied.'

Uniform Dark-blue blazer, white shirt, grey trousers/blue skirt, school tie. Sixth-formers wear uniform. Very strictly enforced.

Homework Average 14-year-old, six to seven hours a week; 16-year-old, 10 hours.

Vocational qualifications GNVQ, Health and Social Care, Leisure and Tourism, Art and Design.

Primary schools Bredon Hill Middle; St Egwin's CE Middle; Simon de Montfort Middle; Blackminster Middle.

CHEW VALLEY SCHOOL

Chew Lane
Chew Magna
Near Bristol BS18 8QB
Tel (01275) 332272
Fax (01275) 333625

- National ranking 371 (235, 482, 363, 236)
- GCSE 60% (69%)
- A-levels 48% (A/B); 95% (A/E)
- Higher education 77%

- Mixed comprehensive
- Pupils 1,120
- Boys (11–18) 549
- Girls (11–18) 571
- Sixth form 228 (20%)
- Education authority *Bath and North-east Somerset*

Headteacher Kenneth John Biggs, 52, appointed in September 1984. Staff 67 (men 28, women 39).

Motto *None*

Background Opened in 1958 as a small rural secondary school. It has since developed a sixth form, become fully comprehensive and grown to more than 1,000 pupils. Stands on a 30-acre site eight miles south of Bristol in open countryside overlooking Chew Valley Lake. Buildings completed in four stages, intially in 1958 and 1974. New classroom block and library, with newly-converted sixth-form centre, opened in September 1995. Further improvements to science and humanities accommodation opened in 1996–97. Some temporary classrooms remain, but these are progressively being replaced. About 280 applicants for 180 places. Selected as one of first 61 technology schools; activities week for years 7 to 9; work-experience for years 10 and 12. Exchanges with France, Germany, Belgium and Canada. Residential course for all pupils in year 7. Improving standards in school sports teams; community use of school sports facilities since 1993.

Streaming Setting in mathematics and modern languages in year 8; in most subjects from year 9.

Approach to discipline 'Our basic principle is that praise and encouragement are more effective motivators of pupils than any sanctions or punishments.' House points and commendation certificates for good work. Sanctions: 'on report', detention, or exclusion, in extreme cases.

Uniform Green sweatshirt with school badge, grey trousers/skirt. Years 10 and 11 wear black sweatshirt. Strictly enforced; dress code for sixth-formers.

Homework Average 11-year-old, five hours a week; 14-year-old, seven to eight hours; 16-year-old, 10 to 12 hours.

Vocational qualifications GNVQ Advanced, Business and Finance, Art and Design. GNVQ Intermediate, Business and Finance, Health and Social Care (from September 1996).

Inspection April 1994: 'Chew Valley School is an outstanding school. The range of achievement throughout its work and life is consistently very good.'; 'A remarkably high proportion of the teaching is good or very good; only the smallest minority is less than satisfactory.'; 'The premises themselves are intensively used and are insufficient for their purpose. There is insufficient storage space. Some specialist areas are deficient; the temporary accommodation is especially poor.'

Primary schools Bishop Sutton Primary; Cameley Primary; Chew Magna Primary; Chew Stoke CE Primary; Dundry Primary; East Harptree Primary; Felton Primary; Pensford Primary; Stanton Drew Primary; Ubley Primary; Winford Primary.

TADCASTER GRAMMAR SCHOOL

Toulston
Tadcaster
North Yorkshire LS24 9NB
Tel (01937) 833466
Fax (01937) 836086

- National ranking 372 (346, 395, 409, –)
- GCSE 60% (61%)
- A-levels 40% (A/B); 95% (A/E)
- Higher education 85% (Cambridge 1)

- Mixed comprehensive
- Pupils 1,251
- Boys (11–18) 627
- Girls (11–18) 624
- Sixth form 116 (9%)

- Education authority *North Yorkshire*

Headteacher David Impey, 58, appointed in September 1985. Staff 73 (men 42, women 31).

Motto *None*

Background Founded in 1557, originally for the sons of the poor, by Owen Oglethorpe, Bishop of Carlisle and a native of Newton Kyme; merger with Dawson Girls' School at beginning of century; grammar school for 50 years; after second world war, became one of first bilateral schools. Moved to current 70-acre parkland site in 1960; became comprehensive in 1968; modern buildings as well as Toulston Lodge, Dower House of Fairfax family: large assembly hall, with modern stage lighting and amplification; nearly 40 classrooms; science laboratories, technology, home economics, art rooms, libraries and resource centre. Over-subscribed. Sports facilities 'second to none in North Yorkshire': two gymnasiums, seven tennis courts, hockey, soccer and rugby pitches, cricket square, hard-surface athletics track; also cross-country and orienteering. New floodlit Astroturf pitch in October 1995. Strong sporting tradition. Large junior choir, school orchestra, concert band. Combined Cadet Force; Duke of Edinburgh Award Scheme.

Alumni Michael Whitlam, director-general of the British Red Cross.

Streaming In mathematics from year 7; in most other subjects from year 8, based on half-year blocks.

Approach to discipline 'Traditional: pupils are encouraged to show respect for teachers, each other and the school environment.'

Uniform Girls: navy skirt, white blouse, school tie, navy V-neck pullover with logo, white/navy socks or navy tights, black shoes. Boys: black blazer with school badge, black/grey trousers, white shirt, grey V-neck jumper, school tie, dark socks, black shoes.. 'We are a full uniform school, except for the sixth-form.'

Homework Average 11-year-old, five hours a week; 14-year-old, eight hours; 16-year-old, 10 hours.

Vocational qualifications GNVQ Advanced, Business and Finance; RSA Modules in years 10 and 11.

Inspection March 1995: 'A very good school.'; 'Teachers and pupils are highly-motivated, work hard and achieve high standards in lessons and public examinations.'; 'Leadership is of the highest quality and the school is well-managed at all levels.'; 'The school establishes clear values and pupils feel safe and welcomed in an environment where behaviour is exemplary. Extra-curricular activity is extensive and of a high standard. Arrangements for assemblies are excellent and they have a strong spiritual focus.'

Primary schools Copmanthorpe County Primary; Tadcaster Riverside Primary; Bishopthorpe County Primary; Tadcaster East Primary; Appleton Roebuck Primary.

REDBORNE UPPER SCHOOL AND COMMUNITY COLLEGE

Ampthill
Bedfordshire MK45 2NU
Tel (01525) 404462
Fax (01525) 841246

- National ranking 373 (353, 491, 448, –)
- GCSE 60% (61%)
- A-levels 40% (A/B); 90% (A/E)
- Higher education 80% (Cambridge 2)

- Mixed comprehensive
- Pupils 1,150
- Boys (13–18) 565
- Girls (13–18) 585
- Sixth form 300 (26%)
- Education authority *Bedfordshire*

Headteacher Nigel Croft, 39, appointed in April 1994. Staff 70 (men 39, women 31).

Motto *None*

Background Opened in 1970s as upper school and community college serving Ampthill, Flitwick and neighbouring villages. The North and South Schools, the two main groups of buildings that make up the school, stand in 40 acres of grounds, with wide variety of trees, shrubs, flower beds and rock gardens. Rugby, soccer, hockey and cricket pitches, netball, and grass and hard tennis courts; also a three-acre farm. Oversubscribed, with 340 applications for 321 places. Duke of Edinburgh Award Scheme. Foreign exchanges with schools in France, Spain and United States; cultural visits to Italy,

Germany, skiing in Austria, and sporting holiday in the Ardeche. Charity fund-raising, raising more than £40,000 in 10 years.

Streaming In mathematics and languages in year 9; in other subjects in years 10 and 11.

Approach to discipline 'Fair but firm. We emphasise the solid and traditional virtues of hard work, good behaviour and politeness. Reasonable sanctions are used, when required, to back up our standards of discipline.'

Uniform White shirt/blouse, school tie, black school jumper with badge, black trousers/skirt, black shoes. Dress code for sixthformers. Regulations 'strictly adhered to'.

Homework Average 14-year-old, eight to 10 hours a week; 16-year-old, 10 to 12 hours.

Vocational qualifications GNVQ Advanced, Business Studies, Art and Design; GNVQ Intermediate, Leisure and Tourism, Art and Design, Land-based Industries; NNEB Nursery Training.

Inspection Spring 1995: 'A very well-ordered community.'; 'The administration, communication and organisation of the school are excellent and the senior management works well and effectively as a team. Over 80% of lessons are good, with 40% showing very good teaching.'; 'Parents are very supportive of the activities of the school: they considered the range of information they receive as exemplary.'; 'There were examples of good teaching in every subject area, and students' behaviour, motivation and relationships with teachers were always very good.'

Primary schools Woodland Middle; Alomeda Middle; Fulbook Middle.

CHURCHILL COMMUNITY SCHOOL

Churchill Green
Churchill
Bristol BS19 5QN
Tel (01934) 852771
Fax (01934) 853202
E-mail: churchil@rmplc.co.uk
Internet: http://www.rmplc.co.uk/eduweb/
          sites/churchil

- National ranking 374 (349, 276, 420, –)
- GCSE 60% (61%)
- A-levels 37% (A/B); 90% (A/E)
- Higher education 70% (Oxford 2, Cambridge 3)

302 ST ANTHONY'S GIRLS' SCHOOL

- Mixed comprehensive
- Pupils 1,521
- Boys (11–18) 764
- Girls (11–18) 757
- Sixth form 376 (25%)
- Education authority *North Somerset*

Headteacher Brian Kirkup, 56, appointed in April 1992. Staff 101 (men 48, women 53).

Motto Aiming for excellence.

Background Opened as a comprehensive in 1971 to serve the village of Churchill and eight surrounding villages; set in wooded grounds in south of Avon, with Mendip Hills nearby, 10 miles east of Weston-super-Mare and 15 miles south of Bristol; buildings organised as lower, middle and sixth-form schools serving eight faculties. Excellent sports centre on site: swimming pool, sports hall, fitness studio, squash courts; surrounded by extensive playing fields, including all-weather facilities. Over-subscribed, with 300 applications for 232 places. Music and drama 'outstanding': junior and senior orchestra, swing band, folk band, choir, chamber orchestra, jazz; annual performances in Weston-super-Mare Playhouse Theatre. Full programme of competitive team games; county and national honours. Quality of sixth-form education highly praised: 'Teaching and learning across all curriculum areas of a high standard.' Strong links with Europe; close partnership with local businesses and light industry; 'excellent' information technology facilities; whole-school optical fibre network; Learning Resource Centre.

Alumni Helen Hobson, actress; Rob Barton, gold-medallist acrobat; Andrew and Harley Masters, international canoeists; Kati Chappel, international violinist.

Streaming Pupils put in sets in mathematics, science, modern languages; broad bands in technology; extent of setting increases in years 10 and 11.

Approach to discipline 'Discipline is firm and fair with clear expectations laid out for students. Emphasis is on respect for people and property, creating a positive, caring, co-operative, hard-working environment. There are clear rewards and sanctions, with a structured suspension procedure for serious indiscipline. The school is a happy, warm and pleasant place to be.'

Uniform Navy sweatshirt with logo, white shirt/blouse, house tie, dark-grey/black/blue trousers or skirt, black shoes. Firmly enforced. No uniform for sixth-formers, but 'sensible' dress expected.

Homework Average 11-year-old, five to seven hours 30 minutes a week; 14-year-old, seven hours 30 minutes to 10 hours; 16-year-old, 10 to 12 hours 30 minutes.

Vocational qualifications GNVQ Advanced, Health and Social Care, Business, Leisure and Tourism; Avon Youth Award Scheme; RSA, Skills Award.

Inspection February 1997: 'A good school with many very good features and a number of outstanding features.'

Primary schools St Andrew's Junior, Congresbury; Winscombe Woodborough Primary, Winscombe; Wrington CE Primary; Churchill CE Primary, Churchill; Banwell Primary, Banwell.

ST ANTHONY'S GIRLS' SCHOOL

Thornhill Terrace
Sunderland SR2 7JN
Tel (0191) 567 4726
Fax (0191) 565 7944

- National ranking 375 (399, 414, 331, –)
- GCSE 60% (58%)
- A-levels 36% (A/B); 86% (A/E)
- Higher education 85% (Oxford 1)

- Girls' comprehensive
- Pupils 1,285
- Boys *Not applicable*
- Girls (11–18) 1,285
- Sixth form 240 (19%)
- Education authority *Sunderland*

Headteacher Sister Mary Aelred, 52, appointed in September 1993. Staff 78 (men 14, women 64).

Motto Sine labe (Without stain).

Background Originally private convent school; became grant-supported Roman Catholic secondary school in 1906; direct-grant grammar in 1948, before becoming girls' comprehensive in 1972. Buildings near city centre are a mixture of old and new: three adjacent villas, with additions since 1950s. Pupils from all parts of city; over-subscribed, with 1.8 applications per place. School considers library provision and access important. Sporting achievements: national netball champions for two successive years. New swimming pool given by Sisters of Mercy Sunderland to celebrate 150 years in the city. Enterprise Schemes; School–Industry Compact. 'A Christian school recognising individual talents and equal worth, and offering the opportunity to enhance and develop the lives of our students.'

Alumni Angela Piggford, Olympic athlete; Professor Mary Grey, professor of Theology, Southampton University; Helen Lonsdale, England under-21 netball captain.

Streaming Pupils placed in four bands after first half-term, with special group for those with learning difficulties.

Approach to discipline Frequent opportunities for praise and commendation at daily collective worship and clear sanctions for violation of school rules such as neglected homework, lateness, truancy, violence and aggressive language. Heads of year take lead on disciplinary matters; close links with parents, including interviews, consultation and home visits, where desirable.

Uniform Navy blazer with green trim and badge, navy skirt, white blouse, school tie, navy V-neck pullover with school-colour trim. Strictly enforced; financial help for those who need it.

Homework Average 11-year-old, six hours a week; 14-year-old, nine hours; 16-year-old, 12 hours.

Vocational qualifications GNVQ Intermediate, Health and Social Care, Business; GNVQ Advanced, Business; Pilot school for GNVQ Foundation, Part 1, Health and Social Care.

Inspection April 1994: 'A very good school.'; 'Pupils achieve high levels in listening, reading, speaking, writing and numeracy, although information technology is underdeveloped in some subject areas.'; 'The school provides a well-ordered and pleasant environment for learning and teaching. The quality of inter-personal relationships is good, with very high standards of behaviour achieved in and out of classrooms.'; 'The curriculum is broad and balanced, meeting the needs of the national curriculum, although the lack of suitable playing fields restricts the learning opportunities for physical education.'; 'The school's ethos is friendly, orderly and courteous, with a high regard for mutual respect.'

Primary schools English Martyrs RC Primary; St Hilda's RC Primary; St Mary's RC Primary; St Patrick's RC Primary, Ryhope; St John Bosco RC Primary; Montessori School; St Anne's RC Primary; St John and St Patrick's Church Primary; St Benet RC Primary; St Joseph's RC Primary; St Cuthbert's RC Primary; St Leonard's RC Primary.

GARFORTH COMMUNITY COLLEGE

Lidgett Lane
Garforth
Leeds LS25 1LJ
Tel (0113) 286 9091
Fax (0113) 287 2727

- National ranking 376   (352, 359=)
- GCSE 60% (61%)
- A-levels 35% (A/B); 93% (A/E)
- Higher education 65% (Oxford 1, Cambridge 1)

- Mixed comprehensive
- Pupils 1,742
- Boys (11–18) 868
- Girls (11–18) 874
- Sixth form 273 (16%)
- Education authority *Leeds*

Headteacher David John Stephens, 55, appointed in September 1992. Staff 107 (men 51, women 56).

Motto Reaching for excellence.

Background Situated on the east side of Leeds, half a mile from the centre of Garforth (population 30,000). Opened in 1967 with purpose-built accommodation. Attracts pupils from a wide area of east Leeds as well as North Yorkshire. Extensive playing fields on 28-acre site; tree-planting programme. Two sports halls, music suite, technology suite, drama workshop. Over-subscribed, with more than 340 applications for 300 places. County and national success in rugby, football, badminton, swimming, cricket, cross-country, gymnastics and tai kwon do. Art, music (two orchestras) and science among strengths. 'High expectations and work ethic. Traditional standards of behaviour. Secure environment with firm but fair management of young people.'

Alumni Karen Brennan, Camelot marketing director.

Streaming Generally mixed-ability; setting in

mathematics (years 8 to 11), science (year 9), and modern foreign languages (years 8 and 9).

Approach to discipline 'Having laid down a minimum of rules for the community, we expect them to be observed either through self-discipline or imposed discipline.'

Uniform Boys: Navy tailored trousers, white shirt, college pullover, college tie, black/grey socks, black shoes. Girls: Navy tailored skirt/dress/trousers, white blouse, college pullover/cardigan, college tie, black shoes, white socks. 'High standards of dress are positively promoted. We mean what we say!'

Homework Average 11-year-old, 10 hours a week; 14-year-old, 15 hours; 16-year-old, 20 hours.

Vocational qualifications BTEC National Diploma Business and Finance, Science; Childhood Studies; GNVQ Advanced, Leisure and Tourism, Business; GNVQ Intermediate, Business, Science, Health and Social Care; NVQ Level 2, Sport and Recreation; RSA Practical Skills Profile, Word-processing; Community Sports Leadership Award.

Inspection November 1993: 'Garforth Community College provides a very high standard of education for all pupils.'; 'There is scope for the college to develop the quality of learning even more by refining teaching methods in order to extend the range of stimulus in the classroom and to make increased demands upon pupils' learning and creativity.'; 'Standards of literacy are high and they are evident in all areas of the curriculum. Pupils use both written and oral skills with confidence. Standards in mathematics are also high, but there is less cross-curricular use and confidence with mathematical and computational skills.'; 'The behaviour of pupils, their work ethic, and their attitudes to everything they are asked to do is excellent. This is encouraged by the excellent pastoral support system in the college and the high quality of the relationships between staff and pupils.'

Primary schools Ninelands Primary; West Garforth Junior; East Garforth Primary; Garforth Green Lane Primary; Kippax North Primary.

THE WEALD SCHOOL

Station Road
Billingshurst
West Sussex RH14 9RY
Tel (01403) 783123
Fax (01403) 782305
E-mail: 9384025.mailbox@dialnet.co.uk

- National ranking 377 (348, 289, 385, 363)
- GCSE 60% (61%)
- A-levels 34% (A/B); 91% (A/E)
- Higher education 74%

- Mixed comprehensive
- Pupils 1,481
- Boys (11–18) 794
- Girls (11–18) 687
- Sixth form 309 (21%)
- Education authority West Sussex

Headteacher Virginia Holly, 47, appointed in April 1991. Staff 93 (men 40, women 53).

Motto None

Background Built in the 1950s as a secondary modern, buildings have since been added to the 25-acre site on the edge of the village of Billingshurst. School serves a 140-square-mile area. Not over-subscribed: 220 applications for 240 places. Proud of physical education facilities and achievements; sporting strengths include basketball and rugby. Noted for drama department, which teaches A-level in theatre studies; drama exchange with France; strong special needs department; continental work-experience for sixth-formers in France and Germany. Generally sufficient places to satisfy applications.

Streaming Pupils in sets according to ability in English, mathematics, modern languages and science.

Approach to discipline Agreed policy explained carefully to parents and pupils; follows recommendations of government's Elton Report on discipline. Eight-point code of conduct.

Uniform Black trousers/skirt, school tie, V-neck jumper with school logo, pinstriped shirt/blouse, school tie, black shoes. 'A school policy to which parents agree before sending their child to the Weald.'

Homework Average 11-year-old, seven hours 30 minutes a week; 14-year-old, 10 hours; 16-year-old, 12 hours 30 minutes.

Vocational qualifications BTEC First; BTEC National; RSA.

Primary schools Billingshurst Junior; St Mary's CE Primary, Pulborough; Rudgwick County Primary; Wisborough Green County Primary; Kirdford County Junior.

OAKLANDS ROMAN CATHOLIC SCHOOL

Stakes Hill Road
Waterlooville
Hampshire PO7 7BW
Tel (01705) 259214
Fax (01705) 230317

- National ranking 378 (410, 283, 352, 336)
- GCSE 60% (57%)
- A-levels 34% (A/B); 87% (A/E)
- Higher education 94% (Oxford 1)

- Grant-maintained
- Mixed comprehensive
- Pupils 1,062
- Boys (11–18) 543
- Girls (11–18) 519
- Sixth form 125 (12%)
- Education authority *Hampshire*

Headteacher Chris Whitfield, 52, appointed in January 1985. Staff 68 (men 27, women 41).

Motto *None*

Background Originally a girls' independent grammar school with small boarding element until 1971, when it became local authority comprehensive; open rural surroundings; substantial building programme in 1973: sports hall, art and technology block, mathematics and science block. Extensive landscaping to create sports fields; 1992 modular building for sixth form; 1993 modular building to replace temporary classrooms and a base for year 11, including tutor rooms, conference room, and teaching rooms for history and geography. Over-subscribed, with two applications per place; many applications from families of other Christian denominations. Concert hall helps sustain 'excellent reputation' for creative arts. Wide range of sporting activities. Christian ethos.

Streaming Setting by subject gradually introduced from year 8.

Approach to discipline High standards and expectations; Christian aims and atmo-

sphere. 'The prime rule that underlines all others is that Oaklands students are expected to act at all times in a sensitive, responsible manner, showing kindness, consideration, honesty and respect for others and their property.'

Uniform Blue shirt/blouse, grey trousers/skirt, grey jumper/cardigan with school motif. School sells main items to ensure consistency; worn without exception by years 7 to 11.

Homework Average 11-year-old, six hours a week; 14-year-old, nine hours; 16-year-old, 15 hours.

Vocational qualifications GNVQ Intermediate and Advanced, Health and Social Care, Leisure and Tourism.

Inspection October 1994: 'A good school with many excellent features.'; 'It has a clear Christian philosophy which is put into practice in the day-to-day life of the school and commands the support of staff, parents and pupils.'; 'The school serves the great majority of its pupils very well indeed, but pupils of high ability do not always have sufficient demands placed upon them.'; 'Pupil involvement in school activities outside the classroom is excellent. The support of parents for the school is another outstanding feature.'; 'Pupils respect one another and are committed to their work. The school meets the high expectations of parents almost completely.'

Primary schools St Peter's RC Primary; St Thomas More's RC Primary, Bedhampton; St Paul's RC Primary, Paulsgrove; St Jude's Catholic Primary, Fareham.

BISHOP RAMSEY CHURCH OF ENGLAND SCHOOL

Hume Way
Ruislip
Middlesex HA4 8EE
Tel (01895) 639227
Fax (01895) 622429

- National ranking 379 (327, 258, 479, 272)
- GCSE 60% (62%)
- A-levels 33% (A/B); 91% (A/E)
- Higher education 61% (Cambridge 1)

- Mixed comprehensive
- Pupils 1,109

- Boys (11–18) 558
- Girls (11–18) 551
- Sixth form 196 (18%)
- Education authority *Hillingdon*

Headteacher Michael Udall, 52, appointed in January 1992. Staff 69 (men 25, women 44).

Motto *None*

Background Founded in September 1977; based on two sites in suburbs of Ruislip: lower school (years 7 to 9) and upper school (years 10 to 13). Sixth-form wing and information technology centre at upper school, where there are also extensive playing fields. New sports hall, technology block, science laboratories and classrooms in 1994. Voluntary-aided; over-subscribed, with two applications for each place; takes pupils from Harrow, Brent, Ealing, Hillingdon, Hertfordshire and Buckinghamshire. Reputation for creative arts, with numerous festivals, concerts and drama productions. House system. Sporting achievements: regular winners of local championships and many representative honours. Service to the community emphasised. Worship plays an important part in the life of the school.

Streaming Separate arrangements for each subject, but setting begins in year 7.

Approach to discipline High standards of appearance, courtesy and discipline outlined in school's code of conduct; appropriate sanctions employed. 'Praise and reward are also an important part of school life.' Variety of certificates for achievement, effort or community service.

Uniform Brown blazer with gold-and-brown badge, grey trousers/brown skirt, beige shirt, brown-and-gold tie, dark shoes. No uniform for sixth-formers. Enforced 'without exception'.

Homework Average 11-year-old, five to seven hours 30 minutes a week; 14-year-old, 10 hours; 16-year-old, 15 hours.

Vocational qualifications BTEC National Diploma; GNVQs, Art and Design, Business, Leisure and Tourism.

Inspection April 1996: 'A successful school where the Christian ethos is demonstrated through emphasis on the development of the whole individual, good relationships, meaningful worship and a high regard for community service. Admissions are based on patterns of family worship and links with parents are good.'; 'Lessons are often lively, with built-in elements of individual and collaborative learning, research and enjoyment. Opportunities for spiritual, moral and social development are a strong feature.'; 'Across the school pupils are well-motivated, confident and articulate. They are happy and positive about the school and their work and are keen to do well. This positive atmosphere is generated by good teaching in a large number of lessons, but the range of teaching strategies and learning opportunities should be extended across the school.'; 'Despite the difficulties of the split site, the school is well-organised and purposeful.'; 'The school buildings remain a problem, especially in the lower school. There are a number of health and safety matters which cause concern on both sites. The quality and range of learning resources, including the libraries, are inadequate to provide pupils with sufficient opportunities for independent learning.'

Primary schools Bishop Winnington Ingram CE Primary; Sacred Heart RC Primary; Dr Triplett's CE Primary; Edward Betham CE Primary; St John's CE Primary.

DEYES HIGH SCHOOL

Deyes Lane
Maghull
Merseyside L31 6DE
Tel (0151) 526 3814
Fax (0151) 526 3713
E-mail: deyeshigh@campus.bt.com

- National ranking 380 (427, 193, 401, –)
- GCSE 60% (55%)
- A-levels 32% (A/B); 82% (A/E)
- Higher education 70% (Cambridge 3)

- Mixed comprehensive
- Pupils 1,470
- Boys (11–18) 745
- Girls (11–18) 725
- Sixth form 300 (20%)
- Education authority *Sefton*

Headteacher Peter Middleton, 56, appointed in September 1992. Staff 90 (men 50, women 40).

Motto Primus inter pares (First among equals).

Background On attractive campus in residential area of Maghull; well-served by public transport, and close to junction of M57 and M58. Sports hall and swimming pool on site. A 'most attractive' feature is school quadrangle, inhabited by peafowl, other birds and small animals. Over-subscribed, with more than 170 applications for 130 places. 'The school offers a broad and balanced curriculum, with strengths in all areas. There is a wide range of sporting activities, and music and drama play an important part in the life of the school.' Flourishing exchange link with a lycée in Le Havre. Duke of Edinburgh Award Scheme. Schools Curriculum Award in 1990. Investors in People 1996. Parent and Friends' Association.

Streaming 'Pupils are placed in mixed-ability tutor-groups. Some teaching is done in these groups, but there is also a substantial degree of subject setting by ability.'

Approach to discipline Based on charter of values agreed by pupils, staff and governors, and a published code of conduct. Policy of rewarding achievement as well as sanctions.

Uniform Black blazer, school pullover, black skirt/trousers, school tie.

Homework Average 11-year-old, five hours a week; 14-year-old, seven hours 30 minutes; 16-year-old, 10 hours.

Vocational qualifications GNVQ Intermediate, Art Science and Design, Business; GNVQ Advanced, Business.

Inspection April 1994: 'A clearly-defined ethos and strong sense of community pervades the school. The evidence for this can be seen from strategic planning through to daily encounters between staff and pupils.'; 'The values encouraged by the school are characterised by a respect for others which fosters personal growth and development, and encourages independence.'; 'Standards of behaviour throughout the school are generally excellent.'; 'Pupils talk about their school with pride and parental satisfaction is high.'

Primary schools St Andrew's CE Primary, Maghull; Northway County Primary, Maghull; Lydiate County Primary; St Thomas CE Primary, Lydiate; Summerhill County Primary, Maghull; Green Park County Primary, Maghull.

THE HAYFIELD SCHOOL

**Hurst Lane
Auckley
Doncaster
South Yorkshire DN9 3HG
Tel (01302) 770589
Fax (01302) 770179
E-mail: debbie@hayfield.demon.co.uk**

- National ranking 381 (397, 413, 403, –)
- GCSE 60% (58%)
- A-levels 30% (A/B); 83% (A/E)
- Higher education 95% (Oxford 1, Cambridge 1)

- Grant-maintained
- Mixed comprehensive
- Pupils 1,150
- Boys (11–18) 575
- Girls (11–18) 575
- Sixth form 195 (17%)
- Education authority *Doncaster*

Headteacher Tony Storey, 58, appointed in August 1971. Staff 70 (men 36, women 34).

Motto *None*

Background Opened in 1971 on 42-acre rural site south of Doncaster; pupils from commuter villages, market town of Bawtry and southern suburbs of Doncaster. Still has original headteacher, with OBE for work in education. Grant-maintained since April 1995; awarded Charter Mark in November 1995; Associate Technology College status since 1996. Over-subscribed, with 270 applications for 180 places. Curriculum strengths include technology and business studies, English, mathematics, performing arts, science, languages and humanities. Strong residential field courses; music and drama productions. Sporting achievements, with national representatives in some sports; basketball, netball, soccer, rugby, athletics, cricket, swimming, hockey, table tennis. Environmentalists' Club; Parent-Teacher Association. Strong links with industry. Investor in People Award. Identified for praise in 1997 annual Ofsted report.

Streaming In mathematics, French and German in year 8; in science in year 9; GCSE sets in years 10 and 11.

Approach to discipline 'Firm but fair': clear guidelines set out and followed; high expectations; 'excellent' staff–pupil relationships;

caring for individuals.

Uniform Brown sweater, brown trousers/skirt, white shirt/blouse, school tie. Sixth-formers required to wear sensible 'professional' dress. Firmly enforced, with sensitivity in sixth form or where a family problem.

Homework Average 11-year-old, six hours a week; 14-year-old, eight to 10 hours; 16-year-old, 10 to 15 hours.

Vocational qualifications Technology, Business and Industrial Studies to A-level; Information Technology link course; GNVQ, Business Studies.

Inspection March 1995: 'The Hayfield is a very good school.'; 'It provides a very good standard of education for its pupils.'; 'It has very good management and a strong team of teachers.'; 'The school has, with justification, a high reputation in the community.'

Primary schools Finningley CE Primary; Hayfield Lane Primary; Bawtry Mayflower Primary; Auckley Primary; St Wilfrid's CE Primary, Branton.

THE GREY COAT HOSPITAL

Greycoat Place
London SW1P 2DY
Tel (0171) 828 0968
Fax (0171) 828 2697
E-mail: tgchosp@mailbox.rmplc.co.uk

- National ranking 382
- GCSE 60%
- A-levels 25% (A/B); 90% (A/E)
- Higher education 80%

- Girls' comprehensive
- Pupils 950
- Boys (16–18) 30
- Girls (11–18) 920
- Sixth form 210 (22%)
- Education authority *Westminster*

Headteacher Marion Muriel Parsons, 53, appointed in January 1988. Staff 61 (men 8, women 53).

Motto God give the increase.

Background Founded in 1698; upper school in original school building in heart of Westminster; only the seventh headteacher since 1874. Voluntary-aided Church of England school. Split site following 1977 amalgamation with St Michael's Secondary Modern, a

mile and a half away; pupils with wide variety of backgrounds, not affluent and most have some affiliation to Christian religion. Recent staff changes resulted in younger, well-qualified teachers. Over-subscribed, with three applications per place. Proud of 'very active' art, music and drama department; physical education team helped school win 1991 *Evening Standard* award for doing most for sport in London. Sporting achievements: school has national basketball player, gymnasts, athletes, fencers, swimmers. Three choirs, several music groups; recent improvement to technology; information technology facilities 'probably some of the finest in London'. Christian ethos; weekly communion services; strong religious education department. Work-shadowing; Duke of Edinburgh Award Scheme. Old Greys' Association.

Alumni Nicola Kutapan, chairman of the 300 Group; Frances Dimond, curator of Royal Photographic Archive; Sarah Greene, television personality and former *Blue Peter* presenter; Caroline Glyn, schoolgirl author of the 1960s.

Streaming Mixed-ability in year 7; school draws pupils from 120 primary schools. Setting of pupils for languages in year 8; in science in year 9. Constant review.

Approach to discipline Strong Christian ethos. Local inspectors reported: 'The school has high expectations for pupils' behaviour and good standards of discipline'; also 'excellent' pastoral system. Code of conduct; part-time school counsellor; detentions and daily report cards as well as plethora of rewards for achievement, effort and improvement.

Uniform Grey blazer, blue/green patterned school blouse, grey skirt, grey/white/black socks, black shoes. Detailed regulations very strictly enforced.

Homework Average 11-year-old, nine hours a week; 14-year-old, 12 to 15 hours; 16-year-old, minimum 18 hours.

Vocational qualifications BTEC, Business and Finance, Science, Care, French for Business, Sport and Recreation, Care in the Community.

Inspection February 1995: 'A very good school. Its success derives from a strong basis of Christian values, excellent leadership by the headteacher, the two deputy headteachers and a strong senior management team, as well as the commitment and the quality of its staff.'; 'The pupils at Grey Coat Hospital are well-motivated and develop good attitudes to learning as they move through their years of schooling. They are happy, they are proud of their school, and their attitudes towards their schoolwork are a credit both to themselves and to their teachers. The quality of their learning improves in the upper school and particularly in the sixth form.'; 'Pupils are taught in a caring atmosphere by hard-working and well-qualified teachers. Some departments in the school have limited experience of recent educational ideas and initiatives.'; 'There is an exceptionally wide range of extra-curricular activities provided by the school staff.'

Primary schools St Peter's CE Primary; Burdett Coutts Primary; St Gabriel's CE Primary; St George's CE Primary; St Mary's CE Primary.

DAVISON CHURCH OF ENGLAND HIGH SCHOOL FOR GIRLS

Selborne Road
Worthing
West Sussex BN11 2JX
Tel (01903) 233835
Fax (01903) 211417

- National ranking 383 = (302 =, 359 =)
- GCSE 60% (63%)
- A-levels *Not applicable*
- Higher education *Not applicable*

- Girls' comprehensive
- Pupils 850
- Boys *Not applicable*
- Girls (12–16) 850
- Sixth form *Not applicable*
- Education authority *West Sussex*

Headteacher Sheila Wallis, appointed in January 1988. Staff 50 (men 8, women 42).

Motto Ora et labora (Prayer and work).

Background In 1812, William Davison created the country's first free school in Worthing; the school still seeks to provide 'a secure Christian environment within which girls are encouraged to achieve their full potential'. Traditional values 'with contemporary education expertise'. Current building opened in 1960, occupying a pleasant site to the east of Worthing between the sea and the South Downs. Facilities include large

sports hall, gymnasium, fitness suite, dance studio, new science laboratories, refurbished library and music suite. Noted for its pioneering crèche facilities, in partnership with the Midland Bank, for teachers in the area. Clubs programme offers girls a choice of 103 options. Over-subscribed, with three applications per place. A 'caring, outward-looking' school which lists among its strengths performing arts and opportunities offered for leadership and responsibility roles.

Alumni Charlotte Mason, founder of Charlotte Mason Teacher Training College in Cumbria.

Streaming Broad bands for two years, with some setting, including small teaching groups for special needs pupils in national curriculum subjects.

Approach to discipline 'Firm but fair.'

Uniform Navy blazer, navy skirt, navy jumper, white blouse, red-and-navy tie, red hat.

Homework Average 14-year-old, nine hours a week; 16-year-old, 14 hours.

Vocational qualifications RSA Computer Literacy and Information Technology.

Inspection March 1996: 'A very good school with many outstanding features. It successfully provides a very high quality of education within a caring and supportive environment, offering pupils of all abilities very good opportunities to realise their full potential in their academic and personal development.'; 'Pupils' standards of achievement in public examinations are high overall and very high in English, German, art, physical education and business studies.'; 'The commitment and positive attitudes shown by pupils to their work are outstanding features of the school and contribute strongly to their very high quality of learning. Pupils show good learning skills in the great majority of subjects. They concentrate and cooperate well, listen carefully to advice and readily reflect on their own progress. Pupils with special educational needs make good progress.'; 'Teachers have a good command of their subjects and challenge pupils appropriately in lessons that are well planned to meet their needs. Occasionally, opportunities to develop higher order skills are not fully exploited.'; 'Staff morale and commitment are high.'

Primary schools Thomas A'Becket Middle;

Chesswood Middle; Downsbrook Middle; The Vale Middle; Broadwater CE Middle; St Nicolas and St Mary CE Middle, Shoreham-by-Sea.

HEALING COMPREHENSIVE SCHOOL

Low Road
Healing
Grimsby
Lincolnshire DN37 7QD
Tel (01472) 882882
Fax (01472) 885571

- National ranking 383= (401=, 416=, 374=, –)
- GCSE 60% (58%)
- A-levels *Not applicable*
- Higher education *Not applicable*

- Mixed comprehensive
- Pupils 758
- Boys (11–16) 406
- Girls (11–16) 352
- Sixth form *Not applicable*
- Education authority *North East Lincolnshire*

Headteacher Charles Edward Maurice Pritchard, 60, appointed in January 1975. Staff 41 (men 23, women 18).

Motto *None*

Background Has grown and developed from village school on outskirts of Grimsby. Oversubscribed, with 1.5 applications per place. Records of Achievement. Individuals have represented the county at cricket, athletics, judo and football. Work-experience in year 10. Duke of Edinburgh Award Scheme. Prefect system. 'Hard-working and caring institution, fostering enjoyment and high personal standards.' Identified by Ofsted in 1996 as 'a good and improving school'.

Streaming Two broad bands, with targeted special needs support.

Approach to discipline 'Very firm, fair and well-structured.'

Uniform Dark-grey/black trousers or black skirt, white shirt/blouse, black V-neck pullover, red-gold-and-black striped tie. Regulations enforced 'totally'.

Homework Average 11-year-old, five to six hours a week; 14-year-old, eight to 10 hours; 16-year-old, 10 to 12 hours.

Vocational qualifications *None*

Inspection March 1995: 'This is a good school, some aspects of which are outstanding.'; 'Standards of teaching and learning are good and the school has succeeded in creating a culture of achievement. Pupils have positive attitudes to learning and they work hard.'; 'Moral awareness is greatly enhanced by the ethos of the school and pupils respect people and property.'; 'The school is an orderly community, behaviour is very good and relationships are excellent.'

Primary schools Healing Primary; Stallingborough CE Primary; Keelby Primary; Laceby Acres Primary.

LIGHT HALL SCHOOL

Hathaway Road
Shirley
Solihull
West Midlands B90 2PZ
Tel (0121) 744 3835
Fax (0121) 733 6148

- National ranking 383= (446=, 401=)
- GCSE 60% (54%)
- A-levels *Not applicable*
- Higher education *Not applicable*

- Mixed comprehensive
- Pupils 1,159
- Boys (11–16) 582
- Girls (11–16) 577
- Sixth form *Not applicable*
- Education authority *Solihull*

Headteacher David Robert Scard, 57, appointed in January 1984. Staff 71 (men 31, women 40).

Motto *None*

Background Established in 1964 as a boys' secondary modern; girls first admitted in 1967; became comprehensive in 1972. Buildings added because of increased numbers; 'magnificent setting in its own extensive grounds'. Four football pitches, one rugby pitch, two all-weather areas (one with floodlights), newly-refurbished sports hall, new all-weather cricket strip, four tennis courts. Recent additions include new library, new classroom block, new careers suite and four computer rooms; school has more than 150 computers. 1992 and 1997 Schools Curriculum Award; Royal Anniversary Trust silver medal for community work; praised in 1995 annual Ofsted report; environment awards from Conoco and BT. Strong industry and community links; partnership school with Land Rover; community centre on site and luncheon club for the elderly. Heavily over-subscribed, with more than 100 applications refused. Notable for 'major and minority sporting achievement'. Proud of 'a very special ethos often commented upon by our many visitors'. Open, caring and disciplined environment. 'We celebrate pupil success in all areas of school activity, not least in community work and charities.'

Streaming Each year-group divided into two equal-ability bands for timetabling. Setting in most subjects from October of first term, becoming more refined as pupils progress through school.

Approach to discipline 'Self-discipline is encouraged. We have high expectations of attendance, punctuality, appearance and behaviour. Pupils appreciate these expectations and know that those who transgress will be punished. Parents are fully involved, with partnership the keynote.'

Uniform Boys: black blazer and badge, dark-grey trousers, grey/white shirt, school tie, black socks/shoes. Girls: black blazer and badge, bottle-green skirt (lower school) or black skirt (upper school), white blouse, school tie, green sweater (lower school) or black sweater (upper school), black shoes. Very strictly enforced, but few problems reported: 'Pupils wear their uniform with pride.'

Homework Average 11-year-old, three hours a week; 14-year-old, five hours; 16-year-old, 10+ hours.

Vocational qualifications RSA; Pitman; Basic Tests in Health Hygiene and Safety.

Inspection December 1993: 'This is a very good school which provides high-quality education for its pupils.'; 'The quality of pupils' learning is good. Pupils are well-motivated, enthusiastic and hardworking.'; 'Teachers are well-qualified, competent and confident.'; 'Teachers' relationships with pupils are very good and they set high standards for pupils' behaviour and work. Much of the teaching is good, but in many lessons the range of approaches and styles is too narrow, this limits pupils' learning.'; 'The school is well-managed and organised, and the headteacher provides excellent leadership.'

Primary schools St James CE Primary; Shirley Heath Primary; Haslucks Green Primary; Mill Lodge Primary; Peterbrook Primary; Chilcote Primary.

LOWTON HIGH SCHOOL

Newton Road
Lowton
Warrington
Greater Manchester WA3 1DU
Tel (01942) 767040
Fax (01942) 767053

- National ranking 383= (428=, 448=, 295=, –)
- GCSE 60% (55%)
- A-levels *Not applicable*
- Higher education *Not applicable*

- Mixed comprehensive
- Pupils 1,040
- Boys (11–16) 518
- Girls (11–16) 522
- Sixth form *Not applicable*
- Education authority *Wigan*

Headteacher Susan Elizabeth Crosdale, 50, appointed in September 1991. Staff 64 (men 29, women 35).

Motto *None*

Background Opened in 1977 as first community high school to be built by Wigan education authority; 'attractive and innovative architectural design', designed along lines of small village: 10 separate teaching blocks, large sports hall, drama studio, lecture theatre, music suite, information technology suite and community bar. General classrooms are carpeted and all rooms equipped to highest standards. Over-subscribed, with 238 applications for 208 places. Some temporary buildings. Plans for new science block being considered. School serves Lowton St Mary's, Lowton St Luke's and parts of Golborne and Leigh. Extra support for pupils with special needs; records of achievement for all pupils; close links with industry; careers programme, with work-experience and practice job interviews for upper-school students. Pastoral system based on form-tutor group. Floodlit all-weather tennis courts/multi-sports areas. Identified by Ofsted in 1996 as 'a good and improving school'; winner of Powergen Award for School

Science; Schools Curriculum Award.

Streaming Mixed-ability teaching for all subjects in lower school. Gradual introduction of setting in mathematics (year 9) and English, science and modern languages (year 10).

Approach to discipline 'The school has a firm, clear code of conduct. It is based on the notions of care and courtesy. Respect for individuals is encouraged.' Aim for punishment to be appropriate to offences, often socially-useful task or extra work. Allowance made for individual offender and circumstances of offence.

Uniform Royal-blue blazer with school badge, charcoal-grey skirts/trousers, pale-blue shirt with school tie.

Homework Average 11-year-old, five to six hours a week; 14-year-old, seven hours 30 minutes to eight hours; 16-year-old, 10+ hours.

Vocational qualifications *None*

Inspection March 1995: 'This is a popular and successful school with many strengths. Good standards are achieved by pupils of all abilities, including those with special educational needs.'; 'Pupils have good, positive attitudes to their work and make good progress in both key stages. The quality of their learning is a particular strength of the school. Teachers have high expectations and good command of their subjects.'; 'The headteacher provides the school with effective leadership and has established very good working relationships and staff involvement at all levels. The school's planning and priority setting are, however, less effective.'; 'Socially, pupils are confident and courteous and demonstrate responsibility and initiative.'

Primary schools Gilded Hollins Primary; Christ Church CE Primary; Lowton Primary; Lowton West County Primary; St Mary's CE Primary; St Luke's CE Primary.

MULLION SCHOOL

Meaver Road
Mullion
Cornwall TR12 7EB
Tel (01326) 240098
Fax (01326) 241382

- National ranking 383= (495=, 334=)

- GCSE 60% (49%)
- A-levels *Not applicable*
- Higher education *Not applicable*

- Mixed comprehensive
- Pupils 538
- Boys (11–16) 285
- Girls (11–16) 253
- Sixth form *Not applicable*
- Education authority *Cornwall*

Headteacher Victoria Morley, 50, appointed from September 1997. Staff 34 (men 22, women 12).

Motto *None*

Background Purpose-built comprehensive opened in 1978 to provide education for all children living on the Lizard Peninsula; designed for a four-form entry, it has capacity for up to 600 pupils; all facilities accessible to disabled pupils in wheelchairs; specialist facilities for children with hearing difficulties; close links with nine primary schools. Full curriculum, with special arrangements to ensure basic skills such as English and mathematics are mastered. Extra-curricular activities 'to extend the able, tutor the talented, and harness the enthusiasm of all'. High proportion of year 10 enrol for Duke of Edinburgh (Bronze) Award Scheme; vocal and instrumental ensembles. Annual drama production. County under-13 soccer champions (1995). Not over-subscribed, but 21% of pupils come from outside the catchment area. Sound and video-recording equipment and projectors for all departments; information technology networked in every classroom from the school's computer centre; CD-Rom in the library, which also has fax/modem facilities. Outdoor pursuits: lightweight camping equipment, three 14-foot Falmouth Bass boats. The school has its own 45-seat bus, bought and maintained by thriving association of parents and friends. The school has won six awards for its community work; Charter Mark 'for excellence in the public service' renewed in 1995. Applauded by Times Educational Supplement for annual report to parents in 1993, 1994 and 1996.

Alumni Andrew Butterrill, awarded the British Empire Medal for bravery during the Gulf War; Stephen Hagget, Royal Historical Society award-winner; David Roberts, Northamptonshire and England under-19 cricketer.

Streaming Pupils remain in mixed-ability groups for most subjects in years 7 to 9. From year 8, some subjects, including foreign languages, are re-grouped into bands; others, including mathematics, are reorganised into sets.

Approach to discipline 'Firm and fair, with the emphasis on self-discipline and respect for others. Sanctions range from detention to exclusion (very rare).' Golden rule: 'Do the right and reasonable thing.' Emphasis on the '4Cs': care, courtesy, concern, co-operation.

Uniform Navy V-neck jumper (badge optional), white shirt, tie optional, blue/black trousers or skirt/slacks. Same colour socks/stockings with black 'sensible' shoes. PE and sportswear colours are also defined. 'Fully enforced.' Bursary fund for hardship cases.

Homework Average 11-year-old, five hours a week; 14-year-old, six hours; 16-year-old, seven hours.

Vocational qualifications Preliminary certificate in modern languages for work (French).

Inspection February 1993: 'A good school with high expectations and a positive working ethos.'; 'Pupils produce good quality written work, most read competently and fluently, and standards of oracy are generally sound.'; 'Learning takes place in a purposeful manner and pupils are set challenging work which is undertaken in an atmosphere characterised by good relationships between teachers and pupils.'; 'The school has excellent links with parents and the local community and has been awarded both the Schools Curriculum Award and the Charter Mark.'; 'The school buildings and grounds are exemplary in their care and condition, and much of the display work is of high quality.'; 'The school has successfully established a happy, hard-working and caring community where the contributions of all pupils and adults are valued, and where all are dedicated to the achievements of the highest standards of work and behaviour.' November 1996: 'Mullion School serves its community extremely well, achieving good standards of teaching and a very good response from well-behaved pupils in a happy, well-ordered environment.'; 'There is a very good support for pupils with special educational needs.'; 'The inspection team found the views of parents very helpful; one parent encapsulated the majority view: "an excellent school – approachable, caring,

achieving high standards and turning out well-mannered, likeable young people."'

Primary schools Coverack Primary; Cury CE Primary; Garras Primary; Landewednack Primary; Grade Ruan Primary; Manaccan Primary; Mullion Primary; St Keverne Primary; St Martin-in-Meneage Primary.

RICARDS LODGE HIGH SCHOOL

Lake Road
Wimbledon
London SW19 7HB
Tel (0181) 946 2208
Fax (0181) 971 9700

- National ranking 383 = (489 =, –, 455 =, –)
- GCSE 60% (50%)
- A-levels *Not applicable*
- Higher education *Not applicable*

- Girls' comprehensive
- Pupils 840
- Boys *Not applicable*
- Girls (12–16) 840
- Sixth form *Not applicable*
- Education authority *Merton*

Headteacher Sheila Catherine Oviatt Ham, 47, appointed in April 1997. Staff 43 (men 7, women 36).

Motto Quality education for girls.

Background Original Ricards Lodge was built in 1875 and remains part of current complex; Wimbledon Day Commercial School moved to site in 1950; became Ricards Lodge High School in 1969; beautiful school in residential area of Wimbledon, not far from Wimbledon Lawn Tennis Club; modern buildings added to Victorian lodge in open grounds with trees and shrubs. Over-subscribed, with 225 applications for 210 places. Electronic registration of pupils with 'swipe' cards. Personal and social education is highly valued, with all staff taking part. High number of pupils selected to be Wimbledon ball girls; success at local, county and national level in competitions: athletics, gymnastics, hockey, cross-country and football. Strong focus on music: performance at regular concerts. Annual drama production; students go on to work with National Youth Theatre. School trips in England and abroad. 'Overall, Total Quality Management is our major focus.

Policies and procedures are clearly defined and regularly reviewed. We place great value on our human resources, developing and training both staff and students, and affording as many opportunities as possible for consultation within an "evaluation and review" culture.' Winners of 1995 Merton Curriculum Award.

Streaming Sets for mathematics, science and languages in all years; other subjects taught in mixed-ability groups.

Approach to discipline Firm; high expectations; Code of Conduct and Behaviour, which pupils and parents are required to sign; fair: 'Sanctions do not include humiliation, but miscreants pay in terms of community services. Sanctions include detentions, community service and exclusions.' Also rewards; parents kept informed. Effective anti-bullying policy, with student-managed and staff-supervised anti-bullying council.

Uniform Navy sweatshirt with school logo, navy skirt/trousers/culottes, white shirt, black/navy shoes. Strictly enforced, 'but notes from parents may excuse a short-term difficulty'.

Homework Average 12-year-old, seven hours a week; 14-year-old, 10 hours; 16-year-old, 12 to 14 hours.

Vocational qualifications Piloting GNVQ units, Health and Social Care.

Inspection November 1995: 'Ricards Lodge is a good school which provides well for its students. They achieve well overall and behave with self-discipline and courtesy. Working relationships within the school are positive and the school enjoys the support and confidence of parents. The school is effectively managed and the governors and senior management provide clear leadership.'; 'Among the factors which support the sound achievement of students are their well-developed skills in reading, writing, speaking and listening, the system of student review and target-setting, an orderly and harmonious school environment, the good behaviour of students in class and around the school, and good standards of teaching.'; 'The comparatively low uptake of double science at GCSE may be limiting the access of some girls to science-based careers.'

Primary school Park House Middle; Wimbledon Chase Middle; Priory Middle; Hillcross Middle; Bushey Middle.

SAWSTON VILLAGE COLLEGE

New Road
Sawston
Cambridge
Cambridgeshire CB2 4BP
Tel (01223) 832217
Fax (01223) 836680

- National ranking 383 = (366 = , 378 =)
- GCSE 60% (60%)
- A-levels *Not applicable*
- Higher education *Not applicable*

- Grant-maintained
- Mixed comprehensive
- Pupils 1,133
- Boys (11–16) 534
- Girls (11–16) 599
- Sixth form *Not applicable*
- Education authority *Cambridgeshire*

Headteacher Kevin McMullen, 48, appointed in September 1994. Staff 65 (men 32, women 33).

Motto *None*

Background Created by Henry Morris, the pioneer of community education. Built in 1930, the heart of the college is the listed Fountain Court. Students attracted from broad catchment area stretching from the Cambridge boundaries to borders of Essex. Originally for 400 pupils, 'Even the addition of a science block, sports hall, swimming pool and technology facilities has been unable to meet the needs of this popular school'. More building planned. Extensive community programme, with more than 5,000 adults using educational, cultural and sports facilities each week. Fully-subscribed, above planned admission limit: 'The school caters for a well-defined rural catchment area and normally attracts about 30 pupils a year from outside the catchment area.' High standard of music; on-site squash, shooting and multi-gym facilities. 'Trust best epitomises the college ethos. Students are given open access to the whole site at all times of the day. They are considered to be partners in the learning process and respond with a mature sense of self-respect.'

Streaming Ability sets for most subjects.

Approach to discipline 'Standards of behaviour are set by the tradition of trust and mutual respect which underpins activities inside and outside the classroom. Students are involved in policy and planning via the Student Council. Breaches of discipline are rare, but students who impair the learning process are held to account.'

Uniform Maroon sweatshirt with college emblem, white sports shirt underneath. 'The uniform was designed by the pupils and is essentially casual; therefore, enforcement is not a significant issue.'

Homework Average 11-year-old, seven hours a week; 14-year-old, eight to 12 hours; 16-year-old, 12 to 15 hours.

Vocational qualifications *None*

Inspection April 1995: 'The standards of achievement at Sawston Village College are good'; 'There is under-achievement among some less able pupils.'; 'Pupils' capabilities in using information technology are developing but there is room for improvements here.'; 'The motivation of pupils is very good; the vast majority are keen to learn. Most lessons proceed at a good pace and provide pupils with good levels of challenge. The college is very successful in developing pupils' learning skills and constructive attitudes to learning.'; 'The teachers are competent, committed and work enthusiastically.'; 'A major feature is the high level of expectation which teachers have of their pupils, which is often matched by diligence and commendable rates of progress.'; 'The leadership and management of the college are good.'

Primary schools John Paxton Primary, Sawston; William Westley CE Primary, Whittleford; Icknield Primary, Sawston; Stapleford Community Primary, Stapleford; Great and Little Shelford CE Primary, Great Shelford; Duxford CE Community Primary, Duxford.

ST JOSEPH'S ROMAN CATHOLIC HIGH SCHOOL

Chorley New Road
Horwich
Bolton
Greater Manchester BL6 6HW
Tel (01204) 697456
Fax (01204) 669018

- National ranking 383= (428=, 253=, 279=, –)

- GCSE 60% (55%)
- A-levels *Not applicable*
- Higher education *Not applicable*

- Mixed comprehensive
- Pupils 732
- Boys (11–16) 367
- Girls (11–16) 365
- Sixth form *Not applicable*
- Education authority *Bolton*

Headteacher Leo Conley, 41, appointed in August 1995. Staff 43 (men 18, women 25).

Motto Iustitia sine timore (Be just and fear not).

Background Built in the mid-1960s as a secondary modern school; became comprehensive during local re-organisation in 1970s. Extensive playing fields; £1.3m building programme completed in 1993: sports hall, various refurbishments, conversion of large block into learning resource centre and five classrooms. Over-subscribed, with 165 applications for 140 places. 'Excellent' sporting tradition, enabling pupils to reach county and national standards in variety of sports: netball, soccer, swimming, athletics, cross-country, volleyball, cricket and rugby. Vibrant music department: 110-member girls' choir, boys' choir, full orchestra and various ensembles. Public-speaking is integral part of curriculum, with local and regional success.

Alumni Philip Clarke, rugby league international.

Streaming 'Some subjects set according to departmental policy; others remain mixed-ability.'

Approach to discipline 'Firm but fair in a caring environment, with the character of a family based on the Gospel message and the teachings of the Church.'

Uniform Years 7 and 8: blazer, tie, pullover, white shirt, grey trousers/skirts. Years 9 and 10: royal-blue pullover with school badge, tie, white shirt, grey trousers/skirt. Year 11: black pullover, white shirt, navy trousers/skirt. Regulations enforced 'very strictly'.

Homework Average 11-year-old, five hours a week; 14-year-old, nine hours; 16-year-old, 12 to 14 hours.

Vocational qualifications RSA, Typing, Wordprocessing, Information Technology; City and Guilds, Sports and Recreation.

Inspection May 1996: 'A good school with a number of features from which the pupils gain considerable benefit.'; 'The ethos of the school is rooted in its values as a Catholic community, characterised by respect and concern for others and a recognition of the importance of spiritual and moral education. The attitudes which pupils display towards their work, to members of staff and to one another are very positive.'; 'Relationships between staff and pupils are excellent.'; 'Work is carefully planned, teachers have a good command of their subjects, there are expectations of high standards of work made of pupils, and time and resources are used effectively.'; 'The school is well led, daily administration is effective and the school is well supported by its clerical, technical and ancillary staff.'; 'The accommodation, although sufficient for current members, will not be adequate if higher numbers continue to be admitted.'

Primary schools St Mary's RC Primary, Horwich; Sacred Heart RC Primary, Westhoughton; St Joseph's RC Primary, Anderton; Our Lady's RC Primary, Aspull; Holy Family RC Primary, New Springs.

ST THOMAS A BECKET ROMAN CATHOLIC SCHOOL

Barnsley Road
Sandal
Wakefield
West Yorkshire WF2 6EQ
Tel (01924) 250408/252431
Fax (01924) 254714

- National ranking 383 = (460 =, 293 =, 414 =, −)
- GCSE 60% (53%)
- A-levels *Not applicable*
- Higher education *Not applicable*

- Mixed comprehensive
- Pupils 752
- Boys (11–16) 375
- Girls (11–16) 377
- Sixth form *Not applicable*
- Education authority *Wakefield*

Headteacher Paul Heitzman, 41, appointed in January 1995. Staff 40 (men 19, women 21).

Motto Esse quam videri (To be rather than seem to be).

Background Originally a 400-pupil secondary modern school built in 1963 in residential suburb of Sandal south of Wakefield. Modern buildings, well-maintained; extensive playing fields to rear. Over-subscribed and still growing, with 1.3 applications per place. Sporting representatives at city, county and national level; cricket for boys and girls. Sign-language group; award for work with local industry; Duke of Edinburgh Award Scheme; road safety competition; local music and drama groups.

Alumni David Ward, Leeds and England rugby league captain.

Streaming Mixed-ability in lower school; setting in mathematics, science and modern languages.

Approach to discipline 'There is strong emphasis in the school on attendance, care and discipline. We encourage all pupils to live by Christian values.' Pastoral heads monitor behaviour and liaise with tutors, teachers, parents, welfare agencies.

Uniform Black blazer, grey pullover/cardigan, grey trousers/skirt, maroon tie and badge. 'Simple, inexpensive and effective. Strictly enforced.'

Homework Average 11-year-old, five hours a week; 14-year-old, 10 hours; 16-year-old, more than 10 hours as required.

Vocational qualifications RSA; Youth Award Scheme.

Inspection December 1993: 'St Thomas A Becket School offers Catholic education of good quality.'; 'Standards of achievement in lessons are satisfactory or better across the whole curriculum. In English, mathematics and history they are good. Pupils' attitudes to learning are good. They work hard and are well-motivated.'; 'Longer term planning and identification of priorities are unsatisfactory.'; 'The behaviour of pupils is excellent.'

Primary schools St Austin's RC Primary; English Martyrs RC Primary; St Ignatius RC Primary, Ossett; St Mary's RC Primary, Leeds.

WOODHEY HIGH SCHOOL

Bolton Road West
Ramsbottom
Bury
Lancashire BL0 9QZ

Tel (01706) 825215
Fax (01706) 825989

- National ranking 383 = (366 =, 481, 337 =, –)
- GCSE 60% (60%)
- A-levels *Not applicable*
- Higher education *Not applicable*

- Mixed comprehensive
- Pupils 989
- Boys (11–16) 524
- Girls (11–16) 465
- Sixth form *Not applicable*
- Education authority *Bury*

Headteacher Frank Bennett, 59, appointed in September 1979. Staff 53 (men 20, women 33).

Motto Excellentia (Excellence).

Background Opened in 1979 as custom-built six-form entry comprehensive in semi-rural area on edge of Ramsbottom town. Three blocks of buildings, including a sports hall. Addition of two new laboratories, making a total of seven; also new library and information technology resources centre in 1994. Recently-renovated sports fields. Prides itself on examination results, quality of teaching staff and smart appearance of pupils. Over-subscribed, with 270 applications for 192 places. Three in four (76%) continue their education after 16. 1987 Schools Curriculum Award; 1988 Children of Achievement Award. Laptop computers available for use in all subjects. Overseas visits: Switzerland, Austria, Italy, France, Spain. Clubs: drama, photography, meteorology, aerobics, electronic music; school choir, chamber choir, band, guitar-playing for beginners. Main sports include soccer, rugby, basketball, netball, badminton, hockey, cross-country, athletics, cricket. Annual theatrical production. Duke of Edinburgh Award Scheme.

Streaming Mixed-ability for first half-term in year 7. Pupils then assessed and put in sets for all academic subjects.

Approach to discipline 'Rules kept to a minimum with pupils simply being asked to observe the principles of courtesy and common sense, to respect both people and property, and to do all in their power to enhance both their own and the school's reputation. Good order is achieved by praising achievement, and setting relevant and achievable goals. When necessary, misbeha-

viour is punished by restriction of liberty and, if necessary, consultation with parents.'

Uniform Maroon sweater (optional), charcoal-grey trousers/skirt, white shirt/blouse, maroon tie with crest, black/grey socks (or white for girls), black shoes.

Homework Average 11-year-old, eight hours a week; 14-year-old, 12 hours; 16-year-old, 12 hours.

Vocational qualifications GNVQ, Hairdressing, Beauty Therapy, Business Administration, Information Technology.

Inspection January 1994: 'This is a school in which achievement is afforded a high priority and where pupils are encouraged to strive for excellence. Teaching is generally competent and effective. It is usually well-organised and is always founded on mutual respect between teachers and pupils. In some subjects tasks are not always well-matched to pupils' abilities, particularly for the least able pupils at Key Stage 4. Learning is of good quality overall but opportunities for pupils to develop independence in learning are limited in some subjects.'

Primary schools St Andrew's CE Primary; St Paul's CE Primary; Peel Brow Primary; Hazlehurst Primary; Greenmount Primary; Holcombe Brook Primary; St Mary's CE Primary, Hawkshaw; Summerseat Methodist Primary; Emmanuel CE Primary, Holcombe.

CHIPPING CAMPDEN SCHOOL

Cider Mill Lane
Chipping Campden
Gloucestershire GL55 6HU
Tel (01386) 840216
Fax (01386) 840498

- National ranking 393 (167, 268 =, 410, –)
- GCSE 59% (84%)
- A-levels 45% (A/B); 93% (A/E)
- Higher education 65% (Oxford 1, Cambridge 2)

- Grant-maintained
- Mixed comprehensive
- Pupils 936
- Boys (11–18) 468
- Girls (11–18) 468
- Sixth form 119 (13%)
- Education authority *Gloucestershire*

Headteacher Jeffrey Price, 46, appointed in

September 1994. Staff 53 (men 25, women 28).

Motto 550 years of achievement.

Background Foundation school dating from 1440 in middle of one of Cotswolds' most beautiful and historic towns; takes pupils from large geographical area of north Cotswolds, also from Oxfordshire, Warwickshire, Herefordshire and Worcestershire; occupies pleasant site, with original 1920s classrooms plus large additions in 1960s and 1970s; new science block and refurbished classrooms in 1994; new design and information technology block in September 1997; surrounded by ample playing fields on edge of countryside. Foundation funds used to supplement school budget. Over-subscribed, with 220 applications for 172 places. Sports facilities: indoor heated swimming pool, large sports hall, gym and purpose-built fitness centre; district council sports centre on site from September 1995. Emphasis on traditional competitive games, alongside individual achievement. Particularly notable examination results in science, mathematics, technology and English. 'Excellence' in creative arts, art and drama. Traditional pastoral system: three houses and heads of house. 'The school is, above all, a caring institution with a respect for the individual and a sincere aim for all students to achieve their full potential, no matter what their ability.'

Alumni Robert Payne-Smith, Dean of Canterbury and Regius Professor of Daventry (1865–71); Professor Evan Parker, professor of physics, Warwick University; David Stanley, chief education officer of Hereford and Worcestershire.

Streaming Mixed-ability, with in-class support in year 7; in years 8 and 9, six classes divided into two, with top, bottom and middle sets. 'Each main subject area sets pupils independently, allowing for considerable flexibility.'

Approach to discipline 'The school has a traditional approach to school discipline, insisting on high standards of courtesy and behaviour. Departments run lunch-time detention systems. Evening detentions are used in some cases and the school operates a successful system of internal suspension before a pupil would finally be excluded from school.'

Uniform Simple and practical: navy jumper/

sweatshirt with school badge in gold embroidery, charcoal trousers for boys and navy skirt or trousers for girls, school/house tie for boys. Uniform rules are strictly enforced by pastoral staff.'

Homework Average 11-year-old, four to five hours a week; 14-year-old, five to six hours; 16-year-old, six to 10 hours.

Vocational qualifications GNVQ Intermediate, Leisure and Tourism.

Inspection November 1993.

GUILDFORD COUNTY SCHOOL

Farnham Road
Guildford
Surrey GU2 5LU
Tel (01483) 504089
Fax (01483) 300849
E-mail: 106272.310@compuserve.com

- National ranking 394 (314, 484, 312, 285)
- GCSE 59% (62%)
- A-levels 41% (A/B); 92% (A/E)
- Higher education 83% (Oxford 2)

- Grant-maintained
- Mixed comprehensive
- Pupils 962
- Boys (11–18) 478
- Girls (11–18) 484
- Sixth form 202 (21%)
- Education authority *Surrey*

Headteacher David N. Smith, 57, appointed in September 1977. Staff 60 (men 19, women 41).

Motto *None*

Background Established as a girls' grammar school just after the turn of the century on the shoulder of the Hogs Back close to centre of Guildford. Became a comprehensive in the late 1970s, when a new building was added to allow further growth to 750 pupils from age of 12 to 18. Grant-maintained from September 1990; pupils admitted at 11 from September 1993; further growth not expected. New developments: library, specialist rooms for music and information technology and some general classrooms. Over-subscribed, with 1.7 applications per place.

Streaming Lessons taught in ordered classes formed according to pupils' ability, re-grouped for different parts of curriculum. Regularly reviewed.

Approach to discipline Clear, well-tried standards of conduct set for all pupils; good and courteous behaviour required. 'Praise and approval are no less important than reprimand and sanction, but poor behaviour or effort is firmly and effectively checked. We support the belief that school discipline will not be completely successful unless it encourages boys and girls to make a fresh start "tomorrow".'

Uniform Boys: navy blazer with badge, grey trousers, white shirt, navy-and-red tie, navy V-neck pullover. Girls: Navy blazer, apple-green blouse, navy skirt, navy V-neck pullover.

Homework Average 11-year-old, seven hours a week; 14-year-old, 10 hours 30 minutes; 16-year-old, 10 hours 30 minutes.

Vocational qualifications Book-keeping and Accounts, Word-processing, Typing; Computer Literacy and Information Technology; Pre-vocational education course validated by Guildford College of Higher and Further Education.

Inspection February 1993: 'Standards of achievement and learning were satisfactory or better in approximately 85% of the lessons. The majority of pupils of all ages and abilities make steady progress.' 'Pupils have good opportunities to develop their social and cultural education within the curriculum and through a range of well-supported extra-curricular activities.'; 'The school effectively promotes the spiritual and moral development of the pupils. Relationships in the school are supportive but firm. Pupils show respect for each other and for authority. Generally, pupils behave very well.'

Primary schools Queen Eleanor's CE Junior; Holy Trinity CE Junior; Northmead Junior; Stoughton Grange Junior; Tillingbourne County Junior.

SACKVILLE SCHOOL

Lewes Road
East Grinstead
West Sussex RH17 5RF
Tel (01342) 410140
Fax (01342) 315544

- National ranking 395 (378, 409, 277, 326)

- GCSE 59% (59%)
- A-levels 37% (A/B); 89% (A/E)
- Higher education 83% (Oxford 2)

- Mixed comprehensive
- Pupils 1,570
- Boys (11–18) 800
- Girls (11–18) 770
- Sixth form 270 (17%)
- Education authority West Sussex

Headteacher David Hywel Bennett, 53, appointed in January 1994. Staff 93 (men 41, women 52).

Motto Deeds not words.

Background The school was founded by public subscription in 1859 as a national church school on a site provided by Countess Amherst, a descendant of Thomas Sackville. Moved to current site close to town centre in 1964; became comprehensive in 1970; attracts pupils from throughout East Grinstead and Kent, Surrey and East Sussex. Well-stocked lending and reference library open during school day and after school for supervised study. Noted for sporting achievements: Sussex county finalists or champions in cricket, football, hockey, rugby and swimming. Also known for public performances of music and drama. Average of 1.2 applications for each place. Prides itself on care of individual pupils: 'A division into three separate "schools" ensures that personal contact between staff, parents and pupils provides the basis for an outstanding education.'

Alumni Lance Price, BBC political correspondent.

Streaming Setting by ability in each subject introduced from year 7 and covering most subjects by year 9.

Approach to discipline Aim is for structured, disciplined society where young people stimulated to develop lively, enquiring minds capable of independent judgment and action. High standards expected in and out of school.

Uniform Boys: dark-grey trousers, light-blue shirt, navy pullover/cardigan with logo, navy school tie, dark socks, black shoes. Girls: navy skirt/trousers, light-blue blouse, navy pullover/cardigan with logo, navy/white socks or navy/white/natural tights. Strictly enforced for years 7 to 11; dress code for sixth-formers.

Homework Average 11-year-old, seven hours 30 minutes a week; 14-year-old, 10 hours; 16-year-old, 15 hours.

Vocational qualifications GNVQ Level 2.

Primary schools The Meads Primary; Halsford Park Primary; Blackwell Primary; St Mary's CE Primary; Estcots Primary.

BEECHEN CLIFF SCHOOL

Alexandra Park
Bath BA2 4RE
Tel (01225) 420366
Fax (01225) 314025

- National ranking 396 (467, 415, 373, –)
- GCSE 59% (52%)
- A-levels 36% (A/B); 91% (A/E)
- Higher education 66% (Cambridge 2)

- Grant-maintained
- Boys' comprehensive
- Pupils 996
- Boys (11–18) 971
- Girls (16–18) 25
- Sixth form 170 (17%)
- Education authority *Bath and North East Somerset*

Headteacher Roy Alfred Ludlow, 52, appointed in April 1990. Staff 61 (men 43, women 18).

Motto *None*

Background Formerly City of Bath Boys' Grammar School; became comprehensive following amalgamation with Oldfield Boys' School in 1971; in 'magnificent' setting on southern side of Bath, surrounded by own grounds that include two rugby pitches, cricket square, all-weather pitch; main building made from Bath stone and dates from 1931. Additions: suites of rooms for science, technology, humanities, sixth-form teaching block, spacious sports centre; school has outdoor activities cottage in Brecon Beacons. Over-subscribed, with average of 1.6 applications per place. 'All-round' curriculum strength; 'formidable' reputation in sport, especially rugby and cricket (annual match with MCC, and annual entry in Wisden); soccer, hockey and athletics strong. Outdoor pursuits. Music: annual concert in February. Success in public-speaking competitions; drama also 'very strong'. 'Beechen Cliff is about high stan-

dards, principally in academic work but also in music, sport, drama and public-speaking. The school takes pride in a scholarly, purposeful atmosphere, in which all pupils are valued and encouraged to aim high. High aspirations for all are seen as vital.'

Alumni Sir Roger Bannister, athlete and former master of Pembroke College, Oxford; Arnold Ridley, actor; Raymond Leppard, conductor; Dr Richard Roberts, 1993 Nobel prizewinner for medicine; John Hall, Bath and England rugby player.

Streaming Pupils put in sets from year 8.

Approach to discipline 'We believe in praise and encouragement, wherever possible. However, we consider good discipline to be vital. The school maintains firm discipline and has an excellent reputation in this respect.'

Uniform Black blazer with badge, charcoal-grey trousers, white shirt, school tie, grey V-neck pullover, grey socks, black shoes.

Homework Average 11-year-old, five hours a week; 14-year-old, seven hours 30 minutes; 16-year-old, 10 hours.

Vocational qualifications One-year sixth-form pre-vocational course.

Inspection October 1993: 'The school provides a very effective education for pupils.'; 'The extensive provision of extra-curricular activities is of considerable benefit to the intellectual, sporting and social development of students. Many staff give much extra time to these activities and parents also make valuable contributions as appropriate. The teaching is generally good, committed and often scholarly. Pupils are well-motivated in class and relationships are mainly good. The leadership of the school is strong and positive, although the systems of management are unnecessarily complex.'; 'Pupils are polite and take a pride in their appearance. Discipline is mainly good, though there are some minor lapses.'

Primary schools Newbridge Junior; Moorlands Junior; South Twerton Junior; St Stephen's CE Primary; Weston All Saints CE Primary.

KENNET SCHOOL

Stoney Lane
Thatcham
Berkshire RG19 4LL

Tel (01635) 862121
Fax (01635) 871814

- National ranking 397 (400, 470, 429, –)
- GCSE 59% (58%)
- A-levels 27% (A/B); 93% (A/E)
- Higher education 61%

- Mixed comprehensive
- Pupils 1,382
- Boys (11–18) 693
- Girls (11–18) 689
- Sixth form 215 (16%)
- Education authority *Berkshire*

Headteacher Paul G. Dick, 42, appointed in January 1989. Staff 87 (men 42, women 45).

Motto Excellence through endeavour.

Background Opened in 1957 to serve growing population of Thatcham; set on eastern perimeter of town; introduced sixth-form in 1970; grew to eight-form entry in 1990. Building modernisation and expansion to meet growing demand. Extensive pitches, floodlit courts and fully-equipped sports hall; swimming pool added; shared facilities with Kennet Sports Centre; new library and study block. Over-subscribed, with 262 applications for 227 places. Unit for physically-handicapped pupils. Science and English regarded among academic strengths; also modern languages, and a humanities course for year 7. 'We seek excellence for all, both academically and socially. We aim to produce well-qualified, fully-developed young adults. The high expectations in the classroom are complemented by an enormous range of educational visits, both local and national.' Identified for praise in 1996 annual Ofsted report.

Streaming In mathematics from year 7; languages, science, humanities from year 9; English in years 10 and 11.

Approach to discipline 'A condition of attendance is the willingness to contribute to a calm, purposeful atmosphere. Pupils are expected to give of their best in class and in behaviour and dress. Our expectations are met.'

Uniform Jumper with badge, blue shirt/blouse, grey/black trousers for boys or blue skirt for girls, black shoes. Very strictly enforced.

Homework Average 11-year-old, six hours a week; 14-year-old, six hours; 16-year-old,

eight hours.

Vocational qualifications GNVQ Level 2, Health and Social Care, Travel and Tourism; GNVQ Level 3, Business, Art.

Inspection September 1994: 'A good school which sets and achieves high standards, in academic performance and personal development.'; 'Pupils consistently demonstrate good learning skills and make clear progress in their lessons.'; 'Pupils use information technology in many subject areas, with confidence and skill.'; 'Pupils benefit from an excellent system of pastoral care and support and a range of extra-curricular activities.'; 'The school benefits from strong leadership and effective senior management.'

Primary schools Francis Baily Primary; St Mary's Primary; Parsons Down Primary; Spurcroft Primary; Whitelands Park Primary.

LUTTERWORTH GRAMMAR SCHOOL AND COMMUNITY COLLEGE

Bitteswell Road
Lutterworth
Leicestershire LE17 4RS
Tel (01455) 554101
Fax (01455) 553725

- National ranking 398 (329, 445, 353, –)
- GCSE 59% (62%)
- A-levels 24% (A/B); 83% (A/E)
- Higher education 75% (Oxford 1, Cambridge 1)

- Mixed comprehensive
- Pupils 1,195
- Boys (14–19) 613
- Girls (14–19) 582
- Sixth form 345 (29%)
- Education authority *Leicestershire*

Headteacher Christopher John Henstock, 48, appointed in August 1995. Staff 110 (men 51, women 59).

Motto Sapere aude (Dare to be wise).

Background Re-founded as a grammar school in 1880; developed as small market-town selective school of 400 in 1930s; became comprehensive and community college for ~1,700 in late 1960s and early 1970s. Buildings on extensive campus. Specialist accommodation: modern library and resources centre, 15 science laboratories, seven computer laboratories, workshops and design studios, sports hall, weights room, swimming pool, sixth-form centre (in 'splendid manor house'), television studio, drama studio, small theatre, business centre. Regular individual and team success in national sporting competitions. Music and drama: choir regularly tour performing Masses; drama productions from Greek theatre to *West Side Story*. 'We are a school which bases itself upon its traditional and well-established strengths. We believe in the importance of young people learning, within a positive, structured and well-ordered environment, those rigorous and varied skills necessary for the modern world.' Regular homework; wide range of extra-curricular activities; compulsory uniform; pastoral system.

Alumni John Cooper, Olympic hurdler; Nick Cooke, England cricketer; Nigel Briers, Leicestershire cricket captain.

Streaming Teaching groups are generally based upon parallel settings within subjects.

Approach to discipline 'We believe in developing the good sense and consideration of our students. As they are aged 14 to 19, it is reasonable to expect individual and group self-discipline and thoughtfulness. That is what they extensively give. Relationships are positive and purposeful.'

Uniform Navy V-neck jumper, black/grey trousers or navy/black skirt or trousers, blue/white shirt/blouse. Sixth-formers are expected to dress 'in a business-like manner'.

Homework Average 14-year-old, 15 hours a week; 16-year-old, 18 hours.

Vocational qualifications GNVQ, Business and Finance, Performing and Media Arts.

Inspection January 1996: 'The school is very successful. Students achieve good examination results in virtually all subjects. Staff have established a very good working ethos and there are good professional relationships between all participants. Students respond with maturity, both in their work and as young citizens.'; 'Students make good progress in acquiring knowledge and skills. The challenge and pace of lessons is particularly good in the sixth form. However, across the school there are shortcomings in the teaching in about one-eighth of lessons; in most of these cases the work is not sufficiently well matched to the needs of the students.'

CIRENCESTER KINGSHILL SCHOOL

Kingshill Lane
Cirencester
Gloucestershire GL7 1HS
Tel (01285) 651511
Fax (01285) 885652
E-mail: cksgm@rmplc.co.uk

- National ranking 399= (302=, 334=, 233=, 337=)
- GCSE 59% (63%)
- A-levels *Not applicable*
- Higher education *Not applicable*

- Grant-maintained
- Mixed comprehensive
- Pupils 680
- Boys (11–16) 376
- Girls (11–16) 304
- Sixth form *Not applicable*
- Education authority *Gloucestershire*

Headteacher Mike Redman, 48, appointed in September 1987. Staff 39 (men 17, women 22).

Motto Striving for excellence.

Background Founded 1976; moved to current site in 1977 as purpose-built comprehensive on eastern edge of Cirencester in semi-rural open setting. Draws pupils from Cirencester and surrounding parishes. Buildings semi-open plan; no corridors; new four-room language block and two new food technology rooms to open in May 1998. Consistently over-subscribed since 1988, with about 160 applications for 156 places; admission limit increased due to popularity; nine in 10 pupils continue with education after 16. Proud of modern languages and foreign exchanges; German and French taught from year 7 from September 1997; noted for pioneering work in science and design; developing reputation for expressive arts, with many musical and drama events; more than 200 pupils play musical instruments; emphasis on independent learning and use of resources. Full range of sports; new tennis courts and artificial cricket wicket. New science and technology building completed in spring 1995. Investor in People Award in 1996. Increasing level of extra-curricular activities include adventure holiday for year 10 pupils and residential visits to Wales, France and Germany.

Streaming Pupils in sets in modern languages

and mathematics from year 8.

Approach to discipline Firm and fair. 'Emphasis on praise, cooperation and contribution of pupils to the school. Serious indiscipline is rare but is firmly dealt with.' Sanctions: community service, detention and exclusion. Parents and governors supportive.

Uniform Boys: white/pale-blue/navy/red shirt, navy/dark-grey trousers, navy/red sweatshirt/sweater/cardigan/navy blazer. Girls: white/pale-blue/navy/red blouse, navy dress/skirt/trousers, navy/red sweatshirt/sweater/cardigan/blazer. Uniform rules deliberately give pupils a degree of choice.

Homework Average 11-year-old, five to 10 hours a week; 14-year-old, 10 hours; 16-year-old, 10 to 15 hours.

Vocational qualifications *None*

Inspection March 1994: 'This is a good school in which examination achievement is high, relationships are excellent and all members of the school community treat each other with respect.'; 'Pupils respond well to the trust which is given to them, with the result that the controlled and orderly feeling in the community is achieved with a light touch.'

Primary schools Cirencester County Junior; Ann Edwards Primary, South Cerney; Powell's CE Primary; Ashton Keynes Primary; Watermoor CE Primary.

GILLOTT'S SCHOOL

Gillott's Lane
Henley-on-Thames
Oxfordshire RG9 1PS
Tel (01491) 574315
Fax (01491) 410509

- National ranking 399= (290=, 278=, 432=, 364=)
- GCSE 59% (64%)
- A-levels *Not applicable*
- Higher education *Not applicable*

- Mixed comprehensive
- Pupils 885
- Boys (11–16) 461
- Girls (11–16) 424
- Sixth form *Not applicable*
- Education authority *Oxfordshire*

Headteacher John Lockyer, 56, appointed in January 1987. Staff 47 (men 16, women 31).

Motto *None*

Background The only secondary school in Henley, serving not only the town, but also attracting pupils from as far as Watlington and over the county boundary at Marlow. Buildings in 40-acre parkland setting on fringe of town. Offices in large Victorian house, but other buildings all new since 1960: specialist suites for main subjects, special needs area, music centre, dance/drama studio, gymnasium, fitness room, assembly hall, kitchens and dining area. Joint-use sports centre on site, with full-size swimming pool, squash courts; extensive playing fields include tennis courts. Over-subscribed, with 1.2 applications per place. More than eight in 10 school-leavers (85%) go on to full-time further education. Performing arts and sports among strengths; rugby team are frequently county champions; many pupils achieve county and national sports honours.

Streaming Pupils are increasingly put in sets from year 7.

Approach to discipline 'The emphasis is on firm boundaries and self-discipline. We believe that good relationships between pupils, staff and parents are crucial.'

Uniform Navy jumper with badge, grey trousers/skirt. Regulations firmly enforced.

Homework Average 11-year-old, three hours a week; 14-year-old, five hours; 16-year-old, seven hours.

Vocational qualifications Youth Award Scheme.

Inspection March 1996: 'A very good school. Many good features are demonstrated across the range of the work at the school and pupils achieve high standards in many aspects of the curriculum.'; 'Pupils respond well to the high expectations of work and behaviour consistently applied by all staff.'; 'Teachers are well-qualified, talented and hard-working. They are supported well by a number of skilled non-teaching staff.'; 'Governors are involved fully in the work of the school and the headteacher and deputies provide effective leadership.'

Primary schools Trinity CE Primary; Valley Road Primary; Burford County Combined; Stokenchurch Middle.

HOPE VALLEY COLLEGE

Castleton Road
Hope
Via Sheffield
Derbyshire S30 2RD
Tel (01433) 620555
Fax (01433) 620054
E-mail: hvcollege@aol.com
Internet: http://members.aol.com/
hvcollege

- National ranking 399= (382=, 401=)
- GCSE 59% (59%)
- A-levels *Not applicable*
- Higher education *Not applicable*

- Mixed comprehensive
- Pupils 429
- Boys (11–16) 214
- Girls (11–16) 215
- Sixth form *Not applicable*
- Education authority *Derbyshire*

Headteacher Linda Norah Hudson, 49, appointed in January 1995. Staff 23 (men 12, women 11).

Motto *None*

Background Within the Peak National Park, the school serves a catchment area of 90 square miles; almost all pupils transported by bus. Established in the 1960s in the style of the 'Village Colleges' in Cambridgeshire. Strong community dimension, with site used by adults during the day and at night. Not oversubscribed; 93 applications for 106 places. Drama is 'particularly outstanding'; school performances 'verge on the professional'. Also two modern languages up to the age of 14; almost all pupils get a GCSE grade in a foreign language. There is an emphasis on the individual and a respect for the personal views of the students. Lessons tend to be interactive and academic achievement is high. The college management team, apart from the principal and vice-principal, is an elected body.'

Streaming Setting in some subjects after year 7.

Approach to discipline Firm boundaries, but rules kept to a minimum; students involved in school's behaviour policy. 'We have excellent relationships with parents, who are very supportive of the college.'

Uniform Grey/blue sweatshirt with college logo.

Homework Average 11-year-old, three hours a week; 14-year-old, five hours; 16-year-old, 12 hours.

Vocational qualifications *None (under review)*

Inspection October 1993: 'Pupils achieve good standards at this school.'; 'The school provides a good quality of education through a committed and experienced staff, effective planning and competent management.'; 'The school ethos encourages openness and pupil participation in decision-making, and there is an emphasis on pupils developing both their own values and an appreciation of the values of others.'

Primary schools Hathersage St Michael's CE Primary; Bamford Primary; Eyam CE Primary; Grindleford Primary; Bradwell Junior; Hope Primary; Castleton CE Primary; Edale CE Primary.

LAURENCE JACKSON SCHOOL

Church Lane
Guisborough TS14 6RD
Tel (01287) 636361
Fax (01287) 610309

- National ranking 399= (279=, 416=)
- GCSE 59% (65%)
- A-levels *Not applicable*
- Higher education *Not applicable*

- Mixed comprehensive
- Pupils 1,449
- Boys (11–16) 720
- Girls (11–16) 729
- Sixth form *Not applicable*
- Education authority *Redcar and Cleveland*

Headteacher Chris Lord, 54, appointed in September 1986. Staff 79 (men 28, women 51).

Motto *None*

Background Situated on the edge of Guisborough, about six miles from the coast and a couple of miles from the North York Moors National Park. Opened in 1958 as Guisborough County Modern School; became the Laurence Jackson School in 1970; extensive expansion in 1970s and 1980s; buildings extensively used by the Evening Institute and many local organisations. Dual-use sports centre on the site. Seven feeder primary schools, but with increasing number of pupils from outside catchment area. Oversubscribed, with 335 applications for 302 places in September 1997. 'Very strong' in sport, music and drama; wide range of subjects: 27 in years 10 and 11; proud of learning support scheme for children with special needs; 'excellent' careers provision, one of only 37 schools to win Education-Industry Partnership Award in 1994. 'A busy and purposeful community in which we try to be aware of, respect and cater for the needs of everyone – young people and adults – who make up this community.'

Alumni Selina Scott, former head girl (1966–67) and television personality; Bob Champion, Grand National-winning jockey.

Streaming Some streaming, particularly in core subjects; measure of departmental autonomy.

Approach to discipline 'Firm but fair. Code of conduct generally well-supported by pupils and parents. Merit points for praiseworthy contributions in all areas of school life for years 7 to 9; commendations in years 10 and 11.

Uniform Dark-grey/black trousers or bottle-green skirt, white shirt, black V-neck cardigan/pullover, school tie, black/grey/white socks or beige/black/white tights, plain 'sensible' shoes.

Homework Average 11-year-old, five hours a week; 14-year-old, seven hours; 16-year-old, 10 hours.

Vocational qualifications RSA; GNVQs.

Inspection September 1995: 'Laurence Jackson School provides a good education for its pupils. The quality of teaching and learning in the school is enhanced by the arrangements that are made for pupils' welfare guidance. The school has a high reputation in the local community.'; 'Throughout the school, lessons are well-planned with clear aims which are communicated to pupils. In the great majority of lessons, teachers have appropriate expectations, and the support they provide for pupils is well-judged. Good relationships between teachers and pupils provide the basis for a positive working atmosphere.'; 'For most pupils, homework is regularly set. Some pupils find it difficult to manage the demands that are made on them and the work does not always foster real learning beyond the school day.'

Primary schools Belmont Primary; Galley Hill Primary; Kemplah County Primary; Newstead Primary; Normanby Primary.

NUNTHORPE SCHOOL

Guisborough Road
Middlesbrough TS7 0LA
Tel (01642) 310561
Fax (01642) 325672
E-mail: nunthorpeschool@campus.bt.com

- National ranking 399 = (331 = , 401 = , 318 = , –)
- GCSE 59% (62%)
- A-levels *Not applicable*
- Higher education *Not applicable*

- Mixed comprehensive
- Pupils 1,300
- Boys (11–16) 660
- Girls (11–16) 640
- Sixth form *Not applicable*
- Education authority *Redcar and Cleveland*

Headteacher John Rowling, 56, appointed in April 1984. Staff 74 (men 27, women 47).

Motto *None*

Background On southern edge of Teesside conurbation, next to North Yorkshire moors; draws most of pupils from relatively prosperous residential areas: 'Parents are supportive and they, and the staff, have high expectations of the students.' Well-maintained, internally pleasant building; wide corridors allowing displays to be a feature. Over-subscribed, with 1.5 applications per place. Proud of 'excellent' examination results: English, mathematics, drama, art, history, business studies, modern languages and science. Three separate sciences offered for most able pupils: 'There is a clear policy that provides for very able students as well as a well-developed support system for students of lower academic ability.' Strong music tradition, with girls' choir with international reputation; recently produced professional CD. Sport thrives: winners of national gymnastic competitions; national representatives. Two national athletics champions in 1996

Streaming *None*

Approach to discipline 'The school has a strong policy on social, moral, spiritual and cultural dimensions. Courtesy and respect are expected and offered by students. Bullying is dealt with severely.'

Uniform 'The school has a sensible uniform that has wide acceptance among students, who conform readily.'

Homework Average 11-year-old, six to seven hours a week; 14-year-old, 10 to 12 hours; 16-year-old, 14 to 16 hours.

Vocational qualifications City and Guilds; GNVQ.

Inspection April 1995: 'Nunthorpe is a well-established good school, with many exceptional qualities. Its reputation in the local community is justifiably high.'; 'Relationships within the school are very good.'; 'The overall quality of teaching is good. Teachers generally have a good command of their subjects and they develop the enthusiasm of the pupils. Work given to pupils is matched accurately to their abilities in the majority of cases. There is evidence that tasks having more challenge could be given in some instances.'; 'The leadership shown by the governing body is very effective. The headteacher and senior management team provide clear, direct and demanding leadership which at times can place pressure on staff'.

Primary schools Captain Cook's Primary, Marton; The Avenue Primary, Nunthorpe; Chandler's Ridge Primary, Nunthorpe; Nunthorpe Primary; Ormesby Primary.

ST URSULA'S CONVENT SCHOOL

Crooms Hill
Greenwich
London SE10 8HN
Tel (0181) 858 4613
Fax (0181) 305 0560

- National ranking 399= (401=, 401=, 279=, 198)
- GCSE 59% (58%)
- A-levels *Not applicable*
- Higher education *Not applicable*

- Girls' comprehensive
- Pupils 600
- Boys *Not applicable*
- Girls (11–16) 600
- Sixth form *Not applicable*
- Education authority *Greenwich*

Headteacher Anne Stephanie Fulton, appointed in April 1994. Staff 39 (men 5, women 34).

Motto Serviam (I serve).

Background Sited next to Greenwich Park and facing Blackheath in spacious grounds with hill-top view across the Thames and the City of London. School was founded in 1877 by the Ursuline sisters as a grammar school and became a comprehensive 100 years later. Original Georgian house progressively extended: five science laboratories; three computer network rooms; design and technology unit, and food technology unit. A new wing houses lower school and includes music suite. Voluntary-aided; Christian community; pupils from families 'of modest means'. GCSE in 16 subjects. On average, 2.5 applications per place; 98% go on to post-16 education. Inter-school matches in netball, rounders, hockey, and tennis; 'lively' music department with seven visiting instrumental staff; more than 120 girls learn an instrument; pupils entered for Guildhall drama examinations.

Streaming Pupils placed on entry in overlapping streams. Almost all subjects taught in these groups throughout.

Approach to discipline Friendly, family-like atmosphere. Stress on controlled behaviour and consideration for others. 'There is a close partnership with parents and all share the same Christian values. Rules are few and simple. It is expected they will be observed easily and co-operatively.'

Uniform Blazer, navy skirt, white blouse, school tie, navy coat, black shoes. 'All pupils are expected to wear the uniform and to wear it well. Enforcement is consistent and regular.'

Homework Average 11-year-old, five hours to seven hours 30 minutes a week; 14-year-old, seven hours 30 minutes to 10 hours; 16-year-old, at least 12 hours 30 minutes.

Vocational qualifications *None*

Inspection May 1996: 'A very good school; pupils achieve high standards of attainment in relation to their prior attainment. Its most significant strengths are its concerns for all aspects of its pupils' development. There are no major weaknesses.'; 'Pupils show interest in their lessons because the teaching is interesting and engaging. They enjoy their work and make good progress. Relationships between teachers and pupils are always constructive.'; 'Attendance and punctuality are excellent.'; 'Moral and social development are intrinsic to many subjects and are conscientiously promoted through personal and social education and the extra-curricular programme. There are insufficient opportunities for the pupils to undertake responsibilities.'

Primary schools Total of 48 feeder schools.

WOODCOTE HIGH SCHOOL

Meadow Rise
Coulsdon
Surrey CR5 2EH
Tel (0181) 668 6464
Fax (0181) 660 9038

- National ranking 399= (495=, 516=, 432=, –)
- GCSE 59% (49%)
- A-levels *Not applicable*
- Higher education *Not applicable*

- Mixed comprehensive
- Pupils 904
- Boys (11–16) 470
- Girls (11–16) 434
- Sixth form *Not applicable*
- Education authority *Croydon*

Headteacher Ian Wilson, 46, appointed in April 1992. Staff 50 (men 20, women 30).

Motto *None*

Background Originally an 11–14 school; changed when Croydon re-organised in 1988; most buildings date from late 1950s, with large new block completed in 1988; 47 acres at southern tip of Croydon. Facilities include sports hall, drama hall, music studios and instrumental practice rooms; new music and art block added in 1995, with second music studio and practice rooms. Over-subscribed, with three applications per place. Won all four leagues in Croydon Cricket Association in 1993; in 1995, reached finals in all five Croydon Soccer Cup competitions, winning three of them; competitive teams in all sports. Nearly 160 pupils receive regular instrumental tuition: two choirs, orchestra, bands, ensembles. All pupils involved in community service in year 10. Latin taught to all pupils in year 8; several groups study it to GCSE. 'A traditional, hard-working ethos, with an expectation of good academic results and with a commitment to a wide range of extra-curricular activities.'

Streaming Pupils placed in sets for English,

science, modern languages from year 7; further setting, such as in mathematics, from year 9.

Approach to discipline 'A traditional firm approach. There is a simple code of conduct, emphasising acceptable behaviour and describing expectations of staff and those which pupils may reasonably hold.'

Uniform Royal-blue blazer with school badge, white shirt/blouse, grey trousers/skirt, school tie, black shoes. No boots or trainers. Very strictly enforced.

Homework Average 11-year-old, six hours a week; 14-year-old, 12 hours; 16-year-old, 15 to 20 hours.

Vocational qualifications *None*

Inspection December 1996: 'A sound school with a number of strengths. GCSE grades are above national averages, there is a wide and popular range of extra-curricular activity, the pupils' moral and social development is very good and their spiritual and cultural development good.'; 'Pupils with special educational needs make unsatisfactory progress in a number of subjects.'; 'Most teachers have good subject expertise in the areas which they teach and have high expectations of the pupils. They maintain good or very good control, they employ very good learning routines and explain clearly what pupils are expected to do. Teachers use a variety of approaches, including good humour and effective use of resources.'; 'The school has a good ethos and clear sense of purpose, appreciated by pupils and their parents as well as the staff.'

Primary schools Woodcote Junior; Smitham Primary; Chipstead Valley Primary; Byron Junior.

THE CASTLE SCHOOL

Park Road
Thornbury
South Gloucestershire BS12 1HT
Tel (01454) 416363
Fax (01454) 414536
E-mail: castle-edu@msn.com

- National ranking 406 (375, 369, 313, –)
- GCSE 58% (59%)
- A-levels 56% (A/B); 96% (A/E)
- Higher education 84% (Oxford 2, Cambridge 2)

- Mixed comprehensive
- Pupils 1,449
- Boys (11–18) 769
- Girls (11–18) 680
- Sixth form 270 (19%)
- Education authority *South Gloucestershire*

Headteacher Adrian Verwoert, 49, appointed in September 1985. Staff 82 (men 35, women 47).

Motto *None*

Background Set in expanding market town 12 miles north of Bristol; largely built in 1964; well-maintained buildings on two sites, sixth-form centre and former grammar school. Main site: specialist accommodation for science and design technology, extensive sports fields, sports hall, swimming pool, information technology rooms, purpose-built music suite. Over-subscribed, with about 340 applications for 240 places; most pupils from Thornbury and surrounding villages, but increasing number from Bristol. Drama productions 'very high standard', also dance and music; designed garden for 1994 Chelsea Flower Show; year 11 pupil represented England in international cross-country in Beijing in 1994. 'A caring environment in which all students are encouraged to achieve their potential. Although academic performance is seen as important, each pupil is treated as an individual, and the achievements of those with special educational needs valued just as highly.'

Alumni Alison Gill, Olympic rowing medallist.

Streaming Mixed-ability in year 7; banded subject by subject as appropriate from year 8: languages and mathematics, from year 8; English, not until year 10.

Approach to discipline 'No pupil must be allowed to disrupt the education of others. Politeness to staff and peers, and respect for property and the environment are demanded.'

Uniform Navy skirt/grey trousers, white blouse/shirt, navy V-neck jumper with crest, school tie. 'Enforced rigidly.'

Homework Average 11-year-old, at least five hours a week; 14-year-old, at least 10 hours; 16-year-old, as long as necessary.

Vocational qualifications GNVQ Levels 2 and 3, Business and Finance, Art and Design, Leisure and Tourism, Manufacturing and Health and Social Care; pilot for GNVQ Part One for Business and Finance, Health and Social Care.

Inspection January 1996: 'A very good school. It has many strengths, most notably in its academic achievement and the quality of relationships within the school.'; 'Pupils are good learners. The quality of learning is sound or better in around 90% of lessons, at all stages.'; 'The school is well-managed. The governing body is effective and has very good links with all areas of the school.'; 'Pupils gain from well-motivated and trained teachers.'; 'Pupils are well cared for, and their progress is thoughtfully considered. Behaviour and attendance are generally good.'

Primary schools Manorbrook Primary; St Mary's CE Primary; Crossways Junior; Gillingstool County Primary; Christ the King RC Primary.

THE RIDINGS HIGH SCHOOL

High Street
Winterbourne
Bristol
South Gloucestershire BS17 1JL
Tel (01454) 772347
Fax (01454) 250404
E-mail: ridingshigh@campus.bt.com
Internet: http://members.aol.com/
      theridings/index.htm

- National ranking 407 (362, 487, 390, –)
- GCSE 58% (60%)
- A-levels 42% (A/B); 88% (A/E)
- Higher education 74% (Oxford 1)

- Mixed comprehensive
- Pupils 1,774
- Boys (11–18) 909
- Girls (11–18) 865
- Sixth form 271 (15%)
- Education authority *South Gloucestershire*

Headteacher Dr Robert Stephen Gibson, 43, appointed in September 1995. Staff 102 (men 54, women 48).

Motto Maximising potential through partnership.

Background Situated in 'suburban village' of Winterbourne in an expanding area northeast of Bristol; opened in premises of former Gloucestershire Modern School in 1969;

pupils regularly drawn from more than 30 local primary schools; many 'out-of-area' applications. Over-subscribed, with 1.3 applications per place. Three in four pupils (76%) stay on in full-time education at 16. 'Exceptional' examination results in mathematics and English. Open-access sixth-form. 'By their active participation in the wide range of curricular and extra-curricular activities which we offer, pupils will enhance their inter-personal skills, they will gain greater knowledge and understanding, and they will obtain personal enjoyment and satisfaction.' BT Link status; recognised by local and national businesses as 'centre of excellence for academic and vocational results.'; NCVQ inspection recognised GNVQ courses as among 'the best in the country'.

Alumni Christine Guy, national breaststroke champion; Gary Megson, assistant manager of Norwich City FC; Scott Cameron, national moto-cross champion; Channon Hazell, British rackets champion; Richard Lewis, producer of BBC Television's *Telly Addicts;* James McIlwrath, managing director of Inch's Cider Company; Graham and Colin McIntyre, orienteering world champions; Mark Zanaker, member of Red Arrows display team; Alison Dare, national point-to-point champion; Steve Dunn, FIFA referee.

Streaming 'Groups may be broad-banded, mixed-ability or setted. Differentiated learning/teaching strategies operate in all subject areas.' Open-access sixth-form.

Approach to discipline School Discipline Policy Statement lists detailed aims and objectives. 'Discipline is essential for learning: although self-discipline is the best kind of discipline, there are occasions when the school has to act to preserve good order. Privileges may be removed or sanctions imposed.'

Uniform Light-blue blouse/shirt, black sweatshirt, school tie, black trousers/skirt/culottes, black/light-blue socks, black footwear and black outside garments. 'Lack of co-operation considered breach of school discipline.'

Homework 'Homework is set on a regular basis and a student planner is issued to pupils. The length of the homework is not rigidly stipulated because pupils work at different rates and because the homework is not always a piece of written work.'

Vocational qualifications RSA, Computer Literacy and Information Technology; GNVQ Intermediate and Advanced, Business Studies, Health and Social Care, Leisure and Tourism.

Inspection January 1994: 'The Ridings High School is a good school which provides well for its pupils.'; 'There is some work of high quality in most curriculum areas, notably in English, mathematics and history, although outstanding performance is rare. Standards achieved by special need pupils in relation to their ability and potential are uneven.'; 'Praise and encouragement are used effectively to create a climate conducive to learning, but the match of expectations to the abilities of pupils is not always well-judged. The quality of relationships within the school is significantly good and contributes to the school's aim to be a caring and active community.'

Primary schools Elm Park Primary; Frampton Cotterell CE Primary; Frenchay Primary; Hambrook Primary; Highcroft Primary; Iron Acton Primary; The Manor Primary; St Michael's CE Primary, Winterbourne. Total of 49 feeder schools.

BRIDGEWATER COUNTY HIGH SCHOOL

Broomfields Road
Appleton
Warrington
Cheshire WA4 3AE
Tel (01925) 263919/266973
Fax (01925) 861434

- National ranking 408 (–, 362, –)
- GCSE 58%
- A-levels 32% (A/B); 90% (A/E)
- Higher education 75% (Oxford 2)

- Mixed comprehensive
- Pupils 1,478
- Boys (11–18) 715
- Girls (11–18) 763
- Sixth form 170 (12%)
- Education authority *Cheshire*

Headteacher Christopher Marks, 44, appointed in September 1994. Staff 91 (men 45, women 46).

Motto *None*

Background Based on two campuses, half-a-mile apart, following amalgamation of schools in 1987 in residential area of north Cheshire on southern side of Warrington:

Appleton Hall, purpose-built in 'splendid' grounds in the 1960s, houses years 7 and 8; upper school at Broomfields Road, with sixth-form centre and 'first-class' leisure centre, with swimming pool, squash courts, large sports hall, sauna and fitness training room, and a large all-weather flood-lit games area. Lower School building pro-gramme has provided eight new classrooms for languages and humanities; some im-provements to drama and music facilities completed in September 1996. 'The care and nurture of the individual would be the school's hallmark. Perhaps because our buildings are adapted to educate those from the Warrington area with physical ability, the school has a very strong focus on maximis-ing potential from all its pupils. We are greatly concerned to ensure that every scrap of academic potential is developed from all children, all the time.'

Alumni Timothy Firth, playwright; Terry Waite, Archbishop of Canterbury's former special envoy (when schools were separate).

Streaming Mixed-ability in early year 7. Some setting in latter part of year 7; increases up the school.

Approach to discipline Formal statement on discipline and five-point code of conduct. 'We believe that within the school, discipline should be seen in a positive light. Where sanctions are required for those who trans-gress the code of conduct, these will be fair, reasonable and positive, with emphasis on redressing that which was wrong.'

Uniform White shirt/blouse, grey trousers/ skirt, navy jumper/cardigan, navy/grey/ white socks, school tie, black/grey shoes. Regulations enforced 'strictly'.

Homework Average 11-year-old, five hours a week; 14-year-old, seven hours 30 minutes; 16-year-old, 10 hours.

Vocational qualifications GNVQ Advanced.

Inspection January 1996: 'Pupils' attitudes to learning are very positive. Cooperation with each other and with their teachers is a strong feature.'; 'The ethos and high expectations of the school promote good moral and social standards effectively. The school is a calm, purposeful and orderly community.'; 'Les-sons are well-planned with clear objectives. many teachers show a good awareness of individual needs. Pupils are regularly in-formed of expectations. Teachers have a good command of their subject, and their enthusiasm and commitment ensure pupils do well, especially in examinations.'; 'The headteacher provides the school with excel-lent leadership.'

Primary schools Broomfields Junior; St Tho-mas' CE Primary; Moore Primary; Appleton Thorn Primary; Stockton Heath Primary; St Matthew's CE Primary; Daresbury Primary; St Wilfrid's CE Primary.

ST PAUL'S ROMAN CATHOLIC SCHOOL

Oathall Avenue
Haywards Heath
West Sussex RH16 3ET
Tel (01444) 415418
Fax (01444) 417042)

- National ranking 409 (242, 186)
- GCSE 58% (68%)
- A-levels 11% (A/B); 91% (A/E)
- Higher education 78%

- Mixed comprehensive
- Pupils 634
- Boys (11–18) 333
- Girls (11–18) 301
- Sixth form 93 (15%)
- Education authority West Sussex

Headteacher John F. Flower, 49, appointed in September 1986. Staff 39 (men 20, women 19).

Motto Domine ut serviam (Lord, that I may serve).

Background Opened as a Catholic secondary school in 1963; became a comprehensive 10 years later. The only school in the area with its own sixth form. Situated in pleasant surroundings, close to the centre of Hay-wards Heath; housed in modern buildings with full range of facilities. Preference given to applications from Catholics, but one in four pupils are non-Catholics. Over-sub-scribed, with 153 applications for 124 places; applications from children attending 32 schools within a 20-mile radius. 'The quality of teaching and learning across all areas of the curriculum is high. All depart-ments are strong and successful.' All pupils study a second modern language; particular emphasis on religious education. Musical opportunities 'wide and varied'; high pro-portion of pupils learning a musical instru-ment. Sporting strengths: netball, basketball, football, athletics and tennis.

Streaming Setting in many subjects, including mathematics, science and languages.

Approach to discipline 'St Paul's is a place of reconciliation where consideration for one's fellow students should be manifest at all times. We aim to develop self-discipline and respect for authority. Where there are behavioural problems which cannot be resolved, despite considerable support and guidance by the staff, sanctions will be applied. We also believe a well-developed rewards system lessens the need to discipline.'

Uniform White shirt/blouse, school tie, grey trousers/skirt, royal-blue jumper. Regulations enforced 'very strictly, without being seen to be unreasonable'.

Homework Average 11-year-old, five to seven hours 30 minutes a week; 14-year-old, seven hours 30 minutes to 10 hours; 16-year-old, 10 to 15 hours.

Vocational qualifications GNVQ Advanced, Leisure and Tourism; GNVQ Intermediate, Leisure and Tourism, Health and Social Care, Business Studies, Art and Design.

Inspection November 1993: 'The quality of learning across the school is good. Pupils are very well-motivated, show good consideration, are responsive to the challenges set by their teachers and make satisfactory progress.'; 'The school enjoys effective leadership and is well-organised. Available resources are generally managed efficiently and financial controls are good.'; 'The school has a strong ethos which positively affects the quality of education provided. Standards of behaviour and relationships within the school are high and the spiritual, moral, social and cultural development of pupils is good. Standards of pastoral care and pupil guidance are good. The school enjoys strong support and commitment from governors, parents, staff and pupils. Pupils have a strong sense of loyalty to the school.'

Primary schools St Joseph's RC Primary, Haywards Heath; St Wilfrid's RC Primary, Burgess Hill; St Pancras RC Primary, Lewes; Harlands Primary, Haywards Heath; St Wilfrid's CE Primary, Haywards Heath.

BISHOP HEBER HIGH SCHOOL

Chester Road
Malpas
Cheshire SY14 8JD

Tel (01948) 860571
Fax (01948) 860962
E-mail: bheber@mail.rmplc.co.uk

- National ranking 410 (223, 287, 389, –)
- GCSE 58% (70%)
- A-levels 27% (A/B); 83% (A/E)
- Higher education 80% (Oxford 1)

- Mixed comprehensive
- Pupils 1,064
- Boys (11–18) 544
- Girls (11–18) 520
- Sixth form 202 (19%)
- Education authority *Cheshire*

Headteacher Michael Carding, 48, appointed in September 1986. Staff 64 (men 32, women 32).

Motto Pret d'accomplir (Ready to accomplish).

Background Rural comprehensive in market town (pop. 2,000), serving large area of southwest Cheshire and attracting more than 200 pupils from North Shropshire and Clwyd; oldest building dates from 1960s; significant extension in 1975 included community sports hall and library. Recent extension opened by Duke of Gloucester in 1991: creative arts, language and science facilities. Extensive playing fields overlook Cheshire sandstone ridge and Dee valley. Not over-subscribed; about 175 applications for 180 places. Particular strengths include sport, especially rugby, hockey, tennis and athletics, as well as music, with nearly one in five pupils playing an instrument; three groups in National Festival of Music for Youth. 1992 Schools Curriculum Award. Language College from September 1996: five foreign languages taught, including French, German and Spanish to A-level. 'Pupils encouraged to be pro-European and broaden their horizons'; state-of-the-art language centre from September 1997. A 24-place unit for pupils with learning difficulties and support for pupils with special needs throughout the school. 'We value honesty, loyalty, tolerance, compassion, teamwork and achievement. We believe in equality of opportunity.'

Streaming 'Each subject has the facility to set by ability independent of other subjects. Mathematics and science set at the beginning of year 7; most subjects set by the beginning of year 8.'

Approach to discipline Prospectus emphasises importance of healthy relationships, good discipline, high standards of behaviour. School is 'very orderly community': 'Behaviour in lessons is invariably of a very high standard and this greatly contributes to effective learning.' Mutual respect between staff and pupils; code of conduct widely followed.

Uniform Girls: navy/black blazer (optional), navy skirt, navy V-neck pullover/cardigan, navy/white socks or tights, black shoes, school tie. Boys: black/navy blazer (compulsory), grey trousers, grey/white shirt, school tie, grey socks, black shoes. 'Considered locally to be very smart; relaxation to "colour code" for sixth-formers.'

Homework Average 11-year-old, six to eight hours a week; 14-year-old, 10 to 12 hours; 16-year-old, 15 hours.

Vocational qualifications GNVQ Intermediate, Business, Art and Design, Health and Social Care; GNVQ Advanced, Business, Art and Design.

Inspection February 1994: 'Pupils respond well to praise and encouragement.'; 'There are numerous opportunities for pupils to enrich their social and cultural development through an outstandingly wide range of extra-curricular activities and community links.'; 'There is a strong, positive and generous ethos that is based upon encouraging the total development of each individual pupil.'; 'Pupils, staff, parents and governors all share a strong sense of loyalty to the school and show great pride in its achievements.'; 'Good behaviour, courteous relationships and other indications of high moral standards are invariably evident.'

Primary schools Malpas Alport Endowed Primary; Farndon County Primary; The Park County Primary, Tattenhall; Shocklach Oviatt CE Primary; Bickerton CE Primary; Clutton CE Primary; Harthill County Primary; Huxley CE Primary.

HETHERSETT HIGH SCHOOL

Queen's Road
Hethersett
Norfolk NR9 3DB
Tel (01603) 810924
Fax (01603) 812697
E-mail: hhsit@rmplc.co.uk

- National ranking 411 = (302 = , 511 = , 337 = , –)
- GCSE 58% (63%)
- A-levels *Not applicable*
- Higher education *Not applicable*

- Mixed comprehensive
- Pupils 583
- Boys (12–16) 309
- Girls (12–16) 274
- Sixth form *Not applicable*
- Education authority *Norfolk*

Headteacher Marian Chapman, 54, appointed in January 1991. Staff 42 (men 19, women 23).

Motto Aiming high – Achieving together.

Background Purpose-built in large village on outskirts of Norwich in 1979 for 600 pupils; campus consists of nine pavilions, each containing curriculum-linked departments; 'excellent' facilities include lifts and ramps for students in wheelchairs. Spacious grounds to rear for sports; ecological site near science department. Not over-subscribed. Strong music department: wind band, jazz band, orchestra. 'We have very high expectations for all students and expect them to be attained by hard work and cooperation. Parental involvement is valued greatly, with 90% average attendance at parents' evening.' Identified in 1997 annual Ofsted report for achieving 'high performance or being highly effective.'

Streaming Mixed-ability in year 8; setting introduced in year 9 and increased in years 10 and 11.

Approach to discipline Firm but fair; very high expectations of courtesy and behaviour; close parental involvement if necessary.

Uniform Navy sweatshirt with school logo, white shirt/blouse, grey trousers for boys or navy skirt/trousers for girls, school tie for boys. 'Very high standards achieved.'

Homework Average 14-year-old, 10 to 15 hours a week.

Vocational qualifications Diploma of Vocational Education.

Inspection March 1996: 'A good school. The strong work ethic and the good standards of behaviour evident in the school have a significant impact on pupils' achievements. The school is a very orderly community and pupils respond well to the opportunities provided for them.'; 'The most able pupils require further challenges.'; 'The quality of teaching and learning throughout is most often good and occasionally very good.'; 'The leadership provided by the headteacher is good and management overall is satisfactory, although stronger links are needed between senior and middle management to ensure aspects of the school's work are coordinated more effectively.'; 'The school is a very orderly and purposeful community, and pupils are courteous and polite. Good personal and social relationships exist at all levels and teachers are perceived by pupils as caring.'

Primary schools Hethersett Middle; Mulbarton Middle; Cringleford Middle; Blackdale Middle.

HIGHAM LANE SCHOOL

Shanklin Drive
Nuneaton
Warwickshire CV10 0BJ
Tel (01203) 388123
Fax (01203) 370550

- National ranking 411= (382=, 205=, 205=, 315=)
- GCSE 58% (59%)
- A-levels *Not applicable*
- Higher education *Not applicable*

- Mixed comprehensive
- Pupils 1,211
- Boys (11–16) 606
- Girls (11–16) 605
- Sixth form *Not applicable*
- Education authority *Warwickshire*

Headteacher Dr Ramsey Thomas Tetlow, 46, appointed in January 1990. Staff 61 (men 22, women 39).

Motto *None*

Background Original building dates from 1939; on 10-acre site in residential area about a mile northeast of Nuneaton town centre. Facilities include recently-refurbished library and resources centre, fitness suite, community room, design technology suite, networked information technology rooms, and a farm; two additional science laboratories from September 1994. Provides for physically-disabled pupils; has a growing community profile. Over-subscribed, with 1.2 applications per place. Strong sporting

and music traditions; 'excellent' art; 1994 winners of Midland Schools Debating Society competition and winners of Midlands Youth Parliament competition; half-termly newspaper produced by pupils. Pupils study two out of three languages: French, German and Spanish. School trips: theatre, art exhibitions, youth hostelling. Duke of Edinburgh Award Scheme. Overseas visits: skiing in France, Russia, Germany and Spain; yearly exchange to linked school in California. Elected school council. Traditional values encouraged. School expanded to 11–16 in September 1996.

Streaming Flexible setting for English, mathematics, humanities and modern languages; all other subjects taught in mixed-ability groups until years 10 and 11, where pupils also put in sets for science.

Approach to discipline Based on consideration for others and respect for the environment. Emphasis on praising good behaviour and rewarding it with house points; encourages collective responsibility; well-publicised code of sanctions. 'Some discipline problems are discussed with the school council (pupil representatives) and their ideas are often sought. Anti-bullying policy, for example.'

Uniform Red shirt with school tie, black trousers/skirt, black pullover, black/white socks, black shoes. Regulations enforced 'very strictly and seldom abused'.

Homework Average 14-year-old, five hours a week; 16-year-old, seven hours.

Vocational qualifications *None*

Inspection March 1993: 'The school's ethos is one of openness and trust. The positive values and attitudes for which the school stands are reflected in its daily life and work, and warmly endorsed by its parents.' November 1996: 'A very good school in which pupils attain high levels of achievement and personal development.'; 'In English, and all other subjects, across both key stages, pupils listen remarkably well and are attentive to teachers' talk, the ideas of other pupils and reading aloud. A great many pupils read confidently, understanding texts in all subjects, although research skills are given too little practice.'; 'Although pupils have relatively little opportunity to develop independent study, when this is offered, both in lessons and in extra-curricular activities, they show themselves capable of work of high quality.'; 'Behaviour around the school is excellent.'

Primary schools Milby Junior; Weddington Junior; Chetwynd Junior; Queen's CE Junior.

ST CHRISTOPHER'S CHURCH OF ENGLAND HIGH SCHOOL

Queen's Road West
Accrington
Lancashire BB5 4AY
Tel (01254) 232992
Fax (01254) 234775

- National ranking 411 = (428 =, 502 =, 432 =, -)
- GCSE 58% (55%)
- A-levels *Not applicable*
- Higher education *Not applicable*

- Mixed comprehensive
- Pupils 845
- Boys (11–16) 374
- Girls (11–16) 471
- Sixth form *Not applicable*
- Education authority *Lancashire*

Headteacher Alasdair David Coates, 45, appointed in January 1993. Staff 46 (men 21, women 25).

Motto Ad gloriam dei (To the glory of God).

Background Opened in 1958, serving east Lancashire; open site to the north of Accrington, with extensive views of hills surrounding the town. Strong links with parishes and clergy, many of whom visit regularly. Significant additions to original buildings to accommodate pupils at increasingly popular school. Over-subscribed, with 300 applications for 168 places. Strong extra-curricular life. Music: school orchestra, choir, many ensembles, especially the recorder group, regular concerts. Sport: district football champions, strong netball and hockey. Young Enterprise: winners of Best Product for East Lancashire in three successive years. Winners of 1994 senior and junior local debating competition. 'We seek to promote the spiritual, moral, cultural, mental and physical development of each of our pupils within a caring and supportive community, preparing them as Christians for the opportunities, responsibilities and experiences of their adult life.'

Streaming After one term in mixed-ability groups, pupils are placed in sets according to their ability in each subject. Regularly reviewed to take account of progress made.

Approach to discipline 'Firm, fair discipline is applied, according to traditional Christian principles. A code of conduct has been drawn up, according to which good behaviour is rewarded and sanctions imposed when standards of behaviour fall short of those set out in the code.'

Uniform Navy blazer, navy skirt/black trousers, white shirt/blouse, school tie, navy V-neck pullover/cardigan, black/navy shoes and socks. Rigidly enforced: 'Any pupil arriving in clothing which doesn't conform, or with an extravagant hairstyle, is sent home.'

Homework Average 11-year-old, seven hours 30 minutes a week; 14-year-old, 10 hours; 16-year-old, 12 hours 30 minutes to 15 hours.

Vocational qualifications *None*

Primary schools All Saints CE Primary, Clayton-le-Moors; St John's CE Primary, Accrington; St Bartholomew's CE Primary, Great Harwood; Peel Park Primary, Accrington; St John's CE Primary, Baxenden.

THE KINGSWINFORD SCHOOL

Water Street
Kingswinford
West Midlands DY6 7AD
Tel (01384) 296596
Fax (01384) 401098
E-mail: gpallot@kingford.demon.co.uk

- National ranking 411 = (489 =, 278 =, 414 =, 337 =)
- GCSE 58% (50%)
- A-levels *Not applicable*
- Higher education *Not applicable*

- Grant-maintained
- Mixed comprehensive
- Pupils 849
- Boys (11–16) 425
- Girls (11–16) 424
- Sixth form *Not applicable*
- Education authority *Dudley*

Headteacher Geoffrey James Harrison, 52, appointed in September 1986. Staff 51 (men 23, women 28).

Motto *None*

Background Opened in 1939 as county senior school in what was then part of the county of Staffordshire; absorbed into Dudley as part of 1960s local government re-organisation; became comprehensive for pupils aged 12–16 in 1975; further re-organisation to 11–16 in 1991; became grant-maintained in April 1993, serving Kingswinford and Wall Heath on western edge of Dudley. Over-subscribed, with two applications per place. More than seven in 10 school-leavers (74%) continue full-time education after 16; a further 25% enter training. Extracurricular activities: weight-training, Christian Union, photography, debating, Languages Club, Science Club.

Alumni Stuart Lampitt, Worcestershire cricketer; Jack Flavell, former Worcestershire and England cricketer.

Streaming Pupils in sets for mathematics and science from year 8; and in English from year 9.

Approach to discipline Code of conduct given to all pupils and parents. 'The expectation is that everyone will act with courtesy and consideration to others at all times. Discipline is seen to be firm but fair.'

Uniform Black blazer with gold-embroidered badge, black or grey trousers/skirt/culottes, blue shirt/blouse, black-blue-and-gold striped tie, black/grey shoes. No exceptions made.

Homework Average 11-year-old, five hours a week; 14-year-old, nine to 10 hours; 16-year-old, 15 hours.

Vocational qualifications *None*

Primary schools St Mary's RC Primary; Blanford Mere Primary; Church of the Ascension Primary; Dawley Brook Primary; Maidensbridge Primary.

CAMDEN SCHOOL FOR GIRLS

Sandall Road
London NW5 2DB
Tel (0171) 485 3414
Fax (0171) 284 3361
E-mail: camden@rmplc.co.uk

- National ranking 415 (220, 387, 223, –)
- GCSE 57% (70%)

- A-levels 41% (A/B); 93% (A/E)
- Higher education 80% (Oxford 3, Cambridge 3)

- Girls' comprehensive
- Pupils 879
- Boys (16–18) 85
- Girls (11–18) 794
- Sixth form 314 (36%)
- Education authority *Camden*

Headteacher Geoffrey Michael Fallows, 55, appointed in June 1989. Staff 53 (men 10, women 43).

Motto Onwards and upwards.

Background Founded in 1871 by Frances Mary Buss, Victorian pioneer of girls' education; current site was occupied until the war by the North London Collegiate School, Buss's first foundation. Severe bomb damage caused major rebuilding in 1950s when school was a grammar; became comprehensive in 1976; buildings are 'motley collection' of older, new and temporary on site which 'though cramped, has real character'. Over-subscribed, with 1.7 applications per place. The only school in the education authority to offer Classics, which is thriving; A-level groups in Latin and Classical Civilisation as well as occasional Greek. Outstanding results in art have been constant feature; remarkable orchestral tradition. 'The school has a strong tradition for encouraging independence and individuality, and for maintaining the founder's wish that girls should aspire to as high achievement as their abilities make possible.' Relaxed atmosphere; teacher–pupil relationships based on respect and tolerance. Identified by Ofsted as 'outstandingly successful'.

Alumni Emma Thompson, actress; Sophie Thompson, actress; Kate Saunders, journalist; Sara Kestleman, actress; Beeban Kidron, film director; Julia Cleverdon, Business in the Community.

Streaming *None*

Approach to discipline 'The key is self-discipline and responsibility. We aim to persuade rather than coerce, but tough sanctions are considered if bad behaviour has bad effect on learning of others. If girls are well-known by tutors and parents are supportive, discipline is not a serious concern.'

Uniform *None*

Homework Average 11-year-old, six hours a week; 14-year-old, eight hours; 16-year-old, 10 hours.

Vocational qualifications GNVQ Health and Social Care; NVQ, Business Administration.

Inspection May 1995: 'The pupils at Camden School receive a good quality of education. The standards reached in all subjects are at least sound and standards in aesthetic subjects are exceptional. The school realises its aim to develop and maintain the school's traditions and to encourage in pupils a sense of self-worth and consideration for others.'; 'Teachers are well-qualified, confident in their subject areas and they plan their lessons well.'; 'The school provides an attractive learning environment, improved by good decoration in some areas and enhanced by attractive and informative displays of pupils' work.'; 'Pupils' behaviour is good and most respond well to the combination of freedom and responsibility which the school provides.'

Primary schools Brecknock Primary; Torriano Primary; Kentish Town CE Primary; Hungerford Primary.

GUILSBOROUGH SCHOOL

West Haddon Road
Guilsborough
Northampton
Northamptonshire NN6 8QE
Tel (01604) 740641
Fax (01604) 740136

- National ranking 416 (–, 515, 247, –)
- GCSE 57%
- A-levels 39% (A/B); 93% (A/E)
- Higher education 70%

- Mixed comprehensive
- Pupils 1,084
- Boys (11–18) 573
- Girls (11–18) 511
- Sixth form 184 (17%)
- Education authority *Northamptonshire*

Headteacher Stuart Arthur Marson, 46, appointed from September 1995. Staff 61 (men 27, women 34).

Motto Striving for excellence.

Background Founded in 1958, the school became a comprehensive in 1967; new buildings added in 1976 on rural site on edge of village. Most pupils come from the surrounding 30 villages and hamlets. Two main teaching blocks include hall, gym and administrative areas; also technology and design block; sport, drama and music block; all-weather sports area and extensive fields. Not over-subscribed. 1992 Schools Curriculum Award. Range of residential visits and exchanges with schools in l'Isle-Jourdain (Vienne) in France, Marburg in Germany and Washington DC. Sporting activities: badminton, tennis, soccer, rugby, hockey, weight-training, cricket, netball, basketball, trampolining, athletics, cross-country, golf, sailing, and climbing. School band competes nationally; proud of orchestral and drama productions. Duke of Edinburgh Award Scheme. Elected School Council.

Alumni Tony Birtley, ITN journalist; Ruthie Drewitt, BBC *Panorama* journalist; Gerald Perryman, soccer player; Ben Henegan, composer.

Streaming Pupils put in sets in modern languages from year 8; in mathematics from year 9.

Approach to discipline Aim is school community marked by care, courtesy and consideration for others: 'We do not tolerate bullying, bad language, aggressive behaviour, vandalism or disrespect.' Aim to help students to accept responsibility for actions to ensure no repetition; graded scale of sanctions include service to school and placing 'on report'; close co-operation with parents.

Uniform White shirt/blouse, school tie for boys (except in summer), black trousers/skirt, silver-grey sweatshirt with royal-blue school logo. Sixth-formers not required to wear uniform. 'School dress is a requirement of attendance at the school.'

Homework Average 11-year-old, five hours to seven hours 30 minutes a week; 14-year-old, seven hours 30 minutes to 10 hours; 16-year-old, 10 to 15 hours.

Vocational qualifications GNVQs Intermediate and Advanced.

Inspection September 1994: 'Guilsborough School has made considerable progress towards translating school aims, which focus on the all-round development of pupils, into practice. The standards achieved by pupils of all abilities are good; they are articulate and they read well.'; 'Pupils are competent learners. They are capable of exercising a high degree of responsibility for their own learning and, when given the opportunity, they work cooperatively and independently. In some lessons, more opportunities should be taken to challenge pupils to use their learning skills. Teachers are well-qualified and have a good command of their subjects. Some examples of outstanding teaching were seen.'; 'The school provides a caring and secure environment for its pupils, in which relationships are good.'

Primary schools Long Buckby Primary; Guilsborough CE Primary; Crick Primary; West Haddon Primary; Clipston Endowed Primary.

NORTHGATE HIGH SCHOOL

Sidegate Lane West
Ipswich
Suffolk IP4 3DL
Tel (01473) 210123
Fax (01473) 281084
E-mail: noriplib@rmplc.co.uk
Internet: http://www.rmplc.co.uk/eduweb/sites/noriplib

- National ranking 417 (398, 412)
- GCSE 57% (58%)
- A-levels 35% (A/B); 88% (A/E)
- Higher education 86% (Oxford 3, Cambridge 4)

- Mixed comprehensive
- Pupils 1,626
- Boys (11–18) 755
- Girls (11–18) 871
- Sixth form 595 (37%)
- Education authority *Suffolk*

Headteacher Neil Robert Watts, 45, appointed in April 1992. Staff 101 (men 50, women 51).

Motto High expectations.

Background The 'flagship' of Suffolk education; a comprehensive proud of its grammar school foundations which 'seeks to combine the very best of old and new'. 'New' school opened in March 1992 after being largely rebuilt in £8m project started in 1986. Offers 'some of the finest facilities for staff, pupils and students of any school in the country': joint-use sports centre and arts centre; new purpose-built accommodation for all curriculum areas. Over-subscribed, with 300 applications for 205 places. All

areas of the school are 'equally strong'. Music, drama and sporting activities grow in number each year: 14 drama/music performances; 1st XI in national under-19 semi-finals. 'The Northgate ethos has always focused on opportunity, challenge and striving for excellence, coupled with self-discipline, responsibility and respect for others.' Praised in 1995 annual Ofsted report.

Alumni Trevor Nunn, director emeritus of the Royal Shakespeare Company; Jane Lapotaire, actress; Alison Hamilton, Olympic athlete and doctor; Sally Dearman, RAF's first woman pilot.

Streaming Mixed-ability tutor-groups form the basis of many teaching groups in years 7 and 8. Grouping by ability increases significantly in older age-groups.

Approach to discipline 'A positive approach to discipline is followed, with self-discipline stressed. Sanctions, if used, are clear, firm and consistent.'

Uniform Navy V-neck jumper, white shirt/blouse, school tie, mid-grey trousers/skirt, white/navy/grey socks, black shoes. No uniform for sixth-formers. Regulations strictly enforced.

Homework Average 11-year-old, seven hours a week; 14-year-old, 11 hours; 16-year-old, 14 hours.

Vocational qualifications GNVQ Intermediate, Business Studies.

Inspection March 1995.

Primary schools Rushmere Hall Primary; Sidegate Primary; St Helen's Primary; St John's CE Primary; St Margaret's CE Primary; St Matthew's CE Primary.

FRAMWELLGATE MOOR COMPREHENSIVE SCHOOL

Newton Drive
Framwellgate Moor
Durham
County Durham DH1 5BQ
Tel (0191) 386 6628
Fax (0191) 383 0917
E-mail: framcomp@rmplc.co.uk

- National ranking 418 (441, 462, 465 =, –)
- GCSE 57% (54%)
- A-levels 35% (A/B); 84% (A/E)
- Higher education 64% (Cambridge 1)

- Mixed comprehensive
- Pupils 1,341
- Boys (11–18) 721
- Girls (11–18) 620
- Sixth form 271 (20%)
- Education authority *Durham*

Headteacher Austin Michael McNamara, 44, appointed in January 1995. Staff 76 (men 41, women 35).

Motto A quality education at Framwellgate.

Background Operating as a comprehensive since 1971; in pleasant semi-rural position on northern side of Durham City; occupies building that opened in 1965, with four newer ones that opened in 1976; playing fields and a 400m running track on 45-acre site; site close to university, a large college of further education, a college of agriculture and a rapidly-expanding business park. 'The very distinct vertical pastoral care system, which each day integrates students of all abilities and age ranges, reflects the school's commitment to these values.' Oversubscribed, with about 230 applications for 210 places. Range of extra-curricular activities. Particular strengths: music (150 participants), sport (400 participants), five foreign exchange visits each year. School newspaper, with a 6,000 circulation. Duke of Edinburgh Award Scheme.

Streaming Mixed-ability groups in year 7; setting is introduced in mathematics and languages in year 8; pupils in either sets or bands in most subjects in year 9.

Approach to discipline Dialogue between pupils, parents and teachers and 'a holistic view of education'. Pupils have their own representative groups at house and whole-school level; they are encouraged 'to take responsibility for their own education, in the widest sense'. 'We seek to reward positive participation and achievement, whilst nevertheless taking a firm approach to pupils who lack self-discipline and thereby disrupt the education of others.'

Uniform White shirt, house tie, school sweater, navy/black trousers or skirt, formal black/brown/navy shoes. 'All pupils, except sixth-formers, must conform to uniform.

Homework 'Homework is set according to pupil need. Time allocation is not specifically age-related. Hours of homework steadily increase for years 7 to 11 to match the increasing maturity of the student and the demands of the curriculum.'

Vocational qualifications GNVQ Foundation, Business, Health and Social Care, Leisure and Tourism, Art and Design; GNVQ Intermediate and Advanced, Business, Health and Social Care, Leisure and Tourism.

Inspection March 1995: 'The school provides a very good education for its pupils and students.'; 'Standards in English, mathematics and science are high, although a minority of pupils under-achieves in aspects of English and mathematics at Key Stage 3.'; 'Pupils' and students' learning is sound or good at all levels. They acquire a good range of knowledge and skills. They are competent learners. They are generally well-motivated and work hard. Teaching is sound overall and in many instances it is good. Teachers have good subject knowledge and give lessons at a brisk pace. They sometimes over-direct pupils, restricting independent learning.'

Primary schools Durham Blue Coat CE Junior; Finchale Primary; Framwellgate Moor Primary; Nettlesworth Primary.

THE KING'S SCHOOL

Ottery St Mary
Devon EX11 1RA
Tel (01404) 812982
Fax (01404) 812982

- National ranking 419 (485, 354, 257, –)
- GCSE 57% (50%)
- A-levels 33% (A/B); 90% (A/E)
- Higher education 69% (Oxford 1)

- Mixed comprehensive
- Pupils 880
- Boys (11–18) 440
- Girls (11–18) 440
- Sixth form 119 (14%)
- Education authority *Devon*

Headteacher John Barrymore Teare, 51, appointed in April 1989. Staff 50 (men 27, women 23).

Motto Schola regia de Ottery (Royal school of Ottery).

Background Founded by Bishop John de Grandisson in 1337; became The King's School in 1545; celebrated 450th anniversary in 1995. Set on outskirts of rural town with views of Otter Valley looking towards coast. Main 1911 building extended in three phases to accommodate expansion; some temporary accommodation. Extensive grounds provide 'excellent' facilities. Slightly over-subscribed. The school has not attempted to specialise, but rather to provide 'a very good all-round education'. Sporting tradition, with numerous fixtures and many representative honours; looking to build on success in creative arts. 'The King's School is proud to be a true comprehensive serving all the children from the local community. It aims to encourage pupils of all abilities to achieve their best. Within that context, academic excellence and superb examination results are valued along with a pleasant working atmosphere and a full and varied programme of opportunities.'

Alumni Samuel Taylor Coleridge, poet; Henry, Josiah and Thomas Wedgwood, potters.

Streaming Pupils put in sets in some subjects: mathematics from year 7; French from year 8; English from year 9.

Approach to discipline 'There is a well-structured system based on a balance of rewards and sanctions. The school ethos promotes the basic principles of consideration, courtesy and respect towards others in conjunction with recognising achievements and setting personal targets.'

Uniform Years 7 to 9: blazer with badge, grey/black skirt or trousers, grey/white shirt, school tie. Blazer optional for years 10 and 11; pupils can wear burgundy school V-neck sweater with badge. Sixth-formers wear smart casual wear. Regulations enforced 'very strictly, within practical application for parents'.

Homework Average 11-year-old, five hours 30 minutes a week; 14-year-old, eight hours; 16-year-old, 11 hours.

Vocational qualifications GNVQ Intermediate, Business, Leisure and Tourism; GNVQ Advanced, Health and Social Care.

Inspection March 1993: 'The King's School is popular with parents and is appropriately valued for the range, breadth and general quality of educational experience that is provided.' January 1997: 'A good school with particular strength in the very good relationships within the school and its extra-curricular programme.'; 'Attainment in the key skills of literacy, numeracy and information technology is high, as is that

in the core subjects of English, mathematics and science.'; 'Progress is satisfactory in general in the sixth form and good in several subjects, but is not as marked as in earlier years.'; 'At all stages, pupils respond very well in their lessons. They are keen to learn and behave well in class. They have positive relationships with the teachers and each other. They volunteer information readily and join willingly in activities. Around the school, they are friendly and responsive.'; 'The headteacher and senior staff provide warm and committed leadership.'; 'Though staffing, equipment and accommodation are not generous, the school makes very good use of the resources available to it.'

Primary schools Ottery St Mary Primary; Feniton CE Primary; West Hill Primary; Payhembury Primary; Tipton St John Primary.

WESTLANDS HIGH SCHOOL

Holmes Chapel Road
Congleton
Cheshire CW12 4NH
Tel (01260) 273604
Fax (01260) 297557

- National ranking 420 (331, 452, –)
- GCSE 54% (61%)
- A-levels 40% (A/B); 84% (A/E)
- Higher education 89% (Oxford 1, Cambridge 2)

- Mixed comprehensive
- Pupils 685
- Boys (11–18) 331
- Girls (11–18) 354
- Sixth form 106 (15%)
- Education authority *Cheshire*

Headteacher Richard Haigh, 45, appointed in September 1993. Staff 40 (men 15, women 25).

Motto *None*

Background Established as girls' grammar in 1957; became co-educational comprehensive in 1979; in West Heath residential suburb of Congleton; grounds include sports field, all-weather pitch, tennis courts. Buildings extended over the years; latest addition was art block built in 1990s. Not over-subscribed. Study suggested the school was ranked 15th out of 100 schools in northern England in survey of 'value-added' examination performance. 'Strong tradition of excellence in creative arts'. Lists three main characteristics: consistently good academic performance in all subjects; small school able to work closely with parents and provide pupils with individual pastoral care and guidance; commitment to rich programme of extra-curricular activity.

Alumni Ian and David Brightwell, Manchester City soccer players and sons of Robbie Brightwell and Ann Packer, the athletes.

Streaming Mixed-ability form-groups on entry; setting begins in year 8 and increases through the school. Personal timetables in years 10 to 13.

Approach to discipline 'Our code of conduct applies to everyone in the organisation. It stresses the importance of personal responsibility, care for people and property. Pupils are expected to behave in such a way that teachers can teach and pupils can learn.'

Uniform Blazer with badge, grey trousers/navy skirt, white shirt, school tie. Sixth-formers do not wear uniform. Regulations enforced 'very' strictly.

Homework Average 11-year-old, five hours a week; 14-year-old, seven hours; 16-year-old, nine hours.

Vocational qualifications GNVQ Intermediate, Business, Leisure, Care; GNVQ Advanced, Business, Art.

Inspection January 1996: 'Westlands High School is a happy, popular and successful school with many strengths and which provides a very good standard of education. The pupils are well-behaved, achieve well and examination results are good. The school is very well managed and gives good value for money and deserves its high reputation.'; 'The quality of learning is predominantly good and often outstanding.'; 'Lessons are well planned so that pupils understand clearly what is required of them. Teachers are well qualified, highly competent and hard-working.'; 'Homework is set regularly and makes a contribution to the achievement of high standards.'

FORMBY HIGH SCHOOL

Freshfield Road
Formby
Liverpool L37 3HW

Tel (01704) 873100/877383
Fax (01704) 831748
E-mail: formby.high@campus.bt.com

- National ranking 421 (330, 312, 232, –)
- GCSE 57% (62%)
- A-levels 29% (A/B); 88% (A/E)
- Higher education 91% (Oxford 1)

- Mixed comprehensive
- Pupils 751
- Boys (11–18) 412
- Girls (11–18) 339
- Sixth form 111 (15%)
- Education authority *Sefton*

Headteacher Peter George Baldock, 58, appointed in September 1987. Staff 46 (men 24, women 22).

Motto *None*

Background Original secondary school building dates from 1938; mixed comprehensive since 1968; in spacious grounds in middle of 'dormitory town' on coast midway between Liverpool and Southport; surrounded by green fields, pine woods and sea on three sides. Separate blocks added since 1968: classroom block, sports block, practical block, drama/music, science and administrative. Not over-subscribed: 132 applications for 189 places. 'Particularly strong' in athletics and drama. Local, regional and national representatives in various sports. Aim: 'The provision of a secure, caring environment in which a firm, fair discipline underpins the pursuit of high academic achievement for all, and in which all pupils are encouraged to take advantage of opportunities in and out of school to develop their talents, abilities and skills in a positive way.'

Alumni Angela Eagle, Labour MP for Wallasey; Adrian Mills, presenter on BBC Television's *That's Life* programme.

Streaming Setting in mathematics and French from year 8; science and English from year 9.

Approach to discipline Implementation of 'Positive Discipline' programme, which recognises openly the 'excellent' conduct of overwhelming majority of pupils. In every lesson, pupils able to collect bronze, silver and gold certificates; rewards counterbalanced by sanctions for those failing to conform to expected standards.

Uniform Black blazer with school badge, grey

trousers/skirt, white shirt, school tie. Regulations enforced 'very strictly'.

Homework Average 11-year-old, seven to eight hours a week; 14-year-old, 10 hours; 16-year-old, 12 to 14 hours.

Vocational qualifications *None*

Inspection September 1994: 'This is a school with some considerable strengths which achieves good examination results within a very positive and supportive ethos.'; 'Teaching is enhanced by the positive attitudes to work of pupils who are generally well-motivated and responsive. Lessons are well-planned and when specialists are teaching their subjects the quality of teaching is usually sound and often good.'; 'The school has a clear set of values that are strongly supported by its parents and governors.'; 'Behaviour is conducive to a positive working atmosphere, and regular attendance and punctuality are effectively promoted.'

Primary schools St Peter's CE Primary; Freshfield Primary; Redgate Primary; Holy Trinity CE Primary.

ST PETER'S COLLEGIATE SCHOOL

Compton Park
Compton Road West
Wolverhampton
West Midlands WV3 9DU
Tel (01902) 756444
Fax (01902) 751952
E-mail: speters@rmplc.co.uk

- National ranking 422 (277, 226, 310, –)
- GCSE 57% (65%)
- A-levels 26% (A/B); 87% (A/E)
- Higher education 90% (Oxford 1)

- Mixed comprehensive
- Pupils 1,055
- Boys (11–18) 515
- Girls (11–18) 540
- Sixth form 255 (24%)
- Education authority *Wolverhampton*

Headteacher Peter M. Crook, 45, appointed in January 1989. Staff 64 (men 35, women 29).

Motto *None*

Background Situated on parkland site on western borders of Wolverhampton and Staffordshire countryside; one of three aided secondary schools in Lichfield diocese; one of only a few state schools affiliated to Woodard Foundation of Church Schools. Founded in 1847 in buildings next to St Peter's Collegiate Church in town centre; moved in 1965; oldest state educational institution in Wolverhampton 'with a tradition of academic, cultural and sporting excellence nourished by Christian spiritual and moral values'. Over-subscribed, with three applications per place. Technology college; links with industry; successful art and music. Extensive on-site sports facilities; also new theatre, chapel and sixth-form centre. 'By combining the best of our traditions with considered innovation, we offer each student the opportunity to discover the keys to success through the realisation of personal potential.' Highlighted for praise in 1995 and 1996 annual Ofsted reports; recognised by Education Extra for extra-curricular activities 'of merit'.

Streaming Mixed-ability in year 7; pupils put in ability sets in each subject in years 8 to 11.

Approach to discipline 'Each child has the right to a safe, secure environment in which purposeful study can be pursued. School rules apply Gospel values to everyday life.'

Uniform Boys: black blazer with school badge, grey trousers, white shirt, school tie. Girls: navy blazer/jumper, navy skirt, pink-check blouse. Sixth-form boys wear distinctive tie and girls wear white blouses. Very strictly enforced.

Homework Average 11-year-old, five hours a week; 14-year-old, six hours 15 minutes; 16-year-old, seven hours 30 minutes.

Vocational qualifications GNVQ, Health and Social Care, Leisure and Tourism, Business.

Inspection May 1994: 'St Peter's Collegiate School is very popular and successful. It is deservedly held in high regard by parents, the wider community it serves, and by its pupils and staff. The staff are very hard-working, loyal and highly-committed to providing the best opportunities for the pupils in and beyond the school.'; "Teachers have a thorough command of their subjects and are both confident and competent in their work with pupils.'; 'Behaviour and discipline in and around the school is very good.'

Primary schools Uplands Junior; Christ Church CE Junior; St Jude's CE Junior; St Andrew's CE Junior; St Bartholomew's CE Junior; St Michael's CE Primary; St Paul's CE Primary.

AMERY HILL SCHOOL

Amery Hill
Alton
Hampshire GU34 2BZ
Tel (01420) 84545
Fax (01420) 84137

- National ranking 423= (428=, 471=, 455=, –)
- GCSE 57% (55%)
- A-levels *Not applicable*
- Higher education *Not applicable*

- Mixed comprehensive
- Pupils 806
- Boys (11–16) 409
- Girls (11–16) 397
- Sixth form *Not applicable*
- Education authority *Hampshire*

Headteacher Alun Parry-Jones, 58, appointed in April 1980. Staff 48 (men 17, women 31).

Motto *None*

Background Built in 1939 in centre of market town with catchment area extending to villages in west; buildings enlarged over the years. Close links with Alton College for tertiary education; more than eight in 10 pupils continue education at 16. Fully-subscribed. Reputation for music and art. Special programmes for particularly able students. Regular visits at home and abroad, including established French and German exchanges. Regional winners in National Science Week Festival of Chemistry in 1994. Recent successes in Hansard Society and National Youth Parliament competitions. 'The school enjoys a relaxed but purposeful atmosphere. Our children are generally well-behaved and happy. Staff are highly-professional and caring.'

Alumni Jimmy Dickinson, former England and Portsmouth soccer player.

Streaming Setted by ability in various subjects during year 7.

Approach to discipline 'We have a well-ordered community. A "non-repressive" regime aims to encourage courtesy, consideration and self-discipline. A range of rewards and punishments is used as appropriate.'

Uniform Blue shirt, blue jumper (school crest optional), school tie (dark-blue with light-blue stripe), grey trousers for boys or blue trousers/skirt for girls. Strictly enforced.

Homework Average 11-year-old, six to eight hours a week; 14-year-old, eight to 10 hours; 16-year-old, 10+ hours.

Vocational qualifications *None*

Inspection May 1995: 'This is a good school which has excellent relationships between all members of its community. Pupils' behaviour is very good. There is a culture of trust and the work ethos is strong, which leads to highly-motivated pupils whose quality of learning is generally good. Standards are generally sound or better. Generally the more able pupils and pupils with special educational needs achieve above expectations. There is some under-achievement by pupils in the middle range of ability.'; 'The leadership of the school is caring and effective, and the daily pattern of organisation runs smoothly.'

Primary schools Anstey Primary; Butts Primary; St Lawrence's CE Primary; Wootey Primary; Medstead Primary; Bentworth CE Primary; Chawton CE Primary; Selborne CE Primary.

CHAILEY SCHOOL

Mill Lane
South Chailey
East Sussex BN8 4PU
Tel (01273) 890407
Fax (01273) 890893

- National ranking 423= (495=, 448=, 392=, –)
- GCSE 57% (49%)
- A-levels *Not applicable*
- Higher education *Not applicable*

- Mixed comprehensive
- Pupils 486
- Boys (11–16) 241
- Girls (11–16) 245
- Sixth form *Not applicable*
- Education authority *East Sussex*

Headteacher Vivian Howell, 49, appointed in September 1991. Staff 33 (men 15, women 18).

Motto *None*

Background Founded in 1958; on 17.5-acre site in heart of rural Sussex. Most pupils come from six or seven villages surrounding the school; many from rural background: children of gamekeepers, farmers, farmworkers and estate workers, as well as London commuters; new housing developments in locality. Fully-subscribed; proud of 'added value', with exam results higher than might be expected from ability of intake. 'Our buildings are perhaps best described as attractively functional'; 25 classrooms, laboratories, workshops, school hall, stage, library-cum-learning resource centre, administrative centre, and 'state-of-art' sports hall. New music suite with multi-track recording studio, new drama studio, new science laboratory and home economics centre. 'The outside may be 1958, but inside it's all 1990s.' New learning support suite; new wing for design technology department, incorporating computer-aided design facilities. Strong traditions in music and sport; planning permission for floodlit, all-weather playing field for school and community use. Good all-round 'though particular strength in the arts'; well-established choir and orchestra. Notable success by hockey teams over past few years; individuals have won many county caps. Parent-Teacher Association; Former Pupils' Association. 'We want all our pupils to become fulfilled, responsible members of society, whatever their career choice may be. It is our task to bring the best out of every pupil in our care.'

Alumni Piers Morgan, editor of *The Mirror*; John Trower, national javelin coach.

Streaming Children are streamed in core subjects, beginning with modern languages in year 8.

Approach to discipline 'We encourage pupils to take responsibility for their own behaviour within a clear framework of rules and guidelines. We have a well-established pastoral system, and strong parental support and involvement in our school.'

Uniform Navy trousers/skirt, navy V-neck sweater with school motif, light-blue shirt/blouse, school tie for boys, brown/black shoes. 'Pupils are expected to wear uniform.'

Homework Average 11-year-old, six to seven hours a week; 14-year-old, seven to eight hours; 16-year-old, nine to 10 hours.

Vocational qualifications *None*

Inspection September 1996: 'A successful school that provides a good education for its pupils within a caring and pleasant environment.'; 'Pupils demonstrate positive attitudes towards their work in class and are fully involved in lessons. Behaviour around the school and in class is good.'; 'Teachers have high expectations of pupils, plan their lessons well and manage their classes effectively.'; 'There is too little emphasis on the wider cultural dimension and pupils display limited understanding of the diversity and richness of cultures other than their own.'; 'The headteacher and governing body give strong leadership in the management of the school.'

Primary schools Barcombe CE Primary; St Peter's County Primary; Danehill's County Primary; Fletching CE Primary; Hamsey County Primary; Newick County Primary; Plumpton County Primary; Wivelsfield Primary.

CIRENCESTER DEER PARK SCHOOL

Stroud Road
Cirencester
Gloucestershire GL7 1XB
Tel (01285) 653447
Fax (01285) 640669
E-mail: headcdps@rmplc.co.uk

- National ranking 423= (354=, 448=, 374=, –)
- GCSE 57% (61%)
- A-levels *Not applicable*
- Higher education *Not applicable*

- Grant-maintained
- Mixed comprehensive
- Pupils 1,043
- Boys (11–16) 516
- Girls (11–18) 527
- Sixth form *Not applicable*
- Education authority *Gloucestershire*

Headteacher David A. Crossley, 41, appointed in September 1991. Staff 59 (men 27, women 32).

Motto Dona praesentis rape laetus horae (Make the most of life's gifts).

Background Established as 11–18 comprehensive in 1966, combining grammar school dating back to 13th century, and boys' and girls' secondary schools; became 11–16 school in 1991, sharing campus with Cirencester College. Attractive site, with Earl of Bathurst's Park and Cirencester Royal Agricultural College as neighbours: new Expressive Arts Centre and new science centre; industry-standard PC network. In association with English Table Tennis Association and Cirencester Table Tennis League, new sports hall completed in May 1995 and a new library/learning centre in September 1996. Over-subscribed, with average of 1.5 applications for each place. Nearly nine in 10 pupils stay on in education after 16, most attending Cirencester Tertiary College, which shares campus. Music: 200 pupils learning instruments; choir, jazz band, Saturday Music Centre for primary pupils based on site, recording studio. Enrichment activities: scientist in residence, poet in residence, dance troupe, India exchange, annual 'enrichment week', European visits, outdoor pursuits, work experience for year 10 pupils. Sport: 40 clubs or teams; 1994 under-13 county cup finalists, under-15 area finalists; many county/national representatives; basketball among sporting strengths. Earned Investor in People Award for training and staff development. 'Deer Park is a lively, demanding and challenging environment in which to work and learn. Our first aim is to convince pupils that they can achieve more than they first thought.' Technology college from April 1995.

Streaming Pupils in sets from year 8 according to needs of subject, notably in languages, science, English and mathematics.

Approach to discipline 'Schools Standards Booklet clearly outlines expectations, issued to all pupils and parents; reflect the fact that pupils behave reasonably most of time, but some need to be treated differently some of the time.'

Uniform Navy sweatshirt/V-neck pullover, white shirt, navy school polo shirt, school tie. 'A clear school standard that is enforced.'

Homework Average 11-year-old, five hours a week; 14-year-old, seven hours; 16-year-old, 10 hours.

Vocational qualifications Mostly offered at Cirencester College: wide range of .BTEC, GNVQ, NVQ and other courses. Piloting option GNVQ in conjunction with college.

Primary schools Chesterton Primary; Powells CE Primary; Stratton CE Primary; Watermoor CE Junior; Cirencester County Junior.

THE FITZWIMARC SCHOOL

Hockley Road
Rayleigh
Essex SS6 8EB

Tel **(01268) 743884**
Fax **(01268) 742877**

- National ranking 423 (477 = , 502 = , 318 = , 295 =)
- GCSE 57% (51%)
- A-levels *Not applicable*
- Higher education *Not applicable*

- Grant-maintained
- Mixed comprehensive
- Pupils 1,250
- Boys (11–16) 639
- Girls (11–16) 611
- Sixth form *Not applicable*
- Education authority *Essex*

Headteacher David Cox, 53, appointed in 1987. Staff 68 (men 32, women 36).

Motto Procedens (Going forward).

Background Founded in 1937 on outskirts of Rayleigh; considerably enlarged and improved; became eight-form entry co-educational comprehensive in 1967. Grounds include hard playing areas and a playing field for hockey, rugby, soccer, rugby, cricket, rounders and athletics; also five hard tennis courts and netball courts. Became grant-maintained in January 1993; over-subscribed, with 346 applications for 244 places; more than eight in 10 pupils (85%) continue their education after 16, mainly to local sixth-form college, with usually 40 former pupils going on to higher education. Facilities include eight science laboratories, four art and craft studios that include pottery kilns and photographic unit, two music rooms with three practice studios, six craft, design, and technology workshops with computer suite, four home economics areas, five computer rooms, business studies centre, drama studio, two gymnasia and health and fitness room, large sports hall, careers room, library and resources centre. All of school decorated in past three years; science and technology areas extensively remodelled and re-equipped. New history block in September 1994. Sporting achievements include 50 school teams in national finals in past eight years, with five athletics teams being national champions since 1991. One of 11 schools to receive Excellence Award for sport in 1997. Youth orchestra; drama productions.

Streaming Pupils are put in sets according to ability in each subject from year 8, unless mixed-ability groups thought to be advantageous, such as in religious education.

Approach to discipline High expectations with as few rules as possible; guiding principles of common sense, courtesy, concern for welfare of others and recognised need to uphold standards; pupils provided with opportunities to exercise self-discipline and to socialise freely and in civil manner. 'The vast majority of pupils react positively and maturely, and the friendly, relaxed but purposeful atmosphere is frequently commented on by visitors.'

Uniform Scarlet jumper, black trousers/skirt, white shirt/blouse. 'Simple, inexpensive and smart. All pupils wear the full school uniform.'

Homework Average 11-year-old, six hours a week; 14-year-old, seven hours; 16-year-old, 10 hours.

Vocational qualifications GNVQ, Manufacturing.

Primary schools Grove Primary; Edward Francis Primary; Wyburns Primary; Rayleigh County Junior; Downhall County Primary.

NOTRE DAME ROMAN CATHOLIC SCHOOL FOR GIRLS

Looseleigh Lane
Plymouth
Devon PL6 5HN
Tel (01752) 775101
Fax (01752) 768120
E-mail: ndrcs@aol.com
Internet: http://www.members.aol.com/ndrcs

- National ranking 427 (438, 519, 274, –)
- GCSE 56% (54%)
- A-levels 38% (A/B); 92% (A/E)
- Higher education 94%

- Girls' comprehensive
- Pupils 764
- Boys (16–18) 2
- Girls (11–18) 762
- Sixth form 126 (15%)
- Education authority *Devon*

Headteacher Sister Maureen Lomax, 54, appointed in September 1992. Staff 44 (men 14, women 30).

Motto Ah! Qu'il est bon, le bon Dieu (How good God is!).

Background Founded in 1865 as first girls' school in Plymouth; next to cathedral until bombed in Second World War; in 1966, new school built and pupils moved to semi-rural site; in 1981, amalgamation of Notre Dame High School with Cardinal Vaughan Secondary School. Over-subscribed, with 1.3 applications per place; pressure on places would be even greater if Roman Catholic pupils living in Cornwall received free travel to what is their nearest Catholic state secondary. Curriculum strengths include English, art, history, music, religious studies and drama; 'excellent' personal, social and moral education programme. 'In spite of limited PE facilities, children do well': hockey, cross-country, netball. National success in public-speaking competitions. Charity fund-raising. Duke of Edinburgh Award Scheme; language exchanges; school news magazine for parents and local community.

Streaming Pupils placed in sets for mathematics from year 7; for science and French from year 8; for English and religious studies from year 10.

Approach to discipline Firm but caring: 'Notre Dame encourages all its members to show courtesy and respect for each other and all whom they meet, to value honesty and truth, and to accept responsibility for self and others. It is vital that parents and teachers are seen to hold the same values.' Code of conduct posted in each form room; rewards and sanctions; early contact with parents in discipline procedure.

Uniform Mid-grey, knife-pleated skirt (knee-length or longer), blouse (different colours for different year-groups), black blazer with badge, royal-blue V-neck pullover with crest, school tie, grey/white socks or tights (black tights only for year 11 pupils), 'suitable' black shoes. No make-up. Regulations enforced 'quite strictly'.

Homework Average 11-year-old, seven hours 30 minutes a week; 14-year-old, 12 hours 30 minutes to 15 hours ; 16-year-old, 17 hours 30 minutes.

Vocational qualifications GNVQ, Business and Finance, Health and Social Care.

Inspection May 1995: 'This is a good school which provides an effective education for its pupils. The pupils, staff, parents and the wider community are proud to be identified with their school and the Notre Dame heritage of which it is part.'; 'The teaching is proficient and in almost all lessons it is judged to be sound or better, and in half it is good or very good. Lessons are generally well-planned and, in the best lessons, goals are made clear, the teachers' subject knowledge is good, their expectations are high, work is mainly well-matched to the pupils' abilities and relationships are very good. The insufficiency of support for pupils with special educational needs impedes the progress of the least able. The slow pace of some lessons and their lack of variety in activities holds back the most able.'

Primary schools St Peter's RC Primary; St Paul's RC Primary; Keyham Barton RC Primary; Holy Cross RC Primary; Bickleigh Down CE Primary.

TEESDALE SCHOOL

Prospect Place
Barnard Castle
County Durham DL12 8HH
Tel (01833) 638166/637507
Fax (01833) 695127

- National ranking 428 (507, 479, 481, –)
- GCSE 56% (46%)
- A-levels 33% (A/B); 73% (A/E)
- Higher education 80%

- Mixed comprehensive
- Pupils 822
- Boys (11–18) 398
- Girls (11–18) 424
- Sixth form 136 (17%)
- Education authority *Durham*

Headteacher Paul Harrison, 43, appointed from September 1996. Staff 49 (men 19, women 30).

Motto *None*

Background Rural area, drawing pupils from a large part of southwest Durham; formed in 1976 by the amalgamation of Barnard Castle Grammar School and Baliol Secondary Modern School; half the pupils come from the market town of Barnard Castle, with the rest from surrounding villages and farms. Not over-subscribed, but one in four pupils come from 'non-catchment' primary schools. School has the only post-16 education facility in the Teesdale district. New technology rooms opened in September 1993; each of the school's three blocks has full-size computer room and several computer clusters. Strong in cross-country championships, providing several county representatives each year. 'Traditional (uniform and annual prize-giving) and progressive (curriculum development and pastoral guidance).'

Alumni Professor John Burns, geneticist; Brian Fletcher, former Grand National jockey; Eric Gates and David Thomas, former England footballers.

Streaming Setting in most subjects from year 7.

Approach to discipline 'Emphasis is on good behaviour, rewarded by merits and gold star awards, which are given for good academic work and behaviour. The school has a central detention system and parents are notified of all detentions, as well as merits.'

Uniform Navy sweatshirt with embroidered school badge or white/navy shirt, with badge, for summer, navy skirt/trousers. Sixth-formers wear dress similar to that of the staff. 'Uniform is encouraged and worn by most students in years 7 to 11.'

Homework Average 11-year-old, three hours 30 minutes a week; 14-year-old, five hours; 16-year-old, seven hours 30 minutes.

Vocational qualifications GNVQ, Manufacturing, Business, Leisure and Tourism; Health and Social Care.

Inspection October 1996: 'Teesdale School is on the threshold of change. It has become a complacent school where professional debate and discussion have not flourished. Most staff sense that their contributions and ideas for the future development of the school have not been valued. The school has laudable aims. It is successful in maintaining good levels of examination success. It has a healthy budget and an energetic new senior management team and staff willing to contribute to the successful development of the school.'

Primary schools Barnard Castle CE Primary; Middleton Primary, Middleton-in-Teesdale; Montalbo Primary, Barnard Castle; Gainford CE Primary; St Mary's Primary, Barnard Castle; Cothersone Primary.

MAGDALEN COLLEGE SCHOOL

Waynflete Avenue
Brackley
Northamptonshire NN13 6AF

Tel (01280) 703911
Fax (01280) 704953
E-mail: mcsbrak@mailbox.rmplc.co.uk

- National ranking 429 (409, 522, 407, –)
- GCSE 56% (57%)
- A-levels 29% (A/B); 93% (A/E)
- Higher education 72%

- Mixed comprehensive
- Pupils 1,219
- Boys (11–18) 628
- Girls (11–18) 591
- Sixth form 247 (20%)
- Education authority *Northamptonshire*

Headteacher Elaine Ruth Wotherspoon, 47, appointed in January 1993. Staff 81 (men 43, women 38).

Motto Sicut lilium (As lilies).

Background Split-site school in small market town; one site is modern, while other dates from 15th century, with school celebrating 450th anniversary of its founding in 1998; distinctive setting includes school chapel and lake. Over-subscribed. Music is 'very strong': chapel choir sings Evensong in school chapel; youth choir undertakes European tours; junior choir, orchestra, jazz band. School has designated special provision for students with moderate or specific learning difficulties. 'We are a caring institution in which the quality of learning is paramount, but one which also places emphasis on mutual respect and care for others.'

Streaming Mixed-ability in year 7; some setting in some subjects in years 8 to 11.

Approach to discipline 'Emphasis on self-discipline and accountability for one's behaviour.'

Uniform Navy sweatshirt/cardigan, with Magdalen College Oxford lily embroidered on garments and on school tie. All students in years 7 to 11 wear uniform.

Homework Average 11-year-old, five hours a week; 14-year-old, seven hours 30 minutes; 16-year-old, 10 hours.

Vocational qualifications GNVQ, Business, Science, Leisure and Tourism, Health and Social Care.

Inspection November 1995: 'Magdalen College School cares for its pupils well and they achieve good standards in most subjects.

Examination results are well above the national average. The school is increasingly popular with parents.'; 'Staff are well-qualified and the teaching is often good, and sometimes outstanding. However, there are shortcomings in about a sixth of lessons. Teaching sometimes does not provide sufficiently demanding work for the most able pupils.'; 'Pupils make good progress and have excellent attitudes to learning; they show maturity and motivation. Extra-curricular activities enhance learning and are enjoyed by many pupils.'

Primary schools Southfield County Primary; Bracken Leas Primary; Brackley CE Primary; Croughton CE Primary; Helmdon Primary; Newbottle and Charlton CE Primary; Syresham CE Primary.

BINGLEY GRAMMAR SCHOOL

Keighley Road
Bingley
West Yorkshire BD16 2RS
Tel (01274) 562557/567688
Fax (01274) 510136

- National ranking 430 (444, 398, 480, –)
- GCSE 56% (54%)
- A-levels 26% (A/B); 80% (A/E)
- Higher education 85% (Cambridge 1)

- Grant-maintained
- Mixed comprehensive
- Pupils 1,074
- Boys (13–18) 547
- Girls (13–18) 527
- Sixth form 256 (24%)
- Education authority *Bradford*

Headteacher Ian Plimmer, 59, appointed in January 1984. Staff 63 (men 37, women 26).

Motto Lampada tradare nostrum est (It is for us to pass on the light).

Background School is an old foundation dating to 1529, when a house and schoolmaster's salary were endowed in Bingley; serves same catchment area of Bingley and surrounding villages; moved to current site in early Victorian times, but bulk of building took place in the 1930s; in attractive grounds, with some of its playing fields on site; substantial laboratory expansion in the 1960s. More recent building has included a new technology and dining block, renovation and expansion of sixth-form accommodation; new laboratory block in 1994, together with dual-use sports centre. Oversubscribed, with average of 1.5 applications per place. 'Outstanding' extra-curricular opportunities. Particular strengths in music (annual Continental performance) and games (rugby and netball); wide range of outdoor activities, community work. 'Traditionally rooted, with a modern curriculum; close links with families and the community; high expectations of pupils, high reputation locally, very successful in placing schoolleavers; committed, loyal and supportive staff.' Highlighted for praise in annual Ofsted report in 1995.

Alumni Austin Mitchell, Labour MP for Great Grimsby; John Briggs, pianist; Fred Hoyle, astronomer and writer.

Streaming Setting in English, mathematics, modern languages, science.

Approach to discipline 'Firm, plenty of common sense, high expectations of pupils.'

Uniform 'Bingley red' blazer and sweaters. No uniform in sixth-form, but code of dress applies. Regulations enforced 'reasonably'.

Homework Average 13-year-old, seven to 10 hours a week; 14-year-old, 10 to 12 hours; 16-year-old, 15 hours.

Vocational qualifications GNVQ Intermediate and Advanced.

Inspection November 1993: 'A good school with some outstanding features.'; 'Pupils make good progress and their attitudes to their work are very good.'; 'The headteacher provides strong and highly-effective leadership, ably supported by the deputy headteachers and a well-organised governing body which is greatly involved with the school.'; 'There is a strong ethos and a very clear sense of overall purpose within the school. Pupils' behaviour is good. The school is orderly as a community, and attendance and punctuality are good.'; 'The accommodation has been considerably improved by the provision of new science laboratories and a sports hall, but there is a shortage of suitable classroom accommodation in some subject areas, notably mathematics.'

Primary schools Gilstead Middle; Ryshworth Middle; Parkside Middle; Stoney Lee Middle; Nab Wood Middle.

BURSCOUGH PRIORY HIGH SCHOOL

Trevor Road
Burscough
Ormskirk
Lancashire L40 7RZ
Tel (01704) 893259
Fax (01704) 893307

- National ranking 431= (446=, 378=, 482=, –)
- GCSE 56% (54%)
- A-levels *Not applicable*
- Higher education *Not applicable*

- Mixed comprehensive
- Pupils 738
- Boys (11–16) 360
- Girls (11–16) 378
- Sixth form *Not applicable*
- Education authority *Lancashire*

Headteacher Roger Noel Leighton, 48, appointed in January 1985. Staff 40 (men 19, women 21).

Motto E pluribus unum (One from the many).

Background Close to centre of Burscough; draws pupils from town and surrounding villages and rural area within distance of about nine miles. Opened in 1958; re-organisation in mid-1970s; 'enjoys pleasant, open site and clean, spacious buildings and extensive, adjacent playing fields are key features'. Over-subscribed. Many clubs and activities; French and German exchanges; Young Enterprise. Orienteering: in 1994, school team was sixth in British championships. 'Priory High School is a caring and challenging community. We aim to develop confidence, tolerance and respect for each individual in his or her own right. We encourage collaboration and co-operation, whilst at the same time fostering individual initiative and leadership to allow each pupil to maximise his or her potential.' Identified by Ofsted in 1996 as a 'good and improving school'.

Alumni Colin Brown, chief political correspondent of *The Independent*; Craig Winrow, international 800m athlete.

Streaming Pupils are placed in all-ability classes in year 7 and are streamed progressively as they advance up the school, beginning in year 8 for mathematics and modern languages.

Approach to discipline 'Pupils are expected to conform to a high standard of behaviour and are encouraged to develop a respect for others as well as themselves. Discipline is firm but fair. Emphasis is placed on rewarding pupils for effort and attainment in their school work, for regular attendance and for service to the school and community.'

Uniform Black V-neck jumper with school crest, white shirt/blouse, school tie, black trousers/skirt. In year 11, students suggest their own colour for the jumper. 'School uniform is worn by all pupils.'

Homework Average 11-year-old, six hours a week; 14-year-old, eight hours; 16-year-old, 10 hours.

Vocational qualifications *None*

Inspection February 1994: 'This is a good school with considerable strengths. It provides a good education for its pupils.'

Primary schools Burscough Lordsgate CE Primary; Burscough St John's CE Primary; Burscough Bridge Methodist Primary; Burscough County Primary; Newburgh CE Primary; Parbold Douglas CE Primary; Rufford CE Primary; Richard Durning's Endowed Primary, Bispham.

LITTLEOVER COMMUNITY SCHOOL

Pastures Hill
Littleover
Derby
Derbyshire DE23 7BD
Tel (01332) 513219
Fax (01332) 516580

- National ranking 431= (495=, 494=, 455=, –)
- GCSE 56% (49%)
- A-levels *Not applicable*
- Higher education *Not applicable*

- Mixed comprehensive
- Pupils 1,118
- Boys (11–16) 584
- Girls (11–16) 534
- Sixth form *Not applicable*
- Education authority *Derbyshire*

Headteacher David Nichols, 44, appointed in April 1993. Staff 71 (men 32, women 39).

Motto Bene consulendo (Achievement through contemplation).

Background Opened in 1949, since when original buildings have doubled in size; plans submitted to restore sixth-form, which was removed in 1989 reorganisation. Situated four miles southwest of Derby in semi-rural surroundings, with extensive grounds and 'excellent facilities for academic and sporting activities'. Always over-subscribed, with average of 1.5 applications per place. School is proud of all-round academic success and wealth of extra-curricular activities. School teams regularly compete in football, netball, cricket, hockey and athletics; many county representatives; currently has Derbyshire boys' and girls' golf champions. Regular music and drama events; members of school orchestra play with East of England orchestra; steel band has won national competitions and toured many countries.

Streaming Setting according to ability progressively introduced from year 8.

Approach to discipline 'The school code of conduct is known and understood by all pupils.'

Uniform Black pullover/sweatshirt with school logo, white shirt/blouse, grey skirt/trousers, black shoes. Regulations enforced 'very strictly': 'Governors made uniform compulsory in 1994.'

Homework Average 11-year-old, eight hours a week; 14-year-old, 10 hours; 16-year-old, 13 hours.

Vocational qualifications City and Guilds Diploma.

Inspection October 1993: 'The good quality of relationships contributed towards purposeful learning experiences. Parents are fully supportive of the ethos of the school and are appreciative of the way in which the school is developing good patterns of behaviour in pupils.'; 'Discipline is firm but unobtrusive. There is a graduated system of rewards and sanctions in operation which helps to promote good behaviour.'

Primary schools Brookfield Primary; St Peter's CE Junior; Wren Park Primary; Dale Primary.

RINGMER COMMUNITY COLLEGE

Lewes Road
Ringmer
East Sussex BN8 5NE

Tel **(01273) 812220**
Fax **(01273) 813961**
E-mail: **ringmer@pavilion.co.uk**

- National ranking 431 = (331 = , 242 = , 295 = , –)
- GCSE 56% (62%)
- A-levels *Not applicable*
- Higher education *Not applicable*

- Mixed comprehensive
- Pupils 836
- Boys (11–16) 413
- Girls (11–16) 423
- Sixth form *Not applicable*
- Education authority *East Sussex*

Headteacher John William Wakely, 55, appointed in April 1983. Staff 56 (men 24, women 32).

Motto Achieving, caring, contributing.

Background Original school opened in 1958; became comprehensive in 1976; opened as community college in 1988. Rural comprehensive school in 17 acres of grounds in Sussex Downs, about four miles northeast of Lewes. Three principal buildings: administrative departments, classrooms, hall, dining area, swimming pool; the Clark building, named after former headteacher, houses art, drama and technology departments; languages building completed in September 1993. Over-subscribed, with 1.1 applications per place. Special mention of arts: art, music, dance and drama; music department features stage band, wind band, training band, orchestra, junior and senior choirs, rock groups, guitar ensemble, recorder ensembles and various chamber ensembles. Instrumental tuition to about 200 pupils 'as a result of the outstanding quality of the East Sussex Music Service'. Strong traditions of competitive sport: inter-house and inter-school competitions in rugby, football, cricket, netball, hockey, cross-country, stoolball and athletics. Integrated youth service programme. Identified by Ofsted in 1996 as one of 32 'outstandingly successful' schools.

Streaming In mathematics, languages and science banding gives way to setting as pupils proceed up through the college.

Approach to discipline 'The essential basis of the college's discipline is the careful communication to pupils of a clear-cut code of expectations and reasons for this code.'

Positive counselling, encouragement of self-discipline, positive reinforcement of good behaviour with system of rewards. Otherwise, sanctions range from short lunchtime detention to exclusion.

Uniform Plain mid-grey skirt/trousers, white shirt, green-and-silver striped tie, dark-green sweatshirt with college logo, black shoes. Regulations renewed biennially in consultation with parent-teacher association and student council.

Homework Average 11-year-old, five hours a week; 14-year-old, eight to 10 hours; 16-year-old, up to 15 hours.

Vocational qualifications Diploma of Vocational Education.

Inspection September 1993: 'The college provides a very effective education. The standards achieved by pupils in most subjects are predominantly good in lessons and good in public examinations.'; 'Teaching is effective and provides pupils with opportunities to develop a good range of learning skills. Pupils are well-motivated and relationships are excellent. Praise and encouragement are used to create a climate which promotes learning.'

Primary schools Ringmer County Primary; South Malling CE Primary; Laughton County Primary; East Hoathly CE Primary; Chiddingly CE Primary; Blackboys CE Primary; Firle CE Primary.

THE DORMSTON SCHOOL

Millbank
Sedgley
Dudley
West Midlands DY3 1SN
Tel **(01384) 816395**
Fax **(01384) 816396**
E-mail: **info@dormston.dudley.gov.uk**
Internet: **http://www.edu.dudley.gov. uk/schools/dormston**

- National ranking 431 = (489 = , 524, 482 = , –)
- GCSE 56% (50%)
- A-levels *Not applicable*
- Higher education *Not applicable*

- Mixed comprehensive
- Pupils 1,121
- Boys (11–16) 562
- Girls (11–16) 559

- Sixth form *Not applicable*
- Education authority *Dudley*

Headteacher Barbara H. O'Connor, 58, appointed in June 1983. Staff 60 (men 20, women 40).

Motto Progress through partnership.

Background Serves residential area in Sedgley, on northern edge of Dudley; opened in 1937 and was originally two small single-sex secondary moderns; became mixed comprehensive (11 to 16) in early 1970s; became 11-to-16 school in 1991. Over-subscribed, with 1.5 applications per place. 'Our overall aims and objectives try to reflect the needs of the pupils growing up in a rapidly-changing technological society'; keeps pace with developments in information technology and micro-electronics. Facilities include: purpose-built performing arts centre; music, dance, drama, art studios; 'state-of-the-art' information technology rooms, science laboratories and technology rooms. As well as national curriculum subjects, all pupils study: two foreign languages up to 14; one language up to 16; full range of arts up to GCSE; technology and information technology to 16. Post-16 centre linked with Dudley College of Technology from September 1996.

Alumni Martin Clarke, snooker player.

Streaming Pupils are placed in mixed-ability teaching groups in most subjects in year 7. Thereafter they may be placed in teaching groups according to their ability in English, mathematics, science, modern languages and humanities.

Approach to discipline Code of conduct 'based on common sense and consideration for others'; pupils told and reminded of it. Aim at helping pupils to become disciplined, mature adults, able to take increasing responsibility for their own work and behaviour: 'Expected standards of behaviour are regularly discussed with pupils through the form-tutor and year-head.'

Uniform Black blazer, school badge, white shirt/blouse, grey trousers/skirt, grey pullover/cardigan, black shoes. Regulations enforced '100%'.

Homework Average 11-year-old, five hours a week; 14-year-old, seven hours 30 minutes; 16-year-old, 10 hours.

Vocational qualifications GNVQs being introduced.

Inspection May 1993: 'The school is a mature, self-regulating community. Pupils respect each other and maintain positive relationships with staff.'; 'The quality of teaching is mostly sound and often good. Teachers are knowledgeable and enthusiastic'; 'Pupils show a mature and responsible attitude to learning.'; 'This is a good school with a distinct and positive ethos. It provides a secure, well-ordered and pleasant environment for learning and teaching. Pupils behave well and relationships are good. Review and guidance sessions provide valuable opportunities for pupils to talk individually to tutors and to review their progress.' October 1996: 'A good school with many very good features and a very strong caring ethos. The staff are hard-working and deeply committed to the well-being and education of all pupils.'; 'Overwhelmingly, the quality of teaching is at least satisfactory, frequently good and occasionally very good. There is much good practice in the school, but this is not consistent within and across the departments.'; 'The school has strong leadership and a clear educational direction for its work.'; 'Much progress has been made since the last inspection in meeting the requirements of the key issues raised.'

Primary schools Alder Coppice Primary; Cotwall End Primary; Queen Victoria Primary; Hurst Green Primary.

UPPINGHAM COMMUNITY COLLEGE

London Road
Uppingham
Rutland
Leicestershire LE15 9TJ
Tel (01572) 823631
Fax (01572) 821193
E-mail: uppcom@rmplc.co.uk
Internet: http://www.uppingham.demon.co.uk

- National ranking 431= (422=, 471=, 432=, –)
- GCSE 56% (56%)
- A-levels *Not applicable*
- Higher education *Not applicable*

- Grant-maintained
- Mixed comprehensive
- Pupils 680
- Boys (11–16) 330
- Girls (11–16) 350
- Sixth form *Not applicable*

- Education authority *Rutland*

Headteacher Peter MacDonald-Pearce, appointed in September 1988. Staff 40 (men 20, women 20).

Motto Non videri sed esse (Not seem, but be).

Background Opened in 1920 to serve small rural community of southwest Rutland; built for 600 pupils, but owing to increased pressure on places, £870,000 expansion programme under way. Admission limit increased from 120 to 162; 'idyllic' setting overlooking Welland Valley; became technology college in April 1995; technology curriculum enhanced to 48%. One in 10 pupils learning musical instruments up to Grade 8. Senior orchestra, junior orchestra, recorder consort, concert band, string quartet. Sports: football, rugby, basketball, hockey, rounders, netball, cross-country, cricket and volleyball; representatives at county and regional level.

Streaming Pupils are set for mathematics throughout; some setting in modern languages from year 8; also some setting in years 10 and 11 for certain subjects.

Approach to discipline Printed code of conduct: 'Discipline is based on the premise that all should take responsibility for their own actions. A strong emphasis is laid on "No pupil should stop a teacher from teaching nor another pupil from learning".'

Uniform Navy V-neck sweatshirt (available with college logo), jumper, cardigan, white shirt/blouse, navy skirt/trousers for girls, grey/black trousers for boys, grey/black/white socks or navy/black/flesh tights, tie, black shoes. 'Pupils are expected to adhere strictly to the requirements.'

Homework Average 11-year-old, five hours a week; 14-year-old, six hours; 16-year-old, 10 hours.

Vocational qualifications Catering; GNVQs being considered.

Inspection April 1996: 'Students at Uppingham Community College enjoy a very good education. This is well-balanced and contains a wider range of experiences than is usual. Leadership is very effective and the college provides a well-organised, orderly and caring community. The attitudes of students to their learning is a strength.'; 'A high level of concentration and courteous attention is paid in class.'; 'Very effective leadership is given by the principal. This has established a distinctive curriculum and an imaginative approach to the college day.'; 'Accommodation is managed well within the limitations of the existing buildings.'

Primary schools Uppingham CE Primary; Leighfield County Primary; North Luffenham CE Primary; Edith Weston County Primary; Gretton CE Primary; Hallaton CE Primary; Tugby County Primary; Bringhirst County Primary.

DURHAM JOHNSTON COMPREHENSIVE SCHOOL

Crossgate Moor
Durham City DH1 4SU
Tel (0191) 384 3887
Fax (0191) 384 5771
E-mail: johnston@rmplc.co.uk

- National ranking 436 (395, 428, 236, –)
- GCSE 55% (58%)
- A-levels 61% (A/B); 97% (A/E)
- Higher education 76% (Oxford 4, Cambridge 3)

- Mixed comprehensive
- Pupils 1,478
- Boys (11–18) 765
- Girls (11–18) 722
- Sixth form 290 (20%)
- Education authority *Durham*

Headteacher John Dunford, 50, appointed in September 1982. Staff 87 (men 43, women 44).

Motto Sapere aude (Dare to be wise).

Background The school, which was founded in 1899, became comprehensive in 1979 on amalgamation of the grammar school with two secondary moderns; on two sites 2.5 miles apart, with years 7 and 8 on lower-school site. Both sites overlook Durham Cathedral, where the school's annual carol service is held. Over-subscribed, with about 300 applications for 232 places; intake increased to 269. Upper school has spacious grounds; extra buildings planned to make it single-site school. Reputation for drama, music and arts. Winners of *Observer* Mace and Cambridge Union debating competitions in 1993. Regular exchanges with schools in France, Germany, Japan,

United States and Russia. 'Activity Time' on Friday afternoons; 'good balance' of age and experience on staff. 'There is a strong working ethos in the school, which aims at providing a secure environment in which children can learn. The school provides a wide range of opportunities for children of all abilities. It has a particularly high reputation for the achievements of its sixth-formers.'

Streaming Mixed-ability in year 7; two broad bands in years 8 and 9; streamed for core subjects in years 10 and 11.

Approach to discipline 'Firm, fair discipline, with an increasing degree of self-discipline expected as the children get older.'

Uniform Black blazer with badge, white shirt/blouse, grey trousers/skirt, school tie. 'Uniform is insisted upon.'

Homework Average 11-year-old, seven hours a week; 14-year-old, 10 hours; 16-year-old, 14 hours.

Vocational qualifications *None*

Inspection October 1994: 'A very successful school, despite the inevitable constraints imposed by a split site, highly valued by parents and the community.'; 'Pupils are well taught within an ethos which is conducive to effective learning. There is a need, however, in some areas of the curriculum to introduce greater variation in the teaching approaches used. Relationships, both within the classroom and elsewhere, are excellent, as are the standards of behaviour.'; 'The school benefits from sound leadership from the senior staff and governors.'

Primary schools Bowburn Junior; Shincliffe CE Primary; St Margaret's CE Primary; Neville's Cross County Primary; Langley Moor County Primary; Brandon Junior; Browney County Primary.

WAINGEL'S COPSE SCHOOL

Denmark Avenue
Woodley
Berkshire RG5 4RF
Tel (0118) 969 0336
Fax ((0118) 944 2843
Email: waingels@aol.com
Internet: http://users.aol.com/waingels

National ranking 437 (324, 377, 350, 325)

- GCSE 55% (62%)
- A-levels 50% (A/B); 96% (A/E)
- Higher education 60% (Oxford 1, Cambridge 2)

- Mixed comprehensive
- Pupils 1,448
- Boys (11–18) 758
- Girls (11–18) 690
- Sixth form 245 (17%)
- Education authority *Berkshire*

Headteacher Richard Green, 44, appointed from September 1996. Staff 81 (men 38, women 43).

Motto Quality in all.

Background Opened in 1971 in purpose-built accommodation on 28-acre site in semi-rural setting, serving suburb to east of Reading. Over-subscribed, with 300+ applications for 240 places. School proud of well-stocked, well-used library and sixth-form library. Strong tradition of drama, drama workshops, visits to London theatres. Sporting success at county level: under-19 basketball, badminton as well as netball, hockey, cricket, soccer and rugby. After-school activities: music, chess, bridge, art, technology and astronomy. Balance between arts and science: 54% of pupils going on to higher education study science-related subjects, 44% on arts/social science courses.

Alumni Duncan Prescott, clarinettist.

Streaming Pupils in sets in most academic subjects throughout. The most able pupils in mathematics take GCSE early.

Approach to discipline Widely-published codes of conduct are well-observed. 'If breaches of discipline do occur, they are firmly dealt with by academic staff and head of year.'

Uniform Bottle-green pullover with school crest, dark-grey trousers/bottle-green skirt, white shirt, school tie. 'Pupils may only attend in school uniform.'

Homework Average 11-year-old, five hours a week; 14-year-old, 10 hours; 16-year-old, 15 hours.

Vocational qualifications BTEC First, Business and Finance; GNVQ Intermediate. Further courses planned: Art and Design, Health and Social Care, Advanced Business and Finance.

Inspection January 1996: 'Waingel's Copse is a good school. It has a positive ethos which promotes pupils' academic and personal development. Pupils achieve good standards and have positive attitudes to their work. The school is well-organised; relationships and behaviour are good; the environment is well-maintained and supports learning. Staff are hard-working and effective.'

Primary school Woodley CE Primary; Willow Bank Primary; Rivermead Primary; St Dominic Savio RC Primary.

THE BEAUCHAMP COLLEGE

Ridge Way
Oadby
Leicester
Leicestershire LE2 5TP
Tel (0116) 271 5809
Fax (0116) 271 5454
E-mail: mc@bcoll.demon.co.uk
Internet: http://www.beauchamp.leics.
    sch.uk

- National ranking 438 (377, 434, 309, –)
- GCSE 55% (59%)
- A-levels 39% (A/B); 90% (A/E)
- Higher education 80% (Oxford 2, Cambridge 3)

- Mixed comprehensive
- Pupils 1,603
- Boys (14–18) 795
- Girls (14–18) 808
- Sixth form 680 (42%)
- Education authority *Leicestershire*

Headteacher Maureen Cruickshank, 55, appointed in April 1981. Staff 90 (men 50, women 40).

Motto *None*

Background Founded by Warwick the King-maker 600 years ago; in 1964 the school moved from Kibworth Beauchamp to new buildings in Oadby four miles south of Leicester city centre, changing from a grammar school to an upper school for pupils aged 14 to 18 and a community college. Additions in last five years: new suite of physics laboratories, physical education building with classrooms, office and well-equipped fitness room, five new classrooms and new music suite; new drama, economics and media studies building. Over-subscribed, with more than one third of pupils from outside catchment area; 460 applications for 450 places. Eight in 10 pupils stay into sixth form; total of 33 A-level subjects

offered, and five Intermediate and four Advanced GNVQ courses. French exchanges; overseas work-experience; annual ski trips and exchanges with Salzburg; many A-level residential visits. Sixth-formers represented Britain at 1993 European Youth Parliament in Budapest. Drama, music and religious education among other strengths. Celebrates cultural diversity of pupils. Technology College status from April 1996; sponsorship and government funding to enhance learning opportunities. Feeder high schools include Gartree High, Manor High and Bushloe High.

Alumni John Deacon, bass guitarist with Queen.

Streaming 'Individual departments and faculties set as they think best for their subjects.'

Approach to discipline 'Our approach is to encourage self-discipline and respect.'

Uniform 'Students enjoy their own choice of clothes.'

Homework Average 14-year-old, 10 hours a week; 16-year-old, 15 hours.

Vocational qualifications RSA; GNVQ.

Inspection September 1993: 'Beauchamp is a very effective school with high standards of achievement in public examinations in most areas of the curriculum. Students' attitudes to learning are excellent, but there is a range of research skills which are not fully developed. Students are well-motivated and relationships are excellent. Most students work hard.'; 'The college is strongly led and well managed.'; 'The college has clear values which lead to excellent behaviour and a very orderly atmosphere.'

KATHARINE LADY BERKELEY'S SCHOOL

Kingswood Road
Wotton-under-Edge
Gloucestershire GL12 8RB
Tel (01453) 842227
Fax (01453) 845480

- National ranking 439 (376, 356, 451, –)
- GCSE 55% (59%)
- A-levels 36% (A/B); 95% (A/E)
- Higher education 80% (Oxford 2, Cambridge 1)

- Grant-maintained
- Mixed comprehensive

- Pupils 1,263
- Boys (11–18) 666
- Girls (11–18) 597
- Sixth form 165 (13%)
- Education authority *Gloucestershire*

Headteacher John Law, 55, appointed in September 1982. Staff 77 (men 31, women 46).

Motto Non palma sine pulvere (No victory without hard work).

Background Formerly endowed by Katharine, wife of Thomas, Lord Berkeley in 1384; old school buildings built in 1726; moved to new buildings on current site in 1963; extensions in 1973 when school became comprehensive; second phase completed in 1975; became grant-maintained in September 1992. Over-subscribed, with 1.5 applications per place. Accommodation consists of eight main areas, including humanities building, technology area, science centre, sports hall and gymnasium. Staying-on rate for A-level is up to 50%: 'Many children of average ability are taking two or three A-levels and achieving much.' Language College status from 1996: French, German, Russian, Spanish, Japanese, Chinese, Italian and Latin offered; 20 pupils (9%) admitted on evidence of linguistic ability; Investors in People Award in January 1995.

Streaming Two bands in year 7, with some setting; setting in most subjects in years 8 to 11.

Approach to discipline Strict but fair. Emphasis on concepts of right and wrong. Strong views on drugs, bullying, and so on; much money spent on in-service training for staff on these subjects.'

Uniform Maroon blazer, white shirt, grey trousers/skirt, school tie. Very strictly enforced.

Homework Average 11-year-old, eight hours a week; 14-year-old, 10 hours; 16-year-old, 14 hours.

Vocational qualifications GNVQ; NVQ.

Inspection December 1993: 'This is a good school. Standards of work are generally good, sometimes very good.'; 'Pupils are mainly well-motivated and relationships are good. There are some areas of excellence, which include music, art and hockey. The quality of learning and teaching is high

and good attitudes to work ensure progress in all bands of ability. There is an unusually high degree of co-operation between pupils throughout the school and particularly so in the sixth-form.'; 'Behaviour of pupils is generally good, often excellent.'

Primary schools British Primary; Blue Coat CE Primary; Charfield Primary; Alexander Hosea Primary; Wickwar Primary; Hawkesbury Upton Primary.

BROOKFIELD COMMUNITY SCHOOL

Chatsworth Road
Chesterfield
Derbyshire S40 3NS
Tel (01246) 568115
Fax (01246) 566827

- National ranking 440 (–, 469, 477, –)
- GCSE 55%
- A-levels 34% (A/B); 88% (A/E)
- Higher education 72%

- Mixed comprehensive
- Pupils 1,158
- Boys (11–18) 574
- Girls (11–18) 584
- Sixth form 237 (20%)
- Education authority *Derbyshire*

Headteacher Liz Thomas, 54, appointed in April 1990. Staff 57 (men 30, women 27).

Motto *None*

Background Opened in 1991, with teachers joining from 11 different schools; housed on two sites, with catchment area covering most of southwest Chesterfield and extending into town centre. Over-subscribed, with about 1.3 applications per place. 'It is a school which celebrates excellence in all things. At Brookfield people matter and everyone in the school is valued. The school's pastoral structure and discipline are rooted in care, friendliness and good humour, and great stress is placed on the partnership between school and home.'

Streaming Two 'express' sets in science in each year-group in years 10 and 11; setting by ability in mathematics.

Approach to discipline Code of conduct displayed and discussed with students at start of school year. When high standards not met, counselling is followed by: extra work, detention with 24 hours' notice to parents, 'on report' system for daily monitoring, exclusion for serious misbehaviour that may be either permanent or temporary.

Uniform Girls: black/grey skirt, trousers or culottes, white/pale-grey/pale-blue school blouse, black/grey sweater or sweatshirt, school tie, black shoes. Boys: black/grey trousers, white/pale-grey/pale-blue shirt, black/grey sweater/sweatshirt, black shoes.

Homework Average 11-year-old, five hours a week; 14-year-old, seven hours; 16-year-old, 10 hours.

Vocational qualifications *None*

Inspection May 1994: 'This is a good school which has made significant advances from its formation in 1991 and has overcome many of the inherent problems associated with re-organisation. It is an orderly school with good relationships based on mutual respect of teachers and pupils. The school generally provides a good standard of education. Standards achieved by pupils are consistently good throughout the school.'; 'Pupils are well-motivated and dedicated staff set high professional standards.'

Primary schools Holymoorside Primary; Old Hall Junior; Whitecotes Primary; Brockwell Junior; Abercrombie Primary; Brampton Junior.

COOMBE DEAN

Charnhill Way
Elburton
Plymouth
Devon PL6 5AU
Tel (01752) 406961
Fax (01752) 482140

- National ranking 441 (486, 486, 371, –)
- GCSE 55% (50%)
- A-levels 29% (A/B); 91% (A/E)
- Higher education 73% (Oxford 1, Cambridge 1)

- Mixed comprehensive
- Pupils 892
- Boys (11–18) 440
- Girls (11–18) 452
- Sixth form 160 (18%)
- Education authority *Devon*

Headteacher Peter Reid, 51, appointed in 1988. Staff 49 (men 25, women 24).

Motto Achieving their full potential.

Background Opened in 1976 in new purpose-built buildings in Plymstock, suburb south-east of Plymouth; attracts pupils from all over the city as well as neighbouring villages in the South Hams. Every pupil studies two foreign languages in years 7 to 9; also creative arts option in years 10 and 11. Over-subscribed, with 1.2 applications per place. Purpose-built community sports hall; dual-use library. Business Centre funded by grant of £47,000 from Gleason Memorial Fund, an American charity, in 1991. Computer facilities 'second to none in the area'. Annual activities week, with pupils travelling to wide range of centres; includes water sports. Sporting success, particularly volleyball; members in England squad. Many representatives in city and county teams.

Streaming Setting is introduced from year 8 across most subjects.

Approach to discipline 'Governors, parents and pupils contribute to the school's code of conduct. A clear six-step procedure which involves parents means that discipline problems are rare.'

Uniform Royal-blue V-neck jumper with school crest, grey trousers/skirt, white shirt/blouse, school tie. Trainers, denim jackets and other variations are not allowed: 'The school's standard of dress is very high and parents are quickly involved if there is any variation.'

Homework Average 11-year-old, five hours a week; 14-year-old, seven hours 30 minutes; 16-year-old, 10 hours.

Vocational qualifications GNVQ Advanced, Health and Social Care, Business and Finance; about 30 NVQs through Tamar Valley Consortium.

Inspection February 1996; 'This is a good school, with many very good features. The school's reputation in the local community is justifiably high.'; 'The allocation of time to subjects is sufficient except for art, music and RE. The quality of learning is generally sound or better and improves from Key Stage 3 through to post-16. Pupils are usually enthusiastic and reponsive. Teachers are well-qualified, knowledgeable about their subject and most are suitably deployed.'; 'The headteacher and senior management team provide good leadership.'

Primary schools Wembury Primary; Goosewell Primary; Salisbury Road Primary; Hyde Park Primary; Montpelier Primary.

YATELEY SCHOOL

School Lane
Yateley
Hampshire GU46 6NW
Tel (01252) 879222
Fax (01252) 872517

- National ranking 442 (344, 302, 225, –)
- GCSE 55% (61%)
- A-levels 28% (A/B); 92% (A/E)
- Higher education 55% (Oxford 1, Cambridge 2)

- Mixed comprehensive
- Pupils 1,528
- Boys (11–18) 771
- Girls (11–18) 757
- Sixth form 256 (17%)
- Education authority *Hampshire*

Headteacher Dr Ian Goodall, 50, appointed in April 1988. Staff 100 (men 42, women 58).

Motto Nihil nisi verum (Nothing but the truth).

Background Founded in 1968 as the first purpose-built comprehensive school in Hampshire; Yateley is pleasant town bordering Hampshire countryside but within reach of west London, Reading, Camberley, and Farnham; modern buildings, well-maintained and well-equipped; landscaped 45-acre site. Over-subscribed, with average of 1.1 applications per place. Swimming pool, squash courts, fitness suite, tennis courts. Spanish, Latin and Classical civilisation taught to A-level; art and drama 'outstanding'. Duke of Edinburgh Award Scheme. Emphasis on discipline within caring environment: 'First priority is that pupils feel happy and secure so that they will achieve well academically. Pupils are expected to be courteous and helpful, and to develop as whole individuals by taking part in a wide range of extra-curricular and community service.'

Alumni Kerry Shacklock, Olympic swimmer; Christina Cahill, Olympic athlete.

Streaming Pupils put in sets according to ability in each subject from year 8.

Approach to discipline 'We take a firm line on discipline, but try to develop self-discipline. Pupils are occasionally expelled for serious misbehaviour.'

Uniform Navy sweater with embroidered school badge, grey trousers/navy skirt or trousers, white shirt/blouse, black shoes. Regulations enforced 'very strictly'. Casual dress allowed for sixth-formers.

Homework Average 11-year-old, eight hours a week; 14-year-old, 12 hours; 16-year-old, 15 hours.

Vocational qualifications Diploma of Vocational Education; GNVQ, Business, Leisure and Tourism, Health and Social Care.

Inspection March 1993: 'Standards of achievement are generally good, although in some areas able pupils could be challenged more effectively.'; 'Pupils respond well to teaching which is generally effective and often good.'; 'The school runs within a civilised working atmosphere which is reflected by the good relationships between the pupils and their teachers based on a clearly understood code of behaviour, and an appropriate tutorial and personal and social education programme.' November 1996: 'A highly-successful school which continually strives for improvement. Pupils are well-taught in a purposeful and orderly environment, and they achieve high standards.'; 'Pupils have an excellent attitude to learning and their response in lessons is one of the school's real strengths.'; 'Teaching is a particular strength of the school and makes a significant impact on pupils' attainment and progress.'; 'Teachers are committed, hard-working and conscientious.'

Primary schools Westfields Junior; Newlands Primary; Charles Kingsley CE Primary; St Peter's Junior.

CHOSEN HILL SCHOOL

Brookfield Road
Churchdown
Gloucester
Gloucestershire GL3 2PL
Tel (01452) 713488
Fax (01452) 714976
E-mail: chosen.hill@dialnet.co.uk

- National ranking 443 (419, 348, 276, –)
- GCSE 55% (56%)
- A-levels 26% (A/B); 89% (A/E)
- Higher education 95% (Oxford 2, Cambridge 1)

- Grant-maintained
- Mixed comprehensive
- Pupils 1,191
- Boys (11–18) 556
- Girls (11–18) 635
- Sixth form 189 (16%)
- Education authority *Gloucestershire*

Headteacher Alan Winwood, 55, appointed in September 1988. Staff 69 (men 30, women 39).

Motto *None*

Background In the village of Churchdown, midway between Cheltenham and Gloucester in semi-rural surroundings. Opened in 1960 as selective grammar-technical school; became comprehensive in 1970; grant-maintained since 1992. Wide range of 'excellent' modern facilities: large library, 10 science laboratories including four that opened in 1993, language laboratory, design and technology suite, two gymnasia, purpose-built music suite, art rooms and professional recording studio. Well-equipped hall for acclaimed concerts and drama productions; extensive computer network. Over-subscribed, with more than three applications per place. One week work-experience for year 10 and sixth-formers; also one day a week work-experience for one year of sixth-formers. Record 'second to none' in sport, drama and music; most recent production was *Cabaret* in March 1996; regional and national sporting representatives; drama productions throughout the year, with chance for all pupils to participate. Choirs, bands, orchestras and ensembles perform in school and local venues; annual concert in Gloucester Cathedral. Technology College status from September 1997.

Alumni Rod Thomas, Welsh footballer; Eleanor Rawling, former national president of Geographical Association.

Streaming Two equal-ability bands; ability setting in all subjects.

Approach to discipline Aim to provide secure, safe working environment based on respect and consideration for others and their property: 'When a pupil's behaviour does not conform to an acceptable standard a range of appropriate sanctions may be used, after consultation with parents. The school is highly regarded within the community for the excellent standard of pupil behaviour.'

Uniform Green blazer with school badge, white blouse/shirt, school tie, green skirt/ grey trousers. Sixth-formers: black blazer for boys, white shirt, sixth-form tie, grey trousers or grey/black skirt or culottes. 'Uniform is 100% throughout the school, including sixth-form.'

Homework Average 11-year-old, five hours a week; 14-year-old, seven hours; 16-year-old, 10 hours.

Vocational qualifications GNVQ Intermediate and Advanced, Business, Health and Social Care; Foreign Languages at Work, Background to Business; RSA; Keyboarding; Computer Literacy and Information Technology.

Inspection November 1995: 'A very good school.'; 'There are no subjects where standards are consistently less than satisfactory.'; 'High-quality special needs provision is making a significant contribution to the progress of less able pupils.'; 'These results are related to good quality teaching, high expectations of pupils and a general expectation that all pupils are capable of good achievement.'; 'The timetable and lesson length have recently been changed and some adjustments may be needed in the future to allow for more appropriate grouping of students by ability.'; 'Relations between pupils and staff are excellent; mutual respect is evident in classrooms and around the school and pupils are spontaneously helpful and considerate. Attendance is good and behaviour is excellent. There is a very positive feel to the school.'

Primary schools Churchdown Village Junior; Warden Hill Primary, Cheltenham; Dinglewell Junior; Longlevens Junior; Hillview Primary.

ALL SAINTS CHURCH OF ENGLAND SCHOOL

Sunnyside Road
Wyke Regis
Weymouth
Dorset DT4 9BJ
Tel (01305) 783391
Fax (01305) 785291

- National ranking 444= (428=, 494=, 455=, –)
- GCSE 55% (55%)
- A-levels *Not applicable*
- Higher education *Not applicable*

- Mixed comprehensive
- Pupils 807
- Boys (11–16) 399
- Girls (11–16) 408
- Sixth form *Not applicable*
- Education authority *Dorset*

Headteacher Timothy Peter Balmforth, 43, appointed in September 1997. Staff 44 (men 20, women 24).

Motto *None*

Background Founded in 1957 as a Church of England secondary school; became comprehensive in 1985 upon local re-organisation, when substantial building programme extended the original buildings; on pleasant site at Wyke Regis, two miles west of Weymouth. Over-subscribed, with 200 applications for 150 places. Third school in the country to achieve Investors in People standard. Orchestra, band, choir. Annual Shakespeare production. Duke of Edinburgh Award Scheme. ICL Centre of Excellence for Computing. 'All Saints seeks to provide a Christian environment within which pupils are encouraged to work to the full extent of their abilities. It is our aim that each child should feel valued as an individual with an important contribution to make to our community and that, in turn, each pupil will learn to value others.' Close links with Weymouth College for tertiary education; nine in 10 pupils continue education at 16.

Streaming Setting in most subjects from year 8; all-ability tutor-groups.

Approach to discipline 'Pupils are expected to behave with common sense, courtesy and decency at all times; to respect the rights of others and to treat school facilities with care and respect. Appropriate sanctions are used when the code of conduct is breached.'

Uniform Grey skirt/trousers, white blouse/shirt, school tie, wine V-neck sweater with school name, black/brown shoes. 'All pupils are expected to observe the regulations with regard to sensible school dress and personal appearance.'

Homework Average 11-year-old, five hours a week; 14-year-old, seven hours 30 minutes; 16-year-old, 10+ hours.

Vocational qualifications *None*

Inspection October 1996: 'A good school with some very good features, which include good attainment in external examinations, excellent relationships with its community, a very friendly and welcoming ethos and well-behaved, articulate pupils.'; 'Leadership is very purposeful and the school has successfully managed difficult changes in recent years.'; 'The school, with the support of the local education authority, has made provision for a wider range of special needs than in most schools and is developing ways to enable pupils with special educational needs to make progress.'; 'There are many contraints in the buildings, not least the narrow and twisting corridors and entranceways, but the school deals with them very well and has resigned itself to the non-availability of extra accommodation in the near future.'

Primary schools Wyke Regis CE Junior; Holy Trinity CE Junior; St Augustine's RC Primary; St Andrew's CE Primary.

HODGSON HIGH SCHOOL

Moorland Road
Poulton-le-Fylde
Blackpool
Lancashire FY6 7EU
Tel (01253) 882815
Fax (01253) 899971
E-mail: hodgson@rmplc.co.uk

- National ranking 444 = (401 = , 416 = , 414 = , 275 =)
- GCSE 55% (58%)
- A-levels *Not applicable*
- Higher education *Not applicable*

- Mixed comprehensive
- Pupils 1,010
- Boys (11–16) 514
- Girls (11–16) 496
- Sixth form *Not applicable*
- Education authority *Lancashire*

Headteacher Peter Simon Wood, 39, appointed in April 1997. Staff 55 (men 26, women 29).

Motto *None*

Background Serves towns of Poulton-le-Fylde, Thornton Cleveleys and surrounding Wyre villages. Opened in 1932, the school has been significantly extended; set in pleasant grounds with 'excellent' sporting facilities. Over-subscribed, with 1.2 applications per place. Technology College. Major building programme in 1996/7. Musical activities include two school bands, orchestra and choir; in sports, pupils regularly compete at county and national level. Numerous contacts with Europe, including exchanges with schools in Germany, France and Ukraine; eight different groups visited Europe in 1995/6. One in three pupils go on to higher education after sixth-form college; three to Oxford in 1993. National finalists: 1993 Nuclear Electric 'Science Challenge'; 1994 athletics cup; cross-country championships. British Aerospace link school. Investors in People accreditation.

Streaming Pupils placed in one of four ability sets in each subject; flexible system meaning a pupil can be in different level for different subjects. Regularly reviewed.

Approach to discipline 'Fairly traditional approach.' Misbehaviour punished through formal detention system. Parents involved at early stage when problems occur. Good work and behaviour rewarded. Responsibility encouraged through prefect system in year 11 in which vast majority voluntarily participate.

Uniform Royal-blue blazer, navy sweater, navy skirt/trousers, pale-blue/white shirt or blouse, school tie, blue/black/brown shoes. Fully enforced.

Homework Average 11-year-old, five hours a week; 14-year-old, seven hours 30 minutes; 16-year-old, 10 to 12 hours.

Vocational qualifications GNVQ Part One (from September 1996).

Inspection January 1995: 'A very successful and caring school where pupils of all abilities realise their potential within a stimulating, cultural ethos.'; 'The quality of education is high for pupils of all ages and abilities.'; 'Well-qualified and committed teachers have high expectations of all pupils and this, combined with generally good and often outstanding teaching, ensures progress in learning and positive pupil attitudes and motivation.'; 'The school is popular and in a period of growth.'; 'The headteacher provides thoughtful, skilful and supportive leadership.'; 'Good and often exemplary behaviour makes a significant contribution to the standards and the quality of pupils' learning.'

Primary schools Stanah Primary, Thornton Cleveleys; Breck Primary, Poulton-le-Fylde; Carleton Green Primary, Poulton-le-Fylde; Copp CE Primary, Great Eccleston; Manor Beach County Primary, Thornton Cleveleys.

SCALBY SCHOOL

Fieldstead Crescent
Newby
Scarborough
North Yorkshire YO12 6TH
Tel (01723) 362301
Fax (01723) 369226

- National ranking 444= (252=, 293=, 432=, −)
- GCSE 55% (67%)
- A-levels *Not applicable*
- Higher education *Not applicable*

- Mixed comprehensive
- Pupils 1,038
- Boys (11–16) 527
- Girls (11–16) 511
- Sixth form *Not applicable*
- Education authority *North Yorkshire*

Headteacher David Christopher Pynn, 49, appointed in September 1988. Staff 62 (men 32, women 30).

Motto Steadfast.

Background Situated to north of Scarborough with catchment area that includes 100 square miles of North York Moors; three in 10 pupils come from rural areas. Opened in 1942; became comprehensive in 1973; six-acre site, with buildings improved and extended several times. Eight science laboratories, modern technology suite, three art rooms, sports hall, gymnasium, learning resources centre, hall, dining hall, general classrooms. Over-subscribed, with 1.2 applications per place; more than eight in 10 pupils (83%) continue full-time education at 16. International reputation of music groups, including jazz orchestra; concert band has regularly performed at National Festival of Music for Youth and National Concert Band Festival; one in eight pupils (13%) learn musical instrument. In sport, the school has won national schools' badminton championship three times in four years, at different age-groups. Emphasis on special needs: pupils with learning difficulties and the very able; unit for hearing-impaired children; school adapted to meet needs of pupils with physical difficulties; also for visually-impaired children.

Alumni Colin Appleton, former Leicester City soccer player; Peter Brooke, puppet animator with Jim Henson, creator of The Muppets;

SOHAM VILLAGE COLLEGE 361

Christopher Bruce, Ballet Rambert director; Ralph Pixton, Hong Kong radio broadcaster; Toby Jepson, Bruce and Jim Dickinson in 'The Little Angels' rock group.

Streaming Pupils in sets for mathematics from year 7; in English, languages and science from year 8. Technology, performing arts and humanities are taught in randomised groups.

Approach to discipline 'Responsibility and high standards are encouraged at all times. Positive rewards are used extensively and clear guidelines are set down for behaviour and work. Close and open contacts with families are promoted.'

Uniform Boys: black blazer with school badge (oak leaves and acorns), charcoal-grey trousers, white shirt, petrol-blue tie with oak-leaf motif. Girls: black blazer with school badge, petrol-blue skirt and jersey, white shirt, tie. Very strictly enforced.

Homework Average 11-year-old, seven hours 30 minutes a week; 14-year-old, 11 hours; 16-year-old, 15 hours.

Vocational qualifications *None*

Inspection October 1995: 'A good, efficiently-run school. It has a substantial tradition of success. A strong positive ethos combined with a meticulous attention to detail contribute to the quality of education and attainments achieved.'; 'The quality of, in particular, music and sports extra-curricular activities is excellent and provides a well-established point of interaction between the school and the community.'; 'Pupils listen intelligently and intently. Many have a good grasp of number but its application across different subjects is limited. The use of information technology to raise standards is appropriate in English but there is substantial scope for expansion generally.'

Primary schools Newby Primary; Northstead Primary; Barrowcliff Junior; Lindhead Primary; St Martin's CE Primary.

SOHAM VILLAGE COLLEGE

Sand Street
Soham
Ely
Cambridgeshire CB7 5AA
Tel (01353) 720569
Fax (01353) 624854

- National ranking 444 = (382 =, 359 =)
- GCSE 55% (59%)
- A-levels *Not applicable*
- Higher education *Not applicable*

- Grant-maintained
- Mixed comprehensive
- Pupils 1,172
- Boys (11–16) 543
- Girls (11–16) 629
- Sixth form *Not applicable*
- Education authority *Cambridgeshire*

Headteacher Dr Alan Bullock, appointed in January 1985. Staff 69 (men 38, women 31).

Motto Non nobis sed omnibus (Not only for us, but for everyone).

Background Original village college built in 1958; amalgamated with boys' grammar school in 1972 to serve the communities in and around Soham. Buildings stand in extensive grounds 'with an arboretum ambience'. New science block, music suite and library resource centre in 1991. Well-resourced, with fibre-optic network throughout the campus. Became grant-maintained in 1993; became technology college in 1994. Over-subscribed, with 283 applications for 240 places. Eight in 10 pupils continue with education at 16. 'We seek to foster a climate within which every boy and girl can develop his or her talents to the fullest. At the same time, pupils become aware of the importance of community generally, where mutual respect between pupils and staff is shown, where initiative and originality can flourish, and where young people develop as individuals.'

Streaming Broad bands, with setting in subjects such as mathematics and modern languages.

Approach to discipline 'Fair but firm discipline. The key objective is to attain pupil self-discipline. A distinctive ethos of achieving excellence with care is a motivator in academic, sporting and all other activities. Punishments are rarely needed, but when they are they 'fit the pupil not the misdemeanour.'

Uniform Boys: blazer, grey trousers, year tie. Girls: blouse, jumper, skirt. The school colours are royal blue and grey. Fully enforced; grants available for those needing help.

Homework Average 11-year-old, seven hours

30 minutes a week; 14-year-old, 10 hours; 16-year-old, 10 hours.

Vocational qualifications GNVQ, Health and Social Care.

Inspection March 1997.

Primary schools Fordham CE Primary; Isleham CE Primary; Kennett Primary; St Andrew's CE Primary; Weatheralls County Primary.

SOUTH AXHOLME SCHOOL

Burnham Road
Epworth
Doncaster
South Yorkshire DN9 1BY
Tel (01427) 872121
Fax (01427) 875028

- National ranking 444= (411=, 520, 482=, −)
- GCSE 55% (57%)
- A-levels *Not applicable*
- Higher education *Not applicable*

- Mixed comprehensive
- Pupils 803
- Boys (11–16) 414
- Girls (11–16) 389
- Sixth form *Not applicable*
- Education authority *North Lincolnshire*

Headteacher Malcolm Dennis Toms, 47, appointed in September 1990. Staff 44 (men 24, women 20).

Motto To better things.

Background Established in 1961 in pleasant grounds and occupying quiet rural site close to centre of small town of Epworth on the A161 Goole to Gainsborough; open countryside backs onto school playing fields. Comprehensive range of facilities: well-stocked library, suite of music rooms, science laboratories, specially-adapted rooms for information technology, learning support suite, on-site dual-use leisure centre. School 'in excellent state of repair and is well-furnished'. Oversubscribed, with 194 applications for 172 places. French and German exchanges, skiing trips, educational visits to European cities; music and drama 'strong'; national finalists in Barclay's Youth Drama Awards, with one pupil winning top individual prize. School newspaper. Wide range of sport: reputation for cricket, and track and field athletics.

Streaming Pupils are placed in sets by ability for mathematics in year 7; setting is then introduced in languages in year 8 and science and English in year 9.

Approach to discipline 'Low-key and unobtrusive, but very firm. There are clear sanctions which are applied consistently. Our philosophy is to anticipate problems and hence defuse them before they become serious.'

Uniform Black V-neck jumper/cardigan, black trousers/skirt, white shirt/blouse, school tie, black/grey/white socks or black tights, black shoes; distinctive tie for year 11 pupils. Very strictly enforced.

Homework Average 11-year-old, five hours a week; 14-year-old, six hours; 16-year-old, eight hours.

Vocational qualifications RSA, Information Studies.

Primary schools Epworth Primary; Wroot Travis Charity Primary; Belton CE Primary; West Butterwick CE Primary; Westwoodside CE Primary; Haxey CE Primary; Misterton Primary; St Martin's CE Primary; Walkeringham Primary.

ST MICHAEL'S CHURCH OF ENGLAND HIGH SCHOOL

Astley Road
Chorley
Lancashire PR7 1RS
Tel (01257) 264740
Fax (01257) 230177

- National ranking 444= (354=, 448=, 355=, −)
- GCSE 55% (61%)
- A-levels *Not applicable*
- Higher education *Not applicable*

- Mixed comprehensive
- Pupils 1,045
- Boys (11–16) 514
- Girls (11–16) 531
- Sixth form *Not applicable*
- Education authority *Lancashire*

Headteacher Robert H. Hardwick, 52, appointed in September 1991. Staff 57 (men 22, women 35).

Motto Therefore Choose . . . (Deuteronomy 30).

Background Opened in 1964 and re-organised in 1972 to take six forms of entry covering whole ability range; admits 208 pupils annually, mix of rural and urban children. Buildings in well-maintained grounds in residential area: three computer suites, sports hall, gymnasium, seven science laboratories, music suite, range of design and technology rooms, fine library. Significant development of hall, dining room, science and technology areas in 1993. Over-subscribed, with 240 applications for 208 places. Music and drama 'very strong', with regular productions involving very large numbers of pupils; many choirs, orchestras and wind bands. Tradition of outdoor education; residential week for all year 9 pupils. Learning support for the very able as well as those with difficulties; strong pastoral care system. 'The value of every individual in the sight of God is kept in mind in all the school's work. Visitors frequently comment on the warmth of relationships and the purposeful, friendly atmosphere of the school.' Schools Curriculum Award 1997.

Streaming Setting by ability in most subjects: 'A pupil's progress in one subject is not restricted because of his or her ability in another.'

Approach to discipline 'The school's motto indicates a key aim of the school, which is to develop personal autonomy in young people based on Christian values and on mutual respect. A code of conduct has been re-negotiated in 1994, involving children through Forum (pupil council), which makes those values and expectations explicit. The school takes firm action against anyone who threatens the learning, safety, security or happiness of other pupils.'

Uniform Maroon jumper with school emblem, white shirt, grey skirt/trousers, black shoes. Years 10 and 11 wear black jumpers. 'Regulations produced after major consultation two years ago. Vigorously upheld, although with care and concern for any parent or pupil in difficult circumstances.'

Homework Average 11-year-old, five hours a week; 14-year-old, seven hours 30 minutes; 16-year-old, 10 hours.

Vocational qualifications GNVQ.

Inspection January 1996: 'This is a successful school which achieves high standards for all its pupils in a supportive and stimulating learning environment.'; 'The school has a well-defined ethos, enjoys strong leadership and has a committed and dedicated staff. Its reputation in the local community is justifiably high.'; 'There is a strong sense of corporate identity and a shared ethos which contributes to the quality of education provided by the school.'; 'The headteacher provides strong leadership and a clear strategic vision for the school.'; 'The school is an orderly community in which relationships are characterised by mutual respect, tolerance and good humour.'

Primary schools St Laurence's CE Primary, Chorley; St Peter's CE Primary, Chorley; Whittle St John CE Primary; Clayton Back Lane CE Primary, Clayton Le Woods.

GUISELEY SCHOOL

Fieldhead Road
Guiseley
West Yorkshire LS20 8DT
Tel (01943) 872315
Fax (01943) 872287
E-mail: guiseley_school_ed@msn.com

- National ranking 450 (275, 319, 423, –)
- GCSE 54% (65%)
- A-levels 49% (A/B); 85% (A/E)
- Higher education 67% (Oxford 1, Cambridge 3)

- Mixed comprehensive
- Pupils 1,132
- Boys (11–18) 594
- Girls (11–18) 538
- Sixth form 192 (17%)
- Education authority *Leeds*

Headteacher Tony Thornley, 49, appointed in 1989. Staff 72 (men 33, women 39).

Motto In giving we receive.

Background School origins in early 19th century; transferred to current site in 1963; intake is 'genuinely comprehensive', with more than average proportion of able pupils because relatively few use independent sector. Over-subscribed, with 1.2 applications per place. New wing: purpose-built drama area, two business studies rooms, six mathematics rooms, food and fabrics suite. Proud of high standard of extra-curricular activities: music, drama, sport, outdoor activities. Links with a French lycée and German gymnasium, through which exchanges arranged. In technology, winners of Careers Industries Training Board competition; past finalists of Young Business Award. 'The school achieves excellent academic results within a caring and supportive framework.' Technology College from September 1996; technology department students won section of 1996 'Odyssey of the Mind' national design competition. Named in 1996 Ofsted list of 'good and improving' schools.

Alumni Neil Metcalfe, Commonwealth Games bronze-medallist.

Streaming Pupils are put in sets in all subjects according to ability from year 8.

Approach to discipline 'Pupils learn by the ethos set both within and outside the classroom. We take a firm and consistent line, are reasonable, have a sense of humour, are fair, and above all make it clear to pupils that we believe they matter as individuals.'

Uniform Girls: white blouse, navy skirt/trousers, school tie, navy V-neck pullover/cardigan, dark socks, dark shoes. Boys: white shirt, dark-grey trousers, school tie, navy V-neck pullover/cardigan, dark socks, dark shoes. Sixth-formers have freedom to choose clothing provided it is 'neat and appropriate'. 'Very strictly enforced.'

Homework Average 11-year-old, four to five hours a week; 14-year-old, six to eight hours; 16-year-old, 15 + hours.

Vocational qualifications GNVQ Foundation, Intermediate and Advanced, Health and Social Care, Business, Leisure.

Inspection December 1994: 'A good school with outstanding features of particular merit.'; 'At all levels of the school, pupils benefit from teaching which is of a high standard; nearly all lessons are taught by specialist subject teachers and skilful selection of both content and method indicates a high degree of teacher expertise.'; 'Attendance and punctuality are very good. Pupils cooperate willingly and are generally well-behaved. They are supportive of each other and nearly all subscribe to the community values promoted by the school.'

Primary schools Tranmere Park Primary; St Oswald's CE Primary; Manston Primary; Hawkesworth CE Primary; Queensway Primary.

SEAFORD HEAD COMMUNITY COLLEGE

Arundel Road
Seaford
East Sussex BN25 4LX
Tel (01323) 891623
Fax (01323) 492576
E-mail: seahorse@rmplc.co.uk
Internet: http://www.rmplc.co.uk/eduweb/sites/seahorse/index.html

- National ranking 451 (505, 499, 427, –)
- GCSE 54% (47%)
- A-levels 48% (A/B); 86% (A/E)
- Higher education 80%

- Mixed comprehensive
- Pupils 1,274
- Boys (11–18) 635
- Girls (11–18) 639
- Sixth form 197 (15%)
- Education authority *East Sussex*

Headteacher Robin Precey, 47, appointed in January 1992. Staff 83 (men 36, women 47).

Motto Success for all.

Background Comprehensive for 25 years; became community college responsible for adult education and youth service in May 1993. Lower school is 200 yards from the sea at foot of Seaford Head; new music and technology suites in 1995; new extension planned for September 1999. Upper school is 800 yards away on attractive campus with some buildings, including a library, opened only recently. Over-subscribed, with 268 applications for 210 places. Indoor swimming pool; 'state-of-the-art' information technology; special facility for dyslexic children of high ability; 'broad, balanced curriculum with high levels of achievement'.

Streaming Mainly mixed-ability in years 7 and 8, with setting introduced gradually in the upper school.

Approach to discipline Clear conduct code based on courtesy, consideration and common sense: 'Discipline is firm but fair, with an emphasis on students achieving self-discipline in the senior part of the upper school.'

Uniform Black college sweatshirt, tie, white shirt, grey or black trousers/skirt/culottes. No uniform in sixth form. Very strictly enforced, 'but personal circumstances taken into account'.

Homework Average 11-year-old, five hours a week; 14-year-old, eight hours; 16-year-old, 10+ hours.

Vocational qualifications NVQ and GNVQ, Care, Business and Administration.

Inspection November 1993: 'Pupils attending the college are receiving a sound education.'; 'Good standards are achieved in classwork and homework in all subjects. Pupils are working at or beyond the levels which could be expected by their abilities at intake. High expectation and high achievement are characteristics of the college.'; 'The college is providing good-quality education in all subjects.'

Primary schools Seaford County Primary; Chyngton Primary; Alfriston Primary; Annecy RC Primary; Cradle Hill County Primary.

ALL SAINTS' ROMAN CATHOLIC SCHOOL

Mill Mount Lane
York
North Yorkshire YO2 3UE
Tel (01904) 647877
Fax (01904) 647877
E-mail: c686@ielnet.es.ur

- National ranking 452 (503, 322, 372, –)
- GCSE 52% (47%)
- A-levels 39% (A/B); 90% (A/E)
- Higher education 85%

- Mixed comprehensive
- Pupils 1,009
- Boys (11–18) 471
- Girls (11–18) 538
- Sixth form 148 (15%)
- Education authority York

Headteacher Dr Adrian Elliott, 53, appointed in September 1985. Staff 63 (men 28, women 35).

Motto *None*

Background Founded in 1985 following amalgamation of three Catholic schools, one of which was the oldest girls' school in the country; on two sites about 300 yards apart in attractive buildings in middle of city; separate playing fields about a mile away. Over-subscribed, with 1.3 applications per place. Three languages taught to A-level:

French, German and Spanish; Latin taught to GCSE; no pupil has failed A-level Theology since the school opened. Duke of Edinburgh Award Scheme. School soccer teams won two out of four local leagues, came second in other two, finalists in two cups in 1993/4. 'Very wide social intake': pupils travelling up to 25 miles to and from school, from Ampleforth, Maltby, Thirsk, Tadcaster, Pocklington.

Streaming Pupils put in sets in mathematics from Christmas in year 7; from year 8, in sets for all subjects.

Approach to discipline 'We place great emphasis on reward through merit and records of achievement. Sanctions are used, particularly detention, contact with parents and exclusion.'

Uniform Dark trousers or dark-blue skirt, blue pullover/cardigan, white/blue shirt or blouse, school tie. Regulations enforced 'strictly but with common sense and sensitivity.'

Homework Average 11-year-old, five hours a week; 14-year-old, seven hours 30 minutes; 16-year-old, 15 hours.

Vocational qualifications GNVQ; City and Guilds.

Inspection October 1994: 'A very good school in which the outcomes successfully fulfil the aims of its mission statement. Pupils and teachers work hard in an atmosphere founded upon mutual respect and cooperation. The ethos, which is firmly rooted in the principles of the Catholic faith, is challenging as well as supportive and caring.'; 'The standards of achievement of pupils with special educational needs are excellent.'; 'The quality of learning is excellent and pupils demonstrate high levels of motivation, concentration and enthusiasm.'

Primary schools St Aelred's RC Primary; English Martyrs' RC Primary; St George's RC Primary; Our Lady's RC Primary; St Wilfrid's RC Primary.

KNUTSFORD HIGH SCHOOL

Bexton Road
Knutsford
Cheshire WA16 0EA
Tel (01565) 633294/632277
Fax (01565) 633796
E-mail: 9064163.depot@dialnet.co.uk

- National ranking 453 (442, 396)
- GCSE 54% (54%)
- A-levels 37% (A/B); 90% (A/E)
- Higher education 91% (Oxford 1, Cambridge 1)

- Mixed comprehensive
- Pupils 1,435
- Boys (11–18) 713
- Girls (11–18) 722
- Sixth form 266 (19%)
- Education authority *Cheshire*

Headteacher Kevin Hollins, 42, appointed in March 1997. Staff 93 (men 38, women 55).

Motto *None*

Background Formed in 1973; lower school (years 7 and 8) and upper school (years 9 to 13) quarter of a mile apart, joined by link path. Rural setting with extensive grounds on the edge of Knutsford. 'Excellent' accommodation, including extensive science provision, European language laboratory, purpose-built art, design and technology area, joint-use sports complex with swimming pool, sports hall, floodlit Astroturf pitch. Purpose-built sixth-form centre with new study and social areas. New information technology suites in both main buildings. All years have their own social areas. Oversubscribed, with 410 applications for 240 places; many pupils attracted from outside catchment area. Broad and balanced curriculum; thrice-winner of Schools Curriculum Award. Outstanding sporting achievements: county champions in every age group in one of the major sports in 1994 and 1995. Strong music and dance tradition, with reputation for quality of art. 'A happy as well as successful school where all are encouraged to develop themselves fully whilst always showing respect and consideration for everyone else in the school and wider community.' Supportive parents. Investor in People Award in 1997.

Streaming Pupils taught in mixed-ability groups in year 7; in sets for mathematics and modern languages from year 8; in other subjects, from year 9 or 10.

Approach to discipline 'The school implements a policy of assertive discipline, where good behaviour is rewarded but where clear and universal sanctions are applied for any inappropriate behaviour.'

Uniform Boys: blue shirt, dark-grey trousers, blue jumper, tie, dark shoes. Girls: blue blouse, skirt, jumper, tie, dark shoes. Strictly applied.

Homework Average 11-year-old, five hours a week; 14-year-old, seven hours 30 minutes; 16-year-old, 10 hours.

Vocational qualifications GNVQ Intermediate, Business, Leisure and Tourism, Hospitality and Catering; GNVQ Advanced, Business, Art and Design.

Inspection March 1996. 'The school provides a good standard of education within a caring environment. Pupils of all abilities achieve well, they enjoy attending school, obtaining good examination results and develop into responsible adults. The split-site causes some loss of efficiency, but overall the school provides good value for money.'; 'Work of a consistently high standard is evident in technology, art, physical education and performing arts.'; 'The quality of learning and teaching throughout the school is predominantly sound or good in approximately equal proportions. A significant proportion of lessons contain outstanding features.'; 'The headteacher and other staff in positions of responsibility provide the school with effective leadership and manage the day-to-day running of the school well.'; 'A significant loss of teaching time arises from the movement of teaching staff and pupils between sites and from the limited range of accommodation on each of the two sites.'; 'Pupils are generally happy and purposefully engaged at school and this is reflected in their levels of attendance.'

Primary schools Bexton Primary; Egerton Primary; Manor Park Primary; Mobberley CE Primary; Stamford Park Primary.

HELE'S SCHOOL

Seymour Road
Plympton
Plymouth
Devon PL7 4LT
Tel (01752) 337193
Fax (01752) 331460

- National ranking 454 (420, 333, 478, –)
- GCSE 54% (56%)
- A-levels 35% (A/B); 96% (A/E)
- Higher education 88% (Oxford 1, Cambridge 1)

- Mixed comprehensive
- Pupils 1,300
- Boys (11–18) 658
- Girls (11–18) 642
- Sixth form 250 (19%)
- Education authority *Devon*

Headteacher Michael Uglow, 50, appointed in January 1994. Staff 77 (men 39, women 38).

Motto *None*

Background Founded in 1658 and endowed by Sergeant Maynard and Elize Stert, surviving trustees of Elize Hele; Old Grammar School building in Plympton St Maurice completed in 1671; recognised as co-educational Devon county grammar in 1921; moved in 1937 to current site on north-eastern edge of Plymouth and close to fringes of Dartmoor. New extensions in 1970, with further building completed in 1983; became comprehensive in 1983 and adopted current name. Over-subscribed, with 245 applications for 211 places. Almost all pupils take nine GCSEs; £500,000 building project, including sixth-form centre, completed in 1995; music practice rooms in 1996. Combined Cadet Force; Duke of Edinburgh Award Scheme.

Alumni Sir Joshua Reynolds, painter and first president of the Royal Academy; James Northcote, artist; Benjamin Haydon, artist; Sir Charles Eastlake, first director of National Gallery; Paul Rogers, actor; Jane Drabble, assistant managing director BBC Network Television; Baroness Hallis of Heigham, opposition front-bench spokesperson on social security, local government and housing.

Streaming Year 7, mixed-ability; year 8, mixed-ability except modern languages, where the most able take second foreign language; year 9, setting in mathematics, science languages; years 10 and 11, setting in all subjects either by ability or option choice.

Approach to discipline Clear code of conduct; a positive system is emphasised for rewarding students: 'Rules are simple, defensible and manageable. They are reinforced when necessary by a clearly-understood and agreed system of sanctions aimed at maintaining good personal relationships and valuing people.'

Uniform Black blazer with gold-coloured braid and badge, charcoal-grey trousers/black skirt, white/grey/cream shirt or white blouse, school tie, grey/black V-neck pullover for boys or navy for girls.

Homework Average 11-year-old, five hours a week; 14-year-old, six to seven hours; 16-year-old, 10 hours.

Vocational qualifications Extensive range of post-16 NVQs; GNVQ Advanced, Business Studies, Leisure and Tourism; GNVQ Intermediate, Health and Social Care.

Inspection January 1994: 'Hele's is a good school. Of the lessons seen, some 91% were judged to be satisfactory or better.'; 'Competence in reading, writing, speaking and listening, and numeracy were all judged to be generally satisfactory. Pupils, however, should be given more opportunity to think and speak for themselves. Pupils are well-motivated to learn, although a greater use of differentiated materials would be beneficial to learning.'; 'The school has a well-ordered, disciplined and harmonious atmosphere. There are clear codes of conduct and relationships are respectful. Pupils co-operate well within the school community and they are given opportunities to exercise some responsibility.'

Primary schools Boringdon Primary; Old Priory Junior; Woodford Junior; Glen Park Primary; Chaddlewood Junior.

WYMONDHAM HIGH SCHOOL

Folly Road
Wymondham
Norfolk NR18 0NT
Tel (01953) 602078
Fax (01953) 605518

- National ranking 455 (341, 342, 318=, 295=)
- GCSE 54% (61%)
- A-levels 34% (A/B); 88% (A/E)
- Higher education 82% (Cambridge 3)

- Mixed comprehensive
- Pupils 907
- Boys (11–18) 466
- Girls (11–18) 441
- Sixth form 99 (11%)
- Education authority *Norfolk*

Headteacher David Robert Walker, 52, appointed in May 1989. Staff 59 (men 32, women 27).

Motto *None*

Background The school, which has occupied current 20-acre site since 1939, has evolved alongside Wymondham, a thriving market town (population: 11,000) whose abbey towers can be seen from the A11; Norwich is 10 miles to the east. Over-subscribed, with three applications for every two places. Recent developments include a sixth-form wing (sixth form launched in September 1992, first A-level results in 1994); up to eight in 10 pupils (80%) continue their education after 16; sixth form currently targeted at those wishing to take at least three A-levels and intending to continue into higher education. High-technology music suite and practice rooms; specialist library and resource centre; £1.4m sports centre with five badminton courts, squash courts, rock-climbing facilities and all-weather floodlit area; work begun on six-lane competition-size swimming pool; two dedicated computer rooms and three new science laboratories. Intake is cross-section from rural or semi-rural areas and dormitory suburbs. All parents and pupils interviewed before joining the school. School runs weekly 'helplines' so that pupils can receive further guidance and help with self-study. Each house has a local patron; strong commitment to charity fund-raising and community service; additional transport arrangements to enable all students to enjoy extra-curricular activities. Regular exchanges to France and Germany; expedition to Switzerland each summer. 'Visitors to the school comment on the calm and quiet atmosphere which exists within the buildings. While walking round they comment on how tasks are being entered into in a business-like fashion with enthusiasm and purpose.'

Streaming Pupils timetabled into departments in half-year groups (of about 100 pupils). Each department sets pupils according to ability in particular subject. Continually reviewed throughout year.

Approach to discipline Direct and easily understood. Strong house system; traditional values retained. 'High standards of behaviour and conduct are expected.'

Uniform Navy blazer with badge, navy skirt/grey trousers, pale-blue shirt, school tie. Requirements 'rigorously maintained'.

Homework Average 11-year-old, five hours a week; 14-year-old, five to 10 hours; 16-year-old, 10 hours.

Vocational qualifications *None*

Primary schools Morley CE Primary; Wicklewood Primary; Hingham County Primary; Barnham Broom CE Primary; Barford County Primary; Spooner Row County Primary; Robert Kett Middle; Mulbarton Middle.

ST MARY REDCLIFFE AND TEMPLE SCHOOL

Somerset Square
Bristol BS1 6RT
Tel **(0117) 929 3931**
Fax **(0117) 925 0347**

- National ranking 456 (361, 447)
- GCSE 54% (60%)
- A-levels 30% (A/B); 90% (A/E)
- Higher education 80%

- Mixed comprehensive
- Pupils 1,100
- Boys (11–18) 545
- Girls (11–18) 555
- Sixth form 200 (18%)
- Education authority *Bristol*

Headteacher David McGregor, 50, appointed from September 1996. Staff 66 (men 33, women 33).

Motto Steadfast in faith.

Background Current school established in 1966 on amalgamation of St Mary Redcliffe Boys' School (founded in 1571) and Temple Colston Girls' School (founded in 1709). Single city-centre site, with playing fields on the outskirts of Bristol. Attracts pupils from four counties around Bristol within a 25-mile radius; pupils from more than 80 primary schools; selection almost entirely on the grounds of church connection. Over-subscribed, with two applications per place. Long rugby tradition, resulting in 21 England caps. Departments picked out for special praise by school inspectors: science, modern languages and religious education. Indoor heated swimming pool. Nearly nine in 10 (87%) of pupils go on to sixth form at the school or education elsewhere. 'Caring, purposeful with underlying Christian philosophy. Each child is valued in his or her own right and school seeks to develop skills, interests, knowledge and abilities to the maximum extent.'

Streaming Initially in mixed-ability groups; setting according to ability in most subjects in years 7 and 8. Each year-group is divided into two half-year bands which are further sub-divided within subjects.

Approach to discipline 'Friendly but firm. The school is conscious of its reputation for good discipline. It is clearly necessary in a large school on a small site in the centre of a busy city.'

Uniform Boys: black blazer with badge and tie. Girls: white blouse, grey skirt/black trousers. Regulations enforced 'quite strictly'.

Homework Average 11-year-old, five to seven hours 30 minutes a week; 14-year-old, seven hours 30 minutes to 10 hours; 16-year-old, .10 to 15 hours.

Vocational qualifications GNVQ Intermediate and Advanced, Business, Leisure and Tourism, Art and Design.

Inspection May 1994: 'A good school and effective in most respects. Notable features are the caring attitudes which are fostered and sustained.'; 'Nevertheless there is some academic potential which is not fully realised, particularly by boys. Some individual pupils achieve well in sport at county and occasionally national level.'; 'Learning is satisfactory or better in the majority of lessons and pupils are mainly responsive to the teaching.'; 'The majority of teaching is carried out by qualified specialists and the quality of specialist knowledge is usually satisfactory or better.'; 'It is a caring Christian community in which pupils display a noticeable sense of spiritual and moral awareness which is reflected in considerate attitudes to one another.'

Primary schools Westbury-on-Trym CE Primary; Henleaze Junior; St Mary Redcliffe CE Primary; Knowle Junior; Horfield CE Primary.

ST BERNARD'S HIGH SCHOOL

Milton Road
Westcliff-on-Sea
Essex SS0 7JS
Tel (01702) 343583
Fax (01702) 390201

- National ranking 457 (458, 277, –, 331 =)
- GCSE 54% (53%)
- A-levels 18% (A/B); 79% (A/E)

- Higher education 57%

- Grant-maintained
- Girls' comprehensive
- Pupils 733
- Boys (16–18) 16
- Girls (11–18) 717
- Sixth form 100 (14%)
- Education authority *Essex*

Headteacher Victoria Squirrell, 44, appointed in September 1995. Staff 43 (men 17, women 26).

Motto Dieu mon abri (The Lord is my shelter).

Background Founded by Bernardine Cistercian Sisters in 1910; became voluntary-aided after 1944 Education Act; ceased being a convent in 1983, but traditional emphasis on Catholic values maintained. Set on small site in residential area near sea front; buildings are a mixture of traditional and early 19th century, to which additions have been made. New wing housing resource area and second computer room was built in 1971. Over-subscribed, with two applications per place. Broad curriculum, with most pupils taking 10 GCSEs (including religious education); 'open' sixth form; school prides itself on musical and stage productions; full participation in local and national sports encouraged.

Alumni Anne Stallybrass, actress; Gemma Craven, actress; Helen Mirren, actress.

Streaming Mixed-ability groups in year 7 followed by setting by ability in modern languages, mathematics and science.

Approach to discipline 'Self-discipline is aimed for. A short code of conduct is in place. Emphasis is laid on high expectations based on gospel values. Where pupils repeatedly fall short of these expectations, sanctions are imposed. Positive encouragement for good work and behaviour in the Merit Award Scheme. Parental involvement is an underlying principle.'

Uniform Navy skirt, navy pullover with logo, blue/white check blouse. Dress code for sixth-formers. 'Strict adherence insisted upon.'

Homework Average 11-year-old, five hours a week; 14-year-old, seven hours 30 minutes; 16-year-old, 10 hours.

Vocational qualifications GNVQ Intermediate,

Business, Leisure and Tourism, Health and Social Care; Cambridge Modular Information Technology course.

Primary schools St Helen's RC Primary; St George's RC Primary, Shoeburyness; Sacred Heart RC Primary, Southend; Our Lady of Lourdes RC Primary, Leigh-on-Sea; St Teresa's RC Primary, Rochford; St Joseph's RC Primary, Canvey Island; Holy Family RC Primary, Benfleet; Our Lady of Ransom RC Primary, Rayleigh.

PENSBY HIGH SCHOOL FOR GIRLS

Irby Road
Heswall
Wirral
Merseyside L61 6XN
Tel (0151) 648 1941/5684
Fax (0151) 648 8103

- National ranking 458 (459, 501, 413, –)
- GCSE 54% (53%)
- A-levels 15% (A/B); 88% (A/E)
- Higher education 88%

- Girls' secondary modern
- Pupils 845
- Boys *Not applicable*
- Girls (11–18) 845
- Sixth form 122 (14%)
- Education authority *Wirral*

Headteacher Stephen Hyden, 46, appointed in January 1992. Staff 48 (men 9, women 39).

Motto Live to learn; learn to live.

Background Opened in 1953; well-maintained building in rural setting, with open fields behind. Over-subscribed, with two applications per place. Facilities include extensive playing fields, gymnasium, dance/drama studio, music suite, language laboratory, six science laboratories, art and pottery rooms, computerised library. 'Excellent' sporting achievements, with girls regularly representing area and district; volleyball players have reached national standard. Reputation for expressive and performing arts; pupils have reached finals in national science competitions. 'Pensby High School for Girls is a modern, forward-looking school that also believes firmly in the traditional values of hard work, good manners and self-discipline. It provides a blend of the very best in traditional education, sound teaching, high standards of courtesy, regular homework, and has a well-qualified, experienced staff who provide a caring, structured environment for every child's development.'

Streaming Pupils are put in sets in mathematics in the first term of year 7; different subject sets as pupils get older.

Approach to discipline 'School rules are rigorously applied, but praise and achievement are highlighted.'

Uniform Navy blazer, navy jumper, white shirt, navy skirt, school tie, white socks, black shoes. Very strictly enforced.

Homework Average 11-year-old, four hours a week; 14-year-old, eight hours; 16-year-old, 10 hours.

Vocational qualifications GNVQ Intermediate, Science, Hospitality and Catering; GNVQ Intermediate and Advanced, Health and Social Care, Business, Information Technology, Leisure and Tourism.

Inspection October 1995: 'The school succeeds in its aim of promoting the intellectual, moral, social and physical developments of all pupils. It provides a calm working environment in which girls learn effectively, with enthusiasm and a commitment to their studies. All pupils receive a very good education. Some outstanding work was seen in classes across a number of subjects. The school's high reputation with parents is well deserved.'; 'Pupils enjoy coming to school and this is encouraged by the strong support provided by parents.'

Primary schools Heswall County Primary; Pensby County Primary; Greasby Junior; St Peter's CE Primary; Pensby Park County Primary; Thingwall County Primary; Black Horse Hill County Primary; Dawpool CE Primary; Gayton County Primary.

ARCHBISHOP BLANCH SCHOOL

Mount Vernon Road
Liverpool L7 3EA
Tel (0151) 709 1452
Fax (0151) 709 2940
E-mail: archblan@liv.ac.uk

- National ranking 459 (443, 430)
- GCSE 54% (54%)
- A-levels 15% (A/B); 86% (A/E)
- Higher education 61%

- Girls' comprehensive
- Pupils 855
- Boys (16–18) 10
- Girls (11–18) 845
- Sixth form 155 (18%)
- Education authority *Liverpool*

Headteacher Kathleen Anne Zimak, 54, appointed in April 1987. Staff 51 (men 11, women 40).

Motto *None*

Background City-centre location on elevated site overlooking the Anglican and Catholic cathedrals and the Liver Building. Formed in 1981 from two smaller, well-established schools with sound reputations: Liverpool Girls' College and St Edmund's. Recently-constructed buildings on one site 'with developing facilities catering more than adequately for the whole curriculum': 'excellent' sports facilities and craft, design technology workshop. Over-subscribed, with three applications per place. Large sports hall. Music: choir appearing at Eisteddfod to represent England. Young Enterprise winners. Merseyside hockey and netball champions. Winners of several national art competitions. 'This is a Church of England foundation, believing in a caring, supporting atmosphere in which students are encouraged to excel in an appropriate skill or talent. We encourage the contribution which all faiths can make.'

Alumni Diane Allahgreen, junior Olympic athletics champion; Caroline Smith, cross-Channel swimmer.

Streaming Setting in year 8 in mathematics, languages and science.

Approach to discipline 'Students are encouraged to take responsibility for their own actions and infringement of agreed rules is dealt with fairly.'

Uniform Years 7 to 11: Navy skirt, light-blue shirt, navy tie with purple-and-gold stripes, navy pullover, navy blazer and badge. Years 12 and 13: grey skirt, lilac shirt, black jacket. Strictly enforced.

Homework Average 11-year-old, 11 hours 30 minutes a week; 14-year-old, 14 hours; 16-year-old, 15+ hours.

Vocational qualifications GNVQ, Business Studies; RSA and Pitman, secretarial qualifications; Youth Award Scheme.

Inspection September 1994: 'A good school which provides a high quality of education for its pupils.'; 'Pupils' skills of reading, writing and listening are generally good. They are able to express themselves clearly, but need to develop greater confidence in speaking. Pupils' skills of numeracy are sound, but further opportunities are needed to develop numeracy in subjects other than mathematics. The provision of resources is inadequate and restricts the quality of pupils' learning. In particular, the number of computers is unsatisfactory, and therefore the skills and use of information technology across the curriculum are adversely affected.'; 'Pupils' attitude to learning is a major strength in the school and the quality of learning is good. Pupils approach their work with interest and enthusiasm and are keen to succeed. Relationships are good and pupils work co-operatively and productively, making effective progress in most lessons.'; 'The quality of teaching is generally sound or good.'; 'The school is an orderly and caring environment. It is a strong Christian community which provides a positive framework for the development of good relationships and behaviour.'

Primary schools Mosspits Primary; Booker Avenue Junior; Blackmoor Park Junior; Gilmour County Primary; West Derby CE Primary.

CARDINAL ALLEN ROMAN CATHOLIC HIGH SCHOOL

Melbourne Avenue
Fleetwood
Lancashire FY7 8AY
Tel (01253) 872659
Fax (01253) 772143

- National ranking 460= (411=, 471=, 432=, 337=)
- GCSE 54% (57%)
- A-levels *Not applicable*
- Higher education *Not applicable*

- Mixed comprehensive
- Pupils 799
- Boys (11–16) 401
- Girls (11–16) 398
- Sixth form *Not applicable*
- Education authority *Lancashire*

Headteacher John O'Brien, 53, appointed in

May 1982. Staff 44 (men 14, women 30).

Motto *None*

Background Opened in 1963 and named after Cardinal William Allen, who had local associations; founded to serve families and parishes of North Fylde in Diocese of Lancaster. Voluntary-aided; Christian ethos; over-subscribed, with 190 applications for 150 places. More than three in four school-leavers (77%) continue their education after 16. Clubs and societies: school choirs, instrumental tuition, foreign language clubs, chess, drama, gymnastics, badminton, library, theatre visits, foreign travel, computers.

Streaming Separate sets in English and mathematics in year 7; other subjects follow. Progress reviewed in years 7 to 9.

Approach to discipline Special responsibility of year-tutors and form-teachers. 'Pupils are expected to achieve high standards of courtesy and behaviour both in school, and travelling to and from school.' Punishments: sanctions or loss of privileges; extra written work, 'on report', or detention.

Uniform Black blazer with badge, dark-grey trousers/royal-blue skirt, grey/pale-blue/white shirt or pale-blue blouse, school tie, grey or cherry-red pullover, black shoes.

Homework Average 11-year-old, five to seven hours 30 minutes a week; 14-year-old, seven hours 30 minutes; 16-year-old, 10 hours.

Vocational qualifications Diploma of Vocational Education.

Inspection February 1994: 'This is a school whose firm adherence to the values of its Catholic foundation is evident in all aspects of its corporate life: parents are strongly supportive of the school; teachers set high standards and pupils feel secure in an environment where their welfare has a high priority. As a consequence, relationships at every level in the school are good. Pupils are respected as individuals, and so most of them learn to respect others. The staff work hard and are anxious for pupils to succeed. The school is well led. All this contributes to high standards of achievement and an atmosphere of mutual trust.'

Primary schools St Edmund's RC Primary; St Mary's RC Primary; St Wulstan's RC Primary; Sacred Heart RC Primary, Thornton Cleveleys; St Teresa's RC Primary, Thornton Cleveleys; St John's RC Primary, Poulton-le-Fylde; St Bernadette's RC Primary, Bispham; St William's RC Primary, Pilling.

CHARLTON (G.M.) SCHOOL

Severn Drive
Wellington
Telford
Shropshire TF1 3LE
Tel (01952) 223257
Fax (01952) 222117
E-mail: charlgm@rmplc.co.uk

- National ranking 460= (401=, 314=)
- GCSE 54% (58%)
- A-levels *Not applicable*
- Higher education *Not applicable*

- Grant-maintained
- Mixed comprehensive
- Pupils 824
- Boys (11–16) 388
- Girls (11–16) 436
- Sixth form *Not applicable*
- Education authority *Shropshire*

Headteacher Kay Cheshire, appointed in September 1993. Staff 47 (men 19, women 28).

Motto Scientia veritas est (Knowledge is truth).

Background Originally built in the 1960s as a girls' school. Situated on the northern edge of Telford; became grant-maintained in September 1993; extensive playing fields and large, well-equipped hall. New technology suite opened in January 1996. Over-subscribed, with 1.5 applications per place. Although an 11–16 school, pupils can take AS-levels in English and computing. 'Very active' physical education department with extensive extra-curricular activities. Main sports: rugby, hockey, netball. Large orchestra and choir; many musical, dramatic and dance evenings. Strong links with school in Magdeburg in Lithuania; school exchanges. Particular curriculum strengths include science, English, drama and music. Firm links with local employers; participants in many community events.

Streaming Pupils are set according to ability in different subject areas.

Approach to discipline 'Firm and fair. Our aim is to know each child well enough to support him or her as a learner. We have high expectations and a remarkable prefect system.'

Uniform Dark-blue trousers/skirt and jumper, tie, black shoes. Regulations enforced 'very strictly'.

Homework Average 11-year-old, five hours a week; 14-year-old, eight hours; 16-year-old, 10 hours.

Vocational qualifications *None*

Inspection November 1994: 'Consistent expectations of pupils, a committed, able staff and increasingly strong support from its governing body are characteristics of this good school, in which standards of achievement have reached impressive levels.'; 'Pupils talk well and with confidence, are supportive of the academic achievements of their peers, but feel able to criticise aspects of the organisation of the school, using reasoned argument.'; 'Good skills gained in information technology lessons are under-used in the curriculum as a whole. Standards of achievement in a number of subjects are restricted by the limitations of the accommodation.'; 'Most pupils show enthusiasm for their studies and work conscientiously. A greater variety of learning experiences and increased responsibility for their own learning could enhance quality.'; 'The school enjoys purposeful leadership.'

Primary school Dothill Junior; Apley Wood County Primary; Bratton St Peter's CE Primary; Park County Junior; Leegomery County Junior.

THE CAVENDISH SCHOOL

Eldon Road
Eastbourne
East Sussex BN21 1UE
Tel (01323) 731340
Fax (01323) 739572
E-mail: cavendsh@pavilion.co.uk

- National ranking 460= (302=, 471=, 295=, −)
- GCSE 54% (63%)
- A-levels *Not applicable*
- Higher education *Not applicable*

- Mixed comprehensive
- Pupils 966
- Boys (11–16) 510
- Girls (11–16) 456
- Sixth form *Not applicable*
- Education authority *East Sussex*

Headteacher Arthur Christian Cornell, appointed in September 1978. Staff 55 (men 29, women 26).

Motto Courtesy.

Background Secondary modern until 1979; re-organisation involved re-siting of school and almost doubling in size. Mathematics and technology block added in 1981; dual-use sports hall in 1983; £1m extension for expressive art block and refurbishment of main building in 1993. Off-site facility for boys' games, 'but still a soccer school of excellence'. Development Trust created in 1992. Regularly over-subscribed since 1979, with 1.1 applications per place: 'But we have worked to reduce over-subscription because of the disappointment and frustration it creates.' Proud of special reputation in mathematics, English, drama, music and soccer. Extra-curricular activities also include subject workshops; exchanges in French and German, as well as bi-annual skiing trips, music tours and competitive weekend sporting tournaments at home and abroad.

Streaming Mixed-ability tutor-groups; target mixed ability in year 7 with possibility of setting after Christmas in mathematics, science and languages. In years 8 and 9, whole-year setting in mathematics, science, languages and humanities. In years 10 and 11, whole-year setting in core subjects with possibility of 7-10 GCSEs supported by vocational courses.

Approach to discipline 'The school works on a behaviour policy based on three principles. All members of the community are entitled: to be treated fairly, with respect and courtesy; to be allowed to succeed; to work in safe and pleasant surroundings.' House system, with 'parenting' and 'buddy' strategies.

Uniform Navy V-neck pullover with house motif, charcoal-grey/navy/black trousers or navy skirt/trousers for girls, white shirt, house tie, black/brown shoes. Distinctive sweater for year 11.

Homework Average 11-year-old, two hours a week; 14-year-old, five hours; 16-year-old, 10 hours.

Vocational qualifications City and Guilds Pre-Vocational Diploma of Vocational Education.

Inspection September 1995: 'Cavendish is a good school in which children learn effectively. The school provides a good education for its pupils within a well-ordered community. A major strength of the school is the caring and supportive ethos and the positive relationships of staff and pupils.'; 'Pupils are well-behaved, work hard and attend regularly. Punctuality is good.'; 'Pupils are encouraged to achieve to the best of their ability. Pupils are happy and secure and have positive attitudes to learning.'

Primary schools Ocklynge County Primary; Bourne County Primary; Stafford County Primary; Meads CE Primary; St Thomas à Becket RC Primary.

HAWARDEN HIGH SCHOOL

The Highway
Hawarden
Deeside
Flintshire CH5 3DJ
Tel (01244) 532103/534412
Fax (01244) 534699
E-mail: head@hdnhigh.u-net.com

- National ranking 463 (436, 509, 467, –)
- GCSE 53% (54%)
- A-levels 40% (A/B); 91% (A/E)
- Higher education 76% (Cambridge 1)

- Mixed comprehensive
- Pupils 1,052
- Boys (11–18) 570
- Girls (11–18) 482
- Sixth form 142 (13%)
- Education authority *Flintshire*

Headteacher Chris Harvey, 57, appointed in September 1981. Staff 63 (men 29, women 34).

Motto Labor omnia vincit (Toil conquers all).

Background Became a comprehensive in 1967; origins back through Hawarden Grammar School to its foundation in 1606; occupies buildings that range in age from late Victorian to late 20th century; six miles from Chester and 10 miles from Wrexham; 'highly-Anglicised' border area of north-east Flintshire is mainly residential. Over-subscribed, with average of 1.1 applications per place. 1990 Schools Curriculum Award; Prince of Wales Award for work in creating four-acre nature reserve in school grounds; Environmental Enterprise Award in 1990 and 1995; under-16 Welsh netball champions. Young Enterprise; foreign travel; French exchange. Investors in

People Award; Technology Schools Initiative. 'Mutual respect is encouraged and demonstrated in the daily life of the school.'

Alumni Gary Speed, Wales and Leeds United footballer.

Streaming Year 7 pupils in mixed-ability groups; year 8, set only in mathematics; most pupils taught in sets from year 9.

Approach to discipline 'The school aims to create an orderly and tension-free atmosphere that encourages learning and self-discipline. Unsatisfactory conduct is dealt with in a variety of ways: extra duties, being on report, detention or exclusion. Parents are informed of any serious or persistent behavioural problem.'

Uniform School tie, white shirt/blouse, mid-grey trousers/skirt, jumper. 'Tactfully and firmly enforced.'

Homework Average 11-year-old, five hours a week; 14-year-old, seven hours 30 minutes; 16-year-old, 10 hours.

Vocational qualifications GNVQ.

Primary schools Rector Drew Primary; Penarlag Primary; Ewloe Green Primary; Sandycroft Primary; Northop Hall Primary.

MONTSAYE SCHOOL

Greening Road
Rothwell
Kettering
Northamptonshire NN14 2BB
Tel (01536) 418844
Fax (01536) 418282

- National ranking 464 (502, –, 361, –)
- GCSE 53% (47%)
- A-levels 39% (A/B); 91% (A/E)
- Higher education 82% (Cambridge 3)

- Mixed comprehensive
- Pupils 1,115
- Boys (11–18) 599
- Girls (11–18) 516
- Sixth form 202 (18%)
- Education authority *Northamptonshire*

Headteacher Lawrence Dale, 60, appointed in January 1982. Staff 66 (men 31, women 35).

Background Developed from a secondary modern, receiving first comprehensive intake in 1976; doubled in size from 1976 to 1981 on 20-acre site on edge of small town with its own playing fields. Several building programmes: sports hall, swimming pool; upgraded technology facilities in 1993. Not over-subscribed. Schools Curriculum Award; links with European Union; drama, technology and music among strengths. 'The school believes in the value of the comprehensive system and curricular entitlement, and therefore aims for all-round excellence.'

Streaming Some mixed-ability and a variety of setting, with each departmental area organising pupils as appropriate. All pupils are setted at some stage.

Approach to discipline 'The aim is to create a well-structured, secure environment, to develop self-esteem and, from that, self-discipline, a respect for others and the school environment. In such an environment, all should be able to reach their full potential.

Uniform Red sweatshirt with school crest (black for upper school), white shirt/blouse, black trousers/skirt, black school tie with red-and-white stripe. 'Smart dress' for sixth-formers.

Homework Average 11-year-old, four hours a week; 14-year-old, six hours; 16-year-old, 10 hours.

Vocational qualifications GNVQ Intermediate and Advanced.

Inspection November 1996: 'A successful school which provides a very good quality of education for its pupils.'; 'English becomes a real strength of the school at GCSE and A-level examinations; results are above the national average.'; 'Students are very good listeners and attain a good standard in speaking, although opportunities to develop as confident speakers are inconsistent across the curriculum. They are good readers.'; 'Students have a very positive and responsible attitude to their work at Montsaye School. Their application is a real strength. They are co-operative, collaborate well with teachers and each other in lessons and when moving around the school site. This is an orderly and well-ordered school where students pay attention, concentrate and persevere with their learning tasks.'; 'The quality of care and concern for the welfare of students is another important strength of this school.'; 'There is a powerful commitment to equal opportunities and it is the driving ethos at the school.'; 'Strong, effective and determined guidance and leadership are provided by the headteacher.'

Primary schools Rothwell Junior; Havelock Junior, Desborough; Loatlands Primary, Desborough; Wilbarston Primary; Braybrooke Primary.

THE SANDON SCHOOL

Molrams Lane
Chelmsford
Essex CM2 7AQ
Tel (01245) 473611
Fax (01245) 478554

- National ranking 465 (500, 480, 474, –)
- GCSE 53% (48%)
- A-levels 29% (A/B); 84% (A/E)
- Higher education 71%

- Grant-maintained
- Mixed comprehensive
- Pupils 1,058
- Boys (11–18) 534
- Girls (11–18) 524
- Sixth form 137 (13%)
- Education authority *Essex*

Headteacher Sian Carr, 37, appointed in January 1997. Staff 70 (men 28, women 42).

Motto Vincit qui se vincit (The victor is he who conquers himself).

Background Serves socially-diverse suburban and semi-rural area south of Chelmsford; attracts pupils from wide area and 'proportion of pupils from high socio-economic households is significantly greater than the national average.' Centre for training of teachers in partnership with Cambridge University. Music, sports, outdoor pursuits are strongly encouraged. Gained national reputation in girls' basketball; two international players. Variety of regional and national awards for technology. 'Students demonstrate a genuine sense of belonging to the school community and share the values of mutual responsibility, openness and trust, courtesy, co-operation and respect. However, above all we are not complacent. We are continually evaluating our effectiveness and seeking improvement.'

Alumni Charlie Lee-Potter, BBC journalist,

Streaming 'Students work in all-ability groupings initially. As they progress through the school, changes are made to those groupings as is felt appropriate by each subject area.'

Approach to discipline 'Central to the school's

aim is the pursuit of excellence. Initiative and self-discipline are therefore encouraged alongside developing an awareness of the responsibilities of being a member of a community. Very high standards of personal conduct are therefore expected; bullying and unsociable behaviour are unacceptable and are dealt with swiftly and severely.'

Uniform Navy blazer with school badge, navy skirt/charcoal-grey trousers, pale-blue shirt, navy jumper with school crest, school tie, black shoes.

Homework Average 11-year-old, 10 hours a week; 14-year-old, 10 hours, plus coursework; 16-year-old, 15 hours, plus coursework.

Vocational qualifications GNVQ Intermediate, Business Studies.

Inspection December 1993: 'Overall, Sandon provides a good quality of education for its pupils. The school places considerable emphasis on the creation of a strong community.'; 'Most lessons are well-planned and have clear goals.'; 'The headteacher provides strong and effective leadership and is supported by staff who show a clear professional commitment to the school. The governors operate effectively and share with the staff a commitment to the continuing improvement of standards and the quality of provision.'

Primary schools Baddow Hall Junior, Great Baddow; Priory Primary, Bicknacre; Danbury St John, Danbury; Danbury Park Primary, Danbury; Great Totham Primary; East Hanningfield CE Primary.

HOLY CROSS ROMAN CATHOLIC HIGH SCHOOL

Burgh Lane
Chorley
Lancashire PR7 3NT
Tel (01257) 262093
Fax (01257) 232878

- National ranking 466 = (472 =, 448 =)
- GCSE 52% (52%)
- A-levels *Not applicable*
- Higher education *Not applicable*

- Mixed comprehensive
- Pupils 730
- Boys (11–16) 379
- Girls (11–16) 351
- Sixth form *Not applicable*

- Education authority *Lancashire*

Headteacher Francis Anthony Charnock, appointed in September 1983. Staff 40 (men 22, women 18).

Motto For a better tomorrow.

Background Catholic comprehensive serving the town of Chorley and surrounding rural areas; formed in 1973 through the amalgamation of two single-sex schools which occupied the same site on the southwest of the town; the two sections are connected by a path across playing fields; school hopes to move onto single site by 1997. Not oversubscribed. 'A school based on gospel values, striving constantly in partnership with parents to achieve the highest standards. We value all pupils as individuals and seek to help them grow and develop within a caring and supportive Christian environment.' Identified by Ofsted in 1996 as a 'good and improving' school.

Alumni Phil Cool, television comedian; Mickie Walsh, Republic of Ireland soccer player.

Streaming Setting in English, mathematics, science and modern languages.

Approach to discipline 'The key to good order is self-discipline. Holy Cross pupils are expected to take responsibility for their actions. We try to be positive in approaching problems. There is a pupil code of behaviour which was drawn up in consultation with pupils. This is displayed throughout the school.'

Uniform White shirt, school tie, black school sweater with badge, black trousers/skirt. 'All pupils are expected to wear uniform.'

Homework Average 11-year-old, five to six hours a week; 14-year-old, seven to eight hours; 16-year-old, nine to 10 hours.

Vocational qualifications *None*

Inspection May 1994: 'Secure in its Catholic foundation, Holy Cross is a very successful and happy school where principled leadership and the commitment of staff enable pupils to achieve good standards consistent with their abilities.'; 'Teachers expect the best from their pupils, both in terms of their behaviour and their academic progress. Pupils respond positively to this encouragement with courtesy, affection and respect. Little bullying occurs; attendance levels are high; the programme of extra-curricular activities is rich and varied; relationships at all levels are friendly; opportunities are given for pupils to take on responsibilities and to serve the community; the school enjoys the confidence of parents.'

Primary schools St Mary's RC Primary; St Gregory's RC Primary; Sacred Heart RC Primary; St Oswald's RC Primary; St Joseph's RC Primary.

LAVINGTON SCHOOL

The Spring
Market Lavington
Devizes
Wiltshire SN10 4EB
Tel (01380) 812352
Fax (01380) 818492

- National ranking 466= (477=, 253=, –, 295=)
- GCSE 53% (51%)
- A-levels *Not applicable*
- Higher education *Not applicable*

- Grant-maintained
- Mixed comprehensive
- Pupils 564
- Boys (11–16) 271
- Girls (11–16) 293
- Sixth form *Not applicable*
- Education authority *Wiltshire*

Headteacher Martin Watson, appointed from September 1997. Staff 31 (men 14, women 17).

Motto *None*

Background On western edge of village of Market Lavington, six miles south of Devizes. Main school building dates from 1962 when the school opened; further additions in 1976. Substantial building programme completed in March 1995: new science/technology block; all temporary buildings removed. Over-subscribed, with 1.25 applications per place. More than one in three places taken by pupils outside designated area. Nearly nine in 10 (86%) go on to further education. Formal links with Dauntsey's, local private school; working farm and horticultural unit on site, which operate as business as well as teaching resource, all pupils have opportunity to learn musical instrument. Latin, French

and German on offer to all pupils; all follow a modern language to GCSE.

Streaming No streaming. Setting for certain subjects from year 7; simultaneous teaching for as many subjects as possible so that teaching groups can be compiled appropriately.

Approach to discipline 'It is our fundamental belief that every member of the school community has the right to be treated with respect. Pupils are encouraged to develop a self-discipline within the parameters set out in the school's code of conduct.'

Uniform Grey skirt/trousers, grey monogrammed pullovers, white shirt/blouse, black tie with red stripe (optional in summer), black/grey shoes. Regulations enforced 'absolutely'.

Homework Comprehensive homework policy: 'essential part of the school's curriculum for all students'. Extra work or detention for failure to make satisfactory attempt. All homework to be marked and returned within fortnight at most. Homework diaries, regular monitoring by senior staff.

Vocational qualifications BTEC Business and Communication Studies.

Inspection October 1993: 'The school provides an effective education.'; 'The teaching is competent. Pupils are well-motivated and relationships are excellent. Sound progress is made in the great majority of lessons.'; 'The school has clear, established values which promote an orderly and harmonious environment. Pupils display responsible attitudes towards the fabric and corporate body of the school, and respond well to strong moral and spiritual leadership.'

Primary schools St Barnabas CE Primary; Holy Trinity CE Primary; Dauntsey's Primary; Worton and Marston Primary; Chirton CE Primary; Urchfont CE Primary; St Thomas à Becket Primary.

TESTBOURNE COMMUNITY SCHOOL

Micheldever Road
Whitchurch
Hampshire RG28 7JF
Tel (01256) 892061
Fax (01256) 896796

- National ranking 466= (401=, 416=, 355=, –)

- GCSE 53% (58%)
- A-levels *Not applicable*
- Higher education *Not applicable*

- Grant-maintained
- Mixed comprehensive
- Pupils 513
- Boys (11–16) 282
- Girls (11–18) 231
- Sixth form *Not applicable*
- Education authority *Hampshire*

Headteacher Trevor Richard Thomas Pankhurst, 60, appointed in April 1983. Staff 31 (men 14, women 17).

Motto Integrity.

Background Rural community school, first in Hampshire, in ample grounds in small county town; first in area to become grant-maintained; favourable staff–pupil ratio; buildings undergoing extensive refurbishment. Not over-subscribed. Computers in almost all departments; older machines being replaced by industry-standard PCs. Two information technology suites, well-stocked library. 'Excellent' sports facilities: swimming pool, new tennis court, multigym, sauna, large sports hall, gymnasium. Close links with local industry; 1991 national award. Mixture of traditional and modern: 'The school is small enough to know all its pupils well, but large enough to offer a broad curriculum with effective ability grouping.'

Streaming Pupils are put in sets by achievement in all subjects during or at the end of year 7. Setting in mathematics after one term in year 7.

Approach to discipline 'The atmosphere is friendly but purposeful. Discipline is firm but not oppressive. We benefit from having an experienced staff, many of whom have, or have had, children in the school. Our behaviour policy states: 'Everyone will act with courtesy and consideration to others at all times.' A range of rewards and sanctions is used to encourage good behaviour.'

Uniform Navy blazer, black/dark-grey trousers or navy pleated skirt, school tie. Regulations enforced 'very strictly': 'All pupils are in uniform.'

Homework Average 11-year-old, 30 minutes per subject per week; 14-year-old, 45 minutes per subject per week; 16-year old, one to two hours per subject per week.

Vocational qualifications *None*

Inspection September 1996: 'Pupils of all abilities make sound progress in relation to their prior attainment in most subjects.'; 'The behaviour of pupils in lessons and around the school is good. Pupils' attitudes are very positive in lessons. They are very responsive and diligent when given opportunities to work with others or take responsibility for their own work. The atmosphere in the school is calm, orderly and friendly.'; 'Many pupils take part enthusiastically in a wide range of extra-curricular activities such as sport and drama which significantly enhance their personal development.'; 'The quality of teaching in English and drama was of a particularly high standard.'; 'Across the school as a whole, limited use is made of the assessment of previous work when planning lessons and seeking to improve the standards attained by pupils.'

Primary schools Whitchurch Primary; Overton Primary, Basingstoke; St Mary Bourne Primary, Andover; Barton Stacey Primary, Winchester; Oakley CE Junior, Basingstoke; Longparish Junior, Andover.

THE GRANGE SCHOOL

Grange Lane
Pedmore
Stourbridge
West Midlands DY9 7HS
Tel (01384) 816660
Fax (01384) 816661

- National ranking 466= (446=, 471=, 432=, –)
- GCSE 52% (54%)
- A-levels *Not applicable*
- Higher education *Not applicable*

- Mixed comprehensive
- Pupils 825
- Boys (11–16) 397
- Girls (11–16) 428
- Sixth form *Not applicable*
- Education authority *Dudley*

Headteacher Barry Thomas Wratton, 42, appointed in January 1997. Staff 46 (men 24, women 22).

Motto Realising the potential of your child.

Background Opened in 1939 as a small mixed secondary modern; became 11-to-16 comprehensive in 1976 and has twice been substantially extended; occupies elevated site overlooking Black Country and rolling hills. Range of facilities includes swimming pool funded by parent-teacher association in 1970; new food technology and information technology areas. Over-subscribed, with 219 applictions for 182 places. The most academically-able pupils take 11 GCSEs; in 1995, 27% of pupils gained eight or more GCSEs at grades A to C. 'Excellent performing arts are a particular feature of the school.' Identified by Ofsted in 1996 as 'a good and improving school'.

Streaming Full range of arrangements, according to subject: setting, banding, mixed-ability. Tutor groups are mixed-ability.

Approach to discipline 'We encourage the pupils to accept that nothing less than the best is good enough. We expect orderly behaviour as an important part of consideration for others.'

Uniform Black blazer, charcoal-grey trousers/skirt, white shirt, black shoes. Very strictly enforced.

Homework Average 11-year-old, five hours a week; 14-year-old, 10 hours; 16-year-old, 12 hours.

Vocational qualifications GNVQ.

Inspection February 1994: 'The school provides an effective education. It has a commitment to achievement and has high expectations of pupils in all aspects of school life.'; 'The great majority of pupils are achieving at the level of their capability.'; 'The quality of teaching is consistently satisfactory and pupils are well-motivated and responsive. The learning environment is positive and conducive to learning. The staff are committed and hard-working.'

Primary schools Ham Dingle Primary; Hob Green Primary; Rufford Primary; Wollescote Primary; Pedmore Primary; Oldswinford Primary.

THE SACRED HEART ROMAN CATHOLIC COMPREHENSIVE SCHOOL

Derwent Road
Redcar TS10 1PJ
Tel (01642) 473221
Fax (01642) 473741
E-mail: sacred.redcar.se@campus.bt.com .

- National ranking 466= (460=, 416=)
- GCSE 53% (53%)
- A-levels *Not applicable*
- Higher education *Not applicable*

- Mixed comprehensive
- Pupils 720
- Boys (11–16) 357
- Girls (11–16) 363
- Sixth form *Not applicable*
- Education authority *Redcar and Cleveland*

Headteacher Kevin Mitchell, 47, appointed in September 1993. Staff 41 (men 18, women 23).

Motto Semper fidelis (Ever faithful).

Background Shares 'pleasant' site with Catholic primary school in a residential area of Redcar. Modern buildings: assembly hall, gymnasium, library, religious education department; specialist accommodation for technology, home economics and art; four science laboratories, music room, lower-school teaching block, tennis courts, playing fields including rugby, soccer, hockey and cricket pitches. Five feeder primary schools; two in three pupils travel significant distances to attend the school. Over-subscribed, with 1.2 applications per place. 'Carmel' ethos: 'Catholic, Academic, Rewarding, Managed well, Equal opportunity, Life and love.'

Streaming Mostly mixed-ability in lower school; limited banding in upper school.

Approach to discipline Promotes self-discipline; code of conduct 'clear and communicated'; various rewards and sanctions to promote 'a rewarding and working ethos'.

Uniform Boys: black blazer, black V-neck jumper, white shirt, black trousers, school tie, plain black shoes. Girls: navy skirt, navy V-neck jumper, school blouse, black shoes. Strictly enforced.

Homework Average 11-year-old, three hours a week; 14-year-old, five hours; 16-year-old, 10 hours.

Vocational qualifications *None*

Inspection March 1996.

Primary schools St Bede's RC Primary, Marske-by-the-Sea; St Alban's RC Primary; St Dominic's RC Primary; St Joseph's RC Primary, Loftus; St Paulinus RC Primary, Guisborough.

THE SUMMERHILL SCHOOL

Lodge Lane
Kingswinford
West Midlands DY6 9XE
Tel (01384) 816165
Fax (01384) 816166

- National ranking 466= (422=, 259=, 318=, –)
- GCSE 53% (56%)
- A-levels *Not applicable*
- Higher education *Not applicable*

- Mixed comprehensive
- Pupils 1,008
- Boys (11–16) 530
- Girls (11–16) 478
- Sixth form *Not applicable*
- Education authority *Dudley*

Headteacher Jill Stuart, 41, appointed in January 1996. Staff 56 (men 23, women 33).

Motto Success through caring.

Background Well-equipped school in modern accommodation on south Staffordshire border: specialist design block, science block, two main teaching blocks, humanities building that incorporates purpose-built music rooms, music practice rooms, recording studio and drama complex. Sporting facilities include heated indoor swimming pool, six tennis courts, 20 acres of land. Serves Kingswinford, Wordsley and Wall-Heath. Over-subscribed, with 350 applications for 195 places. Duke of Edinburgh Award Scheme. School newspaper; strong modern languages, with trips to other European countries; mini-enterprise scheme. Music: woodwind, drum and choral groups, brass band, big band concerts. Sporting success includes rugby, hockey, netball and football; outstanding individual performances in athletics, golf, cricket, swimming and table tennis.

Streaming Mixed-ability teaching in most subjects. From early in year 7, streaming in mathematics and French; broad ability bands in German.

Approach to discipline Friendly but firm framework; most situations handled in classroom and then regarded as finished. Detention sometimes appropriate; parents given 24 hours' notice. 'Ultimately, we are striving to help pupils as they grow physically and mentally to become self-disciplined in their own lives.'

Uniform Navy V-neck jumper/sweatshirt with school logo, charcoal-grey/black trousers or navy skirt/trousers/culottes for girls, light-blue shirt for boys or blue-and-white striped blouse, school tie, white/navy/black socks or tights, black shoes. Very strictly enforced.

Homework Average 11-year-old, five hours a week; 14-year-old, five hours; 16-year-old, 10 hours.

Vocational qualifications NVQ.

Inspection March 1994: 'This is a good school.'; 'The quality of teaching is judged to be satisfactory or better in more than 90% of the lessons observed. This is also true for the quality of pupils' learning. Even higher standards might be achieved if the information gained from assessment were more effectively used to help pupils further to improve their work and to help teachers plan, pace and differentiate the learning more precisely.'; 'The school provides a caring, secure and civilised environment for learning. Pupils are well-behaved and are aware of and share the values that the school seeks to promote.'

Primary schools Glynne Primary; Dawley Brook Primary; Belle Vue Primary; Church of the Ascension Primary; Maidensbridge Primary.

THE TEST VALLEY SCHOOL

Roman Road
Stockbridge
Hampshire SO20 6HA
Tel (01264) 810555
Fax (01264) 810173

- National ranking 466= (382=, 488=, 295=, –)
- GCSE 52% (59%)
- A-levels *Not applicable*
- Higher education *Not applicable*

- Mixed comprehensive
- Pupils 600
- Boys (11–18) 300
- Girls (11–18) 300
- Sixth form *Not applicable*
- Education authority *Hampshire*

Headteacher Wendy Morrish, 43, appointed in January 1994. Staff 34 (men 12, women 22).

Motto In pursuit of personal excellence.

Background Established in 1961; on outskirts of village of Stockbridge in quiet rural area, with outstanding views of countryside surrounding River Test; serves large area covering many villages. Three main buildings; full-size open-air swimming pool with diving facilities, playing fields and tennis courts. Development of music, drama and art facilities underway. Fully subscribed. Enters competitive sports with success, despite being small school; individual representatives at district and county level. 'The balance of good results and maximum participation is encouraged.' National Duracell Technology Awards in 1993 and 1994; finalists in 1995 Young Engineer for Britain. Residential and local visits for all pupils: foreign exchanges, work experience in France, curriculum and activity days. Wide extra-curricular activities. Close links with local primary schools; Test Valley Association is 'a particular strength'.

Streaming Setting introduced in subjects where appropriate.

Approach to discipline 'A high standard of behaviour is considered to be of the greatest importance to provide the structured framework and atmosphere for learning. The school aims to promote an increasing sense of self-discipline, high standards of behaviour, a sense of values and responsibility for others.'

Uniform Dark-grey trousers/skirt, white shirt, school tie, bottle-green V-neck jumper with school emblem for years 7 to 9; grey jumper for years 10 and 11. 'Uniform is regarded as important and rules are enforced.'

Homework Average 11-year-old, five hours a week; 14-year-old, eight hours; 16-year-old, at least 10 hours.

Vocational qualifications RSA; Pitman; Rural Science course.

Primary school Wallop CE Primary; Stockbridge Primary; Wherwell Primary; King's Somborne CE Primary; Broughton Primary.

WILLIAM FARR CHURCH OF ENGLAND COMPREHENSIVE SCHOOL

Lincoln Road
Welton
Lincolnshire LN2 3JB
Tel (01673) 860225/862832

Fax (01673) 862660
E-mail: wfarr.school@argonet.co.uk

- National ranking 466= (411=, 416=)
- GCSE 52% (57%)
- A-levels *New sixth form*
- Higher education *New sixth form*

- Grant-maintained
- Mixed comprehensive
- Pupils 1,088
- Boys (11–18) 552
- Girls (11–18) 536
- Sixth form 152 (14%)
- Education authority *Lincolnshire*

Headteacher Paul Strong, 51, appointed in November 1986. Staff 60 (men 26, women 34).

Motto Striving for excellence.

Background Founded in 1952 by the Rev William Farr, the local vicar, on the site of wartime bomber station Dunholme Lodge; on 35-acre site six miles north of Lincoln. Grant-maintained since 1992; consistently over-subscribed, with applications from parents in preference to local grammar schools; 1.2 applications per place; pupils from an area of 400 square miles and more than half from outside catchment area. New buildings: technology and sports (1990); mathematics and information technology (1994); geography and history building (1996); further developments for information technology, music, art and drama being planned; major £400,000 investment in information technology in progress. Sixth form from September 1995, with wide curriculum. 'Excellent' sporting achievements at local, regional and national level. High standard of art; numerous musical groups, with about three in 10 pupils learning a musical instrument. Resources centre, with more than 200 computers throughout the school; number set to double by 1999 on whole-school network. Increasing social and curricular links with France, Germany, United States and Australia; adventure and skiing trips in United Kingdom and Europe. Buildings adapted for disabled pupils; winners of Grant-Maintained Schools Award of Excellence for this initiative. Charity fund-raising 'essential part of school life'; support programme for small primary schools in Jamaica. Duke of Edinburgh Award Scheme, with more participants than any other school in Lincoln. 'An environment of change and innovation within the traditional academic and moral values of hard work, self-discipline, responsibility towards others and healthy competition.' House system promotes competition throughout curriculum. Care and guidance through a 'year' system; detailed personal, social and moral education at the heart of the school's basic principles.

Streaming Year 7: mixed-ability, except mathematics (two half-year bands in sets). Year 8: mixed-ability only in English, technology, art and music. Year 9: mixed-ability only in technology, art and music. Years 10 and 11: all subjects in sets. 'As a principle, pupils are gradually moved into appropriate ability groups year on year.'

Approach to discipline 'Firm but fair, based on a code of conduct of responsibility to others. Inconsiderate behaviour is not tolerated. Parents are regarded as crucial partners in the enforcement of discipline.' Care and guidance are at the core of the school's ethos.

Uniform Years 7 to 11: black blazer with badge and House colour, saxe-blue shirt/blouse, school tie, grey pullover with badge, grey skirt/trousers. All uniform to agreed school pattern. Dress code for sixth-formers 'appropriate to study and membership of whole school community of a high standard'. Strictly enforced.

Homework Average 11-year-old, seven to eight hours a week; 14-year-old, eight to 10 hours; 16-year-old, 10 to 12 hours.

Vocational qualifications RSA, Computer Literacy and Information Technology (to all year 11 pupils); RSA, Environmental Studies, Graphics and Media Studies. GNVQ from September 1998.

Inspection October 1995: 'William Farr School is a good school which provides a high quality of education for its pupils. A good working environment has been created which allows pupils to learn effectively. Pupils are encouraged to develop a sense of social responsibility and they respond well to the opportunities provided.'; 'The school has a caring and supportive ethos. The behaviour of pupils is very good and has a positive impact on standards of achievement.'

Primary schools Welton St Mary's CE Primary; Nettleham CE Primary; Dunholme CE Primary; Ellison Boulters Scothern CE Primary; Hackthorn CE Primary; Pollyplatt CE Primary; Scampton CE Primary; Ingham CE Primary; Sturton-by-Stow Primary.

UCKFIELD COMMUNITY COLLEGE

Downsview Crescent
Uckfield
East Sussex TN22 3DJ
Tel (01825) 764844
Fax (01825) 762946
E-mail: ucc@pavilion.co.uk

- National ranking 474 (360, 432, 244, –)
- GCSE 51% (60%)
- A-levels 30% (A/B); 86% (A/E)
- Higher education 63% (Oxford 2, Cambridge 2)

- Mixed comprehensive
- Pupils 1,300
- Boys (11–18) 693
- Girls (11–18) 607
- Sixth form 250 (19%)
- Education authority *East Sussex*

Headteacher David Henry James Rebbitt, 58, appointed in January 1978. Staff 79 (men 31, women 48).

Motto Realising potential.

Background Serves small country town and ring of surrounding villages. A £3m building programme started in 1995 because of rising numbers, particularly among sixth-formers: significant extensions to science block as well as new classroom block. Community college responsible for 1,500 part-time adult students; also youth work. Two sets of playing fields. Over-subscribed, with 200+ applications for 186 places. Shared use of well-equipped leisure centre and indoor swimming pool. Average of six students per computer; machines are PC-compatible and all are networked. Strong international links: Romania, France, Germany and United States. Local education authority inspection in 1992: 'Examination achievement is very impressive, especially when the ability profile of the pupils is taken into consideration. The review team were very aware of an atmosphere of energy and enterprise.'

Streaming Mixed-ability groups for most subjects in year 7; grouped by ability in most subjects from year 8.

Approach to discipline 'Standards of discipline are high and the consideration and care extended to pupils is exceptional. We have clearly-defined policies on, and strategies for dealing with, bullying.'

Uniform White/blue blouse or shirt, navy skirt/trousers, navy pullover/cardigan or sweatshirt with college logo, college tie, white/blue tights/socks, black/brown shoes. 'We expect and receive parental support.'

Homework Average 11-year-old, six hours 30 minutes a week; 14-year-old, six hours 30 minutes; 16-year-old, at least l4 hours, plus project work.

Vocational qualifications GNVQ Levels 2 and 3.

Inspection May 1995: 'Standards are good in art and physical education, but there is too much underachievement in technology and modern languages. Standards in information technology are variable.'; 'A good range of extra-curricular activities and excellent links with the community and industry provide additional experiences and opportunities.'; 'The leadership of the college is strong and the principal and senior staff work closely with the governors.'; 'The students are open, pleasant and courteous. The atmosphere in the college is happy and caring and relationships are good. Students receive a sound moral education, are given opporunities to display initiative and take responsibilities.'

Primary schools Manor County Primary; Holy Cross CE Primary; Rocks Park Primary; St Philip's Primary; Buxted Primary; Maresfield Primary; Nutley CE Primary; Little Horsted CE Primary.

WINDSOR GIRLS' SCHOOL

**Imperial Road
Windsor
Berkshire SL4 3RT
Tel (01753) 861410
Fax (01753) 868117**

- National ranking 475 (476, 429)
- GCSE 51% (51%)
- A-levels 27% (A/B); 91% (A/E)
- Higher education 86%

- Girls' comprehensive
- Pupils 607
- Boys *Not applicable*
- Girls (13–18) 607
- Sixth form 118 (19%)
- Education authority *Berkshire*

Headteacher Carole Diane Chevalley, 50, appointed in September 1995. Staff 38 (men 9, women 29).

Motto *None*

Background School dates from the 1920s, when it was a girls' grammar school. Moved to current purpose-built site on edge of Windsor near the Great Park in 1950; later became a 13–18 comprehensive. 'Light and spacious' building, with landscaped grounds containing many mature trees and grassed areas. First school in Berkshire to receive an Investors in People Award. Over-subscribed with 189 applications for 157 places. Particular emphasis on science, mathematics and technology, particularly design work, as well as arts and humanities. Girls encouraged to see all subjects as open to them. 'Strong' drama and music; many pupils participate in sports at county and national level. 'Keen to be involved in the community in a spirit of contribution and service. Academic attainment is important and all ability ranges are developed to reach their full potential. There is a particular interest in provision for the able child and a good record of university entrance. The school is keen to equip girls for good careers and leadership roles in adult life.'

Streaming Setting in English, mathematics, French and science. Additional setting in geography in years 10 and 11.

Approach to discipline 'The school expects good order at all times, especially in class, where standards of behaviour are very good. The approach is based on courtesy to others and self-discipline, although swift action is taken when behaviour falls short of the standard.' Several teachers are trained counsellors; staff-student committee and prefects involved in developing acceptable codes of behaviour.

Uniform Dark-green skirt and jacket, dark-green V-neck jumper, white blouse, green/white socks or tights, black school shoes. Dark-green/black coat. No jewellery. Regulations enforced 'very strictly'.

Homework Average 14-year-old, 10 hours a week; 16-year-old, 12 or 13 hours.

Vocational qualifications GNVQ Intermediate, Business Studies, Leisure and Tourism, Art and Design, Hospitality and Catering; GNVQ Advanced, Business Studies.

Inspection February 1996: 'Pupils have a well-developed sense of what is right and wrong, which is reflected in their general behaviour. They relate positively to adults and to one another. Pupils are well-supported by a very good pastoral care system which enables them to approach their work feeling valued and secure.'

Primary schools Dedworth Middle; Trevelyan Middle; St Peter's CE Middle; St Edward's Royal Free Ecumenical Middle.

THE COLONEL FRANK SEELY SCHOOL

Flatts Lane
Calverton
Nottinghamshire NG14 6JZ
Tel (0115) 965 2495
Fax (0115) 965 5723
E-mail: cfseely@inotts.co.uk
Internet: http://www.inotts.co.uk/cfseely

- National ranking 476 (456, 397, 335, –)
- GCSE 50% (53%)
- A-levels 28% (A/B); 89% (A/E)
- Higher education 58%

- Mixed comprehensive
- Pupils 1,218
- Boys (11–18) 629
- Girls (11–18) 589
- Sixth form 172 (14%)
- Education authority *Nottinghamshire*

Headteacher Paul Sykes, 53, appointed in 1992. Staff 67 (men 32, women 35).

Motto Ut prosim (In order that we may serve).

Background School named after Colonel Frank Seely, a philanthropist born in 1864, chairman of Babbington Collieries, the family business; represented Calverton as county councillor. Full almost to capacity. Strong sporting tradition; wide extra-curricular programme. Duke of Edinburgh Award Scheme. Reputation for work with pupils with physical disabilities. Separate sixth-form centre on campus. Over-subscribed, with 1.2 applications per place.

Streaming Setting by ability in some subjects.

Approach to discipline 'A code of conduct and high expectations.'

Uniform Blazer, white shirt/blouse, grey/black trousers or skirt, black shoes, house tie; dress code for sixth-formers. Regulations enforced 'strictly'.

Homework Average 11-year-old, up to four hours 30 minutes a week; 14-year-old, up to eight hours; 16-year-old, up to eight hours.

Vocational qualifications City and Guilds, Diploma of Vocational Education; GNVQ Intermediate (Consortium).

Inspection November 1993: 'The school develops confidence in pupils and they relate well to each other and to staff. Notable is the sensitive way in which pupils with disabilities are helped and supported by other pupils. Pupils display a strong sense of belonging and loyalty to the school community.'

Primary schools St Wilfrid's Primary; Sir John Sherbrooke Primary; Lambley Primary; Woodborough Wood's Foundation School; Lowdham CE Primary.

CROFTON HIGH SCHOOL

High Street
Crofton
Wakefield
West Yorkshire WF4 1NF
Tel (01924) 862201/862470
Fax (01924) 865258

- National ranking 477= (489=, 516=, 392=, –)
- GCSE 50% (50%)
- A-levels *Not applicable*
- Higher education *Not applicable*

- Mixed comprehensive
- Pupils 920
- Boys (11–16) 460
- Girls (11–16) 460
- Sixth form *Not applicable*
- Education authority *Wakefield*

Headteacher John Malcolm Myers, 49, appointed in July 1990. Staff 50 (men 23, women 27).

Motto *None*

Background Moved to current buildings in 1964, ending 10 years of temporary accommodation; in 1974, Crofton High School opened after re-organisation with 700 pupils and 40 teachers; high point of 1,200 in mid-1980s; new buildings added in 1974, 1979 and 1984. Rolls have since fallen, although they are expected to rise again to more than 800 by end of decade. Nearly fully-subscribed, with 205 applications for 175 places. Nearly nine in 10 (87%) continue education after 16. Sporting tradition: rugby league, cricket, hockey, netball and athletics. Links with industry and community; several curriculum awards. The school bases its philosophy on a child-centred approach to education, supported by a warm, caring relationship between members of the school community. Everyone here has rights supported by responsibilities; everyone supports each other's entitlement. We are striving to create an Achievement Curriculum that recognises and celebrates work of quality where it is found.'

Alumni Mark Pearson, Great Britain rugby league player; John Wood, Durham cricketer.

Streaming In mathematics and languages, and where subject departments think best; other subjects have either banding or mixed-ability groups.

Approach to discipline 'Firm. A clear code of conduct has been published, which governors, teachers, pupils and parents are aware of. The code was produced in consultation with these parties.'

Uniform Burgundy sweater/cardigan/sweatshirt, white/grey shirt/blouse, grey/black trousers or skirt, burgundy-and-grey striped tie, black/white/grey socks or tights, black/brown shoes. Enforced 'firmly and within bounds of reason and good sense'.

Homework Average 11-year-old, seven hours 30 minutes a week; 14-year-old, seven hours 30 minutes; 16-year-old, not less than 10 hours.

Vocational qualifications None

Inspection February 1993.

Primary schools Crofton Junior; Crofton Shay Lane Primary; Sharlston Primary; Walton Junior; Ackworth Junior; Ryhill Primary.

ST MARY'S ROMAN CATHOLIC HIGH SCHOOL

Lugwardine
Hereford HR1 4DR
Tel (01432) 850416
Fax (01432) 850110

- National ranking 477 = (501, 242 =, 337 =, –)

- GCSE 50% (48%)
- A-levels *Not applicable*
- Higher education *Not applicable*

- Mixed comprehensive
- Pupils 608
- Boys (11–16) 285
- Girls (11–16) 323
- Sixth form *Not applicable*
- Education authority *Hereford and Worcester*

Headteacher Wiktor Daron, 43, appointed in September 1993. Staff 36 (men 15, women 21).

Motto Per Mariam (Through Mary).

Background Well-established school that prides itself on 'excellent' local reputation; original foundation of the school was in village of Lower Bullingham by four members of Order of the Sisters of Charity of St Vincent de Paul; all-girls school moved to current site in Lugg Valley, two miles from Hereford, in 1954; became co-educational in 1966; buildings 'in very good order'; new block added in 1990. Grounds include rugby, hockey and soccer pitches, outdoor swimming pool, tennis courts. Over-subscribed, with 160 applications for 120 places. Well-equipped classrooms, with two specialist information technology rooms, drama studio, music room, and recently-refurbished science and textiles areas. Large number of extra-curricular activities, school productions, all major sports, and numerous educational visits and exchanges.

Alumni Kevin Sheedy, Everton soccer player; Kim Lock, athlete.

Streaming Banding and streaming according to ability in most subjects from year 8.

Approach to discipline 'The school's ethos is rooted in Gospel values and this is reflected in the care for others.'

Uniform Blue blazer, white shirt/blouse, grey trousers/blue skirt, black shoes. 'All pupils are expected to adhere to the rules and spirit of school uniform at all times. The school is noted for its high standards in this respect.'

Homework Average 11-year-old, four to five hours a week; 14-year-old, at least six hours; 16-year-old, at least nine hours.

Vocational qualifications RSA, Computer Literacy and Information Technology.

Inspection November 1993: 'The school provides a good education for its pupils.'; 'Pupils are orderly, well-behaved and courteous in class and around the school. Relationships are excellent at all levels and the positive atmosphere in lessons supports learning. Pupils are well-dressed and the vast majority wear their uniform with pride.'

Primary schools St Francis Xavier's RC Primary; Our Lady's RC Primary; St Joseph's RC Primary, Ross-on-Wye; St Joseph's RC Primary, Malvern. More than 25 other feeder schools.

THE COUNTY HIGH SCHOOL, LEFTWICH

Granville Road
Northwich
Cheshire CW9 8EZ
Tel (01606) 41511
Fax (01606) 331483
E-mail: 9064134.depot@dialnet.co.uk

- National ranking 477= (477=, 359=, 248=, 230=)
- GCSE 50% (51%)
- A-levels *Not applicable*
- Higher education *Not applicable*

- Mixed comprehensive
- Pupils 810
- Boys (11–16) 427
- Girls (11–16) 383
- Sixth form *Not applicable*
- Education authority *Cheshire*

Headteacher Trevor Hodkinson, 52, appointed in April 1991. Staff 46 (men 22, women 24).

Motto Ad altaria tendamus (Striving for excellence).

Background Founded as Northwich Girls' Grammar School in 1957, the school was enlarged in readiness for the change to a comprehensive in 1978. Extensive grounds on southern boundary of market town of Northwich. Takes pupils from wide area of central Cheshire, from Antrobus and Whitley in the north to Winsford and Middlewich in the south. Not over-subscribed; 185 applications for 199 places. More than three in four school-leavers continue with their education, with four in 10 studying for degrees. 'Excellent' facilities for science, technology, languages and drama; English, sciences, art, history and business studies also among curriculum strengths. Most pu-

pils go on residential courses each year. Strong European links, including Dole in France and a twin school in Germany; French work-experience for year 11 pupils.

Streaming Pupils are set by subject from year 8; mathematics in year 7.

Approach to discipline Standards based on self-respect and respect for others and their property. 'Relationships in the school are good; staff know their pupils and deal with them firmly yet fairly, and with courtesy.' Wide parental support.

Uniform Pale-blue shirt/blouse, maroon sweater with school logo, maroon and pale-blue striped tie, grey trousers/skirt, black shoes. Worn by all pupils.

Homework Average 11-year-old, seven to eight hours a week; 14-year-old, eight to nine hours; 16-year-old, 12 to 15 hours.

Vocational qualifications RSA, Computer Literacy and Information Technology.

Inspection January 1994: 'This is a good school with considerable strengths in many areas. Standards of achievement are very good.'; 'The quality of pupils' learning is consistently good across subjects and key stages. Teaching was satisfactory in over 85% of lessons seen, and good or very good in almost half.'; 'Pupils' spiritual, moral, social and cultural development is well supported by very good standards of behaviour and good relationships which make the school a safe and secure community.'

Primary schools Moulton County Primary; Davenham CE Primary; Leftwich County Primary; Comberbach County Primary; Witton Church Walk CE Primary; Whitley County Primary; St Mark's GM Primary, Antrobus; Great Budworth CE Primary.

WHITBURN COMPREHENSIVE SCHOOL

Nicholas Avenue
Whitburn
Tyne and Wear SR6 7EA
Tel (0191) 529 3712
Fax (0191) 529 5569

- National ranking 477= (489=, 448=)
- GCSE 50% (50%)
- A-levels *Not applicable*
- Higher education *Not applicable*

- Mixed comprehensive

- Pupils 739
- Boys (11–16) 354
- Girls (11–16) 385
- Sixth form *Not applicable*
- Education authority *South Tyneside*

Headteacher Alan Michael Love, 40, appointed in January 1994. Staff 44 (men 20, women 24).

Motto *None*

Background Opened as all-age school in 1932; became secondary modern after 1944 Education Act; became comprehensive in 1977. Clifftop site overlooking North Sea within village of Whitburn, serving suburbs of South Tyneside; pupils usually come from Whitburn, Cleadon, Marsden, Seaburn and from the more distant feeder schools in South Shields and Sunderland. Older buildings upgraded in 1995, including refurbished art department. Fully-subscribed. Nearly three in four pupils (73%) go on to A-levels or vocational courses. Regular participants in essay, mathematical and environment competitions, with many first places. Strong Community Association on site sharing school facilities. Wide range of sports facilities include squash courts, weights room, sauna, drama hall. Visits at home and abroad; outdoor activities include sailing, skiing and fell-walking; theatre and historical visits are regular features. 'A generally happy school with a good standard of behaviour and discipline. Considerable staff involvement in extra-curricular activities.' Wide range of extra-curricular activities each day from 3.30pm to 5.30pm.

Streaming Streaming occurs after Christmas in year 7. Pupils grouped by ability in core subjects. Movement between groups after termly assessments.

Approach to discipline 'Our guidance policy includes "Assertive Discipline", in which positive rewards are seen as important as following a set of school and class rules, agreed by both parents and staff. As a principle we encourage good relationships between everyone in school based on positive rewards, careful monitoring and firm action against those who do not respect other people.'

Uniform Black trousers/skirt, white shirt, school tie, black jumpers, socks and shoes. PE kit purchased through the school.

Homework Average 11-year-old, five hours a week; 14-year-old, eight hours; 16-year-old, 15 hours.

Vocational qualifications GNVQ, Health and social Care, as year 10 option; GNVQ Leisure and Tourism, from September 1998.

Inspection October 1993: 'The GCSE results show that in almost all areas of the curriculum girls significantly outperform boys and that in many subjects the school is not reaching the national averages.'; 'The quality of teaching is mostly satisfactory and is occasionally very good. However, there are significant variations in the quality of learning within year-groups.'; 'Leadership is open and responsive, but there are areas where it is not strong.'; 'Behaviour is usually good in lessons. Pastoral support is sound and a wide variety of extra-curricular activities provide a range of social and cultural contexts for pupil development.' *The school reports it has completed its Ofsted action plan, dealing with all points made in the inspection report.*

Primary schools Whitburn Junior; Cleadon Village Junior; Marsden Primary.

BEVERLEY GRAMMAR SCHOOL

Queensgate
Beverley
East Yorkshire HU17 8NF
Tel (01482) 881531
Fax (01482) 881564
E-mail: 101575.1252@compuserve.com

- National ranking 481 (475, 507, 446, –)
- GCSE 49% (51%)
- A-levels 45% (A/B); 90% (A/E)
- Higher education 80% (Oxford 2, Cambridge 2)

- Boys' comprehensive
- Pupils 701
- Boys (11–18) 701
- Girls *Not applicable*
- Sixth form 91 (13%)
- Education authority *East Yorkshire*

Headteacher Barry Hunton Roger, 50, appointed in April 1989. Staff 43 (men 30, women 13).

Motto Adolescentiam alunt senectutem oblectant (Nurture youth, solace old age).

Background Founded in AD 721 by St John of Beverley; claims to be the third oldest school of its kind in the country; strong links with Beverley Minster and vicar is a school governor. The school was originally sited at the minster, now in extensive, open grounds on west side of the town. Over-subscribed, with 1.2 applications per place. Sporting tradition, with main sports being soccer in winter and cricket in summer; many others, too; soccer teams won three of five East Riding leagues in 1993; 1994 under-16 Humberside champions; one pupil is English under-16 golf champion; one international schoolboy hockey player; county representatives at soccer, cricket, athletics, cross-country, golf, rugby union, tennis and bowls. Thriving school orchestra. 'Very strong' Old Boys' Association. 'We encourage success, no matter what the level.' Joint sixth form with Beverley High School.

Alumni St John Fisher, Bishop of Rochester; John Alcock, Lord High Chancellor and Bishop of Ely; Thomas Percy, co-conspirator with Guy Fawkes; Neil Mallender, England cricketer.

Streaming Initially, five mixed-ability classes based on house system; setting takes place further up the school in some subjects.

Approach to discipline 'Firm! We expect self-discipline and have strict sanctions for those who do not meet our expectations. Anyone caught bullying, fighting, being violent to others or smoking is automatically sent home and does not return until parents have been seen. All know this, and the need to take this action is rare. Generally, the atmosphere at the school is quiet and orderly.'

Uniform Black/grey jumper, black/grey trousers, white/grey/blue shirt, black-and-white striped school/house tie, black/brown shoes. No denim, t-shirts or earrings. Regulations enforced 'rigidly': 'Persistent offenders are sent home.'

Homework Average 11-year-old, five hours a week; 14-year-old, seven hours 15 minutes; 16-year-old, 10 hours.

Vocational qualifications GNVQ Advanced.

Primary schools Beverley Minster CE Primary; Beverley St Nicholas Primary; Walkington Primary; Tickton CE Primary; Parkstone Primary, Hull.

ST JOAN OF ARC CATHOLIC SCHOOL

High Street
Rickmansworth
Hertfordshire WD3 1HG
Tel (01923) 773881
Fax (01923) 897545

- National ranking 482 (455, 251, –, 345=)
- GCSE 49% (66%)
- A-levels 40% (A/B); 96% (A/E)
- Higher education 98% (Oxford 3)

- Grant-maintained
- Mixed comprehensive
- Pupils 951
- Boys (11–18) 423
- Girls (11–18) 528
- Sixth form 120 (13%)
- Education authority *Hertfordshire*

Headteacher Anthony Sumner, 47, appointed in September 1992. Staff 66 (men 22, women 44).

Motto Fidelis ad mortem (Faithful unto death).

Background Established in Rickmansworth in 1905 by the Religious, the Daughters of Jesus, a congregation founded in Brittany in 1834. Until 1975 a Convent Girls' Grammar School, it then became a six-form entry co-educational comprehensive catering for Catholic children. High street frontage within short walk of Rickmansworth station; administrative block was formerly large Georgian house belonging to George Eliot; set in 12 acres of gardens surrounded by lakes; within grounds is a moat that is central feature of the school. Over-subscribed. Extensive playing fields, with pitches for soccer, rugby, hockey, athletics track, cricket wickets; gymnasium, outdoor courts for tennis, netball and basketball. Off-site sports facilities in nearby towns include swimming, sailing, canoeing, dry-slope skiing and squash courts; many pupils have represented school at district and county level in wide range of sports. Complete range of musical tuition; many pupils learning two instruments, with termly concerts. Separate block for arts facilities, with three studios built in 1980s; proud of grades at A-level and GCSE, with yearly exhibitions for parents and the public. Catholic ethos and aims: 'To ensure that each individual is cared for spiritually, morally, intellectually, physically, socially and emotionally.'

Streaming 'We are committed to valuing all members of the school equally and to equal opportunities for all. Each year-group is subdivided into six groups of mixed ability. Setting in ability groups is introduced progressively as heads of departments indicate the need, especially in mathematics and science.'

Approach to discipline 'It is our policy to expect high standards of behaviour and work from every pupil. Discipline is firm but positive. We believe in encouraging all our students to respect all aspects of community: respect for others, for themselves and for the environment.'

Uniform Maroon blazer, grey trousers/maroon skirt, maroon sweater and jumper with school logo. Very strictly enforced.

Homework Average 11-year-old, six hours a week; 14-year-old, eight hours; 16-year-old, 15 hours.

Vocational qualifications *None*

Inspection October 1994: 'This is a good school. Most pupils were seen to be achieving at or above their perceived ability; in some cases considerably so. The school has a very caring and committed staff who are well-qualified.'; 'Pastoral care is particularly effective. There are excellent relationships between pupils and staff and throughout the school community. Pupils are happy and secure; their behaviour is good. The spiritual, moral, social and cultural development of pupils is very good.'

Primary schools Holy Rood RC Primary, Watford; St Anthony's RC Primary, Watford; St Joseph's RC Primary, Watford; St John's RC Primary, Rickmansworth; Sacred Heart RC Primary, Ruislip; St John Fisher RC Primary, Pinner.

CHESTERTON COMMUNITY COLLEGE

Gilbert Road
Cambridge
Cambridgeshire CB4 3NY
Tel (01223) 578188
Fax (01223) 300786
E-mail: chestertoncollege@a4029.
camcnty.gov.uk

• National ranking 483 = (460 =, 448 =)

• GCSE 46% (53%)
• A-levels *Not applicable*
• Higher education *Not applicable*

• Mixed comprehensive
• Pupils 970
• Boys (11–16) 454
• Girls (11–16) 516
• Sixth form *Not applicable*
• Education authority *Cambridgeshire*

Headteacher Howard Gilbert, 40, appointed in September 1993. Staff 52 (men 20, women 32).

Motto *None*

Background Set in residential area to the north of Cambridge. Separate girls' and boys' schools were established on the site in 1935; amalgamated in 1972; re-organised into a comprehensive in September 1974. Considerable alterations to buildings over the years, of which the most important was completed in 1992: impressive resource centre, information technology suite, and music block. Extensive playing fields, indoor swimming pool, gymnasium, all-weather floodlit tennis courts. Fully-subscribed. Pupils entered early for GCSE in mathematics and modern languages; renowned centre for musical excellence; 'huge' pupil participation in extra-curricular activities; one in four boys plays for a school soccer team.

Alumni Dina Carroll, singer.

Streaming Mixed-ability form groups in year 7; then separate sets for each subject, reviewed termly.

Approach to discipline 'The school aims to develop a self-assured, self-disciplined and caring attitude in pupils. It is important to celebrate success and to have a few simple, clearly-understood principles of behaviour which we encapsulate in our code of conduct.'

Uniform Years 7 to 9: college clothes must be in college colours of grey, maroon and black. Years 10 and 11: pupils 'exercise their judgment in choosing clothes which are appropriate to the formality of the work at college'.

Homework Average 11-year-old, five hours a week; 14-year-old, 10 hours; 16-year-old, 10 hours.

Vocational qualifications *None*

Inspection January 1996: 'Chesterton is a successful community college where students enjoy a good quality of education in a caring learning environment. Tolerance, respect for each other and valuing the individual are promoted well alongside raising achievement. Standards are sound or good in all subjects and very good in some subjects. Parents share the college's aspirations and value its work with their children and the wider community.'

Primary schools Milton Road Junior; Mayfield Primary; St Luke's CE Primary; Arbury Primary; St Andrew's CE Junior.

IAN RAMSEY CHURCH OF ENGLAND SCHOOL

Green's Lane
Fairfield
Stockton-on-Tees TS18 5AJ
Tel (01642) 585205
Fax (01642) 570488
E-mail: ian.ramsey@campus.bt.com

- National ranking 483= (460=, 378=)
- GCSE 46% (53%)
- A-levels *Not applicable*
- Higher education *Not applicable*

- Mixed comprehensive
- Pupils 1,214
- Boys (11–16) 592
- Girls (11–16) 622
- Sixth form *Not applicable*
- Education authority *Stockton-on-Tees*

Headteacher Barry Alan Winter, 52, appointed in January 1991. Staff 66 (men 25, women 41).

Motto None

Background Situated to the west of Stockton-on-Tees; Church of England aided comprehensive, the only one in the Diocese of Durham, occupying two main buildings: former Stockton Grammar School in Fairfield Road and former Fairfield Secondary School 100 yards away in Green's Lane. Between the two buildings is the school's technology block. Extensive grounds include soccer, rugby pitches, a cricket square and six tennis courts; also a swimming pool. Over-subscribed, with 1.2 applications per place. 'The school tries to put Christianity at the centre of all that goes on.' Strong sporting tradition: rugby, cricket, soccer and hockey. School orchestra recently toured United States. 'We aim to create an open and cooperative climate, underpinned by Christian values, which provides high-quality opportunities and experience as a basis for lifelong learning to all members of the school community.'

Alumni Barry Unsworth, writer and Booker Prize winner; Steven Hackney, under-19 England rugby union international and Barbarians player; Alison Curbishley, international 400m hurdler.

Streaming Setting left to discretion of 'Curriculum Areas': in mathematics, from year 7 to 11. Mixed-ability throughout in English. 'Areas operate systems which they feel serve our pupils best.'

Approach to discipline 'We keep rules to a minimum. The main codes are to have common-sense and exercise consideration and courtesy for others at all times. Discipline is important. Infringements of school rules or standards may result in detention or, in extreme cases, exclusion.'

Uniform Navy/charcoal-grey trousers or navy skirt, white/blue shirt, navy sweater/cardigan (badge optional), school tie, navy/white socks, navy/black/natural tights, navy/black shoes. Regulations 'strictly enforced'. The occasional warning letter is required.

Homework Average 11-year-old, five hours a week; 14-year-old, seven hours; 16-year-old, 14 hours.

Vocational qualifications Northern Partnership for Record of Achievement; Foreign Languages in Tourism; GNVQs under investigation.

Inspection November 1994: 'A good school in which most pupils achieve well.'; 'Pupils and parents value the school highly. There is a vibrant sense of community and pupils work hard. They respond with enthusiasm and maturity when given opportunities to share in the management of their learning and in the organisation of the school. The staff are enthusiastic and loyal. Teachers have very good subject knowledge and secure classroom skills.'; 'The school enjoys strong and responsive leadership.'; 'The school is on an attractive site and is well-maintained, but despite careful management the numbers of pupils place pressure on the available space.'; 'A range of opportunities during the school day and in extra-curricular activities, most notably in sport and music, contribute to the spiritual, moral, social and cultural development of pupils.'

Primary schools Hartburn Primary; Holy Trinity CE Junior; Bowesfield Lane Primary; St Mark's CE Junior; The Glebe Primary, Norton.

THE MARCHES SCHOOL

Morda Road
Oswestry
Shropshire SY11 2HD
Tel (01691) 652959
Fax (01691) 671515
E-mail: marches.tech.coll@campus.bt.com

- National ranking 483= (506, 437=)
- GCSE 48% (47%)
- A-levels Not applicable
- Higher education Not applicable

- Mixed comprehensive
- Pupils 1,160
- Boys (11–16) 600
- Girls (11–16) 560
- Sixth form Not applicable
- Education authority Shropshire

Headteacher Alan Cooper, 51, appointed in April 1988. Staff 71 (men 36, women 35).

Motto Achievement Through Caring.

Background Formed as a result of the amalgamation of two smaller schools in 1988; a £3.5m building programme, lasting four years, has enabled the school to be housed on one site in purpose-built accommodation. Set on 30-acre site just south of Oswestry; serves the town and surrounding villages. 'Outstanding' facilities for mathematics, science and technology. Almost fully-subscribed, with 262 applications for 272 places. Information technology 'a major strength'; Technology College status from April 1996. Regular music and drama productions; wide range of instrumental tuition, flourishing choirs, bands, orchestras. Sporting achievements: regular county cup successes in soccer, cricket, hockey, netball, swimming and athletics. 'The school provides a secure and caring environment in which the highest possible attainment is encouraged and expected from every child in all areas of school life. There is an emphasis on positive and shared values. The school aims to achieve a partnership with parents and within the local community, enabling children to grow towards responsible adulthood.'

Streaming Mixed-ability in year 7; in sets according to ability in particular subjects from year 8 in mathematics, science, languages; from year 9, in geography, history and English.

Approach to discipline 'Discipline is firm but fair. There is a clear written code of conduct which is widely used and reinforced. The positive is emphasised and good practice is regularly praised and rewarded in and around school and in assemblies.'

Uniform White shirt/blouse, red-and-white school tie, blue school sweater (black in year 11), grey trousers/skirt, 'sensible' shoes. No trainers. Regulations 'very strictly' enforced: 'Parents are contacted over infringements and we aim to work with parents to maintain the standards we all want.'

Homework Average 11-year-old, four to five hours a week; 14-year-old, seven to 10 hours; 16-year-old, 10+ hours.

Vocational qualifications GNVQs.

Primary schools Woodside Junior; Beechgrove CE Junior; Trefonen CE Primary; St Oswald's RC Primary; Bryn Offa CE, Pant; Whittington CE Primary; The Meadows Primary; Selattyn CE Primary; Morda Primary; Maesbury Primary.

THE DEEPINGS SCHOOL

Park Road
Deeping St James
Peterborough
Lincolnshire PE8 8NF
Tel (01778) 342159
Fax (01778) 380590

- National ranking 486 (494, 493, 469, –)
- GCSE 45% (49%)
- A-levels 32% (A/B); 95% (A/E)
- Higher education 63% (Oxford 1)

- Mixed comprehensive
- Pupils 1,299
- Boys (11–18) 650
- Girls (11–18) 649
- Sixth form 188 (14%)
- Education authority Lincolnshire

Headteacher Dr David Anthony Bryars, 49, appointed in September 1988. Staff 76 (men 39, women 37).

Motto *None*

Background Located on border with Cambridgeshire; formed in 1972, with 450 pupils; shares large dual-use leisure centre on site, including swimming pools. 'It is justifiably proud of its sporting achievements, its innovative approach to information technology, and its successful examination results.' Over-subscribed, with average of 1.2 applications per place. Strong sporting and music traditions; success in district, county and national sporting competitions; large A-level AS-level music group, as well as performing groups for orchestral and pop music. More than 100 computers used on site. 'The central purpose of the Deepings School is to help all pupils to develop their unique potential to the full.'

Alumni Anne and Julie Hollman, England athletes.

Streaming Pupils can be set within subjects by ability. This varies by subject from setting across an entire year-group to mixed-ability grouping.

Approach to discipline 'The school emphasises a pupil–teacher relationship based on caring and mutual respect. Positive rewards are used to encourage pupils to work hard and success is always noted. The school rarely needs to use negative sanctions.'

Uniform Mid-grey skirt/trousers, school tie, school jumper, white shirt, black footwear. 'The school enforces its uniform policy firmly with the support of parents.'

Homework Average 11-year-old, five hours a week; 14-year-old, seven hours 30 minutes; 16-year-old, 10 hours.

Vocational qualifications Diploma of Vocational Education; GNVQ.

Inspection October 1996: 'Pupils behave well, their attendance is very good, and they generally enjoy being at school. The headteacher provides effective leadership and gives the school a clear educational direction and a positive ethos. The school's administration runs smoothly, pupils are well cared for and they have equality of opportunity.'; 'The best lessons incorporate imaginative and inspiring teaching and a richness in the use of language. However, the planning and delivery of lessons do not always cater for the different abilities of pupils.'; 'The excellent range of extra-curricular activities is well supported by pupils and staff. Time in lessons is usually spent effectively, but the form and tutor periods are not always used well.'

Primary schools Market Deeping County Primary; William Hildyard CE Primary; Deeping St James County Primary; Linchfield County Primary.

FISHGUARD HIGH SCHOOL

Heol Dyfed
Fishguard
Dyfed SA65 9DT
Tel (01348) 872268
Fax (01348) 872716

- National ranking 487 (470, –, 400, –)
- GCSE 44% (52%)
- A-levels 30% (A/B); 90% (A/E)
- Higher education 90% (Oxford 2)

- Mixed comprehensive
- Pupils 760
- Boys (11–18) 358
- Girls (11–18) 402
- Sixth form 130 (17%)
- Education authority *Pembrokeshire*

Headteacher Eryl Parry, 54, appointed in September 1985. Staff 50 (men 30, women 20).

Motto Labor omnia vincit (Work conquers everything).

Background Opened in new buildings in 1954; occupies 'superb campus' overlooking Fishguard bay, with playing fields on site. Buildings are 'spacious and extensive': swimming pool, gym and sports hall; teaching facilities, particularly IT, being continuously developed; large hall and sixth-form centre. Not over-subscribed; large catchment area, with about half the pupils arriving on buses. Winners in 1992 of inaugural Sainsbury's Award for Arts Education after devising and presenting a bilingual musical play; 1994 Prince of Wales Award. Regularly fields sporting teams for all age-groups; since 1986, nine pupils have represented Wales at under-18 level. Orchestra and pupils regularly progress to the National Youth Orchestra of Wales and the National Youth Theatre of Wales. 'We are a community school aiming to serve the needs of all the children in our locality. We are an organised and friendly community, which aims for high academic standards within a friendly, supportive environment.'

Streaming Pupils taught in sets based on ability. 'In general, a single group of sets may service up to three different subjects.'

Approach to discipline 'We hold high expectations of our pupils. In general, they find it easy to meet these. Any pupils who fall below the required standards are dealt with firmly and with understanding. We are keen to involve parents.' Working groups looking at both bullying and discipline.

Uniform Black sweater (green in sixth form), white shirt/blouse, black trousers/skirt, black shoes/boots. Regulations enforced 'persistently and firmly'.

Homework Average 11-year-old, six to seven hours a week; 14-year-old, seven hours; 16-year-old, nine to 10 hours.

Vocational qualifications Diploma of Vocational Education; GNVQ Intermediate and Advanced. All vocational courses begin in year 12.

Inspection April 1994.

Primary schools Fishguard Junior; Goodwick Primary; Holy Name RC Primary; Letterston Primary; Bro Ingli School, Newport; Dinas Primary; Wolfscastle Primary; Puncheston Primary; Mathry Primary.

BRIMSHAM GREEN SCHOOL

Broad Lane
Yate
Bristol BS17 5LB
Tel (01454) 310977
Fax (01454) 323465

- National ranking 488 (457, 375, 471, –)
- GCSE 43% (53%)
- A-levels 24% (A/B); 84% (A/E)
- Higher education 68%

- Mixed comprehensive
- Pupils 885
- Boys (11–18) 427
- Girls (11–18) 458
- Sixth form 132 (15%)
- Education authority *South Gloucestershire*

Headteacher Richard E. Warrillow, 49, appointed in September 1991. Staff 54 (men 26, women 28).

Motto *None*

Background Modern school buildings opened in 1978; on northern outskirts of Yate, about 11 miles from Bristol; 'excellent' specialist facilities; 'very extensive' playing fields on site, including floodlit athletics track and Astroturf hockey pitch. Over-subscribed, with average of 1.3 applications per place. Unit for physically-handicapped pupils; all pupils fully integrated in mainstream classes and follow full curriculum. School teams in usual sports provide steady stream of county representatives. 'Excellent' music department, with orchestra and three school bands; 80-member concert band undertakes European tour every other year. 'Friendly and hard-working pupils; young and committed staff.'

Streaming Mixed-ability in year 7; some setting introduced in some subjects from year 8.

Approach to discipline 'Firm and fair, based upon mutual respect. We use rewards and punishments to ensure a proper working atmosphere in lessons and around the school.'

Uniform Maroon school pullover, white shirt, school tie, black trousers/skirt. Strictly enforced.

Homework Average 11-year-old, three hours a week; 14-year-old, five hours; 16-year-old, seven hours.

Vocational qualifications GNVQ Intermediate and Advanced.

Inspection March 1996: 'Brimsham Green is a welcoming and orderly school which is moving forward under good management. It is a thinking and reviewing school where standards of work are usually sound and sometimes good. The provision for pupils with special education needs is outstanding. The school is well-staffed and provides good value for money.'; 'Standards of achievement are usually sound and sometimes good. Very little work is poor.'; 'The quality of marking varies, but the best is well-judged, consistent and helpful to pupils. Relationships in classes are cordial and supportive, especially to those with special educational needs. Where lessons in several subjects are less successful, particularly at Key Stage 3, the expectations of teachers and pupils could be raised further; there is some lack of challenge, stimulus and enjoyment, all of which are present in the best lessons. The setting and quality of homework are inconsistent. The quality of learning is mainly sound and often good, especially in the sixth form.'

Primary schools St Mary's CE Primary; Ridge Junior; North Road Primary; Frome Bank Primary; Raysfield Junior.

UPPER NIDDERDALE HIGH SCHOOL

Low Wath Road
Pateley Bridge
North Yorkshire HG3 5HL
Tel (01423) 711246
Fax (01423) 711859

- National ranking 489 (511, 526 = , 432 = , –)
- GCSE 43% (42%)
- A-levels *Not applicable*
- Higher education *Not applicable*

- Mixed comprehensive
- Pupils 341
- Boys (11–16) 164
- Girls (11–16) 177
- Sixth form *Not applicable*
- Education authority *North Yorkshire*

Headteacher Neville Metcalfe, 52, appointed in April 1988. Staff 23 (men 10, women 13).

Motto Personal progress in a caring community.

Background Founded in 1875, occupying buildings in centre of small Nidderdale town of Pateley Bridge; moved into purpose-built premises on greenfield site just outside the town in 1980; well-equipped, especially in information technology, despite small size; also well-furnished, carpeted and with sports hall. Extensive grounds, surrounded by open fields, sheep farms, moors and river. Over-subscribed, with average of 1.4 applications per place. Particular strength in outdoor education and information technology; all teaching rooms and offices are networked, also with two suites of computers. 'Our strengths lie in knowing each student very well and in meeting each student's educational needs.

We are firmly based in a community where the individual matters, and the values of that community are reflected in all we do.'

Streaming Pupils in sets according to ability; each subject setted independently.

Approach to discipline 'Good behaviour and a high standard of work is encouraged through praise, a positive and creative atmosphere, the merit system, and records of achievement.' Code of Conduct; high expectations: 'Discipline is fair, firm, consistent, and no child is allowed to disrupt the education and lives of others.'

Uniform Grey/black trousers or skirt, white/mid-grey shirt, school tie, grey/maroon V-neck pullover/cardigan, dark socks/tights, dark shoes. Enforced 'very firmly'.

Homework Average 11-year-old, five hours a week; 14-year-old, eight to 10 hours; 16-year-old, 10 to 15 hours.

Vocational qualifications *None*

Inspection February 1995: 'Upper Nidderdale High School is a good school and is an asset to the community. It provides an education which is mostly of good quality across a range of work that is only limited by its size.'; 'Learning was at least sound in 95 per cent of the lessons inspected and good or very good in almost two thirds of these lessons. A range of learning skills is being developed and pupils display good, often exemplary, attitudes to their learning. They are willing, motivated and keen to do well.'; 'Given more space and sufficient challenge, and a wider range of opportunities in some lessons, pupils – particularly the more able – would achieve yet higher standards. Formal strategies for monitoring and evaluating the quality of learning and teaching are not in place.'; 'The ethos of the school is purposeful, orderly and supportive. The behaviour of pupils is excellent and attendance is very good.'

Primary schools St Cuthbert's CE Primary; Kirkby Malzeard Primary; Summerbridge Primary; Dacre Braithwaite Primary; Fountains CE Primary; Birstwith CE Primary; Glasshouses Primary.

Scotland

ABOYNE ACADEMY

Bridgeview Road
Aboyne
Aberdeenshire AB34 5JN
Tel (013398) 86222
Fax (013398) 86922
E-mail: 101535.3145@compuserve.com

- Standard grade 49% (1/2); 88% (1/4)
- Higher grade 27%
- Higher education 34%

- Mixed comprehensive
- Pupils 557
- Boys (11–17) 298
- Girls (11–17) 259
- Sixth form 37 (7%)
- Education authority *Aberdeenshire*

Headteacher Sheena M. M. Cooper, appointed in October 1983. Staff 64 (men 23, women 41).

Motto Scientia et societas (School and community)

Background Aboyne Academy and Deeside community Education Centre is purpose-built academy in rural Royal Deeside; current building opened in 1975, although there has been a school in Aboyne since 17th century. Well-equipped with swimming pool, games hall, theatre, squash court, gymnasium, and on-site outdoor centre. Catchment area embraces whole of Upper Deeside, stretching more than 60 miles. Not over-subscribed. Balanced curriculum, with special attention to art, music, drama and physical education; strong information technology. 'The aim of Aboyne Academy is to provide a friendly, happy and supportive environment in which students are encouraged to identify and develop all of their talents as fully as possible and in which they can form healthy, responsible and well-balanced attitudes to school, family and society.'

Alumni Jack Maitland, international distance runner and triathlete; Pamela Wright, golfer; Julie Forbes, golfer; Gary Forbes, golfer.

Streaming Elements of banding from S1; large team to support pupils with learning difficulties.

Approach to discipline 'The school operates a Code of Appropriate Behaviour that applies both in and out of class. Staff and pupils are encouraged to act fairly and with consideration as members of the community.'

Uniform Grey/navy/black trousers/skirt, navy/grey sweatshirt with school badge, white/pale-blue polo shirt with school badge. 'It is not possible to enforce regulations, but pupils are actively encouraged to wear uniform.'

Homework Average 11-year-old, three to five hours a week; 14-year-old, eight to 10 hours; 16-year-old, up to 12 hours.

Vocational qualifications Scotvec modules; School Group Award.

Primary schools Aboyne Primary; Torphins Primary; Kincardine O'Neil Primary; Tarland Primary; Ballater Primary; Braemar Primary; Logie Coldstone Primary; Crathie Primary; Lumphanan Primary; Finzean Primary.

AITH JUNIOR HIGH SCHOOL

Aith
Bixter
Shetland ZE2 9NB
Tel (01595) 810206
Fax (01595) 810297

- Standard grade 60% (1/2); 90% (1/4)
- Higher grade *Not applicable*
- Higher education *Not applicable*

- Mixed comprehensive
- Pupils 153
- Nursery 15
- Primary 67
- Secondary 71
- Education authority *Shetland Islands Council*

Headteacher Glenda Valerie Moffat, appointed in October 1993. Staff 17 (men 8, women 9).

Motto *None*

Background Well-maintained school is 15 years old and overlooks pasture land 'amidst a settled and supportive community'; has primary and secondary wing, gymnasium, swimming pool, playing fields, offices, dining/leisure areas. Not over-subscribed. In rural setting near local marina; nautical courses offered. 'Happy, secure, well-disciplined atmosphere; relaxed, caring yet well-structured, allowing pupils growth and development towards a mature, responsible adulthood; an open-door policy supported by caring parents and community; an attractive, aesthetically pleasing environment backed by a supportive authority.'

Alumni Robert Alan Jamieson, author.

Streaming Setting for Standard Grade French.

Approach to discipline 'Positive. Clear guidelines and code of behaviour, shared responsibility with self-discipline built into primary and secondary social courses.'

Uniform 'Aith School has its own clear identity. There is no need of school uniform and it would not be appropriate in our community.'

Homework Variable.

Vocational qualifications Introductions to small boats, computers, computer application packages, vehicle layout, use and care of hand tools in motor vehicle engineering, craft practices for vehicle trades.

ANDERSON HIGH SCHOOL

Twageos Road
Lerwick
Shetland Isles ZE1 0BA
Tel (01595) 692306
Fax (01595) 695688

- Standard grade 60% (1/2); 90% (1/4)
- Higher grade 5%
- Higher education 70%

- Mixed comprehensive
- Pupils 850
- Boys (11–18) 415
- Girls (11–18) 435
- Sixth form 360 (42%)
- Education authority *Shetland Islands Council*

Headteacher Ian William Spence, 50, appointed in August 1995. Staff 82 (men 46, women 36).

Motto Do weel and persevere.

Background Formerly the Anderson Educational Institute; opened in 1862 as the gift of Arthur Anderson, co-founder of P & O; aims were to provide elementary education for poor children and higher education for children whose parents could pay fees. Largest secondary school in Shetland (population 22,500); takes pupils transferring from junior high schools throughout the islands as well as those living in and around Lerwick. 'A caring, tolerant establishment, of which each person is recognised as a unique, valued participating member.'

Alumni Sir Robert Stout, New Zealand prime minister.

Streaming Only to limited degree in mathematics. 'Mixed-ability is seen to be educationally and socially desirable.'

Approach to discipline 'Discipline is the prime responsibility of the class teacher. A school code of discipline is detailed in the school handbook, with clear guidelines from classroom to department to assistant headteacher to headteacher. The school strives to create an atmosphere that is pleasant and relaxed yet ordered and secure, where pupils feel happy to learn and teachers feel happy to teach.'

Uniform *None*

Homework Average 11-year-old, four to five hours a week; 14-year-old, seven to eight hours; 16-year-old, regular revision and private study. 'It is neither possible nor desirable to set prescribed time limits for homework. Much depends on the individual student.'

Vocational qualifications Scotvec courses.

Primary schools Lerwick Sound Primary; Bells Brae Primary; Quarff Primary; Bressay Primary.

BALERNO HIGH SCHOOL

5 Bridge Road
Balerno
Edinburgh EH14 7AQ
Tel (0131) 477 7788
Fax (0131) 477 7707
E-mail: rory.mackenzie@balernochs.edin.sch.uk
Internet:http://www.balernochs.edin.sch.uk

- Standard grade 47% (1/2); 87% (1/4)
- Higher grade 24%
- Higher education 45% (Oxford 1, Cambridge 1)

- Mixed comprehensive
- Pupils 886
- Boys (12–18) 429
- Girls (12–18) 457

- Sixth form 240 (27%)
- Education authority *City of Edinburgh*

Headteacher Rory Mackenzie, 48, appointed in April 1995. Staff 63 (men 31, women 32).

Motto *None*

Background Modern buildings opened in 1983 on south-western fringe of Edinburgh; serves communities of Balerno, Kirknewton and Ratho as well as the intervening rural areas. School's community programme operates seven days a week, 8am to 10pm, for almost 50 weeks a year: 'The priorities, nevertheless, remain child-centred and the community programme is community-led.' Over-subscribed, with 1.2 applications per place. Strong emphasis on sports, music and information technology; opportunities for all ages in broad range of activities. National Sportslink Award; Schools Curriculum Award. Musical activities are a strong feature. Learning Support Service for pupils throughout the school. Interactive Technology Centre for accelerated learning. 'The general tone is academic.'

Streaming Mixed-ability throughout S1 and S2. Thereafter teaching sets are formed according to the level of Standard Grade classes being taken.

Approach to discipline 'Pupils are encouraged to appreciate the value of a safe, comfortable and attractive environment, and contribute to this end by being thoughtful and caring in their attitude to other pupils and staff, as well as to the fabric and furnishings of the building.' Sanctions 'applied firmly'; 'parents play an important part in maintaining an appropriate climate for successful teaching and learning.' Range of opportunities for various posts of responsibility in senior school.

Uniform White shirt, dark-grey trousers/navy skirt, navy tie with red-and-silver stripes. 'Uniform is strongly encouraged, but is non-mandatory in line with the policy of the local authority.'

Homework Average 12-year-old, three hours 45 minutes to five hours a week; 14-year-old, five to 10 hours; 16-year-old, 12 hours 30 minutes.

Vocational qualifications Wide range of Scottish Qualifications Agency modules; all pupils required to take part in work-experience in each of years 4 to 6.

Inspection 'The school was well-managed, with clear educational aims for both the long and short term which had gained the support of staff and parents.'; 'The headteacher and his deputy were easily accessible to the staff and knew the pupils well. The unity of purpose in the school and the loyalty of the staff reflected well on the senior promoted staff. This was a good and successful school.'

Primary schools Dean Park Primary; Ratho Primary; Kirknewton Primary; Curriehill Primary; Bonaly Primary.

BRAE HIGH SCHOOL

Brae
Shetland ZE2 9QG
Tel (01806) 522370
Fax (01806) 522734
E-mail: brae.high@zetnet.co.uk
Internet: http://www.zetnet.co.uk/sigs/schools/brae

- Standard grade 42% (1/2); 85% (1/4)
- Higher grade 4%
- Higher education 40%

- Mixed comprehensive
- Pupils 420
- Boys (3–18) 198
- Girls (3–18) 222
- Sixth form 53 (13%)
- Education authority *Shetland Islands Council*

Headteacher Joseph Irvine, 53, appointed in August 1988. Staff 40 (men 16, women 24).

Motto *None*

Background A small primary school had existed in Brae for about 100 years, with a secondary department added in about 1950. The population increase brought about by the building of the Sullom Voe oil terminal caused a rapid expansion in the school roll; a nursery and primary department was opened in 1976; secondary department expanded to have its own fifth form (1993) and sixth form (1994). Not over-subscribed. Good sporting and leisure facilities, including new all-weather pitch. School lists music department among its strengths, with successful school orchestra. 'A pleasant, well-resourced learning environment where pupils and staff are on the whole happy at their work.'

Streaming Some setting in S3 and S4 in mathematics; otherwise mixed-ability teaching.

Approach to discipline 'We try to encourage a friendly and relaxed atmosphere within the school, but insist on standards of behaviour that ensure the safety and well-being of pupils, and maximum achievement by them.'

Uniform *None*

Homework Average 11-year-old, two hours 30 minutes a week; 14-year-old, five hours; 16-year-old, eight hours.

Vocational qualifications Various Scotvec national certificate short courses.

Primary schools North Roe Primary; Urafirth Primary; Mossbank Primary; Olnafirth Primary; Lunnasting Primary; Brae Junior High.

FARR HIGH SCHOOL

Bettyhill
By Thurso
Caithness KW14 7SS
Tel (01641) 521217
Fax (01641) 521203

- Standard grade 40% (1/2); 92% (1/4)
- Higher grade 8%
- Higher education 33%

- Mixed comprehensive
- Pupils 78
- Boys (11–18) 33
- Girls (11–18) 45
- Sixth form 17 (22%)
- Education authority *Highland*

Headteacher Jim A. Johnston, 46, appointed in December 1991. Staff 11 (men 6, women 5)

Motto To go the extra mile.

Background In Bettyhill, a crofting township that is central to the rugged and remote north coast of Sutherland; school serves area of 531 square miles making up parishes of Tongue and Farr. Building dates from 1964; built as junior secondary, upgraded to four-year status in 1969, and has had fifth and sixth year since 1988; has 47-pupil primary department. Active in outdoor education; annual outdoor activities week each summer since 1980. Annual skiing week; takes part in sports when possible; in 1989, primary girls' soccer team played at

Hampden Park and were runners-up in national seven-a-side competition; technical department among strengths. Officially upgraded to high school status in 1997.

Streaming Impractical, inappropriate and anathema to school's philosophy.

Approach to discipline 'The school fosters an attitude of consideration towards others. With the small number of pupils, the expectation of good behaviour is usually sufficient to see that it occurs.'

Uniform *None*

Homework Average 11-year-old, two hours a week; 14-year-old, four hours; 16-year-old, at least four hours.

Vocational qualifications Wide variety of Scotvec modules.

Primary schools Tongue Primary; Farr Primary; Melvich Primary; Altnaharra Primary.

FORTROSE ACADEMY

Academy Street
Fortrose
Ross-shire IV10 8TW
Tel (01381) 620310
Fax (01381) 621699

- Standard grade 43% (1/2); 90% (1/4)
- Higher grade 8%
- Higher education 24%

- Mixed comprehensive
- Pupils 650
- Boys (12–18) 335
- Girls (12–18) 315
- Sixth form 160 (25%)
- Education authority *Highland*

Headteacher John Douglas Simpson, 46, appointed in May 1989. Staff 51 (men 23, women 28).

Motto *None*

Background Founded in 1791; opened in 1892 on current site on the Black Isle; original building still in use; substantial extensions in 1933, 1967 and 1973, since when 12 further 'demountable' classrooms added. Catchment area comprises whole of Black Isle peninsula, a rural area of small towns, villages and scattered communities to the north of Inverness; fairly prosperous area with well-developed farming industry. Oversubscribed. Has performed well in Young

Enterprise: Scottish champions and runners-up in European Trade Fair. Strong musical tradition. Recent HMI report described by education official as 'most positive he had ever read'.

Streaming Setting of pupils in S2 in mathematics and modern languages; classes in S3 arranged according to subject choice.

Approach to discipline 'The school actively encourages self-discipline and many opportunities are given to youngsters to demonstrate this quality. Where pupils consistently fail to comply with the school's reasonable requirements then sanctions are immediate and severe.'

Uniform Grey/black/navy trousers/skirt, white or blue shirts/blouse, school tie, cardigan/pullover. 'School dress is actively "encouraged" but as long as pupils are reasonably smart no disciplinary action is taken.'

Homework Average 11-year-old, two hours a week; 14-year-old, six to eight hours; 16-year-old, eight to 10 hours.

Vocational qualifications Variety of Scotvec modules.

Inspection March 1993: 'The school had many strengths. It was effectively led by the headteacher and his senior management team. Staff had shown a high degree of loyalty to the school, and strong commitment to the education and well-being of the pupils. Pupils were attentive and behaved well in school, in conditions which afforded them little social space. The way forward for this very good school is to maintain and further extend challenge for pupils of all abilities.'

Primary schools Avoch Primary; Cromarty Primary; Munlochy Primary; Culbokie Primary; Kessock Primary.

GAIRLOCH HIGH SCHOOL

Achtercairn
Gairloch
Ross-shire IV21 2BP
Tel (01445) 712275
Fax (01445) 712318
e-mail: gairloch_high@wester_ross.fc.uhi.
      ac.uk

Standard grade *63% (1/2); 95% (1/4)
Higher grade 45%

- Higher education 50%

- Mixed comprehensive
- Pupils 212
- Boys (12–18) 114
- Girls (12–18) 98
- Sixth form 24 (11%)
- Education authority *Highland*

Headteacher Neil Keith Wilkie, 58, appointed in June 1978. Staff 26 (men 12, women 14).

Motto *None*

Background On western seaboard of Ross-shire amid magnificent scenery, within walking distance of impressive beaches; formerly a two-year secondary school, which was upgraded to four-year status in 1979 and six-year status in 1985. Roll has since risen steadily, serving catchment area of 700 square miles and eight associated primary schools. A number of pupils travel a daily round-trip of over 100 miles to and from school; some pupils from outside normal catchment area. New £5m school with sporting facilities completed in 1994. Playing fields include new all-weather pitch. Not over-subscribed, because of geographical isolation. Sporting success has included winners of McPhail and Malloch football trophies; runners-up in Ross/Sutherland Hockey Championships; winners for third successive year of Anne Mackinnon Cup for Athletics (for school with fewer than 500 pupils), and West Ross Tourist Board Cup for Athletics. More than 50 pupils involved in Duke of Edinburgh Award Scheme. Foreign Awareness Programme includes twinning with two schools in Denmark and Germany; pupil and staff exchanges. Winners in 1996 of Cameron Quaich for Senior Debating, open to all 54 secondary schools in Grampian and Highland. Successful participation in Gaelic Mods: vocals and instrumental, including bagpipes and clarsach. In 1997, two pupils represented Highland schools at commemoration service for return of Stone of Destiny at St Giles Cathedral, Edinburgh. Breadth of curriculum commended by HMI school inspectors, who described it as a 'highly-effective' school: 'It provides a lively, purposeful and productive learning environment within which pupils' needs and preferences are professionally and sympathetically identified and met.'

Streaming S1 and S2: mixed-ability common

course with purposeful differentiation; all pupils study two languages, with exception of special needs pupils, who study French and Gaelic/German. S3 and S4: Standard Grade, mixed ability and setting where appropriate; French remains compulsory, while Gaelic/German optional. S5 and S6: Streaming for Higher Grade pupils and mixed ability for modular courses.

Approach to discipline 'A high priority is given to self-discipline, self-respect, respect for others and for authority. Prefects are given additional responsibilities.'

Uniform Boys: grey trousers, white shirt, school tie. Girls: navy skirt/slacks, white blouse, school tie. Blazers are popular but optional.

Homework Average 11-year-old, five hours a week; 14-year-old, seven hours 30 minutes; 16-year-old, 10 hours.

Vocational qualifications More than 50 Scotvec modules.

Primary schools Gairloch Primary; Bualnaluib Primary; Kinlochewe Primary; Inverasdale Primary; Poolewe Primary; Shieldaig Primary; Torridon Primary; Scoraig Primary.

*Statistics refer to proportion of pupils gaining 3+ Standard or Higher Grades.

KINGUSSIE HIGH SCHOOL

Ruthven Road
Kingussie
Inverness-shire PH21 1ES
Tel (01540) 661475
Fax (01540) 661123

- Standard grade 24% (1/2); 79% (1/4)
- Higher grade -
- Higher education 33%

- Mixed comprehensive
- Pupils 400
- Boys (12–18) 200
- Girls (12–18) 200
- Sixth form 96 (24%)
- Education authority *Highland*

Headteacher Dr Tom Taylor, appointed in 1990. Staff 38 (men 21, women 17).

Motto Gu Dichiollach (With diligence).

Background Schooling in the area dates from Columban missionaries; situated next to River Spey, looking across at Cairngorms;

new secondary building in 1970; extended with eight temporary classrooms, new floodlit playing field, new technology extension; special education department. School's geographic location prevents over-subscription. Full outdoor education programme. Link with German school in Rhineland. Musical tradition: concerts, ceilidhs, hosts local annual music festival. More than 20 extracurricular activities normally offered each year, including Duke of Edinburgh Award Scheme. Wide sporting activities, with regular local and national successes in shinty, orienteering and skiing, in which individual pupils compete internationally. Pupil groups regularly involved in social and community activities, as well as with industry/commerce, including Young Enterprise team competitive successes. Scottish and European winners of European Business Game (Ravenna 1996); winners of 1996 British Schools Orienteering Championship; gold medal won by folk group at 1996 Festival of Festivals, Queen Elizabeth Hall in London.

Streaming In some subjects from S3.

Approach to discipline 'In a school of approximately 400 pupils, discipline problems of a major kind are very uncommon.'

Uniform White shirt, grey/black trousers or skirt. 'Voluntary but expected in S6.'

Homework 'Policy specifies increasing amount as pupils progress throughout the school.'

Vocational qualifications Scotvec modules.

Primary schools Alvie Primary; Aviemore Primary; Dalwhinnie Primary; Kingussie Primary; Newtonmore Primary.

KIRKWALL GRAMMAR SCHOOL

Kirkwall
Orkney KW15 1QN
Tel (01856) 872102
Fax (01856) 872911
E-mail: kirkgramsch@campus.bt.com

- Standard grade 27% (1/2); 85% (1/4)
- Higher grade 3%
- Higher education 80% (Cambridge 1)

- Mixed comprehensive
- Pupils 878
- Boys (11–18) 422
- Girls (11–18) 456
- Sixth form 96 (11%)

● Education authority *Orkney Islands Council*

Headteacher Eric Sinclair, 48, appointed in March 1991. Staff 75 (men 40, women 35).

Motto *None*

Background Modern buildings on attractive campus in Kirkwall, capital of Orkney. Catchment area includes rural mainland Orkney and all north isles, most of south isles and town of Kirkwall. More than 100 pupils live in school hostel. 'Very active and supportive' School Board. Aims to build confidence in pupils as independent learners; comprehensive pastoral care; special needs pupils fully integrated into school; further education college on site; close links with local business and industry; comprehensive work-experience programme and close links with local Enterprise Company. School newspaper entitled *The Kirkwallian*; weekly column by school in *The Orcadian* local newspaper. Close links with Norway and Germany; well-established European dimension in curriculum; school commended in 1995 by the Central Bureau and a travel bursary was awarded to a senior pupil. The school's own charitable trust, the Grammar School Enrichment Fund, established in January 1994. Statement of Values, agreed between staff and pupils, and discussed with parents, includes: 'All pupils and members of staff should feel that they are valued as individuals regardless of who they are, where they come from, their beliefs, the colour of their skin, or their academic ability.'

Streaming S1 and S2 largely mixed-ability, with setting in mathematics. Arrangements vary from subject to subject in years S3 to S6.

Approach to discipline Rules in four basic categories: showing consideration for others in school community; respecting school and personal property; ensuring safety and well-being of staff and pupils; making sure school runs smoothly.

Uniform Grammar school sweatshirt available, with logo designed by pupil. Optional.

Homework Interactive Homework and Study Diary issued to parents and pupils: 'The nature of homework varies with subjects and age-groups.' All subjects have homework policy that is regularly reviewed. All pupils given lessons in study skills.

Vocational qualifications Scotvec modules in

most subject areas; further education college on site.

Primary schools Papdale Primary; Glaitness Primary; Hope Primary; St Andrews Primary; Orphir Primary; Bũrray Primary; Flotta Primary; Eday Primary; North Ronaldsay Primary; Shapinsay Primary; Rousay Primary; Egilsay Primary.

MALLAIG HIGH SCHOOL

Mallaig
Inverness-shire PH41 4RG
Tel (01687) 462107
Fax (01687) 462219

● Standard grade 43% (1/2); 97% (1/4)
● Higher grade –
● Higher education 32%

● Mixed comprehensive
● Pupils 155
● Boys (12–18) 78
● Girls (12–18) 77
● Sixth form 5 (3%)
● Education authority *Highland*

Headteacher J. Forbes Jackson, 59, appointed in August 1985. Staff 18 (men 10, women 8).

Motto *None*

Background Upgraded from a junior secondary school in temporary accommodation in August 1989 to sixth-year status in a purpose-built building overlooking the Sound of Sleat. Specialist classrooms throughout. Features include assembly hall, canteen, gym hall, all-weather playing field and adjacent swimming pool; 15% of pupils placed by parental request. Small school with favourable teacher/pupil ratio gives a family atmosphere.

Streaming Mixed-ability teaching in S1 and S2. Setting for mathematics and French in S3 and S4. Other subjects are mixed-ability from S1 to S4.

Approach to discipline Policy clearly distinguishes between discipline and the need for support. Emphasises the need for relevant and stimulating teaching to motivate pupils.

Uniform Pupils are encouraged to wear red or grey sweatshirts. Clothing promoting alcohol or bearing offensive logos is banned.

Inspection October 1996: 'Teaching and non-teaching staff showed a commendable commitment to the school. Within a quiet, purposeful atmosphere there was a strong sense of community. Staff knew the pupils as individuals and had high expectations of behaviour. Discipline was good. Pupils related well to each other and, with few exceptions, responded positively to their teachers. They were acquiring a sense of responsibility by assisting with some whole-school activities and by contributing to community service. Their involvement in the pupil council and supported study sessions was worthy of development. Staff organised a good range of extra-curricular clubs and inter-house sporting activities. The school was exploring ways of improving provision for competitive sport with other schools.'

Primary schools Mallaig Primary; Lady Lovat Primary; Arisaig Primary; Acharacle Primary.

PIEROWALL JUNIOR HIGH SCHOOL

Westray
Orkney KW17 2DW
Tel (01857) 677353
Fax (01857) 677310

- Standard grade 40% (1/2); 93% (1/4)
- Higher grade *Not applicable*
- Higher education *Not applicable*

- Mixed comprehensive
- Pupils 102
- Boys (4–16) 56
- Girls (4–16) 46
- Sixth form *Not applicable*
- Education authority *Orkney Islands Council*

Headteacher Alistair Scott Sangster, 48, appointed in August 1988. Staff 16 (men 8, women 8).

Motto *None*

Background Small school catering for whole of relatively remote island; pupils transfer to Orkney mainland at end of either S2 or S4, according to pupil or parental choice. School depends on some itinerant teachers who fly out daily from Kirkwall. Original building dates from 1874; upgradings in 1960 and 1987, when a community wing was added, and 1991, when a swimming pool was added. 'Because we are small, we are able to achieve high academic standards and have high levels of discipline. There is something of a hot-house atmosphere, which enables pupils to attain high standards in the range of school activities.'

Streaming Individual attention in small classes.

Approach to discipline 'Firm but fair, although discipline is not an issue in school. We all (apart from itinerants) live and work together on the island.'

Uniform *None*

Homework Average 11-year-old, five hours to seven hours 30 minutes a week; 14-year-old, seven hours 30 minutes to 10 hours; 16-year-old, seven hours 30 minutes to 10 hours.

Vocational qualifications Limited number of Scotvec modules.

Inspection December 1992: 'Overall, the school had progressed well and had many strengths. Most pupils made satisfactory progress and attained good standards. Staff had sustained an impressive commitment to developing courses to Standard Grade and gave pupils good encouragement and support. The school should build on its considerable good practice and should focus on the clear priorities in the development plan.'

Primary schools Papa Westray Primary.

PORTREE HIGH SCHOOL

Viewfield Road
Portree
Isle of Skye IV51 9ET
Tel (01478) 612030/612973
Fax (01478) 612154

- Standard grade 40% (1/2); 84% (1/4)
- Higher grade 8%
- Higher education 36%

- Mixed comprehensive
- Pupils 676
- Boys (11–18) 345
- Girls (11–18) 331
- Sixth form 64 (9%)
- Education authority *Highland*

Headteacher David Meek, 43, appointed in January 1994. Staff 63 (men 29, women 34).

Motto *None*

Background The school was established in the

summer of 1763 by the decision of Sir James MacDonald of Sleat. Its first headteacher was Alexander Campbell, who later became minister of the parish of Portree. The school has become the sole secondary school on the island and now takes pupils only from some of the Inner Hebridean Islands: Raasay, Canna, Eigg and Soay. However, a number of pupils from the mainland attend because of the parents' charter. Many pupils leave for school around 7am, since they can have an 80-mile round-trip. Others stay in the school hostel for a week or even a term at a time. Adaptations have recently been completed which allow the school to cater for disabled pupils. An increasing proportion of the pupils have had their primary education taught fully through the medium of Gaelic and the school offers a range of subjects in Gaelic: mathematics, personal and social education, history and home economics. The sporting side of the school is particularly strong: hockey, shinty and basketball are played against many schools and over the years a significant number of pupils have competed at national level. School excursions are also vital; recent trips to Strasbourg, Prague and Morocco. It gains tremendously from the strength of the local community; school and community complement each other extremely well.

Streaming Pupils are, for the most part, grouped in mixed-ability sections. This does not mean they will always be taught as a single class, but different teaching and learning strategies will be used to ensure that every pupil is working to his or her full potential.

Approach to discipline 'The pupils must be thoroughly educated into knowing, understanding and observing the school rules. Members of staff, both individually and collectively, must be consistent at all times in their dealings with the pupils. This requires us to set them an example of courteous and responsible behaviour, praising and encouraging their meritorious initiatives and condemning in no uncertain voice all actions that sink below the norms of decent conduct.'

Uniform Pupils are expected to wear the school uniform: maroon blazer or navy sweatshirt, pullover with school badge, white shirt/blouse, school tie, dark trousers/skirt.

Inspection March 1996: 'The school had many strengths, including a headteacher with a clear vision of the priorities needed for the school; generally good teaching, well-motivated pupils and positive relationships established between teachers and pupils; good levels of success at Standard and Higher Grade; a good variety of extra-curricular activities and an impressive range of foreign visits and exchanges; and also some extremely effective links with the local community.' The report suggested that there was some good use of homework, but there was also 'a need for further demand and challenge for some pupils, particularly the most able'.

Primary schools Portree Primary; Broadford Primary; Dunvegan Primary; Staffin Primary; Uig Primary; Kyleakin Primary; Carbost Primary; Edinbane Primary; Sleat Primary; Borrodale Primary; Elgol Primary; Kensaleyre Primary; Kilmuir Primary; Knockbreck Primary; Macdiarmid Primary; Struan Primary; Raasay Primary; Soay Primary.

SIR EDWARD SCOTT SCHOOL

Harris
Isle of Harris
Western Isles HS3 3BG
Tel (01859) 502339
Fax (01859) 502014

- Standard grade 43% (1/2); 100% (1/4)
- Higher grade -
- Higher education 53%

- Mixed comprehensive
- Pupils 140
- Boys (11–18) 60
- Girls (11–18) 80
- Sixth form 20 (14%)
- Education authority *Western Isles*

Headteacher Donald Murray, appointed in October 1981. Staff 21 (men 15, women 6).

Motto Dilseachd, Dicheall, Dealas.

Background Established in 1872; separate secondary and primary sites; recently upgraded to include provision for S5 and S6; first Higher Grade in 1993; mixture of original and subsequent buildings; well-maintained, well-resourced. Neighbouring football field, swimming pool, excellent natural environment for outdoor education. Only secondary school in Harris; 1991 HMI report: 'The school has a vital and positive ethos. Supportive links with parents, the School Board and the community had been well developed; commendable attention was paid to emphasising local tradition, culture and language in the life of the school. Staff were committed and demonstrated a close concern for the needs of pupils; pupils were responsive, applied themselves willingly, worked hard and achieved good results.'

Streaming The small number of pupils does not allow streaming. All classes are mixed-ability.

Approach to discipline Good conduct inside and outside classroom is essential prerequisite for effective teaching and sound learning. Clear duty of school to prevent disruptive behaviour. 'Rules formed accordingly and strictly enforced.' Staff-Pupil Council; School Board and Parent Committees.

Uniform Informal: navy shirt with white collar, navy tie with school logo. Formal: white shirt/blouse, navy tie wiith school logo.

Homework Average 11-year-old, four hours a week; 14-year-old, seven hours; 16-year-old, 10 hours.

Vocational qualifications Wide range of Scotvec National Certificate courses.

STEWARTON ACADEMY

Cairnduff Place
Stewarton
Kilmarnock KA3 5QF
Tel (01560) 482342
Fax (01560) 485339

- Standard grade 34% (1/2); 83% (1/4)
- Higher grade 13%
- Higher education 54%

- Mixed comprehensive
- Pupils 900
- Boys (12–18) 417
- Girls (12–18) 483
- Sixth form 105 (12%)
- Education authority *East Ayrshire*

Headteacher Derek Mathieson, 49, appointed in April 1994. Staff 62 (men 33, women 29).

Motto Be courteous.

Background Occupied new £3.3m single two-storey building in 1985; on elevated site in rural landscape on eastern boundary of Stewarton. Playing fields: football, rugby, hockey and running track. Total of 23 upper-floor classrooms grouped into suites according to subjects; seven science laboratories, two music rooms with practice areas, two business studies rooms and computer room. Ground floor: administrative accommodation, gymnasium, games hall, four technical subjects rooms, three home economics rooms, open-plan art area with pottery and photography rooms, lecture theatre, library-resource centre, dining room/cafeteria. Over-subscribed, with average of 1.2 applications per place. Extra-curricular activities form an important part of school life. Achievements in 1997 range from gold-medallists in British Wind Band Championships to Scottish Curling Champions. Foreign trips and exchanges. 'We seek a well ordered, pleasant environment in which learning, in its broadest sense, will flourish; an environment in which all our young people can develop their individual potential to the full, educationally, socially and in cultural, sporting and leisure activities.'

Streaming English and mathematics from S3.

Approach to discipline 'The essence of good discipline lies in prevention rather than cure and the entire school works very hard towards this goal. Where necessary, "the cure" must be appropriate and firm.'

Uniform Black blazer with badge, white shirt/blouse, black trousers/skirt, school tie, black V-neck sweater/cardigan. Pupils 'strongly encouraged' to wear uniform 'within the policy of the authority'.

Homework Average 11-year-old, five to six hours a week; 14-year-old, 10 to 12 hours; 16-year-old, three hours per week for each subject studied. All times are only recommended.

Vocational qualifications Scottish Qualifications Authority examinations.

Primary schools Nether Robertland Primary; Lainshaw Primary; Dunlop Primary; Kilmaurs Primary.

Index (i) by school name

The number in brackets refers to the school's national ranking (Scottish schools are unranked). The number in italics indicates the page reference.

Abbey Grammar School (104), *85*

Aboyne Academy *397*

Adams' Grammar School (89), *73*

Aith Junior High School *397*

All Hallows Catholic High School (290), *233*

All Saints' Church of England School (444=), *358*

All Saints Roman Catholic School (452), *365*

Alsager School (223), *178*

Altrincham Grammar School for Boys (105), *86*

Altrincham Grammar School for Girls (37=), *32*

Amery Hill School (423=), *342*

Anderson High School *398*

Anglo-European School (231), *185*

Ansford Community School (350=), *282*

Antrim Grammar School (135), *109*

Archbishop Blanch School (459), *370*

Archbishop Tenison's Church of England High School (184), *146*

Arden School (173), *138*

Arnewood School, The (256=), *210*

Aylesbury Grammar School (43), *38*

Aylesbury High School (20), *19*

Backwell School (197), *157*

Bacup and Rawtenstall Grammar School (142), *114*

Balerno High School *398*

Banbridge Academy (35), *31*

Barton Court Grammar School (157), *126*

Beaconsfield High School (83), *68*

Beal High School (296), *238*

Beauchamp College, The (438), *354*

Beechen Cliff School (396), *320*

Bennett Memorial Diocesan School (180), *143*

Bentley Wood High School (350=), *282*

Benton Park School (348), *280*

Beverley Grammar School (481), *387*

Beverley High School (289), *232*

Bewdley High School (322), *260*

Bexley Erith Technical High School (122), *99*

Bingley Grammar School (430), *347*

Bishop Challoner RC School (207), *166*

Bishop Heber High School (410), *331*

Bishop Luffa School (178), *141*

Bishop of Hereford's Bluecoats School, The (225=), *181*

Bishop of Llandaff Church-in-Wales High School, The (235), *188*

Bishop Ramsey Church of England School (378), *305*

Bishop Stopford School (202), *162*

Bishop Vesey's Grammar School (159), *127*

Bishop Walsh School (312), *251*

Bishop Wordsworth's School (25), *22*

Bishop's Stortford High School, The (234), *187*

Bishopston Comprehensive School (212=), *170*

Blue Coat Church of England Comprehensive School, The (271), *217*

Blue Coat School, The (54), *46*

Bohunt Community School (361=), *291*

Borden Grammar School (123), *100*

Boston Grammar School (124), *100*

Boston High School (150), *121*

Bottisham Village College (333=), *269*

Bourne Grammar School (94), *77*

Bournemouth School (76=), *63*

Bournemouth School for Girls (51), *44*

Brae High School *399*

Bramhall High School (361=), *291*

Brentwood County High School (345), *277*

Brentwood Ursuline Convent High School (204), *163*

Bridgewater County High School (408), *329*

Brimsham Green School (488), *393*

Brine Leas High School (256=), *204*

Brookfield Community School (440), *355*

Broughton High School (361=), *292*

Broxbourne School, The (347), *279*

Bullers Wood School (191), *152*

Burgate School, The (277=), *226*

Burscough Priory High School (431=), *348*

Caereinion High School (341), *274*

Caerleon Comprehensive School (291), *234*

Caistor Grammar School (56=), *48*

Calday Grange Grammar School (130), *105*

Camden School for Girls (415), *335*

Campion Roman Catholic School for Boys, The (203), *163*

Cams Hill School (277=), *222*

Canon Slade School (276), *221*

Cape Cornwall School (333=), *269*

Cardiff High School (303), *243*

Cardinal Allen Roman Catholic High School (460=), *371*

Cardinal Vaughan Memorial School, The (170), *135*

Carre's Grammar School (121), *98*

Castle School, The (Taunton) (256=), *211*

Castle School, The (Bristol) (406), *327*

Cavendish School, The (460=), *373*

Chailey School (423=), *342*

Charlton (G.M.) School (460=), *372*

Charters School (210), *168*

Chatham Grammar School for Girls (149), *120*

Chatham House Grammar School (153), *123*

Cheadle Hulme High School (277=), *223*

Chelmsford County High School for Girls (4), *5*

Chesham High School (118), *96*

Chesterton Community College (483=), *389*

Chew Valley School (371), *299*

Chichester High School for Girls (321), *259*

Chipping Campden School (393), *317*

Chislehurst and Sidcup Grammar School (63), *53*

Chosen Hill School (443), *357*

Christian Brothers Grammar School (119), *97*

Christleton High School (249), *199*

Churchill School (374), *301*

Churston Grammar School (69), *58*

Cirencester Deer Park School (423=), *343*

Cirencester Kingshill School (399=), *322*

Clarendon House Grammar School for Girls (154), *124*

Claverham Community College (277=), *224*

Cleeve School (254), *202*

Clitheroe Royal Grammar School (28), *25*

Colchester County High School for Girls (6), *7*

Colchester Royal Grammar School (8), *9*

Collingwood College (306), *246*

Colonel Frank Seely School, The (476), *384*

Colyton Grammar School (14=), *14*

Comberton Village College (256=), *205*

Conyers School (253), *202*

Coombe Dean (441), *356*

Copthall School (252), *201*

Corfe Hills School (219), *175*

Cotham Grammar School (218), *174*

Cottenham Village College (297=), *239*

County High School, Leftwich, The (477=), *386*

Cowbridge School (230), *184*

Cranbrook School (100), *82*

Crofton High School (477=), *384*

Crofton School (256=), *206*

Crompton House School (326=), *263*

Crossley Heath School, The (93), *76*

Dame Alice Owen's School (165), *132*

Dane Court Grammar School (109), *89*

Dartford Grammar School (85), *70*

Dartford Grammar School for Girls (103), *84*

Davenant Foundation School (328), *265*

Davison Church of England High School (383=), *309*

Deanery Church of England High School, The (349), *281*

Debenham Church of England High School (212=), *170*

Deepings School, The (486), *391*

Desborough School (293), *235*

Devonport High School for Boys (116), *94*

Devonport High School for Girls (44), *39*

Deyes High School (380), *306*

Dormston School, The (431=), *350*

Dover Grammar School for Boys (47), *40*

Down High School (114), *93*

Downs School, The (361=), *298*

Dr Challoner's Grammar School (21), *19*

Dr Challoner's High School (71), *59*

Durham Johnston Comprehensive School (436), *352*

East Bergholt High School (277=), *224*

Ecclesbourne School, The (185), *147*

Egglescliffe School (310), *250*

Ermysted's Grammar School (1), *3*

Fairfield High School (333=), *270*

Fallibroome High School (285), *228*

Farmor's School (324), *261*

Farr Secondary School *400*

Fernwood Comprehensive School (350=), 283

Finham Park School (272), 218

Fishguard High School (487), 392

Fitzwimarc School, The (423=), 344

Folkestone School for Girls, The (97), 79

Formby High School (421), 341

Fort Pitt Grammar School (166), 132

Fortismere School (305), 245

Fortrose Academy 400

Framwellgate Moor Comprehensive School (418), 337

Frogmore Community School (295), 237

Gairloch High School 400

Garforth Community College (376), 303

Gillott's School (399=), 323

Glyn ADT Technology School (330), 266

Goffs School (186=), 148

Gordano School (356), 287

Grammar School for Girls Wilmington, The (138), 111

Grange School, The (466=), 378

Gravesend Grammar School for Boys (112), 92

Gravesend Grammar School for Girls (95), 78

Grays Convent High School (297=), 240

Green School for Girls, The (294), 236

Greensward School, The (225=), 182

Grey Coat Hospital, The (382), 308

Guildford County School (394), 318

Guilsborough School (416), 336

Guiseley School (450), 363

Gumley House Convent School (269), 215

Haberdashers' Aske's Hatcham College (346), 276

Hadleigh High School (361=), 293

Handsworth Grammar School (140=), 112

Harrogate Grammar School (179), 142

Hartford High School (361=), 294

Hartismere High School (297=), 240

Harvey Grammar School, The (91=), 75

Hasmonean High School (175), 139

Hawarden High School (463), 374

Haybridge High School (181), 144

Hayfield School, The (381), 307

Healing Comprehensive School (383=), 310

Heart of England School (315), 254

Heckmondwike Grammar School (96), 79

Hele's School (454), 366

Henrietta Barnett School, The (3), 4

Henry Beaufort School, The (256=), 212

Herschel Grammar School (206), 165

Hethersett High School (411=), 332

High School for Girls (101), 83

High Storrs School (237), 189

Higham Lane School (411=), 333

Highcliffe School (225=), 180

Highsted School (137), 110

Highworth Grammar School for Girls (80), 66

Highworth Warneford School (333=), 271

Hodgson High School (444=), 359

Holbrook High School (333=), 272

Holt School, The (192), 153

Holy Cross Roman Catholic High School (466=), 376

Hope Valley College (399=), 324

Howard of Effingham School (195), 156

Hummersknott School (333=), 272

Huntington School (304), 244

Ian Ramsey Church of England School (483=), 390

Ilford County High School (99), 81

Ilkley Grammar School (244), 195

JFS (Jews' Free School) (242), 193

John Fisher School, The (238), 190

John Hampden Grammar School (66), 56

John Henry Newman School (320), 258

John Taylor High School (233), 186

Joseph Rowntree School, The (308), 248

Judd School, The (41), 36

Katharine Lady Berkeley's School (439), 354

Kendrick Girls' School (13), 13

Kennet School (397), 320

Kesteven and Grantham Girls' School (91=), 74

Kesteven and Sleaford High School (146), 117

King David High School (182), 144

King Edward VI Aston School (61), 52

King Edward VI Camp Hill School for Boys (9), 10

King Edward VI Camp Hill School for Girls (37=), 33

King Edward VI Five Ways (27), 24

King Edward VI Grammar School (49), 42

King Edward VI Handsworth School (33), 29

King Edward VI School (Louth) (128), 103

King Edward VI School (Stratford) (30), 27
King Edward VI School, Lichfield (270), 216
King's School, The (Grantham) (87), 71
King's School, The (Ottery St Mary) (419), 338
King's School, The (Peterborough) (147), 118
Kings of Wessex Community School, The (344), 277
Kingswinford School Grant-Maintained, The (411=), 334
Kingussie High School 402
Kirkwall Grammar School 402
Knutsford High School (453), 365
Lady Manners School (232), 185
Lady Margaret School (158), 127
Lancaster Girls' Grammar School (42), 37
Lancaster Royal Grammar School (10), 11
Langley Grammar School (160), 128
Langley Park School for Boys (239), 191
Langley Park School for Girls (205), 164
Latymer School, The (32), 28
Laurence Jackson School (399=), 324
Lavington School (466), 377
Lawrence Sheriff School (111), 91
Light Hall School (383=), 310
Limavady Grammar School (117), 95
Linton Village College (247=), 198
Littleover Community School (431=), 349
Lord Williams's School (314), 253
Lowton High School (383=), 311
Lutterworth Grammar School and Community College (398), 321
Lymm High School (325), 262
Magdalen College School (429), 346
Maiden Erlegh School (199), 159
Maidstone Grammar School (102), 83
Mallaig High School, 403
Malmesbury School (326=), 264
Marches School, The (483=), 391
Marling School, The (139), 112
Methodist College Belfast (70), 59
Millais School (225=), 180
Minster School, The (251), 200
Montsaye School (464), 374
Mullion School (383=), 312
Nailsea School (292), 235
Newlands School (189), 151
Newport Free Grammar School (275), 220
Newport Girls' High School (17), 17
Newstead Wood School for Girls (2), 3

Noadswood School (317=), 256
Nonsuch High School for Girls (59), 50
North Halifax Grammar School, The (88), 72
Northgate High School (417), 337
Norton Knatchbull School, The (48), 41
Notre Dame Roman Catholic School for Girls (427), 345
Nower Hill High School (350=), 284
Nunthorpe School (399=), 325
Oaklands Roman Catholic School (378), 305
Oakwood Park Grammar School (167), 133
Oathall Community College (240=), 192
Olchfa School (323), 260
Old Swinford Hospital (86), 70
Omagh Academy (127), 103
Ormskirk Grammar School (273), 219
Our Lady and St Patrick's College, Knock (73), 61
Our Lady's Grammar School (113), 93
Oxted County School (288), 231
Painsley Roman Catholic High School (277=), 225
Parkstone Grammar School (29), 26
Parmiter's School (287), 230
Pate's Grammar School (19), 18
Penair School (333=), 273
Pensby High School for Girls (458), 370
Philip Morant School, The (256=), 212
Pierowall Junior High School 404
Piggott School (224), 179
Plymouth High School for Girls (152), 122
Poole Grammar School (84), 69
Portadown College (56=), 49
Portree High School 404
Poynton County High School (246), 197
Presdales School (201), 151
Prince Henry's High School (370), 298
Queen Elizabeth's Girls' School (Barnet) (332), 268
Queen Elizabeth's Grammar School (Horncastle) (76=), 64
Queen Elizabeth's Grammar School, Faversham (109), 89
Queen Elizabeth's Grant-Maintained Grammar School (169), 134
Queen Elizabeth's High School (Gainsborough) (136), 109
Queen Elizabeth High School (Hexham) (309), 249

Queen Elizabeth Royal Free Grammar School of Spalding (161), *129*

Queen Elizabeth School (Carnforth) (268), *215*

Queen Mary's Grammar School (39), *34*

Queen Mary's High School (55), *47*

Radyr Comprehensive School (208), *167*

Rainford High School (342), *275*

Rainham Mark Grammar School (82), *67*

Ranelagh School (176), *140*

Range High School (220), *176*

Reading School (7), *8*

Redborne Upper School and Community College (373), *301*

Ribston Hall High School (163), *130*

Ricards Lodge High School (383=), *313*

Ridings High School, The (407), *328*

Ringmer Community College (431=), *349*

Ripon Grammar School (53), *46*

Robert May's School (222), *177*

Rochester Grammar School for Girls, The (75), *62*

Romsey School, The (350=), *285*

Rosebery (250), *200*

Royal Belfast Academical Institution, The (125), *101*

Royal Grammar School, The (16), *16*

Royal School, Armagh, The (162), *129*

Royal School, Dungannon, The (144), *115*

Rugby High School (46), *40*

Sackville School (395), *319*

Sacred Heart Roman Catholic Comprehensive School, The (466=), *379*

Sale Grammar School (131), *106*

Sandbach High School (216), *173*

Sandon School, The (463), *375*

Sawston Village College (383=), *314*

Scalby School (444=), *360*

Seaford Head Community College (451), *364*

Sexey's School (171), *136*

Sharnbrook Upper School and Community College (311), *250*

Silverdale School (190), *151*

Simon Langton Grammar School for Boys (40), *35*

Sir Edward Scott School *405*

Sir Henry Floyd Grammar School (107), *88*

Sir Joseph Williamson's Mathematical School (115), *94*

Sir Roger Manwood's School (156), *125*

Sir Thomas Rich's School (148), *119*

Sir William Borlase's Grammar School (62), *53*

Skegness Grammar School (110), *90*

Skinners' School, The (26), *23*

Skipton Girls' High School (23), *21*

Slough Grammar School (133), *107*

Soham Village College (444=), *361*

South Axholme School (444=), *362*

South Wilts Grammar School for Girls (81), *67*

Southend High School for Boys (65), *55*

Southend High School for Girls (64), *54*

St Aidan's Church of England High School (196), *157*

St Andrew's School (177), *141*

St Anne's Convent School (215), *172*

St Anthony's Girls' School (375), *302*

St Augustine's School (183), *145*

St Bartholomew's School (329), *266*

St Bede's Roman Catholic High School (Ormskirk) (361=), *295*

St Bede's School (Redhill) (221), *176*

St Bernard's Convent School (140=), *113*

St Bernard's High School (457), *369*

St Christopher's Church of England High School (411=), *334*

St Edward's School (331), *267*

St Gabriel's Roman Catholic High School (361=), *296*

St Gregory's Catholic Comprehensive School (Bath) (297=), *241*

St Gregory's Catholic Comprehensive School (Tunbridge Wells) (307), *247*

St Gregory's Roman Catholic High School (256=), *207*

St Hilda's Church of England High School (274=), *220*

St Hilda's Roman Catholic Girls' High School (240=), *193*

St James' Roman Catholic High School (361=), *297*

St Joan of Arc Catholic School (482), *388*

St John Fisher Roman Catholic High School (343), *276*

St Joseph's Roman Catholic High School (383=), *315*

St Laurence School (243), *194*

St Louis Grammar School (74), *61*

St Mark's Catholic School (316), *255*

St Mary Redcliffe and Temple School (456), *368*

St Mary's Roman Catholic High School (Chesterfield) (200), *160*

St Mary's Roman Catholic High School (Hereford) (477=), *385*

St Michael's Catholic Grammar School (22), *20*

St Michael's Church of England High School (444=), *362*

St Michael's College (120), *98*

St Monica's Roman Catholic High School (256=), *208*

St Nicholas Roman Catholic High School (209), *167*

St Olave's Grammar School (5), *6*

St Patrick's Girls' Academy (12), *12*

St Patrick's Grammar School (151), *121*

St Paul's Roman Catholic School (409), *330*

St Peter's Catholic School (313), *252*

St Peter's Collegiate School (422), *341*

St Peter's Roman Catholic High School (198), *158*

St Philomena's Catholic High School for Girls (255), *203*

St Thomas A Becket Roman Catholic School (383=), *316*

St Thomas More Catholic High School (212=), *171*

St Thomas More School (340), *273*

St Ursula's Convent School (399=), *326*

Stewarton Academy *406*

Stokesley School (217), *173*

Strabane Grammar School (168), *134*

Stratford-upon-Avon Grammar School for Girls (18), *17*

Strathearn School (24), *22*

Stretford Grammar School (172), *137*

Stroud High School (143), *115*

Summerhill School, The (466=), *380*

Sutton Coldfield Girls' School (72), *60*

Swavesey Village College (256=), *209*

Tadcaster Grammar School (372), *300*

Tanbridge House School (317=), *256*

Teesdale School (428), *346*

Test Valley School, The (466=), *380*

Testbourne Community School (466=), *377*

Thomas Mills High School (236), *189*

Thornden School (193=), *154*

Tiffin Girls' School, The (50), *43*

Tiffin School (79), *65*

Tolworth Girls' School (245), *196*

Tonbridge Grammar School for Girls (34), *30*

Torquay Boys' Grammar School (76=), *64*

Torquay Grammar School for Girls (68), *57*

Townley Grammar School for Girls (58), *50*

Trinity Catholic High School (186=), *149*

Tudor Grange School (193=), *155*

Tunbridge Wells Girls' Grammar School (36), *32*

Tunbridge Wells Grammar School for Boys (45), *39*

Turton High School (286), *229*

Twynham School (277=), *227*

Uckfield Community College (474), *382*

Upper Nidderdale High School (489), *394*

Uppingham Community College (431=), *351*

Urmston Grammar School (132), *106*

Waingel's Copse School (437), *353*

Waldegrave School for Girls (297=), *242*

Wallington High School for Girls (67), *56*

Wallington School (126), *116*

Warden Park School (247=), *198*

Wardle High School (317=), *257*

Watford Grammar School for Boys (174), *138*

Watford Grammar School for Girls (155), *124*

Weald of Kent Grammar School for Girls (31), *27*

Weald School, The (377), *304*

Weaverham High School (277=), *228*

Wellsway School (267), *214*

West Kirby Grammar School for Girls (106), *87*

Westcliff High School for Boys (134), *108*

Westcliff High School for Girls (52), *45*

Westgate School, Winchester, The (256=), *213*

Westlands High School (420), *339*

Wetherby High School (360), *290*

Wheatley Park School (358), *289*

Whickham School (357), *288*

Whitburn Comprehensive School (477=), *386*

Whitley Bay High School (359), *289*

William Farr Church of England Comprehensive School (466=), *381*

Wilmington Grammar School for Boys (164), *131*

Wilson's School (145), *116*

Windsor Girls' School (475), *383*

Wirral County Grammar School for Girls (89), *74*

Wirral Grammar School (129), *104*

Wolverhampton Girls' High School (14=), *15*

Woodcote High School (399=), *327*

Woodford County High School (98), *80*

Woodhey High School (383=), *316*

Woodlands Community School (350=), *286*

Wycombe High School (11), *12*

Wymondham College (188), *150*

Wymondham High School (455), *367*

Yateley School (442), *357*

Ysgol Gyfun Bro Myrddin (211), *169*

Ysgol Gyfun Gwyr (225=), *183*

Ysgol-y-Preseli (302), *243*

Index (ii) by location

Aboyne	Aboyne Academy 397
Accrington	St Christopher's Church of England High School 334
Alton	Amery Hill School 342
Altrincham	Altrincham Grammar School for Boys 86
Altrincham	Altrincham Grammar School for Girls 32
Amersham	Dr Challoner's Grammar School 19
Ampthill	Redborne Upper School and Community College 301
Antrim	Antrim Grammar School 109
Armagh	Royal School, Armagh, The 129
Armagh	St Patrick's Grammar School 121
Ascot	Charters School 168
Ashford	Highworth Grammar School for Girls 66
Ashford	Norton Knatchbull School, The 41
Aylesbury	Aylesbury Grammar School 38
Aylesbury	Aylesbury High School 19
Aylesbury	Sir Henry Floyd Grammar School, The 88
Bakewell	Lady Manners School 185
Balerno	Balerno High School 398
Ballymena	St Louis Grammar School 61
Banbridge	Banbridge Academy 31
Barnard Castle	Teesdale School 346
Barnet	Copthall School 201
Barnet	Hasmonean High School 139
Barnet	Henrietta Barnett School, The 4
Barnet	Queen Elizabeth's Girls' School 268
Barnet	St Michael's Catholic Grammar School 20
Basingstoke	Bishop Challoner RC School 166
Bath	Beechen Cliff School 320
Bath	St Gregory's Catholic Comprehensive School 241
Battle	Claverham Community College 224
Beaconsfield	Beaconsfield High School 68
Bebington	Wirral County Grammar School for Girls 74
Bebington	Wirral Grammar School 104
Beckenham	Langley Park School for Boys 191
Beckenham	Langley Park School for Girls 164
Bedford	Sharnbrook Upper School and Community College 250
Belfast	Methodist College Belfast 59
Belfast	Our Lady and St Patrick's College, Knock 61
Belfast	Royal Belfast Academical Institution, The 101
Belfast	Strathearn School 22
Bettyhill	Farr Secondary School 400
Beverley	Beverley Grammar School 387
Beverley	Beverley High School 232
Bewdley	Bewdley High School 260
Bexley	Bexley Erith Technical High School 99
Bexleyheath	Townley Grammar School for Girls 50
Billingshurst	Weald School, The 304

Bingley	Bingley Grammar School 347
Birmingham	Handsworth Grammar School 112
Birmingham	King Edward VI Aston School 52
Birmingham	King Edward VI Camp Hill School for Boys 10
Birmingham	King Edward VI Camp Hill School for Girls 33
Birmingham	King Edward VI Five Ways 24
Birmingham	King Edward VI Handsworth School 29
Bishop's Stortford	Bishop's Stortford High School, The 187
Bixter	Aith Junior High School 397
Blackpool	Hodgson High School 359
Bolton	Canon Slade School 221
Bolton	St Joseph's Roman Catholic High School 315
Bolton	Turton High School 229
Boston	Boston Grammar School 100
Boston	Boston High School 121
Bourne	Bourne Grammar School 77
Bournemouth	Bournemouth School 63
Bournemouth	Bournemouth School for Girls 44
Brackley	Magdalen College School 346
Bracknell	Ranelagh School 140
Bradford-on-Avon	St Laurence School 194
Brentwood	Brentwood County High School 277
Brentwood	Brentwood Ursuline Convent High School 163
Bristol	Backwell School 157
Bristol	Brimsham Green School 393
Bristol	Churchill School 301
Bristol	Cotham Grammar School 174
Bristol	Gordano School 287
Bristol	Ridings High School, The 328
Bristol	St Mary Redcliffe and Temple School 368
Bristol	Wellsway School 214
Brixham	Churston Grammar School 58
Broadstairs	Dane Court Grammar School 89
Broadstone	Corfe Hills School 175
Broxbourne	Broxbourne School, The 279
Bruton	Sexey's School 136
Burnley	St Hilda's Roman Catholic Girls High School 193
Burton-on-Trent	John Taylor High School 186
Bury	St Gabriel's Roman Catholic High School 296
Bury	Woodhey High School 316
Calverton	Colonel Frank Seely School, The 384
Camberley	Collingwood College 246
Camberley	Frogmore Community School 237
Cambridge	Bottisham Village College 269
Cambridge	Chesterton Community College 389
Cambridge	Comberton Village College 205
Cambridge	Cottenham Village College 239
Cambridge	Linton Village College 198
Cambridge	Sawston Village College 314
Cambridge	Swavesey Village College 209
Camden	Camden School for Girls 335

Camden	JFS (Jews' Free School) 193	
Canterbury	Barton Court Grammar School 126	
Canterbury	Simon Langton Grammar School for Boys 35	
Cardiff	Bishop of Llandaff Church-in-Wales High School, The 188	
Cardiff	Cardiff High School 243	
Cardiff	Radyr Comprehensive School 167	
Carmarthen	Ysgol Gyfun Bro Myrddin 169	
Carnforth	Queen Elizabeth School 215	
Carshalton	St Philomena's Catholic High School for Girls 203	
Castle Cary	Ansford Community School 282	
Chandlers Ford	Thornden School 154	
Chatham	Chatham Grammar School for Girls 120	
Chatham	Fort Pitt Grammar School 132	
Cheadle	Cheadle Hulme High School 223	
Cheam	Nonsuch High School for Girls 50	
Cheddar	Kings of Wessex Community School, The 277	
Chelmsford	Chelmsford County High School for Girls 5	
Chelmsford	King Edward VI Grammar School 42	
Chelmsford	Sandon School, The 375	
Cheltenham	Cleeve School 203	
Cheltenham	Pate's Grammar School 18	
Chesham	Chesham High School 96	
Cheshunt	Goffs School 148	
Chester	Christleton High School 199	
Chesterfield	Brookfield Community School 355	
Chesterfield	St Mary's Roman Catholic High School 160	
Chew Magna	Chew Valley School 299	
Chichester	Bishop Luffa School 141	
Chichester	Chichester High School for Girls 259	
Chipping Campden	Chipping Campden School 317	
Chislehurst	Bullers Wood School 152	
Chorley	Holy Cross Roman Catholic High School 376	
Chorley	St Michael's Church of England High School 362	
Christchurch	Highcliffe School 180	
Christchurch	Twynham School 227	
Cirencester	Cirencester Deer Park School 343	
Cirencester	Cirencester Kingshill School 322	
Clitheroe	Clitheroe Royal Grammar School 25	
Colchester	Colchester County High School for Girls 7	
Colchester	Colchester Royal Grammar School 9	
Colchester	East Bergholt High School 225	
Colchester	Philip Morant School, The 273	
Colyton	Colyton Grammar School 14	
Congleton	Westlands High School 339	
Coulsdon	Woodcote High School 327	
Coventry	Finham Park School 218	
Coventry	Heart of England School 254	
Cowbridge	Cowbridge School 184	
Cranbrook	Cranbrook School 82	
Crewe	St Thomas More Catholic High School 171	
Croydon	Archbishop Tenison's Church of England High School 146	

Croydon	St Andrew's School	141
Crymych	Ysgol-y-Preseli	243
Darlington	Hummersknott School	272
Dartford	Dartford Grammar School	70
Dartford	Dartford Grammar School for Girls	84
Dartford	Wilmington Grammar School for Boys	131
Derby	Ecclesbourne School, The	147
Derby	Littleover Community School	349
Derby	Woodlands Community School	286
Devizes	Lavington School	277
Doncaster	Hayfield School, The	307
Doncaster	South Axholme School	362
Dover	Dover Grammar School for Boys	40
Downpatrick	Down High School	93
Dudley	Dormston School, The	350
Dungannon	Royal School, Dungannon, The	115
Dungannon	St Patrick's Girls' Academy	12
Durham	Durham Johnston Comprehensive School	352
Durham	Framwellgate Moor Comprehensive School	337
East Grinstead	Sackville School	319
Eastbourne	Cavendish School, The	373
Edmonton	Latymer School, The	28
Effingham	Howard of Effingham School	156
Ely	Soham Village College	361
Enniskillen	St Michael's College	98
Epsom	Glyn ADT Technology School	266
Epsom	Rosebery	200
Evesham	Prince Henry's High School	298
Eye	Hartismere High School	240
Fairford	Farmor's School	261
Fareham	Cams Hill School	222
Fareham	Crofton School	206
Faversham	Queen Elizabeth's Grammar School, Faversham	89
Fishguard	Fishguard High School	392
Fleetwood	Cardinal Allen Roman Catholic High School	371
Folkestone	Folkestone School for Girls, The	79
Folkestone	Harvey Grammar School, The	75
Fordingbridge	Burgate School, The	226
Formby	Formby High School	340
Formby	Range High School	176
Fortrose	Fortrose Academy	400
Fulham	Lady Margaret School	130
Gainsborough	Queen Elizabeth's High School	109
Gairloch	Gairloch High School	401
Garforth	Garforth Community College	303
Gateshead	St Thomas More School	273
Gillingham	Rainham Mark Grammar School	67
Gloucester	Chosen Hill School	357
Gloucester	High School for Girls	83
Gloucester	Ribston Hall High School	130
Gloucester	Sir Thomas Rich's School	119

Grantham	Kesteven and Grantham Girls' School 74
Grantham	King's School, The 71
Gravesend	Gravesend Grammar School for Boys 92
Gravesend	Gravesend Grammar School for Girls 78
Grays	Grays Convent High School 240
Greenwich	St Ursula's Convent School 326
Grimsby	Healing Comprehensive School 310
Guildford	Guildford County School 318
Guisborough	Laurence Jackson School 324
Guiseley	Guiseley School 363
Hagley	Haybridge High School 144
Halifax	Crossley Heath School, The 76
Halifax	North Halifax Grammar School, The 72
Harrogate	Harrogate Grammar School 142
Harrogate	St Aidan's Church of England High School 157
Harrogate	St John Fisher Roman Catholic High School 276
Hawarden	Hawarden High School 374
Haywards Heath	Oathall Community College 192
Haywards Heath	St Paul's Roman Catholic School 386
Haywards Heath	Warden Park School 198
Heckmondwike	Heckmondwike Grammar School 79
Henley-on-Thames	Gillott's School 323
Hereford	Bishop of Hereford's Bluecoats School, The 181
Hereford	Fairfield High School 270
Hereford	St Mary's Roman Catholic High School 385
Heswall	Pensby High School for Girls 370
Hexham	Queen Elizabeth High School 249
High Wycombe	John Hampden Grammar School 56
High Wycombe	Royal Grammar School, The 16
High Wycombe	Wycombe High School 12
Hockley	Greensward School, The 182
Hook	Robert May's School 177
Hope	Hope Valley College 324
Horncastle	Queen Elizabeth's Grammar School 64
Hornchurch	Campion Roman Catholic School for Boys, The 163
Horsham	Millais School 180
Horsham	Tanbridge House School 256
Hounslow	St Mark's Catholic School 255
Ilford	Beal High School 238
Ilford	Ilford County High School 81
Ilkley	Ilkley Grammar School 195
Ingatestone	Anglo-European School 185
Ipswich	Hadleigh High School 293
Ipswich	Holbrook High School 272
Ipswich	Northgate High School 337
Isle of Harris	Sir Edward Scott School 405
Isleworth	Green School for Girls, The 236
Isleworth	Gumley House Convent School 215
Kensington	Cardinal Vaughan Memorial School, The 135
Kettering	Bishop Stopford School 162
Kettering	Montsaye School 374

Kilmarnock	Stewarton Academy 406
Kingston upon Thames	Tiffin Girls' School, The 43
Kingston upon Thames	Tiffin School 65
Kingswinford	Kingswinford School Grant-Maintained, The 334
Kingswinford	Summerhill School, The 380
Kingussie	Kingussie High School 402
Kirkwall	Kirkwall Grammar School 402
Knutsford	Knutsford High School 365
Lancaster	Lancaster Girls' Grammar School 37
Lancaster	Lancaster Royal Grammar School 11
Langley	Langley Grammar School 128
Leeds	Benton Park School 280
Lerwick	Anderson High School 398
Lewisham	Haberdashers' Aske's Hatcham College 278
Lichfield	King Edward VI School, Lichfield 216
Limavady	Limavady Grammar School 95
Lincoln	Caistor Grammar School 48
Liphook	Bohunt Community School 291
Little Chalfont	Dr Challoner's High School 59
Liverpool	Archbishop Blanch School 370
Liverpool	Blue Coat School, The 46
Liverpool	King David High School 144
Liverpool	St Hilda's Church of England High School 220
Loughton	Davenant Foundation School 265
Louth	King Edward VI School 103
Lutterworth	Lutterworth Grammar School and Community College 321
Lymm	Lymm High School 262
Macclesfield	All Hallows Catholic High School 233
Macclesfield	Fallibroome High School 228
Maghull	Deyes High School 306
Maidenhead	Desborough School 235
Maidenhead	Newlands School 151
Maidstone	Invicta Grammar School for Girls 51
Maidstone	Maidstone Grammar School 83
Maidstone	Oakwood Park Grammar School 133
Mallaig	Mallaig High School 403
Malmesbury	Malmesbury School 264
Malpas	Bishop Heber High School 331
Manchester	Stretford Grammar School 137
Manchester	Urmston Grammar School 106
Marlow	Sir William Borlase's Grammar School 53
Middlesbrough	Nunthorpe School 325
Middlesbrough	Stokesley School 173
Mullion	Mullion School 312
Muswell Hill	Fortismere School 245
Nailsea	Nailsea School 235
Nantwich	Brine Leas High School 204
New Milton	Arnewood School, The 210
Newbury	Downs School, The 298
Newbury	St Bartholomew's School 266
Newcastle upon Tyne	Whickham School 288

Newport	Adams' Grammar School 73	
Newport	Caerleon Comprehensive School 234	
Newport	Newport Girls' High School 17	
Newry	Abbey Grammar School 85	
Newry	Our Lady's Grammar School 93	
Norfolk	Hethersett High School 332	
Northampton	Guilsborough School 336	
Northwich	County High School, Leftwich, The 386	
Northwich	Hartford High School 294	
Northwich	St Nicholas Roman Catholic High School 167	
Nottingham	Fernwood Comprehensive School 283	
Nuneaton	Higham Lane School 333	
Oadby	Beauchamp College, The 354	
Oldham	Blue Coat Church of England Comprehensive School, The 217	
Oldham	Crompton House School 263	
Omagh	Christian Brothers Grammar School 97	
Omagh	Omagh Academy 103	
Ormskirk	Burscough Priory High School 348	
Ormskirk	Ormskirk Grammar School 219	
Ormskirk	St Bede's Roman Catholic High School 295	
Orpington	Newstead Wood School for Girls 3	
Orpington	St Olave's Grammar School 6	
Oswestry	Marches School, The 391	
Ottery St Mary	King's School, The 338	
Oxford	Wheatley Park School 289	
Oxted	Oxted County School 231	
Pateley Bridge	Upper Nidderdale High School 394	
Penrith	Queen Elizabeth Grammar School 134	
Penzance	Cape Cornwall School 269	
Peterborough	Deepings School, The 391	
Peterborough	King's School, The 118	
Pinner	Nower Hill High School 284	
Plymouth	Coombe Dean 356	
Plymouth	Devonport High School for Boys 94	
Plymouth	Devonport High School for Girls 39	
Plymouth	Hele's School 366	
Plymouth	Notre Dame Roman Catholic School for Girls 345	
Plymouth	Plymouth High School for Girls 122	
Poole	Parkstone Grammar School 26	
Poole	Poole Grammar School 69	
Portadown	Portadown College 49	
Portree	Portree High School 404	
Potters Bar	Dame Alice Owen's School 132	
Preston	Broughton High School 292	
Prestwich	St Monica's Roman Catholic High School 208	
Purley	John Fisher School, The 190	
Ramsgate	Chatham House Grammar School 123	
Ramsgate	Clarendon House Grammar School for Girls 124	
Rayleigh	Fitzwimarc School, The 344	
Reading	Kendrick Girls' School 13	
Reading	Maiden Erlegh School 159	

Reading	Piggott School 179
Reading	Reading School 8
Redcar	Sacred Heart Roman Catholic Comprehensive School, The 379
Redhill	St Bede's School 176
Rickmansworth	St Joan of Arc Catholic School 388
Ringmer	Ringmer Community College 349
Ripon	Ripon Grammar School 46
Rochdale	Wardle High School 257
Rochester	Rochester Grammar School for Girls, The 62
Rochester	Sir Joseph Williamson's Mathematical School 94
Romford	St Edward's Church of England School 267
Romsey	Romsey School, The 285
Rugby	Lawrence Sheriff School 91
Rugby	Rugby High School 40
Ruislip	Bishop Ramsey Church of England Comprehensive School 305
Saffron Walden	Newport Free Grammar School 220
Sale	Sale Grammar School 106
Salisbury	Bishop Wordsworth's School 22
Salisbury	South Wilts Grammar School for Girls 67
Sandbach	Sandbach High School 173
Sandwich	Sir Roger Manwood's School 125
Scarborough	Scalby School 360
Seaford	Seaford Head Community College 364
Sheffield	High Storrs School 189
Sheffield	Silverdale School 151
Shetland	Brae High School 399
Sidcup	Chislehurst and Sidcup Grammar School 53
Sittingbourne	Borden Grammar School 100
Sittingbourne	Highsted School 110
Skegness	Skegness Grammar School 90
Skipton	Ermysted's Grammar School 3
Skipton	Skipton Girls' High School 21
Sleaford	Carre's Grammar School 98
Sleaford	Kesteven and Sleaford High School 117
Slough	Herschel Grammar School 165
Slough	Slough Grammar School 107
Slough	St Bernard's Convent School 113
Solihull	Arden School 138
Solihull	Light Hall School 310
Solihull	St Peter's Catholic School 252
Solihull	Tudor Grange School 155
South Chailey	Chailey School 342
Southampton	Noadswood School 256
Southampton	St Anne's Convent School 172
Southend-on-Sea	Southend High School for Boys 55
Southend-on-Sea	Southend High School for Girls 54
Southwell	Minster School, The 200
Spalding	Queen Elizabeth Royal Free Grammar School of Spalding 129
St Helens	Rainford High School 275
Stanmore	Bentley Wood High School 282
Stevenage	John Henry Newman School 258

Stockbridge	Test Valley School 380
Stockport	Bramhall High School 291
Stockport	Poynton County High School 197
Stockport	St James' Roman Catholic High School 297
Stockton-on-Tees	Egglescliffe School 250
Stockton-on-Tees	Ian Ramsey Church of England School 390
Stoke-on-Trent	Alsager School 178
Stoke-on-Trent	Painsley Roman Catholic High School 225
Stourbridge	Grange School, The 378
Stourbridge	Old Swinford Hospital 70
Stowmarket	Debenham Church of England High School 17
Strabane	Strabane Grammar School 134
Stratford-upon-Avon	King Edward VI School 27
Stratford-upon-Avon	Stratford-upon-Avon Grammar School for Girls 17
Stroud	Marling School 112
Stroud	Stroud High School 115
Sunderland	St Anthony's Girls' School 302
Surbiton	Tolworth Girls' School 196
Sutton Coldfield	Bishop Vesey's Grammar School 127
Sutton Coldfield	Bishop Walsh School 251
Sutton Coldfield	Sutton Coldfield Girls' School 60
Swansea	Bishopston Comprehensive School 170
Swansea	Olchfa School 260
Swansea	Ysgol Gyfun Gwyr 183
Swindon	Highworth Warneford School 271
Tadcaster	Tadcaster Grammar School 300
Taunton	Castle School, The 211
Telford	Charlton (G.M.) School 372
Thame	Lord Williams's School 253
Thatcham	Kennet School 320
Thornbury	Castle School, The 327
Tonbridge	Judd School, The 36
Tonbridge	Tonbridge Grammar School for Girls 30
Tonbridge	Weald of Kent Grammar School for Girls 27
Torquay	Torquay Boys' Grammar School 64
Torquay	Torquay Grammar School for Girls 57
Trowbridge	St Augustine's School 145
Truro	Penair School 273
Tunbridge Wells	Bennet Memorial Diocesan School 143
Tunbridge Wells	Skinners' School, The 23
Tunbridge Wells	St Gregory's Catholic Comprehensive School 247
Tunbridge Wells	Tunbridge Wells Girls' Grammar School 32
Tunbridge Wells	Tunbridge Wells Grammar School for Boys 39
Twickenham	Waldegrave School for Girls 242
Uckfield	Uckfield Community College 382
Uppingham	Uppingham Community College 351
Wakefield	Crofton High School 384
Wakefield	St Thomas A Becket Roman Catholic School 316
Wallington	Wallington High School for Girls 56
Wallington	Wilson's School 116
Walsall	Queen Mary's Grammar School 34

Walsall	Queen Mary's High School 47
Ware	Presdales School 161
Warrington	Bridgewater County High School 329
Warrington	Lowton High School 311
Warrington	St Gregory's Roman Catholic High School 207
Waterfoot	Bacup and Rawtenstall Grammar School 114
Waterlooville	Oaklands Roman Catholic School 305
Watford	Parmiter's School 230
Watford	Watford Grammar School for Boys 138
Watford	Watford Grammar School for Girls 124
Weaverham	Weaverham High School 228
Welshpool	Caereinion High School 274
Welton	William Farr Church of England Comprehensive School 381
West Kirby	Calday Grange Grammar School 105
West Kirby	West Kirby Grammar School for Girls 87
Westcliff-on-Sea	St Bernard's High School 369
Westcliff-on-Sea	Westcliff High School for Boys 108
Westcliff-on-Sea	Westcliff High School for Girls 45
Westminster	Grey Coat Hospital, The 308
Westray	Pierowall Junior High School 404
Wetherby	Wetherby High School 290
Weymouth	All Saints Church of England School 358
Whitburn	Whitburn Comprehensive School 386
Whitchurch	Testbourne Community School 377
Whitley Bay	Whitley Bay High School 289
Wigan	Deanery Church of England High School, The 281
Wigan	St Peter's Roman Catholic High School 158
Wilmington	Grammar School for Girls Wilmington, The 111
Wimbledon	Ricards Lodge High School 313
Winchester	Henry Beaufort School, The 212
Winchester	Westgate School, Winchester, The 213
Windsor	Windsor Girls' School 383
Wokingham	Holt School, The 153
Wolverhampton	St Peter's Collegiate School 341
Wolverhampton	Wolverhampton Girls' High School 15
Woodbridge	Thomas Mills High School 189
Woodford Green	Trinity Catholic High School 149
Woodford Green	Woodford County High School 80
Woodley	Waingel's Copse School 353
Worthing	Davison Church of England High School 309
Wotton-under-Edge	Katharine Lady Berkeley's School 354
Wymondham	Wymondham College 150
Wymondham	Wymondham High School 367
Yarm	Conyers School 202
Yateley	Yateley School 357
York	All Saints' Roman Catholic School 365
York	Huntington School 244
York	Joseph Rowntree School, The 248

Index (iii) by education authority

Barnet
Copthall School 201
Hasmonean High School 139
Henrietta Barnett School, The 4
Queen Elizabeth's Girls' School 268
St Michael's Catholic Grammar School 20

Bath and North East Somerset
St Gregory's Catholic Comprehensive School 241
Beechen Cliff School 320
Chew Valley School 299
Wellsway School 214

Bedfordshire
Redborne Upper School and Community College 301
Sharnbrook Upper School and Community College 250

Belfast Education and Library Board
Methodist College Belfast 59
Royal Belfast Academical Institution, The 101
Strathearn School 22

Berkshire
Charters School 168
Desborough School 235
Downs School, The 298
Herschel Grammar School 165
Holt School, The 153
Kendrick Girls' School 13
Kennet School 320
Langley Grammar School 128
Maiden Erlegh School 159
Newlands School 151
Piggott School 179
Ranelagh School 140
Reading School 8
Slough Grammar School 107
St Bartholomew's School 266
St Bernard's Convent School 113
Waingel's Copse School 353
Windsor Girls' School 383

Bexley
Bexley Erith Technical High School 99
Chislehurst and Sidcup Grammar School 53
Townley Grammar School for Girls 50

Birmingham
Bishop Vesey's Grammar School 127
Bishop Walsh School 251
Handsworth Grammar School 112
King Edward VI Aston School 52
King Edward VI Camp Hill School for Boys 10
King Edward VI Camp Hill School for Girls 33
King Edward VI Five Ways 24
King Edward VI Handsworth School 29
Sutton Coldfield Girls' School 60

Bolton
Canon Slade School 221
St Joseph's Roman Catholic High School 315
Turton High School 229

Bournemouth
Bournemouth School 63
Bournemouth School for Girls 44

Bradford
Bingley Grammar School 347
Ilkley Grammar School 195

Bristol
Cotham Grammar School 174
St Mary Redcliffe and Temple School 368

Bromley
Bullers Wood School 152
Langley Park School for Boys 191
Langley Park School for Girls 164
Newstead Wood School for Girls 3
St Olave's Grammar School 6

Buckinghamshire
Aylesbury Grammar School 38
Aylesbury High School 19

Beaconsfield High School 68
Chesham High School 96
Dr Challoner's Grammar School 19
Dr Challoner's High School 59
John Hampden Grammar School 56
Royal Grammar School, The 16
Sir Henry Floyd Grammar School, The 88
Sir William Borlase's Grammar School 53
Wycombe High School 12

Bury
St Gabriel's Roman Catholic High School 296
St Monica's Roman Catholic High School 208
Woodhey High School 317

Calderdale
Crossley Heath School, The 76
North Halifax Grammar School, The 72

Cambridgeshire
Bottisham Village College 269
Chesterton Community College 389
Comberton Village College 205
Cottenham Village College 239
King's School, The 118
Linton Village College 198
Sawston Village College 314
Soham Village College 361
Swavesey Village College 209

Camden
Camden School for Girls 335
JFS (Jews' Free School) 193

Cardiff
Bishop of Llandaff Church-in-Wales High School, The 188
Cardiff High School 243
Radyr Comprehensive School 167

Carmarthenshire
Ysgol Gyfun Bro Myrddin 169

Cheshire
All Hallows Catholic High School 233
Alsager School 178
Bishop Heber High School 331
Bridgewater County High School 329
Brine Leas High School 204

Christleton High School 199
County High School, Leftwich, The 386
Fallibroome High School 228
Hartford High School 294
Knutsford High School 365
Lymm High School 262
Poynton County High School 197
Sandbach High School 173
St Gregory's Roman Catholic High School 207
St Nicholas Roman Catholic High School 167
St Thomas More Catholic High School 171
Weaverham High School 228
Westlands High School 339

Cornwall
Cape Cornwall School 269
Mullion School 312
Penair School 273

Coventry
Finham Park School 218

Croydon
Archbishop Tenison's Church of England High School 146
St Andrew's School 141
Woodcote High School 327

Cumbria
Queen Elizabeth Grammar School 134
Queen Elizabeth School 215

Darlington
Hummersknott School 272

Derbyshire
Brookfield Community School 355
Ecclesbourne School, The 147
Hope Valley College 324
Lady Manners School 185
Littleover Community School 349
St Mary's Roman Catholic High School 160
Woodlands Community School 286

Devon
Churston Grammar School 58
Colyton Grammar School 14
Coombe Dean 356
Devonport High School for Boys 39

Devonport High School for Girls *94*
Hele's School *366*
King's School, The *338*
Notre Dame Roman Catholic School for Girls *345*
Plymouth High School for Girls *122*
Torquay Boys' Grammar School *64*
Torquay Grammar School for Girls *57*

Doncaster
Hayfield School, The *307*

Dorset
All Saints Church of England School *358*
Corfe Hills School *175*
Highcliffe School *180*
Parkstone Grammar School *26*
Poole Grammar School *69*
Twynham School *227*

Dudley
Dormston School, The *350*
Grange School, The *378*
Kingswinford School Grant-Maintained, The *334*
Old Swinford Hospital *70*
Summerhill School, The *380*

Durham
Durham Johnston Comprehensive School *352*
Framwellgate Moor Comprehensive School *337*
Teesdale School *346*

East Sussex
Cavendish School, The *373*
Chailey School *342*
Claverham Community College *224*
Ringmer Community College *349*
Seaford Head Community College *364*
Uckfield Community College *382*

East Yorkshire
Beverley Grammar School *389*
Beverley High School *232*

Enfield
Latymer School, The *28*

Essex
Anglo-European School *185*

Brentwood County High School *277*
Brentwood Ursuline Convent High School *163*
Chelmsford County High School for Girls *5*
Colchester County High School for Girls *7*
Colchester Royal Grammar School *9*
Davenant Foundation School *265*
Fitzwimarc School, The *344*
Grays Convent High School *240*
Greensward School, The *182*
King Edward VI Grammar School *42*
Newport Free Grammar School *220*
Philip Morant School, The *213*
Sandon School, The *375*
Southend High School for Boys *55*
Southend High School for Girls *54*
St Bernard's High School *369*
Westcliff High School for Boys *108*
Westcliff High School for Girls *45*

Flintshire
Hawarden High School *394*

Gateshead
St Thomas More School *273*
Whickham School *288*

Gloucestershire
Chipping Campden School *317*
Chosen Hill School *357*
Cirencester Deer Park School *343*
Cirencester Kingshill School *322*
Cleeve School *203*
Farmor's School *261*
High School for Girls *83*
Katharine Lady Berkeley's School *354*
Marling School *112*
Pate's Grammar School *18*
Ribston Hall High School *130*
Sir Thomas Rich's School *119*
Stroud High School *115*

Grampian
Aboyne Academy *397*

Greenwich
St Ursula's Convent School *326*

Hammersmith and Fulham
Lady Margaret School *127*

Hampshire
Amery Hill School 342
Arnewood School, The 210
Bishop Challoner School 166
Bohunt Community School 291
Burgate School, The 226
Cams Hill School 222
Crofton School 206
Frogmore Community School 237
Henry Beaufort School, The 212
Noadswood School 256
Oaklands Roman Catholic School 305
Robert May's School 177
Romsey School, The 285
St Anne's Convent School 172
Test Valley School 380
Testbourne Community School 377
Thornden School 154
Westgate School, Winchester, The 213
Yateley School 357

Haringey
Fortismere School 245

Harrow
Bentley Wood High School 282
Nower Hill High School 284

Havering
Campion Roman Catholic School for Boys,
   The 163
St Edward's Church of England
   Comprehensive School 267

Hereford and Worcester
Bewdley High School 260
Bishop of Hereford's Bluecoats School, The
   181
Fairfield High School 270
Haybridge High School 144
Prince Henry's High School 298
St Mary's Roman Catholic High School 385

Hertfordshire
Bishop's Stortford High School, The 187
Broxbourne School, The 279
Dame Alice Owen's School 132
Goffs School 148
John Henry Newman School 258
Parmiter's School 230
Presdales School 161

St Joan of Arc Catholic School 388
Watford Grammar School for Boys 138
Watford Grammar School for Girls 124

Highland
Farr Secondary School 400
Fortrose Academy 400
Gairloch High School 400
Kingussie High School 402
Mallaig High School 403
Portree High School 404

Hillingdon
Bishop Ramsey Church of England
   School 305

Hounslow
Green School for Girls, The 236
Gumley House Convent School 215
St Mark's Catholic School 255

Kensington and Chelsea
Cardinal Vaughan Memorial School, The 135

Kent
Barton Court Grammar School 126
Bennet Memorial Diocesan School 143
Borden Grammar School 100
Chatham Grammar School for Girls 120
Chatham House Grammar School 123
Clarendon House Grammar School for Girls
   124
Cranbrook School 82
Dane Court Grammar School 89
Dartford Grammar School 70
Dartford Grammar School for Girls 84
Dover Grammar School for Boys 40
Folkestone School for Girls, The 79
Fort Pitt Grammar School 132
Grammar School for Girls Wilmington, The
   111
Gravesend Grammar School for Boys 92
Gravesend Grammar School for Girls 78
Harvey Grammar School, The 75
Highsted School 110
Highworth Grammar School for Girls 66
Invicta Grammar School for Girls 51
Judd School, The 36
Maidstone Grammar School 83
Norton Knatchbull School, The 41
Oakwood Park Grammar School 133

Queen Elizabeth's Grammar School 88
Rainham Mark Grammar School 67
Rochester Grammar School for Girls, The 62
Simon Langton Grammar School for Boys 35
Sir Joseph Williamson's Mathematical School 94
Sir Roger Manwood's School 125
Skinners' School, The 23
St Gregory's Catholic Comprehensive School 247
Tonbridge Grammar School for Girls 30
Tunbridge Wells Girls' Grammar School 32
Tunbridge Wells Grammar School for Boys 39
Weald of Kent Grammar School for Girls 27
Wilmington Grammar School for Boys 131

Kingston upon Thames
Tiffin School 65
Tiffin Girls' School, The 43
Tolworth Girls' School 196

Kirklees
Heckmondwike Grammar School 79

Lancashire
Bacup and Rawtenstall Grammar School 114
Broughton High School 292
Burscough Priory High School 348
Cardinal Allen Roman Catholic High School 371
Clitheroe Royal Grammar School 25
Hodgson High School 359
Holy Cross Roman Catholic High School 376
Lancaster Girls' Grammar School 36
Lancaster Royal Grammar School 11
Ormskirk Grammar School 219
St Bede's Roman Catholic High School 295
St Christopher's Church of England High School 334
St Hilda's Roman Catholic Girls High School 193
St Michael's Church of England High School 362

Leeds
Benton Park School 280
Garforth Community College 303
Guiseley School 363
Wetherby High School 290

Leicestershire
Beauchamp College, The 354
Lutterworth Grammar School and Community College 321

Lewisham
Haberdashers' Aske's Hatcham College 278

Lincolnshire
Boston Grammar School 100
Boston High School 121
Bourne Grammar School 77
Caistor Grammar School 48
Carre's Grammar School 98
Deepings School, The 391
Kesteven and Grantham Girls' School 74
Kesteven and Sleaford High School 117
King Edward VI School 103
King's School, The 71
Queen Elizabeth Royal Free Grammar School of Spalding 129
Queen Elizabeth's Grammar School 64
Queen Elizabeth's High School 109
Skegness Grammar School 90
William Farr Church of England Comprehensive School 381

Liverpool
Archbishop Blanch School 370
Blue Coat School, The 46
King David High School 144
St Hilda's Church of England High School 220

Lothian
Balerno High School 398

Merton
Ricards Lodge High School 313

Newport
Caerleon Comprehensive School 234

Norfolk
Hethersett High School 332
Wymondham College 150
Wymondham High School 367

North East Lincolnshire
Healing Comprehensive School 310

North Eastern Education and Library Board
Antrim Grammar School 109
St Louis Grammar School 61

North Lincolnshire
South Axholme School 362

North Somerset
Backwell School 157
Churchill Community School 301
Gordano School 287
Nailsea School 235

North Tyneside
Whitley Bay High School 289

North Yorkshire
Ermysted's Grammar School 3
Harrogate Grammar School 142
Ripon Grammar School 46
Scalby School 360
Skipton Girls' High School 21
St Aidan's Church of England High School 157
St John Fisher Roman Catholic High School 276
Stokesley School 173
Tadcaster Grammar School 300
Upper Nidderdale High School 394

Northamptonshire
Bishop Stopford School 162
Guilsborough School 336
Magdalen College School 346
Montsaye School 374

Northumberland
Queen Elizabeth High School 249
Colonel Frank Seely School, The 384
Fernwood Comprehensive School 283
Minster School, The 200

Oldham
Blue Coat Church of England Comprehensive School, The 217
Crompton House School 263

Orkney
Kirkwall Grammar School 402
Pierowall Junior High School 404

Oxfordshire
Gillott's School 323
Lord Williams's School 253
Wheatley Park School 289

Pembrokeshire
Fishguard High School 392
Ysgol-y-Preseli 243

Powys
Caereinion High School 274

Redbridge
Beal High School 238
Ilford County High School 81
Trinity Catholic High School 149
Woodford County High School 80

Redcar and Cleveland
Laurence Jackson School 324
Nunthorpe School 325
Sacred Heart Roman Catholic Comprehensive School, The 379

Richmond upon Thames
Waldegrave School for Girls 242

Rochdale
Wardle High School 257

Rutland
Uppingham Community College 351
Deyes High School 306
Formby High School 341
Range High School 176

Sheffield
High Storrs School 189
Silverdale School 151

Shetland Islands Council
Aith Junior High School 397
Anderson High School 398
Brae High School 399

Shropshire
Adams' Grammar School 73
Charlton (G.M.) School 372
Marches School, The 391
Newport Girls' High School 17

Solihull
Arden School 138
Heart of England School 254
Light Hall School 310
St Peter's Catholic School 252
Tudor Grange School 155

Somerset
Ansford Community School 282
Castle School, The 211
Kings of Wessex Community School, The 277
Sexey's School 136

South Eastern Education and Library Board
Down High School 93
Our Lady and St Patrick's College, Knock 61

South Gloucestershire
Brimsham Green School 393
Castle School, The 327
Ridings High School, The 328

South Tyneside
Whitburn Comprehensive School 386

Southern Education and Library Board
Abbey Grammar School 85
Banbridge Academy 31
Our Lady's Grammar School 93
Portadown College 49
Royal School, Armagh, The 129
Royal School, Dungannon, The 115
St Patrick's Girls' Academy 12
St Patrick's Grammar School 121

St Helens
Rainford High School 275
John Taylor High School 186
King Edward VI School, Lichfield 216
Painsley Roman Catholic High School 225

Stockport
Bramhall High School 291
Cheadle Hulme High School 223
St James' Roman Catholic High School 297

Stockton-on-Tees
Conyers School 202
Egglescliffe School 250
Ian Ramsey Church of England School 390

Strathclyde
Stewarton Academy 406

Suffolk
Debenham Church of England High School 170
East Bergholt High School 224
Hadleigh High School 293
Hartismere High School 240
Holbrook High School 272
Northgate High School 337
Thomas Mills High School 189

Sunderland
St Anthony's Girls' School 302

Surrey
Collingwood College 246
Glyn ADT Technology School 266
Guildford County School 318
Howard of Effingham School 156
Oxted County School 231
Rosebery 200
St Bede's School 176

Sutton
John Fisher School, The 190
Nonsuch High School for Girls 50
St Philomena's Catholic High School for Girls 203
Wallington High School for Girls 56
Wallington School 116
Wilson's School 116

Swansea
Bishopston Comprehensive School 170
Olchfa School 260
Ysgol Gyfun Gwyr 183

Swindon
Highworth Warneford School 271

Trafford
Altrincham Grammar School for Boys 86
Altrincham Grammar School for Girls 32
Sale Grammar School 106
Stretford Grammar School 137
Urmston Grammar School 106

Vale of Glamorgan
Cowbridge School 184

Wakefield
Crofton High School *384*
St Thomas A Becket Roman Catholic School *316*

Walsall
Queen Mary's Grammar School *34*
Queen Mary's High School *47*

Warwickshire
Higham Lane School *333*
King Edward VI School *27*
Lawrence Sheriff School *91*
Rugby High School *40*
Stratford-upon-Avon Grammar School for Girls *17*

West Sussex
Bishop Luffa School *141*
Chichester High School for Girls *259*
Davison Church of England High School *309*
Millais School *180*
Oathall Community College *192*
Sackville School *319*
St Paul's Roman Catholic School *330*
Tanbridge House School *256*
Warden Park School *198*
Weald School, The *304*

Western Education and Library Board
Christian Brothers Grammar School *97*
Limavady Grammar School *95*
Omagh Academy *103*
St Michael's College *98*
Strabane Grammar School *134*

Western Isles
Sir Edward Scott School *405*

Westminster
Grey Coat Hospital, The *308*

Wigan
Deanery Church of England High School, The *281*
Lowton High School *311*
St Peter's Roman Catholic High School *158*

Wiltshire
Bishop Wordsworth's School *22*
Lavington School *377*
Malmesbury School *264*
South Wilts Grammar School for Girls *67*
St Augustine's School *145*
St Laurence School *194*

Wirral
Calday Grange Grammar School *105*
Pensby High School for Girls *370*
West Kirby Grammar School for Girls *87*
Wirral County Grammar School for Girls *74*
Wirral Grammar School *104*

Wolverhampton
St Peter's Collegiate School *341*
Wolverhampton Girls' High School *15*

York
All Saints' Roman Catholic School *365*
Huntington School *244*
Joseph Rowntree School *248*